PENGUIN BOOKS

CLASSIC SATYAJIT RAY

Satyajit Ray was born on 2 May 1921 in Calcutta. After graduating from Presidency College, Calcutta, in 1940, he studied art at Rabindranath Tagore's university, Shantiniketan. By 1943, Ray was back in Calcutta and had joined an advertising firm as a visualizer. He also started designing covers and illustrating books brought out by Signet Press. A deep interest in films led to his establishing the Calcutta Film Society in 1947. During a six-month trip to Europe in 1950, Ray became a member of the London Film Club and managed to see ninety-nine films in only four and a half months.

In 1955, after overcoming innumerable difficulties, Satyajit Ray completed his first film, *Pather Panchali*, with financial assistance from the West Bengal government. The film was an award winner at the Cannes Film Festival and established Ray as a director of international stature. Together with *Aparajito* (The Unvanquished, 1956) and *Apur Sansar* (The World of Apu, 1959), it forms the Apu trilogy and perhaps constitutes Ray's finest work. Ray's other films include *Jalsaghar* (The Music Room, 1958), *Charulata* (1964), *Aranyer Din Ratri* (Days and Nights in the Forest, 1970), *Shatranj Ke Khilari* (The Chess Players, 1977), *Ghare Baire* (The Home and the World, 1984), *Ganashatru* (Enemy of the People, 1989), *Shakha Proshakha* (Branches of a Tree, 1990) and *Agantuk* (The Stranger, 1991). Ray also made several documentaries, including one on Tagore. In 1987, he made the documentary *Sukumar Ray* to commemorate the birth centenary of his father, perhaps Bengal's most famous writer of nonsense verse and children's books. Satyajit Ray won numerous awards for his films. Both the British Federation of Film Societies and the Moscow Film Festival Committee named him one of the greatest directors of the second half of the twentieth century. In 1992, he was awarded the Oscar for Lifetime Achievement by the Academy of Motion Picture Arts and Science and, in the same year, was also honoured with the Bharat Ratna.

Apart from being a film-maker, Satyajit Ray was a writer of repute. In 1961, he revived the children's magazine *Sandesh* which his grandfather, Upendrakishore Ray, had started and to which his father used to contribute frequently. Satyajit Ray contributed numerous poems, stories and essays to *Sandesh*, and also published several books in Bengali, most of which became bestsellers. In 1978, Oxford University awarded him its DLitt degree.

Satyajit Ray died in Calcutta in April 1992.

Gopa Majumdar has translated several works from Bengali to English, the most notable of these being Ashapurna Debi's *Subarnalata*, Taslima Nasrin's *My Girlhood* and Bibhutibhushan Bandyopadhyay's *Aparajito*, for which she won the Sahitya Akademi Award in 2001. She has translated several volumes of Satyajit Ray's short stories, a number of Professor Shonku stories and all of the Feluda stories for Penguin Books India. She is currently translating Ray's cinematic writings for Penguin.

CLASSIC SATYAJIT RAY

Translated from the Bengali by the author and Gopa Majumdar

PENGUIN BOOKS

PENGUIN BOOKS
Published by the Penguin Group
Penguin Books India Pvt. Ltd, 11 Community Centre, Panchsheel Park, New Delhi 110 017, India
Penguin Group (USA) Inc., 375 Hudson Street, New York, New York 10014, USA
Penguin Group (Canada), 90 Eglinton Avenue East, Suite 700, Toronto, Ontario, M4P 2Y3, Canada (a division of Pearson Penguin Canada Inc.)
Penguin Books Ltd, 80 Strand, London WC2R 0RL, England
Penguin Ireland, 25 St Stephen's Green, Dublin 2, Ireland (a division of Penguin Books Ltd)
Penguin Group (Australia), 250 Camberwell Road, Camberwell, Victoria 3124, Australia (a division of Pearson Australia Group Pty Ltd)
Penguin Group (NZ), 67 Apollo Drive, Rosedale, Auckland 0632, New Zealand (a division of Pearson New Zealand Ltd)
Penguin Group (South Africa) (Pty) Ltd, 24 Sturdee Avenue, Rosebank, Johannesburg 2196, South Africa

Penguin Books Ltd, Registered Offices: 80 Strand, London WC2R 0RL, England

First published by Penguin Books India 2012

10 9 8 7 6 5 4 3 2 1

ISBN 9780143418610

Typeset in Sabon by Suman Srinivasan, Gurgaon
Printed at Anubha Printers, Noida

CONTENTS

Bonku Babu's Friend

No one had ever seen Bonku Babu get cross. To tell the truth, it was difficult to imagine what he might say or do, if one day he did get angry.

It was not as if there was never any reason for him to lose his temper. For the last twenty-two years, Bonku Babu had taught geography and Bengali at the Kankurgachhi Primary School. Every year, a new batch of students replaced the old one, but old or new, the tradition of teasing poor Bonku Babu continued among all the students. Some drew his picture on the blackboard; others put glue on his chair; or, on the night of Kali Puja, they lit a 'chasing-rocket' and set it off to chase him.

Bonku Babu did not get upset by any of this. Only sometimes, he cleared his throat and said, 'Shame on you, boys!'

One of the reasons for maintaining his calm was simply that he could not afford to do otherwise. If he did lose his temper and left his job in a fit of pique, he knew how difficult it would then be to find another, at his age. Another reason was that in every class, there were always a few good students, even if the rest of the class was full of pranksters. Teaching this handful of good boys was so rewarding that, to Bonku Babu, that alone made life as a teacher worth living. At times, he invited those boys to his house, offered them snacks and told them tales of foreign lands and exciting adventures. He told them about life in Africa, the discovery of the North Pole, the fish in Brazil that ate human flesh, and about Atlantis, the continent submerged under the sea. He was a good storyteller, he had his audience enthralled.

During the weekend, Bonku Babu went to the lawyer, Sripati Majumdar's house, to spend the evenings with other regulars. On a number of occasions, he had come back thinking, 'Enough, never again!' The reason was simply that he could put up with the pranks played by the boys in his school, but when grown, even middle-aged men started making fun of him, it became too much to bear. At these meetings that Sripati Babu hosted in the evenings, nearly everyone poked fun at Bonku Babu, sometimes bringing his endurance to breaking point.

Only the other day—less than two months ago—they were talking about ghosts. Usually, Bonku Babu kept his mouth shut. That day, for some unknown reason, he opened it and declared that he was not afraid of ghosts. That was all. But it was enough to offer a golden opportunity to the others. On his way back later that night, Bonku Babu was attacked by a 'spook'. As he was passing a tamarind tree, a tall, thin figure leapt down and landed on his back. As it happened, this apparition had smeared black ink all over itself, possibly at the suggestion of someone at the meeting.

Bonku Babu did not feel frightened. But he was injured. For three days, his neck ached. Worst of all—his new kurta was torn and it had black stains all over. What kind of a joke was this?

Other 'jokes', less serious in nature, were often played on him. His umbrella or his shoes were hidden sometimes; at others, a paan would be filled with dust instead of masala, and handed to him; or he would be forced to sing.

Even so, Bonku Babu had to come to these meetings. If he didn't, what would Sripati Babu think? Not only was he a very important man in the village, but he couldn't do without Bonku Babu. According to Sripati Majumdar, it was essential to have a butt of ridicule, who could provide amusement to all. Or what was the point in having a meeting? So Bonku Babu was fetched, even if he tried to keep away.

On one particular day, the topic of conversation was high-flying—in other words, they were talking of satellites. Soon after sunset, a moving point of light had been seen in the northern sky. A similar light was seen three months ago, which had led to much speculation. In the end, it turned out to be a Russian satellite, called Khotka—or was it Phoshka? Anyway, this satellite was supposed to be going round the earth at a height of 400 miles, and providing a lot of valuable information to scientists.

That evening, Bonku Babu was the first to spot that strange light. Then he called Nidhu Babu and showed it to him. However, he arrived at the meeting to find that Nidhu Babu had coolly claimed full credit for being the first to see it, and was boasting a great deal. Bonku Babu said nothing.

No one knew much about satellites, but there was nothing to stop them from offering their views. Said Chandi Babu, 'You can say what you like, but I don't think we should waste our time worrying about satellites. Somebody sees a point of light in some obscure corner of the sky, and the press gets all excited about it. Then we read a report, say how clever it all is, have a chat about it in our living rooms, perhaps while we casually chew a paan, and behave as if we have achieved something. Humbug!'

Ramkanai countered this remark. He was still young. 'No, it may not be any of us here, but it is human achievement, surely? And a great achievement, at that.'

'Oh, come off it! Of course it's a human achievement . . . who'd build a satellite except men? You wouldn't expect a bunch of monkeys to do that, would you?'

'All right,' said Nidhu Babu, 'let's not talk of satellites. After all, it's just a machine, going round the earth, they say. No different from a spinning top. A top would start spinning if you got it going; or a fan

would start to rotate if you pressed a switch. A satellite's the same. But think of a rocket. That can't be dismissed so easily, can it?'

Chandi Babu wrinkled his nose. 'A rocket? Why, what good is a rocket? All right, if one was made here in our country, took off from the maidan in Calcutta, and we could all go and buy tickets to watch the show . . . well then, that would be nice. But . . .'

'You're right,' Ramkanai agreed. 'A rocket has no meaning for us here.'

Bhairav Chakravarty spoke next. 'Suppose some creature from a different planet arrived on earth . . . ?'

'So what? Even if it did, you and I would never be able to see it.'

'Yes, that's true enough.'

Everyone turned their attention to their cups of tea. There did not seem to be anything left to be said. After a few moments of silence, Bonku Babu cleared his throat and said gently, 'Suppose . . . suppose they came here?'

Nidhu Babu feigned total amazement. 'Hey, Bunkum wants to say something! What did you say, Bunkum? Who's going to come here? Where from?'

Bonku Babu repeated his words, his tone still gentle: 'Suppose someone from a different planet came here?'

As was his wont, Bhairav Chakravarty slapped Bonku Babu's back loudly and rudely, grinned and said, 'Bravo! What a thing to say! Where is a creature from another planet going to land? Not Moscow, not London, not New York, not even Calcutta, but here? In Kankurgachhi? You do think big, don't you?'

Bonku Babu fell silent. But several questions rose in his mind. Was it really impossible? If an alien had to visit the earth, would it really matter where it arrived first? It might not aim to go straight to any other part of the world. All right, it was highly unlikely that such a thing would happen in Kankurgachhi, but who was to say for sure that it could not happen at all?

Sripati Babu was silent so far. Now, as he shifted in his seat, everyone looked at him. He put his cup down and spoke knowledgeably: 'Look, if someone from a different planet does come to earth, I can assure you that he will not come to this God-forsaken place. Those people are no fools. It is my belief that they are sahibs, and they will land in some western country, where all the sahibs live. Understand?'

Everyone agreed, with the sole exception of Bonku Babu.

Chandi Babu decided to take things a bit further. He nudged Nidhu Babu silently, pointed at Bonku Babu and spoke innocently: 'Why, I think Bonku is quite right. Isn't it natural that aliens should want to come to a place where there's a man like our Bonkubihari? If they wanted to take away a specimen, could they find anything better?'

'No, I don't think so!' Nidhu Babu joined in. 'Consider his looks, not to mention his brains . . . yes, Bunkum is the ideal specimen!'

'Right. Suitable for keeping in a museum. Or a zoo,' Ramkanai chipped in.

Bonku Babu did not reply, but wondered silently: if anyone were to look for a specimen, weren't the others just as suitable? Look at Sripati Babu. His chin was so much like a camel's. And that Bhairav Chakravarty, his eyes were like the eyes of a tortoise. Nidhu Babu looked like a mole, Ramkanai like a goat, and Chandi Babu like a flittermouse. If a zoo really had to be filled up . . .

Tears sprang to his eyes. Bonku Babu had come to the meeting hoping, for once, to enjoy himself. That was clearly not to be. He could not stay here any longer. He rose to his feet.

'Why, what's the matter? Are you leaving already?' Sripati Babu asked, sounding concerned.

'Yes, it's getting late.'

'Late? Pooh, it's not late at all. Anyway, tomorrow is a holiday. Sit down, have some more tea.'

'No, thank you. I must go. I have some papers to mark. Namaskar.'

'Take care, Bonkuda,' warned Ramkanai, 'it's a moonless night, remember. And it's a Saturday. Very auspicious for ghosts and spooks!'

Bonku Babu saw the light when he was about halfway through the bamboo grove. Poncha Ghosh owned that entire area. Bonku Babu was not carrying a torch or a lantern. There was no need for it. It was too cold for snakes to be out and about, and he knew his way very well. Normally, not many people took this route, but it meant a short-cut for him.

In the last few minutes he had become aware of something unusual. At first, he could not put his finger on it. Somehow, things were different tonight. What was wrong? What was missing? Suddenly, he realized that the crickets were silent. Not one was chirping. Usually, the crickets sounded louder as he delved deeper into the bamboo grove. Today, there was only an eerie silence. What had happened to the crickets? Were they all asleep?

Puzzled, Bonku Babu walked another twenty yards, and then saw the light. At first, he thought a fire had broken out. Bang in the middle of the bamboo grove, in the clearing near a small pond, quite a large area was glowing pink. A dull light shone on every branch and every leaf. Down below, the ground behind the pond was lit by a much stronger pink light. But it was not a fire, for it was still.

Bonku Babu kept moving.

Soon, his ears began ringing. He felt as if someone was humming loudly—a long, steady noise—there was no way he could stop it. Bonku Babu broke into goosepimples, but an irrepressible curiosity drove him further forward.

As he went past a cluster of bamboo stems, an object came into view. It looked like a giant glass bowl, turned upside-down, covering the pond completely. It was through its translucent shade that a strong, yet gentle pink light was shining out, to turn the whole area radiant.

Not even in a dream had Bonku Babu witnessed such a strange scene.

After staring at it for a few stunned minutes, he noticed that although

the object was still, it did not appear to be lifeless. There was the odd flicker; and the glass mound was rising and falling, exactly as one's chest heaves while breathing.

He took a few steps to get a better look, but felt suddenly as if an electric current had passed through his body. In the next instant, he was rendered completely immobile. His hands and feet were tied with an invisible rope. There was no strength left in his body. He could move neither forward, nor backward.

A few moments later, Bonku Babu—still standing stiffly on the same spot—saw that the object gradually stopped 'breathing'. At once, his ears ceased ringing and the humming stopped. A second later, a voice spoke, shattering the silence of the night. It sounded human, but was extraordinarily thin.

'Milipi-ping kruk! Milipi-ping kruk!' it said loudly.

Bonku Babu gave a start. What did it mean? What language was this? And where was the speaker?

The next words the voice spoke made his heart jump again.

'Who are you? Who are you?'

Why, these were English words! Was the question addressed to him? Bonku Babu swallowed. 'I am Bonkubihari Datta, sir. Bonkubihari Datta,' he replied.

'Are you English? Are you English?' the voice went on.

'No, sir!' Bonku Babu shouted back. 'Bengali, sir. A Bengali kayastha.'

This was followed by a short pause. Then the voice came back, speaking clearly: 'Namaskar!'

Bonku Babu heaved a sigh of relief and returned the greeting. 'Namaskar!' he said, suddenly realizing that the invisible bonds that were holding him tightly had disappeared. He was free to run away, but he did not. Now his astounded eyes could see that a portion of the glass mound was sliding to one side, opening out like a door.

Through that door emerged a head—like a plain, smooth ball—and then the body of a weird creature.

Its arms and legs were amazingly thin. With the exception of its head, its whole body was covered by a shiny, pink outfit. Instead of ears, it had a tiny hole on each side of its head. On its face were two holes where it should have had a nose, and another gaping hole instead of a mouth. There was no sign of hair anywhere. Its eyes were round and bright yellow. They appeared to be glowing in the dark.

The creature walked slowly towards Bonku Babu, and stopped only a few feet away. Then it gave him a steady, unblinking stare. Automatically, Bonku Babu found himself folding his hands. Having stared at him for nearly a minute, it spoke in the same voice that sounded more like a flute than anything else: 'Are you human?'

'Yes.'

'Is this Earth?'

'Yes.'

'Ah, I thought as much. My instruments are not working properly. I was supposed to go to Pluto. I wasn't sure where I had landed, so I spoke to you first in the language they use on Pluto. When you didn't reply, I could tell I had landed on Earth. A complete waste of time and effort. It happened once before. Instead of going to Mars, I veered off and went to Jupiter. Delayed me by a whole day, it did. Heh heh heh!'

Bonku Babu did not know what to say. He was feeling quite uncomfortable, for the creature had started to press his arms and legs with its long, slim fingers. When it finished, it introduced itself. 'I am Ang, from the planet Craneus. A far superior being than man.'

What! This creature, barely four feet tall, with such thin limbs and weird face, was superior to man? Bonku Babu nearly burst out laughing. Ang read his mind immediately. 'There's no need to be so sceptical. I can prove it. How many languages do you know?'

Bonku Babu scratched his head. 'Bengali, English and . . . er . . . Hindi . . . a little Hindi . . . I mean . . .'

'You mean two and a half?'

'Yes.'

'I know 14,000. There isn't a single language in your solar system that I do not know. I also know thirty-one languages spoken on planets outside your system. I have been to twenty-five of them. How old are you?'

'I am fifty.'

'I am 833. Do you eat animals?'

Bonku Babu had had meat curry only recently, on the day of Kali Puja. How could he deny it?

'We stopped eating meat several centuries ago,' Ang informed him. 'Before that, we used to eat the flesh of most creatures. I might have eaten you.'

Bonku Babu swallowed hard.

'Take a look at this!' Ang offered him a small object. It looked like a pebble. Bonku Babu touched it for an instant, and felt the same electric current pass through his body. He withdrew his hand at once.

Ang smiled. 'A little while ago, you could not move an inch. Do you know why? It was only because I had this little thing in my hand. It would stop anyone from getting closer. Nothing can be more effective than this in making an enemy perfectly powerless, without actually hurting him physically.'

Now Bonku Babu felt genuinely taken aback. His mind was feeling far less stunned.

Ang said, 'Is there any place that you have wished to visit, or a scene that you have longed to see, but never could?'

Bonku Babu thought: why, the whole world remained to be seen! He taught geography, but what had he seen except a few villages and towns in Bengal? There was so much in Bengal itself that he had never had the chance to see. The snow-capped Himalayas, the sea in Digha, the forests in the Sunderbans, or even that famous banyan tree in Shibpur.

However, he mentioned none of these thoughts to Ang. 'There is so much I would like to see,' he finally admitted, 'but most of all . . . I think I would like to visit the North Pole. I come from a warm country, you see, so . . .'

Ang took out a small tube, one end of which was covered by a piece of glass. 'Take a look through this!' Ang invited. Bonku Babu peered through the glass, and felt all his hair rise. Could this be true? Could he really believe his eyes? Before him stretched an endless expanse of snow, dotted with large mounds, also covered with ice and snow. Above him, against a deep blue sky, all the colours of a rainbow were forming different patterns, changing every second. The Aurora Borealis! What was that? An igloo. There was a group of polar bears. Wait, there was another animal. A strange, peculiar creature . . . Yes! It was a walrus. There were two of them, in fact. And they were fighting. Their tusks were bared—large as radishes—and they were attacking each other. Streams of bright red blood were running on the soft white snow . . .

It was December, and Bonku Babu was looking at an area hidden under layers of snow. Still, he broke into a sweat.

'What about Brazil? Don't you wish to go there?' asked Ang.

Bonku Babu remembered instantly—piranhas, those deadly carnivorous fish! Amazing. How did this Ang know what he would like to see?

Bonku Babu peered through the tube again. He could see a dense forest. Only a little scattered sunlight had crept in through the almost impenetrable foliage. There was a huge tree, and hanging from a branch . . . what was that? Oh God, he could never even have imagined the size of that snake. Anaconda! The name flashed through his mind. Yes, he had read somewhere about it. It was said to be much, much larger than a python.

But where was the fish? Oh, here was a canal. Crocodiles lined its banks, sleeping in the sun. One of them moved. It was going to go into the water. Splash! Bonku Babu could almost hear the noise. But . . . what was that? The crocodile had jumped out of the water very quickly. Was . . . could it be the same one that went in only a few seconds ago? With his eyes nearly popping out, Bonku Babu noted that there was virtually no flesh left on the belly of the crocodile, bones were showing through clearly. Attached to the remaining flesh were five fish with amazingly sharp teeth and a monstrous appetite. Pirahnas!

Bonku Babu could not bear to watch any more. His limbs were trembling, his head reeled painfully.

'Now do you believe that we are superior?' Ang wanted to know.

Bonku Babu ran his tongue over his parched lips. 'Yes. Oh yes. Certainly. Of course!' he croaked.

'Very well. Look, I have been watching you. And I have examined your arms and legs. You belong to a much inferior species. There is no doubt about that. However, as human beings go, you are not too bad. I mean, you are a good man. But you have a major fault. You are much too meek and mild. That is why you have made so little progress in life. You must always speak up against injustice, and protest if anyone hurts or insults you without any provocation. To take it quietly is wrong, not just for man, but for any creature anywhere. Anyway, it was nice to have met you, although I wasn't really supposed to be here at this time.

There's no point in wasting more time on your Earth. I had better go.'

'Goodbye, Mr Ang. I am very glad to have made your . . .'

Bonku Babu could not complete his sentence. In less than a second, almost before he could grasp what was happening, Ang had leapt into his spaceship and risen over Poncha Ghosh's bamboo grove. Then he vanished completely. Bonku Babu realized that the crickets had started chirping again. It was really quite late.

Bonku Babu resumed walking towards his house, his mind still in a wondrous haze. Slowly, the full implications of the recent events began to sink in. A man—no, it was not a man, it was Ang—came here from some unknown planet, who knew if anyone had ever heard its name, and spoken to him. How extraordinary! How completely incredible! There were billions and billions of people in the world. But who got the chance to have this wonderful experience? Bonkubihari Datta, teacher of geography and Bengali in the Kankurgachhi Primary School. No one else. From today, at least in this particular matter, he was unique, in the whole wide world.

Bonku Babu realized that he was no longer walking. With a spring in every step, he was actually dancing.

The next day was a Sunday. Everyone had turned up for their usual meeting at Sripati Babu's house. There was a report in the local paper about a strange light, but it was only a small report. This light had been seen by a handful of people in only two places in Bengal. It was therefore being put in the same category as sightings of flying saucers.

Tonight, Poncha Ghosh was also present at the meeting. He was talking about his bamboo grove. All the bamboo around the pond in the middle of the wood had shed all their leaves. It was not unusual for leaves to drop in winter, but for so many plants to become totally bare overnight was certainly a remarkable occurrence. Everyone was talking about it, when suddenly Bhairav Chakravarty said, 'Why is Bonku so late today?'

Everyone stopped talking. So far, no one had noticed Bonku Babu's absence.

'I don't think Bunkum will show his face here today. Didn't he get an earful yesterday when he tried to open his mouth?' said Nidhu Babu.

'No, no,' Sripati Babu sounded concerned, 'we must have Bonku. Ramkanai, go and see if you can get hold of him.'

'OK, I'll go as soon as I've had my tea,' replied Ramkanai and was about to take a sip, when Bonku Babu entered the room. No, to say 'entered' would be wrong. It was as if a small hurricane swept in, in the guise of a short, dark man, throwing everyone into stunned silence.

Then it swung into action. Bonku Babu burst into a guffaw, and laughed uproariously for a whole minute, the like of which no one had heard before, not even Bonku Babu himself.

When he could finally stop, he cleared his throat and began speaking:

'Friends! I have great pleasure in telling you that this is the last time you will see me at your meeting. The only reason I am here today is simply that I would like to tell you a few things before I go. Number one—this is for all of you—you speak a great deal of rubbish. Only fools talk of things they don't know anything about. Number two—this is for Chandi Babu—at your age, hiding other people's shoes and umbrellas is not just childish, but totally wrong. Kindly bring my umbrella and brown canvas shoes to my house tomorrow. Nidhu Babu, if you call me Bunkum, I will call you Nitwit, and you must learn to live with that. And Sripati Babu, you are an important man, of course you must have hangers-on. But let me tell you, from today you can count me out. If you like, I can send my cat, it's quite good at licking feet. And . . . oh, you are here as well, Poncha Babu! Let me inform you and everyone else, that last night, an Ang arrived from the planet Craneus and landed on the pond in your bamboo grove. We had a long chat. The man . . . sorry, the Ang . . . was most amiable.'

Bonku Babu finished his speech and slapped Bhairav Chakravarty's back so hard that he choked. Then he made his exit, walking swiftly, his head held high.

In the same instant, the cup fell from Ramkanai's hand, shattering to pieces, and splattering hot tea on most of the others.

Translated by Gopa Majumdar
First published in Bengali in 1962

The Pterodactyl's Egg

Badan Babu had stopped going to Curzon Park after work. He used to enjoy his daily visits to the park. Every evening he would go straight from his office and spend about an hour, just resting quietly on a bench, beside the statue of Suren Banerjee. Then, when the crowds in the trams grew marginally thinner, he would catch one back to his house in Shibthakur Lane.

Now new tram lines had been laid inside the park. The noise of the traffic had ruined the atmosphere totally. There was no point in trying to catch a few quiet moments here. Yet, it was impossible to go back home straight after office, packed into a bus like sardines in a tin.

Besides, Badan Babu simply had to find some time every day to try and enjoy the little natural beauty that was left in the city. He might be no more than an ordinary clerk, but God had given him a lively imagination. He had thought of so many different stories sitting on that bench in Curzon Park. But there had never been the time to write them down. Had he, indeed, managed to find the time, no doubt he would have made quite a name for himself.

However, not all his efforts had been wasted.

His seven-year-old son, Biltu, was an invalid. Since he was incapable of moving around, most of his time was spent listening to stories. Both his parents told him stories of all kinds—fairy tales, folk tales, funny tales and spooky tales, tales they had heard and tales they had read. In the last three years, he had been told at least a thousand stories. Badan Babu had lately been making up stories himself for his son. He usually did this sitting in Curzon Park.

Over the last few weeks, however, Biltu had made it plain that he no longer enjoyed all his stories. One look at Biltu's face was enough to see that he had been disappointed.

This did not surprise Badan Babu very much. It was not possible to think up a good plot during the day; this time was spent doing his work in the office. And now that the peace of Curzon Park had been shattered, his only chance of sitting there in the evening and doing a bit of thinking was lost forever.

He tried going to Lal Deeghi a few times. Even that did not work. The huge, monstrous communications building next to the Deeghi blocked a large portion of the sky. Badan Babu felt suffocated there.

After that even the park near Lal Deeghi was invaded by tram lines and Badan Babu was forced to look for a different spot.

Today, he had come to the riverside.

After walking along the iron railings for about a quarter of a mile on the southern side of Outram Ghat, he found an empty bench.

There was Fort William, not far away. In fact, he could see the cannon. The cannonball stood fixed at the end of an iron rod, almost like a giant lollipop.

Badan Babu recalled his schooldays. The cannon went off every day at 1 p.m., the boys came rushing out for their lunch break and the headmaster, Harinath Babu, took out his pocket-watch religiously and checked the time.

The place was quiet, though not exactly deserted. A number of boats were tied nearby and one could see the boatmen talking among themselves. A grey, Japanese ship was anchored in the distance. Further down, towards Kidderpore, the skyline was crowded with masts of ships and pulleys.

This was a pleasant place.

Badan Babu sat down on the bench.

Through the smoke from the steamers he could see a bright spot in the sky. Could it be Venus?

It seemed to Badan Babu that he had not seen such a wide expanse of sky for a long time. Oh, how huge it was, how colossal! This was just what he needed for his imagination to soar.

Badan Babu took off his canvas shoes and sat cross-legged on the bench.

He was going to make up for lost time and find new plots for a number of stories today. He could see Biltu's face—happy and excited!

'Namaskar.'

Oh no! Was he going to be disturbed here too?

Badan Babu turned and found a stranger standing near the bench: a man, exceedingly thin, about fifty years old, wearing brown trousers and a jacket, a jute bag slung from one shoulder. His features were not clear in the twilight, but the look in his eyes seemed to be remarkably sharp.

A contraption hung from his chest. Two rubber tubes attached to it were plugged into the man's ears.

'Hope I'm not disturbing you,' said the newcomer with a slight smile. 'Please don't mind. I've never seen you before, so . . .'

Badan Babu felt considerably put out. Why did the man have to come and force himself on him? Now all his plans were upset. What was he going to tell poor Biltu?

'You've never seen me for the simple reason that I have never come here before,' he said. 'In a big city like this, isn't it natural that the number of people one has never seen should be more than the number of people one has?'

The newcomer ignored the sarcasm and said, 'I have been coming here every day for the last four years.'

'I see.'

'I sit here in this very spot every day. This is where I do my experiments, you know.'

Experiments? What kind of experiments could one do in this open space by the riverside? Was the man slightly mad?

But what if he was something else? He could be a hooligan, couldn't he? Or a pickpocket?

Good God—today had been pay day! Badan Babu's salary—two new, crisp hundred-rupee notes—was tied up in a handkerchief and thrust into his pocket. His wallet had fifty-five rupees and thirty-two paise.

Badan Babu rose. It was better to be safe than sorry.

'Are you leaving? So soon? Are you annoyed with me?'

'No, no.'

'Well, then? You got here just now only, didn't you? Why do you want to leave so soon?'

Perhaps Badan Babu was being over-cautious. There was no need to feel so scared. After all, there were all those people in the boats, not far away.

Still Badan Babu hesitated.

'No, I must go. It's getting late.'

'Late? It's only half-past five.'

'I have to go quite far.'

'How far?'

'Right up to Bagbazar.'

'Pooh—that's not very far! It's not as though you have to go to a suburb like Serampore or Chuchrah or even Dakshineshwar!'

'Even so, it will mean spending at least forty minutes in a tram. And then it takes about ten minutes to get to my house from the tram stop.'

'Yes, there is that, of course.'

The newcomer suddenly became a little grave. Then he began muttering to himself, 'Forty plus ten. That makes fifty. I am not very used to calculating minutes and hours. My system is different . . . do sit down. Just for a bit. Please.'

Badan Babu sat down again. There was something in the man's eyes and his voice that compelled him to stay back. Was this what was known as hypnotism?

'I don't ask everyone to sit by me for a chat. But you strike me as a man different from others. You like to think. You're not bound only by monetary considerations like 99.9 per cent of people. Am I right?'

Badan Babu said hesitantly, 'Well, I don't know . . . I mean . . .'

'And you're modest! Good. I can't stand people who brag. If it was all just a question of bragging, no one would have the right to do so more than me.'

The newcomer stopped speaking. Then he took out the rubber tubes from his ears and said, 'I get worried sometimes. If I pressed the switch in the dark accidentally, all hell would break loose.'

At this point, Badan Babu could not help asking the question that was trembling on his lips.

'Is that a stethoscope? Or is it something else?'

The man ignored the question completely. How rude, thought Badan Babu. But, before he could say anything further, the other man threw a counter question at him, in an irrelevant manner.

'Do you write?'

'Write? You mean—fiction?'

'Fiction or non-fiction, it does not matter. You see, that is something I have never been able to do. And yet, so many adventures, such a lot of experience and research . . . all this should be written and recorded for posterity.'

Experience? Research? What was the man talking about? 'How many kinds of travellers have you seen?'

His questions were really quite meaningless. How many people were lucky enough to have seen even one traveller?

Badan Babu said, 'I didn't even know travellers could be of more than one kind!'

'Why, there are at least three kinds. Anyone could tell you that! Those who travel on water, those who travel on land and those who travel in the sky. Vasco-da-Gama, Captain Scott and Columbus fall into the first category; and in the second are Hiuen Tsang, Mungo Park, Livingstone and even our own globe-trotter, Umesh Bhattacharya.

'And in the sky—say, Professor Picquard, who climbed 50,000 feet in a balloon and that youngster, Gagarin. But all of these are ordinary travellers. The kind of traveller I am talking about doesn't move on water or land or even in the sky.'

'Where does he move then?'

'Time.'

'What?'

'He moves in time. A journey into the past. A sojourn in the future. Roaming around freely in both. I don't worry too much about the present.'

Badan Babu began to see the light. 'You're talking about H.G. Wells, aren't you? The time machine? Wasn't that a contraption like a cycle with two handles? One would take you to the past and the other to the future? Wasn't a film made on this story?'

The man laughed contemptuously.

'That? That was only a story. I am talking of real life. My own experiences. My own machine. It's a far cry from a fictitious story written by an Englishman.'

Somewhere a steamer blew its horn.

Badan Babu started and pulled his chadar closer. In just a few minutes from now, darkness would engulf everything. Only the little lights on those boats would stay visible.

In the quickly gathering dusk Badan Babu looked at the newcomer once more. The last rays of the sun shone in his eyes.

The man raised his face to the sky and, after a few moments of silence, said, 'It's all quite funny, really. Three hundred years ago, right here by this bench, a crocodile happened to be stretched in the sun. There was a crane perched on its head. A Dutch ship with huge sails stood where that small boat is now tied. A sailor came out on the deck and shot at the crocodile with a rifle. One shot was enough to kill it. The crane managed to fly away, but dropped a feather in my lap. Here it is.'

He produced a dazzling white feather from his shoulder bag and gave it to Badan Babu.

'What . . . are these reddish specks?'

Badan Babu's voice sounded hoarse.

'Drops of blood from the injured crocodile fell on the bird.'

Badan Babu returned the feather.

The light in the man's eyes had dimmed. Visibility was getting poorer by the second. There had been loose bunches of grass and leaves floating in the river. Now they were practically invisible. The water, the earth and the sky had all become hazy and indistinct.

'Can you tell what this is?'

Badan Babu took the little object in his hand—a small triangular piece, pointed at one end.

'Two thousand years ago . . . right in the middle of the river—near that floating buoy—a ship with a beautifully patterned sail was making its way to the sea. It was probably a commercial vessel, going to Bali or some such place, to look for business. Standing here with the west wind blowing, I could hear all its thirty-two oars splashing in the water.'

'You?'

'Yes, who else? I was hiding behind a banyan tree in this same spot.'

'Why were you hiding?'

'I had to. I didn't know the place was so full of unknown dangers. History books don't often tell you these things.'

'You mean wild animals? Tigers?'

'Worse than tigers. Men. There was a barbarian, about that high,' he pointed to his waist. 'Blunt-nosed, dark as darkness. Earrings hung from his ears, a ring from his nose, his body was covered with tattoo marks. He held a bow and an arrow in his hand. The arrow had a poisonous tip.'

'Really?'

'Yes, every word I utter is the truth.'

'You saw it all yourself?'

'Listen to the rest of the story. It was the month of April. A storm had been brewing for some time. Then it started. Oh, what a storm it was, the likes of which I have never seen again! That beautiful ship disappeared amidst the roaring waves before my eyes.'

'And then?'

'One solitary figure managed to make it to the shore, riding on a broken wooden plank, dodging the hungry sharks and alligators. But as soon as he got off that plank . . . oh, my God!'

'What?'

'You should have seen what that barbarian did to him . . . but then, I didn't stay till the end. An arrow had come and hit the trunk of the banyan tree. I picked it up and pressed the switch to return to the present.'

Badan Babu did not know whether to laugh or cry. How could that little machine have such magical powers? How was it possible?

The newcomer seemed to read his mind.

'This machine here,' he said, 'has these two rubber tubes. All you need to do is put these into your ears. This switch on the right will take you to the future and the one on the left will take you to the past. The little wheel with a needle has dates and years written on it. You can fix the exact date you wish to travel to. Of course, I must admit there are times when it misses the mark by about twenty years. But that doesn't make too much difference. It's a cheap model, you see. So it's not all that accurate.'

'Cheap?' This time Badan Babu was truly surprised.

'Yes, cheap only in a financial sense. Five thousand years of scientific knowledge and expertise went into its making. People think science has progressed only in the west. And that nothing has happened in this country. I tell you, a tremendous lot has indeed happened here, but how many know about it? We were never a nation to show off our knowledge, were we? The true artist has always stayed in the background, hasn't he? Look at our history. Does anyone know the names of the painters who drew on the walls of Ajanta? Who carved the temple of Ellora out of ancient hills? Who created the Bhairavi raga? Who wrote the Vedas? The Mahabharata is said to have been written by Vyasa and the Ramayana by Valmiki. But does anyone know of those hundreds of people who worked on the original texts? Or, for that matter, of those that actually contributed to their creation? The scientists in the west have often made a name for themselves by working on complex mathematical formulae. Do you know the starting point of mathematics?'

'Starting point? What starting point?' Badan Babu did not know.

'Zero,' said the man.

'Zero?'

'Yes, zero.'

Badan Babu was taken aback. The man went on.

'One, two, three, four, five, six, seven, eight, nine, zero. These are the only digits used, aren't they? Zero, by itself, means nothing. But the minute you put it next to one, it gives you ten: one more than nine. Magic! Makes the mind boggle, it does. Yet, we have accepted it as a matter of course. All mathematical formulae are based on these nine digits and zero. Addition, subtraction, multiplication, division, fractions, decimals, algebra, arithmetic—even atoms, rockets, relativity—nothing can work without these ten numbers. And do you know where this zero came from? From India. It went to West Asia first, then to Europe and from there to the whole world. See what I mean? Do you know how the system worked before?'

Badan Babu shook his head. How very limited his own knowledge was!

'They used the Roman system,' said the newcomer. 'There were no digits. All they had were letters. One was I, two was II, three was III, but four became a combination of two letters, IV. Five was again just one letter, V. There was no logic in that system. How would you write 1962? It would simply mean writing four different digits, right? Do you know how many letters you'd need in Roman?'

'How many?'

'Seven, MCMLXII. Does that make any sense at all? If you had to write 888, you would normally need only three digits. To write that in the Roman style, you'd need a dozen. DCCCLXXXVIII. Can you imagine how long it would have taken scientists to write their huge formulae? They would have all gone prematurely grey, or—worse—totally bald! And the whole business of going to the moon would have been delayed by at least a thousand years. Just think—some unknown, anonymous man from our own country changed the whole concept of mathematics!'

He stopped for breath.

The church clock in the distance struck six.

Why did it suddenly seem brighter?

Badan Babu looked at the eastern sky and saw that the moon had risen behind the roof of the Grand Hotel.

'Things haven't changed,' the man continued. 'There are still plenty of people in our country who are quite unknown and will probably always stay that way. But their knowledge of science is no less than that of the scientists of the west. They do not often work in laboratories or need papers and books or any other paraphernalia. All they do is think and work out solutions to problems—all in their mind.'

'Are you one of those people?' asked Badan Babu softly.

'No. But I was lucky enough to meet such a man. Not here, of course. I used to travel a lot on foot when I was younger. Went often to the mountains. That is where I met this man. A remarkable character. His name was Ganitananda. But he didn't just think. He wrote things down. All his mathematical calculations were done on the stones strewn about within a radius of thirty miles from where he lived. Every stone and boulder was scribbled on with a piece of chalk. He had learnt the art of travelling in time from his guru. It was from Ganitananda that I learnt that there had once been a peak higher than the Everest by about 5,000 feet. Forty-seven thousand years ago, a devastating earthquake had made half of it go deeper into the ground. The same earthquake caused a crack in a mountain, from which appeared a waterfall. The river that is now flowing before us began its course from this waterfall.'

Strange! Oh, how strange it all was!

Badan Babu wiped his forehead with a corner of his chadar and said, 'Did you get that machine from him?'

'Yes. Well, no, he didn't actually give it to me. But he did tell me of the components that went into making it. I collected them all and made the machine myself. These tubes here are not really made of rubber. It's the bark of a tree that's found only in the hills. I didn't have to go to a shop or an artisan to get even a single part made. The whole thing is made of natural stuff. I made the markings on the dial myself. But, possibly because it's hand-made, it goes out of order sometimes. The switch meant for the future hasn't been working for sometime.'

'Have you travelled to the future?'

'Yes, once I did. But not too far. Only up to the thirtieth century.'

'What did you see?'

'There wasn't much to see. I was the only person walking along a huge road. A weird-looking vehicle appeared from somewhere and nearly ran me over. I did not try going into the future again.'

'And how far into the past have you travelled?'

'That's another catch. This machine cannot take me to the very beginning of creation.'

'Indeed?'

'Yes. I tried very hard, but the farthest I could go back to was when the reptiles had already arrived.'

Badan Babu's throat felt a little dry.

'What reptiles?' he asked. 'Snakes?'

'Oh no, no. Snakes are pretty recent.'

'Then?'

'Well, you know . . . things like the brontosaurus, tyrannosaurus . . . dinosaurs.'

'You mean you've been to other countries as well?'

'Ah, you're making the same mistake. Why should I have had to go to other countries? Do you think our own did not have these things?'

'Did it?'

'Of course it did! Right here. By the side of this bench.'

A cold shiver ran down Badan Babu's spine.

'The Ganga did not exist then,' said the man. 'This place was full of uneven, stony mounds and a lot of wild plants and creepers. There was a dirty pond where you can now see that jetty. I saw a will-o'-the-wisp rise over it and burn brightly, swaying from side to side. In its light, suddenly, I could see a pair of brilliant red eyes. You've seen pictures of a Chinese dragon, haven't you? This was a bit like that. I had seen its picture in a book. So I knew this was what was called a stegosaurus. It was crossing the pond, chewing on some leaves. I knew it would not attack me for it was a herbivorous animal. But, even so, I nearly froze with fear and was about to press the switch to return to the present, when I heard the flutter of wings right over my head. I looked up and saw a pterodactyl—a cross between a bird, an animal and a bat—swoop upon the stegosaurus. My eyes then fell on a large rock lying nearby and the reason for such aggression became clear. Inside a big crack in the rock lay a shiny, round, white egg. The pterodactyl's egg. Even though I was scared stiff, I couldn't resist the temptation. The two animals began fighting and I pocketed the egg . . . ha, ha, ha, ha!'

Badan Babu did not join in the laughter. Could this kind of thing really happen outside the realm of fiction?

'I would have allowed you to test my machine, but . . .'

A nerve in Badan Babu's forehead began to throb. He swallowed hard. 'But what?'

'The chances of getting a satisfactory result are very remote.'

'Wh-why?'

'But you can try your luck. At least you don't stand to lose anything.'

Badan Babu bent forward. Dear God in heaven—please don't let me be disappointed!

The man tucked the tubes into Badan Babu's ears, pressed a switch and grabbed his right wrist.

'I need to watch your pulse.'

Badan Babu whispered nervously, 'Past? Or the future?'

'The past. 6,000 bc. Shut your eyes as tightly as you can.' Badan Babu obeyed and sat in eager anticipation for nearly a whole minute with his eyes closed. Then he said, 'Why, nothing seems to be . . . happening!'

The man switched the machine off and took it back.

'The chances were one in a million.'

'Why?'

'It would have worked only if the number of hairs on your head was exactly the same as mine.'

Badan Babu felt like a deflated balloon. How sad. How very sad he had to lose such an opportunity!

The newcomer put his hand inside his bag again and brought out something else.

Everything was quite clearly visible now in the moonlight.

'May I hold it in my hand?' asked Badan Babu, unable to stop himself. The other man offered him the shiny, round object.

It was quite heavy, and its surface remarkably smooth.

'All right. Time to go now. It's getting late.'

Badan Babu returned the egg. Heaven knew what else this man had seen. 'Hope you're coming here again tomorrow,' said Badan Babu.

'Let's see. There's such an awful lot to be done. I am yet to test the validity of all that the history books talk about. First of all, I must examine how Calcutta came into being. What a hue and cry has been raised over Job Charnock . . . ! Allow me to take my leave today. Goodbye!'

Badan Babu reached the tram stop and boarded a tram. Then he slipped his hand into his pocket.

His heart stood still.

The wallet had gone.

There was nothing he could do except make an excuse and get down from the tram immediately.

As he began walking towards his house he felt like kicking himself. 'Now I know what happened,' he thought. 'When I closed my eyes and he held my hand . . . what a fool I made of myself!'

It was past 8 p.m. by the time he reached home.

Biltu's face lit up at the sight of his father.

By then, Badan Babu had started to feel more relaxed.

'I'll tell you a good story today,' he said, unbuttoning his shirt.

'Really? You mean it? It won't be a flop like all those others . . .?'

'No, no. I really mean it.'

'What kind of story, Baba?'

'The Pterodactyl's Egg. And many more. It won't finish in a day.' If one considered carefully, the material he had collected today to make up stories for Biltu, to bring a few moments of joy into his life, was surely worth at least fifty-five rupees and thirty-two paise?

Translated by Gopa Majumdar
First published in Bengali in 1962

The Hungry Septopus

There it was again—the sound of someone rattling the knocker on my front door. I gave an involuntary exclamation of annoyance. This was the fourth interruption this evening. How was a man expected to work? There was no sign of Kartik, either. He had left for the market a long time ago.

I was forced to leave my desk and open the door myself. It took me a while to recognize the man who was standing outside. When I did, I felt profoundly startled. Why, it was Kanti Babu!

'What a surprise! Do come in,' I said.

'So you have recognized me?'

'Yes, but it wasn't easy.'

I showed him into the living room and offered him a seat. I had not seen him in ten years. His appearance had undergone a remarkable change in that time. In 1950, I had seen the same man in a forest in Assam, jumping around with a magnifying glass in his hand. He was nearly fifty then, but all his hair was still black. He bubbled all the time with energy and endless enthusiasm. Such vitality would be hard to find even among the young.

'Are you still interested in orchids?' Kanti Babu asked.

There was an orchid in a pot resting on my window-sill. It was, in fact, a gift from Kanti Babu himself. I wasn't really interested in plants any more. It was Kanti Babu who had once aroused my curiosity about them. But after he went abroad, I had lost my interest gradually. There were other hobbies and interests, too, but I had given them up as well. Now my only passion was writing.

Things had changed over the years. Now it was possible to make money just by writing. To tell the truth, my last three books had brought me an income that was almost wholly sufficient to meet my household expenses. Not that I had a big house to run—there was only my widowed mother to take care of, and my servant, Kartik. I still had a job, but was hoping to give it up if my writing continued to bring me success. I would write full-time, and when I could take a break, I would travel. That was my plan.

Suddenly, Kanti Babu shivered. 'Are you feeling cold? Shall I close the window? The winter in Calcutta this year . . .' I began.

'No, no. You saw me shiver? It happens sometimes. I am getting old, you see. So my nerves are no longer . . .'

I wanted to ask a lot of questions. Kartik had returned. I asked him to bring us tea.

'I won't take up a lot of your time,' said Kanti Babu. 'I came across one of your novels recently. So I got in touch with your publisher, took your address, and well, here I am. There is a special reason why I had to see you.'

'Yes? Tell me all about it. But before you do, there's so much I want to know. When did you return? Where were you all these years? Where are you now?'

'I returned two years ago. Before that I was in America. Now I live in Barasat.'

'Barasat?'

'I bought a house there.'

'Does it have a garden?'

'Yes.'

'And a greenhouse?'

In the house that I had visited before, Kanti Babu had a lovely greenhouse, in which he tended, with great care, several of his rare plants. I had seen such a large number of strange and weird plants there! Of orchids alone he had more than sixty varieties. One could easily pass a whole day just looking at and enjoying their different colours and other characteristics.

Kanti Babu paused for a second before saying, 'Yes, there is a greenhouse.'

'So you're still as mad about plants as you were ten years ago?'

'Yes.'

Kanti Babu was staring at the opposite wall. Automatically, I followed his gaze. The wall was covered by the skin of a Royal Bengal tiger, including the head.

'Does it seem familiar to you?' I asked.

'Is it that same tiger?'

'Yes. See that hole close to its left ear? That's where the bullet passed through.'

'You were a remarkable shot. Can you still shoot with such perfect accuracy?'

'I don't know. I haven't used my gun for a long time. I gave up shikar more than five years ago.'

'Why?'

'I had had enough. I mean, I had killed enough animals. After all, I'm not getting any younger. It was time to stop destroying wild life.'

'Really? So have you stopped eating meat? Are you now a vegetarian?'

'No. No, I am not.'

'Why not? Killing a wild animal is just plain killing. Say you destroy a tiger, or a crocodile, or a bison, and then you hang its head, or just its horns on your wall. What happens? Your room acquires a special air, some of your visitors are horrified, others are impressed, and you can relive the moments of your youthful adventures. That's all. But think of the chicken, goats and fish you are not just killing, but also eating every day. It's more than mere destruction, isn't it? Why, it's the digestion of a living creature!'

There was really nothing I could say in reply. So I remained silent. Kartik brought us tea.

Kanti Babu remained lost in thought for a few moments, then suddenly shivered again and picked up his cup. 'It isn't unusual for one particular animal to eat another. Nature made things that way. See that gecko lying in wait over there?' he asked.

Over a calendar on the wall sprawled a gecko, staring unblinkingly at an insect, just a couple of inches away from its mouth. Then it moved slowly, ever so slowly, before springing forward in one leap and swallowing its prey.

'There!' exclaimed Kanti Babu. 'That takes care of his dinner. Eating is all most creatures are concerned with. Just think about it. A tiger would eat a man, a man would eat a goat, and a goat would eat anything! Doesn't it all seem terribly wild, primitive and violent? Yet, that is how nature wills it. Stop this cycle, and the whole natural order would be thrown out of gear.'

'Perhaps being a vegetarian is more . . . er . . . civilized?'

'Who told you that? You think leaves and vegetables and plants are lifeless? Do they not live?'

'Yes, of course they do. Thanks to Jagadish Bose and you, I can never forget about the life of plants. But it's different, isn't it? I mean, animals and plants are not the same, surely?'

'Oh? You think there are a lot of differences between the two?'

'Aren't there? A tree cannot move, walk, make a noise, express thoughts or feelings—in fact, there's no way to find out if a tree has a mind at all. Isn't that true?'

Kanti Babu opened his mouth to speak, then shut it without saying a word. Silently, he finished his tea and sat with his head bowed. Eventually, when he looked up and met my eyes, I suddenly felt afraid to see the look of tragic uncertainty in his. Truly, the change in the man was extraordinary.

When he spoke, his voice was quiet. 'Parimal,' he said, 'I live twenty-one miles away. And I am fifty-eight years old. But despite my age and the long distance I had to travel, I took the trouble to get your address and visit you here. Surely I don't need to tell you now that there is a very important reason behind my visit? You can see that, can't you? Or have you lost all your intelligence in trying to produce popular fiction? Are you looking at me right now and thinking: here's a new type—I can use him in a story?'

I had to look away, flushing with embarrassment. Kanti Babu was right. The thought of using him as a character had indeed occurred to me.

'Remember this,' he went on. 'If you lose touch with the realities of life, whatever you write will simply be lies, empty and hollow. Besides, no matter how lively your imagination is, what emerges from it can never match the surprises real life can come up with. Anyway, I didn't come here to give you a lecture. I came, to tell you the truth, to ask a favour.'

Kanti Babu glanced at the tiger again. What favour was he talking about?.

'Do you still have your gun, or did you get rid of it?'

I gave a slight start, and glanced quickly at him. Why did he mention my gun?

'No, I have still got it. But it may well be rusted. Why do you ask?'

'Can you come to my house tomorrow, with your gun?'

I scanned his face. No, there was not even the slightest sign to imply that he might be joking.

'Of course,' he added, 'you'll need bullets, too. The gun alone won't be good enough.'

I could not immediately think of anything to say in reply to Kanti Babu's request. It even occurred to me once that perhaps he had gone mad, although one could not be sure. He was certainly given to crazy whims. Or else why should he have risked his life in a jungle to look for rare plants?

'I can quite easily take my gun, there's no problem,' I said finally. 'But I am dying to know the reason why it might be needed. Is there an animal bothering the residents in your area? Or perhaps there are burglars and thieves?'

'I will explain everything once you get there. Who knows, we might not even have to use the gun. But even if we do, I can assure you that you will not be arrested!'

Kanti Babu rose to his feet. Then he came closer and laid a hand on my shoulder. 'I came to you because when I last saw you, you had struck me as a man who would welcome a new experience, very much like myself. Besides, I don't know many other people. The number of people I actually visited was always small, and now I see virtually no one. The handful of people I could think of contacting are all very different, you see. None of them has the special qualities that you have.'

Just for a minute, I could feel, in the sudden tightening of my muscles, the same thrill that the mere mention of an adventure used to bring, all those years ago.

'When would you like me to get there? How would I find your house?' I asked.

'I'll tell you. Just go straight down Jessore Road until you get to the railway station in Barasat. Then you need to find a lake called Madhumurali Deeghi. It's another four miles from the station. Anyone there will tell you where it is. Next to the lake is an old and abandoned indigo factory. My house is right behind it. Do you have a car?'

'No, but a friend of mine has.'

'Who is this friend?'

'His name is Abhijit. He and I were in college together.'

'What kind of a man is he? Do I know him?'

'No, I don't think so. But he's a good man. I mean, if you're wondering whether he's reliable, I can tell you that he is. Totally.'

'Very well. You may bring him with you. But please make sure that you reach my house before evening. It's important, needless to say.'

Kanti Babu left. Since I did not have a telephone at home, I went to our local chemist just across the road to ring Abhijit. 'Come to my house at once,' I said to him, 'I've got something urgent to discuss.'

'Urgent? You mean you've got a new story you'd like to read out to me? I'll go to sleep again, let me tell you!'

'No, no. It's not about a story. Something quite different.'

'What is it? Why are you speaking so softly?'

'I've come to know about a pup. Mastiff. The man selling it is sitting in my house, right now.'

I knew Abhijit would not stir out of his house unless I could lure him out by talking of dogs. He had eleven dogs. Each one of them belonged to a different species. Three of those dogs had won prizes. Even five years ago, things were different. But now, Abhijit thought and dreamt of nothing but dogs.

Apart from his love of dogs, there was something else that made him very special. Abhijit had unflinching faith in my talent and judgement. When my first novel was turned down by publishers, it was Abhijit who provided the money to publish it privately. 'Mind you,' he told me, 'I know nothing of books and literature. But if you have written this book, it cannot possibly be absolute garbage. These publishers are complete idiots!' As it happened, things turned out quite well. The book was well received and sold a large number of copies. As a result, Abhijit's faith in me grew stronger.

He turned up soon enough, and gave me a painful punch when he discovered that I had lied about the pup. However, seeing his enthusiasm regarding the real reason for calling him out, I soon forgot the pain.

'We haven't had an outing for long time, have we?' Abhijit said eagerly. 'The last time was when we went snipe-shooting in Shonarpur. But who is this man? What's it all about? Why don't you come clean, my friend?'

'How can I, when he told me nothing? Besides, a little mystery is a good thing. I like it. It should give us the chance to use our imagination.'

'All right, but who is this man? What does he do?'

'His name is Kanticharan Chatterjee. Does that mean anything to you? He was once a professor of botany. Used to teach in Scottish Church College. Then he gave up his job and began looking for rare plants in jungles and forests. Sometimes he wrote about them. He had a wonderful collection of plants, particularly of orchids.'

'How did you get to meet him?'

'I met him in a forest bungalow in Assam. I was there to hunt down a tiger. He was hunting everywhere for a nepenthes.'

'Hunting for what?'

'Nepenthes. It's the botanical name for what is commonly called a pitcher-plant. You can get it in the forests of Assam. It eats insects. I did not see it myself, but Kanti Babu told me about it.'

'Eats insects? A plant? It . . . chomps on insects?'

'You did not ever study botany, did you?'

'No.'

'I have seen pictures of this plant. There is no reason to sound so sceptical. It exists.'

'OK. What happened next?'

'Very little. I finished my shikar and came away. Kanti Babu stayed on. I have no idea whether he found that plant or not. What I was afraid of was that he might be killed by a wild animal, or bitten by a snake. When he set off to look for a plant, he thought of nothing else, not even of the dangers in a forest. After coming back to Calcutta, I met him only a couple of times. But I thought of him often, because for a time I developed quite a passion for orchids. Kanti Babu offered to bring me some good quality orchids from America.'

'America? This man went to America?'

'Yes. One of his articles was published in an English botanical journal. It made him quite well known in those circles. Then he was invited to a conference of botanists in America. That was in 1951, or was it '52? That's when I last saw him.'

'Was he there all this while? What was he doing?'

'No idea. Hopefully, he'll tell us tomorrow.'

'He's not . . . ? I mean, is he perhaps a little eccentric?'

'Not any more than you. I can tell you that much. You fill your life with dogs. He fills his with plants.'

We were now going down Jessore Road in the direction of Barasat, travelling in Abhijit's Standard.

There was a third passenger in the car. It was Abhijit's dog, Badshah. It was my own fault, really. I should have known that, unless otherwise instructed, Abhijit was bound to bring one of his eleven dogs.

Badshah was a Rampur hound, a ferocious animal. He had spread himself out on the back seat and was sitting very comfortably as its sole occupant, looking out of the window at the wide, open rice fields. Each time a stray dog from a local village came into view, Badshah gave a mild, contemptuous growl.

When I saw Abhijit arrive with Badshah, I tried to put up a faint protest. At this, Abhijit said, 'I don't have a great deal of faith in your skill, you see. That's why I brought him along. You haven't handled your gun for years. Should there be trouble, Badshah would probably be of far more use than you. He has an extraordinary sense of smell and is quite, quite fearless.'

Kanti Babu's house was not difficult to find. By the time we got there, it was half past two. A driveway led to the house, which was built in the style of a bungalow. Behind the house was an open space. A huge old shirish tree stood where this space ended. By its side was a structure with a tin roof. It looked like a small factory. In front of the house was a garden, at the end of which a long area was covered by another tin roof. A number of shining glass cases stood there in a row.

Kanti Babu came out to greet us, then frowned slightly as he saw Badshah. 'Is he a trained dog?' he asked.

'He'll listen to everything I say,' Abhijit told him. 'But if there's an untrained dog in the vicinity, and Badshah sees him, well, I couldn't tell you what he might do then. Is there such a dog?'

'No. But for the moment, please tie your dog to one of the bars on that window.'

Abhijit gave me a sidelong glance, winked and did as he was told, like an obedient child. Badshah protested a couple of times, but did not seem to mind too much.

We sat on cane chairs on the front veranda. 'My servant Prayag injured his right hand. So I made tea for you and put it in a flask. Let me know when you'd like some.'

It was a very quiet and peaceful place. I could hear nothing but a few chirping birds. How could there be serious danger lurking somewhere in a place like this? I felt a little foolish, sitting with the gun in my hands. So I propped it up against a wall.

Abhijit could never sit still. He was very much a 'city' man; the beauties of nature offered by the countryside, the leaves on a peepal tree, trembling in a slight breeze, or the call of an unknown bird, did nothing to move him. He looked around, shifted restlessly, and suddenly blurted out, 'Parimal told me that you once went to a forest in Assam looking for some weird plant, and nearly got gobbled up by a tiger. Is that true?'

This was something else Abhijit was wont to do. He could not speak without exaggerating everything. I felt afraid Kanti Babu might be offended. But he just laughed and said, 'Do you always think of a tiger whenever you think of danger? But that's not surprising, many people would do that. No, I never came across a tiger. Leeches in the forest caused me some discomfort, but that was nothing serious, either.'

'Did you find that plant?'

The same question had occurred to me, too.

'Which plant?'

'Oh, that . . . pot? . . . No, pitcher-plant or something?'

'Yes. Nepenthes. Yes, I did find it and, in fact, have still got it. I'll show it to you. I am no longer interested in ordinary plants; now I restrict myself only to carnivorous ones. I've got rid of most of my orchids, too.'

Kanti Babu rose and went indoors. Abhijit and I exchanged glances. Carnivorous plants? Plants that ate meat? A few pages and pictures I had studied fifteen years ago in a book on botany dimly wafted before my eyes.

When Kanti Babu re-emerged, there was a bottle in his hand. It contained house-crickets and a few other insects, still alive. The stopper on the bottle, I noticed, had tiny holes, like those on a pepper-shaker.

'Feeding time!' said Kanti Babu with a smile. 'Come with me.'

We followed Kanti Babu out to the long strip of ground at the back of his garden which contained the glass cases.

Each of the cases held a different plant. I had seen none of them before.

'Except for nepenthes,' Kanti Babu told us, 'not a single one is from our country. One of them is from Nepal, another from Africa. The rest are virtually all from Central America.'

'If that is so,' Abhijit asked, 'how do they survive here? I mean, does the soil here have . . .?'

'No. These plants have nothing to do with the soil.'

'No?'

'No. They do not derive sustenance from the soil. Just as human beings can survive anywhere in the world as long as they are fed properly, so can these plants. Adequate and appropriate food is all they need, no matter where they are kept.'

Kanti Babu stopped before a glass case. In it was an extraordinary plant. Its leaves were about two inches long, their edges were white and were serrated, as if they had teeth.

The front of the case had a kind of door, though it was big enough only for the mouth of the bottle to go through. It was bolted from outside. Kanti Babu unbolted it. Then he removed the stopper from the bottle and quickly slipped the bottle through the 'door'. A house-cricket leapt out into the case. Kanti Babu removed the bottle and replaced the stopper. Then he pushed the bolt back into place.

The house-cricket moved restlessly for a few seconds. Then it went and sat on a leaf. At once, the leaf folded itself and caught the insect. To my complete amazement, I saw that the two sets of teeth had closed in and clamped on each other so tightly that the poor house-cricket had no chance of escaping. I had no idea nature could set such a strange, horrific trap. Certainly, I had never seen anything like it before.

Abhijit was the first to speak. 'Is there any guarantee,' he asked hoarsely, 'that the insect would sit on a leaf?'

'Of course. You see, the plant exudes a smell that attracts insects. This plant is called the Venus fly trap. I brought it from Central America. If you go through books on botany, you may find pictures of this plant.'

I was still staring in speechless amazement at the house-cricket. At first, it was struggling to get out, but now it was just lying in its trap, quite lifeless. The pressure from the leaf's 'teeth' appeared to be getting stronger. This plant was every bit as violent as a gecko.

Abhijit laughed dryly. 'If I could keep such a plant in my house, I'd be safe from insects. At least, I wouldn't have to use DDT to kill cockroaches!'

'No, this particular plant couldn't eat—and digest—a cockroach. Its leaves are too small. There's a different plant to deal with cockroaches. Come this way,' invited Kanti Babu.

The next glass case had a plant whose long, large leaves looked like those of a lily. Each leaf had a strange object hanging from its tip. It looked like a pitcher-shaped bag, complete with a lid. I had already seen its picture. It was not difficult to recognize it.

'This,' Kanti Babu declared, 'is nepenthes, or a pitcher-plant. It requires bigger creatures to survive. When I first found it, there were the crushed remains of a small bird in one of those pitchers.'

'Oh my God!' Abhijit exclaimed. The faint contempt his tone had held earlier was quickly disappearing. 'What does it eat now?'

'Cockroaches, caterpillars, even butterflies. Once I found a rat in my rat-trap. I fed it to that plant, it didn't seem to mind. But sometimes these plants eat more than they can digest, and then they die. They're a greedy lot. There are times when they just can't figure out how much strain their own digestive system can bear!'

We moved on to look at other plants, our astonishment mounting higher. There were butterwort, sundew, bladderwort, arozia—plants whose pictures I had seen. But the others were totally new, completely astounding, perfectly incredible. Kanti Babu had collected at least twenty different species of carnivorous plants, some of which, he said, were not included in any other collection in the world.

The prettiest amongst these was the sundew. It had fine strands of hair around its leaves. A droplet glistened on the tip of each hair. Kanti Babu tied a tiny piece of meat—no bigger than a peppercorn—to a thread and took it close to a leaf. We could see, even from a distance, all the hair rise at once, grasping at the piece of meat greedily. But Kanti Babu removed his hand before the meat could be taken.

'If it did get that piece of meat, it would have crushed it, just like the fly trap. Then it would have absorbed whatever nourishment it could get, and rejected the chewed pulp. Not really that different from the way you and I eat meat, is it?'

We left the shed and came out to the garden. The shirish tree was casting a long shadow. I looked at my watch. It was half past four.

'You will find mention of most of these plants in your books,' said Kanti Babu. 'But no one knows about the one I am now going to show you. It will never get written about, unless I write about it myself. In fact, I called you over here really to show you this plant. Come, Parimal. Come with me, Abhijit Babu.'

This time, Kanti Babu led the way to what looked like a factory behind the shirish tree. The door, made of tin, was locked. There was a window on either side. Kanti Babu pushed one of these open, peered in, then withdrew. 'Have a look!' he said.

Abhijit and I placed ourselves at the window. The room was only partially lit by the sunlight that came in through two skylights set high on the opposite wall.

The object the room contained hardly looked like a plant, or a tree. As a matter of fact, it was more like a weird animal—one with large, thick tentacles. A closer look, however, did reveal a trunk. It rose from the ground by several feet to end at what might be described as a head. About eighteen inches below this head, surrounding it, were tentacles. I counted them. There were seven.

The bark of the tree was pale, but it had round brown marks all over.

The tentacles were hanging limply, resting on the ground. The whole object appeared lifeless. Yet, I could feel my flesh creep.

I noticed something else, as my eyes got used to the dark. The floor around the plant was littered with the feathers of some bird.

Neither Abhijit nor I could speak. How long the silence continued, I cannot tell. It was Kanti Babu's voice that broke it. 'The plant is asleep at this moment. It's almost time for it to wake up.'

'Is it really a plant?' Abhijit asked incredulously.

'Well, it has grown out of the ground. What else would you call it? It doesn't, however, behave like a plant. No botanical reference book, or encyclopaedia, could give you a suitable name for it.'

'What do you call it?'

'Septopus. Because it has seven tentacles.'

We began walking back to the house.

'Where did you find it?' I asked.

'There is a dense forest near Lake Nicaragua in Central America. That's where I found it.'

'You must have had to search the area pretty thoroughly?'

'Yes, but I knew that the plant was available there. You haven't heard of Professor Dunston, have you? He was a botanist and an explorer. He died in Central America, looking for rare plants. But his death was quite mysterious. No one ever found his body, no one knows exactly how he died. This particular plant was mentioned in his diary, towards the very end.

'So I went to Nicaragua at the first opportunity. When I got to Guatemala, I heard people talking about this plant. They called it the Satan's Tree. Eventually, I saw a number of these plants. I saw them eat monkeys, armadillos, and other animals. Then, after many days of careful searching, I found a small sapling and brought it with me. You can see how big it has grown in two years.'

'What does it eat here?'

'Whatever I give it. Sometimes I catch rats in my trap to feed it. Prayag has been told to get hold of dogs and cats that get run over. It has eaten those, too. Sometimes I give it the same things that you and I would eat—chicken or goat. Recently, its appetite seems to have grown quite a lot. I can't keep up with it. When it wakes up in the evening, it gets really restless. Yesterday, something happened . . . it was just terrible. Prayag had gone to feed it a chicken. It has to be fed in much the same way as an elephant. The head of this plant has a kind of lid. First of all, it opens its lid. Then it grabs the food with one of its tentacles, as an elephant picks up its food with its trunk, and places it into the opening in the head. After that, it remains quiet for a while. When it starts swinging its tentacles, that means it wants to eat some more.

'So far, a couple of chickens or a lamb was proving to be quite sufficient for a day's meal. Things have changed since yesterday. Prayag fed it the second chicken, shut the door and came away. When the plant gets restless, it strikes its tentacles against the floor, which creates a noise. Prayag heard this noise even after the second chicken had disappeared. So he went back to investigate.

'I was in my room at the time, making entries in my diary. A sudden scream made me come running here to see what was going on. What I saw was horrible. The plant had grabbed Prayag's right hand with a tentacle. Prayag was trying desperately to free his hand, but another tentacle was raised and making its way to him.

'I had to pick up my stick and strike at that tentacle with all my might, and then put both my arms round Prayag to pull him back. Yes, I rescued him all right, but what I saw the plant do next left me feeling positively alarmed. It had managed to tear off a piece of flesh from Prayag's hand. I saw it remove the lid on its head and put it in. I saw it with my own eyes!'

We had reached the front veranda once again. Kanti Babu sat down on a chair. Then he took out a handkerchief and wiped his forehead. 'I had no idea that the Septopus would wish to attack a human being. But now . . . since there has been such an indication . . . I don't have any option. I have got to kill it. I decided to do so immediately after I saw Prayag being attacked, and I put poison in its food. But that plant has such amazing intelligence, it picked the food up with a tentacle, but threw it away instantly. Now the only thing I can do is shoot it. Parimal, now do you understand why I called you here?'

I remained quiet for a few moments. Then I said, 'Do you know for sure that it will die if it's shot?'

'No, I cannot be sure. But I do believe that it has a brain. Besides, I have proof that it can think and judge. I have gone near it so many times, it has never attacked me. It seems to know me well, just as a dog knows its master. It dislikes Prayag because sometimes Prayag has, in the past, teased it and played tricks on it. He has tempted it with food, then refused to feed it. I have seen Prayag take its food close to its tentacles, then withdraw it before the plant could grasp it. Yes, it most definitely has a brain, and that is where it should be, in its head. You must aim and fire at the spot from which those tentacles have grown.'

This time, Abhijit spoke. 'That's not a problem!' he said casually. 'It will only take a minute. Parimal, get your gun.'

Kanti Babu raised a hand to stop Abhijit. 'If the prey is asleep,' is it right to kill it? What does your hunting code say, Parimal?'

'It is quite unethical to kill a sleeping animal. In this case, the prey is incapable of running away. There is no question of killing it until it wakes up.'

Kanti Babu rose and poured tea out of a flask. The Septopus woke within fifteen minutes of our finishing the tea.

Badshah, in the living room, had grown increasingly restive while we were talking. The sound of his keening and scratching noises made both Abhijit and me jump up and go inside. We found Badshah straining at his leash and trying to bite his collar. Abhijit began to calm him down, but at that moment, we heard a swishing noise coming from the factory. It was accompanied by a sharp, pungent smell. It is difficult to describe it. When I was a child, I had had my tonsils removed. Before the operation, I had smelt chloroform. It was somewhat similar.

Kanti Babu swept into the living room. 'Come on, it's time!' he said.

'What is that smell?' I asked.

'It's coming from the Septopus. That's the smell it spreads to attract ani . . .'

Kanti Babu could not finish. Badshah broke free with a mighty pull at the leash, knocked Abhijit out of the way, and leapt in the direction of the factory, to look for the source of the smell.

'Oh God, no!' cried Abhijit, picking himself up and running after his dog.

I picked up my loaded gun and followed him quickly. When I got there only a few seconds later, Badshah was springing up to the open window, ignoring Abhijit's futile attempts to stop him. Then he jumped into the room.

Kanti Babu ran to unlock the door. We heard the agonized screams of the Rampur hound even as Kanti Babu turned the key in the lock.

We tumbled into the room, to witness a horrible sight. One tentacle was not enough this time. The Septopus was wrapping a second, and then a third tentacle around Badshah, in a deadly embrace.

Kanti Babu shouted, 'Don't get any closer, either of you. Parimal, fire!'

I raised my gun, but another voice yelled: 'Stop!'

Now I realized how precious his dog was to Abhijit. He paid no attention to Kanti Babu's warning. I saw him run to the plant, and clutch with both hands one of the three tentacles that were wrapped around Badshah.

What followed froze my blood.

All three tentacles left Badshah immediately and attacked Abhijit. And the remaining four, perhaps aroused by the prospect of tasting human blood, rose from the ground, swaying greedily.

Kanti Babu spoke again. 'Come on, shoot. Look, there's the head!'

A lid from the top of the head was being slowly removed, revealing a dark cavern. The tentacles, lifting and carrying Abhijit with them, were moving towards that yawning gap.

Abhijit's face looked deathly pale, his eyes were bursting out of their sockets.

At any moment of crisis, I had noticed before, my nerves would become perfectly steady and calm, as if by magic.

I raised my gun, took aim and fired at the head of the Septopus, between two brown circular marks in the centre. My hands did not tremble, and my bullet found its mark.

In the next instant, I remember, thick red blood began spurting out of the wounded plant, gushing forth like a fountain. And the tentacles released Abhijit, hanging low, dropping down to the ground, still and lifeless. The last thing I remember is the smell, which suddenly grew ten times stronger, overwhelming my senses, blocking out consciousness, numbing my thoughts . . .

Four months had passed since that day. I had only recently resumed writing. My novel was still incomplete.

It had proved impossible to save Badshah. But Abhijit had already found a mastiff and a Tibetan pup. He was looking for another Rampur hound, I had learnt. Two of his ribs were fractured as a result of his encounter with the Septopus. It took him two months to recover.

Kanti Babu visited me yesterday. He was thinking of getting rid of all his plants that ate insects, he said.

'It might be a good idea to experiment with vegetables, don't you think? I mean, I could grow courgettes, gourds, marrows, things like that. If you like, I can give you some of my old plants. You did so much for me, I am very grateful to you. Say I give you a nepenthes? It can at least take care of the insects in your house . . .?'

'No, no!' I interrupted him. 'If you wish to get rid of those plants, do. Just throw them out. I don't need a plant to catch my insects.'

This last remark received wholehearted support from the gecko sprawled over the calendar.

'Tik, tik, tik!' it said.

Translated by Gopa Majumdar
First published in Bengali in 1962

The Small World of Sadananda

I am feeling quite cheerful today, so this is a good time to tell you everything. I know you will believe me. You are not like my people; they only laugh at me. They think I am making it up. So I have stopped talking to them.

It is midday now, so there is no one in my room. They will come in the afternoon. Now there are only two here—myself and my friend Lal Bahadur. Lal Bahadur Singh! Oh, how worried I was for his sake yesterday! I couldn't believe he would ever come back to me. He is very clever, so he was able to escape unhurt. Anyone else would have been finished by now.

How silly of me!—I have told you my friend's name, but haven't told you my own.

My name is Sadananda Chakraborty. It sounds like the name of a bearded old man, doesn't it? Actually, I am only thirteen. I can't help it if my name is old fashioned. After all, I didn't choose it; my grandma did.

If only she knew how much trouble it would cause me, she would have surely called me something else. How could she have known that people could pester me by saying, 'Why are you so glum when your name means "ever-happy"?' Such fools! As if laughing like a jackass was the only way to show that one was happy. There are so many ways of being happy even when one doesn't smile.

For instance, suppose there's a twig sticking out of the ground and you find a grasshopper landing on its tip again and again. It would certainly make you happy to see it, but if you burst out laughing at it, people would think you were out of your mind. Like that mad uncle of mine. I never saw him, but I was told that he laughed all the time. Even when they had to put him in chains, he found it so funny that he almost split his sides laughing. The truth is, I get fun out of things which most people don't even notice. Even when I am lying in bed I notice things which make me happy. Sometimes a cotton seed will come floating in through the window. Small wispy things which the slightest breath of air sends wafting hither and thither. What a happy sight it is! If it comes floating down towards you, you blow on it and send it shooting up into the air again.

And if a crow comes and settles on the window, watching it is like watching a circus clown. I always go absolutely still when a crow comes and sits nearby, and watch its antics out of the corner of my eyes.

But if you ask me what gives me the most fun, I would say—watching ants. Of course, it is no longer just funny; it is . . . but no, I mustn't tell everything now or the fun will be spoilt. It's better that I begin at the beginning.

Once, about a year ago, I had fever. It was nothing new, as I am often laid up with fever. I catch a chill rather easily. Mother says it's because I spend so much time out of doors sitting on the grass.

As always, the first couple of days in bed was fun. A nice, chilly feeling mixed with a feeling of laziness. Added to this was the fun of not having to go to school. I lay in bed watching a squirrel climbing up the madar tree outside the window when Mother came and gave me a bitter mixture to drink. I drank it up like a good boy and then took the glass of water, drank some of it and blew the rest out of the window in a spray. I wrapped the blanket around me and was about to close my eyes for a doze when I noticed something.

A few drops of water had fallen on the window-sill, and in one of these drops a small black ant was trying desperately to save itself from drowning.

I found it so strange that I propped myself up on my elbows and leaned forward to bring my eyes up close to the ant.

As I watched intently, it suddenly seemed as if the ant was not an ant any more but a man. In fact, it reminded me of Jhontu's brother-in-law who had slipped down the bank into a pond while fishing and, not being able to swim, wildly thrashed his arms about to keep himself afloat. In the end he was saved by Jhontu's elder brother and their servant Narahari.

As soon as I recalled the incident, I had a wish to save the ant.

Although I had fever, I jumped out of bed, ran out of the room, rushed into my father's study and tore off a piece of blotting paper from his writing pad. Then I ran back into my room, jumped onto the bed and held the blotting paper such that its edge touched the drop of water. The water was sucked up in no time.

The suddenly rescued ant seemed not to know which way to go. It rushed about this way and that for a while, and then disappeared down the drainpipe on the far side of the sill.

No more ants appeared on the sill that day.

The next day the fever went up. Around midday Mother came and said, 'Why are you staring at the window? You should try and get some sleep.'

I shut my eyes to please Mother, but as soon as she left, I opened them again and looked at the drainpipe.

In the afternoon, when the sun was behind the madar tree, I saw an ant poking its head out of the mouth of the pipe.

Suddenly it came out and started to move about briskly on the sill.

Although all black ants look alike, I somehow had the feeling that this was the same ant which had nearly drowned yesterday. I had acted as its friend, so it had come to pay me a visit.

I had made my plans beforehand. I had brought some sugar from the pantry, wrapped it up in paper and put it beside my pillow. I now opened the wrapper, took out a large grain of sugar and put it on the sill.

The ant seemed startled and stopped in its tracks. Then it cautiously approached the sugar and prodded it with its head from all sides. Then it suddenly made for the drainpipe and disappeared into it.

I thought: that's odd. I gave it such a nice grain of sugar and it left it behind. Why did it have to come at all if not for food?

The doctor came in a short while. He felt my pulse, looked at my tongue and placed the stethoscope on my chest and back. Then he said that I must take some more of the bitter mixture and the fever would go in a couple of days. That didn't make me happy at all. No fever meant going to school, and going to school meant not watching the drainpipe in the afternoon when the ants came out. Anyway, as soon as the doctor left, I turned towards the window and was delighted to see a whole army of black ants coming out of the drainpipe onto the sill. The leader must be the ant I knew, and it must have informed the other ants of the grain of sugar and led them to it.

Watching for a while I was able to see for myself how clever the ants were. All the ants now banded together to push the grain towards the drainpipe. I can't describe how funny it was, I imagined that if they had been coolies pushing a heavy weight, they'd have shouted, 'All together, heave ho! A little further, heave ho! That's the spirit, heave ho!'

After my fever was gone, school was a bore for a few days. My thoughts would go back again and again to the window-sill. There must be ants coming there every afternoon. I would leave a few grains of sugar on the sill every morning before going to school, and when I returned in the afternoon I would find them gone.

In the class I used to sit at a desk towards the middle of the room. Beside me sat Sital. One day I was a little late and found Phani sitting in my place. So I had no choice but to sit at the back of the class, in front of the wall. In the last period before recess we read history. In his thin, piping voice Haradhan Babu the history teacher was describing how brave Hannibal was. Hannibal had led an army from Carthage and had crossed the Alps to invade Italy.

As I listened, I suddenly had the feeling that Hannibal's army was in the classroom and was on the march very close to me.

I looked around and my eyes travelled to the wall behind me. Down the wall ran a long line of ants—hundreds of small black ants, exactly like a mighty army on the way to battle.

I looked down and found a crack in the wall near the floor through which the ants were going out.

As soon as the bell rang for the recess, I ran out to the back of our classroom and spotted the crack. The ants were coming out of it and making their way through the grass towards a guava tree.

I followed the ants and found, at the foot of the guava tree, something which can only be described as a castle.

It was a mound of earth with a tiny opening at the base through which the ants entered.

I had a great urge to look inside that castle.

I had my pencil in my pocket, and with its tip I began to dig carefully into the mound. At first I found nothing inside, but on digging a little further, I had the surprise of my life. I found there were countless small chambers inside the mound, and a maze of passages leading from one chamber to another. How very strange! How could the ants build such a castle with their tiny arms and legs? How could they be so clever? Did they have schools where they were taught? Did they also learn from books, draw pictures, build things? Did that mean they were no different from human beings except in looks? How was it that they could build their own house while tigers, elephants, bears and horses couldn't? Even Bhulo, my pet dog, couldn't.

Of course, birds build nests. But how many birds can live in a single nest? Can the birds build a castle where thousands of them can live?

Because I had spoilt a part of the mound, there was a great flurry amongst the ants. I felt sorry for them. I thought: now that I have done them harm, I must make up by doing them a good turn, or they will look upon me as their enemy, which I am not. I was truly their friend.

So the next day I took half of a sweetmeat which Mother gave me to eat, wrapped it up in a sal leaf and carried it in my pocket to school. Just before the bell rang for the classes to begin, I put the sweetmeat by the anthill. The ants would have to travel to find food; today they'd find it right at their doorstep. Surely this was doing them a good turn.

In a few weeks the summer holidays began and my friendship with ants began to grow. I would tell the elders about my observations of how ants behaved, but they paid no attention to me. What really put my back up was that they laughed at me. So I decided not to tell anybody anything. Whatever I did, I would do on my own and keep what I learned to myself.

One day, in the afternoon, I sat by the compound wall of Pintu's house watching a hill made by red ants. People will say that you can't sit near red ants for long because they bite. I had been bitten by red ants myself, but of late I had noticed that they didn't bite me any more. So I was watching them without fear when I suddenly saw Chhiku striding up.

I haven't mentioned Chhiku yet. His real name is Srikumar. He is in the same class as me, but he must be older than me because there's a thin line of moustache above his lips. Chhiku is a bully, so nobody likes him. I usually don't meddle with him because he is stronger than me. Chhiku saw me and called out, 'You there, you silly ass, what are you doing squatting there on the ground?' I didn't pay any attention to him. He came up towards me. I kept my eyes on the ants.

Chhiku drew up and said, 'Well, what are you up to? I don't like the look of it.'

I made no attempt to hide what I was doing and told him the truth. Chhiku made a face and said, 'What do you mean—watching ants? What is there to watch? And aren't there ants in your own house that you have to come all the way here?'

I felt very angry. What was it to him what I did? Why did he have to poke his nose into other people's affairs?

I said, 'I'm watching them because I like doing so. You know nothing about ants. Why don't you mind your own business? Why come and bother me?'

Chhiku hissed like an angry cat and said, 'So you like watching ants, eh? Well–there! There!' Before I could do or say anything, Chhiku had levelled the anthill with three vicious jabs of his heel, thereby squashing at least 500 ants.

Chhiku gave a hollow laugh and was about to walk away when something suddenly happened to me. I jumped up on Chhiku's back, grabbed hold of his hair, and knocked his head four or five times against Pintu's compound wall. Then I let go of him. Chhiku burst into tears and went off.

When I got back home, I learnt that Chhiku had already been there to complain against me.

But I was surprised when at first Mother neither scolded nor beat me. Perhaps she hadn't believed Chhiku, because I had never hit anyone before. Besides, Mother knew that I was scared of Chhiku. But when Mother asked what had happened, I couldn't lie to her.

Mother was very surprised. 'You mean you really bashed his head against the wall?'

I said, 'Yes, I did. And why only Chhiku? I would do the same to anyone who trampled on anthills.' This made Mother so angry that she slapped me.

It was a Saturday. Father came back from the office early. When he heard from Mother what had happened he locked me up in my room.

Although my cheeks smarted from the slaps, I wasn't really sorry for myself. I was very sorry for the ants. Once in Sahibgunge where cousin Parimal lives, there was a collision between two trains which killed 300 people. Today it took Chhiku only a few seconds to kill so many ants!

It seemed so wrong, so very, very wrong.

As I lay in bed thinking of all that had happened, I suddenly felt a little chilly and had to draw the blanket over myself.

And then I went off to sleep. I was awakened by a strange noise.

A thin, high-pitched sound, very beautiful, going up and down in a regular beat, like a song.

My ears pricked up and I looked around but couldn't make out where the sound came from. Probably someone far away was singing. But I had never heard such singing before.

Look who's here! Coming out of the drainpipe while I was listening to the strange sound.

This time I clearly recognized it—the ant I had saved from drowning. It was facing me and salaaming me by raising its two front legs and touching its head with them. What shall I call this black creature? Kali, Krishna? I must think about it. After all, one can't have a friend without a name. I put my hand on the window-sill, palm upwards. The ant brought his legs down from his head and crawled slowly towards my hand. Then it climbed up my little finger and started scurrying over the criss-cross lines on my palm.

Just then I started as I heard a sound from the door, and the ant clambered down and disappeared into the drainpipe.

Now Mother came into the room and gave me a glass of milk. Then she felt my forehead and said I had fever again.

Next morning the doctor came. Mother said, 'He has been restless the whole night, and kept saying "Kali" again and again.' Mother probably thought I was praying to the Goddess Kali, because I hadn't told her about my new friend.

The doctor had put the stethoscope on my back when I heard the song again. It was louder than yesterday and the tune was different. It seemed to come from the window, but since the doctor had asked me to keep still, I couldn't turn my head to see.

The doctor finished his examination, and I cast a quick glance towards the window. Hello there! It was a large black ant this time, and this one too was salaaming me. Are all ants my friends then?

And was it this ant which was singing?

But Mother said nothing about a song. Did it mean that she couldn't hear it?

I turned towards Mother to ask her, and found her staring at the ant with fear in her eyes. The next moment she picked up my arithmetic note-book from the table, leaned over me and with one slap of the book squashed the ant. The same moment the singing stopped.

'The whole house is crawling with ants!' said Mother. 'Just think what would happen if one crawled inside your ear.'

The doctor left after giving me an injection. I looked at the dead ant. He was killed while singing a beautiful song. Just like my great-uncle Indranath. He too used to sing classical songs, which I didn't understand very well. One day he was playing the tanpura and singing when he suddenly died. When he was taken to the crematorium in a procession, a group of keertan singers went along singing songs. I watched it and still remember it, although I was then very small.

And then a strange thing happened. I fell asleep after the injection and dreamed that, like the funeral of great-uncle Indranath, a dozen or so ants were bearing the dead ant on their shoulders while a line of ants followed singing a chorus.

I woke up in the afternoon when Mother put her cool hand on my forehead.

I glanced at the window and found that the dead ant was no longer there.

This time the fever kept on for several days. No wonder, because everyone in the house had started killing ants. How can the fever go if you have to listen to the screaming of ants all day long?

And there was another problem. While the ants were being killed in the pantry, hordes of ants turned up on my window-sill and wept. I could see that they wanted me to do something for them—either stop the killing or punish those who were doing the misdeed. But since I was laid up with fever, I could do nothing about it. Even if I were well, how could a small boy like me stop the elders from what they were doing?

But one day, I was forced to do something about it.

I don't exactly remember what day it was, but I do remember that I had woken up at the crack of dawn and right away heard Mother announcing that an ant had got into Phatik's ear and bitten him.

I was tickled by the news but just then I heard the slapping of brooms on the floor and knew that they were killing ants.

Then a very strange thing happened. I heard thin voices shouting, 'Help us! Help us, please!' I looked at the window and found that a large group of ants had gathered on the sill and were running around wildly.

Hearing them cry out I could no longer keep calm. I forgot about my fever, jumped out of bed and ran out of the room. At first I didn't know what to do. Then I took up a clay pot which was lying on the floor and smashed it. Then I started to smash all the things I could find which would break. It was a clever ruse because it certainly stopped the killing of ants. But it made my parents, my aunt, my cousin Sabi all come out of their rooms, grab hold of me, put me back on my bed and lock the door of my room.

I had a good laugh, though, and the ants on my window kept saying, 'Thank you! Thank you!' and went back into the drainpipe again.

Soon after this I had to leave home. The doctor examined me one day and said I should be sent to hospital for treatment.

Now I am in a hospital room. I've been here these last four days.

The first day I felt very sad because the room was so clean that I knew there couldn't be any ants in it. Being a new room, there were no cracks or holes in the walls. There wasn't even a cupboard for ants to hide under or behind it. But there was a mango tree just outside the window, and one of its branches was within reach.

I thought if there was a place to find ants it would be on that branch.

But the first day I couldn't get near the window. How could I, since I was never alone? Either the nurse, or the doctor, or someone from my house was always in the room. The second day too was just as bad.

I was so upset that I threw a medicine bottle on the floor and broke it. It made the doctor quite angry. He was not a nice doctor, this new one. I could tell that from his bristling moustache and from the thick glasses he wore.

On the third day, something happened. There was only a nurse in my room then, and she was reading a book. I was in bed wondering what to do. I heard a thud and saw that the book had slipped from the nurse's hand and fallen on the floor. The nurse had dozed off.

I got down from the bed and tiptoed to the window.

Leaning out of the window and stretching my body as far as it would go, I grabbed hold of the mango branch and began to pull it towards me.

This made a noise which woke up the nurse, and then the fireworks started.

The nurse gave a scream, came rushing towards me and, wrapping her arms around me, dragged me to the bed and dumped me on it.

Others too came into the room just then, so I could do nothing more.

The doctor promptly gave me an injection.

I could make out from what they were saying that they thought I had meant to throw myself out of the window. Silly people! If I had thrown myself from such a height, all my bones would have been crushed and I would have died.

After the doctor left I felt sleepy. I thought of the window by my bed at home and felt very sorry. Who knew when I would be back home again?

I had nearly fallen asleep when I heard a thin voice saying, 'Sepoys at your service, sir—sepoys at your service!'

I opened my eyes and saw two large red ants standing with their chests out by the medicine bottle on the bedside table.

They must have climbed onto my hand from the mango branch without my knowing it.

I said, 'Sepoys?'

The answer came, 'Yes, sir—at your service.'

'What are your names?' I asked them.

One said, 'Lal Bahadur Singh.' And the other said, 'Lal Chand Pandey.'

I was very pleased. But I warned them to go into hiding when people came into the room, or they might be killed. Lal Chand and Lal Bahadur salaamed and said, 'Very well, sir.' Then the two of them sang a lovely duet which lulled me to sleep.

I must tell you right away what happened yesterday, because it's nearly five and the doctor will be here soon. In the afternoon I was watching Lal Chand and Lal Bahadur wrestling on the table while I lay in bed. I was supposed to be asleep, but the pills and the injection hadn't worked. Or, to be quite truthful, I wilfully kept myself awake. If I slept in the afternoon, when would I play with my new friends?

The two ants fought gamely and it was hard to say who would win when suddenly there was a sound of heavy footsteps. The doctor was coming!

I made a sign and Lal Bahadur promptly disappeared below the table. But Lal Chand had been thrown on his back and was thrashing his legs about, so he couldn't run away. And that was what caused the nasty incident.

The doctor came, saw the ant, and saying some rude words in English, swept it off the table with his hand.

I could tell from Lal Chand's scream that he was badly hurt, but what could I do? By that time the doctor had grabbed my wrist to feel my pulse. I tried to get up, but the nurse held me down.

After the examination, the doctor as usual made a glum face and scratched the edge of his moustache. He was about to turn towards the door when he suddenly screwed up his face, gave a leap and yelled 'Ouch!'

Then all hell broke loose. The stethoscope flew out of his hand, his spectacles jumped off his nose and crashed onto the floor. One of the buttons of his jacket came off as he struggled to take it off, his tie wound tighter around his neck and made him gasp and sputter before at last he managed to pull it free, the hole in his vest showed as he yanked off his shirt, jumping around and yelling all the time. I was speechless.

The nurse said, 'What is the matter, sir?'

The doctor continued to jump about and yelled, 'Ant! Red ant! It crawled up my arm—ouch!'

Well, well, well! I knew this would happen, and it serves you right! Lal Bahadur had taken revenge on his friend's behalf.

If they saw me now they would know how deliriously happy Sadananda could be.

Translated by Satyajit Ray
First published in Bengali in 1962

Anath Babu's Terror

I met Anath Babu on a train to Raghunathpur, where I was going on a holiday. I worked for one of the dailies in Calcutta. The pressure of work over the last few months had been killing. I definitely needed a break. Besides, writing being my hobby, I had ideas for a couple of short stories that needed further thought. And I needed peace and quiet to think. So I applied for ten days' leave and left with a packet of writing paper in my suitcase.

There was a reason for choosing Raghunathpur. An old college mate of mine, Biren Biswas, had his ancestral home there. We were chatting in the Coffee House one evening, talking of possible places where one might spend one's holiday. When he heard that I had applied for leave, Biren promptly offered me free accommodation in Raghunathpur. 'I would have gone with you,' he said, 'but you know how tied up I am at the moment. You won't have any problem, though. Bharadwaj will look after you. He's worked for our family for fifty years.'

Our coach was packed. Anathbandhu Mitra happened to be sitting right next to me. He was around fifty, not very tall, hair parted in the middle, a sharp look in his eyes and an amused smile playing on his lips. But his clothes! He appeared to have dressed for a role in a play set fifty years ago. Nobody these days wore a jacket like that, or such collars, glasses or boots.

We began to chat. It turned out that he, too, was going to Raghunathpur. 'Are you also going on a holiday?' I asked him. But he did not answer and seemed to grow a little pensive. Or it may be that he had failed to hear my question in the racket that the train was making.

The sight of Biren's house pleased me very much. It was a nice house, with a strip of land in front that had both vegetables and flowers growing in it. There were no other houses nearby, so the possibility of being disturbed by the neighbours was non-existent.

Despite protests from Bharadwaj, I chose the room in the attic for myself. It was an airy little room, very comfortable and totally private. I moved my things upstairs and began to unpack. It was then that I realized I had left my razor blades behind. 'Never mind,' said Bharadwaj, 'Kundu Babu's shop is only a five-minute walk from here. You'll get your bilades there.'

I left for the shop soon after tea, at around 4 p.m. It appeared that the place was used more or less like a club. About seven middle-aged men were seated inside on wooden benches, chatting away merrily. One of them was saying rather agitatedly, 'Well, it's not something I have only heard about. I saw the whole thing with my own eyes. All right, so it happened thirty years ago. But that kind of thing cannot get wiped out from one's memory, can it? I shall never forget what happened, especially since Haladhar Datta was a close friend of mine. In fact, even now I can't help feeling partly responsible for his death.'

I bought a packet of 7 O'Clock blades. Then I began to loiter, looking at things I didn't really need. The gentleman continued, 'Just imagine, my own friend laid a bet with me for just ten rupees and went to spend a night in that west room. I waited for a long time the next morning for him to turn up but when he didn't, I went with Jiten Bakshi, Haricharan Saha and a few others to look for him in the Haldar mansion. And we found him in the same room—lying dead on the floor, stone cold, eyes open and staring at the ceiling. The naked fear I saw in those eyes could only mean one thing, I tell you: ghosts. There was no injury on his person, no sign of snake-bite or anything like that. So what else could have killed him but a ghost? You tell me?'

Another five minutes in the shop gave me a rough idea of what they were talking about. There was, apparently, a two-hundred-year-old mansion in the southern corner of Raghunathpur, which had once been owned by the Haldars, the local zamindars. It had lain abandoned for years. A particular room in this mansion that faced the west was supposed to be haunted. Although in the last thirty years no one had dared to spend a night in it after the death of Haladhar Datta, the residents of Raghunathpur still felt a certain thrill thinking of the unhappy spirit that haunted the room. The reason behind this belief was both the mysterious death of Haladhar Datta, and the many instances of murders and suicides in the history of the Haldar family.

Intrigued by this conversation, I came out of the shop to find Anathbandhu Mitra, the gentleman I had met on the train, standing outside, a smile on his lips.

'Did you hear what they were saying?' he asked.

'Yes, I couldn't help it.'

'Do you believe in it?'

'In what? Ghosts?'

'Yes.'

'Well, you see, I have heard of haunted houses often enough. But never have I met anyone who has actually stayed in one and seen anything. So I don't quite . . .'

Anath Babu's smile deepened.

'Would you like to see it?' he said.

'What?'

'That house.'

'See? How do you mean?'

'Only from the outside. It's not very far from here. One mile, at the most. If you go straight down this road, past the twin temples and then turn right, it's only a quarter of a mile from there.'

The man seemed quite interesting. Besides, there was no need to return home quite so soon. So I went with him.

The Haldar mansion was not easily visible. Most of it was covered by a thick growth of wild plants and creepers. Only the top of the gate that towered above everything else was visible a good ten minutes before one reached the house. The gate was really huge. The nahabatkhana over it was a shambles. A long drive led to the front veranda. A couple of statues and the remains of a fountain told us that there used to be a garden in the space between the house and the gate. The house was strangely structured. There was absolutely nothing in it that could have met even the lowest of aesthetic standards. The whole thing seemed only a shapeless heap. The last rays of the setting sun fell across the mossy walls.

Anath Babu stared at it for a minute. Then he said, 'As far as I know, ghosts and spirits don't come out in daylight. Why don't we,' he added, winking, 'go and take a look at that room?'

'That west room? The one . . .?'

'Yes. The one in which Haladhar Datta died.'

The man's interest in the matter seemed a bit exaggerated.

Anath Babu read my mind.

'I can see you're surprised. Well, I don't mind telling you the truth. The only reason behind my arrival in Raghunathpur is this house.'

'Really?'

'Yes. In Calcutta I had heard that the house was haunted. I came all the way to see if I could catch a glimpse of the ghost. You asked me on the train why I was coming here. I didn't reply, which must have appeared rude. But I had decided to wait until I got to know you a little better before telling you.'

'But why did you have to come all the way from Calcutta to chase a ghost?'

'I'll explain that in a minute. I haven't yet told you about my profession, have I? The fact is that I am an authority on ghosts and all things supernatural. I have spent the last twenty-five years doing research in this area. I have read everything that's ever been published on life after death, spirits that haunt the earth, vampires, werewolves, black magic, voodoo—the lot. I had to learn seven different languages to do this. There is a Professor Norton in London who has a similar interest. I have been in correspondence with him over the last three years. My articles have been published in well-known magazines in Britain. I don't wish to sound boastful, but I think it would be fair to say that no one in this country has as much knowledge about these things as I do.'

He spoke very sincerely. The thought that he might be telling lies or exaggerating did not cross my mind at all. On the contrary, I found it quite easy to believe what he told me and even felt some respect for the man.

After a few moments of silence, he said, 'I have stayed in at least three hundred haunted houses all over the country.'

'Goodness!'

'Yes. In places like Jabalpur, Cherrapunji, Kanthi, Katoa, Jodhpur, Azimganj, Hazaribagh, Shiuri, Barasat . . . and so many others. I've stayed in fifty-six dak bungalows, and at least thirty indigo cottages. Besides these, there are about fifty haunted houses in Calcutta and its suburbs where I've spent my nights. But . . .'

Anath Babu stopped. Then he shook his head and said, 'The ghosts have eluded me. Perhaps they like to visit only those who don't want to have anything to do with them. I have been disappointed time and again. Only once did I feel the presence of something strange in an old building in Tiruchirapalli near Madras. It used to be a club during British times. Do you know what happened? The room was dark and there was no breeze at all. Yet, each time I tried to light a candle, someone—or something—kept snuffing it out. I had to waste twelve matchsticks. However, with the thirteenth I did manage to light the candle but, as soon as it was lit, the spirit vanished. Once, in a house in Calcutta, too, I had a rather interesting experience. I was sitting in a dark room as usual, waiting for something to happen, when I suddenly felt a mosquito bite my scalp! Quite taken aback, I felt my head and discovered that every single strand of my hair had disappeared. I was totally bald! Was it really my own head? Or had I touched someone else's? But no, the mosquito bite was real enough. I switched on my torch quickly and peered into the mirror. All my hair was intact. There was no sign of baldness.

'These were the only two ghostly experiences I've had in all these years. I had given up all hope of finding anything anywhere. But, recently, I happened to read in an old magazine about this house in Raghunathpur. So I thought I'd come and try my luck for the last time.'

We had reached the front door. Anath Babu looked at his watch and said, 'The sun sets today at 5.31 p.m. It's now 5.15. Let's go and take a quick look before it gets dark.'

Perhaps his interest in the supernatural was contagious. I readily accepted his proposal. Like him, I felt eager to see the inside of the house and that room in particular.

We walked in through the front door. There was a huge courtyard and something that looked like a stage. It must have been used for pujas and other festivals. There was no sign now of the joy and laughter it must once have witnessed.

There were verandas around the courtyard. To our right lay a broken palanquin, and beyond it was a staircase going up.

It was so dark on the staircase that Anath Babu had to take a torch out of his pocket and switch it on. We had to demolish an invisible wall of cobwebs to make our way. When we finally reached the first floor, I thought to myself, 'It wouldn't be surprising at all if this house did turn out to be haunted.'

We stood in the passage and made some rough calculations. The room on our left must be the famous west room, we decided. Anath Babu said, 'Let's not waste any time. Come with me.'

There was only one thing in the passage—a grandfather clock. Its glass was broken, one of its hands was missing and the pendulum lay to one side.

The door to the west room was closed. Anath Babu pushed it gently with his forefinger. A nameless fear gave me goose-pimples. The door swung open.

But the room revealed nothing unusual. It may have been a living-room once. There was a big table in the middle with a missing top. Only the four legs stood upright. An easy chair stood near the window, although sitting in it now would not be very easy as it had lost one of its arms and a portion of its seat.

I glanced up and saw that bits and pieces of an old-fashioned, hand-pulled fan still hung from the ceiling. It didn't have a rope, the wooden bar was broken and its main body torn.

Apart from these objects, the room had a shelf that must once have held rifles, a pipeless hookah, and two ordinary chairs, also with broken arms.

Anath Babu appeared to be deep in thought. After a while, he said, 'Can you smell something?'

'Smell what?'

'Incense, oil and burning flesh . . . all mixed together . . .' I inhaled deeply, but could smell nothing beyond the usual musty smell that comes from a room that has been kept shut for a long time.

So I said, 'Why, no, I don't think I can . . .'

Anath Babu did not say anything. Then, suddenly, he struck his left hand with his right and exclaimed, 'God! I know this smell well! There is bound to be a spirit lurking about in this house, though whether or not he'll make an appearance remains to be seen. Let's go!'

Anath Babu decided to spend the following night in the Haldar mansion. On our way back, he said, 'I won't go tonight because tomorrow is a moonless night, the most appropriate time for ghosts and spirits to come out. Besides, I need a few things which I haven't got with me today. I'll bring those tomorrow. Today I had come only to make a survey.'

Before we parted company near Biren's house, he lowered his voice and said, 'Please don't tell anyone else about my plan. From what I heard today, people here are so superstitious and easily frightened that they might actually try to stop me from going in if they came to know of my plan. And,' he added, 'please don't mind that I didn't ask you to join me. One has to be alone, you see, for something like this . . .'

I sat down the next day to write, but could not concentrate. My mind kept going back to the west room in that mansion. God knew what kind of experience awaited Anath Babu. I could not help feeling a little restless and anxious.

I accompanied Anath Babu in the evening, right up to the gate of the Haldar mansion. He was wearing a black high-necked jacket today.

From his shoulder hung a flask and in his hand he carried the same torch he had used the day before. He took out a couple of small bottles from his pocket before going into the house. 'Look,' he said, 'this one has a special oil, made with my own formula. It is an excellent mosquito repellent. And this one here has carbolic acid in it. If I spread it in and around the room, I'll be safe from snakes.'

He put the bottles back in his pocket, raised the torch and touched his head with it. Then he waved me a final salute and walked in, his heavy boots clicking on the gravel.

I could not sleep well that night. As soon as dawn broke, I told Bharadwaj to fill a thermos flask with enough tea for two. When the flask arrived, I left once more for the Haldar mansion.

No one was about. Should I call out to Anath Babu, or should I go straight up to the west room? As I stood debating, a voice said, 'Here—this way!'

Anath Babu was coming out of the little jungle of wild plants from the eastern side of the house, a neem twig in his hand. He certainly did not look like a man who might have had an unnatural or horrific experience the night before.

He grinned broadly as he came closer.

'I had to search for about half an hour before I could find a neem tree. I prefer this to a toothbrush, you see.'

I felt hesitant to ask him about the previous night.

'I brought some tea,' I said instead. 'Would you like some here, or would you rather go home?'

'Oh, come along. Let's sit by that fountain.'

Anath Babu took a long sip of his tea and said, 'Aaah!' with great relish. Then he turned to me and said with a twinkle in his eye, 'You're dying to know what happened, aren't you?'

'Yes, I mean . . . yes, a little . . .'

'All right. I will tell you everything. But let me just say this one thing right away—the whole expedition was highly successful!'

He poured himself a second mug of tea and began his tale:

'It was 5 p.m. when you left me here. I looked around for a bit before going into the house. One has to be careful, you know. There are times when animals and other living beings can cause more harm than ghosts. But I didn't find anything dangerous. Then I went in and looked into the rooms in the ground floor that were open. None had any furniture left. All I could find was some old rubbish in one and a few bats hanging from the ceiling in another. They didn't budge as I went in, so I came out again without disturbing them.

'I went upstairs at around 6.30 p.m. and began making preparations for the night. I had taken a duster with me. The first thing I did was to dust that easy chair. Heaven knows how long it had lain there.

'The room felt stuffy, so I opened the window. The door to the passage was also left open, just in case Mr Ghost wished to make his entry through it. Then I placed the flask and the torch on the floor and lay down on the easy chair. It was quite uncomfortable but, having spent many a night before under far more weird circumstances, I did not mind.

'The sun had set at 5.30. It grew dark quite soon. And that smell grew stronger. I don't usually get worked up, but I must admit last night I felt a strange excitement.

'I couldn't tell you the exact time, but I guess it must have been around 9 p.m. when a firefly flew in through the window and buzzed around the room for a minute before flying out.

'Gradually, the jackals in the distance stopped their chorus, and the crickets fell silent. I cannot tell when I fell asleep.

'I was awoken by a noise. It was the noise of a clock striking midnight. A deep, yet melodious chime came from the passage. Now fully awake, I noticed two other things—first, I was lying quite comfortably in the easy chair. The torn portion wasn't torn any more, and someone had tucked a cushion behind my back. Secondly, a brand new fan hung over my head; a long rope from it went out to the passage and an unseen hand was pulling it gently.

'I was staring at these things and enjoying them thoroughly, when I realized that from somewhere in the moonless night a full moon had appeared. The room was flooded with bright moonlight. Then the aroma of something totally unexpected hit my nostrils. I turned and found a hookah by my side, the rich smell of the best quality tobacco filling the room.'

Anath Babu stopped. Then he smiled and said, 'Quite a pleasant situation, wouldn't you agree?'

I said, 'Yes, indeed. So you spent the rest of the night pretty comfortably, did you?'

At this, Anath Babu suddenly grew grave and sank into a deep silence. I waited for him to resume speaking, but when he didn't, I turned impatient. 'Do you mean to say,' I asked, 'that you really didn't have any reason to feel frightened? You didn't see a ghost, after all?'

Anath Babu looked at me. But there was not even the slightest trace of a smile on his lips. His voice sounded hoarse as he asked, 'When you went into the room the day before yesterday, did you happen to look carefully at the ceiling?'

'No, I don't think I did. Why?'

'There is something rather special about it. I cannot tell you the rest of my story without showing it to you. Come, let's go in.'

We began climbing the dark staircase again. On our way to the first floor, Anath Babu said only one thing: 'I will not have to chase ghosts again, Sitesh Babu. Never. I have finished with them.'

I looked at the grandfather clock in the passage. It stood just as it had done two days ago.

We stopped in front of the west room. 'Go in,' said Anath Babu.

The door was closed. I pushed it open and went in. Then my eyes fell on the floor, and a wave of horror swept over me.

Who was lying on the floor, heavy boots on his feet? And whose laughter was that, loud and raucous, coming from the passage outside, echoing through every corner of the Haldar mansion? Drowning me in it, paralysing my senses, my mind . . .? Could it be . . .? I could think no more.

When I opened my eyes, I found Bharadwaj standing at the foot of my bed, and Bhabatosh Majumdar fanning me furiously. 'Oh, thank goodness you've come around!' he exclaimed. 'If Sidhucharan hadn't seen you go into that house, heaven knows what might have happened. Why on earth did you go there, anyway?'

I could only mutter faintly, 'Last night, Anath Babu . . .'

Bhabatosh Babu cut me short, 'Anath Babu! It's too late now to do anything about him. Obviously, he didn't believe a word of what I had said the other day. Thank God you didn't go with him to spend the night in that room. You saw what happened to him, didn't you? Exactly the same thing had happened to Haladhar Datta all those years ago. Lying on the floor, cold and stiff, the same look of horror in his open eyes, staring at the ceiling.'

I thought quietly to myself, 'No, he's not lying there cold and stiff. I know what's become of Anath Babu after his death. I might find him, even tomorrow morning, perhaps, if I bothered to go back. There he would be wearing a black jacket and heavy boots, coming out of the jungle in the Haldar mansion, a neem twig in his hand, grinning from ear to ear.'

Translated by Gopa Majumdar
First published in Bengali in 1962

The Two Magicians

'Five, six, seven, eight, nine, ten, eleven.' Surapati finished counting the trunks and turned towards his assistant, Anil. 'All right,' he said, 'Have these loaded into the brake van. Just twenty-five minutes left.'

'I have checked your reservation, sir,' said Anil. 'It's a coupé. Both berths are reserved in your name. It'll be all right.' Then he smiled a little and added, 'The guard is a fan of yours. He's seen your show at the New Empire. Here, sir, come this way!'

The guard, Biren Bakshi, came forward with an outstretched hand and a broad smile. 'Do allow me,' he said, 'to shake the famous hand that has performed all those tricks that gave me so much joy. It is an honour indeed!'

One only had to look at any of Surapati Mondol's eleven trunks to realize who he was. Each bore the legend 'Mondol's Miracles' in large letters both on its sides and its lid. He needed no further introduction. It was barely two months since his last show at the New Empire Theatre in Calcutta, where a large audience, enchanted by his magic show, had expressed genuine appreciation through thunderous applause again and again. The newspapers, too, had carried rave reviews. The week-long show had to be extended to four, on popular demand. Eventually, Surapati had to promise the authorities another show over Christmas break.

'If you need any help, do let me know,' said the guard as he ushered Surapati into his coupé. Surapati looked around and heaved a sigh of relief. He liked the little compartment.

'All right then, sir. May I take your leave?'

'Many thanks.'

The guard left. Surapati settled down by the window and fished out a packet of cigarettes. He felt this was only the beginning of his success. Uttar Pradesh: Delhi, Agra, Allahabad, Varanasi, Lucknow. There were so many other states to visit, so many, many places to go to. A whole new world waited for him. He would travel abroad; and he would show them how a young man from Bengal could be successful anywhere in the world—even in America, the land that had produced the famous Houdini. Oh yes, he would show them all. This was just the beginning.

Anil came panting. 'Everything's fine,' he said.

'Did you check the locks?'

'Yes, sir.'

'Good.'

'I'm in the third bogey from yours.'

'Have they given the "line-clear" signal?'

'They're about to. I'll go now, sir. Would you like a cup of tea at Burdwan?'

'Yes, that would be nice.'

'I'll get it then.'

Anil left. Surapati lit his cigarette and looked out of the window absentmindedly. The sight of the jostling crowds, the porters running about and the sound of the hawker's cry soon melted away. His mind went back to his childhood. He was thirty-three now; on that particular day he could not have been more than eight. By the side of the road in the small village where he lived sat an old woman with a gunny bag in front of her, surrounded by a large crowd. How old could she have been? Sixty? Ninety? It might have been anything. Her age did not matter. What mattered was what she did with her hands. She'd take any object—a coin, a marble, a top, a betel nut, even a guava—and it would vanish before their eyes. The old woman kept up an endless patter until the lost object reappeared out of nowhere. She took a rupee from Kalu Kaka and it disappeared. Much upset, Kalu Kaka began to lose his temper. The old woman giggled and—hey presto—the rupee was there for all to see. Kalu Kaka's eyes nearly popped out.

Surapati could not concentrate on anything much after that day. He never saw that old woman again. Nor did he see such a startling performance anywhere else.

He was sixteen when he came to Calcutta for further studies. The first thing he did upon arrival was to buy as many books on magic as he possibly could and to begin practising the tricks they taught. It meant standing before a mirror for hours with several packs of cards, going through the instructions step by step. But soon, he had mastered them all. Then he began performing at small get-togethers and parties given by friends.

When he was in his second year in college, one of his friends, Gautam, invited Surapati to his sister's wedding. It later proved to be the most memorable evening in the history of Surapati's training as a magician, for that day he met Tripura Babu for the first time.

A huge shamiana stood behind a house in Swinhoe Street. Tripuracharan Mallik sat under it, surrounded by a group of other wedding guests. At the first glance, he seemed quite ordinary. About forty-eight years old, curly hair parted at one side, a smile on his lips, the corners of his mouth streaked with the juice of paan. A man no different from the millions one saw every day. But a closer look at what was happening on the mattress in front of him was enough for one's judgement to undergo a quick change. Surapati, at first, could not believe his own eyes. A silver coin went rolling towards a golden ring kept about a yard away. It stopped beside the ring and then both came rolling back to Tripura Babu. Even before Surapati could recover from the shock, Gautam's uncle accidentally dropped a matchbox on the ground. All the sticks spilled out. 'Don't bother to pick them up,' said Tripura Babu, 'I'll pick them up for you.' With one sweeping movement of his hand, he placed the matchsticks in a heap on the mattress. Then, taking the empty matchbox in his left hand, he began calling, 'Come to me, my dear. Come, come, come . . .' The sticks rose in the air one by one and slipped back into the box as though they were all his pet animals used to obeying their master's command.

Surapati went to him straight after dinner. Tripura Babu seemed very surprised at his interest. 'I have never seen anyone interested in learning magic. Most seem happy simply to see a performance,' he said.

Surapati went to his house a couple of days later. It was, actually, much less than a house. Tripura Babu lived in a small room in an old and dilapidated boarding-house. Poverty stared out of every corner. Tripura Babu told him how he tried to make a living out of his magic shows. He charged fifty rupees per show, but did not get too many invitations. The main reason for this, Surapati soon discovered, was Tripura Babu's own lack of enthusiasm. Surapati could not imagine how anyone so talented could be so totally devoid of ambition. When he mentioned this, Tripura Babu said with a sigh, 'What would be the use of trying to do more shows? How many people would be interested? How many people appreciate the talent of a true artist? Didn't you see for yourself how everyone rushed off at that wedding the minute dinner was announced? Did anyone, with the sole exception of yourself, come back to me?'

Surapati spoke to his friends after this and arranged a few shows. Tripura Babu agreed to teach him his art, possibly partly out of gratitude and partly out of a genuine affection for the boy. 'I do not want any payment,' he said firmly. 'I am only glad that there will be someone to take things forward after I've gone. But remember—you must be patient. Nothing can be learnt in a hurry. If you learn something well, you will know what joy there is in creation. Do not expect a lot of success or fame to come to you immediately. But I know you will do much better in life than I have done, for you have got what I haven't: ambition.'

Slightly nervous, Surapati asked, 'Will you teach me all that you know? Even the one with the coin and the ring?' Tripura Babu laughed. 'You must learn to walk step by step. Patience and diligence are the key words in this form of art. It evolved in ancient times when man's will-power and concentration were far more intense. It is not easy for modern man to get there. You don't know what an effort I had to make!'

Surapati began to go to Tripura Babu regularly. But about six months later, something happened that changed his life completely.

One day on his way to college, Surapati noticed a lot of colourful posters on the walls of Chowringhee: 'Shefallo the Great', they said. A closer look revealed that Shefallo was an Italian magician. He was coming to Calcutta, accompanied by his assistant, Madame Palarmo.

They performed at the New Empire. Surapati sat in a one-rupee seat and watched each item, absolutely entranced. He had only read about these in books. Men disappeared into a cloud of smoke before his eyes, and then reappeared from the same spiralling smoke like the djinn of

Alladin. A girl was placed inside a wooden box. Shefallo sawed the box into two halves, but the girl came out smiling from another box, quite unharmed. Surapati's palms hurt from clapping that night.

He watched Shefallo carefully. He seemed as good an actor as a magician. He wore a shining black suit. In his hand was a magic wand and on his head a top hat. An endless stream of objects kept pouring out of the hat. He put his hand in it once and pulled out a rabbit by its ear. Even before the poor creature had stopped flicking its long ears, out came one pigeon after another—one, two, three, four. They began to flutter around the stage. In the meantime, Shefallo had brought out a lot of chocolates from the hat which he began to throw at the audience.

Surapati noticed one more thing. Shefallo did not stop talking for an instant while he performed. He learnt later that this was what was known as magician's patter. While the audience stayed captivated by his constant flow of words, the magician quietly performed his tricks: the sleight of hand, the little deceptions.

But Madame Palarmo was different. She did not utter a word. How, then, could she deceive everyone? Surapati later learnt the answer to this one. It was possible to show certain items on the stage where the magician's own hands had very little to do. Everything could be controlled by highly mechanized equipment, operated by men from behind a black curtain. To show a man vanish into smoke or to saw a girl in two halves were both such tricks, dependent entirely on the use of equipment. Anyone who had enough money could buy the equipment and perform on stage. But, of course, one had to know the art of presentation, too. One had to have the right flair, the right touch of glamour in the total presentation of the act. Not everyone could do that. Not everyone . . .

Surapati came out of his reverie with a start. The train had just begun to pull out of the station rather jerkily when a man opened the door of his carriage from outside and clambered in. Surapati was about to protest, saying the seats were reserved, but one look at the man's face made him stop short in amazement. Good God—it was Tripura Babu!

Tripuracharan Mallik!

There had been instances in the past when Surapati had had a similar experience. To see an acquaintance in person soon after thinking about him was something that had happened to Surapati before. But finding Tripura Babu in his carriage like this made every other incident of the past pale into insignificance.

Surapati remained speechless. Tripura Babu wiped his forehead with the edge of his dhoti, placed the bundle he was carrying on the bench opposite and sat down. Then he looked at Surapati and smiled: 'Surprised, aren't you?'

Surapati swallowed hard. 'I . . . yes, I'm surprised. In fact, I wasn't sure that you were still alive!'

'Really?'

'Yes. I went to your boarding-house soon after I finished college. I found your room locked. The manager told me you had been run over by a car . . .'

Tripura Babu laughed. 'That would have been rather nice. At least I might have escaped from all my worries and anxieties.'

'Besides,' said Surapati, 'I was thinking of you a little while ago.'

'Oh yes?' a shadow passed over Tripura Babu's face. 'Were you indeed thinking of me? You mean you still do? That's amazing!'

Surapati bit his lip in embarrassment. 'Don't say that, Tripura Babu! How could I forget you? Were you not my first teacher? I was thinking of our days together. This is the first time I am going out of Bengal to perform. I am now a professional magician—did you know that?'

Tripura Babu nodded. 'Yes. I know all about you. That is why I have come to see you today. You see, I have followed your career very closely for the last twelve years. When you had your show at the New Empire, I went there the very first day and sat in the last row. I saw how everyone applauded. Yes, I did feel proud of you. But . . .'

He stopped. Surapati could not find anything to say. There was very little to be said anyway. One could not blame Tripura Babu if he had ended up feeling hurt and left out. After all, if he had not helped Surapati in the very beginning, Surapati could not be where he was today. But what had he done for Tripura Babu in return? Nothing. On the contrary, the memory of Tripura Babu and his early days had grown quite faint in his mind. So had the feeling of gratitude.

Tripura Babu began speaking again. 'Yes, I felt proud of you that day, seeing how successful you were. But I also felt slightly sorry. Do you know why? It was because the path you have chosen is not the right path for a true magician. You may be able to provide entertainment to your audience and even impress them a good deal by using all those gadgets. None of the success would be your own. Do you remember my kind of magic?'

Surapati had not forgotten. He could also remember how Tripura Babu seemed to hesitate when it came to teaching him his best tricks. 'You need a little more time,' he would say. But the right time never came. Shefallo arrived soon afterwards and, two months later, Tripura Babu himself disappeared.

Surapati had felt both surprised and disappointed not to have found Tripura Babu where he lived. But these feelings did not last for very long. His mind was too full of Shefallo and dreams of his own future—to travel everywhere, to have shows in every place, to be a name everyone recognized, to hear only applause and praise wherever he went.

Tripura Babu was staring out of the window, preoccupied. Surapati looked at him a little more closely. He did seem to have hit upon hard times. Practically all his hair had turned grey, his skin sagged, his eyes had sunk very deep into their sockets. But had the look in them dimmed even a little? No! The look in his eyes was startlingly piercing.

He sighed, 'I know of course why you chose this path. I know you believe—and perhaps I am partly responsible for this—that simplicity itself is not often rewarded. A stage performance needs a touch of glamour and sophistication, does it not?'

Surapati did not disagree. Shefallo's performance had convinced him.

Surely a bit of glamour did not do any harm? Things were different today. How much could one achieve by holding simple shows at weddings? How could one claim to be successful if one had to starve? Surapati had every respect for magic in its pure form without any trimmings. But that kind of magic had no future. Surapati knew it and had, therefore, decided to walk a different path.

He said as much to Tripura Babu, who suddenly became agitated. Sitting cross-legged on the bench, he leant forward excitedly. 'Listen, Surapati,' he said, 'if you knew what real magic was, you wouldn't chase what is fake. Magic is not just a sleight of hand, although even that requires years of careful practice. There is so much more to it! Hypnotism! Just think of it—you can control a person completely simply by looking at him. Then there is clairvoyance, telepathy and thought-reading. You can step into someone else's thoughts if you so wish. You can tell what a person is thinking just by feeling his pulse. If you can master this art, you need not even touch a person. All you need to do is just stare at him for a minute and you can read his thoughts. This is the greatest magic of all. Equipment and gadgets have no place in this. What is required is dedication, diligence and intense concentration.'

Tripura Babu stopped for breath. Then he slid closer to Surapati and went on, 'I wanted to teach you all this. But you couldn't wait. A fraud from abroad turned your head. You left the right path and went astray, only to make a fast buck in a world of pomp and show.'

Surapati remained silent. He could not deny any of this.

Tripura Babu seemed to relent a little. He laid a hand on Surapati's shoulder and continued in a milder tone, 'I have come today only to make a request. You may have guessed by now that my financial condition is not a sound one. I know a lot of tricks, but I haven't yet learnt the trick of making money. I know the only reason for this is my lack of ambition. Today I am almost desperate, Surapati. I do not have the strength any more to try to make my own living. All I am sure of is that you will help me, even if it means making a sacrifice. Do this for me, Surapati, and I promise not to bother you any more.'

Surapati was puzzled. What kind of help did the man want?

Tripura Babu went on, 'What I am going to tell you now may strike you as impertinent. But there is no other way. You see, it is not just money that I want. I have got a strange desire in my old age. I want to perform on a stage before a large audience. I want to show them the best trick I know. This may be the first and the last time, but I cannot put the thought out of my mind.'

A cold hand clutched at Surapati's heart. Tripura Babu finally came to the point. 'You are going to perform in Lucknow, aren't you? Suppose you fell ill at the last moment? You cannot, obviously, disappoint your audience. Suppose someone else took your place . . .?'

Surapati felt completely taken aback. What on earth was he saying? He really must be desperate, or he wouldn't come up with such a bizarre proposal.

His eyes fixed on Surapati, Tripura Babu said, 'All you need to do is tell people you cannot perform due to an unavoidable reason, but that your place would be taken by your guru. Would people be very sorry and heartbroken? I don't think so. I do believe they'd enjoy my show. But even so, I propose you take half of the proceeds of the first evening. I would be quite happy with the rest. After that you can go your own way. I will never disturb you again. But you must give me this opportunity, Surapati—just this once!'

'Impossible!' Surapati grew angry. 'What you're suggesting is quite impossible. You don't know what you're saying. This is the first time I'm going to perform outside Bengal. Can't you see how much this show in Lucknow means to me? Do you really expect me to begin my new career with a lie? How could you even think of it?'

Tripura Babu gave him a cool, level look. Then his voice cut across the railway carriage, rising clearly above all the noise: 'Are you still interested in that old trick with the coin and ring?'

Surapati started. But the look in Tripura Babu's eyes did not change.

'Why?' Surapati asked.

Tripura Babu smiled faintly, 'If you accept my proposal, I will teach you the trick. If you don't . . .'

His voice was drowned at this moment in the loud whistle of a Howrah-bound train that passed theirs. Its flashing lights caught the strange brilliance in his eyes.

'And if I don't?' Surapati asked softly once the noise had died down.

'You will regret it. There is something you ought to know. If I happen to be present among the audience, I do have the power to cause a magician—any magician—a lot of embarrassment. I can even make him completely helpless.'

Tripura Babu took out a pack of cards from his pocket. 'Let's see how good you are. Can you take this knave from the back and bring it forward to rest on this three of clubs, in just one movement of your hand?'

This was one of the first things Surapati had learnt. At the age of sixteen it had taken him only seven days to master this one.

And today?

Surapati took the pack of cards and realized that his fingers were beginning to feel numb. Then the numbness spread to his wrist, his elbow and, finally, the whole arm became paralysed. In a daze, Surapati looked at Tripura Babu. His mouth was twisted in a queer smile and his eyes stared straight into Surapati's. The look in them was almost inhuman. Little beads of perspiration broke out on Surapati's forehead. His whole body began to tremble.

'Do you now believe in my power?'

The pack of cards fell from Surapati's hand. Tripura Babu picked it up neatly and said, 'Would you now agree to my proposal?'

Surapati began to feel a little better. The numbness was passing. 'Will you really teach me that old trick?' he asked wearily.

Tripura Babu raised a finger, 'Your guru, Mr Tripuracharan Mallik, shall perform in your place in Lucknow because of your sudden illness. Is that right?'

'Yes.'

'You will give me half of your earnings that evening. Right?'

'Right.'

'Well, then . . .'

Surapati fished out a fifty-paise coin from his pocket and took off his coral ring. Wordlessly, he handed them over to Tripura Babu.

When the train stopped at Burdwan, Anil appeared with a cup of tea and found his boss fast asleep.

'Sir!' said Anil after a few seconds of hesitation. Surapati woke instantly.

'Who . . . what is it?'

'Your tea, sir. Sorry I disturbed you.'

'But . . .?' Surapati looked around wildly.

'What's the matter?'

'Tripura Babu? Where is he?'

'Tripura Babu?' Anil sounded perplexed.

'Oh, no, no. He was run over, wasn't he? Way back in '51. But where is my ring?'

'Which one, sir? The one with the coral is on your finger!'

'Yes, yes, of course. And . . .'

Surapati put his hand in his pocket and took out a coin. Anil noticed that his employer's hands were trembling visibly. 'Anil,' Surapati called, 'come in quickly. Shut the windows. OK. Now watch this.'

Surapati placed the ring at one end of the bench and the coin at the other. 'Help me God!' he prayed silently and turned a deep hypnotic stare fully on the coin, just as he had been taught a few minutes ago. The coin began rolling towards the ring and then both coin and ring rolled back to Surapati like a couple of obedient children.

Anil would have dropped the cup on the floor he was carrying if Surapati had not stretched out a hand miraculously at the last moment and caught it in mid-air.

Surapati began his show in Lucknow by paying tribute to Tripuracharan Mallik, his guru, who was no more.

The last item he presented that evening was introduced as true Indian magic. The trick of the coin and the ring.

Translated by Gopa Majumdar
First published in Bengali in 1963

Shibu and the Monster

'Hey—Shibu! Come here!'

Shibu was often hailed thus by Phatik-da on his way to school. Phatik-da alias Loony Phatik.

He lived in a small house with a tin roof, just off the main crossing, where an old, rusted steamroller had been lying for the last ten years. Phatik-da tinkered with God knew how many different things throughout the day. All Shibu knew was that he was very poor and that people said he went mad because he worked far too hard when he was a student. However, some of Phatik-da's remarks made Shibu think that few people had his intelligence.

But it was indeed true that most of what he said sounded perfectly crazy.

'I say—did you notice the moon last night? The left side seemed sort of extended, as though it had grown a horn!' Or, 'All the crows seem to have caught a cold. Haven't you heard the odd way in which they're cawing?'

Shibu was mostly amused when he heard Phatik-da talk like this, but at times he did get annoyed. Getting involved in a totally meaningless and irrelevant conversation was a waste of time. So he did not always stop for a chat. 'Not today, Phatik-da, I shall come tomorrow,' he would say and skip along to school.

He did not really want to stop today, but Phatik-da seemed more insistent than usual.

'You may come to harm if you do not listen to what I have to say.'

Shibu had heard that insane people, unlike normal people, could sometimes make accurate predictions. He certainly did not want to come to harm. So, feeling a little nervous, he began walking towards Phatik-da's house.

Phatik-da was pouring coconut water into a hookah. 'Have you noticed Janardan Babu?' he said.

Janardan Babu was the new maths teacher in Shibu's school. He had arrived about ten days ago.

'I see him every day,' said Shibu. 'Why—I have maths in the very first period today!'

Phatik-da clicked his tongue in annoyance, 'Tch, tch. Seeing and observing are two different things, do you understand? Look, can you tell me how many little holes your belt has got? And how many buttons are there on your shirt? Try telling me without looking!'

Shibu failed to come up with the correct answers.

Phatik-da said, 'See what I mean? You've obviously never noticed these things, although the shirt and the belt you're wearing are your own. Similarly, you have never noticed Janardan Babu.'

'What should I have noticed? Anything in particular?'

Phatik-da began smoking his hookah. 'Yes, say, his teeth. Have you noticed them?'

'Teeth?'

'Yes, teeth.'

'How could I have noticed them? He doesn't ever smile!'

This was true. Janardan Babu was not exactly cantankerous, but no other teacher was as grave and sombre as him.

Phatik-da said, 'All right. Try to notice his teeth if he does smile. And then come and tell me what you've seen.'

A strange thing happened that day. Janardan Babu laughed in Shibu's class. It happened when, referring to some geometrical designs, Janardan Babu asked what had four arms. 'Gods, sir,' Shankar cried, 'the gods in heaven have four arms!' At this Janardan Babu began chuckling noisily. Shibu's eyes went straight to his teeth.

Phatik-da was crushing some object with a heavy stone crusher when Shibu reached his house that evening. He looked at Shibu and said, 'If this medicine I'm making has the desired effect, I'll be able to change colours like a chameleon.'

Shibu said, 'Phatik-da, I've seen them.'

'What?'

'Teeth.'

'Oh. What did they look like?'

'They were all right, except that they were stained with paan and two of them were longer than the others.'

'Which two?'

'By the side. About here.' Shibu pointed to the sides of his mouth.

'I see. Do you know what those teeth are called?'

'What?'

'Canine teeth. Like dogs have.'

'Oh.'

'Have you ever seen any other man with such large canine teeth?'

'Perhaps not.'

'Who has such teeth?'

'Dogs?'

'Idiot! Why just dogs? All carnivorous animals have large canine teeth. They use them to tear through the flesh and bones of their prey. Especially the wild animals.'

'I see.'

'And who else has them?'

Shibu began racking his brains. Who else? Who had teeth anyway, except men and animals?

Phatik-da dropped a walnut and a pinch of pepper into the mixture he was making and said, 'You don't know, do you? Why, monsters have such teeth!'

Monsters? What had monsters to do with Janardan Babu? And why talk of monsters today? They were present only in fairy tales. They had large, strong teeth and their backs were bent . . .

Shibu started.

Janardan Babu's back was definitely not straight. He stooped. Someone had mentioned that this was so because he had lumbago.

Large teeth, bent backs . . . what else did monsters have?

Red eyes.

Shibu had not had the chance to notice Janardan Babu's eyes for he always wore glasses that seemed to be tinted. It was impossible to tell whether the eyes behind those were red or purple or green.

Shibu was good at maths. LCM, HCF, Algebra, Arithmetic—he sailed through them all. At least, he used to, until a few days ago. During the time of his old maths teacher, Pearicharan Babu, Shibu had often got full marks. But he now began to have problems, although he did try to pull himself together by constantly telling himself, 'It just cannot be. A man cannot be a monster. Not in these modern times. Janardan Babu is not a monster. He is a man.'

He was repeating these words silently in class when a disastrous thing happened.

Janardan Babu was writing something on the blackboard. Suddenly he turned around, took off his glasses and began polishing them absent-mindedly with one end of the cotton shawl he was wearing. He raised his eyes after a while and they looked straight into Shibu's. Shibu went cold with fear. The whites of Janardan Babu's eyes were not white at all. Both eyes were red. As red as a tomato. After this, Shibu got as many as three sums wrong.

Shibu seldom went home straight after school. He would first go to the grounds owned by the Mitters and play with the mimosa plants. After gently tapping each one to sleep, he would go to Saraldeeghi—the large, deep pond. There he would try playing ducks and drakes with broken pieces of earthenware. If he could make a piece skip on the water more than seven times, he would break the record Haren had set. On the other side of Saraldeeghi was a brick kiln. Hundreds of bricks stood in huge piles. Shibu usually spent about ten minutes here, doing gymnastics, and then went diagonally across the field to reach his house.

Today, the mimosa plants seemed lifeless. Why? Had someone come walking here and stepped on them? But who could it be? Not many people came here.

Shibu did not feel like staying there any longer. There was something strange in the air. A kind of premonition. It seemed to be getting dark already. And did the crows always make such a racket—or had something frightened them today?

Shibu took himself to Saraldeeghi. But, as soon as he had put his books down by the side of the pond, he changed his mind about staying. Today was not the day for playing ducks and drakes. In fact, today was not the day for staying out at all. He must get back home quickly. Or else . . . something awful might happen.

A huge fish raised its head from the water and then disappeared again with a loud splash.

Shibu picked up his books. It was very dark under the peepal tree that stood at a distance. He could see the bats hanging from it. Soon it would be time for them to start flying. Phatik-da had offered to explain to him one day why bats' brains did not haemorrhage despite their hanging upside down all the time.

Shibu began walking towards his house.

He saw Janardan Babu near the brick kiln.

There was a mulberry tree about twenty yards from where the bricks lay. A couple of lambs were playing near it and Janardan Babu was watching them intently. He carried a book and an umbrella in his hand. Shibu held his breath and quickly hid behind a pile of bricks. He removed the top two in the pile and peered through the gap.

He noticed Janardan Babu raise his right hand and wipe his mouth with the back of it.

Clearly, the sight of the lambs had made his mouth water, or he would not have made such a gesture.

Then, suddenly, Janardan Babu dropped the book and the umbrella and, crouching low, picked up one of the lambs. Shibu could hear the lamb bleat loudly. He also heard Janardan Babu laugh. That was enough.

Shibu wanted to see no more. He slipped away but, in his haste to climb over the next pile of bricks, tripped and fell flat on the ground.

'Who's there?'

Shibu was going to pick himself up somehow when he found Janardan Babu coming towards him, having put the lamb back on the grass.

'Who is it? Shibram? Are you hurt? What are you doing here?' Shibu could not speak. His mouth had gone dry. But he certainly wanted to ask Janardan Babu what he was doing there. Why did he carry a lamb in his arms? Why was his mouth watering?

Janardan Babu stretched out a hand. 'Here, I'll help you up.'

But Shibu managed to get to his feet without help.

'You live nearby, don't you?'

'Yes, sir.'

'Is that red house yours?'

'Yes, sir.'

'I see.'

'Let me go, sir.'

'Goodness—is that blood?'

Shibu looked at his legs. His knee was slightly grazed and a few drops of blood was oozing from the wound. Janardan Babu was staring at the blood, his glasses glistening.

'Let me go, sir.'

Shibu picked up his books.

'Listen, Shibram.'

Janardan Babu laid a hand on Shibu's back. Shibu could hear his heart beat loudly—like a drum.

'I am glad I found you alone. There is something I wanted to ask you. Are you finding it difficult to follow the maths lessons? Why did you get all those simple sums wrong? If you have any problem, you can come to my house after school. I will give you special coaching. It's so easy to get full marks in maths. Will you come?'

Shibu had to step back to shake off Janardan Babu's hand from his back. 'No, sir,' he gulped, 'I'll manage on my own. I'll be all right tomorrow.'

'OK. But do tell me if there's a problem. And don't be frightened of me. What is there to be frightened of, anyway? Do you think I'm a monster that I'll eat you alive? Ha, ha, ha, ha . . .'

Shibu ran all the way to his house. He found Hiren Uncle in the living-room. Hiren Uncle lived in Calcutta. He was extremely fond of fishing. Very often he came over on weekends and went fishing at Saraldeeghi with Shibu's father.

They would probably go again this time, for he saw that certain preparations had been made. But Hiren Uncle had also brought a gun. There was some talk of shooting ducks. Shibu's father could handle guns, although his aim was not as good as Hiren Uncle's.

Shibu went straight to bed after dinner. He had no doubt now that Janardan Babu was a monster. Thank God Phatik-da had already warned him. If he hadn't, who knows what might have happened at the brick kiln? Shibu shivered and stared out of the window.

Everything shone in the moonlight. He had gone to bed early because he had to wake up early the next morning to study for his exams. Normally, he could not sleep with the light on. But today, if the moonlight had not been so good, he would have left the light on. He felt too frightened today to sleep alone in the dark. The others had not yet finished having dinner.

Shibu was still looking out of the window, half asleep, when the sight of a man made him sit up in terror.

The man was heading straight for his window. He stooped slightly and wore glasses. The glasses gleamed in the moonlight.

Janardan Babu!

Shibu's throat felt parched once more.

Janardan Babu tiptoed his way to the open window; Shibu clutched his pillow tight.

Janardan Babu looked around for a bit and then said somewhat hesitantly, in a strange nasal tone, 'Shibram? Are you there?'

Good God—even his voice sounded different! Did the monster in him come out so openly at night?

He called again, 'Shibram!'

This time Shibu's mother heard him from the veranda and shouted, 'Shibu! There's someone outside calling for you. Have you gone to sleep already?'

Janardan Babu vanished from the window. A minute later, Shibu heard his voice again, 'Shibram had left his geometry book among the bricks. Since it's Sunday tomorrow, I thought I'd come and return it right away. He may need it . . .'

Then he lowered his voice and Shibu failed to catch what he said. But, after a while, he heard his father say, 'Yes, if you say so. I'll send him over to your house. Yes, from tomorrow.'

Shibu did not utter a word, but he screamed silently, 'No, no, no! I won't go, I won't! You don't know anything! He's a monster! He'll gobble me up if I go to his house!'

The next morning Shibu went straight to Phatik-da's house. There was such a lot to tell.

Phatik-da greeted him warmly. 'Welcome! Isn't there a cactus near your house? Can you bring me a few bits and pieces of that plant? I've thought of a new recipe.'

Shibu whispered, 'Phatik-da!'

'What?'

'Remember you told me Janardan Babu was a monster . . .?'

'Who said that?'

'Why, you did!'

'Of course not. You did not notice my words, either.'

'How?'

'I said try to notice Janardan Babu's teeth. Then you came back and said he had large canine teeth. So I said I had heard monsters had similar teeth. That does not necessarily mean Janardan Babu is a monster.'

'Isn't he?'

'I did not say he was.'

'So what do I do now?'

Phatik-da got up, stretched lazily and yawned. Then he said, 'Saw your uncle yesterday. Has he come fishing again? Once a Scotsman called McCurdy killed a tiger with a fishing rod. Have you heard that story?'

Shibu grew desperate, 'Phatik-da, stop talking nonsense. Janardan Babu is really a monster. I know it. I have seen and heard such a lot!'

Then he told Phatik-da everything that had happened over the last two days. Phatik-da grew grave as he heard the tale. In the end he said, 'Hmm. So what have you decided to do?'

'You tell me what I should do. You know so much.'

Phatik-da bent his head deep in thought.

'We have got a gun in our house,' said Shibu suddenly. This annoyed Phatik-da.

'Don't be silly. You can't kill a monster with a gun. The bullet would make an about turn and hit the same person who pulled the trigger.'

'Really?'

'Yes, my dear boy.'

'So what do I do?' Shibu asked again. 'What's going to happen, Phatik-da? My father wants me to start from today . . .'

'Oh, shut up. You talk too much.'

After about two minutes of silence Phatik-da suddenly said, 'Have to go.'

'Where?'

'To Janardan Babu's house.'

'What?'

'I must look at his horoscope. I am not sure yet. But his horoscope is bound to tell me something. And I bet he has it hidden somewhere in his house.'

'But . . .'

'Wait a minute. Listen to the plan first. We will both go in the afternoon. It's Sunday today, so the man will be at home. You will go to the back of his house and call him. Tell him you've come for your maths lesson. Then keep him there for a few minutes. Say anything you like, but don't let him go back into the house. I will try to find the horoscope in the meantime. And then you run away from one side and I from the other.'

'And then?' asked Shibu. He did not like the plan much, but Phatik-da was his only hope.

'Then you'll come to my house in the evening. By then I will have seen his horoscope. If he is indeed a monster, I know what to do about it. And if he's not, there is no cause for anxiety, is there?'

Shibu turned up again at Phatik-da's house soon after lunch. Phatik-da came out about five minutes later and said, 'My cat has started to take snuff. There are problems everywhere!'

Shibu noticed Phatik-da was carrying a pair of torn leather gloves and the bell of a bicycle. He handed the bell to Shibu and said, 'Ring this bell if you feel you're in danger. I will come and rescue you.'

Janardan Babu lived at the far end of town. He lived all alone, without even a servant. It was impossible to tell from the outside that a monster lived there.

Shibu and Phatik made their separate ways to the house. As he began to find his way to the back of the house, Shibu's throat started to go dry again. What if, when he was supposed to call out to Janardan Babu, his voice failed him?

There was a high wall behind the house, a door in the middle of the wall, and a guava tree near the door. Several wild plants and weeds grew around the tree.

Shibu went forward slowly. He must hurry or the whole plan would get upset.

He leant against the guava tree for a bit of moral support and was about to call out to Janardan Babu when he was startled by the sound of something shuffling near his feet. Looking down, he saw a chameleon glide across the ground and disappear behind a bush. There were some white objects lying near the bush. He picked up a fallen twig and parted the bush with it to take a closer look. Oh no! The white objects were bones! But whose bones were they?

Dogs? Cats? Or lambs?

'What are you looking at, Shibram?'

The same nasal voice.

A cold shiver went down Shibu's spine. He turned around quickly and saw Janardan Babu standing at his back door, watching him with a queer look in his eyes.

'Have you lost something?'

'No, sir I . . . I . . .'

'Were you coming to see me? Why did you come to the back door? Well, do come in.'

Shibu tried retracing his steps, but discovered that one of his feet was caught in a creeper.

'I have got a cold, I'm afraid,' said Janardan Babu. 'I've had it since yesterday. I went to your house. You were sleeping.'

Shibu knew he must not run away so soon. Phatik-da could not have finished his job. He might even get caught. Should he ring the bell?

No, he was not really in danger, was he? Phatik-da might get annoyed if he rang it unnecessarily.

'What were you looking at so keenly?'

Shibu could not think of a suitable answer. Janardan Babu came forward.

'This place is very dirty. It's better not to come from this side. My dog brings bones from somewhere and leaves them here. I have often thought of scolding him, but I can't. You see, I'm very fond of animals . . .'

Again, he wiped his mouth with the back of his hand.

'Come on in, Shibram. We must do something about your maths.'

Shibu could not wait any longer. 'Not today, sir. I'll come back tomorrow,' he said and ran away.

He did not stop running until he came to the old and abandoned house of the Sahas, quite a long way away. Goodness—he would never forget what had happened today. He didn't know he had such a lot of courage!

But what had Phatik-da learnt from the horoscope? Shibu went to his house again in the evening. Phatik-da shook his head as soon as he saw Shibu.

'Problems,' he said, 'great problems.'

'Why, Phatik-da? Didn't you find the horoscope?'

'Yes, I did. Your maths teacher is undoubtedly a monster. And a Pirindi monster, at that. These were full-fledged monsters 350 generations ago. But their genes were so strong that even now it's possible to find a half-monster among them. No civilized country, of course, has full monsters nowadays. You can find some in the wild parts of Africa, Brazil and Borneo. But half-monsters are in existence elsewhere in very small numbers. Janardan Babu is one of them.'

'Then where is the problem?' Shibu's voice trembled a little. If Phatik-da could not help, who could?

'Didn't you tell me this morning you knew what to do?'

'There is nothing I do not know.'

'Well, then?'

Phatik-da grew a little grave. Then, suddenly, he asked, 'What's inside a fish?'

Oh no, he had started talking nonsense again. Shibu nearly started weeping, 'Phatik-da, we were talking about monsters. What's that got to do with fish?'

'Tell me!' Phatik-da yelled.

'Intestines?' Phatik-da's yell had frightened Shibu.

'No, no, you ass. With such retarded knowledge, you couldn't even put a buckle on a buck! Listen. I heard this rhyme when I was only two-and-a-half. I still remember it:

Man or animal whichever thou art
Thy life beats in thy own heart
A monster's life lies in the stomach of a fish
Cannot kill him easily, even if you wish.'

Of course! Shibu, too, had read about this in so many fairy tales. A monster's life always lay hidden inside a fish. He should have known.

'When you met him this afternoon, how did he seem?' asked Phatik.

'He said he had a cold and a slight fever.'

'Yes, it all fits in,' Phatik's eyes began to sparkle with enthusiasm. 'It has to. His life's in danger, you see. As soon as the fish is out of water, he gets fever. Good!'

Then he came forward and clutched Shibu by the collar. 'Perhaps it's not too late. I saw your uncle go back to your house with a huge fish. I thought Janardan Monster's life might be in it. Now that you've told me about his illness I'm beginning to feel more sure. We must cut open that fish.'

'But how can we do that?'

'We can, with your help. It won't be easy, but you've got to do it. If you don't, I shudder to think what might happen to you!'

About an hour later Shibu arrived at Phatik-da's house dragging the huge fish by the cord he had tied around it.

'Hope no one saw you?'

'No,' Shibu panted. 'Father was having a bath. Uncle was getting a massage and Mother was inside. It took me some time to find a cord. God—is it heavy!'

'Never mind, you'll grow muscles!'

Phatik-da took the fish inside. Shibu sat marvelling at Phatik-da's knowledge of things. If anyone could rescue him from the danger he was in, it was going to be Phatik-da. Dear God—do let him find what he was looking for.

Ten minutes later, Phatik-da came out and stretched a hand towards Shibu, 'Here. Take this. Keep it with you all the time. Put it under your pillow at night. When you go to school, keep it in your left pocket. If you hold it in your hand, the monster is totally powerless and if you crush it into a powder he'll be dead. In my view, you need not crush it because some Pirindi monsters have been known to turn into normal men at the age of fifty-four. The age of your Janardan Monster is fifty-three years, eleven months and twenty-six days.'

Shibu finally found the courage to look down at what he was holding. A small, slightly damp, white stone lay on his palm, winking in the light of the moon that had just risen.

Shibu put it in his pocket and turned to go. Phatik-da called him back, 'Your hands smell fishy, wash them carefully. And pretend not to know anything about anything!'

The next day, Janardan Babu sneezed once just before entering class and, almost immediately, knocked his foot against the threshold and damaged his shoe. Shibu's left hand, at that precise moment, was resting in his left pocket.

After a long time, Shibu got full marks in maths that day.

Translated by Gopa Majumdar

First published in Bengali in 1963

Patol Babu, Film Star

Patol Babu had just hung his shopping-bag on his shoulder when Nishikanto Babu called from outside the main door. 'Patol, are you in?'

'Oh, yes,' said Patol Babu. 'Just a minute.'

Nishikanto Ghosh lived three houses away from Patol Babu in Nepal Bhattacharji Lane. He was a genial person.

Patol Babu came out with the bag. 'What brings you here so early in the morning?'

'Listen, what time will you be back?'

'In an hour or so. Why?'

'I hope you'll stay in after that. I met my youngest brother-in-law in Netaji Pharmacy yesterday. He is in the film business, in the production department. He said he was looking for an actor for a scene in a film they're now shooting. The way he described the character—fiftyish, short, bald-headed—it reminded me of you. So I gave him your address and asked him to get in touch with you directly. I hope you won't turn him away. They'll pay you, of course.'

Patol Babu hadn't expected such news early in the morning. That an offer to act in a film could come to a fifty-two-year-old non-entity like him was beyond his wildest dreams.

'Well, yes or no?' asked Nishikanto Babu. 'I believe you did some acting on the stage at one time?'

'That's true,' said Patol Babu. 'I really don't see why I should say no. But let's talk to your brother-in-law first and find out some details. What's his name?'

'Naresh. Naresh Dutt. He's about thirty. A strapping young fellow. He said he would be here around ten-thirty.'

In the market, Patol Babu mixed up his wife's orders and bought red chillies instead of onion seeds. And he quite forgot about the aubergines. This was not surprising. At one time Patol Babu had a real passion for the stage; in fact, it verged on obsession. In jatras, in amateur theatricals, in plays put up by the club in his neighbourhood, Patol Babu was always in demand. His name had appeared in handbills on countless occasions. Once it appeared in bold type near the top: 'Sitalakanto Ray (Patol Babu) in the role of Parasar'. Indeed, there was a time when people bought tickets especially to see him.

That was when he used to live in Kanchrapara. He had a job in the railway factory there. In 1934, he was offered higher pay in a clerical post with Hudson and Kimberley in Calcutta, and was also lucky to find a flat in Nepal Bhattacharji Lane. He gave up his factory job and came to Calcutta with his wife. The sailing was smooth for some years, and Patol Babu was in his boss's good books. In 1943, when he was just toying with the idea of starting a club in his neighbourhood, sudden retrenchment in his office due to the war cost him his nine-year-old job.

Ever since then Patol Babu had struggled to make a living. At first he opened a variety store which he had to wind up after five years. Then he had a job in a Bengali firm which he gave up in disgust when his boss began to treat him in too high-handed a fashion. Then, for ten long years, starting as an insurance salesman, Patol Babu tried every means of earning a livelihood without ever succeeding in improving his lot. Of late he had been paying regular visits to a small establishment dealing in scrap iron where a cousin of his had promised him a job.

And acting? That had become a thing of the remote past; something which he recalled at times with a sigh. Endowed with a wonderful memory, Patol Babu would still reel off lines from some of the best parts he had played. 'Listen, O listen to the thunderous twang of the mighty bow Gandiva engaged in gory conflict, and to the angry roar of the mountainous club whizzing through the air in the hands of the great Brikodara!' It sent a shiver down his spine just to think of such lines.

Naresh Dutt turned up at half past twelve. Patol Babu had given up hope and was about to go for his bath when there was a knock on the front door.

'Come in, come in, sir!' Patol Babu almost dragged the young man in and pushed the broken-armed chair towards him. 'Do sit down.'

'No, thanks. I—er—I expect Nishikanto Babu told you about me?'

'Oh yes. I must say I was quite taken aback. After so many years . . .'

'I hope you have no objection?'

'You think I'll be all right for the part?' Patol Babu asked with great diffidence.

Naresh Dutt cast an appraising look at Patol Babu and gave a nod. 'Oh yes,' he said. 'There is no doubt about that. By the way, the shooting takes place tomorrow morning.'

'Tomorrow? Sunday?'

'Yes, and not in the studio. I'll tell you where you have to go. You know Faraday House near the crossing of Bentinck Street and Mission Row? It's a seven-storey office building. The shooting takes place outside the office in front of the entrance. We'll expect you there at eight-thirty sharp. You'll be through by midday.'

Naresh Dutt prepared to leave. 'But you haven't told me about the part,' said Patol Babu anxiously.

'Oh yes, sorry. The part is that of a—pedestrian. An absent-minded, short-tempered pedestrian. By the way, do you have a jacket which buttons up to the neck?'

'I think I do. You mean the old-fashioned kind?'

'Yes. That's what you'll wear. What colour is it?'

'Sort of nut-brown. But woollen.'

'That's all right. The story is supposed to take place in winter, so that would be just right. Tomorrow at 8.30 a.m. sharp. Faraday House.'

Patol Babu suddenly thought of a crucial question.

'I hope the part calls for some dialogue?'

'Certainly. It's a speaking part. You have acted before, haven't you?'

'Well, as a matter of fact, yes . . .'

'Fine. I wouldn't have come to you for just a walk-on part. For that we pick people from the street. Of course there's dialogue and you'll be given your lines as soon as you show up tomorrow.'

After Naresh Dutt left, Patol Babu broke the news to his wife.

'As far as I can see, the part isn't a big one. I'll be paid, of course, but that's not the main thing. The thing is—remember how I started on the stage? Remember my first part? I played a dead soldier! All I had to do was lie still on the stage with my arms and legs spread. And remember where I went from there? Remember Mr Watts shaking me by the hand? And the silver medal which the chairman of our municipality gave me? Remember? This is only the first step on the ladder, my dear! Yes—the first step that would—God willing—mark the rise to fame and fortune of your beloved husband!'

Suddenly, the fifty-two-year-old Patol Babu did a little skip. 'What are you doing?' his wife asked, aghast.

'Don't worry. Do you remember how Sisir Bhaduri used to leap about on the stage at the age of seventy? I feel as if I've been born again!'

'Counting your chickens again before they're hatched, are you? No wonder you could never make a go of it.'

'But it's the real thing this time! Go and make me a cup of tea, will you? And remind me to take some ginger juice tonight. It's very good for the throat.'

The clock in the Metropolitan building showed seven minutes past eight when Patol Babu reached Esplanade. It took him another ten minutes to walk to Faraday House.

There was a big crowd outside the building. Three or four cars stood on the road. There was also a bus loaded with equipment on its roof. On the edge of the pavement there was an instrument on three legs around which a bunch of people were walking about looking busy. Near the entrance stood—also on three legs—a pole which had a long arm extending from its top with what looked like a small oblong beehive suspended at the end. Surrounding these instruments was a crowd of people among which Patol Babu noticed some non-Bengalis. What they were supposed to do he couldn't tell.

But where was Naresh Dutt? He was the only one who knew him.

With a slight tremor in his heart, Patol Babu advanced towards the entrance. It was the middle of summer, and the warm jacket buttoned up to his neck felt heavy. Patol Babu could feel beads of perspiration forming around the high collar.

'This way, Atul Babu!'

Atul Babu? Patol Babu spotted Naresh Dutt standing at the entrance and gesturing towards him. He had got his name wrong. No wonder, since they had only had a brief meeting. Patol Babu walked up, put his palms together in a namaskar and said, 'I suppose you haven't yet noted down my name. Sitalakanto Ray—although people know me better by my nickname Patol. I used it on the stage too.'

'Good, good. I must say you're quite punctual.'

Patol Babu rose to his full height.

'I was with Hudson and Kimberley for nine years and wasn't late for a single day.'

'Is that so? Well, I suggest you go and wait in the shade there. We have a few things to attend to before we get going.'

'Naresh!'

Somebody standing by the three-legged instrument called out.

'Sir?'

'Is he one of our men?'

'Yes, sir. He is—er—in that shot where they bump into each other.'

'Okay. Now, clear the entrance, will you? We're about to start.'

Patol Babu withdrew and stood in the shade of a paan shop.

He had never watched a film shooting before. How hard these people worked! A youngster of twenty or so was carrying that three-legged instrument on his shoulder. Must weigh at least sixty pounds.

But what about his dialogue? There wasn't much time left, and he still didn't know what he was supposed to do or say.

Patol Babu suddenly felt a little nervous. Should he ask somebody? There was Naresh Dutt there; should he go and remind him? It didn't matter if the part was small, but, if he had to make the most of it, he had to learn his lines beforehand. How small he would feel if he muffed in the presence of so many people! The last time he acted on stage was twenty years ago.

Patol Babu was about to step forward when he was pulled up short by a voice shouting 'Silence!'

This was followed by Naresh Dutt loudly announcing with hands cupped over his mouth: 'We're about to start shooting. Everybody please stop talking. Don't move from your positions and don't crowd round the camera, please!'

Once again the voice was heard shouting 'Silence! Taking!' Now Patol Babu could see the owner of the voice. He was a stout man of medium height, and he stood by the camera. Around his neck hung something which looked like a small telescope. Was he the director? How strange!—He hadn't even bothered to find out the name of the director!

Now a series of shouts followed in quick succession—'Start sound!' 'Running!' 'Camera!' 'Rolling!' 'Action!'

Patol Babu noticed that as soon as the word 'Action' was uttered, a car came up from the crossing and pulled up in front of the office entrance. Then a young man in a grey suit and pink make-up shot out of the back of the car, took a few hurried steps towards the entrance and stopped abruptly. The next moment Patol Babu heard the shout 'Cut!' and immediately the hubbub from the crowd resumed.

A man standing next to Patol Babu now turned to him. 'Did you recognize the young fellow?' he asked.

'What, no,' said Patol Babu.

'Chanchal Kumar,' said the man. 'He's coming up fast. Playing the lead in four films at the moment.'

Patol Babu saw very few films, but he seemed to have heard the name Chanchal Kumar. It was probably the same boy Koti Babu was praising the other day. Nice make-up the fellow had on. If he had been wearing a Bengali dhoti and kurta instead of a suit, and given a peacock to ride on, he would make a perfect Kartik, the god considered to be the epitome of good looks. Monotosh of Kanchrapara—who was better known by his nickname Chinu—had the same kind of looks. He used to be very good at playing female parts, recalled Patol Babu.

Patol Babu now turned to his neighbour and asked in a whisper, 'Who is the director?'

The man raised his eyebrows and said, 'Why, don't you know? He's Baren Mullick. He's had three smash hits in a row.'

Well, at least he had gathered some useful information. It wouldn't have done for him to say he didn't know if his wife had asked whose film he had acted in and with which actor.

Naresh Dutt now came up to him with tea in a small clay cup.

'Here you are, sir—the hot tea will help your throat. Your turn will come shortly.'

Patol Babu now had to come out with it.

'If you let me have my lines now . . .'

'Your lines? Come with me.'

Naresh Dutt went towards the three-legged instrument with Patol Babu at his heels.

'I say, Shoshanko.'

A young fellow in short-sleeved shirt turned towards Naresh Dutt. 'This gentleman wants his lines. Why don't you write them down on a piece of paper and give it to him? He's the one who . . .'

'I know, I know.'

Shoshanko now turned to Patol Babu.

'Come along, Dadu. I say, Jyoti, can I borrow your pen for a sec? Grandpa wants his lines written down.'

The youngster Jyoti produced a red ballpoint pen from his pocket and gave it to Shoshanko. Shoshanko tore off a page from the notebook he was carrying, scribbled something on it and handed it to Patol Babu.

Patol Babu glanced at the paper and found that a single word had been scrawled on it—'Oh!'

Patol Babu felt a sudden throbbing in his head. He wished he could take off his jacket. The heat was unbearable.

Shoshanko said, 'What's the matter, Dadu? You don't seem too pleased.'

Were these people pulling his leg? Was the whole thing a gigantic hoax? A meek, harmless man like him, and they had to drag him into the middle of the city to make a laughing stock out of him. How could anyone be so cruel?

Patol Babu said in a voice hardly audible, 'I find it rather strange.'

'Why, Dadu?'

'Just "Oh"? Is that all I have to say?'

Shoshanko's eyebrows shot up.

'What are you saying, Dadu? You think that's nothing? Why, this is a regular speaking part! A speaking part in a Baren Mullick film—do you realize what that means? Why, you're the luckiest of actors. Do you know that till now more than a hundred persons have appeared in this film who have had nothing to say? They just walked past the camera. Some didn't even walk; they just stood in one spot. There were others whose faces didn't register at all. Even today—look at all those people standing by the lamp-post; they all appear in today's scene but have nothing to say. Even our hero Chanchal Kumar has no lines to speak today. You are the only one who has—see?'

Now the young man called Jyoti came up, put his hand on Patol Babu's shoulder and said, 'Listen, Dadu. I'll tell you what you have to do. Chanchal Kumar is a rising young executive. He is informed that an embezzlement has taken place in his office, and he comes to find out what has happened. He gets out of his car and charges across the pavement towards the entrance. Just then he collides with an absent-minded pedestrian. That's you. You're hurt in the head and say "Oh!", but Chanchal Kumar pays no attention to you and goes into the office. The fact that he ignores you reflects his extreme preoccupation—see? Just think how crucial the shot is.'

'I hope everything is clear now,' said Shoshanko. 'Now, if you just move over to where you were standing . . . the fewer people crowding around here the better. There's one more shot left before your turn comes.'

Patol Babu slowly went back to the paan shop. Standing in the shade, he glanced down at the paper in his hand, cast a quick look around to see if anyone was watching, crumpled the paper into a ball and threw it into the roadside drain.

Oh . . . A sigh came out of the depths of his heart.

Just one word—no, not even a word; a sound—'Oh!'

The heat was stifling. The jacket seemed to weigh a ton. Patol Babu couldn't keep standing in one spot any more; his legs felt heavy.

He moved up to the office beyond the paan shop and sat down on the steps. It was nearly half-past nine. Every Sunday morning, devotional songs were sung in Karali Babu's house. Patol Babu went there every week and enjoyed it. What if he were to go there now? What harm would there be? Why waste a Sunday morning in the company of these useless people, and be made to look foolish on top of that?

'Silence!'

Stuff and nonsense! To hell with your 'silence'! They had to put up this pompous show for something so trivial. Things were much better on the stage.

The stage . . . the stage . . . A faint memory was stirring in Patol Babu's mind. Words of advice, given in a deep, mellow voice: 'Remember one thing, Patol; however small a part you're offered, never consider it beneath your dignity to accept it. As an artist your aim should be to make the most of your opportunity, and squeeze the last drop of meaning out of your lines. A play involves the work of many and it is the combined effort of many that makes a success of the play.'

It was Mr Pakrashi who gave the advice. Gogon Pakrashi, Patol Babu's mentor. A wonderful actor, without a trace of vanity in him; a saintly person, and an actor in a million.

There was something else which Mr Pakrashi used to say. 'Each word spoken in a play is like a fruit in a tree. Not everyone in the audience can reach it. But you, the actor, must know how to pluck it, get at its essence, and serve it up to the audience for their edification.'

The memory of his guru made Patol Babu bow his head in obeisance.

Was it really true that there was nothing in the part he had been given today? He had only one word to say—'Oh!', but was that word so devoid of meaning as to be dismissed summarily?

Oh, oh, oh, oh, oh—Patol Babu uttered the word over and over again, giving it a different inflection each time. After doing this for a number of times he made an astonishing discovery. The same exclamation, when spoken in different ways, carried different shades of meaning. A man when hurt said 'Oh' in one way. Despair brought forth a difficult kind of 'Oh', while sorrow provoked yet another kind. In fact, there were so many kinds of Ohs—the short Oh, the long-drawn Oh, Oh shouted and Oh whispered, the high-pitched Oh, the low-pitched Oh, the Oh starting low and ending high, and the Oh starting high and ending low . . . Strange! Patol Babu suddenly felt that he could write a whole thesis on that one monosyllabic exclamation. Why had he felt so disheartened when this single word contained a gold mine of meaning? The true actor could make a mark with this one single syllable.

'Silence!'

The director had raised his voice again. Patol Babu spotted young Jyoti clearing the crowd. There was something he had to ask him. He quickly went over to him.

'How long will it be before my turn comes, bhai?'

'Why are you so impatient, Dadu? You have to learn to be patient in this line of business. It'll be another half an hour before you're called.'

'That's all right. I'll certainly wait. I'll be in that side street across the road.'

'Okay—so long as you don't sneak off.'

'Start sound!'

Patol Babu crossed the road on tiptoe and went into the quiet little side street. It was good that he had a little time on his hands. While these people didn't seem to believe in rehearsals, he himself would rehearse his own bit. There was no one about. These were office buildings, so very few people lived here. Those who did—the shopkeepers—had all gone to watch the shooting.

Patol Babu cleared his throat and began to practise speaking this one-syllable dialogue in various ways. Along with that he tried working out how he would react to the actual collision—how his features would be twisted in pain, how he would fling out his arms, how his body would double up in pain and surprise—all these postures he performed in front of a large glass window.

Patol Babu was called in exactly after half an hour. Now he had got over his apathy completely. All he felt was keen anticipation and suppressed excitement. It was the feeling he used to have twenty years ago just before he stepped on to the stage.

The director, Baren Mullick, called Patol Babu to him. 'I hope you know what you're supposed to do?' he asked.

'Yes, sir.'

'Very good. I'll first say "Start sound". The recordists will reply by saying "Running". That's the signal for the camera to start. Then I will say "Action". That will be your cue to start walking from that pillar, and for the hero to come out of the car and make a dash for the office. You work out your steps so that the collision takes place at this spot, here. The hero ignores you and strides into the office, while you register pain by saying "Oh!", stop for a couple of seconds, then resume walking— okay?'

Patol Babu suggested a rehearsal, but Baren Mullick shook his head impatiently. 'There's a large patch of cloud approaching the sun,' he said. 'This scene must be shot in sunlight.'

'One question please.'

'Yes?'

An idea had occurred to Patol Babu while rehearsing; he now came out with it.

'Er—I was thinking—if I had a newspaper open in my hand, and if the collision took place while I had my eyes on the paper, then perhaps—'

Baren Mullick cut him short by addressing a bystander who was carrying a Bengali newspaper. 'Do you mind handing your paper to this gentleman, just for this one shot? Thanks . . . Now you take your position beside the pillar. Chanchal, are you ready?'

'Yes, sir.'

'Good. Silence!'

Baren Mullick raised his hand, then brought it down again, saying, 'Just a minute. Kesto, I think if we gave the pedestrian a moustache, it would be more interesting.'

'What kind, sir? Walrus, Ronald Colman or butterfly? I have them all ready.'

'Butterfly, butterfly—and make it snappy!'

The elderly make-up man went up to Patol Babu, took out a small grey moustache from a box, and stuck it on with spirit-gum below Patol Babu's nose.

Patol Babu said, 'I hope it won't come off at the time of the collision?'

The make-up man smiled. 'Collision?' he said. 'Even if you wrestle with Dara Singh the moustache will stay in place.'

Patol Babu took a quick glance in the mirror the man was holding. True enough, the moustache suited him very well. Patol Babu silently commended the director's judgement.

'Silence! Silence!'

The business with the moustache had provoked a wave of comments from the spectators which Baren Mullick's shout now silenced.

Patol Babu noticed that most of the bystanders' eyes were turned towards him.'Start sound!'

Patol Babu cleared his throat. One, two, three, four, five—five steps would take him to the spot where the collision was to take place. And Chanchal Kumar would have to walk four steps. So if both were to start together, Patol Babu would have to walk a little faster than the hero, or else—

'Running!'

Patol Babu held the newspaper open in his hand. He had worked out that when he said 'Oh!' he had to mix sixty parts of irritation with forty parts of surprise.

'Action!'

Clop, clop, clop, clop, clop—Wham!

Patol Babu saw stars before his eyes. The hero's head had banged against his forehead, and an excruciating pain robbed him of his senses for a second.

But the next moment, by a supreme effort of will, Patol Babu pulled himself together, and mixing fifty parts of anguish with twenty-five of surprise and twenty-five of irritation, cried 'Oh!' Then after a brief pause, he resumed his walk.

'Cut!'

'Was that all right?' asked Patol Babu anxiously, stepping towards Baren Mullick.

'Jolly good! Why, you're quite an actor! Shoshanko, just take a look at the sky through the dark glass, will you.'

Jyoti now came up to Patol Babu and said, 'I hope Dadu wasn't hurt too badly?'

'My God!' said Chanchal Kumar, massaging his head. 'You timed it so well that I nearly passed out!'

Naresh Dutt elbowed his way through the crowd, came up to Patol Babu and said, 'Please go back to where you were standing. I'll come to you in a short while and do the needful.'

Patol Babu took his place once again by the paan shop. The cloud had just covered the sun and there was a slight chill in the air. Nevertheless, Patol Babu took off his woollen jacket and heaved a sigh of relief. A feeling of complete satisfaction swept over him.

He had done his job well. All those years of struggle hadn't blunted his sensibility. Gogon Pakrashi would have been pleased with his performance. But all the labour and imagination he had put into this one shot—did these people appreciate that? He doubted it. They probably got people off the streets, made them go through a set of motions, paid them for their labours and forgot all about it. Paid them, yes, but how much? Ten, fifteen, twenty rupees? It was true that he needed money very badly, but what was twenty rupees when measured against the intense satisfaction of a small job done with perfection and dedication?

Ten minutes later Naresh Dutt went looking for Patol Babu near the paan shop and found no one there. 'That's odd—the man hadn't been paid yet. What a strange fellow!'

'The sun has come out,' Baren Mullick was heard shouting. 'Silence! Silence!—Naresh, hurry up and get these people out of the way!'

Translated by Satyajit Ray
First published in Bengali in 1963

Bipin Chowdhury's Lapse of Memory

Every Monday, on his way back from work, Bipin Chowdhury would drop in at Kalicharan's in New Market to buy books. Crime stories, ghost stories and thrillers. He had to buy at least five at a time to last him through the week. He lived alone, was not a good mixer, had few friends, and didn't like spending time in idle chat. Those who called in the evening got through their business quickly and left. Those who didn't show signs of leaving would be told around eight o'clock by Bipin Babu that he was under doctor's orders to have dinner at eight-thirty. After dinner he would rest for half an hour and then turn in with a book. This was a routine which had persisted unbroken for years.

Today, at Kalicharan's, Bipin Babu had the feeling that someone was observing him from close quarters. He turned round and found himself looking at a round-faced, meek-looking man who now broke into a smile.

'I don't suppose you recognize me.'

Bipin Babu felt ill at ease. It didn't seem that he had ever encountered this man before. The face seemed quite unfamiliar.

'But you're a busy man. You must meet all kinds of people all the time.'

'Have we met before?' asked Bipin Babu.

The man looked greatly surprised. 'We met every day for a whole week. I arranged for a car to take you to the Hudroo falls. In 1958. In Ranchi. My name is Parimal Ghose.'

'Ranchi?'

Now Bipin Babu realized that it was not he but this man who was making a mistake. Bipin Babu had never been to Ranchi. He had been at the point of going several times, but had never made it. He smiled and said, 'Do you know who I am?'

The man raised his eyebrows, bit his tongue and said, 'Do I know you? Who doesn't know Bipin Chowdhury?'

Bipin Babu now turned towards the bookshelves and said, 'Still you're making a mistake. One often does. I've never been to Ranchi.'

The man now laughed aloud.

'What are you saying, Mr Chowdhury? You had a fall in Hudroo and cut your right knee. I brought you iodine. I had fixed up a car for you to go to Netarhat the next day, but you couldn't because of the pain in the knee. Can't you recall anything? Someone else you know was also in Ranchi at that time. Mr Dinesh Mukerjee. You stayed in a bungalow.

You said you didn't like hotel food and would prefer to have your meals cooked by a bawarchi. Mr Mukerjee stayed with his sister. You had a big argument about the moon landing, remember? I'll tell you more: you always carried a bag with your books in it on your sightseeing trips. Am I right or not?'

Bipin Babu spoke quietly, his eyes still on the books.

'Which month in fifty-eight are you talking about?'

The man said, 'Just before the pujas. October.'

'No, sir,' said Bipin Babu. 'I spent puja in fifty-eight with a friend in Kanpur. You're making a mistake. Good day.'

But the man didn't go, nor did he stop talking.

'Very strange. One evening I had tea with you on the veranda of your bungalow. You spoke about your family. You said you had no children, and that you had lost your wife ten years ago. Your only brother had died insane, which is why you didn't want to visit the mental hospital in Ranchi . . .'

When Bipin Babu had paid for the books and was leaving the shop, the man was still looking at him in utter disbelief.

Bipin Babu's car was safely parked in Bertram Street by the Lighthouse cinema. He told the driver as he got into the car, 'Just drive by the Ganga, will you, Sitaram.' Driving up the Strand Road, Bipin Babu regretted having paid so much attention to the intruder. He had never been to Ranchi—no question about it. It was inconceivable that he should forget such an incident which took place only six or seven years ago. He had an excellent memory. Unless—Bipin Babu's head reeled.

Unless he was losing his mind.

But how could that be? He was working daily in his office. It was a big firm, and he had a responsible job. He wasn't aware of anything ever going seriously wrong. Only today he had spoken for half an hour at an important meeting. And yet . . .

And yet that man knew a great deal about him. How? He even seemed to know some intimate details. The bag of books, wife's death, brother's insanity . . . The only mistake was about his having gone to Ranchi. Not a mistake; a deliberate lie. In 1958, during the pujas, he was in Kanpur at his friend Haridas Bagchi's place. All Bipin Babu had to do was write to—no, there was no way of writing to Haridas. Bipin Babu suddenly remembered that Haridas had not left his address.

But where was the need for proof? If it so happened that the police were trying to pin a crime on him which had taken place in Ranchi in 1958, he might have needed to prove he hadn't been there. He himself was fully aware that he hadn't been to Ranchi—and that was that.

The river breeze was bracing, and yet a slight discomfort lingered in Bipin Babu's mind.

Around Hastings, Bipin Babu had the sudden notion of rolling up his trousers and taking a look at his right knee.

There was the mark of an old inch-long cut. It was impossible to tell when the injury had occurred. Had he never had a fall as a boy and cut his knee? He tried to recall such an incident, but couldn't.

Then Bipin Babu suddenly thought of Dinesh Mukerjee. That man had said that Dinesh was in Ranchi at the same time. The best thing surely would be to ask him. He lived quite near—in Beninandan Street. What about going right now? But then, if he had really never been to Ranchi, what would Dinesh think if Bipin Babu asked for a confirmation? He would probably conclude Bipin Babu was going nuts. No—it would be ridiculous to ask him. And he knew how ruthless Dinesh's sarcasm could be.

Sipping a cold drink in his air-conditioned living room, Bipin Babu felt at ease again. Such a nuisance the man was! He probably had nothing else to do, so he went about getting into other people's hair.

After dinner, snuggling into bed with one of the new thrillers, Bipin Babu forgot all about the man in New Market.

Next day, in the office, Bipin Babu noticed that with every passing hour, the previous day's encounter was occupying more and more of his mind. That look of round-eyed surprise on that round face, the disbelieving snigger . . . If the man knew so much about the details of Bipin Babu's life, how could he be so wrong about the Ranchi trip?

Just before lunch—at five minutes to one—Bipin Babu couldn't check himself any more. He opened the phone book. He had to ring up Dinesh Mukerjee. It was better to settle the question over the phone; at least the embarrassment on his face wouldn't show.

Two-three-five-six-one-six.

Bipin Babu dialled the number.

'Hello.'

'Is that Dinesh? This is Bipin here.'

'Well, well—what's the news?'

'I just wanted to find out if you recalled an incident which took place in fifty-eight.'

'Fifty-eight? What incident?'

'Were you in Calcutta right through that year? That's the first thing I've got to know.'

'Wait just a minute . . . fifty-eight . . . just let me check in my diary.'

For a minute there was silence. Bipin Babu could feel that his heartbeat had gone up. He was sweating a little.

'Hello.'

'Yes.'

'I've got it. I had been out twice.'

'Where?'

'Once in February—nearby—to Krishnanagar to a nephew's wedding. And then . . . but you'd know about this one. The trip to Ranchi. You were there too. That's all. But what's all this sleuthing about?'

'No, I just wanted to—anyway, thanks.'

Bipin Babu slammed the receiver down and gripped his head with his hands. He felt his head swimming. A chill seemed to spread over his body. There were sandwiches in his tiffin box, but he didn't feel like eating them. He had lost his appetite. Completely.

After lunchtime, Bipin Babu realized that he couldn't possibly carry on sitting at his desk and working. This was the first time something like this had happened in his twenty-five years with the firm. He had a reputation for being a tireless, conscientious worker. The men who worked under him all held him in awe. In the worst moments of crisis, even when faced with the most acute problems, Bipin Babu had always kept his cool and weathered the storm. But today his head was in a whirl.

Back home at two-thirty, Bipin Babu shut himself up in his bedroom, lay down in bed and tried to gather his wits together. He knew that it was possible to lose one's memory through an injury to the head, but he didn't know of a single instance of someone remembering everything except one particular incident—and a fairly recent and significant one at that. He had always wanted to go to Ranchi; to have gone there, done things, and not to remember was something utterly impossible.

At seven, Bipin Babu's servant came and announced that Seth Girdhariprasad had come. A rich businessman—and a VIP—this Girdhariprasad. And he had come by appointment. But Bipin Babu was feeling so low that he had to tell his servant that it was not possible for him to leave his bed. To hell with VIPs.

At seven-thirty, the servant came again. Bipin Babu had just dozed off and was in the middle of an unpleasant dream when the servant's knock woke him up. Who was it this time? 'Chuni Babu, sir. Says it's very urgent.'

Bipin Babu knew what the urgency was. Chunilal was a childhood friend of his. He had fallen on bad times recently, and had been pestering Bipin Babu for a job. Bipin Babu had kept fobbing him off, but Chuni kept coming back. What a persistent bore.

Bipin Babu sent word that not only was it not possible for him to see Chuni now, but not in several weeks as well.

But as soon as the servant stepped out of the room, it struck Bipin Babu that Chuni might remember something about the '58 trip. There was no harm in asking him.

He sped downstairs. Chuni had got up to leave. Seeing Bipin Babu, he turned around with a flicker of hope in his eyes.

Bipin Babu didn't beat about the bush.

'Listen, Chuni—I want to ask you something. You have a good memory, and you've been seeing me off and on for a long time. Just throw your mind back and tell me—did I go to Ranchi in fifty-eight?'

Chuni said, 'Fifty-eight? It must have been fifty-eight. Or was it fifty-nine?'

'You're sure that I did go to Ranchi?'

Chuni's look of amazement was not unmixed with worry.

'D'you mean you have doubts about having gone at all?'

'Did I go? Do you remember clearly?'

Chuni was standing up; he now sat down on the sofa, fixed Bipin Babu with a long, hard stare and said, 'Bipin, have you taken to drugs or something? As far as I know, you had a clean record where such things were concerned. I know that old friendships don't mean much to you, but at least you had a good memory. You can't really mean that you've forgotten about the Ranchi trip?'

Bipin Babu had to turn away from Chuni's incredulous stare.

'D'you remember what my last job was?' asked Chunilal.

'Of course. You worked in a travel agency.'

'You remember that and you don't remember that it was I who fixed up your booking for Ranchi? I went to the station to see you off; one of the fans in your compartment was not working—I got an electrician to fix it. Have you forgotten everything? Whatever is the matter with you? You don't look too well, you know.'

Bipin Babu sighed and shook his head.

'I've been working too hard,' he said at last. 'That must be the reason. Must see about consulting a specialist.'

Doubtless it was Bipin Babu's condition which made Chunilal leave without mentioning anything about a job.

Paresh Chanda was a young physician with a pair of bright eyes and a sharp nose. He became thoughtful when he heard about Bipin Babu's symptoms. 'Look, Dr Chanda,' said Bipin Babu desperately, 'you must cure me of this horrible illness. I can't tell you how it's affecting my work. There are so many kinds of drugs these days; isn't there something specific for such a complaint? I can have it sent from abroad if it's not to be had here. But I must be rid of these symptoms.'

Dr Chanda shook his head.

'You know what, Mr Chowdhury,' he said, 'I've never had to deal with a case such as yours. Frankly, this is quite outside my field of experience. But I have one suggestion. I don't know if it'll work, but it's worth a try. It can do no harm.'

Bipin Babu leaned forward anxiously.

'As far as I can make out,' said Dr Chanda, 'and I think you're of the same opinion—you have been to Ranchi, but due to some unknown reason, the entire episode has slipped out of your mind. What I suggest is that you go to Ranchi once again. The sight of the place may remind you of your trip. This is not impossible. More than that I cannot do at the moment. I'm prescribing a nerve tonic and a tranquilizer. Sleep is essential, or the symptoms will get more pronounced.'

It may have been the sleeping pill, and the advice which the doctor gave, which made Bipin Babu feel somewhat better the next morning.

After breakfast, he rang up his office, gave some instructions, and then procured a first-class ticket to Ranchi for the same evening.

Getting off the train at Ranchi next morning, he realized at once that he had never been there before.

He came out of the station, hired a taxi and drove around the town for a while. It was clear that the streets, the buildings, the hotels, the bazaars, the Morabadi Hill were all unfamiliar—with none of these had he the slightest acquaintance. Would a trip to the Hudroo Falls help? He didn't believe so, but, at the same time, he didn't wish to leave with the feeling that he hadn't tried hard enough. So he arranged for a car and left for Hudroo in the afternoon.

At five o'clock the same afternoon in Hudroo, two Gujarati gentlemen from a group of picnickers discovered Bipin Babu lying unconscious beside a boulder. When the ministrations of the two gentlemen brought him around, the first thing Bipin Babu said was, 'I'm finished. There's no hope left.'

Next morning, Bipin Babu was back in Calcutta. He realized that there was truly no hope for him. Soon he would lose everything: his will to work, his confidence, his ability, his balance of mind. Was he going to end up in the asylum at Ranchi . . . ? Bipin Babu couldn't think any more.

Back home, he rang up Dr Chanda and asked him to come over. Then, after a shower, he got into bed with an icebag clamped to his head. Just then the servant brought him a letter which someone had left in the letter box. A greenish envelope with his name in red ink on it. Above the name it said 'Urgent and Confidential'. In spite of his condition, Bipin Babu had a feeling that he ought to go through the letter. He tore open the envelope and took out the letter. This is what he read—

Dear Bipin,
I had no idea that affluence would bring about the kind of change in you that it has done. Was it so difficult for you to help out an old friend down on his luck? I have no money, so my resources are limited. What I have is imagination, a part of which is used in retribution of your unfeeling behaviour.
The man in New Market is a neighbour and acquaintance of mine and a capable actor who played the part I wrote for him. Dinesh Mukerjee has never been particularly well-disposed towards you: so he was quite willing to help. As for the mark on your knee, you will surely recall that you tripped on a rope in Chandpal Ghat back in 1939.
Well, you'll be all right again now. A novel I've written is being considered by a publisher. If he likes it enough, it'll see me through the next few months.
Yours,
Chunilal

When Dr Chanda came, Bipin Babu said, 'I'm fine. It all came back as soon as I got off the train at Ranchi.'

'A unique case,' said Dr Chanda. 'I shall certainly write about it in a medical journal.'

'The reason why I sent for you,' said Bipin Babu, 'is that I have a pain in the hip from a fall I had in Ranchi. If you could prescribe a pain killer . . .'

Translated by Satyajit Ray
First published in Bengali in 1963

The Vicious Vampire

I have always harboured an intense dislike for bats. Whenever a flitter-mouse flits into my room in the house in Calcutta, I feel obliged to drop everything and rush out of the room. Particularly during the summer, I am distinctly uneasy at the thought of one of those creatures knocking against the fan spinning at full speed and dropping to the ground, hurt and injured. So I run out of my room and yell at the cook, Vinod, to come and rescue me. Once, Vinod managed to kill a flitter-mouse with my badminton racquet. To be very honest, my dislike is often mixed with fear. The very sight of a bat puts me off. What peculiar creatures they are—neither birds nor animals, with their queer habit of hanging upside down from trees. I think that the world would have been a far better place to live in if bats did not exist.

My room in Calcutta had been invaded by flitter-mice so many times that I had begun to think they had a strange fondness for me. But I never thought I would find a bat hanging from the ceiling in my room in this house in Shiuri. This really was too much. I could not stay in the room unless it was removed.

My father's friend, Tinkori Kaka, had told me about this house. He was a doctor and had once practised in Shiuri. After retirement, he had moved to Calcutta, but, needless to say, he still knew a lot of people in Shiuri. So I went straight to him for advice when I discovered that I would have to spend about a week there.

'Shiuri? Why Shiuri? What do you want to do there?' he asked. I told him I was working on a research project on old terracotta temples of Bengal. It was my ultimate aim to write a book on this subject. There were so many beautiful temples strewn about the country but no one had ever written a really good book on them.

'Oh, of course! You're an artist, aren't you? So your interest lies in temples, does it? But why do you want to limit yourself just to Shiuri? There are temples everywhere—Shurul, Hetampur, Dubrajpur, Phoolbera, Beersinghpur. But, perhaps, those aren't good enough to be written about?'

Anyway, Tinkori Kaka told me about this house.

'You wouldn't mind staying in an old house, would you? A patient of mine used to live there. He's now shifted to Calcutta. But I believe there is a caretaker in Shiuri to look after the house. It's a fairly large place. I don't think you'll have any problem. And you wouldn't have to pay anything, either. I snatched this man back, so to speak, from the jaws of death as many as three times. He'd be only too pleased to have a guest of mine stay in his house for a week.'

Tinkori Kaka was right. There was no problem in getting to the house. But the minute I got off the cycle rickshaw that brought me from the station and entered my room, I saw the bat.

I called the old caretaker.

'What's your name?'

'Madhusudan.'

'I see. Well, then, Madhusudan—is Mr Bat a permanent resident of this room or has he come here today to give me a special welcome?'

Madhusudan looked at the ceiling, scratched his head and said, 'I hadn't noticed it, sir. This room usually stays locked. It was only opened today because you were coming.'

'But I cannot share a room with a bat.'

'Don't worry about it, sir. It will leave as soon as the sun goes down.'

'All right. But can't anything be done to make sure it doesn't return?'

'No, sir. It won't come back. Why should it? After all, it's not as though it's built a nest here. It must have slipped in last night somehow and couldn't get out for it can't see during the day!'

After a cup of tea, I went and occupied an old cane chair on the veranda. The house was at one end of the town. On the northern side was a large mango grove. Through the trees it was possible to catch glimpses of rice fields that stretched right up to the horizon. On the western side was a bamboo grove and, beyond it, the spire of a church stood tall. This must be the famous ancient church of Shiuri.

I decided to walk round to the church in the evening. I should start working from tomorrow. In and around twenty-five miles of Shiuri at least thirty terracotta temples could be found. I had a camera with me and a large stock of film. Each carving on the walls of these temples should be photographed. The temples might not last very much longer and once these were destroyed, Bengal would lose an important part of its heritage.

It was now 5.30 p.m. The sun disappeared behind the church. I got up, stretched and had just taken a step towards the stairs when something flew past my left ear making a swishing noise, and vanished into the mango grove.

I went into the bedroom and looked at the ceiling. The bat had gone. Thank goodness for that. At least I could work peacefully in the evening. Perhaps I should start writing about the temples I had already seen elsewhere in Burdwan, Bankura and the 24 Parganas.

As soon as darkness fell, I took out my torch and began walking towards the church. The red earth of Birbhum, the uneven terrain, the rows of palms—I loved them all. This was my first visit to Shiuri—I was not really here to look at nature and its beauty, yet the church and its surroundings struck me as beautiful. I passed the church and began walking further west. Then I saw what looked like a park. There was an open space surrounded by a railing. It had an iron gate.

As I came closer, I realized it was not a park but a graveyard. There were about thirty graves in it. A few had carved marble pillars. Others had marble slabs. All were undoubtedly quite ancient. The pillars were cracked. Little plants peeped out of some of these cracks.

The gate was open. I went in and began trying to read some of the hazy, indistinct epitaphs. All were graves of Britons, possibly those who had died in the very early stages of the Raj, as a result of some epidemic or the other.

One particular marble slab seemed to have a slightly more legible inscription. I was about to switch the torch on to read it, when I heard footsteps behind me. I turned around quickly. A short, middle-aged man was standing about ten feet away, smiling at me. He was wearing a black jacket and grey trousers. There was an old, patched up umbrella in his hand.

'You don't like bats, do you?'

I started. How did this stranger know that? The man laughed. 'You must be wondering how I found out. Very easy. When you were telling that caretaker to drive the bat away this morning, I happened to be in the vicinity.'

'Oh, I see.'

Now the man raised his hands in a namaskar.

'I am Jagdish Percival Mukherjee. My family has lived in Shiuri for a long time. Four generations, you know. I like visiting the church and this graveyard in the evening. I am a Christian, you see.'

It was getting darker. I headed back to the house. The man began walking with me. He seemed a bit strange, although he appeared to be harmless enough. But his voice was funny—thin and, at the same time, harsh. In any case, I could never be comfortable with people who made such an obvious attempt to get friendly.

I tried to switch on the torch, but it did not work. Then I remembered I had meant to buy a couple of batteries at the station, and had quite forgotten to do so. How annoying! I could not see a thing. What if there were snakes?

The man said, 'Don't worry about your torch. I am used to moving in the dark. I can see quite well. Careful—there's a pot-hole here!' He pulled me to one side. Then he said, 'Do you know what a vampire is?'

'Yes,' I said briefly.

Who did not know about vampires? Blood-sucking bats were called vampires. They sucked the blood of animals like horses and cows. I did not know whether such bats could be found in India, but I had certainly read about them in books from abroad. And those did not just talk about bats. They even spoke of bodies of dead men that came out of graves in the middle of the night to drink the blood of people who were asleep. Such creatures were also called vampires. The story of Count Dracula was something I had read in school.

It annoyed me to think that the man had raised the subject of vampires in spite of being aware of my aversion to bats.

We both fell silent.

Then we came to the mango grove and the house could be seen quite clearly. Here he stopped abruptly and said, 'It's been a pleasure meeting you. You're going to stay here for some time, aren't you?'

'About a week.'

'Good. Then we shall certainly meet again. Usually, in the evening,' he said, pointing towards the graveyard, 'I can be found there. My forefathers were buried in the same place. I shall show you their graves tomorrow.'

I said silently to myself, 'The less I see of you the better.' Bats I could not bear to look at, anyway. A discussion on those stupid creatures was even worse. There were plenty of other things to think about.

As I climbed up the steps of the veranda, I turned back for a moment and saw the man disappear among the mango trees. By that time, the jackals had started their chorus beyond the rice fields.

It was the month of October; yet, it felt hot and oppressive inside the room. I tossed and turned in my bed after dinner. I even toyed with the idea of opening the door of my room which I had closed for fear of the bat flying in again. In the end, I decided against it, not so much because of the bat, but because of something else. If the caretaker was a light sleeper, perhaps there was no danger of being burgled. But what if a stray dog came in through the open door and chewed up my slippers? This could happen easily in a small mofussil town. In fact, I had already had that kind of experience more than once. So, instead of opening the door, I opened the window that faced the west. A lovely breeze came wafting in.

I soon fell asleep and began to have a strange dream.

In my dream I saw the same man peering through the window of my room and smiling at me. His eyes were bright green and his teeth sharp and narrow. Then I saw the man take a step back, raise his arms and leap through the window. It seemed almost as though it was the sound of his arrival that woke me.

I opened my eyes and saw that dawn had broken. What an awful dream!

I rose and yelled for a cup of tea. I must finish breakfast and leave early, or I would never get all my work done.

Madhusudan seemed a little preoccupied as he placed my tea on the table in the veranda. I asked, 'What's the matter, Madhusudan? Are you unwell? Or didn't you sleep last night?'

Madhu said, 'No, babu. I am quite all right. It's my calf.'

'What happened to your calf?'

'It died last night. Got bitten by a snake probably.'

'What!'

'Yes, sir. It was only a week old. Something bit its throat—God knows if it was a cobra.'

I began to feel uneasy. Bitten on the throat? Where did I . . .? Of course. A vampire bat! Wasn't it only yesterday that I was thinking of the same thing? Vampire bats did suck blood from the throats of animals. But, of course, the calf might indeed have been bitten by a snake. That was perfectly possible, especially if the calf happened to be sleeping.

Why was I trying to link the death of a calf with vampire bats?

I uttered a few words of comfort to Madhusudan and returned to my room. My eyes moved towards the ceiling involuntarily.

The bat was back.

It was my mistake. I should not have left the window open. I decided to keep all the doors and windows closed tonight, no matter how stuffy it became.

I spent a rather enjoyable day among the old terracotta temples. The workmanship of those who had done the carving on the walls was truly remarkable.

I took a bus from Hetampur and returned to Shiuri at about half past four in the evening.

I had to pass the graveyard in order to get home. The busy day had nearly made me forget the man I had met the day before. The sight of the man, standing under a tree just outside the graveyard, therefore, came as a surprise. Perhaps the best thing would be to pretend not to have seen him and walk on. But that was not to be. Just as I bent my head and increased the speed of my walking, he leapt towards me.

'Did you sleep well last night?'

I said 'Yes' without stopping. But it was clear that, like yesterday, he would walk with me. He began walking fast to keep pace with me. 'I have a funny habit, you see,' he said. 'I cannot sleep at night. So I sleep tight during the day and from evening to early morning, I roam around here and there. Oh, I cannot explain to you the joy of walking around at night. You have no idea how many different things are simply crying out to be seen, to be heard in this very graveyard! Have you ever thought of these beings that have spent years and years, lying under the ground, stuffed in a wooden box? Have you wondered about their unfulfilled desires? No one wants to stay a prisoner. Each one of them wants to come out! But not many know the secret of getting out. So, in their sadness, some weep, some wail and others sigh. In the middle of the night, when the jackals go to sleep and the crickets become quiet, those who have sensitive ears—like mine—can hear the soft moaning of these people, nailed into a box. But, as I told you, one would have to have very sharp ears. My eyes and ears work very well at night. Just like a bat's.'

I must ask Madhusudan about this man, I thought. There were a few questions I wanted answered, but I knew there would be no point in asking the man. How long had he really spent in Shiuri? What did he do for a living? Where did he live?

He continued to walk beside me and talk incessantly.

'I don't often make the effort to go and meet people,' he said, 'but I simply had to come and meet you. I do hope you won't deprive me of the pleasure of your company for the remainder of your stay.'

This time I could not control myself. I stopped, turned towards the man and said rather rudely, 'Look, mister, I have come only for a week.

I have a vast amount of work to do. I don't see how I can possibly spend any time with you.'

The man, at first, seemed a little crestfallen at my words. Then he smiled and said in a tone that sounded mild yet oddly firm, 'You may not give *me* your company, but surely I can give you mine? Besides, I was not talking about the time when you'd be busy doing your work—during the day, that is.'

There was no need to waste any more time with him. I said namaskar abruptly and strode towards my house.

'Jagdish Mukherjee? I don't think . . . Oh, wait a minute! Is he short? Wears a jacket and trousers? Is a little dark?'

'Yes, yes.'

'Oh, babu, that man is crazy. Quite mad. In fact, he's only recently been discharged from the asylum. They say he's now cured. How did *you* come across him? I haven't seen him for ages. His father was a priest called Nilmani Mukherjee. A nice man, but I believe he, too, went quite cuckoo before his death.'

I did not pursue the matter. All I said was, 'That bat had come in again. But it was entirely my fault. I had kept the window open. I hadn't realized some of its grills were broken.'

Madhu said, 'Tomorrow morning I shall have those gaps filled. Perhaps during the night you should keep the window closed.'

After dinner, I finished writing notes on the temples I had seen that day. Then I loaded my camera with a new roll. Glancing out of the window, I saw that the clouds of last night had cleared, leaving everything awash in the moonlight.

I went and sat outside on the veranda for a while and returned to my room at around 11 p.m. Then I drank a glass of water and finally went to bed. Jagdish Mukherjee's words were still ringing in my ears. No doubt, in this scientific age, his words were no more than the ravings of a mad man. I must find out which asylum he had gone to and which doctor had treated him.

The clouds having dispersed, the oppressive feeling of the night before had gone. Keeping the window closed was not difficult. In fact, that night I had to use the extra sheet I had brought. I fell asleep soon after closing my eyes. But I woke a little while later, though I could not tell the time nor what it was that had disturbed my sleep. Then I saw a square patch of moonlight on the wall and my heart lurched.

God knew when the window had opened. Light was coming in through the open window. In that patch of light, I saw the shadow of something flying in a circle, again and again.

Holding my breath carefully, I turned my head and looked up. This time I could see the bat.

It kept flying in a circle right over my bed, and slowly began to come down.

I mustered all my courage. It would be disastrous if I lost my will power at a moment like this. Without taking my eyes off the bat, I stretched my right hand towards the bedside table and picked up my large, hardbound notebook. Just as the bat made a final swoop, ready to attack my throat, I struck its head with the notebook, using all my strength.

It went shooting out of the window, knocking once against the broken grills, and landed on the ground outside. The next instant, I thought I heard someone running across the ground.

I rushed to the window and peered out. Nothing could be seen. There was no sign of the bat.

I could not go back to sleep after that.

The first rays of the sun in the morning wiped out the horrors of the night. There was no reason to assume that the bat was a vampire. Yes, it had certainly come very close to me, but how could it be proved that it had done so with the intention of sucking my blood? If that weird character in the graveyard had not raised the subject of vampires, I would not even have dreamt of it. A bat in Shiuri would have struck me as no different from a bat in Calcutta.

I decided to forget the whole thing. There was some work to be done in Hetampur. I finished my cup of tea and left at around half-past-six.

As I approached the graveyard, I came upon a startling sight. A few local people were carrying Jagdish Mukherjee. He appeared to be unconscious and his forehead had a large, black bruise.

'What happened to him?' I asked.

One of the men laughed.

'Fell down from a tree, probably,' he said.

'What! Why should he fall from a tree? What could he have been doing on a tree top?'

'You don't know, babu. This man is totally mad. He seemed to have made a slight recovery lately. Before that, every evening as soon as it got dark, he used to go and hang upside down from trees. Just like a bat!'

Translated by Gopa Majumdar
First published in Bengali in 1964

Indigo

My name is Aniruddha Bose. I am twenty-nine years old and a bachelor. For the last eight years I've been working in an advertising agency in Calcutta. With the salary I get I live in reasonable comfort in a flat in Sardar Shankar Road. The flat has two south-facing rooms and is on the ground floor. Two years ago I bought an Ambassador car which I drive myself. I do a bit of writing in my spare time. Three of my stories have been published in magazines and have been well-appreciated by my acquaintances, but I know I cannot make a living by writing alone.

For the last few months I haven't been writing at all. Instead, I have read a lot about indigo plantations in Bengal and Bihar in the nineteenth century. I am something of an authority on the subject now: how the British exploited the poor peasants; how the peasants rose in revolt; and how, finally, with the invention of synthetic indigo in Germany, the cultivation of indigo was wiped out from our country—all this I know by heart. It is to describe the terrible experience which instilled in me this interest in indigo that I have taken up my pen today.

At this point I must tell you something about my past.

My father was a well-known physician in Monghyr, a town in Bihar. That is where I was born and that is where I did my schooling in a missionary school. I have a brother five years older than me. He studied medicine in England and is now attached to a hospital in a suburb of London called Golders Green. He has no plans to return to India.

My father died when I was sixteen. Soon after his death, my mother and I left Monghyr and came to Calcutta where we stayed with my maternal uncle. I went to St Xavier's College and took my bachelor's degree. Soon after that I got my job with the advertising agency. My uncle's influence helped, but I wasn't an unworthy candidate myself. I had been a good student, I spoke English fluently, and most of all, I had the ability to carry myself well in an interview.

My early years in Monghyr had instilled certain habits in me which I have not been able to give up. One of these was an overpowering desire to go far away from the hectic life of Calcutta from time to time. I had done so several times ever since I bought my car. On weekends I made trips to Diamond Harbour, Port Canning, and Hassanabad along the Dum Dum Road. Each time I had gone alone because, to be quite honest, I didn't really have a close friend in Calcutta. That is why Promode's letter made me so happy. Promode had been my classmate in

Monghyr. After I came away to Calcutta, we continued to keep in touch for three or four years. Then, perhaps it was I who stopped writing. Suddenly the other day when I came back from work, I found a letter from Promode waiting for me on my desk. He had written from Dumka—'I have a job in the Forest Department here. I have my own quarters. Why don't you take a week's leave and come over . . .?'

Some leave was due to me, so I spoke to my boss, and on the twenty-seventh of April—I shall remember the date as long as I live—I packed my bags and set off for Dumka.

Promode hadn't suggested that I go by car; it was my idea. Dumka was 200 miles away, so it would take about five or six hours at the most. I decided to have a big breakfast, set off by ten and reach there before dusk.

At least that was the plan, but there was a snag right at the start. I had my meal and was about to put a paan into my mouth, when my father's old friend Uncle Mohit suddenly turned up. He is a grave old man whom I was meeting after ten years. So there was no question of giving him short shrift. I had to offer him tea and listen to him chat for over an hour.

I saw Uncle Mohit off and shoved my suitcase and bedding into the back seat of my car. Just then, my ground-floor neighbour Bhola Babu walked up with his four-year-old son Pintu in tow.

'Where are you off to all by yourself?' Bhola Babu asked.

When I told him, he said with some concern, 'But that's a long way. Shouldn't you have arranged for a driver?'

I said I was a very cautious driver myself, and that I had taken such care of my car that it was still as good as new—'So there's nothing to worry about.'

Bhola Babu wished me luck and went into the house. I glanced at my wristwatch before turning the ignition key. It was ten minutes past eleven.

Although I avoided Howrah and took the Bally Bridge road, it took me an hour and a half to reach Chandernagore. Driving through dingy towns, these first thirty miles were so dreary that the fun of a car journey was quite lost. But from there on, as the car emerged into open country, the effect was magical. Where in the city did one get to see such a clear blue sky free from chimney smoke, and breathe air so pure and so redolent of the smell of earth?

At about half-past twelve, as I was nearing Burdwan, I began to feel the consequence of having eaten so early. Hungry, I pulled up by the station which fell on the way, went into a restaurant and had a light meal of toast, omelette and coffee. Then I resumed my journey. I still had a 135 miles to go.

Twenty miles from Burdwan, there was a small town called Panagarh. There I had to leave the Grand Trunk Road and take the road to Ilambazar. From Ilambazar the road went via Suri and Massanjore to Dumka.

The military camp at Panagarh had just come into view when there was a bang from the rear of my car. I had a flat tyre.

I got down. I had a spare tyre and could easily fit it. The thought that other cars would go whizzing by, their occupants laughing at my predicament, was not a pleasant one. Nevertheless I brought out the jack from the boot and set to work.

By the time I finished putting the new tyre on, I was dripping with sweat. My watch showed half past two. It had turned muggy in the meantime. The cool breeze which was blowing even an hour ago, and was making the bamboo trees sway, had stopped. Now everything was still. As I got back into the car I noticed a blue-black patch in the west above the treetops. Clouds. Was a storm brewing up? A norwester? It was useless to speculate. I must drive faster. I helped myself to some hot tea from the flask and resumed my journey.

But before I could cross Ilambazar, I was caught in the storm. I had enjoyed such norwesters in the past, sitting in my room, and had even recited Tagore poems to myself to blend with the mood. I had no idea that driving through open country, such a norwester could strike terror into the heart. Claps of thunder always make me uncomfortable. They seem to show a nasty side of nature; a vicious assault on helpless humanity. It seemed as if the shafts of lightning were all aimed at my poor Ambassador, and one of them was sure to find its mark sooner or later.

In this precarious state I passed Suri and was well on my way to Massanjore when there was yet another bang which no one could mistake for a thunderclap. I realized that another of my tyres had decided to call it a day.

I gave up hope. It was now pouring with rain. My watch said half past five. For the last twenty miles I had had to keep the speedometer down to fifteen, or I would have been well past Massanjore by now. Where was I? Up ahead nothing was visible through the rainswept windscreen. The wiper was on but its efforts were more frolicsome than effective. It being April, the sun should still be up, but it seemed more like late evening.

I opened the door on my right slightly and looked out. What I saw didn't suggest the presence of a town, though I could make out a couple of buildings through the trees. There was no question of getting out of the car and exploring, but one thing was clear enough: there were no shops along the road as far as the eye could see.

And I had no more spare tyres.

After waiting in the car for a quarter of an hour, it struck me that no other vehicle had passed by in all this time. Was I on the right road? There had been no mistake up to Suri, but suppose I had taken a wrong turning after that? It was not impossible in the blinding rain.

But even if I had made a mistake, it was not as if I had strayed into the jungles of Africa or South America. Wherever I was, there was no doubt that I was still in the district of Birbhum, within fifty miles of Santiniketan, and as soon as the rain stopped my troubles would be over—I might even find a repair shop within a mile or so.

I pulled out a packet of Wills from my pocket and lit a cigarette. I recalled Bhola Babu's warning. He must have gone through the same trying experience, or how could he have given me such sound advice? In future—Honk! Honk! Honk!

I turned round and saw a truck standing behind. Why was it blowing its horn? Was I standing right in the middle of the road?

The rain had let up a little. I opened the door, got out and found that it was no fault of the truck. When my tyre burst the car had swerved at an angle and was now blocking most of the road. There was no room for the truck to pass.

'Take the car to one side, sir.'

The Sikh driver had by now come out of the truck.

'What's the matter?' he asked. 'A puncture?'

I shrugged to convey my state of helplessness. 'If you could lend a hand,' I said, 'we could move the car to one side and let you pass.'

The Sikh driver's helper came out too. The three of us pushed the car to one side of the road. Then I found out from the two men that I was indeed on the wrong road for Dumka. I had taken a wrong turning and would have to drive back three miles to get back on the right track. I also learnt that there were no repair shops nearby.

The truck went on its way. As its noise faded away, the truth struck me like a hammer blow.

I had reached a dead end.

There was no way I could reach Dumka that night, and I had no idea how and where I would spend the night.

The roadside puddles were alive with the chorus of frogs. The rain had now been reduced to a light drizzle.

I got back into the car and was about to light a second cigarette when I spotted a light through the window on my side. I opened the door again. Through the branches of a tree I saw a rectangle of orange light. A window. Just as smoke meant the presence of fire, a kerosene lamp meant the presence of a human being. There was a house nearby and there were occupants in it.

I got out of the car with my torch. The window wasn't too far away. I had to go and investigate. There was a narrow footpath branching off from the main road which seemed to go in the direction of the house with the window.

I locked the car and set off.

I made my way avoiding puddles as far as possible. As I passed a tamarind tree, the house came into view. Well, hardly a house. It was a small cottage with a corrugated tin roof. Through an open door I could see a hurricane lantern and the leg of a bed.

'Is anybody there?' I called out.

A stocky, middle-aged man with a thick moustache came out of the room and squinted at my torch. I turned the spot away from his face.

'Where are you from, sir?' the man asked.

In a few words I described my predicament. 'Is there a place here where I can spend the night?' I asked. 'I shall pay for it, of course.'

'In the dak bungalow, you mean?'

Dak bungalow? I didn't see any dak bungalow.

But immediately, I realized my mistake. I had followed the light of the lantern, and had therefore failed to look around. Now I turned the torch to my left and immediately a large bungalow came into view. 'You mean that one?' I asked.

'Yes sir, but there is no bedding. And you can't have meals there.'

'I'm carrying my own bedding,' I said. 'I hope there's a bed there?'

'Yes sir. A charpoy.'

'And I see there's a stove lit in your room. You must be cooking your own meal?'

The man broke into a smile and asked if I would care for coarse chapatis prepared by him and urad-ka-dal cooked by his wife. I said it would do very nicely. I liked all kinds of chapatis, and urad was my favourite dal.

I don't know what the bungalow must have been like in its heyday, but now it was hardly what one understood by a dak bungalow. Constructed during the time of the Raj, the bedroom was large and the ceiling was high. The furniture consisted of a charpoy, a table set against the wall on one side, and a chair with a broken arm.

The chowkidar, or the caretaker, had in the meantime lit a lantern for me. He now put it on the table. 'What is your name?' I asked.

'Sukhanram, sir.'

'Has anybody ever lived in this bungalow or am I the first one?'

'Oh, no sir, others have come too. There was a gentleman who stayed here for two nights last winter.'

'I hope there are no ghosts here,' I said in a jocular tone.

'God forbid!' he said. 'No one has ever complained of ghosts.'

I must say I found his words reassuring. If a place is spooky, and old dak bungalows have a reputation for being so, it will be so at all times. 'When was this bungalow built?' I asked.

Sukhan began to unroll my bedding and said, 'This used to be a sahib's bungalow, sir.'

'A sahib?'

'Yes sir. An indigo planter. There used to be an indigo factory close by. Now only the chimney is standing.'

I knew indigo was cultivated in these parts at one time. I had seen ruins of indigo factories in Monghyr too in my childhood.

It was ten-thirty when I went to bed after dining on Sukhan's coarse chapatis and urad-ka-dal. I had sent a telegram to Promode from Calcutta saying that I would arrive this afternoon. He would naturally wonder what had happened. But it was useless to think of that now. All I could do now was congratulate myself on having found a shelter, and that too without much trouble. In future I would do as Bhola Babu had advised. I had learnt a lesson, and lessons learnt the hard way are not forgotten easily.

I put the lantern in the adjoining bathroom. The little light that seeped through the door which I had kept slightly ajar was enough. Usually I find it difficult to sleep with a light on, and yet I did not extinguish the light even though what I badly needed now was sleep. I was worried about my car which I had left standing on the road, but it was certainly safer to do so in a village than in the city.

The sound of drizzle had stopped. The air was now filled with the croaking of frogs and the shrill chirping of crickets. From my bed in that ancient bungalow in this remote village, the city seemed to belong to another planet. Indigo . . . I thought of the play by Dinabandhu Mitra, Nildarpan (The Mirror of Indigo). As a college student I had watched a performance of it in a theatre on Cornwallis Street.

I didn't know how long I had slept, when a sound suddenly awakened me. Something was scratching at the door. The door was bolted. Must be a dog or a jackal, I thought, and in a minute or so the noise stopped.

I shut my eyes in an effort to sleep, but the barking of a dog put an end to my efforts. This was not the bark of a stray village dog, but the unmistakable bay of a hound. I was familiar with it. Two houses away from us in Monghyr lived Mr Martin. He had a hound which bayed just like this. Who on earth kept a pet hound here? I thought of opening the door to find out as the sound seemed quite near. But then I thought, why bother? It was better to get some more sleep. What time was it now?

A faint moonlight came in through the window. I raised my left hand to glance at the wristwatch, and gave a start. My wristwatch was gone.

And yet, because it was an automatic watch, I always wore it to bed. Where did it disappear? And how? Were there thieves around? What would happen to my car then?

I felt beside my pillow for my torch and found it gone too.

I jumped out of bed, knelt on the floor and looked underneath it. My suitcase too had disappeared.

My head started spinning. Something had to be done about it. I called out: 'Chowkidar!'

There was no answer.

I went to the door and found that it was still bolted. The window had bars. So how did the thief enter?

As I was about to unfasten the bolt, I glanced at my hand and experienced an odd feeling.

Had whitewash from the wall got on to my hand? Or was it white powder? Why did it look so pale?

I had gone to bed wearing a vest; why then was I now wearing a long-sleeved silk shirt? I felt a throbbing in my head. I opened the door and went out into the veranda.

'Chowkidar!'

The word that came out was spoken with the unmistakable accent of an Englishman. And where was the chowkidar, and where was his little cottage? There was now a wide open field in front of the bungalow. In the distance was a building with a high chimney. The surroundings were unusually quiet.

They had changed.

And so had I.

I came back into the bedroom in a sweat. My eyes had got used to the darkness. I could now clearly make out the details.

The bed was there, but it was covered with a mosquito net. I hadn't been using one. The pillow too was unlike the one I had brought with me. This one had a border with frills; mine didn't. The table and the chair stood where they did, but they had lost their aged look. The varnished wood shone even in the soft light. On the table stood not a lantern but a kerosene lamp with an ornate shade.

There were other objects in the room which gradually came into view: a pair of steel trunks in a corner, a folding bracket on the wall from which hung a coat, an unfamiliar type of headgear and a hunting crop. Below the bracket, standing against the wall, was a pair of galoshes.

I turned away from the objects and took another look at myself. Till now I had only noticed the silk shirt; now I saw the narrow trousers and the socks. I didn't have shoes on, but saw a pair of black boots on the floor by the bed.

I passed my right hand over my face and realized that not only my complexion but my features too had changed. I didn't possess such a sharp nose, nor such thin lips or narrow chin. I felt the hair on my head and found that it was wavy and that there were sideburns which reached below my ears.

In spite of my surprise and terror, I suddenly felt a great urge to find out what I looked like. But where to find a mirror?

I strode towards the bathroom, opened the door with a sharp push and went in.

There had been nothing there but a bucket. Now I saw a metal bath tub and a mug kept on a stool beside it. The thing I was looking for was right in front of me: an oval mirror fixed to a dressing-table. I looked into it, but the person reflected in it was not me. By some devilish trick I had turned into a nineteenth-century Englishman with a sallow complexion, blond hair and light eyes from which shone a strange mixture of hardness and suffering. How old would the Englishman be? Not more than thirty, but it looked as if either illness or hard work, or both, had aged him prematurely.

I went closer and had a good look at 'my' face. As I looked, a deep sigh rose from the depths of my heart.

The voice was not mine. The sigh, too, expressed not my feelings but those of the Englishman.

What followed made it clear that all my limbs were acting of their own volition. And yet it was surprising that I—Aniruddha Bose—was perfectly aware of the change in identity. But I didn't know if the change was permanent, or if there was any way to regain my lost self.

I came back to the bedroom.

Now I glanced at the table. Below the lamp was a notebook bound in leather. It was open at a blank page. Beside it was an inkwell with a quill pen dipped in it.

I walked over to the table. Some unseen force made me sit in the chair and pick up the pen with my right hand. The hand now moved towards the left-hand page of the notebook, and the silent room was filled with the noise of a quill scratching the blank page. This is what I wrote:

> 27 April 1868
> Those fiendish mosquitoes are singing in my ears again. So that's how the son of a mighty empire has to meet his end—at the hands of a tiny insect. What strange will of God is this? Eric has made his escape. Percy and Tony too left earlier. Perhaps I was greedier than them. So in spite of repeated attacks of malaria I couldn't resist the lure of indigo. No, not only that. One mustn't lie in one's diary. My countrymen know me only too well. I didn't lead a blameless life at home either; and they surely have not forgotten that. So I do not dare go back home. I know I will have to stay here and lay down my life on this alien soil. My place will be beside the graves of my wife Mary and my dear little son Toby. I have treated the natives here so badly that there is no one to shed a tear at my passing away. Perhaps Mirjan would miss me—my faithful trusted bearer Mirjan.
>
> And Rex? My real worry is about Rex. Alas, faithful Rex! When I die, these people will not spare you. They will either stone you or club you to death. If only I could do something about you!

I could write no more. The hands were shaking. Not mine, the diarist's.

I put down the pen.

Then my right hand dropped and moved to the right and made for the handle of the drawer.

I opened it.

Inside there was a pin cushion, a brass paperweight, a pipe and some papers.

The drawer opened a little more. A metal object glinted in the half-light.

It was a pistol, its butt inlaid with ivory.

The hand pulled out the pistol. It had stopped shaking.

A group of jackals cried out. It was as if in answer to the jackals' cry that the hound bayed again.

I left the chair and advanced towards the door. I went out into the veranda.

The field in front was bathed in moonlight.

About ten yards from the veranda stood a large greyhound. He wagged his tail as he saw me.

'Rex!'

It was the same deep English voice. The echo of the call came floating back from the faraway factory and bamboo grove—Rex! Rex!

Rex came up towards the veranda.

As he stepped from the grass onto the cement, my right hand rose to my waist, the pistol pointing towards the hound. Rex stopped in his tracks, his eye on the pistol. He gave a low growl.

My right forefinger pressed the trigger.

As the gun throbbed with a blinding flash, smoke and the smell of gunpowder filled the air.

Rex's lifeless, blood-spattered body lay partly on the veranda and partly on the grass.

The sound of the pistol had wakened the crows in the nearby trees. A hubbub now rose from the direction of the factory.

I came back into the bedroom, bolted the door and sat on the bed. The shouting drew near.

I placed the still hot muzzle of the pistol by my right ear.

That is all I remember.

I woke up at the sound of knocking.

'I've brought your tea, sir.'

Daylight flooded in through the window. Out of sheer habit my eyes strayed to my left wrist.

Thirteen minutes past six. I brought the watch closer to my eyes to read the date, April the twenty-eighth.

I now opened the door and let Sukhanram in.

'There's a car repair shop half an hour down the road, sir,' he said. 'It'll open at seven.'

'Very good,' I said, and proceeded to drink my tea.

Would anyone believe me when they heard of my experience on the night of the hundredth anniversary of the death of an English indigo planter in Birbhum?

Translated by Satyajit Ray
First published in Bengali in 1968

Pikoo's Diary

I am writing my diary. In my new bloo notebook I am writing. Sitting on my bed. Dadu writes diary too but not now bcoz he is sick, so not now. I know the name of his sicknes and that name is coronani thombosi. Baba does not write diary. Not Ma or Dada. Only me and Dadu. My notebook is bigger than Dadu's. Onukul got it, he sed it cost one rupee and Ma paid him. I will write in diary evry day yes when there is no school.

Today I have no school but it is not Sunday. Just there was stryk so no school. Offen we have stryk and no school that is fun. Good this notebook has lines so my writing is strait. Dada can write strait without lines and Baba of corse but it is not holiday for Baba. Or Dada or Ma. Ma does not go to office, only works at home. Now Ma is out with Hiteskaku. She sed she will get me something from New Market. Thees days she gets me many things. A pencil-shapnar a wristwach but it only shows three oclock and a hockee stick and ball. Oh and a book. It is Grims Fairy Tails it has many picturs. God knows what she will get me today may be airgun so lets see.

Dhingra killed a maina with airgun so I will try that sparow. It comes and sits on the raeling evry day. I will aim and pull the triger bang bang it will definitly die. Last nite a bomb went off it made big bang. Baba sed bomb Ma sed no no may be police gun. Baba sed has to be bomb, thees days I hear bang bang offen thru my window. Hey thats a car horn. I know its Hiteskaku's standad heral so it must be Ma come back.

Yesturday Ma gave me airgun but Hiteskaku sed Pikoo babu it is from me not yore Mummy. Hiteskaku bot a band for his wristwach. I sed its name was Tissot but Hiteskaku sed oh no its Tisso bcoz the last t is not spoken. My airgun is very good and in a big box there are bulets lots of them. May be more than hundred. Hiteskaku taut me to fire so I fired in the sky and Onukul scared. That sparow never came yesturday and not today. It is very noughty but tomorow it must come so I will be reddy.

Baba came back from office he saw my airgun he sed why did you get him a gun Ma sed so what. Baba sed we already have bang bang all the time why bring a gun in the house Ma sed it does not matter. But Baba sed you have no sense then Ma sed why are you shoughting you have only just come back from office. Baba sed something yes it was in english and Ma also sed english very quickly like people in the cinema. I saw Jery Louis and Clint Eestwud and a Hindi cinema but it had no fiteing. I saw it with Milu didi oh no I think the ink in my pen is go

I put Baba's green ink it is Quink with a droper in my founten pen. It is Ma's droper she used it to put drops when she had cold. Today I am writing my diary at Baba's desk. Just now the phone went krring krring so I ran and pickd it up and sed halo and guess what it was Baba he sed is that you Pikoo so I sed yes and he sed isnt Ma there I sed no. Baba sed were is she I sed she went out with Hiteskaku. Baba sed oh I see and put the phone down and I did hear it klick. Then I dialled one seven four they told me the time sumtimes I do that to hear the time but what they speak I just cant follow. Today that sparow came. I was reddy with my airgun at the window and the sparow came so I fired it hit a wall and then I saw a hole in Dhingra's wall. The sparow was very scared and flew away. Yesturday Dada has very good aim he put the smallest clay pot on the tank on our roof and fired from far away and the pot was broken. Some peeces fell down on the road I sed oh god if sumone is hurt we are in troubel. Dada is much biger he is biger by twelve years so his aim is so good. Dada goes to collage and I go to school. Dada goes out evry day but I am just at home only sumtimes I go to cinema and I saw one theatar. Dada came back very late last nite so Baba scolded him and Dada shoughted so laud I woke up so I didnt finish my luvly dream. I was rideing a horse and going so fast Dhingra cudnt catch me. Then Hiteskaku gave me a new gun it was a revolvur he sed its name is Fisso and Dadu he was a cowboy like Clint Eestwud he sed lets go to Viktoria Memorial and just then I woke up the dream broke. Now I will go to bathroom.

Yesturday we had a party. No it wasn't my birday or anything just a party. Only old people so I didn't go just wached a littel. Only Baba's frends and Ma's but not Dada's frends not one. Dada is not home he went day before yesturday or may be before that I don't know whare. Dada does politis it is hopeless Baba sed and also Ma. Ma told me dont go whare the party is so I didnt but I ate three sosseges and a cocacola. There was a sahib he was laffing very lowdly ho ho ha ha ho ho and a mem too. And Mister Menon and Mises Menon and one sardar I cud guess immijetly bcoz he had a pugri. Evryone laffed and I cud hear them from my room. Then Ma came in and went to bathroom and then saw her face in the mirror. One more ledy came in too and went to bathroom she was wareing scent a new scent Ma hasnt got that one. Then Ma came in again and sed why dear why are you still awake go to sleep so I sed I was scared alone she sed dont be silly its eleven just close yore eyes and you will sleep. I sed whare is Dada she sed thats enuff just sleep and left. But Baba did not come to my room now Baba and Ma were fiteing they talk in english a lot only sumtimes in bangla. But not in the party they did not fite in the party so the party is good no fiteing only drinks one day sumone was sick Ma sed he wasnt feeling well but Onukul sed he was drinking thats why. We have bottels in our frij when they are emty Ma fills them with water cold water. When they smell Ma scolds Sukdeo she sez why dont you wash them proparly. Sukdeo sez no memsab why does he call her memsab is Ma a mem or is she a sab no its really very funny. Then I fell asleep no one knows how sleep comes. Dadu sez if you die you go on very long sleep and you can dream what you want. only dream all the time.

I hide my diary in a plaice no one knows. It is our old gramofon no one plays it any more bcoz the new one is elktrik it is long playeing so no one touches the old one thats whare I hide my diary and so no one knows I write a diary. I write a lot so my finger pains a littel when Ma was cuting my nails I sed oooh so Ma sed why is it painful I sed no no its nuthing bcoz then she wud know I write my diary. Dadu sed show yore diary to no one only you will write and read it no one else. I have 22 bulets left I counted but that sparow is so noughty it didnt come again. I go to the roof and fire at the tank it makes a tong tong noize and then small rownd rownd marks so I think I will kill pidgeons. Pidgeons just sit and may be walk a littel but they dont fly that much. Dada has bin gone for five days his room is emty only there is a shart a white shart on the rack and a bloo pant and his books and stuff.

I was bloing bubbels yesturday then I herd a horn so I sed thats Hiteskaku and Ma sed darling why dont you go and play with Dhingra its his holiday. I sed Dhingra pulls my hair he hurts me I wont go then Ma sed well you can go to the roof with yore airgun so I sed then I will kill pidgeons. Ma sed oh no not that just fire it at the sky I sed thats no good how can I aim at the sky. Ma sed then go to Onukul I sed Onukul he only plays cards and durwan and Sukdeo and one more man they only play cards all day so I wont go anywhare. Then Ma slaped me hard and I nocked agenst the wood on my bed. So I cried a littel not much tho and Ma left so I cried sum more but not a lot and thot what can I now do. Then I thot lets see whats in the frij there was a creem role and two gulab jamuns I ate them then had water strait from a bottel no I didnt pore in a glass not at all. Then I saw one Illustated Weekly it was on Baba's desk but there was no nice pictur only a donald duk. Then I ran to the varanda and did hi-jump over a small stool that was easy but I tried a bigger stool I fell and got a cut. Only a littel blood but there was detol in the bathroom detol doesnt hurt but tincheridin does so I put detol. Then I ran out bcoz a jet plane went very lowdly I saw when Baba went in a jet I went to dum dum he braught a elektrik shaver from london that was for him and shoes for me and a astronot that was very big but Ronida spoylt it. Now I supose I shud go and do sums.

I am writing my diary agane today. All my bulets are gone why didnt one hit that pidgeon? That gun must be useles. I think I will thro it away. I saw a machbox in Dadas drawer it must mean Dada smokes cigrets or why shud he have machbox. But Dada did not cum back god knows whare he is or may be even god doesnt know. Now if Ma goese too there will be truble bcoz last nite Ma told Baba she will go I had slept in the afternoon so I cudnt sleep I was awake but my eyes were shut tight they thot Pikoo is sleeping so they did talk lowdly. Now there is no one home just me and Dadu whare is Onukul he must be playing cards so only Dadu and me in the house. Dadu lives downstares bcoz Doctor Banarji sed Dadu can not climb stares bcoz he has coronani thombosi. So Dadu has a bell it makes a noize ting ting ting we can all hear it. Today I heard that noize once I was then spitting out of my window making it go far and just then I heard ting ting ting and I cud tell that was Dadu but I tried spitting four times againe one spit went over the wall outside then I thot let me see what Dadu wants. I ran downstares it made such a noize bcoz they are wood stares they make thud thud noize. But Dadu was lying not talking but he wasnt sleeping. So I sed whats the matter Dadu what is it but Dadu sed nuthing he just stared at the fan. It is a Usha only Dadu has Usha evry other fan is GEC. Then I heard the fone ring so I ran and it rang so many times when I sed halo sumone sed is mister shurma there I sed no shurma here wrong number and put it down. It klicked. I was huffing and puffing bcoz I ran so fast so I lay down on the sofa and put my legs up Ma wud scold me but shes not here I saw immijetly my legs ware durty but Ma isnt here anyway. And now I am again writing my diary sitting on my bed but no pages left now and no one in the house only Dadu and me and theres a fly it keeps coming again and again. A very stoopid fly what a bothre and now this page is finished notebook gone all over The End.

Translated by Gopa Majumdar
First published in Bengali in 1970

Ratan Babu and That Man

Stepping out of the train onto the platform, Ratan Babu heaved a sigh of relief. The place seemed quite inviting. A shirish tree reared its head from behind the station house. There was a spot of red in its green leaves where a kite was caught in a branch. There was no sign of busyness in the few people around and a pleasant earthy smell was floating in the air. All in all, he found the surroundings most agreeable.

As he had only a small holdall and a leather suitcase, he didn't need a coolie. He lifted his luggage with both hands and made for the exit.

He had no trouble finding a cycle-rickshaw outside.

'Where to, sir?' asked the young driver in striped shorts.

'You know the New Mahamaya hotel?' asked Ratan Babu.

The driver nodded. 'Hop in, sir.'

Travelling was almost an obsession with Ratan Babu. He went out of Calcutta whenever the opportunity came, though that was not very often. Ratan Babu had a regular job. For twenty-four years he had been a clerk in the Calcutta office of the Geological Survey. He could get away only once a year, when he clubbed his yearly leave with the month-long Puja holidays and set off all by himself. He never took anyone with him, nor would it have occurred to him to do so. There was a time when he had felt the need for companionship; in fact, he had once talked about it to Keshab Babu who occupied the adjacent desk in his office. It was a few days before the holidays; and Ratan Babu was still planning his getaway. 'You're pretty much on your own, like me,' he had said. 'Why don't we go off together somewhere this time?'

Keshab Babu had stuck his pen behind his ear, put his palms together and said with a wry smile, 'I don't think you and I have the same tastes, you know. You go to places no one has heard of, places where there's nothing much to see, nor any decent places to stay or eat at. No sir, I'd sooner go to Harinabhi and visit my brother-in-law.'

In time, Ratan Babu had come to realize that there was virtually no one who saw eye to eye with him. His likes and dislikes were quite different from the average person's, so it was best to give up hopes of finding a suitable companion.

There was no doubt that Ratan Babu possessed traits which were quite unusual. Keshab Babu had been quite right. Ratan Babu was never attracted to places where people normally went for vacations. 'All right,' he would say, 'so there is the sea in Puri and the temple of Jagannath;

you can see the Kanchenjunga from Darjeeling, and there are hills and forests in Hazaribagh and the Hudroo falls in Ranchi. So what? You've heard them described so many times that you almost feel you've seen them yourself.'

What Ratan Babu looked for was a little town somewhere with a railway station not too far away. Every year before the holidays he would open the timetable, pick such a town and make his way there. No one bothered to ask where he was going and he never told anyone. In fact, there had been occasions when he had gone to places he had never even heard of, and wherever he had gone he had discovered things which had delighted him. To others, such things might appear trivial, like the old fig tree in Rajabhatkhaoa which had coiled itself around a kul and coconut tree; or the ruins of the indigo factory in Maheshgunj; or the delicious dal barfi sold in a sweet shop in Moina . . .

This time Ratan Babu had decided on a town called Shini—fifteen miles from Tatanagar. Shini was not picked from the timetable; his colleague Anukul Mitra had mentioned it to him. The New Mahamaya hotel, too, was recommended by him.

To Ratan Babu, the hotel seemed quite adequate. His room wasn't large, but that didn't matter. There were windows to the east and the south with pleasant views of the countryside. The servant Pancha seemed an amiable sort. Ratan Babu was in the habit of bathing twice a day in tepid water throughout the year, and Pancha had assured him that there would be no trouble about that. The cooking was passable, which was all right with Ratan Babu since he was not fussy about food. There was only one thing he insisted on: he needed to have rice with fish curry and chapatis with dal and vegetables. He had informed Pancha about this as soon as he had arrived, and Pancha had passed on the information to the manager.

Ratan Babu was also in the habit of going for a walk in the afternoon when he arrived in a new place. The first day at Shini was no exception. He finished the cup of tea brought by Pancha and set out by four.

After a few minutes' walk he found himself in the open country. The terrain was uneven and criss-crossed with paths. Ratan Babu chose one at random and after half an hour's walk, discovered a charming spot. It was a pond with water lilies growing in it with a large variety of birds flying around. Of these there were some like cranes, snipes, kingfishers and magpies which Ratan Babu recognized; the others were unfamiliar.

Ratan Babu could well have spent all his afternoons sitting beside this pond, but on the second day he took a different path in the hope of discovering something new. Having walked a mile or so, he had to stop for a herd of goats to cross his path. As the road cleared, he went on for another five minutes until a wooden bridge came into view. As he approached it, he realized that a railway line passed below it. He went and stood on the bridge. To the east he could see the railway station; to the west the parallel lines stretched as far as the eye could see. What if a train were suddenly to appear and go thundering underneath? The very thought thrilled him.

Perhaps because he had his eyes on the tracks, he failed to notice another man who had come and stood beside him. Ratan Babu looked around and gave a start.

The stranger was clad in a dhoti and shirt, a snuff-coloured shawl on his shoulder. He wore bifocals and his feet were clad in brown canvas shoes. Ratan Babu had an odd feeling. Where had he seen this person before? Wasn't there something familiar about him? Medium height, medium complexion, a pensive look in his eyes . . . How old could he be? Surely not over fifty.

The stranger smiled and folded his hands in greeting. Ratan Babu was about to return the greeting when he realized in a flash why he had that odd feeling. No wonder the stranger's face seemed familiar. He had seen that face many, many times—in his own mirror. The resemblance was uncanny. The squarish jaw with the cleft chin, the way the hair was parted, the carefully trimmed moustache, the shape of the ear lobes—they were all strikingly like his own. Only, the stranger seemed a shade fairer than him, his eyebrows a little bushier and the hair at the back a trifle longer.

The stranger spoke, and Ratan Babu got another shock. Sushanto, a boy from his neighbourhood, had once recorded his voice in a tape recorder and played it back to him. There was no difference between that voice and the one that spoke now.

'My name is Manilal Majumdar. I believe you're staying at the New Mahamaya?'

Ratanlal—Manilal . . . the names were similar too. Ratan Babu managed to shake off his bewilderment and introduced himself.

The stranger said, 'I don't suppose you'd know, but I have seen you once before.'

'Where?'

'Weren't you in Dhulian last year?'

Ratan Babu's eyebrows shot up. 'Don't tell me you were there too!'

'Yes, sir. I go off on trips every Puja. I'm on my own. No friends to speak of. It's fun to be in a new place all by myself. A colleague of mine recommended Shini to me. Nice place, isn't it?'

Ratan Babu swallowed, and then nodded in assent. He felt a strange mixture of disbelief and uneasiness in his mind.

'Have you seen the pond on the other side where a lot of birds gather in the evening?' asked Manilal Babu.

Ratan Babu said yes, he had.

'Some of the birds I could recognize,' said Manilal Babu, 'others I have never seen before in Bengal. What do you think?'

Ratan Babu had recovered somewhat in the meantime. He said, 'I had the same feeling; I didn't recognize some birds either.'

Just then they heard a booming sound. It was a train. Ratan Babu saw a point of light growing bigger as the train approached from the east. Both the men moved closer to the railing of the bridge. The train hurtled up and passed below them, making the bridge shake. Both of them crossed to the other side and kept looking until the train disappeared from view. Ratan Babu felt the same thrill as he did as a small boy. 'How strange!' said Manilal Babu, 'even at this age watching trains never fails to excite me.'

On the way back Ratan Babu learnt that Manilal Babu had arrived in Shini three days ago. He was staying at the Kalika hotel. His home was in Calcutta where he had a job in a trading company. One doesn't ask another person about his salary, but an indomitable urge made Ratan Babu throw discretion to the wind and put the question. The answer made him gasp in astonishment. How was such a thing possible? Both Ratan Babu and Manilal Babu drew exactly the same salary—437 rupees a month—and both had received exactly the same Puja bonus.

Ratan Babu found it difficult to believe that the other man had somehow found out all about him beforehand and was playing some mysterious game. No one had ever bothered about him before; he kept very much to himself. Outside his office he spoke only to his servant and never made calls on anyone. Even if it was possible for an outsider to find out about his salary, such details as when he went to bed, his tastes in food, what newspapers he read, what plays and films he had seen lately—these were known only to himself. And yet everything tallied exactly with what this man was saying.

He couldn't say this to Manilal Babu. All he did was listen to what the man had to say and marvel at the extraordinary similarity. He revealed nothing about his own habits.

They came to Ratan Babu's hotel first, and stopped in front of it. 'What's the food here like?' asked Manilal Babu.

'They make a good fish curry,' replied Ratan Babu. 'The rest is just adequate.'

'I'm afraid the cooking in my hotel is rather indifferent,' said Manilal Babu. 'I've heard they make very good luchis and chholar dal at the Jagannath Restaurant. What about having a meal there tonight?'

'I don't mind,' said Ratan Babu, 'shall we meet around eight then?'

'Right. I'll wait for you, then we'll walk down together.'

After Manilal Babu left, Ratan Babu roamed about in the street for a while. Darkness had fallen. It was a clear night. So clear that the Milky Way could be seen stretching from one end of the star-filled sky to the other. What a strange thing to happen! All these years Ratan Babu had regretted that he couldn't find anyone to share his tastes and become friends with him. Now at last in Shini he had run into someone who might well be an exact replica of himself. There was a slight difference in their looks perhaps, but in every other respect such similarity was rare even amongst twins.

Did it mean that he had found a friend at last?

Ratan Babu couldn't find a ready answer to the question. Perhaps he would find it when he got to know the man a little better. One thing was clear—he no longer had the feeling of being isolated from his fellow men. All these years there had been another person exactly like him, and he had come to know him quite by chance.

In Jagannath Restaurant, sitting face to face across the table, Ratan

Babu observed that, like him, Manilal Babu ate with a fastidious relish; like him, he didn't drink any water during the meal; and like him, he squeezed lemon into the dal. Ratan Babu always had sweet curd to round off his meals, and so did Manilal Babu.

While eating, Ratan Babu had the uncomfortable feeling that diners at other tables were watching them. Did they notice how alike they were? Was the likeness so obvious to onlookers?

After dinner, the two of them walked for a while in the moonlight. There was something which Ratan Babu wanted to ask, and he did so now. 'Have you turned fifty yet?'

Manilal Babu smiled. 'I'll be doing so soon,' he said, 'I'll be fifty on the twenty-ninth of December.'

Ratan Babu's head swam. They were both born on the same day: the twenty-ninth of December, 1916.Half an hour later, as they were taking leave, Manilal Babu said, 'It has been a great pleasure knowing you. I don't seem to get on very well with people, but you're an exception. I can now look forward to an enjoyable vacation.'

Usually, Ratan Babu was in bed by ten. He would glance through a magazine, and gradually feel a drowsiness stealing over him. He would then put down the magazine, turn off the bedlamp and within a few minutes would start snoring softly. But tonight he found that sleep wouldn't come. Nor did he feel like reading. He picked up the magazine and put it down again.

Manilal Majumdar . . .

Ratan Babu had read somewhere that of the billions of people who inhabited the earth, no two looked exactly alike. And yet every one had the same number of features—eyes, ears, nose, lips and so on. But even if no two persons looked alike, was it possible for them to have the same tastes, feelings, attitudes—as it was with him and his new friend? Age, profession, voice, gait, even the power of their glasses—were identical. One would think such a thing impossible, and yet here was proof that it was not, and Ratan Babu had learnt it again and again in the last four hours.

At about midnight, he got out of bed, poured some water from the carafe and splashed it on his head. Sleep was impossible in his feverish state. He passed a towel lightly over his head and went back to bed. At least the wet pillow would keep his head cool for a while.

Silence had descended over the neighbourhood. An owl went screeching overhead. Moonlight streamed in through the window and onto the bed. Slowly, Ratan Babu's mind regained its calm and his eyes closed of their own accord.

It was almost eight when Ratan Babu woke up the next morning. Manilal Babu was supposed to come at nine. It was Tuesday—the day when the weekly market or haat was held at a spot a mile or so away. The night before, the two had almost simultaneously expressed a wish to visit the haat, more to look around than to buy anything.

It was almost nine when Ratan Babu finished breakfast. He helped himself to a pinch of mouth-freshners from the saucer on the table, came out of the hotel and saw Manilal Babu approaching.

'I couldn't sleep for a long time last night,' were Manilal Babu's first words. 'I lay in bed thinking how alike you and I were. It was five to eight when I woke this morning. I am usually up by six.'

Ratan Babu refrained from comment. The two set off towards the haat. They had to pass some youngsters standing in a cluster by the roadside. 'Hey, look at Tweedledum and Tweedledee!' one of them cried out. Ratan Babu tried his best to ignore the remark and went on ahead. It took them about twenty minutes to reach the haat.

The market was a bustling affair. There were shops for fruits and vegetables, utensils, clothes, and even livestock. The two men wove their way through the milling crowd casting glances at the goods on display.

Who was that? Wasn't it Pancha? For some reason, Ratan Babu couldn't bring himself to face the hotel servant. That remark about Tweedledum and Tweedledee had made him realize it would be prudent not to be seen alongside Manilal Babu.

As they jostled through the crowd a thought suddenly occurred to Ratan Babu. He realized he was better off as he was—alone, without a friend. He didn't need a friend. Or, at any rate, not someone like Manilal Babu. Whenever he spoke to Manilal Babu, it seemed as if he was carrying on a conversation with himself. He knew all the answers before he asked the questions. There was no room for argument, no possibility of misunderstanding. Were these signs of friendship? Two of his colleagues, Kartik Ray and Mukunda Chakravarty, were bosom friends. Did that mean they had no arguments? Of course they did. But they were still friends—close friends.

The thought kept buzzing around his head and he couldn't rid himself of the feeling that it would have been better if Manilal Babu hadn't come into his life. Even if two identical men existed, it was wrong that they should meet. The very thought that they might continue to meet even after returning to Calcutta made Ratan Babu shudder.

One of the shops was selling cane walking sticks. Ratan Babu had always wanted to possess one, but seeing Manilal Babu haggling with the shopkeeper, he checked himself. Manilal Babu bought two sticks and gave one to Ratan Babu saying, 'I hope you won't mind accepting this as a token of our friendship.'

On the way back to the hotel, Manilal Babu spoke a lot about himself—his childhood, his parents, his school and college days. Ratan Babu felt that his own life story was being recounted.

The plan came to Ratan Babu in the afternoon as the two were on their way to the railway bridge. He didn't have to talk much, so he could think. He had been thinking, since midday, of getting rid of this man, but he couldn't decide on a method. Ratan Babu had just turned his eyes to the clouds gathering in the west when a plan suddenly occurred to him with blazing clarity. The vision he saw was of the two of them standing by the railing of the bridge. In the distance a train was approaching. As the engine got within twenty yards, Ratan Babu gathered his strength and gave a hefty push—He closed his eyes involuntarily. Then he opened them again and shot a glance at his companion. Manilal Babu seemed quite unconcerned. But if the two had so much in common, perhaps he too was thinking of a way to get rid of him?

But the man's looks didn't betray any such thoughts. As a matter of fact, he was humming a Hindi film tune which Ratan Babu himself was in the habit of humming from time to time.

The dark clouds had just covered the sun which would in any case set in a few minutes. Ratan Babu looked around and saw they were quite alone. Thank God for that. Had there been anyone else, his plan wouldn't have worked.

It was strange that even though his mind was bent on murder, Ratan Babu couldn't think of himself as a culprit. Had Manilal Babu possessed any traits which endowed him with a personality different from his own, Ratan Babu could never have thought of killing him. But now he felt that there was no sense in both of them being alive at the same time. It was enough that he alone should continue to exist.

The two arrived at the bridge.

'Bit stuffy today,' commented Manilal Babu. 'It may rain tonight, and that could be the start of a cold spell.'

Ratan Babu stole a glance at his wristwatch. Twelve minutes to six. The train was supposed to be very punctual. There wasn't much time left. Ratan Babu contrived a yawn to ease his tension. 'Even if it does rain,' he said, 'it is not likely to happen for another four or five hours.'

'Care for a betel nut?'

Manilal Babu had produced a small round tin box from his pocket. Ratan Babu too was carrying a metal box with betel nuts in it, but didn't mention the fact to Manilal Babu. He helped himself to a nut and tossed it into his mouth.

Just then they heard the sound of the train.

Manilal Babu advanced towards the railing, glanced at his watch and said, 'Seven minutes before time.'

The thick cloud in the sky had made the evening a little darker than usual. The headlight seemed brighter in contrast. The train was still far away but the light was growing brighter every second.

Krrrring . . . krrring.

A cyclist was approaching from the road towards the bridge. Good God! Was he going to stop?

No. Ratan Babu's apprehension proved baseless. The cyclist rode swiftly past them and disappeared into the gathering darkness down the other side of the road.

The train was hurtling up at great speed. It was impossible to gauge the distance in the blinding glare of the headlight. In a few seconds the bridge would start shaking.

Now the sound of the train was deafening.

Manilal Babu was looking down with his hands on the railing. A flash of lightning in the sky and Ratan Babu gathered all his strength, flattened his palms against the back of Manilal Babu, and heaved.

Manilal Babu's body vaulted over the four-foot-high railing and plummeted down towards the thundering engine. That very moment the bridge began to shake.

Ratan Babu wound his shawl tightly around his neck and started on his way back.

Towards the end of his walk he had to break into a run in a vain effort to avoid being pelted by the first big drops of rain. Panting with the effort, he rushed into the hotel.

As soon as he entered he felt there was something wrong.

Where had he come? The lobby of the New Mahamaya was not like this at all—the tables, the chairs, the pictures on the wall . . . Looking around, his eyes suddenly caught a signboard on the wall. What a stupid mistake! He had come into the Kalika hotel instead. Wasn't this where Manilal Babu was staying?

'So you couldn't avoid getting wet?'

Somebody was talking to him. Ratan Babu turned round and saw a man with curly hair and a green shawl—probably a resident of the hotel—looking at him with a cup of tea in his hand. 'Sorry,' said the man, seeing Ratan Babu's face, 'for a moment I thought you were Manilal Babu.'

It was this mistake which raised the first doubts in Ratan Babu's mind. Had he been careful enough about the crime he had committed? Many must have seen the two of them going out together, but had they really noticed? Would they remember what they had seen? And if they did, would the suspicion then fall on him? He was sure no one had seen them after they had reached the outskirts of the town. And after reaching that bridge—oh yes, the cyclist. He must have seen them. But by that time it had turned quite dark and the cyclist passed by at a high speed. Was it likely that he would remember their faces? Certainly not.

The more Ratan Babu pondered, the more reassured he felt. There was no doubt that Manilal Babu's dead body would be discovered. But he just could not believe that it would lead to him being suspected of the crime, and that he would be tried, found guilty, and brought to the gallows.

Since it was still raining, Ratan Babu stayed for a cup of tea. Around seven-thirty the rain stopped and he went directly to the New Mahamaya. He found it almost funny the way he had blundered into the wrong hotel.

At dinner, he ate well and with relish; then he slipped into bed with a magazine, read an article on the aborigines of Australia, turned off the bedlamp and closed his eyes with not a worry in his mind. Once again he was on his own; and unique. He didn't have a friend, and didn't need one. He would spend the rest of his days in exactly the same way he had done so far. What could be better?

It had started to rain again. There were flashes of lightning and claps of thunder. But none of it mattered. Ratan Babu had already started to snore.

'Did you buy that stick from the haat, sir?' asked Pancha when he brought Ratan Babu his morning tea.

'Yes,' said Ratan Babu.

'How much did you pay for it?'

Ratan Babu mentioned the price. Then he asked casually, 'Were you at the haat too?'

Pancha broke into a broad smile. 'Yes, sir,' he said, 'and I saw you. Didn't you see me?'

'Why, no.'

That ended the conversation.

After his tea, Ratan Babu made his way to the Kalika hotel. The curly-haired man was talking to a group of people outside the hotel. He heard Manilal Babu's name and the word 'suicide' mentioned several times. He edged closer to hear better. Not only that, he was bold enough to put a question.

'Who has died?'

The curly-haired man said, 'It was the same man I had mistaken you for yesterday.'

'Suicide, was it?'

'It looks like that. The dead body was found by the railway tracks below the bridge. It seems he threw himself from it. An odd character, he was. Hardly spoke to anyone. We used to talk about him.'

'I suppose the dead body . . .?'

'In police custody. He came here for a change of air from Calcutta. Didn't know anyone here. Nothing more has been found out.'

Ratan Babu shook his head, made a few clucking noises and went off.

Suicide! So nobody had thought of murder at all. Luck was on his side. How simple it was, this business of murder! He wondered what made people quail at the thought.

Ratan Babu felt quite light-hearted. After two days he would now be able to walk alone again. The very thought filled him with pleasure.

It was probably while he pushed Manilal Babu yesterday that a button from his shirt had got ripped and come off. He found a tailor's shop and had the button replaced. Then he went into a store and bought a tube of Neem toothpaste.

As he walked a few steps from the store, he heard the sound of keertan coming from a house. He stood for a while listening to the song, then made for the open terrain outside the town. He walked a mile or so along a new path, came back to the hotel at about eleven, had his bath and lunch, and took his afternoon nap.

As usual he woke up around three, and realized almost immediately that he had to pay another visit to the bridge that evening. For obvious reasons he had not been able to enjoy the sight of the train yesterday. The sky was still cloudy but it didn't seem that it would rain. Today he would be able to watch the train from the moment it appeared till it vanished into the horizon.

He had his afternoon tea at five and went down to the lobby. The manager Shambhu Babu sat at his desk by the front door. He saw Ratan Babu and said, 'Did you know the man who was killed yesterday?'

Ratan Babu looked at Shambhu Babu, feigning surprise. Then he said, 'Why do you ask?'

'Well, it's only that Pancha mentioned he had seen you two together in the haat.'

Ratan Babu smiled. 'I haven't really got to know anyone here,' he said calmly. 'I did speak to a few people in the haat, but the fact is, I don't even know which person was killed.'

'I see,' said Shambhu Babu, laughing. He was jovial by nature and prone to laughter. 'He too had come for a change,' he added. 'He had put up at the Kalika.'

'I see.'

Ratan Babu went out. It was a two-mile walk to the bridge. If he didn't hurry he might miss the train.

Nobody cast suspicious glances at him in the street. Yesterday's youngsters were not in their usual place. That remark about Tweedledum and Tweedledee had nettled him. He wondered where the boys were. The sound of drums could be heard from somewhere close by. There was a puja on in the neighbourhood. That's where the boys must have gone. Good.

At last he was all by himself on the path in the open field. Until he met Manilal Babu, he had been well content with his lot; but today he felt more relaxed than ever before.

There it was—the babla tree. The bridge was only a short distance away. The sky was still overcast, but not with thick black clouds like yesterday. These were grey clouds, and there was no breeze; the sky stood ashen and still.

Ratan Babu's heart leaped with joy at the sight of the bridge. He quickened his pace. Who knows, the train might turn up even earlier than yesterday. A flock of cranes passed overhead. Migratory cranes? He couldn't tell.

As he stood on the bridge, Ratan Babu became aware of the stillness of the evening. Straining his ears, he could hear faint drumbeats from the direction of the town. Otherwise all was quiet.

He moved over to the railing. He could see the signal, and beyond that, the station. What was that now? Lower down the railing, in a crack in the wood was lodged a shiny object. Ratan Babu bent down and prised it out. A small round tin box with betel nuts in it. Ratan Babu smiled and tossed it over the railing. There was a metallic clink as it hit the ground. Who knows how long it would lie there?

What was that light?

Ah, the train. No sound yet, just an advancing point of light. Ratan Babu stood and stared fascinated at the headlight. A sudden gust of wind whipped the shawl off his shoulder. He wrapped it properly around him once more.

Now he could hear the sound. It was like the low rumble of an approaching storm.

Ratan Babu suddenly had the feeling that somebody was standing behind him. It was difficult to take his eyes off the train, but even so he cast a quick glance around. Not a soul anywhere. It was not as dark as the day before, hence the visibility was much better. No, except for himself and that approaching train, there was no one for miles around.

The train was now within a hundred yards.

Ratan Babu edged further towards the railing. Had the train been an old-fashioned one with a steam engine, he couldn't have gone so close to the edge as the smoke would have got into his eyes. This was a smokeless diesel engine. There was only a deep, earthshaking rumble and the blinding glare of the headlight.

Now the train was about to go under the bridge.

Ratan Babu placed his elbows on the railing and leaned forward to watch.

At that very moment a pair of hands came up from behind and gave him a savage push. Ratan Babu went clean over the four-foot-high railing.

As usual, the train made the bridge shudder as it passed under it and sped towards the west where the sky had just begun to turn purple.

Ratan Babu no longer stands on the bridge, but as a token of his presence a small shining object is stuck in a crack in the wooden railing.

It is an aluminium box with betel nuts in it.

•

Translated by Satyajit Ray
First published in Bengali in 1970

Fritz

After having stared at Jayanto for a whole minute, I could not help asking him, 'Are you well? You seem to be in low spirits today.'

Jayanto quickly lost his slightly preoccupied air, gave me a boyish smile and said, 'No. On the contrary, I am feeling a lot better. This place is truly wonderful.'

'You've been here before. Didn't you know how good it was?'

'I had nearly forgotten,' Jayanto sighed. 'Now some of my memories are coming back slowly. The bungalow certainly appears unchanged. I can even recognize some of the old furniture, such as these cane chairs and tables.'

The bearer came in with tea and biscuits on a tray. I poured.

'When did you come here last?'

'Thirty-one years ago. I was six then.'

We were sitting in the garden of the circuit house in Bundi. We had arrived only that morning. Jayanto and I were old friends. We had gone to the same school and college. He now worked in the editorial division of a newspaper and I taught in a school. Although we had different kinds of jobs, it had not made any difference to our friendship. We had been planning a trip to Rajasthan for quite some time. The main difficulty lay in both of us being able to get away together. That had, at last, been made possible.

Most people go to Jaipur, Udaipur or Chittor when they go to Rajasthan; but Jayanto kept talking about going to Bundi. I had no objection for, having read Tagore's poem 'The Fort of Bundi', I was certainly familiar with the name of the place and felt a pleasurable excitement at the prospect of actually seeing the fort. Not many people came to Bundi. But that did not mean that there was not much to see there. It could be that, from the point of view of a historian, Udaipur, Jodhpur and Chittor had a lot more to offer; but simply as a beautiful place, Bundi was perfect.

However, Jayanto's insistence on Bundi did puzzle me somewhat. I learnt the reason on the train when we were coming down. Jayanto's father, Animesh Das Gupta, had worked in the Archaeological Department. His work sometimes took him to historical places, and Jayanto had as a child come to Bundi. He had always wanted to return after growing up, just to see how much the modern Bundi compared to the image he had in his mind.

The circuit house was really rather splendid. Built during the time of the British, it must have been at least a hundred years old. It was a single-storeyed building with a sloping tiled roof. The rooms had high ceilings and the skylights had long, dangling ropes which could be pulled to open and shut them. The veranda faced the east. Right opposite it was a huge garden with a large number of roses in full bloom. Behind these were a lot of trees which obviously housed a vast section of local birds. Parrots could be seen everywhere; and peacocks could be heard, but only outside the compound.

We had already been on a sightseeing tour of the town. The famous fort of Bundi was placed amidst the hills. We had seen it from a distance that day but decided to go back to take a closer look. The only reminders of modern times were the electric poles. Otherwise it seemed as though we were back in old Rajputana. The streets were cobbled, the houses had balconies jutting out from the first floor. The carvings done on these and the wooden doors bore evidence of the work of master craftsmen. It was difficult to believe we were living in the age of machines.

I noticed Jayanto had turned rather quiet after arriving in Bundi. Perhaps some of his memories had returned. It is easy enough to feel a little depressed when visiting a place one may have seen as a child. Besides, Jayanto was certainly more emotional than most people. Everyone knew that.

He put his cup down on the table and said, 'You know, Shankar, it is really quite strange. The first time I came here I used to sit cross-legged on these chairs. It seemed as though I was sitting on a throne. Now the chairs seem both small in size and very ordinary. The drawing-room here used to seem absolutely enormous. If I hadn't returned, those memories would have remained stuck in my mind for ever.'

I said, 'Yes, that's perfectly natural. As a child, one is small in size, so everything else seems large. One grows bigger with age, but the size of all the other things remains the same, doesn't it?'

We went for a stroll in the garden after tea. Jayanto suddenly stopped walking and said, 'Deodar.'

I stared at him.

'A deodar tree. It ought to be here somewhere,' he said and began striding towards the far end of the compound. Why did he suddenly think of a deodar tree?

A few seconds later I heard his voice exclaiming jubilantly, 'Yes, it's here! Exactly where it was before!'

'Of course it's where it was before,' I said. 'Would a tree go roaming about?'

Jayanto shook his head impatiently. 'No, that is not what I meant. All I meant was that the tree is where I thought it might be.'

'But why did you suddenly think of a tree?'

Jayanto stared at the trunk of the tree, frowning. Then he shook his head slowly and said, 'I can't remember that now. Something had brought me near the tree. I had done something here. A European . . .'

'European?'

'No, I can't recall anything at all. Memory is a strange business . . .'

They had a good cook in the circuit house. Later in the evening, while we sat at the oval dining table having dinner, Jayanto said, 'The cook they had in those days was called Dilawar. He had a scar on his left cheek and his eyes were always red. But he was an excellent cook.'

Jayanto's memories began returning one by one soon after dinner when we went back to the drawing-room. He could recall where his father used to sit and smoke a cheroot, where his mother used to knit, and what magazines lay on the table.

And, slowly, in bits and pieces, he recalled the whole business about his doll.

It was not the usual kind of doll little girls play with. One of Jayanto's uncles had brought for him from Switzerland a twelve-inch-long figure of an old man, dressed in traditional Swiss style. Apparently, it was very lifelike. Although it was not mechanized it was possible to bend and twist its limbs. Its face had a smile on it and, on its head, it wore a Swiss cap with a little yellow feather sticking out from it. Its clothes, especially in their little details, were perfect—belt, buttons, pockets, collars, socks. There were even little buckles on the shoes.

His uncle had returned from Europe shortly before Jayanto left for Bundi with his parents. The little old man had been bought in a village in Switzerland. The man who sold him had jokingly said to Jayanto's uncle, 'He's called Fritz. You must call him by this name. He won't respond to any other.'

Jayanto said, 'I had a lot of toys when I was small. My parents gave me practically everything I wanted, perhaps because I was their only child. But once I had Fritz, I forgot all my other toys. I played only with him. A time came when I began to spend hours just talking to him. Our conversation had to be one-sided, of course, but Fritz had such a funny smile on his lips and such a look in his eyes, that it seemed to me as though he could understand every word. Sometimes I wondered if he would actually converse with me if I could speak to him in German. Now it seems like a childish fantasy, but at that time the whole thing was very real to me. My parents did warn me not to overdo things, but I listened to no one. I had not yet been put in a school, so I had all the time in the world for Fritz.'

Jayanto fell silent. I looked at my watch and realized it was 9.30 p.m. It was very quiet outside. We were sitting in the drawing-room of the circuit house. An oil lamp burnt in the room.

I asked, 'What happened to the doll?'

Jayanto was still deep in thought. His answer to my question came so late that, by that time, I had started to think that he had not heard me at all.

'I had brought it to Bundi. It was destroyed here.'

'Destroyed? How?'

Jayanto sighed.

'We were sitting out on the lawn having tea. I had kept the doll by my side on the grass. I was not really old enough to have tea, but I insisted and, in the process, the cup tilted and some of the hot tea fell on my pants. I ran inside to change and came back to find that Fritz had disappeared. I looked around and found quite soon that a couple of stray dogs were having a nice tug-of-war with Fritz. Although he didn't actually come apart, his face was battered beyond recognition and his clothes were torn. In other words, Fritz did not exist for me any more. He was dead.'

'And then?' Jayanto's story intrigued me.

'What could possibly happen after that? I arranged his funeral, that's all.'

'Meaning?'

'I buried him under that deodar tree. I had wanted to make a coffin. Fritz was, after all, a European. But I could find nothing, not even a little box. So, in the end, I buried him just like that.'

At last, the mystery of the deodar tree was solved.

We went to bed at around ten. Our room was a large one and our beds had been neatly made. Not being used to doing a lot of walking, I was feeling rather tired after the day's activities. Besides, the bed was very comfortable. I fell asleep barely ten minutes after hitting the pillow.

A slight noise woke me a little later. I turned on my side and found Jayanto sitting up on his bed. The table lamp by his bed was switched on and, in its light, it was easy to see the look of anxiety on his face.

I asked, 'What is it? Are you not feeling well?'

Instead of answering my question, Jayanto asked me one himself.

'Do you think this circuit house has got small animals? I mean, things like cats or mice?'

'I shouldn't be surprised if it does. Why?'

'Something walked over my chest. That's what woke me.'

'Rats and mice usually come in through drains. But I've never known them to climb on the bed.'

'This is the second time I've woken up, actually. The first time I had heard a shuffling noise near the window.'

'Oh, if it was near the window, it is more likely to be a cat.'

'Yes, but . . .'

Jayanto still sounded doubtful. I said, 'Didn't you see anything after you switched the light on?'

'Nothing. But then, I didn't switch it on immediately after opening my eyes. To tell you the truth, I felt rather scared at first. But when I did switch it on, there was nothing to be seen.'

'That means whatever came in must still be in the room.'

'Well . . . since both the doors are bolted from inside . . .'

I rose quickly and searched under the bed, behind our suitcases and everywhere else in the room. I could not find anything. The door to the bathroom was closed. I opened it and was about to start another search when Jayanto called out to me softly, 'Shankar!'

I came back to the room. Jayanto was staring hard at the cover of his quilt. Upon seeing me, he pulled a portion of it near the lamp and said, 'Look at this!'

I bent over the cloth and saw tiny, brown circular marks on it. I said, 'Well, these could have been made by a cat.'

Jayanto did not say anything. It was obvious that something had deeply disturbed him. But it was two-thirty in the morning. I simply had to get a little more sleep, or I knew I would just keep feeling tired. And we had plans of doing a lot of sightseeing the following day.

So, after murmuring a few soothing words—such as, don't worry, I am here with you and who knows, those marks may have been on your quilt already when you went to bed—I switched off the light once more and lay down. I had no doubt that Jayanto had only had a bad dream. All those memories of his childhood had upset him, obviously, and that was what had led to his dreaming of a cat walking on his chest.

I slept soundly for the rest of the night. If there were further disturbances, Jayanto did not tell me about them. But I could see in the morning that he had not slept well.

'Tonight I must give him one of the tranquillizers I brought with me,' I thought.

We finished our breakfast by nine, as we had planned, and left for the fort. A car had already been arranged. It was almost nine-thirty by the time we reached.

Some of Jayanto's old forgotten memories began coming back again, though—fortunately—they had nothing to do with his doll. In fact, his youthful exuberance made me think he had forgotten all about it.

'There—there's that elephant on top of the gate!' he exclaimed. 'And the turrets! And here is the bed made of silver and the throne. Look at that picture on the wall—I saw it the last time!'

But within an hour, his enthusiasm began to wane. I was so engrossed myself that I did not notice it at first. But, while walking through a hall and looking at the chandeliers hanging from the ceiling, I suddenly realized Jayanto was no longer walking by my side. Where was he?

We had a guide with us. 'Babu has gone out on the terrace,' he told me.

I came out of the hall and found Jayanto standing absent-mindedly near a wall on the other side of the terrace. He did not seem to notice my presence even when I went and stood beside him. He started when I called him by his name.

'What on earth is the matter with you?' I asked. 'Why are you standing here looking morose even in a beautiful place like this? I can't stand it.'

Jayanto simply said, 'Have you finished seeing everything? If so, let's . . .'

Had I been alone, I would definitely have spent a little more time at the fort. But one look at Jayanto made me decide in favour of returning to the circuit house.

A road through the hills took us back to town. Jayanto and I were both sitting in the back of the car. I offered him a cigarette, but he refused. I noticed a veiled excitement in the movement of his hands. One moment he placed them near the window, then on his lap and, immediately afterwards, began biting his nails. Jayanto was quiet by nature. This odd restlessness in him worried me.

After about ten minutes, I could not take it any more.

'It might help if you told me about your problem,' I said. Jayanto shook his head.

'It's no use telling you, for you're not going to believe me.'

'OK, even if I don't believe you, I can at least discuss the matter with you, can't I?'

'Fritz came into our room last night. Those little marks on my quilt were his footprints.'

There was very little I could do at this except catch hold of him by the shoulders and shake him. How could I talk sensibly to someone whose mind was obsessed with such an absurd idea?

'You didn't see anything, did you?' I said finally.

'No. But I could distinctly feel that whatever was walking on my chest had two feet, not four.'

As we got out of the car at the circuit house, I decided that Jayanto must be given a nerve tonic or some such thing. A tranquillizer might not be good enough. I could not allow a thirty-seven-year-old man to be so upset by a simple memory from his childhood.

I said to Jayanto upon reaching our room, 'It's nearly twelve o'clock. Should we not be thinking of having a bath?'

'You go first,' said Jayanto and flung himself on the bed.

An idea came to my mind in the bath. Perhaps this was the only way to bring Jayanto back to normalcy.

If a doll had been buried somewhere thirty years ago and if one knew the exact spot, it might be possible to dig the ground there. No doubt most of it would have been destroyed, but it was likely that we'd find just a few things, especially if they were made of metal, such as the buckle of a belt or brass buttons on a jacket. If Jayanto could actually be shown that that was all that was left of his precious doll, he might be able to rid himself of his weird notions; otherwise, he would have strange dreams every night and talk of Fritz walking on his chest. If this kind of thing was allowed to continue he might go totally mad.

Jayanto seemed to like my idea at first. But, after a little while, he said, 'Who will do the digging? Where will you find a spade?'

I laughed, 'Since there is a garden, there is bound to be a gardener. And that would mean there's a spade. If we offered him a little tip, I have no doubt that he would have no objection to digging up a bit of the ground near the trunk of a tree at the far end of the lawn.'

Jayanto did not accept the idea immediately, nor did I say anything further. He went and had his bath after a little bit of persuasion. At lunch, he ate nothing except a couple of chapatis with meat curry, although I knew he was quite fond of his food.

After lunch we went and sat in the cane chairs on the veranda that overlooked the garden. There appeared to be no one else in the circuit house. There was something eerie about the silence that afternoon. All we could hear was the noise made by a few monkeys sitting on the gulmohar tree across the cobbled path.

Around 3 p.m., we saw a man come into the garden, carrying a watering can. He was an old man. His hair, moustaches and sideburns all were white.

'Will you ask him or should I?'

At this question from Jayanto, I raised a reassuring hand and went straight to the gardener. After I had spoken to him, he looked at me rather suspiciously. Clearly, no one had ever made such a request. 'Why, babu?' he asked. I laid a friendly hand on his shoulder and said, 'Don't worry about the reason. I'll give you five rupees. Please do as you're told.'

He relented, going so far as to give me a salute accompanied by a broad grin.

I beckoned to Jayanto, who was still sitting on the veranda. He rose and began walking towards me. As he came closer, I saw the pallor on his face.

I did hope we would find at least some part of the doll.

The gardener, in the meantime, had fetched a spade. The three of us made our way to the deodar tree.

Jayanto pointed at the ground about a yard from the trunk of the tree and said, 'Here.'

'Are you sure?' I asked him.

Jayanto nodded silently.

'How much did you dig?'

'At least eight inches.'

The gardener started digging. The man had a sense of humour. As he lifted his spade, he asked if there was hidden treasure under the ground and, if so, whether we would be prepared to share it with him. I had to laugh at this, but Jayanto's face did not register even the slightest trace of amusement. It was the month of October and not at all warm in Bundi. Yet the collar of his shirt was soaked in sweat. He was staring at the ground unblinkingly. The gardener continued to dig. Why was there no sign of the doll?

The raucous cry of a peacock made me turn my head for a moment and, in that instant, Jayanto made a strange sound. I quickly looked at him. His eyes were bulging. He raised his right hand and pointed at the hole in the ground with a finger that was visibly trembling.

Then he asked in a voice turned hoarse with fear, 'What . . . what is that?'

The spade slipped from the gardener's hand. I, too, gaped at the ground, open-mouthed in horror, amazement and disbelief.

There lay at our feet, covered in dust, lying flat on its back, a twelve-inch-long, pure white, perfect little human skeleton.

Translated by Gopa Majumdar

First published in Bengali in 1971

Mr Brown's Cottage

I had been looking for an opportunity to go to Bangalore ever since I had found Mr Brown's diary. It happened rather unexpectedly. At the annual re-union of our Ballygunje school, I happened to run into my old classmate, Anikendra Bhowmik. Anik told me he was now working at the Indian Institute of Science in Bangalore. 'Why don't you come and spend your holiday with me?' he asked. 'It's the best place in India! I have a spare room in my house, so you won't have any problem. Will you come?'

Anik and I had been very close friends in school. Then the inevitable happened. He went on to study science and I took up arts. We began moving in opposite directions. After a few years he went to England, and I lost touch with him. This was our re-union after about twelve years.

I said, 'I might. When is the best time to come to Bangalore?'

'Any time. The weather in Bangalore is always pleasant. Why do you think the British were so fond of the place? You can come any time you like. All I need is a week's notice.'

So here was a chance to go and find the house where Mr Brown had lived. But first I must explain about the diary.

I am what is usually described as a bookworm. Old books, especially, fascinate me. I work in a bank and spend at least half my salary on these. Over the last five years I have managed to acquire quite a collection including travel books, shikar tales, autobiographies and diaries. I love their old, faded, brittle, moth-eaten pages. And their smell! The smell of wet earth after the first shower and the smell of old books—I do not think any other smell on earth can match their charm. Not the scent of attar, kasturi, rose, hasnuhana—or even the best perfume in France.

It was my passion for old books that had led me to chance upon the diary of Mr Brown. It was not printed, but a genuine diary, many pages of which were filled with entries, handwritten with a quill. Bound in red leather, it had three-hundred-and- fifty ruled pages and measured six by four-and-a-half inches. The cover had a golden border and in the middle was embossed in gold letters the owner's name: John Middleton Brown. The first page had his signature and his address below it—Evergreen Lodge, Fraser Town, Bangalore. This was followed by a date—January 1858, which meant that the diary was a hundred-and-thirteen years old. I found it together with some other books which also bore Mr Brown's name, and it cost me very little. Maqbool, the bookseller, initially asked for twenty rupees. I offered to pay ten and, in the end, I bought it for twelve. Had Mr Brown been someone famous, this diary would have fetched at least twelve thousand rupees.

I did not expect to find anything other than a description of the life led by a British gentleman in those days. In fact, the first hundred pages offered just that. Mr Brown was a schoolmaster. There was a mention of the school he taught in, descriptions of the city of Bangalore, the trees and flowers he saw, both in his own garden and elsewhere. He mentioned the Viceroy's wife, Lady Canning's visit to Bangalore. Sometimes he talked of his home in Sussex and all the friends and relatives he had left behind. There was also mention of his wife, Elizabeth, though she had died a few years ago.

But the most interesting thing in his diary was the frequent reference to someone called Simon. Whether this was his son or brother or nephew or friend was impossible to tell. But it was clear that Mr Brown was very deeply attached to him. His diary was full of instances of Simon's intelligence, his courage, his anger, his naughtiness and his occasional wayward behaviour. Many of his entries said things like, 'Simon loves to sit in a particular chair'; or 'Simon was not feeling very well today'; 'I feel sad because I have not seen Simon all day'.

Then came the heartbreaking news of Simon's death. On 22nd September, at around 7.30 p.m., Simon was struck by lightning. His body was found the next morning near a charred eucalyptus tree in Mr Brown's garden.

For about a month after Simon's death, he wrote virtually nothing in his diary. Whatever little he did was full of sadness and despair. He thought of going back to Britain, but did not want to leave the place where Simon's soul rested. His health, too, had probably begun to fail. He wrote, 'Today, again I did not go to school', on at least five different occasions. There was mention of a Dr Lucas, who had examined Mr Brown and suggested a course of remedy.

Then, suddenly—on 2nd November—the diary mentioned a strange incident. And it was the description of this incident that made the diary so special.

Mr Brown wrote about the incident in red ink instead of the blue he usually used. 'The most unexpected and extraordinary thing happened today,' he wrote. 'I had gone to Lal Bagh to see if I could find some peace among the trees and the plants. I returned at around 7.30 p.m. As soon as I stepped into the living-room, I saw Simon sitting by the fireside in his favourite high-backed chair! Simon! Was it really Simon? I felt overjoyed. Simon was looking straight at me with such affection in his eyes. But the room was dark. Thomas, that lazy bearer of mine, had forgotten to light a lamp. So I took out my matchbox to see Simon a little better. But—alas!—he vanished the instant I struck a match. This was truly regrettable; but then, I had never hoped to see Simon again. I should be happy if he appears occasionally even as a ghost. What a heavenly day it is today! Simon has not forgotten me even after his death. He even remembers his favourite chair! Please, Simon—do come and visit me sometimes. I don't want anything else from you. I can live happily for the rest of my life if I can see you again.'

Not much was written after this date. But the few entries that followed were full of joy, for Simon came and met Mr Brown every day. His ghost did not disappoint him.

The last entry read, 'The knowledge that he who loved me did not lose his love even after death has given me profound peace.'

Here the diary ended. But my curiosity did not. Did this house of Mr Brown—this Evergreen Lodge in Fraser Town—still exist? And did the ghost of Simon still appear every evening? Would it appear before a stranger? If I went and spent an evening there, would I get to see it?

When I arrived in Bangalore, I mentioned nothing about the diary at first. Anik took me sightseeing all over Bangalore in his Ambassador. We even went to Fraser Town. Bangalore was a really beautiful place, so the praise and appreciation I expressed as we moved around were quite sincerely felt. After the hustle and bustle of Calcutta, such a quiet and peaceful place seemed like something out of a dream.

The next day was Sunday. I raised the subject of Mr Brown's house in the morning as Anik and I sat under a garden umbrella in his house, sipping tea. Anik listened to the whole story without comment. Then he put his cup down on the cane table and said, 'Look, Ranjan, the house you're talking about may still exist. After all, a hundred years is not a very long time. But if you wish to go there simply to lie in wait for a ghost, I fear I cannot join you. I have always been extra sensitive about certain things. I think life at the moment is just fine—I have no problems. But to go ghost hunting now, I think, would be asking for trouble. You must count me out.'

This clearly showed Anik had not changed. He had had a reputation of being very timid and something of a coward in school. I remembered one instance when two other boys had covered themselves in a white sheet and pounced upon poor Anik as he was walking alone one evening. He had been so frightened that the next day his father had come and complained to the headmaster.

Before I could say anything, however, Anik remarked, 'But if you must go, I think I can easily find you company. Hello, Mr Banerjee!'

I turned around and saw a man walking in through the gate and was now coming towards us, smiling a little. He appeared to be around forty-five. Nearly six feet in height, his body seemed both well built and well maintained. He was clad in grey trousers and a dark blue bush-shirt. A black-and- white silk scarf with batik prints was casually wound around his neck.

Anik introduced us. 'This is my friend, Ranjan Sengupta—Mr Hrishikesh Banerjee.'

Mr Banerjee, it turned out, worked in the aircraft factory. He had lived in Bangalore for many years.

Anik offered him a cup of tea and went straight to the subject of the house of Mr Brown. Mr Banerjee broke into such a loud guffaw when he heard the tale that the squirrel that was romping about near our table dashed up the nearest tree and vanished among the leaves.

'Ghosts? Ghosts? You mean you seriously believe in them? Today? In these times?'

I said hesitantly, 'Well, what's wrong with being interested? It may well be that there is a scientific explanation behind the existence of ghosts that has not yet come to light. But who knows—ten years from now someone might hit upon it!'

Mr Banerjee continued to laugh. His teeth, I noticed, were very white and strong.

Finally, Anik said, 'All right, Mr Banerjee. Ghost or no ghost—all I want to know is whether you'd be prepared to go with Ranjan to such a house, if it can be found, and spend an evening there. He is my guest and I cannot allow him to go alone. To tell you the truth, I myself am rather . . . . er . . . . careful about things. If I went with him, I'd be more of a liability than anything else!'

Mr Banerjee took out a pipe from his pocket and began filling it. 'I wouldn't mind,' he said, 'but I would go only on one condition—both of you must come with me.'

He broke into loud laughter again, causing great panic among the birds that were twittering in the vicinity. Anik went slightly pale, but could not refuse.

'What did you say the place was called?' asked Mr Banerjee.

'Evergreen Lodge.'

'In Fraser Town?'

'That's what the diary said.'

'Hmm.' He began smoking his pipe. 'Fraser Town does have a few old British cottages. Anyway—if we must go, why don't we do so this evening? Say I come back here at about four?'

Mr Banerjee may have been an engineer by profession, but he clearly had a military spirit and a strong sense of punctuality. He arrived in his Morris Minor on the dot.

'What are you carrying with you?' he asked, as we got into the car.

Anik gave him the list—a powerful torch, six candles, a first-aid box, some ham sandwiches, a large flask of coffee, a pack of cards, a rug to spread on the floor and a tube of mosquito repellent.

'And arms?'

'Can ghosts be destroyed by arms? Hey, Ranjan—is your ghost a solid one?'

'Never mind,' said Mr Banerjee, 'I have a small revolver. So we needn't worry about whether it's solid or liquid.'

We set off. After a while Mr Banerjee said, 'The place does exist.'

I was surprised, 'You mean you've made enquiries already?'

'I am a very methodical man, Mr Sengupta. Shouldn't one first make sure about the existence of a place before trying to go there? One of my golf mates, Srinivas Deshmukh, lives in that area. I went to his house straight from yours this morning. He told me there is indeed a cottage called Evergreen Lodge in Fraser Town. It has been lying vacant for nearly fifty years. People used to go there for picnics even ten years ago. But no one does so now. Apparently, no one ever lived in that house for very long. However, it does not have a reputation of being haunted. It had some furniture once—but it was all auctioned a few years ago. Col. Mercer bought some of it. He, too, lives in Fraser Town. As far as I can see, we are going to have no more than a picnic ourselves. I am glad Anikendra has brought the cards.'

Driving through the clean, broad roads of Bangalore, it was difficult to imagine the existence of a haunted house. But I could not forget the diary of Mr Brown. Unless one was totally mad, one would not just make up such an extraordinary tale and record it in a diary. Mr Brown did see Simon's ghost—time and again. Would that ghost not appear before us—even once?

I had never been to England, but I had seen pictures of English cottages. The sight of Evergreen Lodge made me feel as though I was standing in front of an old and abandoned house in an English countryside.

There must have been a garden in front of the cottage. Instead of carefully arranged flower beds it now had wild plants and weeds that grew in abundance. There was a small wicket gate through which one had to pass in order to go into the garden. The name of the place was engraved on the gate. But someone—possibly one of the merry picnickers—had added an N before the word Evergreen which now made it Nevergreen.

We began walking towards the house. There were plenty of trees around it. I saw a few eucalyptus trees but failed to recognize the others. The soil of Bangalore was reported to be so good that plants and trees from anywhere in the world could survive here.

There was a portico with a broken tile roof. Creepers covered its pillars. One side of the front door had come off its hinges. Most of the windows were broken. There was such a thick layer of mould on the walls that it was impossible to guess the original colour of the house.

We walked in through the broken door. There was a long passage that led to a room at the far end. There were more rooms on both sides. The one on our right seemed larger than the others. It must have been the living-room. The floor was wooden, although most of it had rotted away. Every step would have to be taken carefully.

We went into the room. The wooden boards creaked under our feet. It seemed very large indeed, possibly because there was no furniture in it. There were windows on the western and the northern sides. The garden could be seen through these on one side, the eucalyptus trees on the other. Was it one of these that was struck by lightning? Simon had been standing under it. Instant death. The thought made me shiver.

I looked at the windowless wall on the southern side. The fireplace was on the left. Simon's favourite chair must have been kept by its side. The ceiling of the room was covered with cobwebs. Evergreen Lodge, that must have been a pretty little cottage once, was obviously in bad shape.

Mr Banerjee was humming a western tune. He stopped to light his pipe and asked, 'What do you usually play? Bridge, poker or rummy?'

Anik was about to sit down, having spread the rug and placed on the floor the stuff he was carrying, when we heard a noise. Someone wearing boots was walking about in one of the other rooms.

I looked at Anik. He had gone quite pale.

The footsteps stopped. Mr Banerjee suddenly took the pipe out of his mouth and yelled, 'Is anybody there?' All of us began to move towards the passage. Anik clutched at my sleeve.

We heard the footsteps again as we reached the passage. Then a man came out from one of the rooms on the right. He stopped short as his eyes fell on us. He was an Indian and, despite a heavy stubble on his face and an unkempt air, undoubtedly an educated gentleman.

'Hello!' he said.

None of us knew what to say.

The newcomer himself answered our unspoken question.

'My name is Venkatesh. I am a painter. Are you the owners of this house? Or have you come to buy it?'

Banerjee smiled and replied, 'Neither. We just happened to stroll in.'

'I see. I was wondering if I could have my studio in this house. I don't mind if it's going to pieces—you wouldn't know who the owner is, would you?'

'I am afraid not,' said Banerjee, 'but you might like to ask Col. Mercer. His house isn't far. Straight down the road and then to the left. Shouldn't take you more than five minutes.'

'Thank you,' said Mr Venkatesh and went out.

We heard the gate open and shut. Mr Banerjee broke into yet another guffaw and said, 'Mr Sengupta, that was not your Simon or some other ghost, was it?'

I had to laugh, 'You cannot expect to see the ghost so soon. It's only a quarter past five. And even if he was a ghost, he couldn't have hailed from the nineteenth century. Such a ghost would wear different clothes.'

We returned to the living-room. Anik sat down on the rug and said, 'You make me nervous with your flights of fancy. Come, let's play cards.'

'Light some of the candles first,' said Banerjee. 'Dusk falls very quickly here.'

We lit two candles and placed them on the wooden floor after which we took turns drinking coffee from the flask. Then it became impossible for me to keep quiet. There was something I had been wondering about, which showed how obsessed I had become with the idea of a ghost. I said to Banerjee, 'You told us Col. Mercer had bought some of the furniture of this house. If he lives so close, couldn't we go and find out about a particular item?'

'What item?'

'A special kind of high-backed chair.'

Anik grew faintly annoyed at this and said, 'Why? Why should we suddenly start looking for a high-backed chair?'

'Well, you see—Mr Brown mentioned this chair in his diary. He said

Simon loved to sit in this chair, even after his death. It used to be kept near that fireplace. So I thought if we could bring it here . . .'

Anik cut me short, 'How will you bring it? In Mr Banerjee's Morris? Or do you suggest the three of us carry it all the way? Have you gone totally mad?'

Banerjee raised his hand at this point and silenced us both.

'That chair was not among the stuff Col. Mercer bought. I go to his house quite often. I would have seen it. As far as I know, he bought two book-cases, two oil paintings, a few flower vases and little knick-knacks for display—you know, art objects.'

I fell silent. Anik began shuffling the cards. Banerjee said, 'Let's play rummy. It should be more interesting if we played with stakes. Do you mind?'

'Not at all,' I replied, 'but I only have a small job in a bank. I cannot afford to lose much.'

The light outside had faded. We began to play. I have never been lucky at cards. Today was no exception. I would have felt happy to see Anik win for I knew he was feeling uncomfortable and nervous. But nothing of the kind happened. It was Mr Banerjee who appeared to have all the luck. He kept humming that western tune and continued to win every game. We were still busy playing when I heard a cat mew. This disappointed me further. A haunted house should not have even a cat living in it. I said as much to Mr Banerjee who laughed, and said, 'But it was a black cat—saw it going down the passage. Black cats go well with ghosts, don't they?'

We went on playing. Only once did we hear the raucous cry of a bird outside. There was no other noise to spoil our concentration.

It was about 6.30 p.m. Daylight had disappeared almost totally. I had finally been favoured by Lady Luck and had won two games, when we heard a strange noise. Someone was knocking at the door. All of us put our cards down and listened. Tap, tap, tap, tap.

Anik went paler then before. My own hands began trembling. But Mr Banerjee was clearly not one to be frightened easily. He broke the silence by demanding loudly, 'Who is it?'

The knock was repeated. Tap, tap, tap.

Banerjee leapt up to go and investigate. I caught the edge of his trousers and pulled him back. 'Don't go alone!' I whispered.

The three of us went out together. We went into the passage and looked towards our left. There was a male figure standing just outside the door, wearing a suit and carrying a stick. It was impossible to distinguish his features in the dark. Anik clutched at my sleeve even more tightly. I looked at him, and, somehow, my courage returned. Meanwhile, Banerjee had taken a few steps forward. Suddenly we heard him exclaim, 'Oh, hello, Dr Larkin! What are you doing here?'

It was now possible to see the middle-aged European. He screwed up his blue eyes slightly behind the golden frame of his glasses and smiled genially, 'Saw your Morris parked outside. Then I noticed candlelight through the windows. So I thought I'd drop in and find out what you're up to.'

Banerjee grinned. 'These two young friends of mine had this weird idea. They dragged me along to play cards here. Just for an adventure!'

'Very good, very good. Youth is the time for doing mad things. Old people like me would only sit at home and reminisce. Well, well. Have a good time!'

Dr Larkin raised his hand in farewell and walked away, tapping his stick on the ground.

Another false alarm. We returned to our game. I had lost about four rupees; now I was beginning to regain some of it. Even if Simon's ghost did not appear, today's outing would be worthwhile if I could manage to win something at cards.

I had been looking at my watch frequently. So I can tell exactly when the real thing happened. Seven-thirty. Mr Brown had mentioned that that was when Simon had died.

I was dealing the cards, Mr Banerjee was lighting his pipe and Anik had just slipped his hand into the packet of sandwiches when the look on his face changed and his whole body became rigid.

His eyes were looking at something beyond the room, in the passage. Banerjee and I automatically followed his gaze. What I saw made me hold my breath.

A pair of brilliant eyes stared at us from the dark passage. They had the pale green and yellow glow of phosphorus and did not flicker.

Mr Banerjee's right hand went into the vest pocket of his coat. And, in that instant, everything fell into place. My voice came back and I said, 'There's no need to take out your revolver, Mr Banerjee. It's that black cat!'

Anik seemed to relax at my words. Banerjee took his hand out of his pocket and said softly, 'How ridiculous!'

The phosphorescent eyes now came closer. As soon as it crossed the threshold, I knew I was right. It was indeed the black cat.

The cat stepped into the room and turned left. Our eyes were following every movement it made. We, too, turned our gaze to the left.

Then all of us made the same sound quite involuntarily. It was the sound one makes when profoundly startled. The reason for this was simple—while we had been sitting playing rummy, a high-backed chair, covered in red velvet, had appeared from somewhere and made its way to the fireplace.

Black as a moonless night, the cat walked silently towards the chair. It stopped for a moment, then jumped on to it neatly and curled up.

At that precise moment, I heard something that froze my blood. An invisible old man was laughing merrily in the room, punctuating his laughter with, 'Simon, Simon, Simon, Simon . . .' There was also the sound of his clapping happily like a child.

A scream told me that Anik had fainted. And Mr Banerjee? He had gathered Anik in his arms and was sprinting towards the main door.

I followed him quickly. The cards, the candles, the food, the rug—everything was left behind. Beyond the door was the main compound and, further down, the gate. We ran like madmen and reached the Morris

Minor parked just outside the gate. Thank goodness Bangalore did not have a lot of traffic. If it did, I shudder to think how many people would have been injured that evening by a speeding maniac.

Anik regained consciousness in the car, but did not utter a single word. Mr Banerjee was the first one to speak as we reached home. He snatched the glass of brandy from Anik's bearer, downed half of it at one go, and said hoarsely, 'So, Simon was a cat!'

I was in no condition to converse either. But I felt in my heart that he was right.

It had to be true. Mr Brown's Simon—that intelligent, whimsical, proud, devoted and affectionate being whom he loved so well—was the black cat we had seen today!

Translated by Gopa Majumdar
First published in Bengali in 1971

Mr Eccentric

I never managed to find out Mr Eccentric's full name. All I did learn was that his surname was Mukherjee. His appearance was quite unforgettable. He was nearly six feet tall, his body was without the slightest trace of fat, his back arched like a bow; and his neck, arms, hands and forehead were covered by innumerable veins that appeared to be bulging out of his skin. What he wore almost every day was a white shirt with black flannel trousers, white socks and white tennis shoes. And he always carried a stout walking stick. Perhaps he needed it because he often walked on uneven, unpaved roads and amongst wild plants.

I met Mr Eccentric ten years ago, when I used to work for a bank. That year, I had taken ten days off in early May, and gone to Darjeeling—my favourite hill town—for a holiday. I saw Mr Eccentric on my very first day.

At about half past four, I had left my hotel for a walk, after a cup of tea. In the afternoon, there had been a short shower. Since there was every chance that it might rain again, I had put on my raincoat before stepping out. As I was walking down Jalapahar Road, the most picturesque and quiet road in Darjeeling, I suddenly spotted a man about fifty yards away. He was standing where the road curved. His body was bent forward, and he was leaning on his walking stick, gazing intently at the grass by the roadside. At first, none of this struck me as unusual. Perhaps he was interested in some wild flower or insect. Perhaps he had seen one of those in the grass. I cast a mildly curious glance in his direction, and kept on walking.

As I got closer, however, I realized that there was something odd about him. It was the intensity of the man's concentration. I was standing only a few feet away, staring at him, but he did not appear to have noticed me at all. He was still bent over the grass, his eyes fixed on it. Now I could not help asking a question: 'Have you lost something?'

There was no reply. Was he deaf?

My curiosity rose. I was determined to see what happened next. So I lit a cigarette, and waited. About three minutes later, life seemed to return to the man's limbs. He bent further forward, and stretched an arm out towards the grass. Then he pushed his fingers into the thick grass, and a second later, withdrew his hand. Between his thumb and index finger was held a small disc. I peered carefully at it. It was a button, nearly as large as a fifty-paise coin. Perhaps it had once been attached to a jacket.

The man brought the button closer to his eyes, scrutinized it thoroughly, turned it around several times, then said 'Tch, tch, tch!' regretfully, before placing it in his shirt pocket, and striding off in the direction of the Mall. He ignored me completely.

Later in the evening, on my way back to the hotel, I ran into an old resident of Darjeeling, Dr Bhowmik. He was standing by the fountain on the Mall. Dr Bhowmik was my father's classmate, and very fond of me. I couldn't help telling him about my encounter with the strange man. When I finished my tale, Dr Bhowmik said, 'Well, from your description, it appears that you met Mr Eccentric.'

'Mr who?'

'Eccentric. It's a sad case, really. I can't remember his first name, his surname is Mukherjee. He's been in Darjeeling for nearly five years. He rents a room in a cottage near Grindlays Bank. Before he came here, he used to teach physics in Ravenshaw College in Cuttack. I believe he was once a brilliant student, and has a German degree in physics. But he left his job, and came to live here. Perhaps he inherited some property, or has some private income, so he gets by.'

'Do you know him?'

'He came to me once, soon after he got here. He had stumbled and fallen somewhere, and cut his knee. It had turned septic. I treated him, and he recovered.'

'But why is he called Eccentric?'

Dr Bhowmik burst out laughing. 'He acquired that name because of his peculiar hobby. I couldn't tell you who was the first to think of that name!'

'What's his hobby?'

'You saw it yourself, didn't you? He picked up a button from the roadside and put it in his pocket. That's his hobby. He'll pick up any old thing and keep it safe in his room.'

'Any old thing? How do you mean?' For some reason, I began feeling increasingly curious about the man.

'Well,' said Dr Bhowmik, 'I call it that, but he claims that every object in his collection is most precious. Apparently, there is a story behind all of them.'

'How does *he* know that?'

Dr Bhowmik glanced at his watch. 'Why don't you ask him yourself?' he suggested. 'He's always pleased to have a visitor, for his stories are endless. All of it is pure nonsense, needless to say, but he's always glad to tell them. Mind you, whether *you* will be glad to hear them or not is a different matter!'

The following morning, I left my hotel soon after breakfast and went looking for Mr Eccentric's house. It proved quite easy to find it, since most people near Grindlays Bank seemed to know where he lived. I knocked on the door of house number seventeen. The man himself answered the door almost at once and, to my astonishment, recognized me immediately.

'You asked me something yesterday, didn't you? But I couldn't reply.

Believe me, I just couldn't speak. At a time like that, if I let my attention wander, it can spell disaster. Do come in.'

The first thing I noticed on entering his room was a glass case. It covered a large portion of a wall. On each shelf was displayed a range of very ordinary objects, not one of which seemed to bear any relationship to the other. One shelf, for instance, had the root of some plant, a rusted padlock, an ancient tin of Gold Flake cigarettes, a knitting needle, a shoe-brush and old torch cells. The man caught me staring at these objects and said, 'None of those things will give you any joy, since only I know what they are worth.'

'I believe there is a story behind everything in your collection?'

'Yes, there certainly is.'

'But that is true of most things, isn't it? Say, if you consider that watch you are wearing . . .' I began, but the man raised a hand and stopped me.

'Yes, there may be a special incident related to many things,' he said. 'But how many of those things would *continue* to carry memories of the past? Of the scene they have witnessed? Only very rarely would you find anything like that. This button that I found yesterday, for example . . . !'

The button in question was placed on a writing desk on the opposite end of the room. Mr Eccentric picked it up and handed it to me. It was a brown button, clearly torn from a jacket. I could see nothing special in it.

'Can you see anything?' he asked.

I was obliged to admit that I could not. Mr Eccentric began speaking, 'That button came from the jacket of an Englishman. He was riding down Jalapahar Road. The man was almost sixty, dressed in riding clothes, hale and hearty, a military man. When he reached the spot where I found that button, he had a stroke, and fell from his horse. Two passersby saw him and rushed to help, but he was already dead. That button came off his jacket as he fell from his horse.'

'Did you see this happen yesterday? I mean, all these past events?'

'Vividly. The more I concentrate, the better do I see.'

'When can you see such things?'

'Whenever I come across an object that has this special power to take me back to the past. It starts with a headache. Then my vision blurs, and I feel faint. Sometimes I feel as if I need support, or else I'd fall down. But almost immediately, various scenes start flashing before my eyes, and my legs become steady once more. When the whole thing's over, my temperature rises. Every time. Last night, until eight o'clock, it was nearly 102. But the fever does not last for more than a few hours. Today, I feel absolutely fine.'

Everything he said sounded far too exaggerated, but I felt quite amused. 'Can you give me a few more examples?' I asked.

'That glass case is packed with examples. See that notebook? It contains a detailed description of every incident. Which one would you like to hear?'

Before I could say anything, he strode over to the glass case and lifted two objects out of it. One was a very old leather glove, the other a spectacle lens. He placed them on a table.

'This glove,' he told me, 'is the first thing I found. It's the first item in my collection. Do you know where I found it? In a wood outside Lucerne, in Switzerland. By then I had finished my studies in Marburg, and was touring the continent before coming back to India. That day, I was out on a morning walk. A quiet and secluded path ran through the wood. After a while, I felt a little tired and sat down on a bench. Almost immediately, my eyes caught sight of only a portion of that glove, sticking out from the undergrowth near the trunk of a tree. At once, my head started throbbing. Then my vision blurred. And then . . . then I could see it all. It was like watching a film. A well-dressed gentleman, possibly an aristocrat, was walking down the same path. In his mouth was a Swiss pipe, on his hands were leather gloves, and he was carrying a walking stick. Suddenly, two men jumped out from behind a bush, and attacked him. The gentleman tried to fight them and, in the struggle, the glove on his right hand came off. Those criminals then grabbed him, killed him mercilessly and looted what money they could find in his pockets, and took his gold watch.'

'Did something like this really happen?'

'I had to spend three days in hospital. I had fever, and was delirious. There were other complications, too. The doctors there could not make a diagnosis. But, a few days later, I recovered as if by magic. After leaving the hospital, I started making enquiries. Eventually, I learnt that two years earlier, a wealthy man called Count Ferdinand was killed at that same spot, exactly as I had seen it. His son recognized the glove.'

The man told this story so easily and naturally that I found it hard not to believe him. 'Did you start building up your collection from that time?' I asked.

'Well, nothing happened for ten years after that first incident. By then I had returned home and was teaching in a college in Cuttack. Sometimes I went on holidays. Once I went to Waltair. That's when the second incident took place. I found this lens stuck between rocks on the beach. A South Indian gentleman had taken his glasses off to go and bathe in the sea. He never returned. He got cramps in his legs as he was swimming, and drowned. I can still see him raising his hands from the water and shouting, 'Help! Help!' It was heartbreaking. This lens, which I found four years after the incident, came off his glasses. Yes, what I saw was true. It was a well-known case of drowning, as I learnt later. The dead man was called Shivaraman. He was from Coimbatore.'

Mr Eccentric replaced the two objects in the glass case and sat down. 'Do you know how many items I have got in my collection? One hundred and seventy-two. I've collected them over thirty years. Have you ever heard of anyone with such a collection?'

I shook my head. 'No, your hobby is unique. There's no doubt about that. But tell me, does each of those objects have something to do with death?'

The man looked grave. 'Yes, so it seems. It isn't just death, but sudden or unnatural death—murder, suicide, death by accident, heart failure, things like that.'

'Did you find all these things simply lying by the roadside, or on beaches, and in woods?'

'Yes, most of them. The rest I found in auctions or antique shops. See that wine jug made of cut glass? I found it in an auction house in Russell Street in Calcutta. Some time in the nineteenth century, wine served out of that jug was poisoned. An Englishman—oh, he was so tall and hefty—died in Calcutta after drinking that wine.'

By this time, I had stopped looking at the glass case, and was looking closely at the man. But I could find nothing in his expression to suggest that he was lying, or that he was a cheat. Was he perhaps insane? No, that did not seem to be the case, either. The look in his eyes did seem somewhat distant, but it was certainly not abnormal. Poets often had that look, or those who were deeply religious and spiritual.

I did not stay much longer. As I said goodbye and started to step out of the room, the man said, 'Please come again. My door is always open for people like you. Where are you staying?'

'The Alice Villa.'

'I see. That's only ten minutes from here. I enjoyed meeting you. There are some people I just cannot stand. You appear to be sympathetic and understanding.'

Dr Bhowmik had invited me to tea that evening. There were two other guests. Over a cup of tea and a plate of savouries, I couldn't help raising the subject of Mr Eccentric. Dr Bhowmik asked, 'How long did you stay there?'

'About an hour.'

'My God!' Dr Bhowmik's eyes widened with amazement. 'You spent nearly an hour listening to that fraud?'

I smiled. 'Well, it was raining so much that I could hardly go out and enjoy myself elsewhere. Hearing his stories was more entertaining than being cooped up in my hotel room.'

'Who are you talking about?'

This question came from a man of about forty. Dr Bhowmik had introduced him to me as Mr Khastagir. When Dr Bhowmik explained about Mr Eccentric, Khastagir gave a wry smile and said, 'Why have you allowed such people to come and live in Darjeeling, Dr Bhowmik? They do nothing but pollute the air!'

Dr Bhowmik gave a slight smile. 'Could the air of such a big place be polluted by just one man? I don't think so!' he remarked.

The third guest was called Mr Naskar. He proceeded to give a short lecture on the influence of frauds and cheats on our society. In the end, I was obliged to point out that Mr Eccentric lived in such isolation that the chances of the society in Darjeeling being influenced by him were extremely remote.

Dr Bhowmik had lived in Darjeeling for over thirty years. Khastagir was also an old resident. After a while, I just had to ask them a question.

'Did an Englishman ever suffer a heart attack while riding a horse on Jalapahar Road? Do you know of any such case?'

'Who, you mean Major Bradley?' Dr Bhowmik replied. 'That happened about eight years ago. He had a stroke—yes, I think it happened on Jalapahar Road. He was brought to the local hospital, but by then it was too late. Why do you ask?'

I told them about the button Mr Eccentric had found. Mr Khastagir seemed outraged. 'You mean that man told you this story, and claimed that he had some supernatural power? He appears to be a crook of the first order! Why, he's spent a few years in Darjeeling, hasn't he? He could easily have heard of Bradley's death. What's supernatural about that?'

To tell the truth, the same thought had already occurred to me. If Mr Eccentric had heard the story from someone in Darjeeling, that was hardly surprising. I changed the subject.

The next few minutes were spent discussing various other topics. When it was time for me to leave, Mr Naskar rose to his feet as well. He had to go past my hotel, he said, so he wanted to walk back with me. We said goodbye to Dr Bhowmik and left. It had started to get dark. For the first time since my arrival in Darjeeling, I noticed that the thick clouds had parted here and there. Through the gaps, the light from the setting sun broke through and fell, like a spotlight, on the city and its surrounding mountains.

Mr Naskar had struck me as a man in good health. But now, it became obvious that he was finding it hard to walk uphill. Nevertheless, between short gasps, he asked me, 'Where does this Eccentric live?'

'Why, do you want to meet him?'

'No, no. Just curious.'

I told him where Mr Eccentric lived. Then I added, 'The man goes out often for long walks. We might run into him, who knows?'

Amazingly, only two minutes later, just as we reached a bend, I saw Mr Eccentric coming from the opposite direction. In one hand, he was holding his heavy walking stick. In the other was a packet wrapped in newspaper. When he saw me, he did not smile; but then, nor did he seem displeased. 'There's something wrong with my electric supply,' he said. 'There's no power at home. So I came out to buy some candles.'

Courtesy made me turn to Mr Naskar. 'This is Mr Mukherjee. And this is Mr Naskar,' I said, making introductions.

Naskar turned out to be quite westernized. Instead of saying 'Namaskar', he offered his hand. Mr Eccentric shook it quietly, without saying a word. Then he appeared to turn into a statue, and just stood there, rooted to the spot. Naskar and I both began to feel uncomfortable. After nearly half a minute, Naskar broke the silence. 'Well, I had better be going,' he said. 'I had heard about you, Mr Mukherjee. Now, luckily, I've had the chance to meet you.'

I had to say something, too. 'Goodbye, Mr Mukherjee!' I said, feeling somewhat foolish. Mr Eccentric seemed truly insane. He was standing in the middle of the road, lost in thought. He did not appear to have heard us, nor did he see us leave. He might have taken a dislike to Naskar, but didn't he behave in a perfectly friendly fashion towards me, only that morning?

We left him behind and continued walking. After a few minutes, I turned my head and looked back. Mr Eccentric was still standing where we had left him. 'From what you told us, I thought the name "Eccentric" might be suitable,' said Naskar, 'but now I think it's a lot more than that!'

It was nine o'clock in the evening. I had just had my dinner, put a paan in my mouth and was toying with the idea of going to bed with a detective novel, when a bearer came and told me that someone was looking for me. I came out of my room and was most surprised to find Mr Eccentric waiting for me. What was he doing in my hotel at nine o'clock? He still looked a little dazed. 'Is there anywhere we can sit and talk privately?' he asked. 'I wouldn't mind talking to you outside, but it's raining again.'

I invited him into my room. He sat down, sighed with relief and said, 'Could you feel my pulse, please?'

I took his hand and gave a start. He was running a fairly high temperature. 'I have got Anacin with me. Would you like one?' I said, concerned.

The man smiled. 'No, no tablet is going to work now. This fever won't go down before tomorrow morning. Then I'll be all right. But I am not worried about my temperature. I have not come to you looking for medical treatment. What I need is that ring.'

Ring? What ring? The perplexed look on my face seemed to irritate Mr Eccentric. 'That man—Laskar or Tusker, whatever his name is!' he said a little impatiently. 'Didn't you see his ring? It's an ordinary, cheap old ring, not set with stones or anything. But I want it.'

Now I remembered. Yes, Naskar did wear a silver ring on his right hand. Mr Eccentric was still speaking. 'When I shook his hand, I could feel that ring brush against my palm. Immediately, I felt as if my whole body would explode. Then the same old thing happened. I went into a trance and began watching the scenes that rose before my eyes. But before the whole thing could finish, a jeep came from the opposite end and ruined everything!'

'So you didn't see the whole episode?'

'No. But what little I did see was bad enough, let me tell you. It was a murder. I did not see the murderer's face. I only saw his hand, moving forward to grasp his victim's neck. On his hand was that ring. The victim was wearing a Rajasthani cap, and glasses with a golden frame. His eyes were bulging, he had just opened his mouth to scream. One of his lower teeth had a gold filling. That's all I saw. I have got to have that ring!'

I stared at Mr Eccentric for a few seconds. Then I said, 'Look, Mr Mukherjee, if you want that ring, why don't you ask Mr Naskar yourself? I don't know him all that well. Besides, I don't think he views your hobby with any sympathy.'

'In that case, what good would it do if I asked him? It might be better if you . . .'

'Very sorry, Mr Mukherjee,' I interrupted him, speaking plainly, 'it wouldn't work even if I went and asked him. Some people are very attached to some of their possessions. Naskar may not wish to part with that ring. If it was something he was not actually using every day, he might have . . .' I broke off.

Mr Eccentric did not waste another second. He sighed, got to his feet and left, disappearing into the dark, damp night. His demand was really weird, I thought to myself. It was one thing to pick up objects from the roadside. But to ask for something someone else was using, just to add one more item to his collection, was certainly wrong. No one could have helped him in this respect. Besides, Naskar did not appear to be a man with any imagination. It was stupid to expect him to understand and just give away his ring.

The next morning, seeing that the clouds had dispersed and the day was bright, I left for a walk after a cup of tea. My aim was to go to Birch Hill. The Mall was full of people. I had to walk carefully to avoid colliding with people on horseback, and others walking on foot, like me. A few minutes later, I found myself in the relatively quiet road to the west of Observatory Hill.

Mr Eccentric's sad face kept coming back to me. If I ran into Naskar by chance, perhaps I would speak to him about that ring. It might not mean a great deal to him, he might not mind giving it to me. I could well imagine the look on Mr Eccentric's face if I handed the ring over to him. When I was a child, I used to collect stamps; so I knew something about a collector's passion. Sometimes, one's passion could turn into an obsession.

Besides, Mr Eccentric did not meddle with anyone, he was happy living alone with his crazy hobby. He was not trying to harm anyone else, and this was probably the first time that he was coveting someone else's possession, although it was nothing valuable. To tell the truth, I had come to the conclusion the previous night that Mr Eccentric had no supernatural powers at all. His collection was based simply on his peculiar imagination. But if that brought him joy and contentment, why should anyone else object?

I spent almost two hours walking near Birch Hill, but did not see Naskar. On my return through the Mall, I had to pick my way through the crowd once again. However, this time many people in the crowd appeared agitated about something. Knots of people were scattered here and there, discussing something excitedly. As I got closer, I heard the words 'police', 'investigation' and 'murder'. I spotted an old gentleman in the crowd and decided to ask him what had happened. 'Oh, they say a suspected criminal fled from Calcutta and came here. The police followed his trail and are looking for him everywhere,' the man told me.

'Do you know his name?'

'I couldn't tell you his real name. I believe he calls himself Naskar.'

My heart jumped into my mouth. There was only one person who could give me more information: Dr Bhowmik!

As it happened, I did not have to go to his house. I ran into him and Khastagir near a rickshaw-stand. 'Just imagine!' Dr Bhowmik exclaimed. 'Only yesterday, the fellow came to my house and had tea. He had come to me some time ago, complaining of a pain in his stomach. Said he was new to the city. So I treated him, and thought I'd introduce him to some other people. That was only yesterday, for heaven's sake. And now this!'

'Has he been arrested?' I asked anxiously.

'No, not yet. The police are looking for him. He's still in Darjeeling, so they'll find him sooner or later, never fear.'

Dr Bhowmik left with Khastagir. My pulse started racing faster. It wasn't just that Naskar had turned out to be a criminal. That was amazing enough. But what about Mr Eccentric? He did say that ring was worn by a murderer. Could it really be that he had some supernatural power, after all?

I had to go and see him. Had he heard the news about Naskar? I must find out.

When I knocked on the door of house number seventeen, no one opened it. I tried again, with the same result. I couldn't really afford to wait outside, for the sky had become overcast again. So I left, and walked briskly back to my hotel. Within half an hour, it began raining very heavily. The bright, sunny morning had become a thing of the past. Where was Naskar hiding? Who had he killed? How had he killed?

At half past three, the manager of my hotel, Mr Sondhi, gave me the news. The police had found the house where Naskar was staying. Right behind it was a deep gorge. In that gorge, Naskar's dead body had been discovered. His head was crushed. Various theories were being put forward, including suicide, momentary insanity, and falling to his death while trying to escape. Apparently, there had been some disagreement with his business partner. Naskar had murdered him, hid his body and run away to Darjeeling. The police had eventually found the body in Calcutta and begun looking for Naskar.

Now I absolutely had to see Mr Eccentric. I could no longer dismiss his words. Events in Switzerland and Waltair might have been made up, he might have heard about Bradley's death in Darjeeling, but how did he know that Naskar was a murderer?

Around five o'clock, the heavy rain settled into a drizzle. I left my hotel and went to Mr Eccentric's house again. This time, the door opened immediately. Mr Eccentric greeted me with a smile, and said, 'Come in, my friend, come in. I was thinking of you.'

I stepped in. It was almost dark. A single candle flickered on the table.

'There's no electricity,' Mr Eccentric explained with a wan smile. 'They haven't yet reconnected the supply.' I took a cane chair, sat down and said, 'Have you heard?'

'About your Tusker? I don't need to hear anything, I already know the whole story. But I am grateful to him.'

'Grateful?' I felt most taken aback.

'He has given me the most important item in my collection.'

'Given you?' My throat suddenly felt dry.

'There it is, on that table. Look!'

I glanced at the table again. Next to the candle was the notebook and, placed on an open page, was Mr Naskar's ring.

'I was recording all the details. Item number 173,' Mr Eccentric said.

A question kept bothering me. 'What do you mean, he gave it to you? When did he do that?'

'Well, naturally he didn't give it to me voluntarily. I had to use force,' Mr Eccentric sighed.

This rendered me completely speechless. In the silence that followed, all I could hear was the clock ticking.

'I am glad you are here. I want to give you something. Keep it with you.'

Mr Eccentric rose and disappeared into a dark corner. I heard a faint clatter, and then his voice: 'This object is certainly worth keeping in my collection, but I cannot bear its effect on me. My temperature keeps shooting higher, and a most unpleasant scene rises before my eyes.'

He emerged from the dark and stood near the candle once more. His right hand was stretched towards me. His fingers were curled around the old, familiar, heavy walking stick.

Even in the faint light from the candle, I could tell that the red stains that covered the handle of that stick were nothing but marks left by dried blood.

Translated by Gopa Majumdar

First published in Bengali in 1972

Khagam

We were having dinner by the light of a petromax lamp. I had just helped myself to some curried egg when Lachhman, the cook and caretaker of the rest house, said, 'Aren't you going to pay a visit to Imli Baba?'

I had to tell him that since we were not familiar with the name of Imli Baba, the question of paying him a visit hadn't arisen. Lachhman said that the driver of the forest department jeep, which had been engaged for our sightseeing, would take us to the Baba if we told him. Baba's hut was in the forest and the surroundings were picturesque. As a holy man he was apparently held in very high regard; important people from all over India came to him to pay their respects and seek his blessings. What really aroused my curiosity was the information that the Baba kept a king cobra as a pet which lived in a hole near his hut and came to him every evening to drink goat's milk.

Dhurjati Babu's comment on this was that the country was being overrun by fake holy men. The more scientific knowledge was spreading in the West, he said, the more our people were heading towards superstition. 'It's a hopeless situation. It puts my back up just to think of it.'

As he finished talking, he picked up the fly swatter and brought it down with unerring aim on a mosquito which had settled on the dining table. Dhurjati Babu was a short, pale-looking man in his late forties, with sharp features and grey eyes. We had met in the rest house in Bharatpur; I was there on my way to Agra from where I was going to my elder brother in Jaipur, with whom I had planned to spend a fortnight's holiday. Both the tourist bungalow and the circuit house being full, I had to fall back on the forest rest house. Not that I regretted it; living in the heart of the forest offers a special kind of thrill along with quiet comfort.

Dhurjati Babu had preceded me by a day. We had shared the forest department jeep for our sightseeing. The previous day we had been to Deeg, twenty-two miles to the east from here, to see the fortress and the palace. That morning we saw the fortress in Bharatpur, and in the afternoon we saw the bird sanctuary at Keoladeo which was something very special. It was a seven-mile stretch of marshland dotted with tiny islands where strange birds from far corners of the globe came and made their homes. I was absorbed in watching the birds, but Dhurjati Babu grumbled and made vain efforts to wave away the tiny insects buzzing around us. These unkis have a tendency to settle on your face, but they are so small that most people can ignore them. Not Dhurjati Babu.

By half-past eight we had finished dinner and were sitting on cane chairs on the terrace and admiring the beauty of the forest in moonlight. 'The holy man the servant mentioned,' I remarked, 'what about going and taking a look at him?'

Flicking his cigarette towards a eucalyptus tree, Dhurjati Babu said, 'King cobras can never be tamed. I know a lot about snakes. I spent my boyhood in Jalpaiguri, and killed many snakes with my own hands. The king cobra is the deadliest, most vicious snake there is. The story of the holy man feeding it goat's milk should be taken with a pinch of salt.'

I said, 'We are going to see the fortress at Bayan tomorrow morning. In the afternoon we have nothing to do.'

'I take it you have a lot of faith in holy men?'

I could see the question was a barbed one. However, I answered calmly.

'The question of faith doesn't arise because I've never had anything to do with holy men. But I can't deny that I am a bit curious about this one.'

'I too was curious at one time, but after an experience I had with one . . .'

It turned out that Dhurjati Babu suffered from high blood pressure. An uncle of his had persuaded him to try a medicine prescribed by a holy man. Dhurjati Babu had done so, and as a result had suffered intense stomach pains. This had caused his blood pressure to shoot up even more. Ever since, he had looked upon ninety per cent of India's holy men as fakes.

I found this allergy quite amusing, and just to provoke him said, 'You said it wasn't possible to tame king cobras; I'm sure ordinary people like us couldn't do it, but I've heard of sadhus up in the Himalayas living in caves with tigers.'

'You may have heard about it, but have you seen it with your own eyes?'

I had to admit that I hadn't.

'You never will,' said Dhurjati Babu. 'This is the land of tall stories. You'll hear of strange happenings all the time, but never see one yourself. Look at our Ramayana and Mahabharata. It is said they're history, but actually they're no more than a bundle of nonsense. The ten-headed Ravana, the monkey-god Hanuman with a flame at the end of his tail setting fire to a whole city, Bhima's appetite, Ghatotkacha, Hidimba, the flying chariot Pushpak, Kumbhakarna—can you imagine anything more absurd than these? And the epics are full of fake holy men as well. That's where it all started. Yet everyone—even the educated—swallows these stories.'

Despite Dhurjati Babu's reservations, the following day we lunched in the rest house after visiting the fortress at Bayan and, after a couple of hours' rest, reached the holy man's hermitage a little after four. Dhurjati Babu didn't object to the trip. Perhaps he too was a little curious about the Baba. The hermitage was in a clearing in the forest below a huge tamarind tree, which is why he was called Imli Baba by the local people, imli being the Hindi word for tamarind. His real name was not known.

In a hut made of date-palm leaves, the Baba sat on a bearskin with a young disciple by his side. It was impossible to guess the Baba's age. There was still an hour or so until sunset, but the dense covering of foliage made the place quite dark. A fire burnt before the Baba, who had a ganja pipe in his hand. We could see by the light of the fire a clothesline stretched across the wall of the hut from which hung a towel, a loincloth, and about a dozen sloughed-off snakeskins.

Dhurjati Babu whispered in my ear: 'Let's not beat about the bush; ask him about the snake's feeding time.'

'So you want to see Balkishen?' asked the Baba, reading our minds and smiling from behind his pipe. The driver of the jeep, Dindayal, had told us a little while ago that the snake was called Balkishen. We told Baba that we had heard of his pet snake and were most anxious to see it drink milk. Was there any likelihood of our wish being fulfilled?

Imli Baba shook his head sadly. He said that as a rule Balkishen came every day in the evening in answer to Baba's call, and had come even two days ago. But since the day before he had not been feeling well. 'Today is the day of the full moon,' said the Baba, 'so he will not come. But he will surely come again tomorrow evening.'

That snakes too could feel indisposed was news to me. And yet, why not? After all, it was a tame snake. Weren't there hospitals for dogs, horses and cows?

The Baba's disciple gave us another piece of news: red ants had got into the snake's hole while it lay ill, and had been pestering it. Baba had exterminated them all with a curse. Dhurjati Babu threw a sidelong glance at me at this point. I turned my eyes towards Baba. With his saffron robe, his long, matted hair, his iron earrings, rudraksha necklaces and copper amulets, there was nothing to distinguish him from a host of other holy men. And yet in the dim light of dusk, I couldn't take my eyes away from the man.

Seeing us standing, the disciple produced a pair of reed mats and spread them on the floor in front of the Baba. But what was the point of sitting down when there was no hope of seeing the pet snake? A delay would mean driving through the forest in the dark, and we knew there were wild animals about; we had seen herds of deer while coming. So we decided to leave. We bowed to the Baba who responded by nodding without taking the pipe away from his mouth. Then we set off for the jeep parked about 200 yards away on the road. Only a little while ago, the place had been alive with the calls of birds coming home to roost. Now all was quiet.

We had gone a few steps when Dhurjati Babu suddenly said, 'We could at least have asked to see the hole where the snake lives.'

I said, 'For that we don't have to ask the Baba; our driver Dindayal said he had seen the hole.'

'That's right.'

We fetched Dindayal from the car and he showed us the way. Instead of going towards the hut, we took a narrow path by an almond tree and arrived at a bush. The stone rubble which surrounded the bush suggested that there had been some sort of an edifice here in the past. Dindayal said the hole was right behind the bush. It was barely visible in the failing light, so Dhurjati Babu produced a small electric torch from his pocket. As the light from it hit the bush we saw the hole. But what about the snake? Was it likely to crawl out just to show its face to a couple of curious visitors? To be quite honest, while I was ready to watch it being fed by the Baba, I had no wish to see it come out of the hole now. But my companion seemed consumed with curiosity. When the beam from the torch had no effect, he started to pelt the bush with clods of dirt.

I felt this was taking things too far, and said, 'What's the matter? You seem determined to drag the snake out, and you didn't even believe in its existence at first.'

Dhurjati Babu now picked up a large clod and said, 'I still don't. If this one doesn't drag him out, I'll know that a cock-and-bull story about the Baba has been spread. The more such false notions are destroyed the better.'

The clod landed with a thud on the bush and destroyed a part of the thorny cluster. Dhurjati Babu had his torch trained on the hole. For a few seconds there was silence but for a lone cricket which had just started to chirp. Now there was another sound added to it; a dry, soft whistle of indeterminate pitch. Then there was a rustle of leaves and the light of the torch revealed something black and shiny slowly slipping out of the hole.

The leaves of the bush stirred, and the next moment, through a parting in them, emerged the head of a snake. The light showed its glinting eyes and its forked tongue flicking in and out of its mouth. Dindayal had been pleading with us to go back to the jeep for some time; he now said, 'Let it be, sir. You have seen it, now let us go back.'

The snake's eyes were fixed on us, perhaps because of the light shining on it. I have seen many snakes, but never a king cobra at such close quarters. And I have never heard of a king cobra making no attempt to attack intruders.

Suddenly the light of the torch trembled and was whisked away from the snake. What happened next was something I was not prepared for at all. Dhurjati Babu swiftly picked up a stone and hurled it with all his strength at the snake. Then he followed it in quick succession with two more such missiles. I was suddenly gripped by a horrible premonition and cried out, 'Why on earth did you have to do that, Dhurjati Babu?'

The man shouted in triumph, panting, 'That's the end of at least one vicious reptile!'

Dindayal was staring open-mouthed at the bush. I took the torch from Dhurjati Babu's hand and flashed it on the hole. I could see a part of the lifeless form of the snake. The leaves around were splattered with blood.

I had no idea that Imli Baba and his disciple had arrived to take their place right behind us. Dhurjati Babu was the first to turn round, and then I too turned and saw the Baba standing with a staff in his hand, a dozen feet behind us. He had his eyes fixed on Dhurjati Babu. It is beyond me to describe the look in them. I can only say that I have never seen such a mixture of surprise, anger and hatred in anyone's eyes.

Then Baba lifted his right arm towards Dhurjati Babu. The index finger shot out towards him. I noticed for the first time that Baba's fingernails were over an inch long. Who did he remind me of? Yes, of a figure in a painting by Ravi Varma which I had seen as a child in a framed reproduction in my uncle's house. It was the sage Durbasha cursing the hapless Sakuntala. He too had his arm raised like that, and the same look in his eyes.

But Imli Baba said nothing about a curse. All he said in Hindi in his deep voice was: 'One Balkishen is gone; another will come to take his place. Balkishen is deathless . . .'

Dhurjati Babu wiped his hands with his handkerchief, turned to me and said, 'Let's go.' Baba's disciple lifted the lifeless snake from the ground and went off, probably to arrange for its cremation. The length of the snake made me gasp; I had no idea king cobras could be that long. Imli Baba slowly made his way towards the hut. The three of us went back to the jeep.

On the way back, Dhurjati Babu was gloomy and silent. I asked him why he had to kill the snake when it was doing him no harm. I thought he would burst out once more and fulminate against snakes and Babas. Instead he put a question which seemed to have no bearing on the incident.

'Do you know who Khagam was?'

Khagam? The name seemed to ring a bell, but I couldn't remember where I had heard it. Dhurjati Babu muttered the name two or three times, then lapsed into silence.

It was half-past six when we reached the guest house. My mind went back again and again to Imli Baba glowering at Dhurjati Babu with his finger pointing at him. I didn't know why my companion had behaved in such a fashion. However, I felt that we had seen the end of the incident, so there was no point in worrying about it. Baba himself had said Balkishen was deathless. There must be other king cobras in the jungles of Bharatpur. I was sure another one would be caught soon by the disciples of the Baba.

Lachhman had prepared chicken curry, daal and chapatis for dinner. A whole day's sightseeing can leave one famished and I found I ate twice as much here as I ate at home. Dhurjati Babu, although a small man, was a hearty eater; but today he seemed to have no appetite. I asked him if he felt unwell. He made no reply. I now enquired of him, 'Do you feel remorse for having killed the snake?'

Dhurjati Babu was staring at the petromax. What he said was not an answer to my question. 'The snake was whistling,' he said in a soft, thin voice. 'The snake was whistling . . .'

I said, smiling, 'Whistling, or hissing?'

Dhurjati Babu didn't turn away from the light. 'Yes, hissing,' he said. 'Snakes speak when snakes hiss . . . yes,

Snakes speak when snakes hiss
I know this, I know this . . .'

Dhurjati Babu stopped and made some hissing noises himself. Then he broke into rhyme again, his head swaying in rhythm.

'Snakes speak when snakes hiss
I know this, I know this.
Snakes kill when snakes kiss
I know this, I know this . . .

What is this? Goat's milk?'

The question was directed at the pudding in the plate before him.

Lachhman missed the 'goat' bit and answered, 'Yes, sir—there is milk and there is egg.'

Dhurjati Babu was by nature whimsical, but his behaviour today seemed excessive. Perhaps he himself realized it, because he seemed to make an effort to control himself. 'Been out in the sun too long these last few days,' he said. 'Must go easy from tomorrow.'

The night was noticeably chillier than usual; so instead of sitting out on the terrace, I went into the bedroom and started to pack my suitcase. I was going to catch the train next evening. I would have to change in the middle of the night at Sawai-Madhopur and arrive in Jaipur at five in the morning.

At least that was my plan, but it came to nothing. I had to send a wire to my elder brother saying that I would be arriving a day later. Why this was necessary will be clear from what I'm about to say now. I shall try to describe everything as clearly and accurately as possible. I don't expect everyone to believe me, but the proof is still lying on the ground fifty yards away from the Baba's hut. I feel a cold shiver just thinking of it, so it is not surprising that I couldn't pick it up and bring it as proof of my story. Let me now set down what happened.

I had just finished packing my suitcase, turned down the wick of my lantern and got into my pyjamas when there was a knock on the door on the east side of the room. Dhurjati Babu's room was behind that door.

As soon as I opened the door the man said in a hoarse whisper: 'Do you have some Flit, or something to keep off mosquitoes?'

I asked: 'Where did you find mosquitoes? Aren't your windows covered with netting?'

'Yes, they are.'

'Well, then?'

'Even then something is biting me.'

'How do you know that?'

'There are marks on my skin.'

It was dark near the door, so I couldn't see his face clearly. I said, 'Come into my room. Let me see what kind of marks they are.'

Dhurjati Babu stepped into my room. I raised the lantern and could see the marks immediately. They were greyish, diamond-shaped blotches.

I had never seen anything like them before, and I didn't like what I saw. 'You seem to have caught some strange disease,' I said. 'It may be an allergy, of course. We must get hold of a doctor first thing tomorrow morning. Try and go to sleep and don't worry about the marks. I don't think they're caused by insects. Are they painful?'

'No.'

'Then don't worry. Go back to bed.'

He went off. I shut the door, climbed into bed and slipped under the blanket. I'm used to reading in bed before going to sleep, but this was not possible by lantern-light. Not that I needed to read. I knew the day's exertions would put me to sleep within ten minutes of putting my head on the pillow.

But that was not to be tonight. I was about to drop off when there was the sound of a car arriving, followed soon by English voices and the bark of a dog. Foreign tourists obviously. The dog stopped barking at a sharp rebuke. Soon there was quiet again except for the crickets. No, not just the crickets; my neighbour was still awake and walking about. And yet through the crack under the door I had seen the lantern either being put out, or removed to the bathroom. Why was the man pacing about in the dark?

For the first time I had a suspicion that he was more than just whimsical. I had known him for just two days. I knew nothing beyond what he had told me about himself. And yet, to be quite honest, I had not seen any signs of what could be called madness in him until only a few hours ago. The comments that he had made while touring the forts at Bayan and Deeg suggested that he was quite well up on history. Not only that: he also knew quite a bit about art, and spoke knowledgeably about the work of Hindu and Muslim architects in the palaces of Rajasthan. No—the man was obviously ill. We must look for a doctor tomorrow.

The luminous dial on my watch showed a quarter to eleven. There was another rap on the east-side door. This time I shouted from the bed.

'What is it, Dhurjati Babu?'

'S-s-s-s-'

'What?'

'S-s-s-s-'

I could see that he was having difficulty with his speech. A fine mess I had got myself into. I shouted again: 'Tell me clearly what the matter is.'

'S-s-s-s-'

I had to leave the bed. When I opened the door, the man came out with such an absurd question that it really annoyed me.

'Is s-s-s-snake spelt with one "s"?'

I made no effort to hide my annoyance.

'You knocked on the door at this time of the night just to ask me that?'

'Only one "s"', he repeated.

'Yes, sir. No English word begins with two s's.'

'I s-s-see. And curs-s-s-e?'

'That's one "s" too.'

'Thank you. S-s-s-sleep well.'

I felt pity for the poor man. I said, 'Let me give you a sleeping pill. Would you like one?'

'Oh no. I s-s-s-sleep s-s-s-soundly enough. But when the s-s-sun was s-s-s-setting this evening—'

I interrupted him. 'Are you having trouble with your tongue? Why are you stammering? Give me your torch for a minute.'

I followed Dhurjati Babu into his room. The torch was on the dressing table. I flashed it on his face and he put out his tongue.

There was no doubt that something was wrong with it. A thin red line had appeared down the middle.

'Don't you feel any pain?'

'No. No pain.'

I was at a loss to know what the matter was with him.

Now my eyes fell on the man's bed. It was apparent that he hadn't got into it at all. I was quite stern about it. I said, 'I want to see you turn in before I go back. And I urge you please not to knock on my door again. I know I won't have any sleep in the train tomorrow, so I want to have a good night's rest now.'

But the man showed no signs of going to bed. The lantern being kept in the bathroom, the bedroom was in semi-darkness. Outside there was a full moon. Moonlight flooded in through the north window and fell on the floor. I could see Dhurjati Babu in the soft reflected glow from it. He was standing in his nightclothes, making occasional efforts to whistle through parted lips. I had wrapped the blanket around me when I left my bed, but Dhurjati Babu had nothing warm on him. If he caught a chill then it would be difficult for me to leave him alone and go away. After all, we were both away from home; if one was in trouble, it wouldn't do for the other to leave him in the lurch and push off.

I told him again to go to bed. When I found he wouldn't, I realized I would have to use force. If he insisted on behaving like a child, I had no choice but to act the stern elder.

But the moment I touched his hand I sprang back as if from an electric shock.

Dhurjati Babu's body was as cold as ice. I couldn't imagine that a living person's body could be so cold.

It was perhaps my reaction which brought a smile to his lips. He now regarded me with his grey eyes wrinkled in amusement. I asked him in a hoarse voice: 'What is the matter with you?'

Dhurjati Babu kept looking at me for a whole minute. I noticed that he didn't blink once during the whole time. I also noticed that he kept sticking out his tongue again and again. Then he dropped his voice to a whisper and said, 'Baba is calling me—"Balkishen!" . . . I can hear him call.' His knees now buckled and he went down on the floor. Flattening himself on his chest, he started dragging himself back on his elbows until he disappeared into the darkness under the bed.

I was drenched in a cold sweat and shivering in every limb. It was difficult for me to keep standing. I was no longer worried about the man. All I felt was a mixture of horror and disbelief.

I came back to my room, shut the door and bolted it. Then I got back into bed and covered myself from head to toe with the blanket. In a while the shivering stopped and I could think a little more clearly. I tried to figure out where the matter stood, and the implication of what I had seen with my own eyes. Dhurjati Babu had killed Imli Baba's pet cobra by pelting it with stones. Immediately after that Imli Baba had pointed to Dhurjati Babu with his finger and said, 'One Balkishen is gone. Another will come to take his place.' The question was: was the second Balkishen a snake or a man?

Or a man turned into a snake?

What were those diamond-shaped blotches on Dhurjati Babu's skin?

What was the red mark on his tongue?

Did it mean that his tongue was about to be forked?

Why was he so cold to the touch?

Why did he crawl under the bed?

I suddenly recalled something in a flash. Dhurjati Babu had asked about Khagam. The name had sounded familiar, but I couldn't quite place it then. Now I remembered. It was a story I had read in the Mahabharata when I was a boy. Khagam was the name of a sage. His curse had turned his friend into a snake. Khagam—snake—curse—it all fitted. But the friend had turned into a harmless non-poisonous snake, while this man . . . Somebody was knocking on the door again. At the foot of the door this time. Once, twice, thrice . . . I didn't stir out of the bed. I was not going to open the door. Not again.

The knocking stopped. I held my breath and waited. There was a hissing sound now, moving away from the door.

Then there was silence, except for my pounding heartbeat.

What was that sound now? A squeak. No, something between a squeak and a screech. I knew there were rats in the bungalow. I had seen one in my bedroom the very first night. I had told Lachhman, and he had brought a rat-trap from the pantry to show me a rat in it. 'Not only rats, sir; there are moles too.'

The screeching had stopped. There was silence again. Minutes passed. I glanced at my watch. A quarter to one. Sleep had vanished. I could see the trees in the moonlight through my window. The moon was overhead now.

There was the sound of a door opening. It was the door of Dhurjati Babu's room which led to the veranda. The door was on the same side as my window. The line of trees was six or seven yards away from the edge of the veranda.

Dhurjati Babu was out on the veranda now. Where was he going? What was he up to? I stared fixedly at my window.

The hissing was growing louder. Now it was right outside my window. Thank God the window was covered with netting!

Something was climbing up the wall towards the window. A head appeared behind the netting. In the dim light of the lantern shone a pair of beady eyes staring fixedly at me.

They stayed staring for a minute; then there was the bark of a dog. The head turned towards the bark, and then dropped out of sight.

The dog was barking at the top of its voice. I heard its owner shouting at it. The barking turned into a moan, and then stopped. Once again there was silence. I kept my senses alert for another ten minutes or so. The lines of a verse I had heard earlier that night kept coming back to me—

Snakes speak when snakes hiss
I know this, I know this.
Snakes kill when snakes kiss
I know this, I know this . . .

Then the rhyme grew dim in my mind and I felt a drowsiness stealing over me.

I woke up to the sound of agitated English voices. My watch showed ten minutes to six. Something was happening. I got up quickly, dressed and came out on the veranda. A pet dog belonging to two English tourists had died during the night. The dog had slept in the bedroom with its owners who hadn't bothered to lock the door. It was surmised that a snake or something equally venomous had got into the room and bitten it.

Instead of wasting my time on the dog, I went to the door of Dhurjati Babu's room at the other end of the veranda. The door was ajar and the room empty. Lachhman gets up every morning at five to light the stove and put the tea-kettle on the boil. I asked him. He said he hadn't seen Dhurjati Babu.

All sorts of anxious thoughts ran in my head. I had to find Dhurjati Babu. He couldn't have gone far on foot. But a thorough search of the woods around proved abortive.

The jeep arrived at half-past ten. I couldn't leave Bharatpur without finding out what had happened to my companion. So I sent a cable to my brother from the post office, got my train ticket postponed by a day and came back to the rest house to learn that there was still no sign of Dhurjati Babu. The two Englishmen had in the meantime buried their dog and left.

I spent the whole afternoon exploring around the rest house. Following my instruction, the jeep arrived again in the afternoon. I was now working on a hunch and had a faint hope of success. I told the driver to drive straight to Imli Baba's hermitage.

I reached it about the same time as we did the day before. Baba was seated with the pipe in hand and the fire burning in front of him. There were two more disciples with him today.

Baba nodded briefly in answer to my greeting. The look in his eyes today held no hint of the blazing intensity that had appeared in them yesterday. I went straight to the point: did the Baba have any information on the gentleman who came with me yesterday? A gentle smile spread over Baba's face. He said, 'Indeed I have! Your friend has fulfilled my hope. He has brought back my Balkishen to me.'

I noticed for the first time the stone pot on Baba's right-hand side. The white liquid it contained was obviously milk. But I hadn't come all this way to see a snake and a bowl of milk. I had come in quest of Dhurjati Babu. He couldn't have simply vanished into thin air. If only I could see some sign of his existence!

I had noticed earlier that Imli Baba could read one's mind. He took a long pull at the pipe of ganja, passed it on to one of his disciples and said, 'I'm afraid you won't find your friend in the state you knew him, but he has left a memento behind. You will find that fifty steps to the south of Balkishen's home. Go carefully; there are thorny bushes around.'

I went to the hole where the king cobra lived. I was not the least concerned with whether another snake had taken the place of the first one. I took fifty steps south through grass, thorny shrubs and rubble, and reached a bel tree at the foot of which lay something the likes of which I had seen hanging from a line in the Baba's hut a few minutes ago.

It was a freshly sloughed-off skin marked all over with a pattern of diamonds.

But was it really a snakeskin? A snake was never that broad, and a snake didn't have arms and legs sticking out of its body.

It was actually the sloughed-off skin of a man. A man who had ceased to be a man. He was now lying coiled inside that hole. He was a king cobra with poison fangs.

There, I could hear him hissing. The sun had just gone down. The Baba was calling: 'Balkishen—Balkishen—Balkishen.'

Translated by Satyajit Ray
First published in Bengali in 1973

Barin Bhowmick's Ailment

Mr Barin Bhowmick got into compartment D as instructed by the conductor and placed his suitcase under his seat. He would not need to open it during his journey. But he must keep the other smaller bag somewhere within easy reach. It contained such essentials as a comb, a hair brush, a toothbrush, his shaving kit, a book by James Hadley Chase to read on the way and several other knick-knacks, including throat pills. If the long train journey in a cold, air-conditioned compartment resulted in a sore throat, he would not be able to sing tomorrow. He quickly popped a pill into his mouth and put his bag on the small table in front of the window.

It was a Delhi-bound vestibule train. There were only about seven minutes left before its departure, and yet there was no sign of the other passengers. Would he be able to travel all the way to Delhi alone? Could he be so lucky? That would indeed be the height of luxury. The very idea brought a song to his lips.

He looked out of the window at the crowd on the platform. Two young men were glancing at him occasionally. Clearly, he had been recognized. This was not a new experience. People often recognized him for they were now familiar not just with his voice but also with his appearance. He had to give live performances at least half-a-dozen times every month. Listen to Barin Bhowmick tonight—he will sing songs written by Nazrul as well as modern hits. Money and fame—both had come to Barin Bhowmick in full measure.

However, this had happened only over the last five years. Before that he had struggled a lot. It was not enough to be a talented singer. He needed a suitable break and proper backing. This came in 1963 when Bhola-da—Bhola Banerjee—invited him to sing in the puja pandal in Unish Palli. Barin Bhowmick had not looked back since then.

In fact, he was now going to Delhi at the invitation of the Bengal Association to sing at their jubilee celebrations. They were paying for his travel by first class and had promised to make all arrangements for his stay in Delhi. He intended spending a couple of days in Delhi. Then he would go to Agra and Fatehpur Sikri and return to Calcutta a week later. After that it would be time for the pujas again and life would become madly hectic.

'Your order for lunch, sir . . .?'

The conductor-guard appeared in the doorway.

'What is available?'

'You are a non-vegetarian, aren't you? You could choose between Indian and western food. If you want Indian, we've got . . .'

Barin Babu placed his order for lunch and had just lit a Three Castles cigarette when another passenger came into his compartment; at the same instant, the train began pulling out of the station.

Barin Babu looked at the newcomer. Didn't he seem vaguely familiar? Barin Babu tried to smile, but his smile vanished quickly as there was no response from the other. Had he made a mistake? Oh, God—how embarrassing! Why did he have to smile like an idiot? A similar thing had happened to him once before. He had thumped a man very hard on the back with a boisterous, 'Hel-lo, Tridib-da! How are you?' only to discover he was not Tridib-da at all. The memory of this incident had caused him much discomfort for days afterwards. God laid so many traps to embarrass one!

Barin Bhowmick looked at the other man once more. He had kicked off his sandals and was sitting with his legs outstretched, leafing through the pages of the latest *Illustrated Weekly*. Again, Barin Babu got the feeling that he had seen him somewhere, and not just for a few minutes. He had spent a long time in this man's company. But when was it? And where? The man had bushy eyebrows, a thin moustache, shiny hair and a little mole in the middle of his forehead. Yes, this face was certainly familiar. Could he have seen this man when he used to work for Central Telegraph? But surely the whole thing could not have been one-sided? His companion was definitely not showing any sign of recognition.

'Your order for lunch, sir?'

The conductor-guard had reappeared. He was a portly, rather amiable gentleman.

'Well,' said the newcomer, 'we'll worry about lunch later. Could I have a cup of tea first?'

'Of course.'

'All I need is a cup and the beverage. I prefer drinking black tea.'

That did it. Barin Bhowmick suddenly began to feel rather unwell. There was a sinking feeling at the pit of his stomach. Then it seemed as though his heart had grown wings and flown straight into his throat. It was not just the man's voice but also the words he uttered with a special emphasis: black tea. That was enough to remove the uncertainties from Barin Babu's mind. Every memory came flooding back.

Barin Babu had indeed seen this man before and that too—strangely enough—in a similar air-conditioned compartment of a train going to Delhi. He himself was going to Patna to attend the wedding of his cousin, Shipra. Three days before he left, he had won a little more than 7,000 rupees at the races. He could, therefore, afford the luxury of travelling first class. This happened nine years ago, in 1964, long before he had become a well-known singer. He could vaguely recall the other man's surname. It began with a 'C'. Chowdhury? Chakravarty? Chatterjee?

The conductor-guard left. Barin Babu realized he could no longer sit facing the other man. He went and stood in the corridor outside, well away from his fellow passenger. Yes, coincidences did occur in life. But this one was unbelievable.

But had 'C' recognized him? If he had not, there might be two reasons for it. Perhaps he had a weak memory. Or perhaps Barin Babu's appearance had undergone significant changes in these nine years. He stared out of the window and tried to recall what these changes might possibly be.

He had gained a lot of weight, so presumably his face now looked fuller than it did before. He did not wear glasses in those days. Now he did. And his moustaches had gone. When did he shave them off? Ah yes. Not very long ago. He had gone to a salon on Hazra Road. The barber was both young and inexperienced. He failed to get the symmetry right while trimming the moustaches. Barin Babu himself did not notice it at first but when everyone in his office from the chatty old liftman, Sukdeo, to the sixty-two-year-old cashier, Keshav Babu, began commenting on it, he shaved his precious moustaches off totally. This had happened about four years ago.

So he had lost his moustaches, but gained a bit of flesh on his cheeks and acquired a pair of glasses. Feeling a little reassured, he returned to his carriage.

A bearer came in with a pot of tea and placed it in front of 'C'. Barin Babu, too, felt the need for a drink, but did not dare speak to the bearer. What if 'C' recognized his voice?

Barin Babu did not even want to think about what 'C' might do to him if he did get recognized. But, of course, everything depended on the kind of man 'C' was. If he was anything like Animesh-da, Barin Babu had nothing to fear. Once, in a bus, Animesh-da realized someone was trying to pick his pocket. But he was too shy to raise a hue-and-cry, so he practically gave away his wallet to the pickpocket, together with four crisp ten-rupee notes. He told his family afterwards, 'A big scene in a crowded bus with me playing a prominent role in it—no, I could not allow that to happen.'

Was this man a bit like that? Probably not. People like Animesh-da were hard to come by. Besides, his looks were not very reassuring. Everything about him—those bushy eyebrows, the blunt nose and that chin that jutted out—seemed to suggest that he would not hesitate at all to plant his hairy hands on Barin Babu's throat and say, 'Are you not the same man who stole my clock in 1964? Scoundrel! I have spent these nine years looking for you! Today, I shall . . .'

Barin Babu dared not think any more. Even in this air-conditioned compartment there were beads of perspiration on his forehead. He stretched himself out on his berth and covered his eyes with his left arm. It was one's eyes that gave one away. In fact, 'C' had seemed familiar only because Barin Babu had recognized the look in his eyes.

He could now recall the incidents vividly. It was not just the matter of stealing 'C''s clock. He could remember every little thing he had stolen in his life since his boyhood. Some were totally insignificant things like a ballpoint pen (Mukul Mama's), or a cheap magnifying glass (his classmate Akshay's), or a pair of bone cuff links that belonged to Chhenida which he did not need at all. He never wore them even once. The only reason he stole these—and, for that matter, all those other things—was that they were near at hand and they belonged to someone else.

Between the ages of twelve and twenty-five, Barin Bhowmick had removed at least fifty different things from various people and made a collection in his house. What could one call it but stealing? The only difference between him and a regular thief was that a thief stole to survive in life; Barin Babu did it out of habit. Nobody ever suspected him. He had, therefore, never been caught. Barin Babu knew that this habit, this strange compulsion to steal things, was a kind of illness. Once he had even learnt the medical term for it from one of his friends who was a doctor, but now he could not remember what it was.

But 'C''s clock was the last thing he had stolen. In the last nine years, he had never experienced that sudden, strong urge. He knew he had got over his illness and was now totally cured.

The difference between stealing 'C''s clock and all the other petty thefts he had indulged in was that he had really wanted that clock. It was a beautiful travelling clock, made in Switzerland. It lay in a blue square box and stood upright the moment the lid was lifted. It was an alarm clock and the sound of the alarm was so sweet that it was a pleasure to wake up to it.

Barin Babu had used that clock consistently over these nine years. He took it with him wherever he went. Even today, the clock was resting within the depths of the bag kept on the table before the window.

'How far are you going?'

Barin Babu gave a violent start. The other man was actually speaking to him!

'Delhi.'

'Pardon?'

'Delhi.'

The first time, in an effort to disguise his voice, Barin Babu had spoken so softly that the man had clearly not heard him.

'Do you find it a bit too cold in here? Is that what's affecting your voice?'

'N-n-no.'

'It can happen, of course. Actually, I would have preferred going by ordinary first class if it wasn't for the dust.'

Barin Babu did not utter a word. He did not want to look at 'C', but his own curiosity forced him to cast frequent glances in 'C''s direction. Was 'C' showing signs of recognition? No. He appeared quite relaxed. Could he be pretending? There was no way of being sure. After all, Barin Babu did not know him well. All he had learnt the last time about his fellow passenger was that he liked having black tea and that he was wont to get down at every station to buy snacks. Thanks to this habit, Barin Babu had had the chance to eat a lot of tasty stuff.

Apart from this, Barin Babu had seen one other side to 'C''s character, just as they were about to reach Patna. This was directly related to the incident involving the clock.

They had been travelling by the Amritsar Mail. It was supposed to reach Patna at 5 a.m. The conductor came and woke Barin Babu at 4.30. 'C', too, was half awake, although he was going all the way to Delhi.

Just about three minutes before the train was to reach Patna, it suddenly screeched to a halt. What could be the reason? There were a few people with torches running about on the tracks. Was it anything serious? Eventually, the guard turned up and said that an old man had been run over by the train while crossing the track. The train would start as soon as his body was removed.

'C' got very excited at this news and clambered down quickly in the dark, still clad in his sleeping suit. Then he went out to see for himself what had happened.

It was during this brief absence that Barin Babu had removed the clock from 'C''s bag. He had seen 'C' wind it the night before, and had felt tempted immediately. But since the likelihood of finding a suitable opportunity was dim, he had told himself to forget the whole thing. However, when an opportunity presented itself so unexpectedly, Barin Babu simply could not stop himself. He had slipped his hand into 'C''s bag and had taken the clock out, then he had dropped it into his own case. It took him fifteen to twenty seconds to do this. 'C' had returned about five minutes later.

'A horrible business! A beggar, you see. The head's been totally severed from the body. I fail to see how an engine can possibly hit somebody despite a cow-catcher being there. Isn't it supposed to push aside all obstacles on the track?'

Barin Babu got off safely at Patna and was met by his uncle. The faint uneasiness at the pit of his stomach vanished the instant he got into his uncle's car and drove off. His heart told him that it was the end of the story. No one could catch him now. The chances of running into 'C' were one in a million, or perhaps even less than that.

But who knew that one day, years later, by such an incredible coincidence, they would meet again? 'A thing like this is enough to make one turn superstitious,' thought Barin Babu to himself.

'Do you live in Delhi? Or Calcutta?' asked 'C'.

He had asked him a lot of questions the last time as well, Barin Babu recalled. He hated people who tried to act friendly.

'Calcutta,' said Barin Babu. Oh no! He had spoken in his normal voice. He really must be more careful.

Good God—why was the man staring so hard at him? What could be the reason for such interest? Barin Babu's pulse began racing again.

'Did your photograph come out in the papers recently?'

Barin Babu realized it would be foolish not to tell the truth. There were other Bengali passengers on the train who might recognize him. There was no harm in telling this man who he was. In fact, if he could be informed that Barin Babu was a famous singer, he might find it difficult to relate him to the thief who had once stolen his clock.

'Where did you see this photograph?' Barin Babu threw a counter question.

'Do you sing?' came another one!

'Yes, a little.'

'Your name . . .?'

'Barindranath Bhowmick.'

'Ah, I see. Barin Bhowmick. That's why you seemed familiar. You sing on the radio, don't you?'

'Yes.'

'My wife is an admirer of yours. Are you going to Delhi to sing at some function?'

'Yes.'

Barin Babu was not going to tell him much. If a simple 'yes' or 'no' could suffice, there was no need to say anything more.

'I know a Bhowmick in Delhi. He's in the finance ministry. Nitish Bhowmick. Is he a relative or something?'

Indeed. Nitish was Barin Babu's first cousin. A man well known for his rigid discipline. A close relative, but not someone who was close to Barin Babu personally.

'No, I'm afraid I don't know him.'

Barin Babu decided to tell this one lie. He wished the man would stop talking. Why did he want to know so many things?

Oh good. Lunch had arrived. Hopefully, the volley of questions would cease, at least for a little while.

And so it did. 'C' obviously enjoyed eating. He began to concentrate on his food and fell silent. Barin Babu no longer felt all that nervous, but still he could not relax completely. They would have to spend at least another twenty hours in each other's company. Memory was such a strange phenomenon. Who could tell what little thing—a gesture, a look, a word—might make some old and forgotten memory come to life?

Black tea, for instance. Barin Babu believed that if those two words had not been uttered, he would never have recognized 'C'. What if something he said or something he did caused 'C' to recognize him?

The best thing, of course, would be not to say or do anything at all. Barin Babu lay down on his berth, hiding his face behind his paperback. When he finished the first chapter, he turned his head cautiously and stole a glance at 'C'. He seemed to be asleep. The *Illustrated Weekly* had dropped from his hand on to the floor. An arm was flung across his eyes, but from the way his chest rose and fell it seemed as though he had fallen into a deep sleep. Barin Babu looked out of the window. Open fields, trees, little huts—the barren landscape of Bihar flashed past. The noise of the wheels came very faintly through the double glass of the windows, sounding like distant drums being beaten in the same steady rhythm: *dha-dhinak, na-dhinak, dha-dhinak, na-dhinak* . . .

Another sound inside the compartment was soon added to this: the sound of 'C''s snoring.

Barin Babu felt a lot more reassured. He began humming a Nazrul song. His voice did not sound too bad. He cleared his throat once and began to sing a bit more loudly. But he had to stop almost immediately.

Something else was making a noise in the compartment. It shocked Barin Bhowmick into silence.

It was the sound of an alarm clock. The alarm on the Swiss clock kept in his bag had somehow been set off. And it continued to ring, non-stop.

Barin Babu discovered he could not move his limbs. They were paralysed with fear. His eyes fixed themselves on 'C'.

'C' moved his arm. Barin Babu stiffened.

'C' was now awake. He removed his arm from his eyes.

'Is it that glass? Could you please remove it? It's vibrating against the wall.'

The noise stopped the instant Barin Babu took the glass out of the iron ring attached to the wall. Before placing it on the table, he drank the water that was in it. This helped his throat, but he was still in no mood to start singing again.

Tea was served a little before they reached Hazaribagh Road. Two cups of hot tea and the absence of any further curious questions from 'C' helped Barin Babu relax more. He looked out once again and began humming softly. Soon, he was able to totally forget the danger he was in.

At Gaya, not unexpectedly, 'C' got down onto the platform and returned with two packets of peanuts. He gave one to Barin Babu. Barin Babu consumed the whole packet with considerable relish.

The sun had set by the time the train left the station. 'C' switched the lights on and said, 'Are we running late? What's the time on your watch?'

Barin Babu realized for the first time that 'C' was not wearing a watch. This surprised him and he could not help but show it. Then he remembered that 'C''s question had not been answered. He glanced at his wristwatch. 'It's 7.35,' he said.

'Then we're running more or less on time.'

'Yes.'

'My watch broke this morning. It was an HMT. . . gave excellent time . . . but this morning someone pulled my bedsheet so hard that the watch fell on the ground and . . .'

Barin Babu did not comment. Any mention of watches and clocks was reprehensible.

'What make is your watch?' asked 'C'.

'HMT.'

'Does it keep good time?'

'Yes.'

'Actually, I have always been unlucky in the matter of clocks.' Barin Babu tried to yawn, simply to assume an unconcerned air, but failed in his attempt. Even the muscles in his jaw appeared to be paralysed. He could not open his mouth. But his ears continued to function. He was forced to hear all that 'C' had to say.

'I had this Swiss travelling clock, you see. Made of gold. A friend of mine had brought it from Geneva. I had used it for barely a month when

I was travelling to Delhi by train—in an air-conditioned compartment like this one. The clock was with me. There were only two of us—another Bengali chap. Do you know what he did? Just think of his audacity! In my absence—while I may have gone to the bathroom or something—he nicked that clock from me! He looked such a complete gentleman. But I suppose I'm lucky he didn't murder me in my sleep. I stopped travelling by train after that. This time, too, I would have gone by air, but the pilots' strike upset my plans . . .'

Barin Bhowmick's throat was dry, his hands felt numb. But he knew if he said absolutely nothing after a tale like that, it would seem odd. In fact, it would seem distinctly suspicious. With a tremendous effort, he forced himself to speak.

'Did . . . did you not look for it?'

'Ha! Can any stolen object be found simply by looking for it? But, for a long time, I could not forget what the man looked like. Even now I have a vague recollection. He was neither fair nor dark, had a moustache and must have been about the same height as you, but slimmer. If I could meet him again, I would teach him a lesson he'd remember all his life. I was a boxer once, you know. A light heavyweight champion. That man is lucky our paths never crossed again . . .'

Barin Babu could now remember the full name of his companion. Chakravarty. Pulak Chakravarty. Strange! The minute he mentioned boxing, his name flashed in Barin Babu's mind like a title on a television screen. Pulak Chakravarty had talked a lot about boxing the last time.

But even if his name had come back to him, what good did that do? After all, it was Barin Babu who was the culprit. And now it had become impossible to carry his load of guilt. What if he went and confessed everything? And then returned the clock? There it was in that bag . . . so near at hand . . .!

No! Was he going mad? How could he entertain such thoughts? He was a famous vocalist. How could he admit to having stooped so low? Would his reputation not suffer? Would anyone ever invite him to sing at their function? What would his fans think? Where was the guarantee that this other man was not a journalist or someone connected with the media? No, there was no question of making a confession.

Perhaps there was no need for it, either. Perhaps he would be recognized, anyway. Pulak Chakravarty was giving him rather odd looks. Delhi was still sixteen hours away. There was every chance of being caught. In Barin Babu's mind flashed a sudden image—his moustaches had grown back, the flesh on his face had worn away, his glasses had vanished. Pulak Chakravarty was staring hard at the face he had seen nine years ago. The look of amazement in his slightly hazel eyes was slowly turning into a look filled with anger. His lips were parting in a slow, cruel smile. 'Ah ha!' he seemed to be saying, 'You are the same man, are you not? Good. I have waited all these years to lay my hands on you. Now I shall have my little revenge . . .'

By 10 p.m., Barin Babu had run up a fairly high temperature, accompanied by intense shivering. He called the guard and asked for an extra blanket. Then he covered himself from head to foot with both blankets and lay flat on his back. Pulak Chakravarty closed the door of their compartment and bolted it. Before switching off the lights, he turned towards Barin Babu and said, 'You appear unwell. I have some very effective pills with me—here, take these two. You're not used to travelling in an air-conditioned coach, are you?'

Barin Babu swallowed the tablets. Well, given his present condition, Pulak Chakravarty might spare him a ruthless punishment. But Barin Babu had made up his mind about one thing. He must transfer that clock to the suitcase of its rightful owner. He must try to get this done tonight, if possible. But he could not move until his temperature went down. His body was still shivering occasionally.

Pulak Chakravarty had switched on the reading lamp over his head. He had a paperback open in his hand. But was he reading it, or was he only staring at a page and thinking of something else? Why did he not turn the page? How long could it take to read a couple of pages?

Suddenly Barin Babu noticed Pulak's eyes were no longer fixed on the book. He had turned his head slightly and was looking at him. Barin Babu closed his eyes. After a long time, he opened one of them cautiously and glanced at Pulak Chakravarty. Yes, he was still staring hard at him. Barin Babu promptly shut his eye again. His heart was jumping like a frog, matching the rhythm of the wheels—*lub dup, lub dup, lub dup*.

A faint click told Barin Babu that the reading light had been switched off. Slightly reassured, he opened both his eyes this time. The light in the corridor outside was coming in through a crack in the door. Barin Babu saw Pulak Chakravarty put his book down on the table beside Barin Babu's bag. Then he pulled his blanket up to his chin, turned on his side, facing Barin Babu, and yawned noisily.

Barin Babu's heartbeats gradually returned to normal. Tomorrow—yes, tomorrow morning he must return the clock. He had noticed Pulak Chakravarty's suitcase was unlocked. He had gone and changed into a sleeping suit a little while ago.

Barin Babu had stopped shivering. Perhaps those tablets had started to work. What were they? He had swallowed them simply so that he would recover in time to be able to sing at that function in Delhi. Applause from an audience was something he had no wish to miss. But had he done a wise thing? What if those pills . . .?

No, he must not think about such things. The incident of the glass vibrating against the wall was bad enough. Obviously, all these strange ideas were simply a result of a sick and guilt-ridden mind. Tomorrow, he must find a remedy for this. Without a clear conscience, he could not have a clear voice and his performance would be a total failure. Bengal Association . . .

The tinkle of tea cups woke Barin Bhowmick in the morning. A waiter had come in with his breakfast: bread, butter, an omelette and tea. Should he be eating all this? Did he still have a slight fever? No, he did not. In fact, he felt just fine. What wonderful tablets those were! He began to feel quite grateful towards Pulak Chakravarty.

But where was he? In the bathroom, perhaps. Or was he in the corridor? Barin Babu went out to take a look as soon as the waiter had gone. There was no one in the corridor outside. How long ago had Pulak Chakravarty left? Should he take a chance?

Barin Babu took a chance, but did not quite succeed in his effort. He had taken the clock out of his own bag and had just bent down to pull out Pulak Chakravarty's suitcase from under his berth, when his fellow passenger walked in with a towel and a shaving kit in his hands. Barin Babu's right hand closed around the clock. He straightened himself.

'How are you? All right?'

'Yes, thank you. Er . . . can you recognize this?'

Barin Babu opened his palm. The clock lay on it. A strange determination had risen in his mind. He had got over the old compulsive urge to steal a long time ago. But this business of playing hide-and-seek, was this not a form of deception? All that tension, those uncertainties, the anxiety over should-I-do-it-or- shouldn't-I, this funny, empty feeling in his stomach, the parched throat, the jumping heart—all these were signs of a malady, were they not? This, too, had to be overcome. There could never be any peace of mind otherwise.

Pulak Chakravarty had only just started to rub his ears with his towel. The sight of the clock turned him into a statue. His hand holding the towel remained stuck to his ear.

Barin Babu said, 'Yes, I am that same man. I've put on a bit of weight, shaved my moustaches and have started wearing glasses. I was then going to Patna and you to Delhi. In 1964. Remember that man who got run over by our train? And you went out to investigate? Well, I took the clock in your absence.'

Pulak Chakravarty's eyes were now looking straight into Barin Babu's. Barin Babu saw him frowning deeply; the whites of his eyes had become rather prominent, his lips had parted as though he wanted to say something but could not find speech.

Barin Babu continued, 'Actually, it was an illness I used to suffer from. I mean, I am not really a thief. There is a medical term for it which escapes me at the moment. Anyway, I am cured now and am quite normal. I used your clock all these years and was taking it with me to Delhi. Since I happened to meet you—it's really a miracle, isn't it?—I thought I'd return it to you. I hope you will not hold any . . . er . . . against me.'

Pulak Chakravarty could do no more than say 'thanks' very faintly. He was still staring at the clock, now transferred to his own hand, totally dumbfounded.

Barin Babu collected his toothbrush, toothpaste, and shaving kit. Then he took the towel off its rack and went into the bathroom. He broke into a song as soon as he had closed the door, and was pleased to note that the old, natural melody in his voice was fully restored.

It took him about three minutes to get N.C. Bhowmick in the finance ministry in Delhi. Then, a deep, familiar voice boomed into his ear.

'Hello.'

'Nitish-da? This is Barin Babu.'

'Oh, so you've arrived, have you? I'm coming this evening to hear you sing. Even you have turned into a celebrity, haven't you? My, my, who would have thought it possible? But anyway, what made you call me?'

'Well—do you happen to know someone called Pulak Chakravarty? He is supposed to have been your batch-mate in college. He was a boxer.'

'Who? Old Pincho?'

'Pincho?'

'Yes, he used to pinch practically everything he saw. Fountain pens, books from the library, tennis racquets from our common room—it was he who stole my first Ronson. It was funny, because it wasn't as though he lacked anything in life. His father was a rich man. It was actually a kind of ailment.'

'Ailment?'

'Yes, haven't you ever heard of it? It's called kleptomania. K-l-e-p . . .'

Barin Babu put the receiver down and stared at his open suitcase. He had only just checked into his hotel and started to unpack. No, there was no mistake. A few items were certainly missing from it. A whole carton of Three Castles cigarettes, a pair of Japanese binoculars and a wallet containing five hundred-rupee notes.

Kleptomania. Barin Babu had forgotten the word. Now it would stay etched in his mind—forever.

Translated by Gopa Majumdar

First published in Bengali in 1973

The Admirer

Arup Babu—Arup Ratan Sarkar—was visiting Puri again after eleven years. He noticed a number of changes—a few new houses, new roads and some new hotels, both large and small. But as he stepped on to the beach, he realized that this was something that would always remain unchanged.

The sea was not visible from Hotel Sagarika where he was staying. But, at night, when all its occupants had gone to bed, it was quite easy to hear the lashing of the waves. Last night the sound of the sea had actually made Arup Babu leave his hotel and come down to the beach. He had arrived in Puri earlier that day, but had gone out to do some shopping. There had been no time during the day to visit the beach. Now he could see the frothy, white waves clearly even in the darkness of a moonless night. He recalled having read somewhere that the water in the sea contained phosphorus, which was why the waves were visible even at night. How lovely the mysterious, luminous waves looked! Nobody in Calcutta would say he was imaginative. Never mind. Arup Babu knew that, deep inside, he had sensitivities that made him different from the average man. He took special care to ensure that the tensions and strife of daily living did not kill those feelings. Occasionally he went to the riverside in Calcutta, or to Eden Gardens. The sight of a rippling river, greenery and flowers could still give him joy. The song of a bird filled his mind with wonder—was it a koel or a cuckoo?

Several minutes of gazing at the waves took away some of the weariness sixteen years of being in a job had bowed him down with.

This evening, Arup Babu had returned to the beach. After walking along the waves for a few minutes, he stopped. There was a saffron-clad figure walking in the distance at great speed. His followers were running after him, unable to keep pace with the holy man. Arup Babu watched this spectacle, an amused smile on his lips. Suddenly, he heard a childish voice behind him.

'Was it you who wrote *The Little Boy's Dream*?' asked the voice. Arup Babu turned around and found a boy of about seven, wearing a white shirt and blue shorts. His arms had a thick layer of sand up to the elbows. He was looking up at him, wide-eyed in wonder.

Before Arup Babu could say anything, the boy continued, 'I have read *The Little Boy's Dream*. Daddy gave it to me on my birthday. I . . . I . . .'

'Go on, say it. Don't be shy!'

This time it was the voice of a woman. It seemed to encourage the boy, who said quickly, 'I liked your book very much!'

Arup Babu glanced at the lady. A pleasant looking woman of about thirty, she was looking straight at him, smiling, and walking slowly in his direction.

Arup Babu addressed the boy, 'No, son. I haven't written any book. I think you've made a mistake.'

The lady was undoubtedly the boy's mother. There was a marked resemblance in their appearances, especially in the cleft on their chins.

Arup Babu's words did not take away the smile from her lips. In fact, it deepened as she came closer and said, 'We have heard of your reluctance to meet people. My brother-in-law had once written to you, asking you to preside over one of their functions. You had replied saying you were not in the least interested in that kind of thing. But you're not going to escape this time. We love your stories. Even we adults enjoy reading what you write for children.'

Arup Babu had no idea who had written *The Little Boy's Dream*, but it was evident that both the boy and his mother admired the writer equally. Who knew he would land in such a tricky situation? Obviously, these people would have to be told they had made a mistake, but he must not sound rude or say anything that might hurt their feelings.

Arup Babu's problem was that he was too soft. Once his dhobi, Gangacharan, had burnt a hole in one of his brand new kurtas. Anyone else would have given the dhobi a tight slap. But just one look at poor Ganga's apologetic face was enough to melt Arup Babu's heart. All he could bring himself to say was, 'Look, you really must be more careful in future.'

It was his kind heart that now made him say mildly, 'Well, how can you be so sure that it was I who wrote *The Little Boy's Dream*?'

The lady raised her eyebrows in surprise and said, 'Didn't your photo come out in the newspaper only recently? We heard on the radio one evening that you had won the academy award for your contribution to children's fiction, and the very next day we saw your photograph. So now a lot of other people know the name of Amalesh Moulik. It's not just us.'

Amalesh Moulik! He had heard the name, but Arup Babu had not seen the photo. Did he look exactly like the man? But, of course, photographs printed in newspapers were usually hazy and unclear.

'The news of your arrival in Puri has spread already,' the lady continued.' We went to Hotel Sea View the other day. One of my husband's friends was staying there until yesterday. The manager of the hotel told him that you'd be coming on Thursday. Today's Thursday, isn't it? Are you staying at the Sea View?'

'Uh . . . well, no. I had . . . er . . . heard that the food there was not very good.'

'Yes, that's quite true. In fact, we were wondering why you had chosen that particular hotel. There are so many better ones. Where did you finally decide to go?'

'I am . . . staying at the Sagarika.'

'I see. That's a new hotel, isn't it? Is it good?'

'Just about OK, I'd say. After all, one hasn't come here to stay for a long time.'

'How long *will* you be staying here?'

'About five days.'

'Then you must come and visit us. We are at the Puri Hotel. You have no idea how many people are waiting to meet you, especially among the children. Look out—your feet are getting wet!'

Arup Babu had not noticed the large wave rushing towards his feet. But, it was not just his feet that were wet; his whole body, he discovered, had started to perspire, despite the strong wind. How did he manage to miss the chance to make a protest, to tell this lady she had indeed made a mistake? It was too late now. But he must remove himself from here and find a quiet corner to consider the possible consequences of his inaction.

'May I . . . now take my leave . . .?'

'You must be writing something new.'

'N-n-no. I am now . . . taking a break.'

'Well, see you soon. I'll tell my husband about you. Will you be coming this way tomorrow?'

Arup Babu beat a quick retreat.

The manager of Sea View, Vivek Roy, had just finished stuffing a large paan into his mouth when Arup Babu arrived at the reception.

'Is Amalesh Moulik expected here?'

'Um.'

'When . . . do you think . . .?'

'Tuezhday. Wai?'

Today was Thursday. Arup Babu was in town until the following Tuesday. If Mr Moulik had sent a telegram, it could only mean that he had had to postpone his arrival at the last minute. The manager confirmed that he was originally scheduled to arrive the same morning.

In reply to Vivek Roy's 'Wai?' Arup Babu said that he had some business with Mr Moulik but would come back on Tuesday. From the Sea View he went straight to the market and found a book shop. Here he managed to find four books by Amalesh Moulik, although *The Little Boy's Dream* was not available. Two were novels and the other two collections of short stories.

By the time he returned to his own hotel, it was about 6.30 p.m. There was a hall at the entrance of the hotel. The manager sat on the left and on the right was a bench and a couple of chairs. On these were sitting two gentlemen; the bench was occupied by two boys and a girl, none more than ten years old. Upon Arup Babu's arrival, the two men smiled and rose to their feet with their hands folded in a namaskar. They nodded at the children, who came forward shyly and touched Arup Babu's feet before he could stop them.

'We are coming from the Puri Hotel,' said one of the men. 'I am Suhrid Sen and this is Mr Ganguly. Mrs Ghosh told us she had met you and this was where you were staying, so . . .'

Thank goodness the man at the book shop had wrapped the books in brown paper. Otherwise God knows what these people might have thought if they found out that an author was buying his own books!

Arup Babu nodded at everything his visitors said, although he knew it was not too late to correct the mistake they were obviously making. All he needed to say was, 'Look, something rather strange is happening. I have not seen Amalesh Moulik's photograph, but I assume he looks a bit like me. Perhaps he, too, has thin moustaches and curly hair and wears glasses just like me. It is also true that he is supposed to be visiting Puri. But, please, for God's sake, I am not that man. I do not write stories for children. In fact, I do not write at all. I work in an insurance company. I have come here simply to have a quiet holiday. Could you please leave me alone? The real Amalesh Moulik is going to arrive here next Tuesday. You can go and check at the Sea View, if you like.'

But would such a speech really help? These people were totally convinced he was Amalesh Moulik and since his initial protests had not worked, how could a telegram lying in the room of the manager of Sea View help? They would assume it was a trick to avoid people. They might even think he was staying at Sagarika under a false name and had sent the telegram to Sea View just to fool everyone.

Besides, there were all these children. One look at them made Arup Babu stop before uttering more protests. All three were staring at him in open admiration. One word of denial would wipe out all their enthusiasm.

'Babun, you can now ask Amalesh Babu what you wanted to know,' said Suhrid Sen, nodding at the older boy.

There was now absolutely no way of backing out. The boy called Babun was looking up at him, his head to one side, his fingers interlinked, ready to ask his question.

'That old man who put the little boy to sleep . . . did he know magic?'

At this crucial moment, Arup Babu discovered that his brain had started to function better than before. He stooped a little and whispered into Babun's ear, 'Well, what do *you* think?'

'I think he did.'

The other two children said simultaneously, 'Yes, yes, he did know magic. We all think he did!'

'Exactly,' Arup Babu straightened up. 'Whatever you think is correct. I wrote what I had to write. Now you must figure out what it means. And what *you* think it means is right. Nothing else matters.'

All the three children seemed very pleased at this answer. Before they left, Suhrid Sen invited him to dinner. There were eight Bengali families staying at Puri Hotel. The group included quite a few children who were regular fans of Amalesh Moulik. Arup Babu did not object for he had realized that he would simply have to play the role of Amalesh Moulik, at least temporarily. There was no point now in worrying about the possible consequences. But there was one thing Arup Babu felt he had to insist upon.

'Look,' he said to Mr Sen, 'I am really not fond of a lot of fuss. I am not used to mixing with people at all. So please may I request you not to spread the news that I am staying here?'

Suhrid Sen promised him that after dinner the following evening, none of them would disturb the peace and quiet Arup Babu was hoping to enjoy. Mr Sen also offered to warn the others to leave him alone as far as possible.

Arup Babu had an early dinner and retired to bed with one of Moulik's books called *Habu's Tricks*. The other three were *Tutul's Adventure*, *Checkmate* and *Sparklers*. The last two were collections of short stories.

It was true that Arup Babu was no authority on literature. However, he had read, in his school days, a number of children's stories written by both Indian and foreign writers. Thirty-nine years later, he realized to his surprise that he still remembered most of what he had read so many years ago. Not only that, he could even find similarities in ideas and plots between Amalesh Moulik's stories and those that he had read as a schoolboy.

All four books, published in large print, amounted to about 125 pages. When Arup Babu put the last one down and switched his light off, the hotel had fallen totally silent. The sea was rumbling in the distance. What time was it? Arup Babu's watch was lying by his pillow. He picked it up. It had once belonged to his father and had a radium dial. It gleamed in the darkness like the foam of the sea. The time was a quarter to one in the morning.

Amalesh Moulik was a well-known author, a popular writer of children's fiction. One had to admit that his language was very lucid and his style unusual. It was difficult to put his books down. But even so, there was not much originality of thought. One heard so many different tales from one's friends; people had such varied experiences. Strange and interesting things could happen even to oneself. Surely all one needed to do was to draw on those experiences and mix them with a bit of imagination? Where was the need to borrow ideas from other authors?

Arup Babu lost a little of his respect for Moulik. At the same time, he felt more relaxed. He was now going to find it easier to pretend to be the famous author.

The admiration of the fans of Amalesh Moulik was considerably enhanced after the dinner at Puri Hotel. Arup Babu had, in the meantime, managed to find a copy of *The Little Boy's Dream* from another shop. It was, therefore, not difficult to answer the thousand questions thirteen small children showered upon him.

By the time the party ended, the children had started calling him 'Honeylick Babu', since he told them that the word *mou* in Bengali meant 'honey' and everyone knew what 'lick' meant in English.

When he heard this, Dr Dasgupta, a guest at the party, remarked, 'You created all the honey and all these children are licking it.' At this, Surangama Devi, his wife, said, 'It's not just the children. Don't forget the adults!'

Two things happened after dinner. The first was that the children asked him to tell them a story. Arup Babu said in reply that he could not make up a story on the spot, but would relate an incident that had occurred in his childhood.

Arup Babu's family used to live in Banchharam Akrur Datta Lane in those days. When he was about five, an expensive clock in his house was found missing. His father called a local pandit, who claimed to have special magical powers. 'I shall find the thief in no time!' he said.

He then brought out a large pair of scissors and, holding them like a pair of tongs, picked up a small cane basket. After chanting a few mantras and throwing handfuls of rice over the basket, he declared the thief was none other than the new servant, Natabar. Arup Babu's uncle caught Natabar by his hair and was about to hit him very hard when the clock slipped out from under a bedsheet.

Everyone clapped when his story ended. Arup Babu rose to take his leave, but was stopped by a chorus of childish voices saying, 'No, no, please wait. Don't go!'

About half a dozen children rushed out of the room and returned with seven books by Amalesh Moulik that they had just bought. 'Please sign these books for us!' they said.

Arup Babu said, 'Well, I don't put my signature on books—ever. Tell you what, I'll take these away and draw a picture in each. Come to my hotel at 4.30 in the evening the day after tomorrow and take your books back.'

The children clapped again.

'Yes, yes, a picture is better than a signature!'

Arup Babu had once won a prize for drawing in school. He had not drawn since then, but surely it would not be impossible to draw some little things in these books if he tried?

The next day was Saturday. Arup Babu left in the morning with the books and his ball point pen. Near the colony of the Nulias, he discovered that there were plenty of things he could sketch. It took him just about an hour to finish his task. In the first book he drew a crab; in the second, three sea shells lying side by side on the sand; and then a couple of crows, a fishing boat, a Nulia's hut, a Nulia child and, finally, a Nulia wearing a hat with a pointed peak, making a fishing net.

Seven little children turned up at his hotel exactly at 4.30 p.m. on Sunday and went away jumping with joy and excitement at the drawings.

That night, when he had retired to his room after dinner, Arup Babu discovered that the feeling of pleasure had given way in his mind to one of anxiety. It was true that not once had he actually said to anyone, 'I am Amalesh Moulik'. But he knew whatever he had done over the last three days could not be seen as anything other than large-scale fraud. The day after tomorrow, on Tuesday, the real Amalesh Moulik was going to arrive. The affection and admiration Arup Babu had received from all those children and their parents was actually meant for this other man. It did not matter whether Mr Moulik wrote well or not. He was obviously a hero to all these people. What on earth would happen when he turned up in person and the manager of Sea View went about telling everyone of his arrival? The thought made Arup Babu feel decidedly uncomfortable.

Should he then try to leave a day earlier? Or else, what was he going to do all day on Tuesday? Where would he hide? Would people not thrash him black and blue when they learnt the truth? What about Mr Moulik himself? He, too, might raise his hand. After all, who could say for sure that all writers were peace-loving and non-violent? And the police? What if the police came to know? Could one be jailed for the kind of thing he had done? Possibly. There was no doubt that what he had done was wrong indeed.

Arup Babu got up and swallowed a sleeping pill for fear of having to spend a sleepless night.

In the end, however, he decided to leave by the night train on Tuesday. The temptation to take a look at the real Amalesh Moulik was too great. He had managed to get a copy of the newspaper that had carried his photograph. Amalesh Moulik did indeed have thin moustaches, curly hair and glasses set in thick frames. But it was necessary to look at the real person to see how far the resemblance went. The picture in the paper was not clear enough.

Arup Babu decided to go to the station not only to look at the man but also to exchange a few words, if possible. It should seem natural enough if he said something like, 'You're Amalesh Moulik, aren't you? Saw your photograph the other day. I enjoy reading your stories . . .' or words to that effect.

He would then leave his luggage at the station and leave for Konark, which he had not yet seen. He could spend the day at the Sun temple in Konark and return in time to catch his train back to Calcutta. There was no better way of hiding.

The Puri Express reached the station twenty minutes late on Tuesday. Arup Babu stood behind a pillar, keeping an eye on the passengers getting down from the first class coaches. A foreigner, clad in shorts, was the first to alight. He was followed by a large Marwari. From the other door an old woman emerged, helped by a young man in white trousers. Behind him came an old man, and after that—yes, there could be no mistake, this was Mr Amalesh Moulik. There were certainly a few basic resemblances in their appearances, but if Arup Babu went and stood beside him, there was positively no danger of being mistaken for his twin. Mr Moulik was shorter by about a couple of inches and his complexion was darker. He even appeared to be older for his side-burns had distinct touches of grey, which was something Arup Babu had not yet acquired.

The man lugged his suitcase off the train and yelled to a coolie. The coolie and Arup Babu went forward together.

'Mr Moulik, I presume?'

The man looked surprised. Then he turned towards Arup Babu and nodded. 'Yes,' he said briefly.

The coolie had picked up the suitcase and placed it on his head. Arup

Babu had a bag and a flask slung from his shoulder. The three began walking towards the main exit.

'I have read your books,' said Arup Babu. 'I saw the news of your winning the academy award and also saw your photograph.'

'Hm.'

'You're booked at the Sea View, aren't you?'

This time Amalesh Moulik looked at Arup Babu rather suspiciously. It was not difficult to guess what he was thinking.

'The manager of Sea View is an admirer of yours, you see,' explained Arup Babu. 'It is he who has spread the news.'

'Ah.'

'A lot of children here are looking forward to your visit.'

'Hm.'

Why did the man say so little? He had now slackened his pace. What could he be thinking of?

Amalesh Moulik came to a halt. Then he turned towards Arup Babu again and asked, 'Have a lot of people learnt about my coming?'

'Yes, so I gathered. Why, will that put you to some inconvenience?'

'No, but I like to be al-al-al—'

'Alone?'

'Yes.'

The man clearly had a stammer. Arup Babu recalled that when Edward VIII of England had decided to step down from the throne, his brother, George, had got quite worried at the thought of becoming king since he had a stammer and being a king inevitably meant having to give speeches.

The coolie was waiting near the exit. Both men hurried their steps.

'This is the p-p-p-rice of f-f-f-ame!'

Arup Babu tried to imagine the reaction of all those children if they met their stammering hero. He did not like what he saw. 'You could do one thing,' he said to Amalesh as they came out of the station.

'What?'

'I don't like the idea of your holiday being spoilt by your fans.'

'Neither do I.'

'Then don't go to Sea View.'

'Wh-wh-at?'

'The food there is awful. I was in Sagarika. My room is now vacant. I suggest you go there.'

'Oh.'

'And don't use your real name. It really would be best if you could shave off your moustaches totally.'

'Mous-s-s—?'

'Immediately. You can go into the waiting room and do it. A matter of no more than ten minutes, I should say. If you do this, no one will recognize you and disturb the peaceful holiday you have no doubt planned for yourself. I can send a telegram from Calcutta tomorrow morning to Sea View and tell them you had to cancel your visit.'

The worried lines on Mr Moulik's forehead took about twenty seconds to disappear. Then a few new creases appeared near his eyes and mouth.

Amalesh Moulik was smiling.

'I d-d-d-on't know how to th-th-th-ank . . .'

'Never mind. But please will you sign these books for me? Let's stand behind that neem tree. No one can spot us there.'

Hidden by the tree, Amalesh Moulik took out his red Parker pen from his pocket and smiled benignly at his admirer. He had put in a lot of effort, right from the day the award was announced, in perfecting his signature. Five signatures on five books. He knew very well that even if his tongue stuttered, his pen could fly smoothly.

Translated by Gopa Majumdar
First published in Bengali in 1974

Fotikchand

1

He was not sure when his eyes had opened. Before he could actually see anything, he could feel that he was cold—he was wet—he was lying on the grass, and there was something hard under his head. Then he felt pain all over his body. Even so, he raised his right arm gingerly and felt under his head. His hand touched a stone, it felt cold. It was a large stone, he could not possibly lift it and move it away. Perhaps moving his head was a better idea. So he moved his head a little, and then lay more comfortably on his back.

Now he was able to see. Until now, it had not been possible to see anything because it was dark, and he was lying under the sky, and the sky was cloudy. Now the clouds were dispersing, revealing bright stars.

He tried to grasp what had happened. It would not be very wise to get on his feet, he realized. It was more important to figure out why he was lying on the grass, why he was in pain, and why his head was throbbing.

What was that noise? It just went on and on, steady and monotonous. He thought for a while, then realized what it was. It was the sound of crickets. Could it be described as a call? No, crickets did not call. They were not birds, but insects. He knew that. Who had told him? That he could not remember.

He tilted his neck. That made his head throb even more painfully. Never mind. He would try not to move, but see as much as possible. He must find out how he came to be here.

What was that? Had the stars in the sky suddenly come down to earth? No. He knew what those were. They were fireflies. They shone in the dark, on and off, and flew in circles. The light that came from them was cool. If you held a firefly in your hand, you wouldn't feel any warmth. Where had he heard that? He had no idea.

But if there were fireflies, there must be trees in the vicinity. Fireflies always fluttered near trees, or bushes. There they were, coming quite close at times, then flying away. He could see some more in the distance. There had to be a lot of trees. What was a large cluster of trees called? It had a name, surely? He knew it, but could not remember the word.

He turned his head in a different direction. Again, he felt a sharp pain. There were several trees on the opposite side as well, fireflies glowing amidst them. The tops of those trees seemed to have merged with the dark sky. The stars were standing still but the fireflies were moving constantly, glittering points of light.

The trees on the other side seemed quite far—a road ran between them. What was that on the road? He had not noticed it before, but now more things were gradually becoming visible.

It was a car, standing in the middle of the road. No. It was not standing, but lying on its side. Whose car was it? Had he been in it? Was he going somewhere? Where was he going? He did not know. Simply could not remember.

For some inexplicable reason the sight of the car made him feel afraid. There was nobody except him, nothing around here except that car and that, too, was lying on the ground with its back to him.

He knew that moving would cause him pain but he got to his feet, nevertheless. He fell down instantly. A few moments later, he made himself get up again. This time, he could walk. He moved slowly towards the trees on the other side of the car.

It was a forest. Yes, that was the word he was looking for. It was still dark, but now he could see well enough to be sure that he was in a forest. So it was possible to see in the light of the stars. Had there been a moon, it would have been easier to see things. And in daylight everything would be clearly visible.

He passed a few trees, then stopped as he reached the next one. There weren't just trees in front of him. There was something else, at some distance. He hid behind a tree, and peered cautiously.

It was a herd of animals. They were walking together, making a rustling noise. They had horns on their heads . . . there went one . . . and another . . . and a third one. They were deer. He knew it. He could remember that word. One of them stopped suddenly, stretching its neck. The others stopped as well. They seemed to be listening intently. A second later, he heard it too. It was a car in the distance—the noise was getting closer.

The deer ran away. They sprang in the air, and were gone in a second. All of them.

The car came closer. Now he could see several other things. The sky was not as dark as before. Treetops were now visible against the skyline. The stars had started to fade. He turned back. Perhaps now he'd be able to see the approaching car. He began walking back towards the road, but discovered that his legs were hurting so much that he could not walk comfortably. He had to limp.

The vehicle came and went. It was not a car, but a truck. It was green, and loaded with goods. It slowed down as it approached the overturned car, but did not stop.

He limped back to the road, and could now see the overturned car. The front was badly damaged. Bits of it looked smashed in. Other parts were totally flattened. The bonnet was half open and tilted at an angle. One of the front doors was open. He could see the head of a man. The man was lying on his back, his head was poking out of the open door. The ground under his head was wet.

There was another man in the back seat. Only his knee was visible through the window. His trousers were black. The car was light blue. There was broken glass—thousands of shards—strewn over a large area around the car. Each tiny piece of glass was reflecting the blue sky above. It was now quite bright.

The crickets had stopped. A bird called somewhere . . . once, twice, thrice . . . it sounded like a shrill whistle.

He looked at the car again, and felt afraid. The broken glass and the red, damp patch on the road also frightened him. Was there red splashed anywhere else? Yes, on his shirt, his arms, and his socks. He should not remain standing here. That road . . . he could see it stretch ahead, winding and curving around bends. In the distance, the trees thinned out. Perhaps that was where the forest ended.

He started walking in that direction. He could make it. It was clear to him that he was not badly hurt. Those other two men were. Or perhaps they were dead. If his head stopped aching, and the cut on his elbow healed, and if he stopped limping, he could quite easily claim to be in perfect health—if anyone were to ask, that is.

What was most puzzling was why he could not remember anything. What had happened before he opened his eyes and saw those stars in the sky? He could not even remember his name. All he knew was that there was a badly damaged car lying on the road with two men in it who were not moving at all. He was walking down a road, there were grassy patches here and there, and the sky was blue. Now it had started to turn red, which meant that the sun was rising, and so it was morning. All this he knew, but nothing else.

He kept walking. The birds were chirping continuously. He could recognize some of the trees. That one was a banyan, and that one was a mango tree, and here was a silk-cotton, and . . . what was that? Guava? Yes, he could see guavas hanging from the branches.

One look at those guavas made him realize he was hungry. He went closer to the tree. Thank goodness he had found it. There was fruit on the mango trees, too. But they were on the higher branches which he could not have climbed with an injured leg. The guavas were well within his reach. He quickly ate two and resumed walking.

The road finally came to an end. It merged into a bigger road, which went in two different directions. Where should he go? He turned right without thinking too much about it. Only a few steps later, he suddenly felt so tired that he had to sit down under a tree. He could not tell what the tree was called, but noticed that its trunk had black and white stripes on it. In fact, all the trees he could see on this side of the road had similar stripes. How had they got there? Who had painted them black and white? He did not know. He could not think.

His head was throbbing once more. He could feel his lips tremble. Then he took a deep breath, and his eyes filled with tears. In the next instant, the road, the trees, the black, the white, the yellow, the green . . .

everything was gone, wiped clean before his eyes as he sank into a dark abyss.

2

There was something moving in front of his eyes. It was the head of a man. There was a turban on his head, and the man had a beard. But no. It wasn't the head that was moving. He was moving himself. The bearded man was shaking him gently.

'*Doodh pee lo, beta, garam doodh*,' the man was saying. In his hand was a glass of milk. Little coils of steam were rising from it.

Now he could see and hear everything clearly. He was lying in the back of a loaded truck. He was lying on one side, on a sheet. Another sheet was draped over him, and under his head, acting as a pillow, was a small bundle of clothes.

He took the glass from the man and sat up. The truck was parked along a road. There was a tea shop on the opposite side. Outside it, a few people were seated on a bench, drinking tea. There were some more shops, one of which was possibly for car repair. Clanking noises came from it. A man was standing next to a black car parked outside this shop. He was wiping his glasses.

The man with the turban had disappeared into the tea shop. Now he reappeared and returned to the truck. With him came all the other men who were sitting on the bench.

'What's your name?' the man asked in Hindi.

'I don't know.' The glass of milk, which he was still holding in his hand, was now half-empty. The milk tasted very good.

'You don't know? What do you mean?'

He remained silent. The man with the turban went on, 'Where are you from? How did you get hurt? Was there anyone else with you? Where did they go?'

'I don't know. I can't remember.'

'What's the matter? Who's this boy?' asked a different voice. The man who was standing by the black car had come forward to enquire. He was not all that old, but his hair was decidedly thin. He was staring hard at the boy, screwing his eyes in concentration. The man with the turban explained quickly. It was all quite simple, really. The man was a truck driver. He had found the boy lying unconscious by the roadside. So he had picked him up, thinking that when he came to, the boy would be able to give his name and address. If he had turned out to be from Calcutta, the truck driver would have taken him to his house.

The other gentleman—a Bengali, as it happened—came closer. 'What is your name?' he asked.

This, of course, was his biggest problem. Why couldn't he remember his name? Once again, he was forced to say, 'I don't know.' The truck driver burst out laughing.

'That's all he's been saying!'

'You don't know your own name? Or do you mean you cannot remember?' the second man asked again.

'I cannot remember.'

Now the gentleman noticed his injured elbow. 'Where else does it hurt?'

The boy pointed at his bruised knees. 'And your head? Did you hurt your head as well?'

'Yes.'

'Let me have a look. Can you bend your head?'

He bent his head obediently. The gentleman examined the part that was swollen. As he touched it briefly, the boy flinched. 'I think there's a cut . . . there's dried blood in your hair. Do you think you could climb down? Let's see. Come on. gently.'

He passed the glass to the truck driver and slid forward. Then he stretched an arm. The second man caught it, and helped him down carefully, making sure it did not hurt him. Then he had a brief chat with the truck driver. Kharagpur was only thirty miles away. The Bengali gentleman would take him there and get him examined by a doctor. Then, once his wounds had been cleaned and dressed, he could be taken to Calcutta.

'Take him straight to a *thana*,' said the truck driver. 'I think there's something wrong somewhere.'

It took the boy a while to grasp the meaning of the word *thana*. Then he heard the word 'police' being mentioned. Suddenly, his heart started beating faster. The police? Didn't they catch thieves and punish them? Was he a thief? He had no idea. What might the police do to him?

The gentleman was going to drive the car himself. He helped him settle into the seat next to the driver. Then he started the car. In a few minutes, the shops and other buildings disappeared. On both sides of the road stretched open fields. Occasionally, he could catch the gentleman looking curiously at him out of the corner of his eye. It did not take him long to start asking questions again.

'Do you live in Calcutta?'

'I don't know.'

'Can't you remember anyone in your family? Your mother? Father? Brothers or sisters? Anyone at all?'

'No.'

Then, purely voluntarily, he offered the man some information. He told him what he did remember, about the previous night, about the broken car, and the two men in it.

'Did you see the number of that car?' he asked.

'No.'

'Can you remember what those men looked like?'

He described a few things he could recall. The gentleman frowned but did not ask him any more questions. His frown remained fixed throughout their journey.

A little later, the boy glanced at the watch the gentleman was wearing. It was now two o'clock. He began to toy with the idea of telling this man that he was hungry. A couple of guavas and a glass of milk were not enough to keep hunger at bay. As things turned out, he did not have to say anything. His companion stopped the car near a stone by the road, which said 'Kharagpur: 12 km'. Then he opened a white cardboard box and took out puris and vegetables from it. He handed some of it to the boy, then finished the rest.

When they had eaten, they set off again. The numbers that appeared on stones grew less and less. The city of Kharagpur became visible in the distance as soon as they passed a stone with the digit two on it. 'Have you ever visited Kharagpur?' asked the gentleman.

The name of the place meant nothing to him. How could he remember whether he had visited it or not? 'There is a big school here called the IIT,' his companion informed him. The word 'IIT' went round and round in his mind, until they reached the heart of town. The increased noise of the traffic wiped it out instantly.

There was a policeman standing at a crossing. Again, his heart began to tremble. 'I don't like the police!' he blurted out.

The gentleman kept his eyes fixed on the road. 'We will have to inform the police. Don't worry about it. It's obvious that you come from a good family. You may have forgotten who your parents are but I am sure they have not forgotten you. If we are to find out where you live, I'm afraid we have got to take help from the police. Only they can make enquiries. There's no reason to be afraid. The police do a lot of good work, too.'

They found a pharmacy. The doctor there bathed his grazed knees with a lotion. Then he cleaned the wound on his elbow, smeared some ointment on a piece of cottonwool, and placed it over the wound. To hold it in place, he put some adhesive plaster over it. Ice was applied to the injury on his head. When this was done, the Bengali gentleman asked the doctor, 'How far is the nearest police station from here?'

Before the doctor could make a reply, the boy said, 'I . . . I would like to use your bathroom.'

'All right. Come with me.' The doctor got to his feet and went out through a rear door. Behind it was a passage. He pointed at a door at the far end. 'That's the bathroom,' he said.

The boy found it, and quickly bolted the door. After using the lavatory, he saw to his relief that there was another door that opened to the street outside. He unbolted it and slipped out.

If he turned right, he realized, he would find himself on the main road. That meant he might be seen and caught. He turned left. Where should he go now? He had no idea, but at least he was not going to be handed over to the police. The thought gave him courage. There were some people in that lane. His bloodstained clothes, the dressing on his elbow, and the way he limped did attract a certain amount of attention. A few people cast curious glances at him, but no one said anything.

He continued to walk. Suddenly, he heard a train whistle.

The lane came to an end. Here was another big road, full of bustling crowds. No one had the time to look at him. On his left was a long iron railing, beyond which lay a number of railway tracks. A freight train was standing on one of these. The whistle he had heard before seemed closer and louder. Now he noticed a pole; a few small horizontal bars with red and green lights on them were fixed at the top. What was it called? It had a name, but he could not remember it.

There, he could now see the station. It was quite big. A train was standing at a platform. Lots of people were getting in and out of it. He limped into the station. The train was right in front of him. The engine whistled again. A voice whispered urgently in his head: 'You must get into that train. Come on. Here's your chance!'

All around him, there were people running, shouting, pulling, pushing. He was nearly knocked over by a large bundle slung across somebody's shoulder, but he managed to recover his balance. In the same instant, he realized that the train had started. The carriages were moving away. He went forward as quickly as he could. But all the doors were shut. How could he get in if he couldn't find an open door?

There, just one door appeared to be open. Could he climb in? No. He was not strong enough. But that voice had become more insistent. 'Go on,' it said, 'do it. You'll never get another chance.'

He stretched out an arm. The handle of the open door was only a few inches away. He would have to run with the train, then grab the handle and jump aboard. If he slipped, he would be . . . it would take only a second . . .

His feet were no longer on the ground. They had not slipped. Someone from the train had stretched out his arm and thrown it across his waist before hoisting him up in one swift motion. He was in the carriage, quite safe.

A voice spoke, sharply and irritably: 'What did you think you were doing? Is this your idea of having fun? Shall I kick your lame leg?'

3

He was sitting on his seat, panting. He was having to breathe so hard that, even if he wished to speak, he could not do so. All he could do was stare at the man who had spoken. Although he had spoken sharply, he did not appear to be all that cross. Or perhaps he had been cross to start with, but a closer look at the injured boy had made him soften. Now, the man's eyes were twinkling. He smiled, his bright white teeth glinting in the sun. It seemed as if the man's head was packed with clever ideas. He could spend a whole lifetime making them work.

There were other people in the carriage, but just the two of them on this seat. Three old men sat opposite them. One of them was fast asleep. The second one took a pinch of some dark powder, held it close to his nostrils and inhaled deeply. The third man was reading a newspaper. As the train rocked and swayed with increasing speed, he had to clutch his paper more firmly and bring it closer to his eyes.

'All right, what's your game?' The man still sounded serious, but the twinkle in his eyes had not gone. He was looking steadily at the boy, as if he could read his mind.

The boy remained silent. His only aim was to avoid the police. But he could not bring himself to say so. To his complete astonishment, the man asked, 'The police? Is it anything to do with them? Are you trying to smuggle rice?'

There was still no answer. The man went on, 'No, I don't think so. You are from a good family. You wouldn't have enough strength to carry a sack of rice.'

The boy stared back in silence. 'What do I have to do to make you talk?' asked the man. 'Look,' he added, moving a little closer and lowering his voice, 'you can tell me. I won't tell anyone else. Trust me. I ran away from home, too. Just like you.'

The boy knew what was going to follow: the now-familiar question regarding his name. So he opened his mouth and asked, 'What's your name?' before the man could say anything.

'Never mind about my name. What's yours?' the man shot back.

By this time, he was tired of saying 'I don't know'. Only a little while ago, opposite the pharmacy in Kharagpur, he had seen a name on a signboard. Painted in black on a white board were the words: Mahamaya Stores. Below it was written 'Prop: Fotikchandra Pal'.

'Fotik,' he said quickly.

'Your name's Fotik? Is that your pet name, or real name?'

'Real name.'

'What's your title?'

'Title?'

'Surname. Can you understand what that means?'

He looked blank. Neither the word 'title' nor 'surname' meant anything to him.

'The word that comes at the end of a name. Like Tagore, after Rabindranath. Look, are you really stupid, or just pretending to be so? It won't take me long to find out, you know.'

Now he began to understand. He knew what 'surname' meant. The words 'at the end of a name' had done the trick. 'Pal,' he said quickly, 'my surname is Pal. That's at the end. In the middle is Chandra. Fotikchandra Pal.'

The man continued to stare for a while. Then he offered his right hand. 'Anyone who can make up a name at the drop of a hat is a gifted artist. Come on, shake hands with Harun, Fotikchandra Pal. Harun, then "al", and then Rashid. Harun-al-Rashid: Emperor of Baghdad, monarch among jugglers.'

He shook hands with the man, but felt a bit put out by his open disbelief. Why couldn't his name be Fotik? How did this man guess it was a false name?

'In the kind of family that you come from, no one would dream of using an old-fashioned name like Fotikchand,' the man declared, giving him a steady look. 'Let me look at your hands.'

Before he could say anything, the man grabbed one of his hands and examined his palm. 'Hm . . . I see. You've never had to travel by public buses, have you? Hanging from a rod like a bat? . . . Your shirt must have cost at least forty-five chips . . . expensive trousers . . . and you've recently had a haircut at a fashionable salon. In Park Street, was it?'

Clearly, he was expected to make a reply. What could he say? 'I cannot remember,' he said truthfully.

Suddenly, the man's eyes narrowed and started glinting strangely. 'Look here,' he said, 'don't try acting funny with the Emperor of Baghdad. Nothing will work here. You go to a good, expensive school, don't you? You meet a lot of other rich boys. So you fell into bad company, and decided to run away from your Dad when the going got tough. You think I can't figure that out for myself? How did you hurt your elbow? Why is your head swollen? Why are you limping? You'll have to tell me everything. Now. Or I'll throw you out on the platform at the next station. I swear. So come on, out with it.'

He began talking. Not because he was afraid of the man's threats, but because suddenly he felt he could trust him. Here was an ally. This man would understand, he would not harm him, nor hand him over to the police. So he told him whatever he could remember, from the moment he opened his eyes in the forest to the moment when he slipped out of the bathroom in the pharmacy.

The man heard him in silence; then he stared out of the window, looking thoughtful. Finally, he shook his head and turned back to him. 'Well, you'll need a place in Calcutta. You couldn't possibly stay where I live.'

'You live in Calcutta?'

'Yes. I've lived there before, and I'm going to live there again. I have a room, in a place called Entally. I travel from time to time, to fairs and festivals. Sometimes, I get called to perform at weddings. Right now, I am coming from Coimbatore. Do you know where it is? It's near Madras. I was there for three weeks—lived purely on idlis and dosas. I've spoken to a circus company. Venkatesh—a trapeze artiste in the Great Diamond Circus—is a friend of mine. He'll let me know as soon as there's a vacancy. But I have to go back to Calcutta for the time being. All indeed is a little patch of grass under Shaheed Minar.'

'On the grass? You'll live on the grass?' the boy sounded puzzled. He could remember lying on the grass for quite a long time.

'No, not live. Work. Perform. See that box under the bench? It's got all my stuff for juggling. I bought none of it. Everything came from my ustad.' The man touched his hand three times to his forehead as he uttered the word 'ustad'. Then he resumed speaking, 'Ustad performed until he was seventy-three years old. Even at that age, half his beard was black. He used to comb his long beard, and wear it parted in the middle. That day . . . I saw him sit on the ground just as he did for his namaz, and throw a top high into the air. Then he spread his palm to catch it as it fell. But, suddenly, he drew his hand back, and clutched at his chest. A second later, he crumpled into a heap, his face buried in the ground. The spinning top landed on his back, between his shoulder blades, and went on spinning. The audience thought it was a new trick, so everyone started clapping. But . . . my ustad never raised his face again.'

The man fell silent, and stared out of the window for a while, possibly thinking of his ustad. Then he said, 'I'll have to talk to Upen-da. Maybe he can do something for you. But let me warn you, the police will be on the lookout.'

The boy's face turned pale instantly. 'Handing you over to the police would really be the correct thing to do,' the man added.

'No, no!' the boy cried in dismay.

'Don't worry,' the man smiled. 'An artist does not always follow the rules. If I was a stickler for rules and routines, I would never have met you like this, in a third-class compartment. Had he stuck to the rules, Arun Mustafi would probably be returning from office at this very minute, driving his own Fiat, from BBD Bagh to Ballygunje.'

A name he had just heard aroused the boy's curiosity. 'Who is Upen-da?' he asked.

'His full name is Upen Gui. He runs a tea shop in Bentinck Street.'

'How can he do something for me?'

'You'll see.'

4

Inspector Dinesh Chand took out his handkerchief once more and wiped the perspiration from his forehead. Then he forced a smile and said, 'Don't be so . . . I mean, don't be like that, sir, we are doing our best, you know. Our investigation is in full swing, I assure you. We . . .'

'Rubbish!' shouted Mr Sanyal. 'You cannot tell me where my son is, or even how he is.'

'No, sir, but . . .'

'Stop. Let me speak. This is what you've learnt so far: a gang of four kidnapped Bablu. They got into a stolen blue Ambassador and were going in the direction of Singbhum.'

'Yes, sir.'

'Don't keep saying "yes, sir". Let me finish. They were hit by a truck on the way. The truck driver ran away, but you caught him afterwards.'

'Yes—' the inspector stopped himself in the nick of time before saying 'sir'.

'Two of those men died on the spot.'

'Bonku Ghosh and Narayan Karmakar.'

'But the leader of the gang is still alive?'

'Yes.'

'What's he called?'

'We don't know his real name.'

'Wonderful! Well, what do you know him as?'

'Samson.'

'And the other one?'

'Raghunath.'

'Is that a pseudonym, too?'

'Could well be.'

'Anyway, you seem to think that Samson and Raghunath are still alive and they ran away from the scene of the accident. You also appear to think that Bablu was somehow thrown out of the car.'

'Yes, because we found a torn sole of a shoe a few yards from the car. That shoe would have fitted a twelve-year-old boy, sir. The road sloped down, you see, towards a forest. That's where we found it. Besides, there were patches of blood. And a new bar of chocolate.'

'But you did not find my son.'

'No, sir.'

'Have you searched the forest? Or are your men too scared of being eaten by tigers?'

The inspector tried to laugh lightly at this, failed, and coughed instead.

'There are no tigers in that forest, sir. It has been searched pretty thoroughly. All the villages nearby—five or six of them—have been searched as well.'

'In that case, what have you come to report? The whole thing is crystal clear to me. Samson and Raghunath took Bablu with them. It's obvious, isn't it?'

The inspector raised a hand to stop Mr Sanyal's reasoning, then thought the better of it, and lowered his hand quickly. 'Sir, we have seen a ray of hope. That's what I . . .'

'A ray of hope? Drop this theatrical language, Inspector, and come to the point.'

Inspector Chand wiped his forehead once again before replying. 'A man called Amarnath Banerjee—he works for the Jute Corporation—was returning to Calcutta from Ghatshila, the day after the accident. He was in his car. He has built a house in Ghatshila, you see, and his wife and son . . .'

'Is that relevant!'

'No, sir. Sorry, sir. About thirty miles from Kharagpur, he saw a young boy in a truck. His arms and legs were injured. The truck driver had found him lying unconscious by the side of the road, about a mile to the north of the accident scene. Mr Banerjee took the boy to Kharagpur and had him checked by a doctor. He gave him first aid, but soon after that, the boy escaped. Mr Banerjee reported the matter to the police.'

The inspector stopped. Mr Sanyal had been listening with his eyes fixed on his massive glasstop table. Now he looked up and asked, 'You know all this, but not the name of that boy?'

'No, sir. There's a problem there, you see. It seems that the boy was suffering from loss of memory.'

'Loss of memory?' Mr Sanyal's whole face twisted in a frown.

'The boy was unable to tell his name, his address, or his father's name. He could not remember a single thing.'

'Nonsense!'

'Yet he fits the description perfectly.'

'How? Did he have a clear complexion, curly hair, was he of medium build?'

'Yes, sir. Besides, he was wearing blue shorts and a white shirt, just like your son.'

'Did anyone see a birthmark on his waist? A mole under his chin?'

'No, sir.'

Mr Sanyal rose from his chair and looked at his watch. 'Today,' he said, 'I have to go to court. I was too worried to work these last three days. Now I have informed my other three sons. One of them is studying at IIT, Kharagpur. He will be here later today. The other two have to travel from Bombay and Bangalore. They'll be here in a day or two. I am most concerned about my mother. Thank goodness Bablu's mother is no more. She could not have endured this shock. Well, I have decided what I want to do. If those two men have still got Bablu, they will demand money, sooner or later. When they do, I am going to pay up and take my son back. After that, whether they are arrested or not is your problem. I don't care.'

So saying, Saradindu Sanyal, one of the most powerful barristers of Calcutta, stormed out of the room, his shoes making loud clicking noises on the marble floor of his library-cum-office. Inspector Chand reached for his handkerchief again.

5

Two men walked into a little-known barber's shop somewhere in north Calcutta, sat in two adjacent chairs and, in a matter of minutes, managed to get their appearances altered quite dramatically. The taller and the heftier of the two had a close-cropped beard, a moustache and long hair that came down to his shoulders. Paresh, the barber, was startled by the hardness of his shoulder muscles. He did as he was told and got rid of both the beard and the moustache. The man's hair was then cut quite short in a style that had been popular ten years ago. The second man lost his sideburns, the parting in his hair moved from the right to the left, and the unkempt beard he sported was wiped clean, leaving only a thin moustache. When they had finished, Paresh and his colleague, Pashupati, were duly paid; but, instead of a tip, what they received in addition was a glance from the first man that nearly stopped their hearts. It commanded them to hold their tongues. No one must know about this particular visit. It was a command neither would dare disobey.

Twenty minutes later, the same men stopped before a decrepit old house in Shobha Bazar and knocked loudly. The front door was opened by a small, somewhat shrivelled old man. The hefty man placed a hand on the old man's chest and pushed him back into the house. The second man followed them in, and bolted the door from inside. It was already dusk—the only light came from a twenty-watt bulb.

'Can you recognize us, Dadu?' asked the hefty one, leaning over the old man. The latter's eyes were bulging. He was trembling so much that his ancient, steel-framed glasses had slipped down his nose.

'Why, n-no, I d-don't th-think . . .' he stammered.

The hefty man smiled menacingly. 'That's because we've shaved. Here, smell this!' He pulled the old man's face down and held it close to his own for a second. 'Can you smell the shaving cream? My name is Samson. Now can you recognize me?'

The old man sat down on a divan, still trembling.

'Were you having a smoke? Is this the time when you smoke your hookah? Sorry to disturb you.' Samson picked up the hookah that stood leaning against the wall, and removed the bowl from its top. There was a small desk on the divan. On this desk lay an open almanac with a marble paperweight on it. Samson removed the paperweight and turned the bowl over. Red-hot pieces of coal slipped out from the bowl and fell on the almanac. Then he threw the bowl away, pulled forward a chair with a broken arm, and sat down, facing the old man.

'Now,' he said, 'tell me this—if you must cheat and swindle, why don't you do so openly? Why pretend to be an astrologer?'

The old man did not know where to look. Smoke rose from his almanac, spiralling upward—the pages were turning black and slowly crumbling away. The smell of burning paper intermingled with the smell of tobacco.

Samson went on speaking, his voice low, but harsh. 'We came here the other day, Dadu, and said we were about to start a big project. So we needed you to find us a suitable day, a good, auspicious day. You looked at your books and said that the seventh of July was a good day. I've heard people say that you, Bhairav Bhattacharya, are so good that if a crow came and sat on your roof, you could work out its future, and you would not be wrong. So we believed you, and you took ten rupees from us and put it in that cash box over there. Well, do you know what happened then?'

The astrologer seemed totally unable to take his eyes off the burning pages of his almanac. It was for this reason that Raghunath placed a hand under his chin and turned his head round, so that he was forced to face Samson. Then he took off the old man's glasses, and pulled his eyes open with his fingers, so that there was no way that he could look away.

'Let me tell you,' Samson went on, 'that the car we were travelling in with all the goods got hit by a truck. It was flattened immediately. Two of our partners died on the spot. I escaped because I am made of steel. But even I nearly dislocated my kneecaps. My partner here was injured pretty badly—even now he cannot sleep on his side. The goods we worked so hard to get . . . well, that's gone, too. Dead. Finished. What I want to know is why you couldn't see any of this happening. Didn't your calculations tell you such a thing was going to happen?'

'N-no, look, we . . . we are not God, after all . . .!'

'Shut up!'

Raghunath released the old man. Samson could now manage on his own. 'Bring it out now. We want ten multiplied by ten.'

'I . . . I . . .'

'Shut up!' Samson shouted. Almost at once, a knife appeared in his hand, its blade flicking out as he pressed a button on its folded, invisible handle. He moved his hand closer to the old man.

'H-here . . . take it, take it!'

Bhairav Bhattacharya's trembling hand fumbled for the key tucked in at his waist, then moved towards the cash box.

6

Fotik had learnt to handle his job quite well in the last five days. Upen Babu was a good man, which had helped a lot. He had agreed to feed him, pay him twelve rupees a month, and find him somewhere to stay. A month's salary had been paid in advance.

Only yesterday, Fotik realized how lucky he was to have Upen Babu to take care of him. He had gone to buy paan for him from a stall nearby. There, he met a boy called Bishu from another tea shop. Bishu had been working there for almost a month. Within a couple of days of starting his job, Bishu had broken a cup. Immediately, his boss, Beni Babu, had uprooted a large chunk of hair from his head and rapped him on the head so sharply that it had swollen up. The swelling, Bishu declared, had become as large as a potato.

Upen Babu was not given to physical violence. He scolded Fotik sometimes, and then went on speaking, showering him with advice. It went on all day, coming out in instalments. When Fotik broke a glass on his second day, at first Upen Babu stared at the pieces in silence. Then, when Fotik began to collect them in a towel, he opened his mouth. 'There, you've broken a glass! It doesn't come for free, you know. Who will have to pay for it? You or I? Try to remember this when you work here—everything costs money. Of course you have to be quick in your job, but that does not mean that you should jump around with a glass in your hand. Things that are used in this shop are not meant for juggling, you know.'

Fotik was embarrassed at first, but then he realized that Upen Babu was speaking more to himself than anyone else. It was certainly not his intention to shout at Fotik in front of everyone. Even as he spoke, his hands continued to work, taking money from the customers and giving them their change. In due course, Fotik realized that Upen Babu never stopped his work even when he launched on his stream of advice.

It was not as if new customers could be spotted every day. Most of those who came were regulars and they always came at a particular time. Their orders never varied, either. Some only wanted a cup of tea, some wanted tea and toast, others asked for tea and eggs and toast. The eggs were either poached or made into omelettes. Fotik had started to recognize some of the regulars and could guess what they might order.

Today, when that thin, perpetually sad looking gentleman arrived and sat down at table number three, Fotik went to him at once and said, 'Tea and dry toast?' The man said, 'So you have learnt that already?' The sad expression on his face did not change even when he spoke to Fotik.

It was fun to be able to recognize people. But he realized he had to tread with caution, for only this afternoon, he had made a mistake. When a man in a yellow shirt turned up, Fotik thought he had recognized him as one of the regulars. So he went up to him and said, 'Tea and a two-egg omelette?' At this, the man removed the newspaper he was holding in front of him and raised his eyebrows. 'Do I have to eat what you would like me to?' he asked dryly.

What pleased Fotik the most was that he was getting used to moving about with plates and cups and saucers in his hands. Harun had said to him, 'You will get the hang of it one day. Then it will come to you naturally like steps in a dance. Actually, this is also an art. Until you get familiar with your art, you will break a few glasses.'

Harun came to see him every evening. He had not told Upen Babu the truth. Fotik had been introduced as a distant cousin from Midnapore. He was supposed to be an orphan with no one in the world except an irritable old uncle, who took ganja and beat him for no reason. 'Look what he did to this poor little boy!' Harun had said to Upen Babu. 'He spanked the boy so hard that he took off the skin from his elbow. See the swelling on his head? He struck him with a log!' Upen Babu seemed perfectly willing to employ Fotik immediately. The boy who worked in the shop before him kept disappearing for days. Only recently, he had missed work for three days to go and watch Hindi films, and he had told endless lies to explain his absence. Upen Babu was glad to get rid of him.

Fotik's appearance had changed a little. Harun had taken him for a haircut and his curly hair was now cut quite short. But Fotik did not mind. On their way back from the barber's shop, Harun had stopped to buy him a pair of shorts, a couple of shirts, two sleeveless vests, and a pair of chappals. 'Wear a vest when you're working,' he said, 'but remember to soak some tea leaves in hot water, and then dip your vests in it. When they are dry, they will not look brand new.'

At this, Fotik had suddenly found himself breaking into goosepimples, possibly because the mention of work had made him think of himself as a grown-up. He knew he would soon get used to the work. He had to start at eight-thirty in the morning and go on until the shop closed at eight o'clock in the evening. These were his hours from Monday to Friday. On Saturdays, the shop closed at four o'clock, and remained closed on Sundays.

Upen Babu had a small room behind the shop. Outside that room, under a tin roof, Fotik had been given a small space to sleep in. Mosquitoes did not let him sleep the first night. He tried covering himself from head to foot with a sheet, but that was suffocating, so he gave up. The next morning, he told Upen Babu about this problem. To his relief, Upen Babu found him a mosquito net. From that day, he had been sleeping quite well. The wound on his elbow had healed. The pain in his head disappeared totally at times but returned occasionally. What did not return at all was his memory. For the life of him, he could not recall anything before the moment of waking up under the stars. 'Don't worry,'

Harun had reassured him. 'You cannot force these things. One day, it will come back to you automatically.'

Harun and he had gone out yesterday, which was a Sunday. Fotik had really enjoyed himself. Harun had told him to wait at the shop. He turned up at two o'clock, a colourful bag hanging from his shoulder. It was a patchwork of many small pieces of cloth placed in rows and stitched together. He took Fotik to Shaheed Minar. They got there in ten minutes.

Fotik could never have imagined such a place. One side of the Minar was packed with people. How could so many people possibly cram themselves together in one place? Harun said, 'If you climbed to the top of the Minar, you would see that this crowd has a pattern. You'd find empty circles here and there, with some artiste or another holding a show, surrounded by an audience.'

'Is this place always so crowded?'

'No, this happens only on Sundays. Come, you must see for yourself. Then you'll understand what I mean.'

Fotik saw, but it would be an exaggeration to say that he understood. What lay before his eyes was so huge, full of so many different types of activities, different languages, different colours and sounds that his eyes, ears and head were overwhelmed. It was not just shows that were being held. On one side, hawkers were selling all kinds of things—toothpowder, ointments for skin diseases, pills for rheumatism, strange herbs and roots, and God knew what else. In one corner, he saw that someone was sitting beside a pile of folded pieces of paper. He also had a parrot. If anyone wished to know his future, the parrot would draw a piece of paper with its beat; on this a prediction would be written. A few yards away stood a man, talking non-stop, praising the remarkable qualities of a certain soap. On his head was a turban, he was wearing khaki shorts, and both his hands were covered by pink foam.

On the other side, a man stood with a very thick and heavy iron chain around his neck. He seemed to be talking quite a lot accompanied by elaborate gestures. Everyone around him appeared to be hanging on to his every word. Close to him, on a paved area, a man was sitting with his legs stretched. His clothes were extremely dirty, his hair was long, unkempt and jet black. He looked like a mad man, but with a piece of chalk in his hand, he was drawing beautiful pictures of characters from the *Ramayana*. People who saw them were throwing coins from all directions, which were landing on the hard surface with a clang, some on the crown on Ram's head, some on Ravan's face, and others on Hanuman's tail. But the man did not seem interested in the money at all.

What appeared to be most popular, Fotik noticed, were 'acts' and shows of various kinds. One particular act caught his attention, and he was so taken aback by it that he could hardly believe his eyes. A small boy—much younger than Fotik—was lying on his back, but his head was buried in a hole in the ground. Another young boy was carefully closing the hole, blocking out every possible passage through which air might pass. The first boy continued to lie still. After a few moments of horrified amazement, Fotik clutched at Harun's sleeve. 'What's he doing? He's going to die!' he exclaimed.

'No. No one comes here to die,' Harun assured him. 'They all come only to live. He'll live, too. What he's doing right now is simply a matter of practice. There's nothing that you can't do if you practise well enough. You'll know what I mean, when you see Harun's special show.'

Harun took him to the spot where he used to hold his shows before. It was now being used by a girl. She was walking on a rope that stretched from one end of a high pole to another. The girl seemed to be having no difficulty in maintaining her balance. 'She's from Madras,' Harun said briefly.

Further on, Fotik saw a number of large iron hoops. Some had been set alight. 'Is someone going to jump through those burning hoops?' Fotik asked eagerly. Harun stopped walking and gave him a sharp look. 'How did you know? Have you seen something like this before? Can you remember?' he asked. Fotik opened his mouth to say 'Yes', but shut it again. Just for a fleeting second, a scene had flashed before his eyes—there were lights, music and a lot of people—but it was gone almost as soon as it had appeared. He was back in the maidan under Shaheed Minar.

Harun began walking again with Fotik in tow. The spot where he finally stopped was quiet, not many people were around. From the crowd they had just left behind them came the sound of a *dugdugi*. Fotik looked back and saw, through a gap in the crowd, the black, hairy legs of a bear. Most performers here used drums to draw attention. But what Harun now took out of his bag was not a drum but a flute. One end was narrow, the other broad with patterns on it. Harun blew into his flute seven times. It rang out, loud and clear, from one end of the maidan to the other.

Then he put the flute away, and startled Fotik considerably by calling out loudly:

'*Chhoo-o-o*!
Chhoo-chhoo-chhoo!'

The sound of the flute and his call was enough to make children come running to him. As soon as he had an audience, Harun clapped his hands, then pirouetted three times before doing a somersault and then jumping quite high in the air. When he finally landed on the ground, he started his chant, the magic rhyme that would bring everyone flocking round to see him:

'*Choo-chhoo-chhoo-oo-oo*!
I know a very good magic spell.
Are you ill? I'll make you well.
Seven seas, and monkeys twelve,
Rats and moles do dig and delve.
Chhoo-chhoo-chhoo-oo-oo!'

Then he played his flute again, blowing into it long and hard. This was quickly followed by another clap and a somersault. Then he picked up the rhyme again:

'Come! Come! Come! Come!
Come-m-m-m!
Come and see my startling act,
Magical tricks, I'm jolly good at.
In this city, I like to play,
I love it best, I have to say.
A longish beard, and nuts and cloves,
Come straight to me, in giant droves.
Come-m-m-m!

Come, commander, wonder-wonder,
Juggler, joker, jumping wonder,
Wonder-Khalif, Harun-Wonder,
Come-m-m-m!

Come boy, good boy, bad boy, fat boy,
Hat boy, coat boy, this boy, that boy,
Calling all-boy, all-boy calling,
Calling . . . calling . . . calling . . . calling,
Come-m-m-m!'

Fotik stood staring, totally amazed by Harun's ability to shout and attract people's attention and interest. Already, a lot of people had left the crowd and come over to join them. Harun stopped and began taking more things out of his bag. The first thing to come out was a bright and colourful mat; this he spread on the ground to sit on. Then out came four gleaming brass balls with red patterns carved on them, two huge tops attached to long strings, three bamboo sticks with red and blue feathers stuck on them, and five different caps of various designs. Harun placed one of these on his head.

Fotik helped him display all the other objects on the grass. 'Thank you,' said Harun, 'that will do. Now look, go and stand in the crowd. Each time I finish an item, you must clap.'

After the first two items, Fotik realized that there was no need for him to lead the general applause. People were clapping spontaneously. To tell the truth, he was so taken aback by the things Harun was doing that he did not even remember to clap. It was not just his hands that moved fast. It seemed as if Harun's whole body had magic in it. Fotik watched, transfixed, as Harun threw his tops high into the air, then pulled them back swiftly, so that they spun in the air and then fell neatly back on his open palm, on the same spot, each time. How did he manage that? Fotik simply could not figure it out.

But it did not end there. Harun placed a top on one end of a bamboo stick that had the red and blue feathers. Even when placed on the stick which was as thin as a pencil, the top continued to spin furiously. Fotik thought that was perhaps the end of the show, this was where he was supposed to clap—but no, suddenly Harun threw his head back and put the bamboo stick on his chin. When he removed his hand, the stick began to spin together with the top, the colourful feathers going round and round. A little later, Fotik noticed that the stick would slow down at times, or even stop moving completely, but the top balanced on it did not stop rotating even for a second.

What brought Harun the maximum applause was his juggling act. He started with two of his brass balls, then picked up a third, and a fourth. The balls caught the evening sun and shone brightly. The light reflected from them, in turn, shone on Harun's face, making it look, every now and then, as if the light was radiating from his face.

The show continued until the sun had set. Towards the end, many more people joined the crowd, leaving what they had been watching earlier. Fotik saw, to his surprise, that even small children were throwing coins around Harun. But Harun did not even glance at them while he was performing. When the show was over, he called Fotik and said, 'Go on, pick them up.'

By the time Harun had replaced every object in his bag, Fotik's job was done. The coins added up to eighteen rupees and thirty-two paise. Harun put the bag back on his shoulder. 'Come on, let's go and have dinner,' he said. 'I'll take you to a Punjabi dhaba. We can have rumali roti and very tasty daal. I bet you've never had anything like it before. Once we've eaten that, we can decide what we'd like for dessert!'

7

Fotik had found a calendar and hung it on the wall in the little place where he slept. At the end of a day, he put a pencil mark on that date, in order to calculate how many days he had spent in his new job. On his eighth day, which was a Thursday, at around half-past twelve, two men walked into the shop and sat at the table that was closest to the door, and farthest from Upen Babu's desk. One of these men was so hefty that Fotik stared at him in surprise. The man who had accompanied him looked quite ordinary.

The hefty looking man shouted, 'Hey!' and Fotik realized he was calling out to him. He was busy clearing another table, recently vacated by one of their regulars, a man with a white mark on his chin, who always came in at about the same time, ordered a cup of tea and then spent half an hour reading the newspaper.

'Two omelettes and tea. Quickly!' added the strong and muscular man.

'Yes, babu,' said Fotik, and stood wondering why, totally unexpectedly, his voice had trembled as he had uttered those words, as had his hand, in which he was holding an empty cup.

But he pulled himself together and went to the kitchen to pass on the new order to Keshto, their cook. Then he put the cup down, and handed over to Upen Babu the money the last customer had paid him. He cast a sidelong glance at the hefty man. He could not recall having seen him before. So why did he react like that on hearing the man's voice? The two men were now talking among themselves. The thin man was holding a lighter for his friend's cigarette.

Fotik looked away, then slowly walked over to another table where Panna Babu sat every day. With a duster, he began clearing the breadcrumbs scattered on it. Panna Babu seemed far better off than any other customer who came here. He always wore good clothes. Upen Babu often left his seat when Panna Babu arrived and exchanged pleasantries with him. There was something else that made Panna Babu different from the others. On two different occasions, he had given Fotik ten paise as a tip. In fact, Fotik had received the second coin only five minutes ago. He had decided to save the extra money to repay Harun for all his kindness.

Keshto began making the omelettes. He had already made the tea, which he now pushed towards Fotik. Fotik took the two cups and walked smartly over to the two men, without spilling a single drop on the saucers. In the last couple of days, he had learnt a special act. He would place part of an order on a table, then mention what remained and add 'Coming!' Today, he said, 'Omelette coming!'

For some unknown reason, his eyes moved towards the hefty man as he spoke. He saw the man's jaw drop. Through his open mouth, the smoke that he forgot to inhale began pouring out, like a ribbon. Curious, Fotik stared at this ribbon of smoke for about five seconds before turning to go. But the man stopped him. 'Oy!' he cried. Fotik stopped. 'How long have you been working here?'

The police! This man had to be from the police, or else why should he ask such a question? Fotik decided at once that he would not give the correct information but he'd have to make sure Upen Babu did not overhear anything. He cast a quick glance at the desk, to discover that Upen Babu was not in the shop. Thank God.

'A long time, babu,' he replied.

'What's your name?'

'Fotik.' This was not his real name, anyway. So there was no harm in saying it.

'When did you have a haircut?'

'A long time ago.'

'Come here. Come closer.'

At this moment, Keshto called from the kitchen to say that the omelettes were ready. 'Let me get your omelettes, babu,' he said quickly.

He brought two laden plates from the kitchen and placed them before the men. Then he went to table number two and got the salt and pepper cellars. The two men were once again talking to each other. They did not look at him. He saw a new customer come in and take table number four. Fotik went over to greet him.

A little later, when the men had finished eating, Fotik had to go back to them to collect the money. 'How did you hurt your arm?' asked the hefty man.

'Grazed it against a wall.'

'How many lies do you tell every day, dear boy?'

Fotik did not reply. He had never seen this man before, but he did not like the way he was speaking to him. Fotik decided to mention this incident to Harun when he saw him next.

'Why don't you answer?'

The man was staring hard at him. Before Fotik could say anything, Upen Babu came back to the shop. He spotted Fotik standing quietly and realized there was something wrong.

'What's the matter?' he asked, stopping by the table.

'Nothing. This babu wanted to know . . .'

'What?'

'How long I've been working here.'

Upen Babu turned to the hefty man. 'Why, sir? Why do you ask?' he said, politely enough.

The man said nothing in reply. He simply put the money on the table, rose and left the shop, followed by his friend.

After this, Fotik got so busy that by the end of the afternoon, he almost forgot the whole episode.

8

Harun arrived at the shop at about four o'clock the same day. He was going to take Fotik with him and show him where he lived. Upen Babu had agreed to let Fotik go at four. Keshto's son, Shotu, was going to work in the shop in Fotik's absence. Shotu was familiar with the job but could not work regularly as he had fever almost thrice a month.

Harun said, as they stepped out, 'I'll show you something new today—a new act I have been practising. I bet you'll be surprised.' At this, Fotik's heart began to dance with joy and excitement, so much so that he failed to notice two men standing outside a paan shop on the opposite pavement. They were the same men who had asked him all those questions earlier.

Harun, it turned out, did not like travelling in crowded buses. 'If I had to clutch a rod and hang from it like a bat, it would damage my hands,' he said. 'And if my hands were damaged, I could never perform and then I'd starve. So let's just walk.'

They went through a number of alleyways and several other broad and narrow roads, before reaching a bridge, under which ran electric trains. Stairs went down from one end of the bridge, leading to a slum. That was where Harun lived. In the distance, Fotik could see chimneys of factories, rising above tall coconut trees. The slum looked as if it had wrapped a blanket of smoke around itself. 'All that smoke has come from the coal stoves people have lit,' Harun explained. 'It's time to start cooking dinner, you see.'

He explained something else. 'In this slum,' he said, climbing down the stairs, 'you will find Hindus and Muslims and Christians, all living together. Some of them are such talented artistes that it takes my breath away. There's a carpenter called Jamal. He sings so well that, listening to him, I often forget where I am. His voice can wipe out all sorrow, all pain. He comes to my room sometimes and sings, and I play the tabla on my wooden cot.'

A small path wound its way through small huts with straw roots towards Harun's room. Fotik kept close to Harun, and walked by his side. Each time they were spotted by a child, Harun was greeted by a big smile. Some called out to him, others jumped joyfully, or clapped. Harun waved at them, and got them to join him. 'Come on!' he said. 'You'll see something new today!'

'Something new? Really? What fun!' cried the children. Fotik had no idea Harun had so many friends.

His room turned out to be small and a little dark. Perhaps that was why he had filled it with colourful objects. There were fabrics, coloured paper, puppets, pictures and kites. Some were hanging on the walls, some were spread on the floor, or simply displayed in quiet corners. Yet, the room did not look cluttered. Not a single piece seemed out of place. Perhaps this was a special kind of art. Fotik also noticed Harun's bag and the box with which he travelled.

Trying to take in so many different things at once, Fotik did not see, at first, the framed picture of a man. His eyes fell on it just as Harun switched on a light. 'Whose picture is that?' Fotik asked. The man was staring out of the photo-frame, looking straight at Fotik. He had a thick moustache, and long, wavy hair. At the bottom of the picture, someone had written in black, clearly and carefully: Enrico Rustelli.

Harun lit a beedi. 'He's my second guru,' he replied, blowing the smoke out. 'I never saw him in person. He's an Italian. He was a juggler too, who lived about a hundred years ago. I found the picture in a magazine and cut it out. You saw me juggle with four balls. Do you know how many he used? Ten. Can you imagine it? Not five, or seven, or eight, but ten! People used to go mad just watching him.'

Fotik felt surprised to learn that Harun had actually studied his subject and read up on juggling. Did that mean he could read English? 'Yes,' Harun replied. 'I went to school, you know. I studied up to class VIII. I am from Chandan Nagore. My father ran a shop—he sold cloth and fabrics. One day, I heard that there was going to be a fair in the next town, and someone was going to hold a magic show. So I went, and saw juggling for the first time in my life. I couldn't believe it. It was so wonderful. I stayed away for two days. When I got back, my father demonstrated some juggling of his own. Have you ever seen the huge scissors that are used to cut cloth from a bale? Well, he used those and here's the result.'

Harun lifted his shirt and showed Fotik a deep scar on his back. 'The wound took three weeks to heal,' he went on. 'I waited until I was better. Then, one day, I found the chance to make my escape. I left home, without telling a soul, with eleven rupees in my pocket, and a small bundle slung over my shoulder. Oh, and I also took a couple of wooden balls that I had bought at the fair, to practise juggling.

'I got into a train without bothering to buy a ticket, without even asking where it was going. Over the next three days, I changed trains three times, and lived on just tea and biscuits. Then, one morning, I peered out of the window of my train, and could see the Taj Mahal. I got off at the next station. I roamed in the city all day, and finally ended up at the fort. There was an open area behind the fort, beyond which was the river Jamuna, and across it, I saw the Taj again. Then I happened to glance in the opposite direction. On the grassy area below the fort, a number of little shows were being held. There were snake charmers and a man with a bear. And in the middle of it all, sat Asadullah. His eyes were blindfolded, but he was juggling with remarkable ease. I was so impressed that I got emotional. It almost brought tears to my eyes. How could an ordinary man have such power?'

'Who else was watching him?' Fotik asked.

'A lot of people, from a balcony in the fort. There were English men and women. Some of them were rolling crisp notes—five or ten-rupee notes—and throwing them down, some at the dancing bear, some at the snake charmers, and others at the juggler. In fact, most of them seemed interested in the juggler. Suddenly, one of those sahibs—obviously a somewhat dimwitted man—threw a note without rolling it first. He meant it for the juggler, but a sudden gust of wind blew it away, and it landed straight in the snake charmer's basket. A cobra sat in it, with a raised hood. The juggler had removed his blindfold by then. The sahib on the balcony began shouting, but I shot forward like a bullet and picked up that note in one swoop, before the snake could move. Then I thrust it into the juggler's hands.

'The man said, "*Shabaash beta, jeete raho*" (well done, son, may you live long). I knew no Hindi at the time, so I could not tell him what I wanted. All I could do was take out the two wooden balls that I had bought before leaving home, and showed them to him. In the last few weeks, I had started to practise juggling. So I also showed him what I had learnt. He smiled, and from that day, I became his pupil. I stayed with him until the day he died. After his death, I've been on my own and shown everything he taught me—except juggling with a blindfold on. Today, that is exactly what I am going to try.'

All the children from the slum were waiting outside. Harun emerged from his room with his bag, with Fotik behind him. They turned left, walking past a number of other rooms, each like Harun's. Then they came to an open space. There was a small pond in one end, across which stood the compound wall of a factory. Harun found a relatively clear spot and spread a durrie. He sat down on it, surrounded by the children, and took out a silk handkerchief from his bag. It was yellow with black dots on it. He passed it to Fotik and said, 'Tie it around my eyes. Make it tight, so it doesn't slip off.' Fotik did as he was told, then stepped back and joined the other children.

Harun folded his hands and saluted his ustad three times. Then he began his act with two brass balls at first, quickly adding a third, and continued with such dexterity and skill that it left Fotik totally speechless. If every memory from his mind was wiped out permanently, leaving only the memory of what he had just witnessed, he felt he could live quite happily for the rest of his life. But Harun did not stop there. He put the balls away, and without taking the blindfold off, took out three knives from his bag. Their blades glittered in the sun, catching reflections of the sky, the trees, the houses and everything else.

A second later, those shiny blades began dancing in Harun's hands. Time and time again, the air was sliced by those knives, but not once did any one of them strike against the other; nor did they damage Harun's hands in any way.

When he finished, the applause that greeted him was deafening. Fotik stepped forward to take the blindfold off, but couldn't. His hands were trembling so much that he failed to untie the knot. Harun realized this, laughed and took it off himself. Then he replaced the knives in his bag and turned to his audience. 'That's all for now, children. You can go back home,' he said. The children disappeared.

Fotik looked at Harun. For some odd reason, he thought Harun was not looking as happy as he should. What was on his mind? Was he sad because all this had reminded him of his days with his ustad?

No. Harun told him the real reason only when they were safely back in his room. 'I saw two men,' he said. 'They were standing at a distance, looking at you. My eyes fell on them just as I took that handkerchief off. They don't live here, I don't think I've seen them before. But I did not like the way they were staring at you.'

Immediately, Fotik was reminded of what had happened earlier in the tea shop. His heart gave a jump. 'Was one of them thin, and the other quite strong?' he asked.

'Yes, yes. So you saw them, too?'

'No, not now. But I saw them this afternoon. They came to the shop.' As he explained quickly Harun's face grew grave. 'Did that hefty looking man have a lot of hair around his ears?' he asked.

Yes! Now that Harun had mentioned it, Fotik remembered clearly. It was, in fact, the man's hairy ears that had first drawn his attention. 'It must be Shyamlal,' Harun said through clenched teeth. 'His body may be hefty, but he is bow-legged. I did notice the shape of his legs, and that's what made me suspicious. He used to have a beard, but he's shaved it off now. Pity he didn't think of getting rid of the hair around his ears. I used to go to a tea shop in Chitpur, a few years ago. That's where I saw him first. He used to drop in with three other men. The four of them . . .' Harun broke off. Fotik saw him frown. 'Didn't you say two men were found dead in the car in the forest?' he asked.

Fotik nodded. Harun's face looked even more grim. 'Then what I feared is true. Your father must be quite wealthy.'

A mention of his father or family made no impact on Fotik's mind. So he remained silent. Harun got up and moved closer to a window. He peered out for a second and said, 'They're still here. I saw one of them light a cigarette.'

Harun sat down again. Fotik had never seen him look so serious. 'Are you worried about my going back to the shop?' he asked.

'No, not really. I could take you back a different way. If we go through that room opposite, we'd be able to find a back alley. Those men will never know that we've slipped out. As far as I can see, they are not that familiar with this area. They simply followed you here today. No, I am not worried about you getting back home tonight. It's your future that worries me.'

Harun stopped and looked straight at Fotik. 'Are you sure you still cannot remember anything?'

'Absolutely. Now I don't even know what "remembering" means.'

Harun did not reply. He patted Fotik's knee, then got to his feet. He left the light on in his room when they went out and locked the door. Instead of going back the way they came, the pair of them slipped into a neighbour's room, and found a different exit.

9

It was the following Sunday. A few people were assembled in barrister Saradindu Sanyal's large drawing room. It was a big house, built nearly sixty years ago, by the man whose portrait hung on the wall. It was Saradindu's father, Dwarkanath Sanyal. He, too, had been a barrister, and an even more successful one. It was said that at one time, Dwarkanath's daily income was a thousand rupees.

Mr Sanyal seemed far more subdued today. The truth was that he was extremely puzzled by the continued silence from his son's captors. No one had sent him a ransom note. This had made him grow more anxious about his son's safety. Today, two other men were present, in addition to Mr Sanyal and the inspector. They were Mr Sanyal's second and third sons, Sudheendra and Preetindra. His eldest son had some important meeting in Delhi, so he had left two days ago.

It was Sudheendra who was talking. He was in his mid-twenties. His sideburns were long, in keeping with the current trend, and he wore glasses set in a thick, black frame.

'But loss of memory isn't that uncommon, Baba,' he was saying. 'It's often written about in foreign magazines. I can't see why you find that so hard to believe. Surely you have read about amnesia?'

Preetindra was silent. He had been the closest to his missing younger brother, Bablu. It was Preetindra who had taught Bablu how to play cricket, helped him with his maths lessons, and had recently taken him to a circus. After his departure to Kharagpur he did not get to see Bablu that often. But now he was sitting silently, striking his forehead with his palm occasionally, in helpless rage and frustration. It was his belief that, had he been at home, no one could have kidnapped his brother. It was difficult to say why he felt like this, for even if he were still in Calcutta, he could hardly have been with Bablu at the time when he was attacked and taken away.

Bablu was returning from school then. His school being within walking distance, he always walked to and from it, unless it happened to be raining. Normally, his friend Parag went with him. Parag lived in the same neighbourhood. However, on that particular day, Bablu was alone. The school was closed, but a few boys had been asked to go and help with preparations for a fete. Bablu was one of them but Parag was not. So, at about half-past five that evening, Bablu was coming back alone from his school. A blue Ambassador stopped briefly by the road, and a gang of hooligans jumped out of if. They grabbed Bablu and dragged him back to the car with them. An old chowkidar witnessed the whole incident from the house opposite, but was unable to help.

'If Bablu has lost his memory,' said Mr Sanyal slowly, 'then he will not remember anything, or recognize anyone, even if he comes back.'

'Amnesia can be treated,' Sudheendra said. 'People can get help to regain lost memory. You can speak to Dr Bose, if you like. If specialists here cannot do anything, I am sure we can consult someone abroad.'

'In that case . . .' began Mr Sanyal. Inspector Chand interrupted him. 'Please do what I suggest, sir,' he said. 'We can safely assume that your son is not with his kidnappers, since they have said and done nothing so far. Besides, if he has lost his memory, he's not going to come back on his own, is he? So I think your best bet is to place an advertisement, offer a reward, then see what happens. It can't do any harm, sir.'

'Have you been able to trace the two men who escaped from that car?' asked Mr Sanyal.

'We believe they are still here somewhere in the city. But we haven't exactly tracked . . . I mean, not yet.'

Mr Sanyal thrust his hands into the pockets of his dressing gown and sighed. 'Very well. Sudheen, see what you can do about an advertisement tomorrow. Pintu is too young to handle this.'

Sudheendra nodded in agreement. Preetindra, miffed at being labelled too young, shifted uneasily in his chair.

'How many newspapers are you thinking of?' Mr Sanyal asked the inspector.

'At least five. Try all the leading ones in English, Bengali and Hindi. If I were you, I would include a few in Urdu and Gurmukhi. After all, we do not know who your son is with at this moment.'

'You will need a photograph, won't you?'

This time, Preetindra opened his mouth. 'I have a photo of Bablu. I took it last year in Darjeeling.'

'Make it a big notice, something that people cannot miss,' said Mr Sanyal. 'Don't worry about expenses.'

10

Fotik was excited all day. Harun was going to include the blindfold juggling act for the first time today at the maidan. Ever since that day when they had been followed by those two men, Harun had called at the shop twice a day to check on Fotik. Although they had reached the shop quite safely that evening with no sign of those men, Harun had become extremely cautious. To be honest, even if Shyamlal and his friend had come after them, they could never have kept up with Harun. Fotik was amazed at his ability to weave his way through a maze of alleyways. He seemed to know the streets of Calcutta better than the back of his hand.

Every time Harun saw Fotik, he asked him if those two men had returned. They had not. Fotik could not tell if they lurked outside the shop, for during his working hours he never got the chance to get out of the shop. His speed and efficiency had improved a lot in the last few days. When he first started, his arms used to feel numb by the time he went to bed. That feeling of numbness had gone now.

These days, he practised juggling with two wooden balls before going to sleep. Harun had given them to him. One was red, and the other yellow. Harun had even taught him how to throw them high in the air, and catch them gently as they came down. 'This art that you are now learning,' he had said, 'was in existence in Egypt five thousand years ago. As a matter of fact, it has been in existence not just for five thousand, but for millions and millions of years, ever since this earth came into being.'

This struck Fotik as an exaggeration. But Harun explained, 'This earth is like a ball, isn't it? Think of the other planets—Mercury, Mars, Venus, Neptune, Jupiter, Saturn. Each one of them is like a ball, and they are revolving around the sun. And the moon? The moon circles the earth. Yet, not once do any one of these collide with other. Can you imagine? It's juggling of the highest order. You'll realize what I mean if you look at the sky at night. Think about it when you practise juggling with your wooden balls.'

Fotik heard all this attentively, but looking at Harun's face, he could sense that he was still worried about those two men. At times, Fotik even felt that it was something more than just anxiety, although he could not put a name to it. Just occasionally, he noticed Harun's bright eyes lose their lustre. What could he be thinking of?

Today, however, none of these thoughts occurred to Fotik when he found himself back at Shaheed Minar with Harun. A lot of people were already gathered where Harun had performed the previous Sunday. Fotik recognized some of them instantly. There was that boy with the pockmarked face. One of his eyes was damaged. And there was that dwarf, who had looked like a child from a distance; but a closer look had revealed his beard and moustache, which had startled Fotik. There was also a tall boy in a lungi, whose teeth were large and protruding. They saw Harun and started clapping loudly.

Harun sat down on the grass, then looked quickly at the sky. Fotik knew why he did this. Clouds had started to gather on the western horizon. If it began raining, everything would be spoilt. Please God, don't let it rain. Please let Harun amaze everyone with his skill, let them see how well he can perform even with his eyes blindfolded. Let him earn more than eighteen rupees and thirty-two paise today. Oh, if only there were sahibs and memsahibs here! Who was going to throw five and ten-rupee notes?

Harun began his show amidst the noise of distant thunder. A little later, he called Fotik closer. A top was still spinning on his palm. 'Open your hand!' he said to Fotik. Then he transferred the spinning top on to Fotik's hand. Fotik felt a slight tickle on his palm and, at the same time, a wave of joy swept over him. Today, he was not just a spectator. He was Harun's assistant, his pupil!

By this time there was another spinning top in Harun's hand. He took the first one back from Fotik and, for as long as the two tops remained in motion, juggled with them with as much ease as he did with the balls.

Then he put the tops away, and called Fotik once more. This time, he took out the dotted silk handkerchief. A murmur rose from the crowd as soon as Fotik tied it around his eyes. It was getting dark, but that would not make any difference to Harun. Fotik knew he did not need any light for this particular item. More people had come and joined the crowd. Today, they were definitely going to make more money than the last time.

Harun rummaged in his bag and took out the balls made of brass. There was another clap of thunder—this time, louder and closer—as Harun quietly saluted his ustad and threw the first ball in the air. All three balls went round, and passed through Harun's hands—one, two, three, four times—and then disaster struck. If the sky had fallen down on his head, Fotik would have felt less upset. God knew what went wrong, but as one of the three balls was going up and another coming down, they struck against each other just above Harun's head, making an ear-splitting noise. Then they flew off in different directions before landing on the grass.

This was bad enough. What was worse was that the same people who had been applauding and cheering so far suddenly turned into monsters and began jeering. Some sneered, others laughed openly, and booed.

That enthusiastic crowd took only a few seconds to disperse. Harun untied the handkerchief himself and began putting everything back in his bag. Fotik bent down to gather the few coins that had been dropped earlier, but Harun forbade him. He then sat on the grass and lit a beedi. Slowly, Fotik walked over to join him. He, too, sat down. He could not bring himself to say anything. Suddenly, everything seemed to have gone quiet. He could hear the traffic in Chowringhee—something he had been totally unaware of even a few minutes ago.

Harun inhaled a couple of times, then threw the beedi away. 'There's such a close link between one's mind and one's hands, Fotik, that if one is preoccupied, the other won't work, either. Today, you saw that happen for yourself. I must make better arrangements for you, and until I do so, no more blind juggling.'

This made no sense to Fotik. What arrangements was Harun talking about? Fotik was just fine in Upen Babu's shop. But Harun was still speaking. '. . . Since that day, I've been thinking. When I saw Shyamlal, I guessed what had happened. Now I can see their whole plan. They had kidnapped you with the intention of asking your father for a big ransom. They would have kept you hidden somewhere until they got what they wanted. But then the car had an accident. Two of their partners died on the spot. Shyamlal and the fourth man escaped, but when they saw you lying unconscious, they assumed that you were also dead. So they left you and ran away. But, only a few days later, they found you purely by chance in Upen-da's shop, and realized that they could still make their plan work.

'When I returned home after dropping you back at the shop that day, those two men were still loitering in my area. I kept an eye on them, and managed to follow them to their hideout. Now, if I told the police, they would be caught. But that would not be the end of the story, would it? Really, I ought to hand you over to the police as well.'

'No, no. Oh, please don't say that, Harun-da!'

'I know. I know how you feel about the police. That's why I haven't yet told them. In any case, there's no point in telling anyone anything until we discover who you really are. Right now, handing you over to the police would be no different from handing over a stray dog.'

This hurt Fotik very much. 'A stray dog?' he cried. 'Can a stray dog juggle? With two wooden balls?'

'You . . . you mean you have been practising?' Harun asked, looking straight at Fotik. For the first time, he smiled.

'Yes, of course!' Fotik replied, still sounding hurt. 'I practise every night, for a whole hour, before going to bed.' He took out the red and yellow balls from his pocket.

'Good,' said Harun. 'All right, let me give it another couple of days. If no one bothers you any more, no one makes any enquiries, I'll take you with me when I go.'

'Go? Where to?' Fotik felt perfectly taken aback. He had no idea Harun was thinking of going anywhere.

'Well, I heard from Venkatesh yesterday. He's my friend in the circus. He's asked me to go to Madras and join him. So I was thinking . . . You see, I don't like living like this any more, depending on what money is thrown at me, picking up coins from the ground. It's been a long time since . . .'

' . . . And who is this young assistant you have got here?'

The question came so unexpectedly that Fotik's heart nearly jumped into his mouth.

The two men were standing nearby. They had just emerged out of the dark. On Fotik's right stood Shyamlal, his bow-legs covered by long trousers. Out of the corner of his eye, Fotik saw the blade of a knife flash, go past his ear and stop somewhere between him and Harun.

'Raghu, pick up those coins. These will be enough to settle some of our debts.' The other man began collecting the coins.

'Why, you didn't answer my ques—' Shyamlal could not finish speaking. Fotik saw Harun's bag—filled with four brass balls, three shining knives, and two large tops—rise from the ground like a rocket, and strike against Shyamlal's chin. Shyamlal staggered back and fell.

'Fotik!' He heard Harun's voice, and realized a second later that, like the bag, he had been swept off the ground. Harun was sprinting, bag and Fotik tucked under his arm. In the meantime, a dust storm had started sweeping across the maidan, covering everything around Shaheed Minar. Most people were rushing towards Chowringhee to escape the rain that was bound to start any minute.

'Can you run?' Harun gasped.

'Sure.'

Fotik found his feet back on solid ground once more. He began running, trying to keep pace with Harun. They made their way to a spot where a lot of cars were parked.

'Taxi!' shouted Harun. Fotik heard the slamming of brakes. A black car stopped. Someone opened the door.

'Central Avenue!' Harun shouted as they got in.

There was a lot of traffic in front of them. They could see Shyamlal and Raghunath at some distance behind their taxi, running desperately to catch them. Daylight had almost totally disappeared. Lights had been switched on in the streets and in all the shops.

Their taxi found a gap in the traffic and started moving. 'Press on the accelerator, please. I'll pay you extra!' said Harun.

The driver turned left into Chowringhee and increased his speed. They came to a crossing with traffic lights. It was the main crossing at Dharamtola. The light changed from red to green just as their taxi reached it. They crossed over, passed the office of the electric board on their left, and found themselves in Central Avenue. The road here was much wider. The traffic here was thinner, thank goodness, it being a Sunday. Fotik could feel the wind rush past his ears.

'Faster, please brother, we're being chased!' said Harun. Fotik turned his head at these words and saw the headlights of another taxi, getting larger and closer every second.

'Harun-da, they'll catch up with us!' he cried in dismay.

'No, they won't.'

The wind was so strong that it nearly blocked his ears. The twin lights were growing smaller now. Then they grew hazy. There were raindrops on the glass at the back. Fotik turned around. The windscreen was wet, too. Through it, he could see more lights, all of them travelling in pairs, come close from the opposite direction, and whoosh past their taxi.

Now, there was a pair of lights coming straight towards him. No, it was not a taxi or a car. It was a bus. A huge bus, like a monster. A demon. Those were its eyes. They were getting bigger, and bigger, and bigger. Suddenly, it was not a bus any more. It had become a truck. The buildings that lined the road had disappeared, as had all the lights. All at once, there was nothing, except darkness, darkness . . . and trees, a lot of trees . . . a forest.

'What is it, Fotik? What's the matter? Are you feeling unwell?' Harun's voice was lost in a sea of all the other noises . . . noises he had heard before. The first thing that came back was the explosion caused by one speeding vehicle hitting another, immediately after which he had felt as if he was flying through the air. As he recalled that feeling, a host of other memories rushed forward, vying with one another for his attention. He was free to choose however many he wanted, for now he could recall almost every day of his life—all twelve years of it. 'Your name is Nikhil,' said some of his memories, 'and you are called Bablu at home. Your father's name is Saradindu Sanyal. You have three brothers, and one sister. All of them are older than you. Your sister Chhaya is married. She lives in Switzerland. You have an old grandmother, too. She spends most of her time in her prayer room, reading an old, thick *Mahabharata*, set in verse. She uses a sing-song tone when she reads it aloud, and rocks herself gently. Her reading glasses are set in a golden frame.'

There was Chhorda—Preetindra—telling him, 'Look, that's how you must use your wrist in order to make a straight drive.' And his maths teacher in school—Mr Shukla—was saying, 'Stop it, Manmohan!' Manmohan was always full of mischief, he had a round face and a very sharp brain. Now he could see Vikram, who sat in front of him. Vikram was sharpening his pencil and placing it on his desk; but Bablu was blowing so hard on it from behind him that it kept rolling off the desk . . . On the night of his sister's wedding, someone was playing *shehnai* on a record, but the record was broken. So the needle got stuck at one particular point, and it went on . . . and on . . . and on . . . until all the guests under the *shamiana* stopped eating and burst into laughter.

He could remember all the holidays he had spent away from home—Darjeeling, and Puri, and before that Mussoorie. And long, long before that, when he was much younger, he had stood on the beach in Waltair. He could feel the sand slipping and moving away from under his feet, which felt as if millions of cold and wet ants were tickling them . . . and then just as his mother said, 'Careful, Bablu darling, you might fall!' he promptly did, with a great thud. His mother? No, he could recall nothing about her. She was just a picture in a frame. Once his house was full of people, but now all his brothers had moved out, his sister was abroad. There used to be an uncle who was now in a mental asylum. Now there were only three people in the whole house.

He was back in the taxi. And he could see all the lights again. Harun . . . yes, there he was . . . rolled the window up on his side. 'Are you scared? Hey Fotik, why don't you speak? They've gone, there's no danger now.'

Fotik could hear their neighbour's Alsatian bark. He was called Duke. Bablu was not afraid of Duke. He was very brave. He slept alone in his room. Once, when he was visiting Darjeeling, he had walked alone on the road to Birch Hill. He had gone a long way, but he did not feel afraid, even when a mist came up and covered everything. He could remember that day very well.

'Are you feeling sick?' Harun asked again. 'Or are you upset?' Fotik shook his head. 'What is it, then?' Harun looked concerned.

Fotik looked at Harun. It was still raining outside. The taxi was going quite fast. All the windows were shut, so there was no need to raise his voice to be heard.

'My memory has come back, Harun-da. I can remember everything,' he said softly.

They were now sitting in a small restaurant in Chitpur, eating rotis and meat curry. Fotik had never eaten at a place like this, and he would not have done so, either, if Harun had not brought him here. On their way to Chitpur, Harun had asked him a lot of questions. This time, Fotik had been able to answer them, and had told him all about himself. He had even described how those four men had kidnapped him on his way back from school.

'Can you show me how to get to Loudon Street, where you say your house is? I don't know that area very well,' said Harun.

Fotik laughed. 'Yes, of course, Harun-da. It's quite easy to find.'

'Hmm.'

Harun thought for a while. Then he said, 'There's no reason to go there straightaway. It's quite late, isn't it? Besides, we must do something about your appearance. It would have been better if you hadn't cut your hair, but now that cannot be helped. Tomorrow, you must wear a clean shirt. I will come to the shop as early as I can. Don't say anything to Upen-da. I will talk to him later.'

Fotik could still not think very clearly. But he did realize that he would have to go back home. There was his father, his grandmother, and their old servant, Harinath. Harinath took very good care of him, although he did sometimes treat him as though he was a baby. There were certain things Fotik was quite capable of handling himself, but Harinath would not let him. This annoyed him at times, but Harinath was an old man, so he did not say anything to him.

Then there was his school to consider. All his friends were there . . . the headmaster . . . the chowkidar, Ramkhilavan . . . Mr Datta, their PT teacher. They had all gone on a school picnic one day, to the Botanical Gardens, riding a steamer from Chandpal Ghat.

Suddenly, his mind switched back to his home, and he remembered something that he felt he had to share with Harun. 'You know, Harun-da,' he said, 'there is an empty room on the ground floor in our house. All it has is a broken cupboard and an old table. If those were removed, you could quite easily live in that room.'

Harun cast him a sidelong glance. Then he tore a piece from his roti and put it in his mouth. 'And will your father let me decorate it as I please? Like my room in the slum?'

Fotik thought about his father and his stern demeanour. The recollection did not inspire a lot of confidence. However, he was not to be daunted. People could change, couldn't they? 'Yes, certainly. Why shouldn't he?'

he said.

'Very well. If your father does allow that, I'll have to admit he has the spirit of an artist. Without that, no one will ever be able to understand the whims of Harun-al-Rashid.'

11

The next morning, the news of a tragic railway accident in Satragachhi covered most of the front page in every newspaper. As a result, most people read only that particular report, thereby failing to notice the advertisement that was printed on the last page. Those whose eyes did fall on it had to admit that the reward offered by Saradindu Sanyal to find his missing son was truly handsome, totally in keeping with his status in society. Five thousand rupees was a lot of money.

Upen Babu did not see the advertisement; nor, as it happened, did Harun, although usually he did glance through the paper every morning when he went to the local restaurant for his first cup of tea. This morning, he was not in the mood to pore over a newspaper. Besides, he was in a hurry. He rose at five-thirty, had a quick cup of tea, and arrived at Upen Babu's shop at seven o'clock, to meet Fotik. Perhaps it was not quite right to call him Fotik any more. But Harun could not possibly think of him as Nikhil, or Bablu, or even Sanyal. For him, he had only one name: Fotikchandra Pal.

'You want to take Fotik somewhere, so early in the morning? Where are you going to take him?' Upen Babu asked, not unreasonably.

'We have to go to Loudon Street. I'll explain when I get back,' Harun said hurriedly. Upen Babu knew Harun did strange things sometimes. But he was a good man, so he said nothing more. He looked at Keshto's son, Shotu, who had just woken up and was stretching lazily. 'Come on!' Upen Babu said to him. 'Stop thrashing your arms about. Go and wash your face—there's work to be done.'

Saradindu Sanyal said to his clerk, Rajani Babu, 'Look at the way they've printed Bablu's photo. I can't recognize my own son! It was such a good photo, too. The quality of printing in our newspapers has become much worse, I have to say. Each is as bad as the other.'

'Have you seen this one, sir?' Rajani Babu offered his boss an English daily. 'The picture is far more clear in this one.'

There was a pile of newspapers in front of Mr Sanyal. Rajani Babu had been instructed to buy every newspaper that carried Bablu's photo. Normally, Rajani Babu arrived at eight-thirty. Today, he was here much earlier than that, in order to help his boss deal with extra visitors. It was Saradindu Sanyal's belief that as soon as people read about the reward being offered, they would storm his house with young boys in tow, claiming to have found Bablu. So he had asked Rajani Babu and his junior, Tapan Sarkar, to join forces with Preetin and their bearer, Kishorilal. They needed all the help they could get to make sure that the whole thing did not get out of control. But Mr Sarkar had not yet turned up, and Preetin was still asleep. He had stayed up late to study for his exams. He was supposed to return to Kharagpur in the afternoon.

A taxi stopped outside their front door. Mr Sanyal put his cup of coffee down on his table and sighed. 'Here we go,' he said. 'That must be the first one.' Little did he know that the first would turn out to be the last.

'Baba!' said a voice. It sounded like Bablu's voice!

Mr Sanyal glanced quickly at the curtain at his door. A second later, Bablu pushed it aside and entered the room. 'You! Where have you been? Who brought you back? What happened? Your hair! What did you do to your hair?' Mr Sanyal asked one question after another without pausing for breath. Then he leaned back in his chair, every taut muscle in his body suddenly relaxing. He heaved a deep sigh of relief. The answers did not matter. What mattered was that his son was back safely.

His eyes went back to the curtain. Through a gap, he could see a man standing outside. 'Please come in,' he invited. He wanted to meet whoever had brought Bablu back. There was the matter of the reward to be settled.

The man stepped in. Mr Sanyal turned to Rajani Babu. 'Please tell the chowkidar not to let anyone in if they try to talk about my missing son. Everyone should be told that he has come back.'

Rajani Babu left. Mr Sanyal looked properly at the man who had just come in. Could he be described as a gentleman? No. His shirt was both cheap and dirty, his chappals worn, and his white cotton trousers badly crushed. Besides, his hair and sideburns . . . here, Mr Sanyal had to stop for a minute. Perhaps the hair and the length of his sideburns might be discounted, for they were no different from what his own sons sported.

'Come closer,' he commanded. 'What's your name?'

'He's Harun-da, Baba. He's a performer. He's just brilliant!' Bablu blurted out.

Mr Sanyal glanced at his son, with whom he had just been reunited. 'Let him speak for himself, Bablu,' he said, sounding faintly annoyed. 'Why don't you go upstairs? Go and see Grandma. She's suffered a lot in the last few days. And wake Preetin. He's still sleeping.'

But Bablu had no wish to leave quite so soon. How could he leave Harun here? He went out of the room but stood in the corridor outside. His father could not see him but Bablu could hear everything that was said. He could even see Harun's back.

Mr Sanyal looked at the man once more. 'Tell me what happened. How did you find my son?'

'I found him in Kharagpur. He was trying to jump into a moving train. I helped him up. He spent the last few days here in Calcutta.'

'Here?'

'Yes, in Bentinck Street. In a tea shop.'

'A tea shop?' Mr Sanyal made no attempt to hide his shock and amazement. 'What was he doing in a tea shop?'

'Working.'

'Working? What kind of work?' Mr Sanyal could hardly believe his ears.

Harun explained. Mr Sanyal had very little hair on his head. Had he had a little more, he would probably have torn each strand.

'What is all this? What are you talking about?' he shouted, rising to his feet. 'You made him work as a waiter in a tea shop? Don't you have any sense at all? Couldn't you see he was from a decent family? Is that what boys from good families do?'

Bablu could no longer contain himself. He rushed back into the room. 'I liked my work. Honestly, I was very good at it!' he cried.

'Stay out of this!' Mr Sanyal roared. 'Didn't I just tell you to go upstairs?'

Bablu had to go out of the room again. He could not have imagined such a thing would happen on his return.

Harun was still standing quietly. When he spoke, his tone was gentle. 'If I knew what kind of a family he came from, I would never have kept him with me. But he could tell me nothing about himself. He did not remember a single thing.'

'And what happened today? All his memories came back the minute you saw the newspaper?' It was clear from the way Mr Sanyal spoke that he did not believe Harun at all.

Harun was surprised. 'The newspaper?' he asked, puzzled. 'I don't know what a newspaper has to do with this, but his memory came back last night. When he told me everything it was late and still raining pretty heavily. So I decided to wait until this morning. Now I have brought him back to you, and my duty is over. There's just one thing I ought to mention before I go. There is a swelling on his head, which causes him pain at times. You may wish to consult a doctor. Goodbye, sir. Hey, Fotik, I am going. Goodbye!'

Harun left. Bablu continued to stand in the corridor, trying to grasp what had just happened. Before he could do so, his father called him back. 'Bablu, come here for a minute.'

He went back to the room and moved closer to his father. Mr Sanyal stretched out an arm. 'Where is it swollen?' Bablu showed him. Harun was right. The swelling had subsided, but was not gone completely. Mr Sanyal did not touch the spot, in case it hurt.

'Did you have a hard time?' he asked his son.

Bablu shook his head, indicating that there had been no problems.

'Very well. Now go upstairs. Tell Harinath to give you a hot bath. I will get Dr Bose to examine you today. If he says everything is all right, you can start going to school from tomorrow. But from now on, you will go everywhere by car. Go on, go and find Harinath.' Bablu left. Mr Sanyal pushed aside the great pile of newspapers on his table and said, 'A tea shop! Pooh!' Rajani Babu had returned some time ago. Mr Sanyal turned to him. 'Can you imagine? My son worked in a tea shop!'

Rajani Babu could think of only one thing, although he did not dare mention it to his employer. The man who had brought Bablu back had obviously not seen the offer of five thousand rupees. Mr Sanyal had simply taken advantage of his ignorance and done nothing to pay him even a single paisa. It was hardly the right thing to do.

About an hour later, Inspector Chand called. 'Did anyone contact you, sir, after seeing your advertisement?' he asked anxiously. When he heard Mr Sanyal's reply, he was astounded. 'This is excellent news, sir, but really, it's all quite incredible. There are times when no solution seems to present itself and then something comes up as if by magic. Your son has been found, and those two culprits have been arrested.'

'What! How did that happen?'

'We received an anonymous call, from a man. He told us where the two were hiding. So we went and picked them up. They were still sleeping. But it did not take them long to wake up when they were brought to the police station. They've now made a full confession.'

The inspector rang off. Within ten minutes, Mr Sanyal was immersed in his work. The whole business of his son's disappearance was wiped out of his mind.

When Bablu went upstairs and found his grandmother, all she could do was hold him close and stroke his head, touching repeatedly the very spot where it hurt the most. 'Thank God! Oh, thank God, my precious. We've got you back, my darling. God is very kind.' She soon rushed back to her prayer room, to offer her thanks yet again. Bablu realized afresh that although his grandmother lived in this house, her mind roamed in a different world.

Preetin left for Kharagpur at two o'clock. Before going, he said, 'I can't believe it. You were in Kharagpur, roaming in the streets, unable to remember either Baba's name or your own and there I was, only a mile away and yet I was clueless. If I could get my hands on those scoundrels . . . one karate chop would have finished them. Anyway, I am going to leave you with some homework. Why don't you write everything down? I mean, now that you can remember what happened, I think you should write a complete account. You are quite good at writing essays, aren't you? Write it up and I will read it on my next visit.'

Left on his own, Bablu felt at a loose end. There was nothing for him to do, or look at. He knew every room, every corridor, every nook and corner of this house. In his own room, there was a damp patch high on the wall that looked a little like the map of Africa. Today, he glanced at it curiously and saw that it had spread somewhat, and now looked like North America.

Dr Bose arrived an hour later. He was plump and cheerful. A smile always seemed to be lurking on his face, even when there was no cause for amusement. Once, Bablu's temperature had shot up to 104 degrees. Even then, when Dr Bose came, he appeared to be smiling. Preetin had told Bablu later that it was simply the structure of Dr Bose's face and his facial muscles that had given him a permanent smile.

Today, Harinath came with him, carrying his bag. Rajani Babu was also there, and Grandma was peering from behind the curtain. His father was still at court. The doctor beamed at Bablu and said, 'Do you know how much you are worth? If there were five of you, you would be the same price as a new Ambassador.'

At first, Bablu failed to get his meaning. Slowly understanding dawned when the doctor finished his examination, patted his back and turned to Rajani Babu. 'Who is the lucky guy?' he asked. 'Five thousand rupees is no joke, is it?' At this, Rajani Babu shifted uncomfortably, cleared his throat and said, 'Well, yes . . . a man brought him back. But . . . er . . . I didn't catch his name.' Dr Bose sensed immediately that there was something wrong, and asked no further questions. 'All right, Bablu, I will come back another time and hear the whole story from you,' he said and took his leave. Rajani Babu and Harinath went with him.

Bablu slowly realized that his father had deceived Harun. Bablu did not read a newspaper every day, but he had read them often enough in the past to know that, in addition to the sports page and information on films and film stars, they sometimes carried advertisements and notices regarding missing people. Cash awards were offered to track them down. Had his father done something similar?

He went downstairs again. All the newspapers were kept in his father's office. It took him only a few minutes to realize that as many as ten papers in five different languages were carrying his picture. It was the one Preetin had taken of him in Darjeeling. Five thousand rupees had been offered to anyone who could bring news of Nikhil Sanyal, age twelve, pet name Bablu.

Harun had not seen this advertisement, so he had not bothered to wait for the payment. But he deserved to be paid. Bablu's father had done something very wrong by not giving him what was rightfully his.

This made Bablu feel so depressed that he had to go out into the garden and sit quietly under the guava tree. He did not feel like talking to anyone. How could his father do this? With five thousand rupees in his pocket, Harun could have bought many more things to add to his show; he could have moved to a better place, found a bigger room. He would not have had to worry about money for a long time. He could have just enjoyed himself.

Perhaps he had seen that notice by now. What would he be thinking?

Bablu returned to the house. Here was their drawing room. It was huge, filled with sofas, chairs, tables, pictures, statues and vases. Everything looked drab, there was no colour anywhere that might lift one's spirits. The covers on the sofas were dirty. No one had changed them for a long time. Had his sister been around, she might have noticed those covers and had them cleaned. There was no one left now to worry about such things.

Bablu sat alone on a sofa for quite some time. The clock on the wall struck four. Duke barked from the house next door. Perhaps he had seen another dog outside in the street. Harun had called him a stray dog. In his present frame of mind, even being a stray appeared to be a better option to Bablu.

12

At four-thirty, Harinath came down with a cup of tea in his hand, and discovered that Bablu was not at home. This did not worry him unduly; he assumed that Bablu had gone to see his friend who lived only three houses away. No doubt he had many things to tell his friend. He would soon be back.

Harinath was right in thinking that Bablu had gone to look for his friend. But it was not the friend who lived nearby. He had given their chowkidar the slip, and sneaked out of the house by climbing over the wall behind their garden. Then he went down Loudon Street, Park Street, Lower Circular Road, and finally found CIT Road. He had to ask a number of people before he could find that bridge. Then he went down the steps, and a little later, saw a tubewell where a lot of women were filling their buckets. He remembered having seen that tubewell before. Harun's room could not be far from here. Only a second later, however, he ran into some of the local boys who recognized him. 'Are you looking for Harun? He's gone!' they said.

Gone? Bablu's heart sank. He could not speak for several seconds. 'Where has he gone?' he finally managed. This time, an old man in a lungi emerged from an equally old house, crumbling with age. 'You want Harun? He's gone to catch a train to Madras. A circus company there wants him.'

Bablu realized he would have to go to Howrah Station. But how was he going to get there? 'You'll need bus number ten,' said one of the boys. Then they took him back to the main road, on the other side of the railway line, and showed him where the bus stop was.

The money Upen Babu had paid him as advance was still in his pocket. He had not spent any of it. Now it came in handy to pay for his bus ticket to Howrah, and to buy a platform ticket at the station.

What if Harun's train had left already?

'Where's the train to Madras? Which platform? Please, someone help me!' Bablu cried, his heart thudding fast.

'Madras? Platform number seven,' answered a voice. 'Look, there it is!'

The train was so long that it covered the entire length of the platform. It appeared to be taking a deep breath before starting its long journey. Dusk had just started to fall. Bablu pushed his way forward, still panting and looking around wildly. This was a third class compartment . . . and another . . . and another . . . and now it said first class . . . where on earth could he find Harun? Bablu kept going, dodging coolies with heavy luggage, jumping over trunks and suitcases, pushing aside people who blocked his way. Then he came to a tea stall and stopped abruptly.

A lot of people were gathered round the stall. Bablu could see three empty teacups rise above their heads, go down and rise again. Everyone was laughing and clapping.

There were a few minutes left before the train's departure. So Harun was holding a little show. Bablu made his way through the crowd, and stood facing him.

'You! What are you doing here?' asked Harun, raising his voice, for his audience was still cheering loudly. Then he returned the cups to the owner of the stall, and turned back to Bablu.

'Did you go to that slum? And they told you I had gone?'

Bablu did not reply. Harun went on speaking. 'Remember that letter from Venkatesh I told you about? Well, I thought things over and decided it would be foolish to miss this chance. They want me to ride a monocycle, and juggle with various objects, with a blindfold on. I need to practise for at least a month. So I had to leave immediately.'

Bablu opened his mouth to tell him about the money he could claim, then thought better of it. Harun had found a new opportunity. Perhaps now he was going to earn a lot more. He seemed cheerful enough. What if a mention of the five thousand rupees caused him grief and disappointment? But what about his own sadness? Should he tell Harun about it? As it turned out, he did not have to. One look at his face told Harun everything.

'You don't like being back home, do you?' he asked.

'No, Harun-da.'

'Fotik keeps coming back, doesn't he? And he says, how nice it would be if you could stay on at the tea shop. You could meet so many people, and you wouldn't have to go to school. And then Harun-da would have taken you to his shows, and both of you could have roamed the streets together. Isn't that what young Fotik has been telling you?'

Harun was absolutely right. Bablu nodded.

'Pay no attention to Fotik,' Harun said firmly. 'If you do not tell him to shut up, he won't let you finish your studies. And that would be a disaster. You cannot imagine how deeply I have regretted not having finished school, or studying further.'

'But how does it matter? You are so gifted. You are an artist.'

'There are different kinds of artists, dear boy. You don't necessarily have to be a juggler. You can stay in your beautiful home, receive a good education, and still be an artist. Art does not begin and end with wooden balls, don't you see? You can play with words, or colour, or music, there are endless possibilities, believe me. When you are older, you will realize which is best for you, you will then develop your own style, and you will know when to . . .'

The guard's whistle rang out, drowning out Harun's remaining words. Bablu could no longer contain himself. He had to tell Harun, he must. So he shouted, interrupting what Harun was still trying to tell him, and said, 'Baba did not pay you the money you deserved, Harun-da! Five thousand rupees. Aren't you going to claim it?'

By this time, Harun had climbed into his coach, but he stopped for a second at the door. Then he turned back and grinned. 'What did they do to your photo?' he asked, leaning forward. 'You looked like a goblin!'

Harun-da knew! He had seen the papers.

The driver blew the whistle this time. Harun went into his compartment but Bablu could still speak to him through a window. 'Tell your father,' Harun said, 'that I would not normally refuse an offer of five thousand rupees. But . . . in the last few days, I have come to look upon you as a brother. Tell me, can anyone sell his brother?'

The train started. Bablu could not think straight. But he could still hear Harun's voice:

'The Great Diamond Circus . . . don't forget the name. When it comes to Calcutta, you must go and see the blind juggler on a cycle!'

'You . . . you will come back here?'

Bablu was now running on the platform, trying to keep pace with the moving train. He would have to give up soon.

'Of course,' Harun replied. 'I will have to. No other city in the whole country appreciates a circus as much as Calcutta does. I will be back, never fear.'

Harun was waving.

He was moving further and further away.

Then he slowly disappeared. The train pulled out of the platform.

There it was—a round, green light. It was called a signal. Bablu could now remember the word easily enough. It meant the line was clear.

He wiped his tears on his sleeve, slowly moving toward the exit. In his pocket were two wooden balls. And in his heart was a man. He would cherish his memories always; he knew that in future this man would help him in whatever he did.

The name of the man was Fotikchandra Pal.

Translated by Gopa Majumdar

First published in Bengali in 1975

Ashamanja Babu's Dog

On a visit to a friend in Hashimara, Ashamanja Babu was able to fulfil one of his long-cherished desires.

Ashamanja Babu lived in a small flat on Mohini Mohan Road in Bhowanipore. A clerk in the registry department of Lajpat Rai Post Office, Ashamanja Babu was fortunate as he could walk to his office in seven minutes flat without having to fight his way into the buses and trains of Calcutta. He lived a rather carefree life as he was not the kind of person to sit and brood about what might have been had Fate been kinder to him. On the whole, he was quite content with his lot. Two Hindi films and a dozen packets of cigarettes a month, and fish twice a week—these were enough to keep him happy. The only thing that perturbed him at times was his lack of companionship. A bachelor with few friends and relatives, he often wished he had a dog to keep him company. It need not be a huge Alsatian like the one owned by the Talukdars, who lived two houses down the lane, it could be any ordinary little dog which would follow him around morning and evening, wag its tail when he came home from work and obey his orders with alacrity. Ashamanja Babu's secret desires were that he would speak to his dog in English. 'Stand up', 'Sit down', 'Shake hands'—how nice it would be if his dog obeyed such commands! Ashamanja Babu liked to believe that dogs belonged to the English race. Yes, an English dog, and he would be its master. That would make him really happy.

On a cloudy day marked by a steady drizzle, Ashamanja Babu went to the market in Hashimara to buy some oranges. At one end of the market, beside a stunted kul tree, sat a Bhutanese holding a cigarette between his thumb and forefinger. As their eyes met, the man smiled. Was he a beggar? His clothes made him look like one. Ashamanja Babu noticed at least five sewn-on patches on his trousers and jacket. But the man didn't have a begging bowl. Instead, by his side was a shoe-box with a little pup sticking its head out of it.

'Good morning!' said the man in English, his eyes reduced to slits as he smiled. Ashamanja Babu was obliged to return the greeting.

'Buy dog? Dog buy? Very good dog.' The man had taken the pup out of the box and had put it down on the ground. 'Very cheap. Very good. Happy dog.'

The pup shook the raindrops off its coat, looked at Ashamanja Babu and wagged its minuscule two-inch tail. Ashamanja Babu moved closer to the pup, crouched on the ground and stretched out his hand. The pup gave his ring finger a lick with its pink tongue. Nice, friendly dog.

'How much? What price?'

'Ten rupees.'

A little haggling, and the price came down to seven-fifty. Ashamanja Babu paid the money, put the pup back in the shoe-box, closed the lid to save it from the drizzle, and turned homewards, forgetting all about the oranges.

Biren Babu, who worked in the Hashimara State Bank, had no idea about his friend's wish to own a dog. He was naturally surprised and a bit alarmed to see what the shoe-box contained. But when he heard the price, he heaved a sigh of relief. He said in a tone of mild reprimand, 'Why come all the way to Hashimara to buy a mongrel? You could easily have bought one in Bhowanipore.'

That was not true; Ashamanja Babu knew it. He had often seen mongrel pups in the streets in his neighbourhood. None of them had ever wagged its tail at him or licked his fingers. Whatever Biren might say, this dog was something special. But the fact that the pup was a mongrel was something of a disappointment to Ashamanja Babu too, and he said so. Biren Babu's retort came sharp and quick. 'But do you know what it means to keep a pedigree dog as a pet? The vet's fees alone would cost you half a month's salary. With this dog you have no worries. You don't even need to give it a special diet. He'll eat what you eat. But don't give him fish. Fish is for cats; dogs have trouble with fish-bones.'

Back in Calcutta, it occurred to Ashamanja Babu that he had to think of a name for the pup. He wanted to give it an English name, but the only one he could think of was Tom. Then, looking at the pup one day, it struck him that since it was brown in colour, Brownie would be a good name for it. A cousin of his had a camera of an English make called Brownie, so the name must be an English one. The moment he decided on the name and tried it on the pup, it jumped off a wicker stool and padded up to him wagging its tail. Ashamanja Babu said, 'Sit down,' and immediately the dog sat on its haunches and opened its mouth in a tiny yawn. Ashamanja Babu had a fleeting vision of Brownie winning the first prize for cleverness in a dog show.

It was lucky that his servant Bipin had also taken a fancy to the dog. While Ashamanja Babu was away at work, Bipin gladly took it upon himself to look after Brownie. Ashamanja Babu had warned Bipin against feeding the dog rubbish. 'And see that he doesn't go out into the street. Car drivers these days seem to wear blinkers.' But however much he might instruct his servant, his worry would linger until he returned from work, and Brownie greeted him ecstatically, his tail wagging fast.

The incident took place three months after returning from Hashimara. It was a Saturday, and the date was November the twenty-third. Ashamanja Babu had just got back from work and sat down on the old wooden chair—the only piece of furniture in the room apart from the bed and the wicker stool—when it suddenly collapsed under him and sent him sprawling on the floor. Naturally, he was hurt and, in fact, was wondering if, like the rickety leg of the chair, his right elbow was also out of commission, when an unexpected sound made him forget all about his pain.

It had come from the bed. It was the sound of laughter or, more accurately, a giggle, the source of which was undoubtedly Brownie, who sat on the bed, his lips still curled up.

If Ashamanja Babu's general knowledge had been wider, he would surely have known that dogs never laughed. And if he had any modicum of imagination, the incident would have robbed him of his sleep. In the absence of either, what Ashamanja Babu did was to sit down with the book *All About Dogs* which he had bought for two rupees from a second-hand book shop in Free School Street. He searched for an hour but found no mention in the book of laughing dogs.

And yet there wasn't the slightest doubt that Brownie had laughed. Not only that, he had laughed because there had been cause for laughter. Ashamanja Babu could clearly recall a similar incident from his own childhood. A doctor had come on a visit to their house in Chandernagore and had sat on a chair which had collapsed under him. Ashamanja Babu had burst out in a fit of laughter, and as a result had his ears twisted by his father.

He shut the book and looked at Brownie. As their eyes met, Brownie put his front paws on the pillow and wagged his tail, which had grown an inch and a half longer in three months. There was no trace of a smile on his face now. Why should there be? To laugh without reason was a sign of madness. Ashamanja Babu felt relieved that Brownie was not a mad dog.

On two more occasions within a week of this incident, Brownie had reason to laugh. The first took place at night, at around nine-thirty. Ashamanja Babu had just spread a white sheet on the floor for Brownie to sleep on when a cockroach came fluttering into the room and settled on the wall. Ashamanja Babu picked up a slipper and flung it at the insect. The slipper missed its target, landed on the mirror hanging on the wall, and sent it crashing to the floor. This time Brownie's laughter more than compensated for the loss of his mirror.

The second time it was not laughter, but a brief snicker. Ashamanja Babu was puzzled, nothing had happened. So why the snicker? His servant Bipin provided the answer when he came into the room. He glanced at his master and said, smiling, 'There's shaving soap right by your ears, sir.' With his mirror broken, Ashamanja Babu had to use one of the window panes for shaving. He now felt with his fingers and found that Bipin was right.

That Brownie should laugh even when the reason was so trifling surprised Ashamanja Babu a great deal. Sitting at his desk in the post office, he found his thoughts turning again and again to the smile on Brownie's face and the sound of the snicker. *All About Dogs* may say nothing about a dog's laughter, but if he could get hold of something like an encyclopaedia of dogs, there was sure to be a mention of laughter in it.

When four book shops in Bhowanipore—and all the ones in New Market—failed to produce such an encyclopaedia, Ashamanja Babu wondered whether he should call on Mr Rajani Chatterji. The retired professor lived not far from his house on the same street. Ashamanja Babu didn't know what subject Rajani Babu had taught, but he had seen through the window of his house many fat books in a bookcase in what appeared to be the professor's study.

So, on a Sunday morning, Ashamanja Babu offered up a silent prayer to goddess Durga for help in this adventure, and made his way to Professor Chatterji's house. He had seen him several times from a distance, and had no idea he had such thick eyebrows and a voice so grating. But since the professor didn't turn him away from the door, Ashamanja Babu took courage and sat himself down on a sofa opposite the professor. Then he gave a short cough and waited. Professor Chatterji put aside the newspaper he was reading and turned his attention to the visitor.

'Your face seems familiar.'

'I live close by.'

'I see. Well?'

'I have seen a dog in your house; that is why . . .'

'So what? We have two dogs, not one.'

'I see, I have one too.'

'Are you employed to count the number of dogs in the city?'

Ashamanja Babu missed the sarcasm in the question. He said, 'I have come to ask if you have something I've been looking for.'

'What is it?'

'I wonder if you have a dog encyclopaedia.'

'No, I don't. Why do you need one?'

'You see, my dog laughs. So I wanted to find out if it was natural for dogs to laugh. Do your dogs laugh?'

Throughout the time it took the wall clock in the room took to strike eight, Professor Chatterji looked steadily at Ashamanja Babu. Then he asked, 'Does your dog laugh at night?'

'Well, yes—even at night.'

'And what are your preferences in drugs? Only ganja can't produce such symptoms. Perhaps you take charas and hashish as well?'

Ashamanja Babu meekly answered that his only vice was smoking—and even that he had had to reduce from three packets a week to two ever since the arrival of his dog.

'And yet you say your dog laughs?'

'I have seen and heard him laugh, with my own eyes and ears.'

'Listen.' Professor Chatterji took off his spectacles, cleaned them with his handkerchief, put them on again and fixed Ashamanja Babu with a hard stare. Then he declaimed in the tones of a classroom lecture:

'I am amazed at your ignorance concerning a fundamental fact of nature. Of all the creatures created by God, only the human species is capable of laughter. This is one of the prime differences between *Homo sapiens* and other creatures. Don't ask me why it should be so, because I do not know. I have heard that a marine species called the dolphin has a sense of humour. Dolphins may be the single exception. Apart from them there are none. It is not clearly understood why human beings should laugh. Great philosophers have racked their brains to find out why; but have not succeeded. Do you understand?'

Ashamanja Babu understood; he also understood that it was time for him to take his leave because the professor had once again picked up his newspaper and disappeared behind it.

Doctor Sukhomoy Bhowmick—some called him Doctor Bow-wow-mick—was a well-known vet. Hoping that a vet might listen to him even if other people didn't, Ashamanja Babu made an appointment on the phone and took Brownie to the vet's residence on Gokhale Road. Brownie had laughed seventeen times in the last four months. One thing Ashamanja Babu had noticed was that Brownie didn't laugh at funny remarks; only at funny incidents. Ashamanja Babu had recited the nonsense-rhyme 'King of Bombardia' to Brownie, and it had produced no effect on him. And yet when a potato from a curry slipped from Ashamanja Babu's fingers and landed in a plate of curd, Brownie had almost choked with laughter. Professor Chatterji had lectured him about God's creatures but here was living proof that the learned gentleman was wrong.

So Ashamanja Babu went to the vet, though he knew that he would be charged twenty rupees for the visit. But even before the vet heard of the dog's unique trait, his eyebrows had shot up at the dog's appearance. 'I've seen mongrels, but never one like this.'

He lifted the dog and placed him on the table. Brownie sniffed at the brass paperweight at his feet.

'What do you feed him?'

'He eats what I eat, sir. He has no pedigree, you see . . .'

Doctor Bhowmick frowned. He was observing the dog with great interest. 'We can tell a pedigree dog when we see one. But sometimes we are not so sure. This one, for instance. I would hesitate to call him a mongrel. I suggest that you stop feeding him rice and daal. I'll make a diet chart for him.'

Ashamanja Babu now made an attempt to come out with the real reason for his visit. 'I—er, my dog has a speciality—which is why I have brought him to you.'

'Speciality?'

'The dog laughs.'

'Laughs—?'

'Yes, laughs, like you and me.'

'You don't say! Well, can you make him laugh now, so I can see?'

Now Ashamanja Babu was stumped. By nature a shy person, he was quite unable to make faces at Brownie to make him laugh, nor was it likely that something funny should happen here at this very moment. So he had to tell the doctor that Brownie didn't laugh when asked to, but only when he saw something funny happening.

After this Doctor Bhowmick didn't have much time left for Ashamanja

Babu. He said, 'Your dog looks distinctive enough; don't try to make him more so by claiming that he laughs. I can tell you from my twenty-two years' experience that dogs cry, dogs feel afraid, dogs show anger, hatred, distrust and jealousy. Dogs even dream, but dogs don't laugh.'

After this encounter, Ashamanja Babu decided that he would never tell anyone about Brownie's laughter again. Why court embarrassment when he could not prove his story? What did it matter if others never knew? He himself knew. Brownie was his dog, his own property. Why drag outsiders into their private world?

But things don't always go according to plans. One day, Brownie's laughter was revealed to an outsider.

For some time, Ashamanja Babu had developed the habit of taking Brownie for a walk in the afternoon near the Victoria Memorial. One April day, in the middle of their walk, a big storm came up suddenly. Ashamanja Babu glanced at the sky and decided that it wasn't safe to try to get back home as the rain would start pelting down any minute. So he ran with Brownie and took shelter below the marble arch with the black equestrian statue on it.

Meanwhile, huge drops of rain had started to fall and people were looking for shelter. A stout man in a white bush shirt and trousers, twenty paces away from the arch, opened his umbrella and held it over his head when a sudden strong gust of wind turned the umbrella inside out with a loud snap.

To tell the truth, Ashamanja Babu himself was about to burst out laughing, but Brownie beat him to it with a loud canine guffaw the sound of which rose above the cacophony of the storm and reached the ear of the hapless gentleman. The man stopped trying to bring the umbrella back to its original shape and stared at Brownie in utter amazement. Brownie was now quite helpless with laughter. Ashamanja Babu had tried frantically to suppress it by clapping his hand over the dog's mouth, but had given up.

The dumbfounded gentleman walked over to Ashamanja Babu as if he had seen a ghost. Brownie's paroxysm was now subsiding, but it was still enough to make the gentleman's eyes pop out of his head.

'A laughing dog!'

'Yes, a laughing dog,' said Ashamanja Babu.

'But how extraordinary!'

Ashamanja Babu could make out that the man was not a Bengali. Perhaps he was a Gujrati or a Parsi. Ashamanja Babu braced himself to answer in English the questions he knew he would soon be bombarded with.

The rain had turned into a heavy shower. The gentleman took shelter alongside Ashamanja Babu, and in ten minutes had found out all there was to know about Brownie. He also took down Ashamanja Babu's address. He said his name was Piloo Pochkanwalla, that he knew a lot about dogs and wrote about them occasionally, and that his experience today had surpassed anything that had ever happened to him, or was likely to happen in the future. He felt something had to be done about it, since Ashamanja Babu himself was obviously unaware of what a priceless treasure he owned.

It wouldn't be wrong to say that Brownie was responsible for Mr Pochkanwalla being knocked down by a minibus while crossing Chowringhee Road soon after the rain had stopped—it was the thought of the laughing dog running through his head which made him a little unmindful of the traffic. After spending two and half months in hospital, Pochkanwalla went off to Nainital to recuperate. He came back to Calcutta after a month in the hills, and the same evening, he made his way to the Bengal Club and described the incident of the laughing dog to his friends Mr Balaporia and Mr Biswas. Within half an hour, the story had reached the ears of twenty-seven other members and three bearers of the club. By next morning, the incident was known to at least a thousand citizens of Calcutta.

Brownie hadn't laughed once during these three and a half months. One good reason was that he had seen no funny incidents. Ashamanja Babu didn't see it as cause for alarm; it had never crossed his mind to cash in on Brownie's unique gift. He was happy with the way Brownie had filled a yawning gap in his life, and felt more drawn to him than he had to any human being.

Among those who got the news of the laughing dog was an executive in the office of the *Statesman*. He sent for reporter Rajat Chowdhury and suggested that he should interview the owner of this laughing dog.

Ashamanja Babu was greatly surprised that a reporter should think of calling on him. It was when Rajat Chowdhury mentioned Pochkanwalla that the reason for the visit became clear. He asked the reporter into his bedroom. The wooden chair had been fitted with a new leg, and Ashamanja Babu offered it to the reporter while he himself sat on the bed. Brownie had been observing a line of ants crawling up the wall; he now jumped up on the bed and sat beside Ashamanja Babu.

Rajat Chowdhury was about to press the recording switch on his tape recorder when it suddenly occurred to Ashamanja Babu that a word of warning was needed. 'By the way, sir, my dog used to laugh quite frequently, but in the last few months he hasn't laughed at all. So you may be disappointed if you are expecting to see him laugh.'

Like many a young energetic reporter, Rajat Chowdhury exuded a cheerful confidence in the presence of a good story. Although he was slightly disappointed, he was careful not to show it. He said, 'That's all right. I just want to get some details from you. To start with, his name. What do you call your dog?'

Ashamanja Babu bent down to speak closer to the mike. 'Brownie.'

'Brownie . . .'

The watchful eye of the reporter had noted that the dog had wagged his tail at the mention of his name. 'How old is he?'

'Thirteen months.'

'Where did you f-f-find the dog?'

This had happened before. Rajat Chowdhury's greatest handicap often showed itself in the middle of interviews, causing him no end of embarrassment. Here, too, the same thing might have happened had it not, unexpectedly, helped in drawing out Brownie's special characteristic. Thus Rajat Chowdhury was the second outsider after Pochkanwalla to see with his own eyes a dog laughing like a human being.

The morning of the following Sunday, sitting in his air-conditioned room in the Grand Hotel, Mr William P. Moody of Cincinnati, USA, read in the papers about the laughing dog and at once asked the hotel operator to put him through to Mr Nandy of the Indian Tourist Bureau. That Mr Nandy knew his way about the city had been made abundantly clear in the last couple of days when Mr Moody had occasion to use his services. The *Statesman* had printed the name and address of the owner of the laughing dog and Mr Moody was very anxious to meet this character.

Ashamanja Babu didn't read the *Statesman*. Besides, Rajat Chowdhury hadn't told him when the interview would appear in print, or he might have bought a copy. It was in the fish market that his neighbour Kalikrishna Dutt told him about it.

'You're a fine man,' said Mr Dutt. 'You've been guarding such a treasure in your house for over a year, and you haven't breathed a word to anybody about it? I must drop in at your place some time this evening and say hello to your dog.'

Ashamanja Babu's heart sank. He could see there was trouble ahead. There were many more like Mr Dutt in and around his neighbourhood who read the *Statesman* and who would want to 'drop in and say hello' to his dog. It was a most unnerving prospect.

Ashamanja Babu quickly made up his mind. He would spend the day away from home. So, with Brownie under his arm, for the first time in his life, he called a taxi and headed to the Ballygunge station where he boarded a train to Port Canning. Halfway there, the train pulled up at a station called Palsit. Ashamanja Babu liked the look of the place and got off. He spent the whole day roaming in the quiet bamboo groves and mango orchards and felt greatly refreshed. Brownie, too, seemed to enjoy himself. The gentle smile that played around his lips was something Ashamanja Babu had never noticed before. This was a benign smile, a smile of peace and contentment, a smile of inner happiness. He had read somewhere that a year in the life of a dog equalled seven years in the life of a human being. And yet he could scarcely imagine such tranquil behaviour in such surroundings from a seven-year-old human child.

It was past seven in the evening when Ashamanja Babu got back home. He asked Bipin if anyone had called. So when Bipin said he had to open the door to callers at least forty times, Ashamanja Babu obviously could not help congratulating himself on his foresight. He had just taken off his shoes and asked Bipin for a cup of tea when there was another knock on the front door. 'Oh, hell!' swore Ashamanja Babu. He went to the door and opened it, and found himself staring at a foreigner. 'Wrong number,' he was at the point of saying, when he caught sight of a young Bengali man standing behind the foreigner. 'Whom do you want?'

'You,' said Shyamol Nandy of the Indian Tourist Bureau. 'That is to say, if the dog standing behind you is yours. He certainly looks like the one described in the papers today. May we come in?'

Ashamanja Babu was obliged to ask them into his bedroom. The foreigner sat on the chair, Mr Nandy on the wicker stool, and Ashamanja Babu on his bed. Brownie, who seemed a bit ill at ease, chose to stay outside the threshold; probably because he had never seen two strangers in the room before.

'Brownie! Brownie! Brownie!' The foreigner leaned towards the dog and called him repeatedly. Brownie, with his eyes fixed on the stranger, was unmoved.

Who were these people, Ashamanja Babu was wondering to himself, when Mr Nandy provided the answer. The foreigner was a wealthy and distinguished citizen of the United States whose main purpose in coming to India was to look for old Rolls-Royce cars.

The American had now got off the chair and, sitting on his haunches, was making faces at the dog.

After three minutes of abortive clowning, the man gave up, turned to Ashamanja Babu and asked, 'Is he sick?'

Ashamanja Babu shook his head.

'Does he really laugh?' asked the American.

In case Ashamanja Babu was unable to follow the American's speech, Mr Nandy translated it for him.

'Brownie laughs,' said Ashamanja Babu, 'but only when he feels amused.'

A tinge of red spread over the American's face when Nandy translated Ashamanja Babu's answer to him. In no uncertain terms he let it be known that he wasn't willing to squander any money on the dog unless he had proof that it really laughed. He refused to be saddled with something which might later prove useless. He further let it be known that in his house he had precious objects from China to Peru, and that he had a parrot which spoke only Latin. 'I have brought my cheque book with me to pay for the laughing dog, but only if I have proof that it actually does so.'

He then proceeded to pull out a blue cheque book from his pocket to prove his statement. Ashamanja Babu glanced at it out of the corner of his eyes. Citibank of New York, it said on the cover.

'You would be walking on air,' said Mr Nandy temptingly. 'If you know a way to make the dog laugh, then out with it. This gentleman is ready to pay up to 20,000 dollars. That's two lakhs of rupees.'

The Bible says that God created the universe in six days. A human being, with his imagination, can do the same thing in six seconds. An image floated into Ashamanja Babu's mind at Mr Nandy's words. It was of himself in a spacious air-conditioned office, sitting in a swivel chair with his legs up on the table, the heady smell of hasu-no-hana wafting in through the window. But the image vanished like a pricked balloon at a sudden sound.

Brownie was laughing.

He had never laughed like this before.

'But he is laughing!'

Mr Moody was down on his knees, tense with excitement, watching the extraordinary spectacle. The cheque book came out again and, along with that, his gold Parker pen.

Brownie was still laughing. Ashamanja Babu was puzzled because he couldn't make out the reason for the laughter. Nobody had stammered, nobody had stumbled, nobody's umbrella had turned inside out, and no mirror on the wall had been hit with a slipper. Why then was Brownie laughing?

'You're very lucky,' commented Mr Nandy. 'I think I ought to get a percentage of the sale—wouldn't you say so?'

Mr Moody rose from the floor and sat down on the chair. He said, 'Ask him how he spells his name.'

Although Mr Nandy relayed the question in Bengali, Ashamanja Babu didn't answer, because he had just seen the light, and the light filled his heart with a great sense of wonder. Instead of spelling his name, he said, 'Please tell the foreign gentleman that if he only knew why the dog was laughing, he wouldn't have opened his cheque book.'

'Why don't you tell me?' Mr Nandy snapped in a dry voice. He certainly didn't like the way events were shaping up. If the mission failed, he knew the American's wrath would fall on him.

Brownie had at last stopped laughing. Ashamanja Babu lifted him up on his lap, wiped his tears and said, 'My dog's laughing because the gentleman thinks money can buy everything.'

'I see,' said Mr Nandy. 'So your dog's a philosopher, is he?'

'Yes, sir.'

'That means you won't sell him?'

'No, sir.'

To Mr Moody, Shyamol Nandy only said that the owner had no intention of selling the dog. Mr Moody put the cheque book back in his pocket, slapped the dust off his knees and, on his way out of the room, said with a shake of his head, 'The guy must be crazy!'

When the sound of the American's car had faded away, Ashamanja Babu looked into Brownie's eyes and said, 'I was right about why you laughed, wasn't I?'

Brownie chuckled in assent.

Translated by Satyajit Ray

First published in Bengali in 1978

Load Shedding

Phoni Babu realized shortly before reaching his bus stop that the entire area was plunged in darkness. Another power cut. More load shedding. By the time he had left his office this evening, having worked over-time, it was already a quarter past eight. It had taken him about thirty-five minutes to get to his area from Dalhousie Square. There was no way of telling how long ago the power cut had started, but he knew that it normally took about four hours for the supply to be restored.

Phoni Babu got off the bus and made his way to the lane where he lived. Not a glimmer of light anywhere. Ironically, things appeared to have improved lately. Why, wasn't it only yesterday that his servant, Nabeen, had asked, 'Should I buy a dozen candles today?' And Phoni Babu had replied, 'No, no. I bet the power cuts will start again the minute you get the candles. Don't buy any now.'

This meant that there were no candles in the house. It was sometimes possible to move about in his room on the second floor, aided by the streetlight. But even the streetlights were out today. Phoni Babu did not smoke, and so did not bother to keep a matchbox in his pocket. He had been toying with the idea of buying a torch for some time, but had not got round to doing so.

A three-minute walk down the lane took him to the house where he lived—number 17/2. Carefully stepping over the three pups that lay near the front door, Phoni Babu went through.

He and Nabeen had moved into this block of apartments only a month ago. Each floor of the house had two flats. Phoni Babu noticed while moving towards the staircase that the flickering yellow light of a candle was falling across the veranda from the window of one of the ground floor flats where Gyan Datta lived. The other flat was in total darkness. No one seemed to be around. It was only two days before the Pujas. Perhaps the occupant, Ramanath Babu, had already left for Madhupur—or was it Ghatshila—to spend his holidays.

'Nabeen!' yelled Phoni Babu as he reached the bottom of the stairs. There was no reply. Clearly, Nabeen was not at home. He often left the house as soon as a power cut began.

Phoni Babu began climbing the stairs without waiting for Nabeen. It was possible to see the first few steps in the candlelight, but beyond that it was pitch dark. Not that it bothered him. He knew there were exactly seventy-two steps to be climbed. He had counted them one day for just such an eventuality.

It was strange, how easy it was to go up a flight of stairs if the lights were on. In the darkness, Phoni Babu shivered as his hand fell on something soft, something very different from the wooden banister. Then he forced himself to put his hand back on the railing and realized it was only a towel someone had carelessly hung on it.

The first floor, too, was completely dark, which meant that both flats were empty. In one of them lived Bijan Babu with his wife and two boys. The younger one was very naughty and a remarkable chatterbox. The other flat was occupied by Mahadev Mandal, who owned a shoe shop in College Street. He might have gone to play cards with his friends. And Bijan Babu must have taken his family to a Hindi film, as he occasionally did.

Phoni Babu continued going up the stairs. As he turned right after the sixtieth step, his foot suddenly knocked against what must have been a metal container. The racket it made caused him to halt in his tracks and wait until his heartbeat returned to normal. The remaining twelve steps had to be negotiated with extreme caution.

Now he had to turn left. An empty cage hung where the stairs ended. It had once contained a mynah. Phoni Babu had often asked his next door neighbour, Naresh Biswas, to have the cage removed. There seemed little point in hanging on to the cage when the mynah had died, but Mr Biswas had paid not the slightest attention to him.

Phoni Babu bent his body like a hunchback in order to avoid banging into the cage and groped his way to the door of his own flat.

From somewhere, not very far away, came the strains of a Tagore song.

Perhaps someone in the house next door was playing a transistor. At a moment like this, in this somewhat spooky, all-engulfing darkness, the sound of music brought a little courage to his mind, though Phoni Babu was certainly not afraid of ghosts.

As his fingers fell on the door, he stopped and took the keys out of his pocket. There were two sets of keys. He kept one and Nabeen had the other. It was easy enough to reach for the padlock but to Phoni Babu's surprise, he discovered there was no padlock at all. This was distinctly peculiar since he could remember quite clearly having locked the house as usual, placing the key in his pocket. Was Nabeen responsible for this? Could he have bolted the door from inside and gone to sleep?

Phoni Babu tried knocking on the door and then stood foolishly as it opened at his touch.

'Nabeen!'

Still no answer. Surely he was not sleeping in the dark?

Phoni Babu crossed the threshold and entered his living room. But perhaps it would be wrong to put it like that for what lay beyond the door was impossible to see. Phoni Babu shut his eyes and opened them again. He could feel no difference. Now he could do what he liked with his eyes closed. The darkness seemed as though it were a solid obstruction that must be physically pushed aside.

The wall to the left had a switchboard. The door to the next room was behind this, and a clothes rack stood near the door. Phoni Babu was carrying an umbrella. This would have to be hung from the rack. And he was feeling hot. So he would need to take his shirt off and place it on the rack as well. But, before he did that, he had to take out his wallet from his pocket and put it in the drawer of the table that stood to the left of the rack.

Phoni Babu reached for the switchboard. Although there was no point now in turning the switches on, he did not want to miss the joy of seeing the whole house light up silently when the power came back.

One of the two switches on the board had a loose head. Nabeen had been groping in the dark recently and had felt an electric shock even during a power cut. Phoni Babu's finger nimbly skipped this particular switch and pressed the second one. It was quite pleasant to hear the switch faintly click into place.

Then he passed the switchboard and slipped through the open door to the next room. The rack was fixed on the wall at about the same height as his own . . .

But no.

His groping hand could find no rack. What it did fall upon was something quite different. Not only that, a miscalculated jab made it slip from the wall and crash to the ground.

A picture? Or was it a mirror? Shards lay all around his feet. He was not worried about his feet as they were protected by the slippers he wore, but where had the rack gone? He stood still, trying to think. There was, of course, a picture of Paramahansa in his room but it should have been hanging on the opposite wall. His mirror usually stood on the table.

Nabeen must have moved the furniture around, as was his habit. Phoni Babu did have to tell him off a number of times for moving his slippers from under the table, where he liked to keep them, and putting them elsewhere.

Still puzzled, Phoni Babu placed his old and worn out umbrella on the floor, carefully balancing it against the wall. Then he took the wallet out of his pocket and began walking towards the invisible table. Pieces of broken glass crunched beneath his feet.

Now all he had to do was find a corner of the table, and then finding the drawer would not be difficult.

But he could not find the table. He took another step forward. It was still impossibly dark. Perhaps if he opened the window that faced the street, it might help.

This time his hand struck against something solid.

Furniture of some kind. Yes, it was wooden. But no, not a table. Was it a cupboard?

Yes, here was the handle. A long, vertical one, made of cut glass. Many old cupboards had handles like that. Phoni Babu did have an old cupboard, but what was its handle made of? He failed to remember.

But this cupboard wasn't locked!

He released the handle. The cupboard gently swung open.

It just didn't make any sense. He never left his cupboard unlocked. God knew he possessed no valuables, but his cupboard did contain all his clothes, some old documents and whatever little cash he had.

Had he forgotten to lock the cupboard this morning?

But where was the table? Could it be—?

Yes, that must be it. Phoni Babu suddenly hit upon an explanation. The day before had been a Sunday. It had rained heavily in the afternoon and a small portion of the ceiling had started to leak. Water had dripped on to his table, which was why Nabeen had spread a few newspapers on it. The building was quite old. He would have to tell the landlord to have the roof repaired. Judging by the puddles he had found on the way, it had rained again during the day. If Nabeen had moved the table near the window and shifted the rack to the opposite wall, one must say he had acted with considerable thoughtfulness.

Phoni Babu returned the wallet to his pocket and moved towards the window. Again he collided with an object.

A chair. Nabeen had obviously moved the chair as well.

Phoni Babu gave up. There was no point in trying to find his way in the dark. He might as well sit in the chair and wait until the lights came back.

He sat down. The chair had arms and the seat was made of cane. Wasn't the chair in his room an armless one? No, he must be mistaken. He had realized today how little one noticed or remembered the details of one's own furniture.

He sat facing the door and could see a small square piece of the sky just over the terrace on the other side. It was reflecting faintly the light from the neighbouring areas as yet unaffected by a power cut.

There were no stars for it was still cloudy but at least it gave him something to look at.

Something was ticking in the room. An alarm clock? There was definitely no alarm clock in his room. So how come—? But before he could think any further, an ear-splitting noise made him nearly fall off his chair.

A telephone.

Just behind his head was a table, and on it a telephone, ringing insistently. It pierced through the silent darkness and stopped finally, after a whole minute of complete cacophony.

Phoni Babu did not have a telephone.

One thing had now become clear to him. This was not his room at all. He had walked into someone else's. And with this realization, everything fell into place.

17/2 and 17/3 were two similar blocks of apartments. Both had three storeys, and both were owned by the same man. Phoni Babu had never been inside 17/3, but obviously its design and plan was identical to that of his house. He was now sitting in a room in one of the two flats on the second floor of 17/3. There was no electricity, the front door was open, the cupboard unlocked.

What could it mean? But whatever the implication of these things,

Phoni Babu was not going to let that worry him. He had realized his mistake and must leave at once. He started to rise, but another noise made him fall back into the chair.

It had come from the left, quite close to where he was sitting. It sounded like a box—a tin suitcase, perhaps—being dragged across the floor.

Phoni Babu's throat began to feel dry and his heart was thudding.

A thief!

There was possibly a bed right next to the chair and, under it, a thief. In his haste to get out, he had clearly banged into a tin suitcase kept under the bed.

It was now easy enough to guess why the door and the cupboard were open.

If the thief was armed, Phoni Babu might be in some danger. His only weapon, his umbrella, was now lying beyond his reach. And, in any case, it was so old that if he hit the thief with it, the umbrella was likely to sustain more injuries.

But the thief was now quiet, possibly as a result of having unwittingly revealed his presence.

Phoni Babu felt like kicking himself. What a stupid mistake to have made and what an impossible situation to be in!

A petty thief was unlikely to carry a revolver, but could well have a knife. But, of course, not all thieves were armed. If it was a question of unarmed combat Phoni Babu was not afraid for he had once been a sportsman. But the biggest problem was this power cut. Even the strongest might feel helpless in such utter darkness.

What on earth was he to do? Should he simply get up and walk away? But what if the lights came back just as he reached the stairs? And what if in that instant, the thief tried to get away from one side and the real owner of the flat turned up from the other? If the owner saw he had been burgled, wouldn't he—

Phoni Babu's thoughts came to an abrupt halt.

There were footsteps coming up the stairs. Slow, measured steps.

Almost unconsciously, Phoni Babu began counting. When the other man reached the forty-ninth step, Phoni Babu began to feel convinced that it was indeed the owner of this flat who was coming up the stairs. And, in a flash, he remembered something else: he knew the owner!

Why hadn't he thought of it before? He had once shared the same taxi with him right up to Dalhousie Square. The man had introduced himself as Adinath Sanyal. He was about fifty years of age. He had a stern demeanour, a fair complexion, and he was clad in a fine cotton kurta—greenish eyes below thick, bushy eyebrows.

Sixty-two, sixty-three, sixty-four . . . the footsteps were getting louder.

There were fresh noises inside the room. Someone scurried across the floor and then came a faint 'Ouch!' Perhaps a piece of broken glass had cut into the thief's foot? Serve him right! The faint patch of light visible in the sky was covered for an instant and then it reappeared. The thief had turned to the right. He had no choice but to jump out of the window and go down the pipe.

The footsteps were now outside on the veranda. Phoni Babu rose, and walked towards the door, taking great care not to step on the shards of glass. Then he picked up his umbrella and went into the living room.

The footsteps stopped just outside the front door. Then, after a few moments of silence, came an explosion, 'What! Why is the door . . .?'

The unmistakable raucous voice of Adinath Sanyal. He had talked quite a lot in the taxi.

There were other things about him that Phoni Babu could now recollect. His own next door neighbour, Naresh Biswas, had once told him that Adinath Sanyal had pots of money stacked away somewhere. Apparently, he owned three houses in Calcutta. All were rented out and he himself lived in these two rooms. The way he earned his living was reportedly not a straightforward one. The drawers of his table and the shelves of his cupboard were supposed to be filled with black money . . .

Mr Sanyal had now gone into the bedroom, breathing heavily and walking all over the broken glass, in the hope of catching the thief red-handed.

Phoni Babu had nothing to fear now. He slipped out of the front door that was still open, and silently went down the seventy-two steps that he had climbed only a few minutes ago. Then he made his way to number 17/2.

As he climbed up the steps of his own house and came to the spot where the empty cage hung, the lights came back. Much relieved, Phoni Babu looked down and found himself clutching a brand-new, fashionable, Japanese umbrella.

Translated by Gopa Majumdar

First published in Bengali in 1978

The Class Friend

It was a quarter past nine in the morning. Mohit Sarkar had just placed his tie round his neck, when his wife entered the room and said, 'Someone's on the phone, asking for you.'

'Who could it be at this time?'

Mohit Sarkar was used to reaching his office on the dot of nine-thirty. A frown appeared between his brows on being told he had to take a phone call just as he was about to leave.

'He says he was in school with you,' his wife told him.

'In school? Just imagine! Did he give his name?'

'Joy. He said that's all you needed to be told, and you'd know who it was.'

Mohit Sarkar had left school thirty years ago. There had been about forty boys in his class. If he thought very carefully, he might be able to recall the names of twenty of those boys, possibly even their faces. Luckily, he could remember Joy—or Joydev—quite clearly, for Joy had been one of the brightest students in his class. He was a handsome young boy, did well in his studies, was good at the high jump, knew a few card tricks, and had once won a medal in a recitation competition. He had recited 'Casablanca'. Mohit Sarkar had never seen him after leaving school. He realized now that it was giving him no great pleasure to learn that an old classmate had called him after so many years.

But he had to pick up the receiver. 'Hello,' he said.

'Who, is that you, Mohit? Can you recognize me? It's Joy, Joydev Bose. Ballygunj School, remember?'

'I cannot recognize your voice. But I remember your face. What can I do for you?'

'You are a big officer now. I am flattered that you remember my name!'

'Never mind all that. What made you call me?'

'Er . . . I need to talk to you. In person, I mean. Could we meet?'

'When?'

'Whenever it's convenient for you. But if it was sooner rather than later, I'd be . . .'

'Very well, let's meet this evening. I'm usually back by six o'clock. Could you come to my house at seven?'

'Certainly. Thank you very much. I'll see you later.'

Mohit Sarkar left in the light blue Standard that he had recently bought. On the way to his office, he tried to remember a few things about his school days. Those were such happy days, despite the stern look in the eyes of Girin Sur, their headmaster with a bad temper. Mohit himself had been a good student. Shankar, Mohit and Joydev—these three boys always vied with one another for the top three positions in their class. Mohit and Joydev became close friends from class six, and studied together in the same class until they left school. At times, they sat next to each other on the same bench. Even when it came to playing football, they found themselves next to each other. Mohit played right-in, and Joydev right-out. At the time, Mohit thought their friendship would last for ever. But they lost touch as soon as they passed out of school.

Mohit's father was wealthy, and a well-known barrister in Calcutta. He got into a good college, and found a well-paid job in a merchant firm within two years of finishing his graduation. Joydev left Calcutta after school and moved to a different town, for his father had a transferable job. Only a short time after his departure, Mohit was surprised to find that he was not missing Joydev any more. He had made new friends who had taken Joy's place.

Eventually, his friends in college were replaced by another set, when he started working. Today, Mohit was one of the four seniormost officers in his company; and his closest friend was one of his colleagues. The only friend from school he saw occasionally at his club was Pragyan Sengupta, who also had a good job in a reputed firm. Strangely enough, Pragyan did not feature anywhere in his memories of school. It was Joydev who featured prominently. The same Joydev, who he had not seen in the last thirty years.

Mohit's office was in Central Avenue. As his car approached the junction where Chowringhee met Suren Banerjee Road, the noise of the traffic broke his reverie and pulled him sharply back to reality. A glance at his watch told him that today he was going to be delayed by three minutes.

When he finished work and returned to his flat in Lee Road in the evening, all thoughts of Ballygunj Government School had disappeared from his mind. To tell the truth, he had forgotten all about Joydev's phone call, and was reminded only when his bearer, Bipin, brought him a folded piece of ruled paper in his sitting room. The paper had been torn out of an exercise book. 'Joydev Bose, as per appointment', it said.

Mohit switched off the BBC news bulletin he had been listening to on the radio, and said to Bipin, 'Ask him to come in.' It suddenly dawned upon him that he should have got some snacks for Joy. After all, he was going to visit him after so many years. Mohit could easily have stopped at Park Street on the way back from his office and bought a cake or something, but he had just not thought about it. Would his wife have arranged something to eat, without being told?

'Remember me?'

The feeling that rose in Mohit Sarkar's mind on hearing the voice, and then beholding its owner, was similar to the feeling one might get if one had finished climbing a flight of stairs, and then taken an extra step, thinking there was one more to go.

The man who had crossed the threshold and entered the room was wearing grey, absurdly loose cotton trousers, and a cheap printed bush shirt, neither of which seemed to have ever seen an iron. The face that stared back at him bore no resemblance at all to the face of Joydev Bose that Mohit Sarkar remembered. This man's eyes were sunken, his skin badly sunburnt, his cheeks hollow. The heavy salt and pepper stubble on his chin was at least three days old, and the top of his head was bald. The few remaining strands of hair around his ears were long and unkempt. Since he had asked the question with a smile, Mohit had caught a glimpse of his teeth, and thought immediately that if someone had such awful teeth, worn and stained by years of chewing paan, then he should never smile without covering his mouth.

'I've changed a lot, haven't I?'

'Sit down.'

Mohit had risen to his feet. He sat down again when his visitor had taken a seat. Mohit had a few old photographs taken when he was in school. If anyone were to compare the face of Mohit at the age of fourteen with the present Mohit Sarkar, they would not find it too difficult to spot some similarities. Why, then, was it so difficult to find anything of his old friend in this man? Could a person's appearance change so completely in thirty years?

'You have not changed all that much,' the visitor went on speaking, 'If I saw you in the street, I'd have recognized you easily enough. The thing is, you see, I have suffered a lot. My father died before I could leave college. So I had to forget about my studies, and look for a job. I needn't tell you how difficult it is to find a good job without knowing anyone in the right places, and without a bit of luck. I mean, for an ordinary . . .'

'Would you like some tea?'

'Tea? Why, yes, thank you.'

Mohit called Bipin and told him to bring two cups of tea. Thank goodness he had not bothered to get cakes or anything fancy. For this man, a plate of biscuits should be enough.

'You cannot imagine,' the man was still speaking, 'how many times I thought today of our days together!' Mohit refrained from admitting that he, too, had spent considerable time reminiscing.

'Do you remember LCM and GCM?' the visitor asked. Mohit had forgotten, but now it came back in a flash. LCM was their PT teacher, Lal Chand Mukherjee; and their maths teacher, Gopen Mitter, was known as GCM.

'Do you remember who made us stand side by side behind the water tank, and took a photo with his box camera?'

Mohit's lips spread in a slight smile to indicate that he did remember. Everything this man was saying had really happened. It was all true. If he was not the real Joydev, how did he know all these things?

'Those five years in school that we spent together were the best time of my life. Those days will never come back. I don't think I could ever be so happy again,' the visitor remarked.

This time, Mohit could not help asking a question: 'As far as I remember, you were the same age as me—'

'Yes, I was younger than you by only three months.'

'—In that case, why do you look so much older? What happened to all your hair?'

'Struggle,' the man replied. 'I've had to struggle so hard. Mind you, there's a history of baldness in my family. My father and grandfather both became bald by the time they were thirty-five. So it's not surprising that I lost my hair. If my cheeks look hollow, it's because of a lack of proper diet, and gruelling hard work. I've never had a desk job, not like you. For seven years, I worked in a factory; then became a medical salesman, then an insurance agent . . . then an agent for various other things. I've never been lucky enough to find a single steady job. Like a shuttlecock I've been thrown around in different directions. So my health suffered . . . that's not surprising, is it?'

Bipin brought the tea, accompanied by samosas and sweets. Mohit's wife was a thoughtful woman. How she might react if she saw this character who was supposed to be his class friend, Mohit could not imagine.

'Won't you have any?'

Mohit shook his head. 'No, I've just eaten.'

'Just one sweet?'

'No, thanks. You eat whatever you want.'

The man picked up a samosa and took a bite. 'My son,' he said, chewing, 'is soon going to have his exams. But I don't even have enough money to pay his exam fees.'

There was no need to hear any more. Mohit had fully grasped the purpose of this visit. In fact, it should have occurred to him before. All his visitor wanted to do was ask for financial assistance. How much would he ask for? If it was no more than ten or twenty, perhaps it would be wise to pay it quietly. If he didn't, where was the guarantee that the man would stop bothering him?

'My son's a bright lad, you know. I hate to think he might have to give up his studies just because I can't find the money. I worry about it so much that at times I cannot sleep at night.' The second samosa also disappeared from the plate. Mohit looked steadily at his visitor, taking every chance he could get to compare his face with that of the young Joydev he had once known. With every passing minute, he began to feel increasingly convinced that this middle-aged man had nothing whatever to do with that adolescent boy.

'. . . So I was wondering,' the visitor concluded, slurping his tea, 'if you could help an old friend out. A hundred, or a hundred and fifty, would be much—'

'Very sorry.'

'What?'

By now, Mohit had decided not to pay a single paisa. But perhaps he need not have been quite so brusque. Somewhat embarrassed, he made himself speak more gently.

'I am sorry. I mean, the problem is that I don't have ready cash at the moment.'

'Then I'll come back tomorrow. Or whenever you say, any time.'

'I have to go out of town tomorrow, for about three days. You can come on Sunday.'

'Sunday?' The man sounded a little disappointed. But Mohit's mind was made up. There was no evidence that this man was the real Joy. A large number of people in Calcutta made a living out of fraud and deception. What if this man was one of them? It could be that he knew the real Joydev. Was it so difficult to speak to someone's old classmate and learn a few things about their school life?

'When should I come on Sunday?'

'In the morning. That would suit me better. Say, between nine and nine-thirty?'

The coming Friday was a holiday. His office would be closed for Id. Mohit had already made plans to go out with his wife, to spend the whole weekend with a friend. They would not be back until Sunday night. So, if this man came in the morning on Sunday, Mohit would not be home.

If Mohit were able to refuse outright to part with his money, this act of deception would have been unnecessary. But he was one of those people who could not be openly rude. If this man returned yet again, even after Sunday, Mohit would find another excuse to avoid him. Hopefully, he would take the hint after that, and never bother him again.

His visitor finished his tea and put the cup down. Almost in the same instant, another man entered the room. It was Banikanto Sen, a close friend of Mohit. Two other men were expected. When they arrived, the four of them would sit down with a pack of cards. They did this every evening.

Banikanto cast a suspicious look at the visitor, which Mohit did not fail to notice. He made no attempt to introduce the two men to each other.

'Well, I guess I had better be off,' the visitor stood up. 'I'll really be grateful if you can do this for me, my dear friend. Truly grateful.'

As soon as he was out of the room, Banikanto glanced at Mohit, frowning. 'Who was that man?' he asked. 'He called you "my dear friend"!'

'Yes. That was for your benefit, I think, to show how well he knew me.'

'Who is he?'

Instead of giving him a reply, Mohit Sarkar went to a bookshelf and picked up an old photo album. Then he opened a particular page and showed it to Banikanto.

'A group photo? Was this taken at your school?' Banikanto wanted to know.

'No, the Botanical Garden. We had gone there for a picnic.'

'Who are these five boys?'

'Can't you recognize me?'

'Wait, let me see.'

Banikanto picked up the album and held it closer to his eyes. He had no difficulty in recognizing his friend.

'Now look at the boy on my right,' Mohit said.

Banikanto peered closer at the photo. 'All right, I've looked,' he said.

'That boy and the man who just left are the same.'

'Tell me, had this boy started gambling even before he had left school?' Banikanto asked, snapping the album shut and throwing it on a sofa. 'I have seen that man at the races at least thirty times.'

'I am not surprised,' Mohit replied, and explained briefly what had happened.

'Inform the police,' Banikanto advised him. 'This city has become a depot for cheats and crooks. That boy in the photo and that gambler who's been visiting you can never be the same. It's impossible!'

Mohit smiled. 'He'll go away, I think, when he comes back on Sunday and finds that I'm out. I don't expect him to cause any more trouble.'

Mohit Sarkar and his wife spent a very pleasant weekend with his friend in a place called Baruipur. The friend owned a farm, so they had fresh fish, fresh eggs from his poultry, and mangoes, coconuts and guavas from his orchard. The afternoons were spent in the shade of a bokul tree, sitting or lying on a durrie, leaning against soft cushions, and playing cards. Much refreshed, both physically and mentally, they returned home at around eleven on Sunday evening. Bipin told him that the gentleman who had visited a few days earlier had come again that morning.

'Did he say anything before he left?'

'No, sir.'

Good. What a relief. The subterfuge had worked, it seemed.

But no. If it had worked, it was only for that day. The following morning at eight o'clock Bipin found his master reading the morning newspaper in his sitting room, and handed him another folded piece of paper. Mohit unfolded it and saw that it was a short letter. It said:

Dear Mohit,

I have sprained my right foot, so I am sending my son to you. If you can give him whatever little you can spare, it will help me enormously. I hope you will not disappoint me.

Yours ever,

Joy.

There could be no escape this time. However, 'little' was all he would offer, Mohit decided. 'Send the boy in,' he said to Bipin.

A boy of about fourteen walked into the room a minute later. He came forward to touch Mohit's feet, then stepped back and stood quietly. Mohit stared at him for a whole minute. Finally, he said, 'Sit down.'

The boy hesitated for a moment, then sat down in one corner of a sofa, holding his hands in his lap.

'I'll be back soon,' Mohit said and went out of the room.

He made his way upstairs to find his wife. The keys to their safe were tied to her pallu. Mohit untied them, opened the safe, and took out four fifty-rupee notes. Then he sealed them in an envelope, locked the safe again, and returned to the living room.

'What's your name?' he asked the boy.

'Sanjay Kumar Bose.'

'This envelope contains money. Do you think you'll be able to take it back to your father?'

The boy nodded.

'Where will you keep it?'

'In the inside pocket of my jacket.'

'Will you take a tram, or a bus?'

'I'll walk.'

'Walk? Where do you live?'

'Mirzapur Street.'

'That's quite far. Will you walk all that way?'

'Baba told me to walk.'

'Well, you can do one thing. Why don't you wait here for another hour, have a cup of tea, and I'll get you something to eat, look at some of my books—I've got heaps of them—and then you can come with me when I leave for my office. My car will drop me first, then take you home. You can show the driver where to go, can't you?'

The boy nodded again.

Mohit called Bipin and told him to get some tea and sweets for the boy. Then he went upstairs again to start getting ready. His heart was feeling a lot lighter. He found himself in a very good mood.

He had failed to recognize Joy; but in his son Sanjay, Mohit Sarkar had rediscovered the class friend he had known thirty years ago.

Translated by Gopa Majumdar

First published in Bengali in 1979

Sahadev Babu's Portrait

Over the last three months, Sahadev Babu had started to make a regular appearance at the auction house owned by Lazarus in Mirza Ghalib Street, previously known as Free School Street.

He had begun his career by hawking booklets—collections of jokes, riddles, popular proverbs, even songs. Then he spent seven years acting as an agent or a broker for various businesses, earning enough commission to start a business of his own. Having spent the last five years selling electrical cables, he had finally reached a point where he could afford a neat and compact flat in Sadananda Road, a Fiat, a telephone, a television, two bearers, a cook and an Alsatian. Those who had known him well in his early days could no longer recognize him easily; and, even if they did, they hesitated to approach him. As a matter of fact, Sahadev Babu himself did not wish to be recognized by his old friends. So he had altered his appearance by growing a moustache, adding an inch to his sideburns, and wearing plain glasses with a golden frame. The glasses were plain, for there was nothing wrong with his eyesight. They were added only for effect.

With his rise in life, he had acquired a new set of friends, who visited him every evening and drank good quality tea, smoked the best cigarettes, played poker with laminated cards, and on weekends, watched Hindi and Bengali films on television.

Anyone entering his drawing room could tell why he had started going to Lazarus. Almost every Sunday, he brought back from there some pretty knick-knack or the other. The clocks, lamps, statues made of brass and china, silver candlesticks, and English landscapes, had all been bought from Lazarus; not to mention tables, chairs, a settee, and the carpet on the floor.

Today, Mihir Babu, who worked for Lazarus, had promised to get him a set of novels by famous British novelists. Mihir Babu had had a lot of experience in this matter, having spent twenty years at the auction house. He could anticipate what his regular clients might like and was familiar with Sahadev Babu's tastes. He had had to meet the demands of the newly rich often enough in the past. He knew very well that many of them were neither well educated, nor particularly fond of reading, but they liked to fill their bookcases with English books in bright jackets.

It was an attractive set of sixteen novels, bound in red leather. One look at it made Sahadev Babu's heart dance with joy. But, in the next instant, something happened that startled him into forgetting all about the novels, at least for the moment. A picture with a gilded frame was hanging on the wall behind the table on which the novels were displayed. Sahadev Babu's eyes fell on it.

It was an oil painting, about 3'x4' in size. In fact, it was a portrait of a Bengali gentleman. That it was quite old was obvious not only from the layer of dust on it, but also from the various objects included in the portrait. The hookah, the kerosene lamp, the silver paan box, the walking stick with an ivory handle, were all reminders of days gone by. Besides, the clothes the subject was wearing were very old fashioned. Who would nowadays wear that kind of kurta with buttons on one side and crinkled sleeves, a dhoti with such a broad border, and such a heavily embroidered Kashmiri shawl? During the time when this portrait had been made, it was customary for wealthy and aristocratic Bengalis to get their portraits done by artists. There was nothing unusual about that. What startled Sahadev Babu was the face of the subject.

'How do you like it?' asked Mihir Babu, strolling across to join him. 'His face is exactly like your own, isn't it?'

The thought had already occurred to Sahadev Babu, but he took a quick look at a fancy mirror kept nearby, waiting to be sold. Now he could be sure. 'True,' he said. 'Whose portrait is this?'

Mihir Babu did not know. 'We got a whole lot of things from a store room in an old house in Chitpur. The house is now going to become a factory. They'll make vests, I believe. This portrait came with all the other stuff,' he said.

'So you don't know who the man was?' Sahadev Babu asked again.

'No, I am afraid not. But I thought of you the minute I saw it. Perhaps he was a zamindar. The artist, I am told, was well known. Sailesh Chatterjee, who was here earlier today—you know, the one who lives in Elgin Road, writes on art and artists sometimes—anyway, he said Paresh Gui, at one time, was a famous painter.'

Sahadev Babu had not failed to notice the name of the artist, written in red in the bottom right hand corner of the painting. 'Is this going to be auctioned, too?' he asked.

'Why, do you want it?'

Strangely enough, getting his own portrait made was one of the many desires Sahadev Babu cherished in his heart. In fact, the idea had come to him one day, here in this shop, upon seeing another oil painting. He had mentioned it to Mihir Babu, whose response had been most encouraging. 'That will be something quite new, won't it?' he had said, 'I mean, it's just not done any more. Yet, a portrait made by a good and experienced artist can change the whole appearance of a room. And just think how long these things last! If you see the oil paintings in art galleries—some of them five hundred years old—they look as if they were painted yesterday. Their colours haven't faded at all.'

Since Sahadev Babu knew no one in the world of art, he was obliged to place an advertisement in the two leading dailies, Ananda Bazar and Jugantar. His neighbour, Sujay Bose, who happened to be a journalist, helped him choose the right words for his ad: 'Wanted: an expert portrait-maker for portrait in oil colours. Write with references to the address below.'

An artist applied. Sahadev Babu asked him to come to his house. He turned out to be about twenty-five years old. His name was Kallol Dasgupta. He had recently passed out of the Government College of Arts, and was looking for work. The certificate his college had given him proved that he had talent. But his appearance put Sahadev Babu off. The young man's long hair, unkempt beard, baggy trousers and garish purple shirt did nothing to inspire confidence. He had to send him away, but the artist returned twice to ask if Sahadev Babu had changed his mind. Perhaps he was very poor indeed, and desperate for work. Still, Sahadev Babu could not hire him. If his appearance was so untidy, how could his work be satisfactory?

Eventually, a business associate recommended a different artist. This one turned out to be presentable in his appearance, so Sahadev Babu told him to go ahead, and even gave a couple of sittings. On the second day, however, he noticed that the face that was emerging on the canvas was looking increasingly like Brajen Datta's who worked in one of the shops in New Market. At this, he had to ask the artist to stop at once. He then thrust five ten-rupee notes in his hand, and bade him goodbye.

Now, in answer to Mihir Babu's question, he said, 'Well, I couldn't get a good artist even after advertising in the papers. And yet, it seems as if this portrait was made specially for me! So, I think . . . well . . .'

'Shall I keep it for you?'

'How much . . . I mean . . .?'

'The price? Oh, I'll charge you as little as possible. But the artist was once quite well known, as I was just saying.'

In the end, Sahadev Ghosh had to pay seven hundred and fifty rupees for the portrait of a man about whom no one knew anything. He brought it home, and hung it on the most prominent place on the wall of his drawing room. The room truly began to look different. There could be no doubt that the artist was remarkably gifted. Every paisley motif on the Kashmiri shawl had been drawn with the utmost care; the diamond in the ring the man was wearing on the third finger of his right hand seemed to glitter; the silver bowl of his hookah looked as if it had just been polished.

Needless to say, Sahadev Babu's friends were as amazed as him when they saw the portrait. At first, many of them thought Sahadev Babu had visited an artist's studio secretly and got the portrait made. When they heard the real story, they could scarcely believe it. It is not often that one finds such striking resemblances between two men, unless they are identical twins. One of his friends, Satyanath Bakshi, asked him outright, 'Are you sure this gentleman isn't one of your ancestors?' That could not be the case, of course, because in the last hundred years, none of Sahadev Babu's ancestors had managed to make any money. His grandfather was the ticket collector at a railway station; and his great-grandfather had worked for a zamindar as a petty clerk.

Nando Banerjee was fond of reading detective novels, and fancied himself as an amateur sleuth. 'I can't rest in peace until I find out who this Babu is,' he declared. 'That diamond ring . . . there's a mystery attached to it, I am sure. I can smell it. What I have to do is consult the encyclopaedia of famous families in Bengal. Nitaida has got all four volumes. Each one is packed with every little detail about various zamindars. There are a lot of pictures, too.'

No one could concentrate on playing poker that evening. There was much talk about other strange coincidences that people had heard of.

That night, Sahadev Babu had a sudden idea. He would let the portrait hang in the drawing room during the day; but, at night, he would bring it to his bedroom. And if he could fix a blue light over it—the kind usually found in railway compartments—it would not interfere with his sleep, but he would be able to see the portrait if he woke in the middle of the night.

The very next day, he called an electrician and had a blue night light installed in his room.

Three days after buying the portrait, Sahadev Babu reduced the length of his sideburns by an inch. That was the only thing that was different from the man's face in the portrait. Then he noticed that the other man's nails were neatly cut, whereas his own were long and dirty. He had never bothered to cut his nails regularly, which often made them grow uncomfortably long. But now he began paying more attention to them.

Other things followed. Sahadev Babu was not in the habit of chewing paan. However, now he bought a silver box like the one in the portrait, got his bearer to stuff paan leaves with masala, and began carrying them in the silver box in his pocket. His humble beginnings and lack of education had not taught him much about social graces or elegant dressing. The portrait of the unknown aristocrat began to influence him to such an extent that, gradually, his whole demeanour changed, and his manners started to acquire a certain polish. As long as he was in his office in Lal Bazar, he remained the same man he had always been. He wore a terylene shirt and terycot trousers to work, smoked Gold Flake cigarettes, drank tea three times a day, and for his lunch, ate a plate of puri-subzi and jalebis, bought from a local sweet shop. All these were old habits.

He changed when he returned home in the evening. The way he walked, or talked, or sat crosslegged with a bolster on his lap, made him a different man. Even the manner in which he raised his voice to call his bearer was new. Naturally, his friends did not fail to notice these changes. 'If that portrait continues to influence you like this, my friend,' they said, 'you will have to leave this flat and find yourself a mansion.' Sahadev Babu smiled a little at such a remark, but said nothing.

He could feel himself drawn closest to the man in the portrait when he switched off all the lights in his room at night, except the blue one. As he lay in his bed, staring at the painting, he truly felt the man in it was none other than himself. At such moments, every night, he felt a strong desire to acquire every object shown in the painting—that embroidered Kashmiri shawl, the fine dhoti and kurta, that chair, that silver hookah, that diamond ring, and the stick with the ivory handle.

Over a period of time, Sahadev Babu fulfiiled this desire, obtaining each object, one by one. The chair and the stick were provided by Mihir Babu. An artisan from Chitpur came specially to make a silver hookah to match the one in the picture. Sahadev Babu bought some high quality tobacco and began to practice smoking a hookah. Getting a kurta made was no problem at all. He also bought golden buttons to go with it.

The shawl came from an old Kashmiri shawlwala. Last winter, this particular man, called Nadir Shah, had visited Sahadev Babu with a great variety of shawls. Sahadev Babu had not bought anything from him then. Nevertheless, he turned up as soon as winter started this year. Sahadev Babu showed him the portrait and asked, 'Can you get me a shawl exactly like this one?'

Nadir Shah took a quick look at the picture. 'It won't be easy to get a jamavar shawl like that,' he said. 'But if you can give me a little time, I can look for one.'

Within three weeks, he returned with a jamavar. The colour was slightly different; but who knew what the real colour of the original shawl had been? It was an old painting, to start with. Besides, who could say with certainty that the oil colour used by the artist was not different from the actual colour of the shawl?

'How much?' asked Sahadev Babu.

'I'll give you a special rate. Four and a half.'

'Four and a half? You mean four hundred and fifty rupees?' Sahadev Babu asked. He had no idea how much a good shawl could cost these days.

'No, sir,' Nadir Shah replied, a crease appearing near his eyes as he smiled, 'I mean four thousand and five hundred.'

Bargaining did not work. His special rate did not get any lower. Sahadev Babu was obliged to write him a cheque for four thousand and five hundred rupees.

There were, even now, a few other items left to be obtained: a marble table with three legs, a kerosene lamp with a round glass shade, and a play by Shakespeare. All of these featured in the picture. Eventually, Sahadev Ghosh got hold of these, too.

Now there was just one thing left on his list: a diamond ring, like the one on the finger of that other man.

When Sahadev Babu had started his own business, he had paid a visit to Naihati, to consult an astrologer called Durgacharan Bhattacharya. He had to find out what was in store for him. The astrologer had predicted enormous success in his new venture and the acquisition of great wealth. In fact, he had written his prediction down on a piece of paper and given it to Sahadev Babu. But in that piece of paper, there was no mention of the heavy losses his business would suffer, within just eight years. Today, Sahadev Babu took it out, tore it, crumpled the pieces into a ball, and threw it out of a window.

Two large orders had been cancelled recently. His losses ran to several lakhs. Although he had started humbly, he had never had to face such difficulties before. His small business had grown and expanded, and he had risen higher and higher in life, without looking back. That was the reason why this sudden setback overwhelmed and horrified him; nor could he tell himself that the problem was only temporary.

He had lost his faith in one astrologer. Yet, distressed as he was, he could not help turning to another. This time, it was someone called Narayan, who lived in Girish Mukherjee Road in Bhowanipore.

Narayan took four and a half minutes to finish his calculations. Sahadev was in for a very bad time, he said. The position of his stars showed that he would have to suffer the whole year. But that was not all. Someone he had trusted in the past had betrayed him.

Sahadev Babu did not even try to work out who this person might be. Had he been warned before, he might have been on his guard. There were plenty of people he had had to trust while running his business. What good would it do now to learn who had betrayed him? What mattered was that all he had built up over the years was about to be destroyed. The rug had been pulled from under his feet.

The first thing that went was his Fiat. Four years ago, he had bought it for thirty-four thousand rupees. Today, he sold it for twelve thousand.

According to an English proverb, a friend in need is a friend indeed. Among his three close friends, only one passed this test. It was Nando Banerjee. He had not yet managed to identify the man in the portrait. One of the four volumes of the encyclopaedia did contain a picture of a zamindar of Selimganj, called Bhutnath Chowdhury, whose clothes and other accessories matched most of the details in Sahadev Babu's portrait; but his face was entirely different. These days, Sahadev Babu found himself depending heavily on Nando's support. Had he not stood by him, God knew what might have happened.

It was the same Nando Banerjee who made the suggestion. 'Look,' he said one day, 'I think you should get rid of that portrait. That's what has brought you all this bad luck. In any case, your appearance has changed so much lately that there are little similarities left between you and that man.'

To tell the truth, the same thought had occurred to Sahadev Babu when he had recently looked into a mirror and compared his own face with the portrait. In the last two months, the hair around his ears had turned grey, there were dark circles under his eyes, his cheeks looked sunken, and his skin had lost its lustre. Yet, the man in the picture looked just the same.

'Go back to Lazarus and return it to them,' Nando Banerjee went on, 'Didn't they say the artist was well known? I'm sure they'll find another buyer. You'll be free from that cursed thing, and be able to earn some money if it is sold.'

That night, Sahadev Babu switched on the blue light and stared once more at the portrait. In a few minutes, the feeling that rose uppermost in his heart was one he had never experienced before. It was fear. The man's lips held a slight smile. Until now, it had always struck him as a pleasant smile. Tonight, it seemed evil. His eyes were looking straight back at him, making him feel as if the smile was intended only for him. How perfectly strange—some ancient artist called Paresh Gui drew the portrait of an unknown man, heaven knew who he was or where he had lived, and yet, the same portrait had ruined his own life! Sahadev Ghosh suddenly thought of all the money he had spent on buying all those extra objects, quite apart from what he had spent on the painting itself. He gave an involuntary shudder. Thank God he did not have the means, even at the time, to buy a diamond ring. Had he bought one, how much more would he have lost?

He could think no more. He switched off the blue light and lay down. His mind was made up. He would get a taxi in the morning and take that portrait back to Lazarus.

'Good morning, sir. What's that you're carrying?'

He was meeting Mihir Babu after nearly a year. It was not a Sunday, so there were no preparations to be made for an auction. Sahadev Babu put the portrait down on the floor. Several sheets from three different newspapers were wrapped tightly around it. He wiped the perspiration from his forehead and explained the matter to Mihir Babu. Naturally, he could not tell him the truth. So he said, 'This portrait has turned me into an object of ridicule, would you believe it? My friends keep saying, "Why did you have to dress up as a zamindar to get your portrait made, when the zamindari system disappeared ages ago?" I'm tired of everyone making fun of me. So I decided to bring it back. See if you can sell it to someone else. Or if it just stays here . . . well, I wouldn't mind!'

'Did I just see you getting out of a taxi? What happened to your car?'

'It's in the workshop. Goodbye.'

Sahadev Babu left. Mihir Babu picked up the telephone directory and found the number of the Academy of Fine Arts. He had to ring his nephew, who was holding an exhibition of his paintings there. Mihir Babu was very fond of this particular nephew.

'Hello, is that Kallol? This is Uncle Mihir. Listen. Do you remember how I'd helped you to earn some money when you came out of college and were looking for work? The very first time? . . . No? Cast your mind back. Didn't you go to a man in Sadananda Road, who had advertised for an artist to make his portrait? And didn't he drive you away? Then you drew his portrait, anyway, simply from memory, but dressed him up as a zamindar? . . . Yes, yes, now do you remember? Well, you see, that same portrait has come back to me. Come and collect it when you can. The shop is absolutely packed, I haven't got enough room here to store it.'

Mibir Babu replaced the receiver and turned his attention to his next client. Mr Aron had arrived to make enquiries about an old chess set that he had seen before.

Now Mihir Babu would have to pass it off as something made in Burma, a hundred and fifty years ago.

Translated by Gopa Majumdar
First published in Bengali in 1979

A Strange Night for Mr Shasmal

Mr Shasmal leant back in his easy chair and heaved a sigh of relief.

He had selected really the most ideal spot, this forest bungalow in northern Bihar. No other place could be more peaceful, quiet or safe. The room, too, was most satisfactory. It was furnished with old, sturdy and attractive furniture, all made during the Raj. The linen neatly spread on a large bed was spotless, and even the attached bathroom was spacious and clean. Through an open window came a cool breeze, and the steady drone of crickets. There was no electricity, but that did not matter. Frequent power cuts in Calcutta had taught him to read by the light of kerosene lamps. He was quite used to it. The lamps in this bungalow had plain glass shades. Possibly for this reason, the light that came from them seemed brighter than the lamps he had at home. He had brought plenty of detective novels, his favourite reading material, with him.

There was no one in the bungalow, except a chowkidar. This, too, suited him very well. It simply meant that he would not have to meet or talk to anyone. Good. About ten days ago, he had visited the tourist office in Calcutta and made a booking. Four days ago, he learnt from a letter from them that his booking was confirmed. He would stay here for at least three days before thinking of moving elsewhere. He had enough money with him to survive, quite easily, at least for a month. He had arrived in his own car which he had driven himself all the way from Calcutta, a distance of 550 kilometres.

True to his word, the chowkidar served him dinner by half past nine: chapatis, arahar daal, some vegetables and chicken curry. The dining room bore signs of the Raj as well. The table, the chairs, the china and a fancy sideboard, all appeared to belong to British times.

'Are there mosquitoes here?' Mr Shasmal asked over dinner. The area where he had his flat in Calcutta was devoid of mosquitoes. He had not had to use a mosquito net in the last ten years. If he did not have to use a net here, either, his happiness would be complete.

The chowkidar said they did get mosquitoes in the winter, but it was now April, so there should not be a problem. However, he knew where a few nets were stored, and could put one up, if need be. At night, he added, it was best to sleep with the door closed. After all, they were in the middle of a forest. A fox or some other wild animal might get into the room if the door was left open. Mr Shasmal agreed. In fact, he had already decided to shut the door before going to bed.

He finished eating. Then he went out on the veranda outside the dining room, with a torch in his hand. He switched it on and directed it towards the forest. It fell on the trunk of a shaal tree. Mr Shasmal moved the beam around, to see if he could spot an animal. There was nothing. The whole forest was totally silent, except for the drone of the crickets. It went on, non-stop.

'I hope there are no ghosts in the bungalow?' asked Mr Shasmal lightly, returning to the dining room. The chowkidar was clearing the table. He stopped briefly on his way to the kitchen, smiled and told him that he had spent the last thirty-five years working here, plenty of people had stayed in the bungalow during that time, but no one had seen a ghost. This made Mr Shasmal's heart lighter.

His own room was the second one after the dining room. He had not bothered to shut the door before going in for his dinner. On his return, he realized that he should not have left it open. A stray dog had found its way there. A thin, scraggy creature, it had a white body with brown spots.

'Hey! Out, get out, shoo!' he cried. The dog did not move, but remained in one corner of the room, looking as if it had every intention of spending the night there.

'Get out, I said!'

This time, the dog bared its fangs. Mr Shasmal stepped back. When he was small, his neighbour's son had been bitten by a mad dog. He could not be saved from getting hydrophobia. Mr Shasmal remembered, in every horrific detail, how that boy had suffered. He did not have the courage to approach a snarling dog. He cast a sidelong glance at the animal, and went out on the veranda again.

'Chowkidar!'

'Yes, Babu?'

'Can you come here for a minute?'

The chowkidar appeared, wiping his hands on a towel. 'There's a dog in my room. Can you get rid of it?'

'A dog?' The chowkidar sounded perfectly taken aback.

'Yes. Why, you mean there isn't a single dog in this area? What's there to be so surprised about? Come with me, I'll show you.'

The chowkidar cast a suspicious look at Mr Shasmal, and entered his room. 'Where is the dog, Babu?'Mr Shasmal had followed him in. There was no sign of the dog. It had left in the few seconds it had taken him to call the chowkidar. Even so, the chowkidar looked under the bed, and checked in the bathroom, just to make sure.

'No, Babu, there's no dog here.'

'Well, may be not now. But it was here, just a minute ago.'

Mr Shasmal could not help feeling a little foolish. He sent the chowkidar back and took the easy chair again. He had almost finished his cigarette. Now he flicked the stub out of the window. Then he raised his arms over his head and stretched lazily, and in so doing, noticed something. The dog had not gone. Or, if it had, it was back again, and was standing once more in the same corner.

How very annoying! If it was allowed to remain, no doubt his new slippers from Bata would be chewed to pieces during the night. Mr Shasmal was well aware of a dog's passion for unattended slippers. He picked them up from the floor and placed them on the table.

So now there was another occupant in the room. Never mind. Let it be there for the moment, he'd try to drive it out once again before he went to bed.

Mr Shasmal stretched an arm and took a novel out of the Indian Airlines bag he had kept on the table. He had folded the page where he had stopped reading. Just as he slipped a finger into that page to open the book, his eyes fell on the corner opposite the dog. Quite unbeknown to him, another creature had slipped into the room.

It was a cat, with stripes all over its body, like a tiger. Curled into a ball, it was staring at him through dim, yellow eyes. Where had he seen a cat like that?

Oh yes. The Kundus, who lived in the house next door, had seven cats. One of them had looked just like this one. That night . . .

The whole thing came back to Mr Shasmal quite vividly.

About six months ago, he had been woken one night by the sound of constant caterwauling. He was already in a foul mood. His business partner, Adheer, had had a violent argument with him just the day before, threatening to go to the police to expose him. It had nearly come to blows. As a result, Mr Shasmal was not finding it easy to sleep. And now this cat was screaming its head off. After half an hour of tolerating the noise, he ran out of patience. Picking up a heavy glass paperweight from his table, he hurled it out of the window, towards the source of the noise. It stopped instantly.

The next morning, the entire household of the Kundus was in an uproar. Someone had brutally murdered one of their cats—the striped tom cat, it was being said. This had amused Mr Shasmal. The murder of a cat? If this could be called a murder, why, people were committing murders every day, without even thinking about it! Memories of another incident came back to him. It had happened many years ago, when he was still in college. He used to stay in the college hostel. One day, he happened to notice a long row of little ants going up a wall in his room. Mr Shasmal had grabbed a newspaper, lit one end of it and run the burning flame down the column of ants. As he watched, each of the tiny insects shrivelled and died, before dropping to the floor. Could that be described as murder?

Mr Shasmal looked at his wristwatch. It was ten minutes to ten. For a whole month, he had had a constant throbbing in his head. That was now gone. He had also been feeling rather hot almost all the time, and had therefore started showering three times a day. That feeling had left him as well.

He opened his book and held it before him. He had read barely a couple of lines, when his eyes fell on the cat once again. Why was it staring so hard at him?

Obviously, there was no chance of being on his own tonight. The only good thing was that the other two occupants were not human. If the two animals behaved well and remained silent, there was no reason not to have a good night's sleep. Sleep was very important to him. He had not slept well over the past few days, for very good reasons. Mr Shasmal was not in favour of the modern practice of swallowing sleeping pills.

He picked up the lamp and put it on the smaller bedside table. Then he took off his shirt, hung it up on a clotheshorse, drank some water from his flask, and went to bed, the book still in his hand. The dog had been sitting at the foot of the bed. Now it rose to its feet. Its eyes were fixed on Mr Shasmal.

The murder of a dog?

Mr Shasmal's heart skipped a beat. Yes, it was murder, in a way. He could recall the incident quite clearly. It took place probably in 1973, soon after he had bought his car. As a driver, he had always been a bit rash. Since it was not possible to drive very fast in the crowded streets of Calcutta, every time he stepped out of the city, the needle of his speedometer shot up automatically. He did not feel satisfied unless he could do at least 70 m.p.h. That was about the speed he was at, when one day, he ran over a dog on the national highway, on his way to Kolaghat. It was an ordinary street dog, white with brown spots. Mr Shasmal realized what he had done, but sped on regardless. His conscience did bother him after a while, but he told himself it did not matter. It was only a stray dog. So thin that you could count all its ribs. What was the point in such a creature staying alive? What good would it have done anyone? Mr Shasmal could remember thinking these things, to remove even the slightest trace of guilt from his mind.

He had succeeded at the time; but tonight, it was the sudden recollection of this incident that completely ruined his peace of mind.

How many animals had he killed in his life? Was each of them going to turn up here? What about that strange black bird he had killed with his first air gun, when he was a child? He did not even know the name of the bird. And then, during a visit to his uncle's house in Jhargram, didn't he use a heavy brick to . . . ?

Yes, it was here.

Mr Shasmal noticed the snake as his eyes moved towards the window. It was a cobra, about eight feet long. Its supple, smooth body had slipped in through the window, and was now climbing the table placed against the wall. Normally, snakes did not appear in April. But this one had. Two-thirds of its body remained on the table. The rest rose from it, the hood spreading out. Its unwavering, cruel eyes glittered in the light of the lamp.

In his uncle's house in Jhargram, Mr Shasmal had crushed a similar snake to death by throwing a brick at its head. The snake had been an old inmate of the house, well known to everyone. It had never done anyone any harm.

Mr Shasmal realized that his throat had gone totally dry. He could not even shout for the chowkidar.

The crickets outside had stopped their racket. A rather eerie silence engulfed everything. His wristwatch ran silently, or he would have heard it ticking. Just for a minute, Mr Shasmal thought he might be dreaming. That had happened to him in the recent past. Even as he lay in his own bed in his room, he had felt as if he was somewhere else, where there were strange people moving about, whispering among themselves. But that weird feeling had not lasted for more than a few moments. Perhaps one imagined such things just before drifting off to sleep. It was possible.

What he was seeing today, however, was not just a dream. He had pinched himself a minute ago, and realized that he was definitely awake. Whatever was happening was for real, and deliberate. It was all meant specifically for him.

Mr Shasmal lay still for nearly an hour. Quite a few mosquitoes had made their way into the room. He had not yet felt them bite, but had seen and heard them hovering around his bed. How many mosquitoes had he killed in his life? Who could tell?

An hour later, seeing that none of the animals were showing signs of aggression, Mr Shasmal began to relax. Perhaps he could try to go to sleep now?

He heard the noise the instant he stretched out an arm to lower the wick of the lamp. The path that ran from the gate of the bungalow to the steps leading to the veranda outside was covered with gravel. Someone was walking along that path. It was no four-legged creature this time. This one had two legs.

Now Mr Shasmal could feel himself sweating profusely, and he could hear his heart pounding in his chest.

The dog and the cat were still staring at him. The mosquitoes had not stopped humming. The cobra's hood was still raised; it was swaying rhythmically from side to side, as if some invisible snake charmer was playing an inaudible flute.

The footsteps had reached the veranda. They were getting closer.

A small, jet-black bird fluttered in through the window and sat on the table: the same bird that he had shot with his airgun. It had fallen off the wall it was perched on, and dropped to the ground into the garden next door.

The footsteps stopped outside his room.

Mr Shasmal knew who it was. Adheer. Adheer Chakravarty, his partner. They were friends once, but of late, they had almost stopped speaking to each other. Adheer did not like the devious way in which Mr Shasmal ran their business. He had threatened to report him to the police. Mr Shasmal, in turn, had told him that it was foolish to be honest when running a business. Adheer could not accept this view. Had he known about Adheer's moral stance, Mr Shasmal would never have made him his partner. It had not taken him long to realize that Adheer had become his biggest enemy. An enemy had to be destroyed. And that was precisely what Mr Shasmal had done.

The previous night, he and Adheer had sat facing each other in Adheer's sitting room. Mr Shasmal had a revolver in his pocket. He had come with the intention of killing his partner. Adheer was sitting only a few feet away. They were arguing once more. When Adheer's voice had reached its highest pitch, Mr Shasmal had taken out his revolver and fired it. Now, as he thought about the expression on the face of the man who had once been a close friend, Mr Shasmal could not help smiling. Adheer had clearly never expected to see him with a firearm in his hand.

Within ten minutes of the incident, he had set off in his car. He had spent the night in the waiting room at the railway station in Burdwan, and started on his journey this morning, to find this forest bungalow that he had booked ten days ago.

Someone knocked on the door. Once, twice, thrice.

Mr Shasmal could only stare at the door. His whole body was trembling. He felt breathless. 'Open the door, Jayant. It's Adheer. Open the door.'

It was the same Adheer he had shot the night before. When he left, Mr Shasmal was not entirely sure whether his partner was dead. Now, there could be no doubt. That dog, that cat, that snake, the bird—and now it was Adheer standing outside the door. If all the other creatures in the room had appeared here after death, it was only logical to assume that Adheer was dead, too.

Someone knocked again. And went on knocking.

Mr Shasmal's vision blurred, but even so, he could see that the dog was advancing towards him, the cat's eyes were only inches away from his own, the snake was gliding down a leg of the table with every intention of going straight for him; the bird flew down to sit on his bed, and on his chest had appeared countless little ants, his white vest was covered with them.

In the end, two constables had to break open the door.

Adheer Babu had brought the police from Calcutta. A letter from the tourist department had been found among Mr Shasmal's papers. That was how they had learnt about his reservation at this bungalow.

When he found Mr Shasmal lying dead, Inspector Samant turned to Adheer Babu. 'Did your partner have a weak heart?' he asked.

'I don't know about his heart. But, recently, his behaviour had struck me as most peculiar. No sane person could possibly have played around with our joint funds, or tried to cheat me, the way he did. I felt convinced that he had actually gone mad when I saw a revolver in his hand. To tell you the truth, when he took it out of his pocket, I simply could not believe my eyes. It took me ten minutes to get over my shock after he fired the gun and ran away. That was when I decided this lunatic must be handed over to the police. If I am alive today, it is really purely by chance.'

Mr Samant frowned. 'But how did he miss, if he fired at close range?'

Adheer Babu smiled, 'How can anyone die, tell me, unless he is destined to do so? The bullet did not hit me. It hit a corner of my sofa. How many people can find their target when it's pitch dark? You see, there was a power cut in our area, and all the lights went off the minute he took out his revolver!'

Translated by Gopa Majumdar
First published in Bengali in 1979

Pintu's Grandfather

Pintu had a great regret in life. Many of his friends had grandfathers, but not one of them was like his own. Raju's grandfather cut ribbons out of red and purple tissue paper to make a long tail for his kite. Pintu himself had seen him do this. Swapan and Sudeep's Dadu—whose red cheeks, beaming smile and snowy white beard always reminded Pintu of Father Christmas—wrote such funny rhymes. Pintu had heard one of them so many times from Swapan that, even now, he could recall a few lines:

London, Madrid, San Francisco
Akbar, Humayun, Harsha, Kanishko
Andes, Kilimanjaro, Fujiyama
Tenzing, Nansen, Vasco-da-Gama
Riga, Lima, Peru, Chile, Chung King, Congo
Hannibal, Tughlak, Taimurlingo . . .

How interesting! One line of geography, and one of history. And he didn't stop at just writing these poems. He set them to music, played the harmonium and sang each one for all the boys.

Then there was Shontu's Dadu. He was so good at shadowgraphy. Using his hands in the light of a candle, he could cast wonderful shadows on the wall. Ateen's Dadu had a fantastic stock of shikar stories. Shubu's Dadu knew of a magic component which he mixed in soapy water to create amazingly strong bubbles. Pintu had once seen one such bubble, as large as a number five football, bounce on the ground seven times before bursting.

Pintu had often thought of his friends' grandfathers, compared them with his own, and sighed.

What his Dadu had was a name that was quite a mouthful: Tridibendra Narayan Guha Majumdar. This was followed by several letters from the alphabet, commas and full stops. These were supposed to be degrees he had obtained. Pintu had heard from his parents that a man so learned and erudite as his Dadu was rare not just in Bengal, but in the whole country. He had passed his matric exam when he was only twelve. Very little had had to be spent on his education, for he had won an amazingly large number of scholarships—a feat few other students could match. There was no end to the number of gold and silver medals that had been given to him. Besides, there were certificates of merit and felicitation presented by various universities, which covered every empty space on the walls of his room. Although he had a sound knowledge of most subjects, what he knew the best was something called philosophy. Dadu had written a book in English on this subject, which was published two years ago. Pintu had seen it. It had 772 pages, and it cost sixty-five rupees.

There was no doubt that he was a learned man. But did being learned and knowledgeable automatically mean that one had to be grave and humourless? Pintu's friends had turned this into a joke. 'Hey, did your Dadu smile today?' they would ask. Pintu could not tell how many times he had heard that question. If he were to say 'Yes' in reply, that would be a lie. In all his eight years, Pintu could not remember a single occasion when his Dadu was seen smiling. This did not, however, mean that he shouted at everyone, or even raised his voice. He did not have to, for no one in the house ever gave him the chance to get cross. If they did, they knew that there would be hell to pay. Pintu could never forget the tale he had heard from his mother. Apparently, before he was born, once their dhobi had accidentally put extra starch in his Dadu's kurta. At this, his Dadu had picked up his sturdy wooden stick and beaten first their dhobi, and then the dhobi's donkey. What the poor donkey had done, no one had dared ask.

Last year, Pintu himself had broken a window pane in Dadu's room. He had been playing danguli with his friends outside, in the open ground. At that moment, Dadu was resting—lying still in his bed, doing the yogic shavasan, after a hard day's work. The little wooden piece had crashed through the glass and landed in his room. Dadu had shortly emerged on the balcony, the piece of wood in his hand. Pintu was still clutching the stick, so it was obvious who was responsible for the damage. Dadu saw him, but showed no sign of anger. He did not scold him. In fact, he did not utter a single word.

When Pintu returned home later in the evening, his mother said, 'Give me that stick you were playing with. It will now remain in your Dadu's room. And for the next seven days, you are not to play any games with your friends.'

Pintu could feel tears come to his eyes. What he minded more than not being allowed to play with his friends for a whole week was the loss of that piece of wood and the stick. Especially the wood. Srinivas had sharpened both ends so beautifully with a sickle. No one in the neighbourhood had such a good piece.

The strange thing was that Pintu knew for sure that his Dadu had not always been like this—at least, not when he was a boy. There was an old photo album in the house. It was made in England, and its thick pages were edged with gold. In it, Pintu had seen a photo of Dadu, taken sixty-two years ago, when he must have been about the same age as Pintu. He was wearing loose shorts, in his hand was a hockey stick, and on his face a big smile. Pintu knew that the boy in that photo looked very much like him. The resemblances in their appearance were really quite striking. How could such a cheerful young boy, who was clearly interested in sports, change so dramatically with age?

Luckily, Dadu did not spend all his time living with them. Pintu's uncle—his father's elder brother—worked in Assam as a senior officer in the forest department. He had a wonderful bungalow in the middle of a forest. Dadu went occasionally to spend a month with him. He always took a suitcase full of notebooks. When he returned, those notebooks were filled with writing.

During his absence, the house took on a totally different air. His sister played the radio loudly to listen to film music; his brother went out to see two films every week (usually with lots of fights and action in them); his father smoked more cigars than usual; and his mother invited all the other ladies in the neighbourhood every afternoon and spent many a happy hour playing cards, or just chatting.

When Dadu returned, things went back to the way they were.

This time, however, things took a different turn.

Dadu went to Assam for a month. Pintu, who slept in the same room as his parents, overheard their conversation one night, shortly before Dadu was expected back home. They were talking about him. He kept his eyes firmly shut, pretending to be asleep, and heard them talk for nearly five minutes. But his father was using such long and difficult English words that Pintu could not understand most of what he was saying. All he managed to gather was that his grandfather had got some sort of a disease.

Two days later, Dadu returned, sick. Dr Rudra, their family physician, went with Pintu's father to receive him at the station. They came back in his father's Ambassador. Dadu got out, helped by Dr Rudra and Pintu's father. They then held him from both sides and took him up the steps to the front veranda, then to the living room, and finally up the main staircase to his own room on the first floor. They even helped him to lie down in his bed.

Pintu was standing at the door of Dadu's bedroom and watching the proceedings, when his mother arrived, laid a hand on his head and said gently, 'Don't stand here. Go downstairs, please.'

'What's the matter with Dadu?' Pintu couldn't help asking. 'He's ill,' his mother replied.

To Pintu, Dadu did not look all that ill. However, he had to admit he had never seen him lean on two people just to walk. Could he have hurt his legs? If he had gone for a walk in the forest where his uncle lived, he could have fallen into a ditch or something. That would not have surprised Pintu at all. Or he might have been bitten by a snake, or a scorpion. That could have made him ill.

Three days passed. Pintu's bedroom was on the ground floor, directly below Dadu's. Since he was not allowed to go upstairs, there was no way he could find out how Dadu was doing. If his older siblings were at home, they might have been able to tell him something. But his sister was in a hostel in Calcutta, and his brother had gone on holiday with a friend to Ranikhet. The previous night, Pintu had heard a bronze glass, or a bowl, fall on the floor in Dadu's room. This morning, there had been other noises to indicate that Dadu was walking about. So, surely he could not be seriously ill?

In the afternoon, Pintu could contain himself no longer. His mother had been upstairs to give Dadu his medicine. She had come down a while ago. His father was in court. A nurse was supposed to come in the evening and take charge, Pintu had heard. But right now, there was no one else in Dadu's room.

Pintu's heart began racing faster. He just had to go upstairs and take a quick look. If Dadu was asleep, he would then go into the room and somehow find his wooden piece and the stick. In Dadu's absence, the room was always kept locked; so he had never had the chance to slip in before.

He did feel a little nervous going up. But Dadu was ill. What could a sick man do to him? The thought gave him courage. Pintu climbed the nineteen steps that led to the first floor, and walked on tiptoes until he came to the door to Dadu's room. It stood on his left. A passage ran ahead, at the end of which was the door to the roof.

The room was totally silent. The smell that greeted Pintu was a familiar one. It was the smell of old books. He loved it. There were some two thousand old books in Dadu's possession. Pintu held his breath and stretched his neck to peer inside. Dadu's bed was empty. Could he have gone out on the balcony?

Pintu raised his right foot to cross the threshold. A noise reached his ears before his foot could touch the floor on the other side.

Clang, clang, clang!

Startled, Pintu took a step backwards. There was another sound. 'Cooo-e-e-e!'

Pintu's eyes turned towards the door to the roof. It was ajar. A face was peeping from the other side.

It was Dadu. But Pintu had never seen him look like this. His whole face was lit up by a smile. His eyes held a mischievous glint. Pintu could only stare at him, totally incredulous.

Then Dadu stretched his right arm from behind the door. In his hand was clasped the wooden stick.

He beckoned in silence, and disappeared from the door. Pintu moved forward to go up to the roof.

It was a large roof. The piece of wood Srinivas had sharpened for him lay in the middle of it. Dadu looked at Pintu, grinned and took aim. Then he struck the piece with the stick. Clang!

He missed the first time. The stick did not touch the piece of wood. Dadu tried again. This time, the stick hit the exact spot it was supposed to, making the piece rise and spin several feet high. Dadu struck it once more with all his might.

The wooden piece flew like a rocket, shooting over the supari tree that stood at least twenty feet to the west. Then it disappeared in the direction of their neighbour's house. Dadu burst into laughter, jumped and clapped his hands.

Pintu moved away, and climbed down the stairs to find his mother. When he told her what he had just seen, she explained that that was the chief symptom of Dadu's illness. Sometimes, apparently, old men caught this disease. When they did, they did not remain old any more. They turned into little boys.

So Dadu had a disease. Never mind. For the first time, Pintu could tell his friends that he had seen his grandfather laugh—uproariously.

Translated by Gopa Majumdar
First published in Bengali in 1979

Big Bill

By Tulsi Babu's desk in his office on the ninth floor of a building in Old Court House Street, there was a window which opened onto a vast expanse of the western sky. Tulsi Babu's neighbour Jaganmoy Dutt had just gone to spit betel juice out of the window one morning in the rainy season when he noticed a double rainbow in the sky. He uttered an exclamation of surprise and turned to Tulsi Babu. 'Come here, sir. You won't see the like of it every day.'

Tulsi Babu left his desk, went to the window, and looked out.

'What do you want me to see?' he asked.

'Why, the double rainbow!' said Jaganmoy Dutt. 'Are you colour-blind?'

Tulsi Babu went back to his desk. 'I can't see what is so special about a double rainbow. Even if there were twenty rainbows in the sky, there would be nothing surprising about that. Why, in that case one can just as well go and stare at the double-spired church on Lower Circular Road!'

Not everyone is endowed with the same sense of wonder, but there was good reason to doubt whether Tulsi Babu possessed any at all. There was only one thing that never ceased to surprise him, and that was the excellence of the mutton kebab at Mansur's. The only person who was aware of this was Tulsi Babu's friend and colleague, Prodyot Chanda.

Therefore, being endowed with this sceptical temperament, when Tulsi Babu found an unusually large egg while looking for medicinal plants in the forests of Dandakaranya, he was not particularly surprised.

Tulsi Babu had been dabbling in ayurvedic medicine for the last fifteen years. His father was a well-known herbalist. Though Tulsi Babu's main source of income was as an upper division clerk in Arbuthnot & Co., he had not been able to discard the family profession altogether. Of late he had started devoting a little more time to it because two fairly distinguished citizens of Calcutta had benefited from his prescriptions, thus giving a boost to his reputation as a part-time herbalist.

The search for these herbs had brought him to Dandakaranya. He had heard that thirty miles to the north of Jagdalpur, there lived a holy man in a mountain cave who knew of some medicinal plants including one for high blood pressure. This plant was supposedly even more efficacious than the more common *Rawolfia serpentina*. Tulsi Babu suffered from hypertension; *serpentina* hadn't worked too well in his case, and he had no faith in homoeopathy or allopathy.

Tulsi Babu took his friend Prodyot Babu with him on a trip to Jagdalpur. Prodyot Babu had often been bothered by his friend's unflappable nature. One day he had been forced to comment, 'All one needs to feel a sense of wonder is a little imagination. You are so devoid of it that even if a full-fledged ghost were to appear before you, you wouldn't be surprised.' Tulsi Babu had replied calmly, 'To feign surprise when one doesn't actually feel it is an affectation. I do not approve of it.'

But this didn't get in the way of their friendship.

The two checked into a hotel in Jagdalpur during the autumn vacation. On the way, in the Madras Mail, two foreign youngsters had got into their compartment. They had turned out to be Swedes. One of them was so tall that his head nearly touched the roof of the compartment. Prodyot Babu had asked him how tall he was and the young man had replied, 'Two metres and seven centimetres.' That was nearly seven feet. Prodyot Babu couldn't take his eyes off this young giant during the rest of the journey; but Tulsi Babu did not register even a flicker of amazement. He said such extraordinary height was simply the result of the diet of the Swedish people, and therefore nothing to wonder about.

They reached the cave of the holy man Dhumai Baba after walking through the forest for a mile or so and then climbing up about 500 feet. The cave was a large one, but since no sunlight penetrated inside, they only had to take ten steps to be engulfed in a darkness thickened by the ever-present smoke from the Baba's brazier. Prodyot Babu was absorbed in watching, by the light of his torch, the profusion of stalactites and stalagmites while Tulsi Babu enquired after his herbal medicine. The tree that Dhumai Baba referred to was known as chakraparna, meaning 'round leaves' in Sanskrit. Tulsi Babu had never heard of it, nor was it mentioned in any of the half-dozen books he had read on herbal medicine. It was not a tree but a shrub, and was found only in one part of the forest of Dandakaranya, and nowhere else. Dhumai Baba gave adequate directions which Tulsi Babu noted down carefully.

Once out of the cave, Tulsi Babu lost no time in setting off in quest of the herb. Prodyot Babu was happy to keep his friend company; he had hunted big game at one time—conservation had put an end to that, but the lure of the jungle persisted.

The holy man's directions proved accurate. Half an hour's walk brought them to a ravine which they crossed and in three minutes they found the shrub seven steps to the south of a neem tree scorched by lightning. It was a waist-high plant with round green leaves, each with a pink dot in the centre.

'What kind of a place is this?' asked Prodyot Babu, looking around.

'Why, what's wrong with it?'

'But for the neem, there isn't a single tree here that I can recognize. And see how damp it is. Quite unlike the places we've passed through.'

It was moist underfoot, but Tulsi Babu saw nothing strange in that. Why, in Calcutta itself, the temperature varied between one neighbourhood and another. Tollygunge in the south was much cooler than Shyambazar in the north. What was so strange about one part of a forest being different from another? It was nothing but a quirk of nature.

Tulsi Babu had just put the bag down on the ground and stooped towards the shrub when a sharp query from Prodyot Babu interrupted him.'What on earth is that?'

Tulsi Babu had seen the thing too, but had not been bothered by it. 'Must be some sort of an egg,' he said.

Prodyot Babu thought it was a piece of egg-shaped rock, but on getting closer he realized that it was a genuine egg: yellow, with brown stripes flecked with blue. What creature could such a large egg belong to? A python?

Meanwhile, Tulsi Babu had already plucked some leafy branches off the shrub and put them in his bag. He wanted to take some more but something happened at that moment which made him stop.

The egg chose that very moment to hatch. Prodyot Babu jumped back at the sound of the cracking shell, but then gathered courage and took a few steps towards it.

The head was already out of the shell. It was not a snake, nor a crocodile or a turtle, but a bird.

Soon the whole body was out. The bird stood on its spindly legs and looked around. It was quite large; about the size of a hen. Prodyot Babu was very fond of birds and kept a mynah and a bulbul as pets; but he had never seen a chick as large as this. It had a big beak and long legs. Its purple plumes were unique, as was its alert behaviour so soon after birth.

Tulsi Babu, however, was not in the least interested in the chick. He had been intent on stuffing his bag with as many leaves from the plant as he could fit in.

Prodyot Babu looked around and commented, 'Very surprising; there seems to be no sign of its parents, at least not in the vicinity.'

'I think that's enough surprises for a day,' said Tulsi Babu, hoisting his bag on his shoulder. 'It's almost four. We must be out of the forest before it gets dark.'

Somewhat reluctantly, Prodyot Babu turned away from the chick and started walking with his friend. It would take at least half an hour to reach the waiting taxi.

A patter of feet made Prodyot Babu stop and turn round. The chick was looking straight at him.

Then it padded across and stopped in front of Tulsi Babu and, opening its unusually large beak, gripped the edge of Tulsi Babu's dhoti.

Prodyot Babu was so surprised that he didn't know what to say, until he saw Tulsi Babu pick up the chick and shove it into his bag. 'What do you think you're doing?' he cried in consternation. 'You put that unknown bird in your bag?'

'I've always wanted to keep a pet,' said Tulsi Babu, resuming his walk. 'Even mongrels are kept as pets. What's wrong with a nameless chick?'

Prodyot Babu saw the bird sticking its neck out of the swinging bag and glancing around with wide eyes.

Tulsi Babu lived in a flat on the second floor of a building in Masjidbari Street. He was a bachelor and besides him, there was only his servant Natabar and his cook Joykesto. There was another flat on the same floor, occupied by Tarit Sanyal, who was the proprietor of the Nabarun Press. Mr Sanyal was a short-tempered man made even more so by repeated power failures in the city which seriously affected the working of his press.

Two months had passed since Tulsi Babu's return from Dandakaranya. He had put the chick in a cage which he had specially ordered immediately upon his return. The cage was kept in a corner of the inner veranda. He had found a name for the chick: Big Bill; soon the Big was dropped and now it was just Bill.

The very first day he had acquired the chick in Jagdalpur, Tulsi Babu had tried to feed it grain but the chick had refused. Tulsi Babu had guessed, and rightly, that it was probably a non-vegetarian, and ever since he had been feeding it moths, cockroaches and whatever other insects he could find. Of late the bird's appetite seemed to have grown. It had started dragging its beak across the bars of the cage showing its immense dissatisfaction. Hence Tulsi Babu had been obliged to feed it meat. Natabar bought meat regularly from the market for its meals, which explained the bird's rapid growth in size.

Tulsi Babu had been far-sighted enough to buy a cage which was several sizes too large for the bird. His instinct had told him that the bird belonged to a large species. The roof of the cage was two and a half feet from the ground. But soon he noticed that when Bill stood straight his head nearly touched the roof, even though he was only two months old; he would soon need a larger cage.

The cry of the bird was a terrible sound. It had made Mr Sanyal choke on his tea one morning while he stood on the veranda. Normally the two neighbours hardly spoke to each other; but that day, after he had got over his fit of coughing, Mr Sanyal demanded to know what kind of an animal Tulsi Babu kept in his cage that yelled like that. It was true that the cry was more beast-like than bird-like.

Tulsi Babu was getting dressed to go to work. He appeared at the bedroom door and said, 'Not an animal, a bird. And whatever its cry, it certainly doesn't keep one awake at night the way your cat does.'

Tulsi Babu's retort put an end to the argument, but Mr Sanyal kept grumbling. It was a good thing the cage couldn't be seen from his flat; one sight of the bird would have led to even more serious consequences.

Although its looks didn't bother Tulsi Babu, they certainly worried Prodyot Babu. The two met rarely outside office hours, except once a week for a meal of kebabs and parathas at Mansur's. Prodyot Babu had a large family and many responsibilities. But since the visit to Dandakaranya, Tulsi Babu's pet was often on his mind. As a result he had started to drop in at Tulsi Babu's from time to time in the evenings. The bird's astonishing rate of growth and the change in its appearance were a constant source of amazement to Prodyot Babu. He was at a loss to see why Tulsi Babu should show no concern about it. Prodyot Babu had never imagined that the look in a bird's eye could be so malevolent. The black pupils in the amber irises would fix him with such an unwavering look that he would feel most uneasy. The bird's beak naturally grew in proportion with its body; shiny black in colour, it resembled an eagle's beak but was much larger in relation to the rest of the body. It was clear, from its rudimentary wings and its long sturdy legs and sharp talons, that the bird couldn't fly. Prodyot Babu had described the bird to many acquaintances, but no one had been able to identify it.

One Sunday Prodyot Babu came to Tulsi Babu with a camera borrowed from a nephew. There wasn't enough light in the cage, so he had come armed with a flash gun. Photography had been a hobby with him once, and he was able to summon up enough courage to point the camera at the bird in the cage and press the shutter. The scream of protest from the bird as the flash went off sent Prodyot Babu reeling back a full yard, and it struck him that the bird's cry should be recorded. Showing the photograph and playing back the cry might help in identifying the species. Something rankled in Prodyot Babu's mind; he hadn't yet mentioned it to his friend, but somewhere in a book or a magazine he had once seen a picture of a bird which greatly resembled this pet of Tulsi Babu's. If he came across the picture again, he would compare it with the photograph.

Later, when the two friends were having tea, Tulsi Babu came out with a new piece of information. Ever since Bill had arrived, crows and sparrows had stopped coming to the flat. This was a blessing because the sparrows would build nests in the most unlikely places, while the crows would make off with food from the kitchen. All that had stopped.

'Is that so?' asked Prodyot Babu, surprised as usual.

'Well, you've been here all this time; have you seen any other birds?'

Prodyot Babu realized that he hadn't. 'But what about your two servants? Have they got used to Bill?'

'The cook never goes near the cage, but Natabar feeds it meat with pincers. Even if he does have any objection, he hasn't come out with it. And when the bird turns nasty, one sight of me calms it down. By the way, what was the idea behind taking the photograph?'

Prodyot Babu didn't mention the real reason. He said, 'When it's no more, it'll remind you of it.'

Prodyot Babu had the photograph developed and printed the following day. He also had two enlargements made. One he gave to Tulsi Babu and the other he took to the ornithologist Ranajoy Shome. Only the other day an article by Mr Shome on the birds of Sikkim had appeared in the weekly magazine *Desh*.

But Mr Shome failed to identify the bird from the photograph. He asked where the bird could be seen, and Prodyot Babu answered with a barefaced lie. 'A friend of mine had sent this photograph from Osaka. He wanted me to identify the bird for him.'

Tulsi Babu noted the date in his diary: February the fourteenth, 1980. Big Bill, who had been transferred from a three-and-a-half-foot cage to a four-and-a-half-foot one only last month, had been guilty of a misdeed the previous night.

Tulsi Babu had been awakened by a suspicious sound in the middle of the night—a series of hard, metallic twangs. But the sound had soon stopped and had been followed by total silence.

Still, the suspicion that something was up lingered in Tulsi Babu's mind. He came out of the mosquito net. Moonlight fell on the floor through the grilled window. Tulsi Babu put on his slippers, took the electric torch from the table, and came out onto the veranda.

In the beam of the torch light he saw that the meshing on the cage had been ripped apart and a hole large enough for the bird to escape had been made. The cage was now empty.

Tulsi Babu's torch revealed nothing on this side. At the opposite end, the veranda turned right towards Mr Sanyal's flat.

Tulsi Babu reached the corner in a flash and swung his torch to the right.

It was just as he had feared.

Mr Sanyal's cat was now a helpless captive in Bill's beak. The shiny spots on the floor were obviously drops of blood. But the cat was still alive and thrashing its legs about.

Tulsi Babu cried out 'Bill' and the bird promptly dropped the cat from its beak.

Then it advanced with long strides, turned the corner, and went quietly back to its cage.

Even in this moment of crisis, Tulsi Babu couldn't help heaving a sigh of relief.

A padlock hung on the door of Mr Sanyal's room; he had left three days ago for a holiday, after the busy months of December and January when school books were printed in his press.

The best thing to do with the cat would be to toss it out of the window on to the street. Stray cats and dogs were run over every day on the streets of Calcutta; this would be just one more of them.

The rest of the night Tulsi Babu couldn't sleep.

The next day he had to absent himself from work for an hour or so while he went to the railway booking office; he happened to know one of the booking clerks which made his task easier. Prodyot Babu had asked after the bird and Tulsi Babu had replied that it was fine. Then he had added after a brief reflection—'I'm thinking of framing the photo you took of it.'

On the twenty-fourth of February, Tulsi Babu arrived in Jagdalpur for the second time. A packing case with Bill in it arrived in the luggage van on the same train. The case was provided with a hole for ventilation.

From Jagdalpur, Tulsi Babu set off with two coolies and the case in a car for the precise spot in the forest where he had found the bird.

At a certain milepost on the main road, Tulsi Babu got off the vehicle and, with the coolies carrying the packing case, set off for the scorched neem tree. It took him nearly an hour to reach the spot. The coolies put the case down. They had already been generously tipped and told that they would have to open the packing case. This was done, and Tulsi Babu was relieved to see that Bill was in fine fettle. The coolies, of course, bolted screaming at the sight of the bird, but that didn't worry Tulsi Babu. His purpose had been served. Bill was looking at him with a fixed stare. Its head already touched the four-and-a-half-foot high roof of the cage.

'Goodbye, Bill.'

The sooner the parting took place the better.

Tulsi Babu started on his journey back.

He hadn't told anybody in the office about his trip, not even Prodyot Babu, who naturally asked where he had been when he appeared at his desk on Monday. Tulsi Babu replied briefly that he had been to a niece's wedding in Naihati.

About a fortnight later, on a visit to Tulsi Babu's place, Prodyot Babu was surprised to see the cage empty. He asked about the bird. 'It's gone,' said Tulsi Babu.

Prodyot Babu naturally assumed that the bird was dead. He felt a twinge of remorse. He hadn't meant it seriously when he had said that the photo would remind Tulsi Babu of his pet when it was no more; he had no idea the bird would die so soon. The photograph he had taken had been framed and was hanging on the wall of the bedroom. Tulsi Babu seemed out of sorts; altogether the atmosphere was gloomy. To relieve the gloom, Prodyot Babu made a suggestion. 'We haven't been to Mansur's in a long while. What about going tonight for a meal of kebabs and parathas?'

'I'm afraid I have quite lost my taste for them.'

Prodyot Babu couldn't believe his ears. 'Lost your taste for kebabs? What's the matter? Aren't you well? Have you tried the herb the holy man prescribed?'

Tulsi Babu said that his blood pressure had come down to normal since he started having the juice of the chakraparna. What he didn't bother to mention was that he had forgotten all about herbal medicines as long as Bill had been with him, and that he had gone back to them only a week ago.

'By the way,' remarked Prodyot Babu, 'the mention of the herb reminds me—did you read in the papers today about the forest of Dandakaranya?'

'What did the papers say?'

Tulsi Babu bought a daily newspaper all right, but rarely got beyond the first page. The paper was near at hand. Prodyot Babu pointed out the news to him. The headline said: 'THE TERROR OF DANDAKARANYA'.

The news described a sudden and unexpected threat to the domestic animals and poultry in the village around the forests of Dandakaranya. Some unknown species of animal had started to devour them. No tigers were known to exist in that area, and proof had been found that something other than a feline species had been causing the havoc. Tigers usually drag their prey to their lairs; this particular beast didn't. The shikaris engaged by the Madhya Pradesh government had searched for a week but failed to locate any beast capable of such carnage. As a result, panic had spread amongst the villagers. One particular villager claimed that he had seen a two-legged creature running away from his cowshed. He had gone to investigate, and found his buffalo lying dead with a sizeable portion of its lower abdomen eaten away.

Tulsi Babu read the news, folded the paper, and put it back on the table.

'Don't tell me you don't find anything exceptional in the story?' said Prodyot Babu.

Tulsi Babu shook his head. In other words, he didn't.

Three days later, a strange thing happened to Prodyot Babu.

His wife had just opened a tin of digestive biscuits at breakfast and was about to serve them to him with his tea when Prodyot Babu abruptly left the dining table and rushed out of the house.

By the time he reached his friend Animesh's flat in Ekdalia Road, he was trembling with excitement.

He snatched the newspaper away from his friend's hands, threw it aside and said panting: 'Where do you keep your copies of *Reader's Digest*? Quick—it's most important!'

Animesh shared with million of others a taste for *Reader's Digest*. He was greatly surprised by his friend's behaviour but scarcely had the opportunity to show it. He went to a bookcase and dragged out some dozen issues of the magazine from the bottom shelf.

'Which number are you looking for?'

Prodyot Babu took the whole bunch, flipped through the pages of a number of issues, and finally found what he was looking for.

'Yes—this is the bird. No doubt about it.'

His fingers rested on a picture of a conjectural model of a bird kept in the Chicago Museum of Natural History. It showed an attendant cleaning the model with a brush.

'Andalgalornis,' said Prodyot Babu, reading out the name. The name meant terror-bird. The article with the picture described it as a huge prehistoric species, carnivorous, faster than a horse, and extremely ferocious.

The doubt which had crept into Prodyot Babu's mind was proved right when in the office next morning Tulsi Babu came to him and said that he had to go to Dandakaranya once again, and that he would be delighted if Prodyot Babu would join him and bring his gun with him. There was too little time to obtain sleeping accommodation in the train, but that couldn't be helped as the matter was very urgent.

Prodyot Babu agreed at once.

In the excitement of the pursuit, the two friends didn't mind the discomfort of the journey. Prodyot Babu said nothing about the bird in the *Reader's Digest*. He could do so later; there was plenty of time for that. Tulsi Babu had in the meantime told him everything. He had also mentioned that he didn't really believe the gun would be needed; he had suggested taking it only as a precaution. Prodyot Babu, on the other hand, couldn't share his friend's optimism. He believed the gun was essential, and he was fully prepared for any eventuality. The morning paper had mentioned that the Madhya Pradesh government had announced a reward of 5,000 rupees to anyone who succeeded in killing or capturing the creature, which had been declared a man-eater ever since a woodcutter's son had fallen victim to it.

In Jagdalpur, permission to shoot the creature was obtained from the conservator of forests, Mr Tirumalai. But he warned that Tulsi Babu and Prodyot Babu would have to go on their own as nobody could be persuaded to go into the forest any more.

Prodyot Babu asked if any information had been received from the shikaris who had preceded them. Tirumalai turned grave. 'So far four shikaris have attempted to kill the beast. Three of them had no success. The fourth never returned.'

'Never returned?'

'No. Ever since then shikaris have been refusing to go. So you had better think twice before undertaking the trip.'

Prodyot Babu was shaken, but his friend's nonchalance brought back his courage. 'I think we will go,' he said.

This time they had to walk a little further because the taxi refused to take the dirt road which went part of the way into the forest. Tulsi Babu was confident that the job would be over in two hours, and the taxi driver agreed to wait that long upon being given a tip of fifty rupees. The two friends set off on their quest.

It was spring now, and the forest wore a different look from the previous trips. Nature was following its course, and yet there was an unnatural silence. There were no bird calls; not even the cries of cuckoos.

As usual, Tulsi Babu was carrying his shoulder bag. Prodyot Babu knew there was a packet in it, but he didn't know what it contained. Prodyot Babu himself was carrying his rifle and bullets.

As the undergrowth became thinner, they could see farther into the forest. That was why the two friends were able to see from a distance the body of a man lying spreadeagled on the ground behind a jackfruit tree. Tulsi Babu hadn't noticed it at first, and stopped only when Prodyot Babu pointed it out to him. Prodyot Babu took a firm grip on the gun and walked towards the body. Tulsi Babu went halfway, and then turned back.

'You look as if you've seen a ghost,' said Tulsi Babu when his friend rejoined him. 'Isn't that the missing shikari?'

'It must be,' said Prodyot Babu hoarsely. 'But it won't be easy to identify the corpse. The head's missing.'

The rest of the way they didn't speak at all.

It took one hour to reach the neem tree, which meant they must have walked at least three miles. Prodyot Babu noticed that the medicinal shrub had grown fresh leaves and was back to its old shape.

'Bill! Billie!'

There was something faintly comic about the call, and Prodyot Babu couldn't help smiling. But the next moment he realized that for Tulsi Babu the call was quite natural. He had succeeded in taming the monster bird, which Prodyot Babu had seen with his own eyes.

Tulsi Babu's call resounded in the forest.

'Bill! Bill! Billie!'

Now Prodyot Babu saw something stirring in the depths of the forest. It was coming towards them, and at such a speed that it seemed to grow bigger and bigger every second.

It was the bird.

The gun in Prodyot Babu's hand suddenly felt very heavy. He wondered if he would be able to use it at all.

The bird slowed down and approached them stealthily through the vegetation.

Andalgalornis. Prodyot Babu would never forget the name. A bird as tall as a man. Ostriches too were tall; but that was largely because of their neck. This bird's back itself was as high as an average man. In other words, the bird had grown a foot and a half in just about a month. The colour of its plumes had changed too. There were blotches of black on the purple now. And the malevolent look in its amber eyes which Prodyot Babu found he could confront when the bird was in captivity, was now for him unbearably terrifying. The look was directed at its ex-master.

There was no knowing what the bird would do. Thinking its stillness to be a prelude to an attack, Prodyot Babu made an attempt to raise the gun with his shaking hands. But the moment he did so, the bird turned its gaze at him, its feathers puffing out to give it an even more terrifying appearance.

'Lower the gun,' hissed Tulsi Babu in a tone of admonition.

Prodyot Babu obeyed. The bird lowered its feathers too and transferred its gaze to its master.

'I don't know if you are still hungry,' said Tulsi Babu, 'but I hope you will eat this because I am giving it to you.'

Tulsi Babu had already brought out the packet from the bag. He now unwrapped it and tossed the contents towards the bird. It was a large chunk of meat.

'You've been the cause of my shame. I hope you will behave yourself from now on.'

Amazed, Prodyot Babu watched as the bird picked up the chunk with its huge beak, and put it inside its mouth.

'This time it really is goodbye.'

Tulsi Babu turned. Prodyot Babu was afraid to turn his back on the bird, and for a while walked backwards with his eyes on the bird. When he found that the bird was making no attempt to follow him or attack him, he too turned round and joined his friend.

A week later the news came out in the papers of the end of the terror in Dandakaranya. Prodyot Babu had not mentioned anything to Tulsi Babu about Andalgalornis, and the fact that the bird had been extinct for three million years. But the news in the papers obliged him to come to his friend. 'I'm at a loss to know how it happened,' he said. 'Perhaps you can throw some light on it.'

'There's no mystery at all,' said Tulsi Babu. 'I only mixed some of my medicine with the meat I gave him.'

'Medicine?'

'An extract of chakraparna. It turns one into a vegetarian. Just as it has done with me.'

Translated by Satyajit Ray

First published in Bengali in 1980

The Attic

If you left National Highway number forty and took a right turn only ten kilometres later, you would find Brahmapur. A few minutes before we reached this turning, I asked Aditya, 'Hey, would you like to visit the place where you were born? You never went back there after you left, did you?'

'No, I didn't. That was twenty-nine years ago. I'm sure our house is now just a pile of rubble. It was nearly two hundred years old when I left it. For that matter, I wonder what happened to my old school? If it's been repaired and renovated extensively, I don't think I'll be able to recognize it. So if I go back there in the hope of reliving childhood memories, I know I'll be disappointed. However, what we could do,' Aditya said, 'is stop at Noga's tea shop and have a cup of tea. That is, if it's still there.'

I turned right and began driving down the road that went to Brahmapur. Aditya's ancestors had once been the local zamindars. His father, Brajendranarayan, left Brahmapur permanently only a year after Independence, and started a business in Calcutta. Aditya remained in Brahmapur until he finished school. Then he moved to Calcutta and went to the university there. I was his classmate in college. When his father died in 1976, Aditya took charge of his father's business. I was now his partner as well as his friend. We were building a new factory in Deodarganj, and were on our way back from there. The car belonged to Aditya. He had driven it on the way to Deodarganj. I was driving it on our return journey. It was now half past three in the afternoon. The month was February, the sunshine pleasantly warm, and there were open fields on both sides, stretching to the horizon. The winter crop had been harvested. It had been a good year for the farmers.

Ten minutes later, we could see buildings and trees. Brahmapur turned out to be a thriving town. Within a few minutes of reaching it, Aditya suddenly said, 'Stop.'

The school building stood on our left. A semi-circular iron frame, fixed over the gate, proclaimed its name in iron letters: Victoria High School, estd. 1892. A driveway ran through the gate, ending before a two-storey building. To the left of the driveway was the sports ground. We parked the car outside, got out and stood at the gate.

'Does it match your memories?' I asked Aditya.

'Not in the least,' Aditya replied. 'Our school did not have a first floor; nor did it have that other building on the right. There used to be an open ground, where we used to play kabaddi.'

'You were a good student, weren't you?'

'Yes, but I always stood second. The top position invariably went to another boy.'

'Do you want to go inside?'

'Are you mad?'

We stood and stared for about a minute before returning to our car. 'Where is that tea shop you mentioned?'

'About three furlongs from here. Straight down that road, near a crossing. A grocery store was next to it, and a Shiva temple just opposite. People from Calcutta used to come to look at it. It was made of terracotta.'

We drove off. 'Where's your house?'

'At the far end of town. I have no wish to see it. I'd only get depressed.'

'Still . . . don't you want to have just one look?'

'OK, may be. I'll think about it. Let's have a cup of tea first.'

We reached the crossing quite soon. The spire of the temple was the first thing we saw. As we approached it, Aditya gave a sudden exclamation. My eyes fell on a signboard at once. 'Nogen's Tea Cabin', it said. The grocery store was also there. Perhaps it was only the appearance of people that was likely to change dramatically in twenty-nine years. Shops and lanes in a town like Brahmapur would never change that much in that time.

It was not just the tea shop that still existed. Its owner, too, was there. He had turned sixty, and had a rather thin and shrivelled appearance. He was clean shaven, but his white hair had been carefully brushed. The lower portion of a blue striped shirt peeped from under a green cotton shawl, draped over a short dhoti.

'Where are you coming from?' he asked, glancing first at the car, then at its two passengers. Naturally, there was no question of his recognizing Aditya.

'Deodarganj,' Aditya replied, 'We're on our way to Calcutta.'

'I see. So why—?'

'We stopped here simply to have a cup of tea in your shop.'

'Good. Do sit down, sir. I can offer you some nice biscuits, too, and chanachur.'

'Thank you. Give us a couple of nankhatai biscuits.'

We took two tin chairs. There seemed to be only one other customer in the shop, sitting at a corner table, though he had neither a cup of tea, nor a plate of biscuits before him. In fact, he appeared to be asleep.

'Mr Sanyal!' Nogen Babu addressed him, raising his voice quite high. 'It's nearly four o'clock. Time you went home, don't you think? I'll soon start getting more people in.' Then he turned to us, winked and said, 'He's deaf. His eyesight's not very good, either. But he cannot afford to get glasses made.'

It became clear that people here liked making fun of this man. But that was not all. From the way Mr Sanyal reacted to Nogen Babu's words, I began to doubt his sanity. He stared at us for a few moments, then suddenly shook himself and burst into poetry. He stretched out his thin right arm, widened his shortsighted eyes, and began reciting:

Hark, there come the plunderers from Maratha,
Get ready to fight them!
Called the Lord of the Ajmer Castle,
Dumoraj was his name.

Starting with these lines, he got to his feet, then went on to recite the whole of Tagore's 'Keeping A Promise'. He ended by folding his hands in a namaskar and bowing his head, without looking at anyone in particular. Then he walked out of the shop rather unsteadily, and went down one of the roads that met at the crossing, possibly to find his own house. There were plenty of people near the crossing. I could see at least ten different people sitting in the sun outside the tea shop, but none of them paid the slightest attention to Mr Sanyal. His recitation of that long poem did not appear to have any effect at all on his audience. The reason was not difficult to guess. Who would want to take any notice of the ravings of a madman?

Having seen many other lunatics before, it did not take me long to get over my surprise at Mr Sanyal's behaviour. But one look at Aditya's face startled me. He seemed to have been stirred by some strong emotion. I asked him what the matter was, but instead of giving me a reply, Aditya turned to Nogen Babu and said, 'Who is that man? What does he do?'

Nogen Babu had brought us tea in two steaming glasses, with a plate of biscuits. 'Shashanka Sanyal?' he asked, placing these before us. 'What can he do? His is truly a cursed life, sir, I can tell you that. I've already told you about his hearing and eyesight. Perhaps his mind is going too. But he has not forgotten anything from his past. He keeps reciting the poems he had learnt in school, and drives everyone up the wall. His father was a school teacher, but he died many years ago. He owned a little land. Most of it had to be sold when Shashanka Sanyal got his daughter married. Then he lost his wife, about five years ago. His only son did his B Com. and was working in Calcutta; but last year, he fell off a mini bus and died. Mr Sanyal changed after that . . . I mean, he's been behaving strangely ever since his son died.'

'Where does he live?'

'Jogesh Kaviraj was his father's friend. Mr Sanyal lives in a room in his house. They feed him, too. He comes to my shop to have tea and biscuits. He never forgets to pay for what he eats here; he still has his pride, you see. But God knows how long he'll be able to go on like this. After all, things don't always remain the same, do they? But, sir, you live in a big city like Calcutta. You would know far more about life and people. Who am I to tell you anything?'

'Jogesh Kaviraj . . . isn't his house to the west of that ground where a big fair is held every year?'

'You know? Are you—?'

'Yes, I had connections here at one time.'

Other customers entered the shop. Nogen Babu had to move away, so the conversation could go no further. We paid for our tea and left the shop.

A group of small boys had gathered round the car. I had to get rid of them before we could get in. This time, Aditya sat in the driver's seat. 'The way to our house is a little complicated. It would be simpler if I drove,' he explained.

'Oh? So you do want to go and see it?'

'It has now become essential.'

The look on his face told me that even if I asked him why he had suddenly changed his mind, he would not speak. His face was set, every muscle tense and taut.

We set off. Aditya took the road that ran east from the crossing. After a few turnings to the left, and some more to the right, we could finally see a house with a high compound wall. In order to reach its old, crumbling front gate, complete with a naubatkhana, we had to negotiate yet another turning.

It was obvious that the three-storey house had once been very impressive, but what remained of it was no more than its basic structure. It might even be haunted, I thought to myself. A broken signboard hung from a wall, from which I gathered that, at some time or another, the house had acted as the office of a development board. It was now totally deserted.

Aditya drove through the gate, then took the car right up the driveway, which was covered with weeds and other wild plants, before stopping at the front door. There was no sign of another human being. It seemed as if no one had bothered to visit this house in the last ten years. There must have been a large garden in front of the house. Now it was a veritable jungle.

'Are you thinking of going inside?' I asked. I was obliged to ask this question, as Aditya had got out of the car and begun walking towards the front door.

'Yes. I couldn't climb up to the roof without going in.'

'The roof . . .?'

'The attic,' replied Aditya, sounding more mysterious than ever.

He was clearly not going to be dissuaded. So I got out, too, and followed him.

The house looked far worse from inside. The beams of the ceiling looked as if they had no wish to go on doing their job; it would not be long before the ceiling caved in. The front room had obviously been where visitors were entertained. Three pieces of broken old furniture were piled in a corner. The floor had disappeared under a thick layer of dust.

A veranda ran behind the front room, at the end of which stood the remains of a large hall. Aditya had told me about the many pujas, jatras, music competitions and other events that used to be held in this hall. Now, its only inhabitants were pigeons, rats, bats and cockroaches. I would not have been surprised if a number of snakes slipped out of the cracks in the wall.

We crossed the hall and turned right. A few feet away was a staircase. We began climbing the steps, removing cobwebs on our way. The top floors were of no interest to us, so we continued climbing until we reached the roof.

'This is the attic,' said Aditya. 'It was my favourite room.' A lot of children have a special fondness for the attic. I did, too. It is the only place in a house where a child can have supreme command.

In this particular attic, a portion of the wall had crumbled away, to create an artificial window. Through it, I could see the sky, the open fields, a portion of a rice mill, and even the spire of the eighteenth-century terracotta temple.

It seemed that this room had suffered more damage than any other in the whole house, for the ravages of time had acted on the top of the house far more strongly than the rooms below. The floor was covered with bird droppings, pieces of straw, dried grass and other rubbish. In one corner stood a broken easy chair, a similarly broken cricket bat, a twisted wicker waste paper basket and a wooden packing crate.

Aditya pulled the packing crate to one side, and said, 'If this thing collapses when I stand on it then you'll have to help me out. Well, here goes . . .!'

There was a niche fairly high up on the wall. Aditya had to stand on the crate in order to reach it. As he began rummaging in it, a couple of sparrows had to suffer a loss, for their freshly built nest got destroyed. It fell to the ground, spreading more rubbish over quite a large area. 'Oh, thank God!' exclaimed Aditya.

This could only mean that he had found whatever he was looking for. One quick glance at the object showed something that looked like a carrom striker. But I failed to see why it had been hidden here, or why it had to be recovered after twenty-nine years.

Aditya rubbed it clean with his handkerchief before putting it in his pocket. When I asked him what it was, he simply said, 'You'll soon find out.'

We climbed down the steps, got back into our car, and went back the way we had come. Aditya stopped the car in front of a shop as we reached the main crossing. We got out once more.

The Crown Jewellers, proclaimed a sign.

We walked into the shop and found the jeweller. 'Could you please take a look at this?' asked Aditya, handing over the object to the owner of the shop. He was an old man, wearing glasses with thick lenses.

The man peered at the disc. Now I could see what it really was. 'This appears to be quite old,' the man said.

'Yes, it is.'

'You don't often get to see such a thing these days.'

'No. Could you please weigh it and tell me how much it's worth?' The old man pulled his scales closer, and placed the grimy disc in it.

Our next stop was the house of Jogesh Kaviraj. A certain suspicion was raising its head in my mind, but looking at Aditya's face, I did not dare ask a single question.

Two young boys, about ten years old, were playing marbles outside the house. They stopped their game and rose to their feet at the sight of a car, looking deeply curious. 'Mr Sanyal?' they said, on being asked where he lived. 'His is the first room on the left, if you go through the front door.'

The front door was ajar. Someone was talking in the room on our left. As we got closer, it became obvious that Mr Sanyal was still reciting poetry, all by himself. It was another long poem by Tagore. He did not stop even when we appeared at his door. He went on, as if he could not see us at all, until he had spoken the last line.

'May we come in?' asked Aditya.

Mr Sanyal turned his eyes to look straight at us. 'No one ever comes here,' he said in a flat voice.

'Would you object to our visiting you?'

'No. Come in.'

We stepped in. There was no furniture in the room except a bed. We remained standing. Mr Sanyal continued to stare at us.

'Do you remember Adityanarayan Choudhury?' Aditya asked.

'Of course,' Mr Sanyal replied, 'A thoroughly spoilt brat from a wealthy family. That's what he was. A good student, but he could never beat me. So he was jealous . . . extremely jealous of me. And he told lies.'

'I know,' Aditya said. Then he took out a small packet from his pocket and handed it to Mr Sanyal. 'Aditya sent this for you,' he added.

'What is it?'

'Money.'

'Money? How much?'

'One hundred and fifty. He said he'd be very pleased if you took it.'

'Really? I hardly know whether to laugh or cry. Aditya has sent me money? Why would he do that?'

'People change with time, don't they? Perhaps the Aditya you once knew does not exist any more.'

'Rubbish! Aditya would never change. I got the prize. A silver medal it was, presented by the barrister, Ramsharan Banerjee. Aditya could not bear it. He took it from me, said he simply wanted to show it to his father. Then it just disappeared. Aditya said there was a hole in his pocket, and the medal had slipped through it. I never got it back.'

'This money is what that medal was worth. You deserve it.'

Mr Sanyal stared, looking absolutely amazed. 'That medal? But it was only a silver medal, worth maybe five rupees, at the most.'

'Yes, but the price of silver has risen. It's now thirty times the price it was when you won that medal.'

'Really? I must admit I didn't know that. But . . .'Mr Sanyal glanced at the fifteen ten-rupee notes he was clutching. Then he raised his face and looked directly at Aditya. His face now wore a strange, changed expression.

'This smacks rather heavily of charity, doesn't it, Aditya?' he said.

We remained silent. Mr Sanyal went on gazing at Aditya. Then he shook his head and smiled. 'When I saw you at the tea shop, I recognized you at once from that mole on your right cheek. But I could see that you had not recognized me. So I decided to recite the same poem for which I had won that medal, in the hope that it might remind you of what you had done. Then, when I saw that you had actually come to my house, I couldn't help saying all those nasty things. It's been many years, but I have not forgotten what you did to me.'

'You are fully justified in feeling the way you do. Everything you said about me is true. Still, if you took the money, I'd be very grateful.'

'No,' Mr Sanyal shook his head again. 'This money will not last for ever, will it? One day, I will have spent it all. I don't want your money, Aditya. What I would like is that medal, if it could be found. If someone gave it to me now, I could forget that one very unpleasant incident that marred my childhood. I would then have no more regrets.'

The medal, hidden in a niche in an attic twenty-nine years ago, finally returned to its rightful owner. The words engraved on it were still clearly legible: 'Master Shashanka Sanyal, special prize for recitation of poetry, 1948'.

Translated by Gopa Majumdar
First published in Bengali in 1981

Bhuto

Naveen came back disappointed a second time. He had failed to get Akrur Babu's support.

It was at a function in Uttarpara that Naveen had first learnt about Akrur Babu's amazing talent—ventriloquism. Naveen did not even know the word. Dwijapada had told him. Diju's father was a professor and had a library of his own. Diju had even taught him the correct spelling of the word.

Akrur Chowdhury was the only person present on the stage but he was conversing with someone invisible, hidden somewhere near the ceiling in the middle of the auditorium. Akrur Babu would throw a question at him. He would answer from above the audience's heads.

'Haranath, how are you?'

'I am fine, thank you, sir.'

'Heard you have become interested in music. Is that true?'

'Yes, sir.'

'Classical music?'

'Yes, sir, classical music.'

'Do you sing yourself?'

'No, sir.'

'Do you play an instrument?'

'That's right, sir.'

'What kind of instrument? The sitar?'

'No, sir.'

'Sarod?'

'No, sir.'

'What do you play, then?'

'A gramophone, sir.'

The auditorium boomed with laughter and applause. Akrur Babu looked at the ceiling to ask a question and then bent his head slightly to catch the reply. But it was impossible to tell that he was answering his own questions.

His lips did not move at all.

Naveen was astounded. He had to learn this art. Life would not be worth living if he did not. Could Akrur Chowdhury not be persuaded to teach him? Naveen was not very interested in studies. He had finished school, but had been sitting at home for the last three years. He simply did not feel like going in for further studies.

Having lost his father in his childhood, he had been brought up by an uncle. His uncle wanted him to join his plywood business. But Naveen was interested in something quite different. His passion lay in learning magic. He had already mastered a few tricks at home. But after having seen a performance by Akrur Chowdhury, all that seemed totally insignificant.

Naveen learnt from the organizers of the show that Akrur Babu lived in Amherst Street in Calcutta. He took a train to Calcutta the very next day and made his way to the house of the man who, in his mind, had already become his guru. But the guru rejected his proposal outright.

'What do you do?' was the first question the ventriloquist asked him. The sight of the man at close quarters was making Naveen's heart beat faster. About forty-five years old, he sported a deep black bushy moustache and his jet black hair, parted in the middle, rippled down to his shoulders. His eyes were droopy, though Naveen had seen them sparkle on stage under the spotlights.

Naveen decided to be honest. 'I've always been interested in magic,' he said, 'but your performance the other day got me passionately interested in ventriloquism.'

Akrur Babu shook his head. 'This kind of art is not for all and sundry. You have to be extremely diligent. No one taught me this art. Go and try to learn it by yourself, if you can.'

Naveen left. But only a week later, he was back again, ready to fall at Akrur Babu's feet. During the last seven days he had dreamt of nothing but ventriloquism.

But this time things got worse. Akrur Babu practically threw him out of his house. 'You should have realized the first time I was not prepared to teach you at all,' he said. 'This clearly shows your lack of perception and intelligence. No one can learn magic without these basic qualities—and certainly not my kind of magic.'

After the first visit Naveen had returned feeling depressed. This time he got angry. Let Akrur Chowdhury go to hell. He would learn it all by himself.

He bought a book on ventriloquism from College Street and began to practice. Everyone—including he himself—was surprised at his patience and perseverance.

The basic rule was simple. There were only a few letters in the alphabet like 'b', 'f', 'm' and 'p' that required one to close and open one's lips. If these letters could be pronounced slightly differently, there was no need to move the lips at all. But there was one other thing. When answering one's own questions, the voice had to be changed. This required a lot of practice, but Naveen finally got it right. When his uncle and some close friends openly praised him after a performance at home, he realized he had more or less mastered the art.

But this was only the beginning.

The days of the invisible audience were over. Modern ventriloquists used a puppet specially designed so that it was possible to slip a hand under it and make its head turn and its lips move. When asked a question, it was the puppet who answered.

Pleased with the progress he had made, his uncle offered to pay for such a puppet for Naveen. Naveen spent about a couple of weeks trying to think what his puppet should look like. Then he hit upon the most marvellous idea.

His puppet would look exactly like Akrur Chowdhury. In other words, Akrur Babu would become a mere puppet in his hands! What a wonderful way to get his own back!

Naveen had kept a photograph of Akrur Babu that he had once found on a hand-poster. He now showed it to Adinath, the puppet maker.

'It must have moustaches like these, a middle parting, droopy eyes and round cheeks.'

What fun it would be to have a puppet like that! Naveen hoped fervently that Akrur Babu would come to his shows.

The puppet was ready in a week. Its clothes were also the same as Akrur Chowdhury's: a black high-necked coat and a white dhoti under it, tucked in at the waist.

Naveen happened to know Sasadhar Bose of the Netaji Club. It was not difficult to get himself included in one of their functions.

He was an instant hit. His puppet had been given a name—Bhutnath, Bhuto for short. The audience thoroughly enjoyed their conversation. Bhuto, Naveen told them, was a supporter of the East Bengal Football Club and he himself supported their opponents, Mohun Bagan. The verbal exchange was so chirpy that no one noticed Bhuto say 'East Gengal' and 'Ohan Agan'.

Naveen became famous practically overnight. Invitations from other clubs began pouring in. He even started to appear on television. There was now no need to worry about his future. He had found a way to earn his living.

At last, one day, Akrur Babu came to meet him.

Naveen had, in the meantime, left Uttarpara and moved into a flat in Mirzapur Street in Calcutta. His landlord, Suresh Mutsuddi, was a nice man. He knew of Naveen's success and treated him with due respect. Naveen had performed recently in Mahajati Sadan and received a lot of acclaim. The organizers of various functions were now vying with one another to get Naveen to perform for them. Naveen himself had changed over the last few months. Success had given him a new confidence and self-assurance.

Akrur Babu had probably got his address from the organizers of his show in Mahajati Sadan. Bhuto and he had talked about the underground railway that evening.

'You know about pataal rail in Calcutta, don't you, Bhuto?'

'No, I don't!'

'That is strange. Everyone in Calcutta knows about it.'

Bhuto shook his head. 'No. I haven't heard of that one. But I do know of hospital rail.'

'Hospital rail?'

'Of course. It's a huge operation, I hear, the whole city's being cut open under intensive care. What else would you call it but hospital rail?'

Today, Naveen was writing a new script on load shedding. He had realized that what the audience liked best were subjects that they could relate to—load shedding, crowded buses, rising prices. His script was coming along quite well when, suddenly, someone knocked on the door. Naveen got up to open it and was completely taken aback to find Akrur Babu standing outside.

'May I come in?'

'Of course.'

Naveen offered him his chair.

Akrur Babu did not sit down immediately. His eyes were fixed on Bhuto.

Bhuto was lying on the table, totally inert.

Akrur Babu went forward, picked him up and began examining his face closely.

There was nothing that Naveen could do. He had started to feel faintly uneasy, but the memory of his humiliation at Akrur Babu's house had not faded from his mind.

'So you have turned me into a puppet in your hands!'

Akrur Babu finally sat down.

'Why did you do this?'

Naveen said, 'That should not be too difficult to understand. I had come to you with great hope. You crushed it totally. But I must say this—this puppet, this image of yours, has brought me all my success. I am able to live decently only because of it.'

Akrur Babu was still staring at Bhuto. He said, 'I don't know if you've heard this already. I had a show in Barasat the other day. The minute I arrived on the stage, the cat-calls began—"Bhuto! Bhuto!" Surely you realize this was not a very pleasant experience for me? I may be responsible, in a way, for your success, but you are beginning to threaten my livelihood. Did you think I would accept a situation like this so easily?'

It was dark outside. There was no electricity. Two candles flickered in Naveen's room. Akrur Babu's eyes glowed in their light just as Naveen had seen them glow on the stage. The little man cast a huge shadow on the wall. Bhutnath lay on the table, as droopy-eyed as ever, silent and immobile.

'You may not be aware of this,' said Akrur Babu, 'but my knowledge of magic isn't limited only to ventriloquism. From the age of eighteen to thirty-eight I stayed with an unknown but amazingly gifted magician, learning his art. No, not here in Calcutta. He lived in a remote place at the foothills of the Himalayas.'

'Have you ever shown on stage any of those other items you learnt?'

'No, I haven't because those are not meant for the stage. I had promised my guru never to use that knowledge simply to earn a living. I have kept my word.'

'But what are you trying to tell me now? I don't understand.'

'I have come only to warn you, although I must admit I have been impressed by your dedication. No one actually taught me the art of ventriloquism. I had to teach myself, just as you have done. Professional magicians do not teach anyone else the real tricks of the trade—they have never done so. But I am not prepared to tolerate the impertinence you have shown in designing your puppet. That is all I came to tell you.'

Akrur Babu rose from his chair. Then he glanced at Bhutnath and said, 'My hair and my moustaches have only recently started to grey. I can see that you have, in anticipation, already planted a few grey strands in your puppet's hair. All right, then. I'll take my leave now.'

Akrur Babu left.

Naveen closed the door and stood before Bhutnath. Grey hair? Yes, one or two were certainly visible. He had not noticed these before, which was surprising since he held the puppet in his hand and spoke to it so often. How could he have been so unobservant?

Anyway, there was no point in wasting time thinking about it. Anyone could make a mistake. He had obviously concentrated only on Bhutnath's face and not looked at his hair closely enough.

But it was impossible to rid himself of a sneaking suspicion.

The next day, he stuffed Bhuto into the leather case made specially for him and went straight to Adinath Pal. There he brought Bhuto out of the case, laid him flat on the ground and said, 'Look at these few strands of grey hair. Did you put these in?'

Adinath Pal seemed quite taken aback. 'Why, no! Why should I? You did not ask for a mixture of black and grey hair, did you?'

'Could you not have made a mistake?'

'Yes, of course. Those few strands might have been pasted purely by mistake. But would you not have noticed it immediately when you came to collect the puppet? You know what I think? I do believe someone has planted these deliberately without your knowledge.'

Perhaps he was right. The whole thing had happened without his knowledge.

A strange thing happened at the function organized by the Friends Club in Chetla.

A clear evidence of Bhuto's popularity was that the organizers had saved his item for the last. In the midst of a rather interesting dialogue on the subject of load shedding, Naveen noticed that Bhuto was uttering words that were not in the script. These included difficult words in English which Naveen himself never used—he hardly knew what they meant.

This was a totally new experience for Naveen, although it made no difference to the show for the words were being used quite appropriately and drawing frequent applause from the crowd. Thank goodness none of them knew Naveen had not ever been to college.

But this unexpected behaviour of his puppet upset Naveen. He kept feeling that some unseen force had assumed control, pushing him into the background.

Upon reaching home after the show, he closed the door of his room and placed Bhuto under a table lamp.

Did Bhuto have that little mole on his forehead before? No, he most certainly did not. Naveen had noticed a similar mole on Akrur Babu's forehead only the other day. It was really quite small, not easily noticeable unless one looked carefully. But now it had appeared on Bhuto's face.

And that was not all. There was something else.

At least ten more strands of grey hair. And deep dark rings under the eyes. These were definitely not there before.

Naveen began pacing up and down impatiently. He was beginning to feel decidedly uneasy. He believed in magic—but his kind of magic was something in which man was in full command. For Naveen, anything to do with the supernatural was not just unacceptable—it was evil. He could see signs of evil in the changes in Bhuto.

At the same time, however, it was impossible to think of Bhuto as anything other than an inert, lifeless object, a mere puppet in his hands despite his droopy eyes and the slight smile on his lips. And yet, his whole appearance was undergoing a change.

It was Naveen's belief that the same changes were taking place in Akrur Babu. He, too, must have started to go grey; his eyes, too, must have got dark circles under them.

Naveen had the habit of talking to Bhuto every now and then, simply to practise his technique. Their conversation went like this:

'It's rather hot today, isn't it, Bhuto?'

'Yes, it's very stuwy.'

'But you have an advantage, don't you? You don't sweat and perspire.'

'How can a ugget sweat and erswire? Ha, ha, ha, ha . . .'

Today, Naveen asked him quite involuntarily, 'What on earth is going on, Bhuto? Why is all this happening?'

Bhuto's reply startled him.

'Karwa, karwa!' he said.

Karma!

The word slipped out through Naveen's lips, just as it would have done on the stage. But he knew he had not said it consciously. Someone had made him utter that word and he felt he knew who that someone might be.

That night, he refused his dinner despite repeated requests from his cook.

Normally, he slept quite well. But tonight he took a pill to help him sleep. At around one in the morning, the pill began to work. Naveen put down the magazine he was reading, switched off the light and fell asleep.

Only a little while later, however, he opened his eyes.

Who had been coughing in the room?

Was it he himself? But he did not have a cough. And yet, it seemed as though someone at close quarters was coughing very softly.

He switched on the lamp.

Bhutnath was still sitting in the same spot, motionless. But he now appeared to be slouching a little with his right arm flung across his chest.

Naveen looked at the clock. It was half past three. The chowkidar outside was doing his rounds, beating his stick on the ground. A dog barked in the distance. An owl flew past his house, hooting raucously. Someone next door obviously had a cough. And a gust of wind must have made Bhuto bend forward slightly. There was no earthly reason to feel scared today, in the twentieth century, living in a busy street of a large city like Calcutta.

Naveen switched off the light and fell asleep once more.

The next day, for the first time in his career, he experienced failure.

The Finlay Recreation Club had invited him to their annual function. A large audience was packed into an enormous hall. As always, his item was the last. Songs, recitations, a Kathak recital and then ventriloquism by Naveen Munshi.

Before setting off from home, he had done all that he always did to take care of his voice. He knew how important it was for a ventriloquist to have a clear throat.

His voice sounded perfectly normal before he went on stage. In fact, he noticed nothing wrong when he asked Bhuto the first question. Disaster struck when it was Bhuto's turn to speak.

His voice sounded hoarse, like that of a man suffering from an acute attack of cough and cold. Naveen knew the audience could not hear a word Bhuto was saying. Strangely enough, it was only Bhuto's voice that seemed to be affected. His own still sounded normal.

'Louder, please!' yelled a few people from the back. Those sitting in the front rows were too polite to yell, but it was obvious that they could not hear anything either.

Naveen tried for another five minutes and then had to withdraw, defeated. Never had he felt so embarrassed.

He declined the organizers' offer to pay him his fee. He could not accept any money under the circumstances. But surely this horrible situation could not last for ever? In spite of his embarrassment, Naveen still believed that soon, things would return to normal.

It was a very hot and sultry night, and over and above there was this new and unpleasant experience. When Naveen returned home at about eleven-thirty, he was feeling positively sick. For the first time, he began to feel a little annoyed with Bhuto, although he knew Bhuto could not really be blamed for anything. His failure was his own fault.

He placed Bhuto on the table and opened one of the windows. There was not much hope of getting a cool breeze, but whatever came in was a welcome relief for there was a power cut again. Today being Saturday, Naveen knew the power supply would not be restored before midnight.

He lit a candle and set it down on the table. Its light fell on Bhuto and Naveen went cold with fear.

There were beads of perspiration on Bhuto's forehead.

But was that all? No. His face had lost its freshness. The cheeks looked sunken. His eyes were red.

Even in a situation like this, Naveen could not help but take a few steps forward towards his puppet. It was as though he had to find out what further shocks and horrors were in store.

But something made him stop almost immediately.

There was a movement on Bhuto's chest, under the high-necked jacket. His chest rose and fell.

Bhuto was breathing!

Could his breathing be heard?

Yes, it could. In the totally silent night, two people breathed in Naveen's room instead of one.

It was perhaps both his fear and amazement that made Naveen exclaim softly, 'Bhuto!'

And, immediately, another voice spoke, the sound of which made Naveen reel back to his bed.

'This is not Bhuto. I am Akrur Chowdhury!'

Naveen knew he had not spoken the words. The voice was the puppet's own. Heaven knows through what magical powers Akrur Chowdhury could make it speak.

Naveen had wanted to turn Akrur Babu into a puppet in his hands. But never did he expect anything like this. It was impossible for him to stay in the same room with a puppet that had come to life. He must leave.

But what was that?

Was the sound of Bhuto's breathing growing faint?

Yes, so it was.

Bhuto had stopped breathing. The beads of perspiration on his forehead had gone. His eyes were no longer red and the dark rings had vanished.

Naveen rose from his bed and picked him up. Something queer had happened in this short time. It was no longer possible to move Bhuto's head or open his lips. The mechanical parts had got jammed. Perhaps a little more force would help.

Naveen tried to twist the head forcibly. It came apart and fell onto the table with a clatter.

In the morning, Naveen ran into his landlord, Suresh Mutsuddi, on the staircase.

'Why, Mr Munshi, you never showed me your magic with the puppet,' he complained, 'ventricollosium or whatever it is called!'

'I've given that up,' said Naveen. 'I'll try something new now. But why do you ask?'

'One of your fellow performers died yesterday. Saw it in the papers this morning. Akrur Chowdhury.'

'Really?'—Naveen had not yet looked at the newspaper— 'What happened to him?'

'Heart attack,' said Suresh Babu. 'Nearly 70 per cent of people seem to die of a heart attack nowadays.'

Naveen knew that if anyone bothered to enquire about the time of his death, they would discover that the man had died exactly ten minutes after midnight.

Translated by Gopa Majumdar
First published in Bengali in 1981

Stranger

Montu had heard his parents discuss, over the last few days, the possibility of a visit by his Dadu. His Chhoto Dadu, that is. Younger grandfather. He was Mother's Chhoto Mama, younger uncle.

Montu happened to be home when Dadu's letter arrived. Mother read it once, then exclaimed softly, 'Just imagine!' Then she raised her voice and called out to Father.

Father was out on the veranda, watching his shoes being repaired. He said, 'What is it?' without even raising his eyes.

Mother came out with the letter and said, 'Mama wants to come here.'

'Mama?'

'My Chhoto Mama. Don't you remember?'

Father turned his head this time, raising his eyebrows. 'Really? You mean he's still alive?'

'Here's a letter from him. Frankly, I didn't even know he could write!'

Father picked up his glasses from the arm of his chair and said, 'Let's have a look.'

After having read the single sheet of paper, he too, said, 'Just imagine!'

Mother had sat down on a stool.

Montu could guess there was something wrong somewhere.

Father was the first to voice his doubts. 'Where do you think he got our address from? And who told him his niece had married a Suresh Bose and they lived here in Mahmudpur?'

Mother frowned a little, 'He might have learnt all that from Shetal Mama.'

'Who's Shetal Mama?'

'Oh God—can't you remember anything? He was a neighbour of all my uncles in Neelkanthapur. A very close friend of the family. You've seen him. He once bet someone that he could eat fifty-six sweets at our wedding. What a laugh we all had!'

'Oh yes, yes. Now I remember.'

'He was very close to Chhoto Mama. I believe, in the beginning, Chhoto Mama used to write only to him.'

'Hasn't Shetal Babu visited us here?'

'Of course, he has. Why—he came to Ranu's wedding, didn't he?'

'Yes, of course. But didn't your Chhoto Mama leave home and turn into a sanyasi?'

'Yes, that's what I thought. I can't figure out why he wants to visit us now.'

Father thought for a minute and said, 'There is no one else he could possibly visit, is there? All your other uncles and aunts are no more, and among the two cousins you have, one is in Canada and the other in Singapore. So who is left here except you?'

'That's true,' said Mother, 'but how shall I recognize a man I have practically never seen? When he left home, I was only two years old and he must have been about seventeen.'

'Didn't you have a photograph in your old album?'

'What good is that? Mama was fifteen when that photo was taken. He must be at least sixty now.'

'Yes, I can see it's going to be a problem.'

'Well, we do have Binu's empty room which we could spare. But who knows what kind of food he likes to eat . . .'

'I wouldn't worry about that. Surely he can have the same as we do?'

'No, not necessarily. If he has indeed become a sadhu he may want to eat only vegetarian food. That would mean making five different dishes every day!'

'The language he's used in the letter is quite normal. I mean, one wouldn't expect a sadhu to talk like this. Look, he's written the date in English and used other English words. Here it is—"unnecessarily"!'

'But he hasn't given us his address.'

'Yes, that's true.'

'And he says he's coming next Monday.'

It was obvious to Montu that both his parents were deeply concerned. It was certainly an odd situation. How could anyone accept a total stranger as an uncle?

Montu had heard of this Dadu barely once or twice before. He knew Dadu had left home even before leaving school.

In the beginning, he wrote to a few people occasionally; but after that there was no news of him. It was Montu's mother's belief that he had died. Montu had wondered a few times about this man and wished he would come back. But he knew that kind of thing happened only in stories. In stories, there were usually people who could recognize such a man. In this case, there was no one. Anyone could arrive and say he was his Dadu. There was no way of being sure.

Dadu was not going to stay for more than ten days. Having spent his childhood in a small town in Bangladesh, he now wanted to see a small town once again. There was no point in going to his own house in Neelkanthapur for no one lived there any more. So he wanted to visit Mahmudpur. At least, there was a niece living there. Montu's father was a lawyer. Montu had an elder sister and a brother. The sister was married and his brother was in Kanpur, studying at IIT.

His mother finished making all the arrangements by Sunday. A room on the first floor was made ready. A new sheet was spread on the bed, the pillows got new covers—even new soaps and towels were provided. Dadu was expected to make his way to their house from the station.

After that . . . well, one would simply have to wait and see. Father had said only this morning, 'Whether or not he's your real uncle, I just hope the man is civilized and well mannered. Otherwise the next ten days will be difficult indeed.'

'I don't like this at all,' grumbled Mother. 'No one knows the man from Adam, and yet we must put up with him. He didn't even send us his address, or we could have written, and made some excuse to put him off!'

But Montu thought otherwise. They had not had a visitor in a long time. His school was closed for the summer holidays and he was home all day. Although there were plenty of friends to play with—Sidhu, Aneesh, Rathin, Chhotka—it was such fun to have someone stay in the house. Who wanted to spend the whole day just with parents? And this whole business of is-he-real-or-not was so intriguing. Just like a mystery. Suppose he did turn out to be an impostor and only Montu learnt the truth about him—how lovely that would be! He would unmask the man and be a hero.

Montu began loitering near the front door from ten-thirty on Monday morning. At a quarter past eleven he saw a cycle rickshaw making its way towards their house. Its passenger had a pot of sweets in his hands and a leather suitcase at his feet. One of his feet was resting on the suitcase.

This man was no sadhu. At least, he was not dressed like one. He was wearing trousers and a shirt. Mother had said he would be around sixty. But he looked younger than that. Most of his hair was still black and though he did wear glasses, they did not appear to be thick ones.

The man paid the rickshawallah, put his suitcase down and, turning to Montu, said, 'Who are you?'

He was clean shaven, had a sharp nose and his eyes, though small, held a twinkle.

Montu picked up the suitcase and replied, 'My name is Satyaki Bose.'

'Which Satyaki are you? The disciple of Krishna? Or the son of Suresh Bose? Can you manage that heavy suitcase? It's got quite a lot of books.'

'Yes, I can.'

'Let's go in then.'

As they came into the veranda, Mother came forward and touched his feet. He handed the pot of sweets to her and said, 'You must be Suhasini?'

'Yes.'

'Your husband is a lawyer, isn't he? He must have gone out on work.'

'Yes.'

'Perhaps I shouldn't have come like this . . . . I did feel hesitant. But then I told myself you wouldn't mind putting up with an old man. After all, it's only a matter of ten days. Besides, Shetal was so full of praise for you. But I do realize your problem. There is no way I can prove that I am your real Mama. So I am not going to expect any special treatment. All you have to do is give an old man a roof over his head for ten days.'

Montu noticed his mother was giving the man occasional sidelong glances. Now she said, 'Would you like to have a bath?'

'Only if it's not inconvenient.'

'No, no, it's not inconvenient at all. Montu, do go and show him the bathroom upstairs. And . . . er . . . I didn't quite know what sort of food you like . . .'

'I eat everything. I should be very happy to have whatever you choose to feed me. I mean it.'

'Do you go to school?' he asked Montu as they began going upstairs.

'Yes. Satyabhama High School. Class VII.'

At this point, Montu could not resist asking a question.

'Are you not a sadhu?'

'Sadhu?'

'Mother said you had become one.'

'Oh, I see. That was a long time ago. I had gone to Haridwar straight from home. I didn't like being at home, so I left. I did, in fact, spend some time with a sadhu in Rishikesh. Then I began to get a bit restless, so I moved on. After that, I never went to a sadhu.'

At lunch, he ate everything with great relish. He clearly did not object to non-vegetarian food for he ate both fish and eggs.

Montu could see his mother relax a little. But she did not once call him 'Mama', though Montu wanted very much to say, 'Chhoto Dadu!'

As he finished his meal and picked up the plate of yoghurt, Mother said, probably only to make conversation, 'You must have had to do without Bengali food for many years.'

The man laughed and said, 'I had some in Calcutta in the last two days. But before that . . . you'll find it difficult to believe if I tell you exactly how many years I've had to do without it.'

Mother said nothing more. Montu wanted to ask—'Why was this? Where did you live?' but stopped himself. If the man was a fraud, he should not be given the chance to cook up stories. One should wait until he came out with the information himself.

But the man did not say anything either. If he had indeed spent more than forty years just roaming around, he ought to have had lots to talk about. Why, then, was he so quiet?

Montu was upstairs when he heard the sound of his father's car. Their guest had retired to bed with a book. Just before that, Montu had spent half an hour with him. He had called out when he saw Montu hovering outside his room.

'Why don't you come in, O disciple of Krishna? Let me show you something.'

Montu went in and stood by the bed.

'Do you know what this is?' asked the man.

'A copper coin.'

'Where from?'

Montu could not read what was written on the coin.

'This is called a lepta. It's a coin used in Greece. And what's this?'

Montu failed to recognize the second coin as well.

'This is one kuru, from Turkey. And this is from Romania. It's called a bani. This coin here is from Iraq—a fil.'

Then he produced coins from at least ten different countries, which Montu had neither seen nor heard of before.

'All these are for you.'

Montu was amazed. What was the man saying? Aneesh's uncle also collected coins and he had explained to Montu that those who did so were called numismatists. But even he did not have so many different coins. Montu was sure of that.

'I knew I would find a grandson where I was going. So I decided to bring these coins for him.'

In great excitement, Montu ran down the stairs to show the coins to his mother. But he stopped short as he heard his father's voice. He was saying something about the man.

'. . . Ten days! That's really too much. We must make it very clear to him that we cannot be fooled so easily. There is no need to give him any special treatment. I think he will leave soon enough if we don't go out of our way to be hospitable. And, of course, we must not take any risks. I spoke to Sudheer today and he gave me the same advice. Keep all your almirahs and cupboards locked. Montu can't be expected to guard the man all the time. He has his friends and he'll go out to play with them. I will go to work. That leaves just you and Sadashiv in the house. I know Sadashiv sleeps most of the time. And you, too, like to have a little rest in the afternoon, don't you?'

'There is something I'd like to tell you,' said Montu's mother.

'What?'

'This man does look a bit like my mother.'

'Do you think so?'

'Yes, he has the same nose and the same look in his eyes.'

'OK, OK, so I'm not saying he's not your Mama. But then, we don't know what this Mama is like. He hasn't had much education, he's led the life of a vagabond without any discipline . . . I tell you, I don't like this business at all.'

Montu went into the room as his father stopped speaking. He did not like what Father had been saying. Even in these few hours he had started to get quite fond of the newcomer. Well, perhaps Father would change his mind when he saw the coins.

'Did he really give you all these?'

Montu nodded.

'Did he say he had actually visited all these places?'

'No, he didn't say that.'

'That's something, then. Coins like these can be bought in Calcutta. There are dealers who sell them.'

The man came downstairs at around half-past four and met Father.

'Your son and I have already made friends,' he said.

'Yes, so he's told me.'

Father shot a few quick glances at him, very much like Montu's mother.

'I can make friends with children quite easily. Perhaps they understand people like me better than adults.'

'Have you roamed around all your life?'

'Yes. I was never one for keeping still in one place.'

'We happen to be different. We can't afford to move about aimlessly. You see, we have a responsibility towards our family, children to look after, a job to keep. You never married, did you?'

'No.'

After a few minutes of silence, the man said, 'Suhasini might not remember this, but one of her great-grandfathers—my grandfather, that is—did a similar thing. He left home at thirteen. I returned at times for a few days. He did not come back at all.'

Montu saw his father turn towards Mother.

'Did you know this?'

'Maybe I did once, but I can't remember anything now,' said Mother.

Something rather interesting happened after tea. Most of Montu's friends knew about the arrival of this strange relative, who might not be a real relative at all. Being very curious, all of them dropped in to have a look at Montu's Dadu. Dadu seemed very pleased to meet this group of boys, all about ten years old.

He reached for his walking stick and took them all out for a walk. They stopped under the kadam tree that stood in a field at some distance. Here they sat down on the ground for a chat.

'Do you know who the Tuaregs are?'

Everyone shook their heads.

'In the Sahara desert,' said Dadu, 'lives a nomadic tribe called the Tuaregs. They are a bold lot who don't stop at anything—even robbing and stealing. Let me tell you the story of a clever man who managed to escape from the clutches of these people.'

The boys listened to his story, utterly spellbound. Montu told his mother later, 'He told the story so well—we felt as though we could actually see it all happen.'

His father overheard him and said, 'This man appears to have read a lot. I have a vague feeling that I have read a similar story in an English magazine.'

Montu had told his parents that he knew Dadu had brought a lot of books in his suitcase, but he did not know if they were all story-books.

Three days passed. Nothing was stolen, the guest gave them no trouble, ate whatever he was given happily, made no demands and did not complain about anything. Some of Father's colleagues and friends began visiting, which was something they rarely did. It was Montu's guess that they only came to check out this old man who might-be-real-and- might-not. His parents seemed to have accepted Dadu's presence. In fact, Montu heard his father say one day, 'Well, one must admit the man is quite simple in his ways. At least he is not trying to be over-friendly. But I fail to see how someone can survive like this. Obviously he left home only to avoid responsibilities. People like him are just parasites. He must have sponged on others all his life.'

Montu happened to call him 'Chhoto Dadu' once. Dadu only looked at him and smiled a little at this, but did not say anything.

Mother had not called him 'Mama' even once. When Montu mentioned this, she said, 'But he doesn't seem to mind! And what if he turns out to be an impostor? Think how embarrassing that would be!'

On the fourth day, their guest said he would go out. 'Isn't there a bus to Neelkanthapur?' he asked.

Father said, 'Yes, a bus leaves every hour from the main market.'

'Then I think I'll go and have a look at the place where I was born. I won't be back until evening.'

'You'll have lunch here, won't you?' asked Montu's mother.

'No. The sooner I leave the better. I'll have lunch somewhere on the way. Don't worry.'

He left before nine.

In the afternoon Montu could not resist the temptation any longer. Dadu's room was empty. Montu was dying to find out what kind of books his suitcase was filled with. Father was not at home and Mother was resting downstairs. Montu went into Dadu's room.

The suitcase was not locked. Clearly the man was not worried about theft.

Montu lifted the lid of the suitcase.

But there were no books inside. Not proper ones, anyway. They were notebooks, at least thirty different ones. About ten of these were bound in hard cover.

Montu opened one of them. There were things written in Bengali.

The writing was neat and clear.

Montu climbed on to the bed with the notebook.

And had to climb down the next instant.

Mother had come upstairs, silently.

'What are you doing here, Montu? Are you messing about with his things?'

Montu put the notebook back into the suitcase like a good boy and came out.

'Go back to your own room. You shouldn't fiddle around with other people's belongings. Go read your own books.'

Their guest returned a little after six in the evening.

The same night, as they sat down to dinner, he made an announcement that took them all by surprise.

'I think I'll go back tomorrow,' he said. 'Your hospitality is beyond reproach, but I simply cannot stay in one place for very long.'

Montu knew his parents were not too sorry to hear this. But he began to feel quite sad.

'Will you go to Calcutta from here?' asked Father.

'Yes, but not for long. I'll go somewhere else soon enough. I have always tried not to be a burden on anyone. I've been totally independent ever since I left home.'

Mother intervened at this point, 'Why do you have to call yourself a burden? We haven't been inconvenienced at all.'

But Montu knew that was not quite true for he had heard Father remark one day on how expensive things were and that it cost a good deal to provide for even one extra person.

This time both Montu and his father went to the station in their car to see their guest off.

Montu could feel the faint uneasiness that still lurked in his father's mind. He knew Father was still wondering, even when the train had actually gone—about whether the man who had stayed with them was indeed the relative he had claimed to be.

A week later, another old man arrived at their house— Montu's mother's Shetal Mama. Montu had seen him only once before, at his sister's wedding.

'Why, it's you, Shetal Mama! What brings you here?'

'The call of duty. Two duties, in fact, not just one. Why else do you think a man of my age would come travelling in a passenger train? I'm going to have lunch here with you—and that's a warning.'

'Of course you must have lunch with us. What would you like to have? We get practically everything here—it's not like Calcutta.'

'Wait, wait. Let me finish doing what I came to do.' He took out a book from his shoulder bag. 'You haven't heard of this book, have you?'

Mother took the book, looked at it and said, 'Why, no!'

'I knew Pulin hadn't told you.'

'Pulin?'

'Your Chhoto Mama! The same man who spent five days here. You didn't even bother to find out his name, did you? Pulin wrote this book.'

'Did he?'

'But don't you read the papers? His name appeared only the other day. Tell me, how many autobiographies of this kind are there in our literature?'

'But, but . . . this is a different name . . .'

'Yes, it's a pseudonym. He's travelled all over the world, yet has stayed so humble.'

'The whole world?'

'I do believe our country has never seen a globe-trotter like Pulin Ray. And he did it all with his own money. He worked as a ship-mate, a coolie, a labourer in the timber trade, sold newspapers, ran a small shop, drove lorries—no work was too small for him. His experiences are stranger than fiction. He's been attacked by a tiger, bitten by a snake, escaped from a violent nomadic tribe in the Sahara, swum to the shore of Madagascar after a shipwreck. He left India in 1939 and made his way through Afghanistan. He says if you can come out of the confines of your house, then the whole world becomes your home. There is no difference then, between whites and blacks and great and small or the civilized and the barbaric.'

'But . . . why didn't he tell us all this?'

'Would you have believed him, insular and parochial as you are? You couldn't even decide whether he was genuine or fake. Not once did you call him "Mama" and you expect him to have talked to you about himself?'

'Oh dear. How awful! Could we not ask him to come back?'

'No. The bird has flown away. He said he hadn't been to Bali, so that is where he'll try to go now. He gave you this book, or rather, he left it for your son. He said, "That boy is still a child. My book may make an impression on his young mind."

'But I haven't yet told you just how crazily he behaved. I asked him so many times to stay for a few more days because I knew this book was bound to win an academy award. They pay ten thousand rupees these days. But he refused to listen to me. Do you know what he said? He said to me, "If some money does come my way, please give it to my niece in Mahmudpur. She looked after me very well." And then he actually put this down in writing. Here's the money—take it.'

Mother took the envelope from Shetal Mama and wiping away her tears, she said in a choked voice, 'Just imagine!'

Translated by Gopa Majumdar
First published in Bengali in 1981

The Maths Teacher, Mr Pink and Tipu

Tipu closed his geography book and glanced at the clock. He had studied non-stop for exactly forty-seven minutes. It was now thirteen minutes past three. There was no harm in going out for a little while, was there? That strange creature had appeared the other day at around this time. Didn't he say that he would come back again if ever Tipu had reason to feel sad? There was a reason now. A very good reason. Should he go out for a minute?

Oh no. Mother had come out to the veranda. He just heard her shoo a crow away. Then the cane chair creaked. That meant she had sat down to sun herself. Tipu would have to wait for a while.

He could remember the creature so well. He had never seen anyone like him—so short, no beard or moustache—yet he was not a child. No child had such a deep voice. But then, the creature was not old either. At least, Tipu had been unable to figure out if he was. His skin was smooth, his complexion the colour of sandalwood tinged with pink. In fact, Tipu thought of him as Mr Pink. He did not know what he was actually called. He did ask, but the creature replied, 'It's no use telling you my name. It would twist your tongue to pronounce it.'

Tipu felt affronted by this. 'Why should I start stuttering? I can say things like gobbledygook and flabbergasted. I can even manage floccinaucinihilipilification. So why should your name be a tongue-twister?'

'You couldn't possibly manage with just one tongue.'

'You mean you have more than one?'

'You need only one to talk in your language.'

The man was standing under the tall, bare shimul tree just behind the house. Not many people came here. There was a large open space behind the tree, followed by rice fields. And behind these, in the distance, stood the hills. Tipu had seen a mongoose disappear behind a bush only a few days ago. Today, he had brought a few pieces of bread with the intention of scattering them on the ground. The mongoose might be tempted to reappear.

His eyes suddenly fell on the man standing under the tree.

'Hello!' said the man, smiling.

Was he a westerner? Tipu knew he could not converse for very long if the man spoke only in English. So he just stared at him. The man walked across to him and said, 'Do you have reason to be sad?'

'Sad?'

'Yes.'

Tipu was taken aback. No one had ever asked him such a question. He said, 'Why, no, I don't think so.'

'Are you sure?'

'Of course.'

'But you're supposed to be sad. That's what the calculations showed.'

'What kind of sadness? I thought I might see the mongoose. But I didn't. Is that what you mean?'

'No, no. The kind of sadness I meant would make the back of your ears go blue. Your palms would feel dry.'

'You mean a very deep sadness.'

'Yes.'

'No, I am not feeling that sad.'

Now the man began to look rather sad himself. He shook his head and said, 'That means I cannot be released yet.'

'Released?'

'Yes, released. I cannot be free.'

'I know what release means,' said Tipu. 'Would you be set free if I felt unhappy?'

The man looked straight at Tipu. 'Are you ten-and-a-half years old?'

'Yes.'

'And your name is Master Tarpan Chowdhury?'

'Yes.'

'Then there is no mistake.'

Tipu could not figure out how the man knew such a lot about him. He asked, 'Does it have to be me? If someone else felt sad, wouldn't that do?'

'No. And it's not enough to feel sad. The cause of sadness must be removed.'

'But so many people are unhappy. A beggar called Nikunja comes to our house so often. He says he has no one in the world. He must be very unhappy indeed.'

'No, that won't do,' the man shook his head again. 'Tarpan Chowdhury, ten years old—is there someone else who has the same name and is of the same age?'

'No, I don't think so.'

'Then it must be you.'

Tipu could not resist the next question.

'What release are you talking about? You appear to be walking about quite freely!'

'This is not my land. I have been exiled here.'

'Why?'

'You ask too many questions.'

'I'm interested, that's all. Look, I've met you for the first time. So naturally I'd like to know who you are, what you do, where you live, who else knows you—things like that. What's wrong with being interested?'

'You'll get jinjiria if you try to learn so much.'

The man did not actually say 'jinjiria'. What he did say sounded so completely unpronounceable that Tipu decided to settle for jinjiria. God knew what kind of an ailment it was.

But who did the man remind him of? Rumpelstiltskin? Or was he one of Snow White's seven dwarfs?

Tipu was passionately fond of fairy tales. His grandfather brought him three or four books of fairy tales every year from Calcutta. Tipu read them all avidly, his flights of fancy taking him far beyond the seven seas, thirteen rivers and thirty-six hills. In his mind, he became a prince, a pearl-studded turban on his head, a sword slung from his waist, flashing diamonds. Some days he would set forth to look for priceless jewels and to fight a dragon.

'Goodbye!' said the man.

Was he leaving already?

'You didn't tell me where you live!'

The man paid no attention. All he said was, 'We shall meet again when you feel sad.'

'But how will you know?'

There was no answer for by then, the man had jumped over a mulberry tree and vanished from sight—having broken all possible world records in high jump.

This had happened about six weeks ago. Tipu did not see the man again. But he needed him now for he was desperately unhappy.

The reason for his sorrow was the new maths teacher in his school, Narahari Babu.

Tipu had not liked him from the very beginning. When he had come to class for the first time he had spent the first two minutes just staring at the boys. How hard he had stared! As though he wanted to kill everyone with that look before he began teaching. Tipu had never seen anyone with such a huge moustache. And his voice! What a deep, loud voice it was! Why did he have to speak so loudly? No one in the class was deaf, after all.

The disaster occurred two days later. It was a Thursday. The sky was overcast and it was cold outside. Tipu did not feel like going out in the lunch break. So he sat in his class reading the story of Dalimkumar. Who was to know the maths teacher would walk past his classroom and come in upon him?

'What book is that, Tarpan?'

One had to admit that the new teacher had a remarkable memory, for he had already learnt the name of each boy.

Tipu felt slightly nervous but took courage from the thought that no one could object to his reading a story-book in the lunch break. '*Tales from Grandma*, sir!' he said.

'Let's have a look.'

Tipu handed the book to his teacher. The latter thumbed its pages for a minute. Then he exploded, 'Kings, queens, princes and demons—birds of pearls on a tree of diamonds, abracadabra—what on earth are you reading? What a pack of nonsense! How do you suppose you'll ever learn mathematics if you keep reading this idiotic stuff?'

'But these are only stories, sir!' Tipu stammered.

'Stories? Shouldn't all stories make sense? Or is it enough simply to write what comes into one's head?'

Tipu was not going to give in so easily.

'Why, sir,' he said, 'even the Ramayana talks of Hanuman and Jambuvan. The Mahabharata, too, is full of tales of demons and monsters.'

'Don't argue,' snarled Narahari Babu. 'Those tales were written by sages more than two thousand years ago. Ganesh with the head of an elephant and the body of a man, and the goddess Durga with ten arms are not the same as the kind of nonsense you're reading. You should read about great men, about explorers, scientific inventions, the evolution of man— things to do with the real world. You belong to the twentieth century, don't you? Foolish, ignorant people in villages might once have enjoyed such absurd stories. Why should you? If you do, you ought to go back to a village school and try learning maths with the help of rhymed couplets. Can you do that?'

Tipu fell silent. He had not realized a small remark from him would trigger off such a tirade.

'Who else in your class reads such books?' his teacher asked.

To tell the truth, no one did. Sheetal had once borrowed *Folk Tales of Hindustan* from Tipu and returned it the very next day, saying, 'Rubbish! Phantom comics are a lot better than this!'

'No one, sir,' Tipu replied.

'Hmm . . . what's your father's name?'

'Taranath Chowdhury.'

'Where do you live?'

'Station Road. At number five.'

'Hmm.' His teacher dropped the book back on Tipu's desk with a thud and left.

Tipu did not go back to his house straight after school. He wandered off beyond the mango grove near the school and found himself in front of Bishnuram Das's house. A white horse was tethered outside it. Tipu leant against a jamrool tree and stared at the horse absent-mindedly. Bishnuram Babu owned a beedi factory. He rode to his factory every day. He was still fit enough to do so, although he had crossed fifty.

Tipu came here often to look at the horse; but today his mind was elsewhere. Deep down in his heart he knew the new maths teacher would try to put a stop to his reading story-books. How would he survive without his books? He read them every day and he enjoyed reading most the ones his teacher had described as stuff and nonsense. His reading such stories had never stopped him from doing well in maths, had it? He had got forty-four out of fifty in the last test. His previous maths teacher Bhudeb Babu had never ticked him off for reading story-books!

The days being short in winter, Tipu knew he had to return home soon, and was about to leave when he saw something that made him hide quickly behind the tree.

His maths teacher, Narahari Babu, was coming towards him, a book and an umbrella under his arm.

Did that mean he lived somewhere close by? There were five other houses next to the one where Bishnuram Babu lived. Beyond these houses was a large, open space known as Hamlatuni's Field. A long time ago, there was a silk factory on the eastern side of the field. Its manager, Mr Hamilton, was reputed to be a hard taskmaster. He worked as manager for thirty-two years and then died in his bungalow, not far from the factory. His name got somewhat distorted and thus the whole area came to be known as Hamlatuni's Field.

In the gathering dusk of the winter evening, Tipu watched Narahari Babu from behind the jamrool tree. He was surprised at his behaviour. Narahari Babu was standing beside the horse, gently patting its back and making a strange chirrupping noise through his lips.

At that very moment, the front door of the house opened and, holding a cheroot in his hand, Bishnuram Babu himself came out.

'Namaskar.'

Narahari Babu took his hand off the horse's back and turned. Bishnuram Babu returned his greeting and asked, 'How about a game?'

'That's precisely why I've come!' said Tipu's teacher. This meant he played chess, because Tipu knew Bishnuram Babu did.

'Nice horse,' said Narahari Babu. 'Where did you get it?'

'Calcutta. I bought it from Dwarik Mitter of Shobhabazar. It used to be a race horse called Pegasus.'

Pegasus? The name seemed vaguely familiar but Tipu could not recall where he had heard it.

'Pegasus,' said the maths teacher. 'What a strange name!'

'Yes, race horses usually have funny names. Happy Birthday, Subhan Allah, Forget-Me-Not . . .'

'Do you ride this horse?'

'Of course. A very sturdy beast. Hasn't given me a day's trouble.'

Narahari Babu kept staring at the horse.

'I used to ride once.'

'Really?'

'We lived in Sherpur in those days. My father was a doctor. He used a horse for making house calls. I was in school then. I used to ride whenever I could. Oh, that was a long time ago!'

'Would you like to ride this one?'

'May I?'

'Go ahead!'

Tipu stared in amazement as his teacher dropped his book and his umbrella on the veranda and untied the horse. Then he climbed onto its back in one swift movement and pressed its flanks with his heels. The horse began to trot.

'Don't go far,' said Bishnuram Babu.

'Get the chessmen out,' said Narahari Babu. 'I'll be back in no time!'

Tipu did not wait any longer. What a day it had been!

But there was more in store.

It was around seven in the evening. Tipu had just finished his homework and was contemplating reading a few stories when his father called him from downstairs.

Tipu walked into their living-room to find Narahari Babu sitting there with his father. His blood froze.

'Your teacher would like to see the books your grandfather has given you,' said Father. 'Go bring them.'

There were twenty-seven books. Tipu had to make three trips to get them all together.

His maths teacher took ten minutes to go through the lot, shaking his head occasionally and saying, 'Pooh!' Finally, he pushed the books aside and said, 'Look, Mr Chowdhury, what I am going to tell you is based on years of thinking and research. Fairy tales or folklore, call it what you will, can mean only one thing—sowing the seed of superstition in a young mind. A child will accept whatever it's told. Do you realize what an enormous responsibility we adults have? Should we be telling our children that the life of a man lies inside a fish and things like that, when the truth is that one's life beats in one's own heart? It cannot possibly exist anywhere else!'

Tipu could not figure out if Father agreed with all that the teacher said, but he did know that he believed in obeying a teacher's instructions.

'A child must learn to obey, Tipu,' he had told him so many times, 'especially what his elders tell him. You can do whatever you like after a certain age, when you have finished your studies and are standing on your own feet. You would then have the right to voice your own opinion. But not now.'

'Do you not have any other books for children?' asked Narahari Babu.

'Oh yes,' said Father, 'they're all here on my bookshelf. I won them as prizes in school. Haven't you seen them, Tipu?'

'I have read them all, Father,' said Tipu.

'Each one?'

'Each one. The biographies of Vidyasagar and Suresh Biswas, Captain Scott's expedition to the South Pole, Mungo Park's adventures in Africa, the story of steel and spaceships . . . you didn't win that many prizes, Father.'

'All right,' said Father, 'I'll buy you some more.'

'If you tell the Tirthankar Book Stall here, they can get you some books from Calcutta,' said Narahari Babu. 'You will read only those from now, Tarpan. Not these.'

Not these! Two little words—but they were enough to make Tipu's world come to an end. Not these!

Father took the books from Narahari Babu and locked them away in his cupboard.

Now they were quite out of reach.

Mother, however, appeared to be on Tipu's side. He could hear her grumble and, while they were having dinner, she went to the extent of saying, 'A man who can say such a thing does not deserve to be a teacher at all!'

Father disagreed, 'Can't you see what he has suggested is for Tipu's good?'

'Nonsense,' said Mother. Then she ruffled Tipu's hair affectionately and said, 'Don't worry. I will tell you stories. Your grandmother used to tell me lots of stories. I haven't forgotten them all.'

Tipu did not say anything. He had already heard a number of stories from his mother and did not think she knew any more. Even if she did, hearing a story from someone was not the same as reading it. With an open book in front of him, he could lose himself in a totally different world. But how could he make his mother see that?

Two days later, Tipu realized he was really feeling sad. It was decidedly the kind of sadness Mr Pink had mentioned. Now he was Tipu's only hope.

Today was Sunday. Father was taking a nap. Mother had left the veranda and was now at her sewing machine. It was three-thirty. Should he try to slip out of the back door? If only the man had told him where he lived! Tipu would have gone to him straightaway.

Tipu tiptoed down the stairs and went out through the back door.

Despite bright sunlight, there was quite a nip in the air. In the distance, the rice fields stretching right up to the hills looked golden. A dove was cooing somewhere and the occasional rustle that came from the shirish tree meant that there was a squirrel hidden in the leaves.

'Hello!'

Oh, what a surprise! When did he arrive? Tipu had not seen him come.

'The back of your ears are blue, your palms seem dry. I can tell you have reason to feel sad.'

'You can say that again,' said Tipu.

The man came walking towards him. He was wearing the same clothes.

The wind blew his hair in tufts.

'I need to know what has happened, or else I'm gobbledygasted.'

Tipu wanted to laugh, but made no attempt to correct what the man had said. Instead, he briefly related his tale of woe. Tears pricked his eyes as he spoke, but Tipu managed to control himself.

'Hmm,' said the man and started nodding. His head went up and down sixteen times. Tipu began to feel a little nervous. Would he never stop? Or was it that he could find no solution to the problem? He felt like crying once more, but the man gave a final nod, stopped and said 'Hmm' again. Tipu went limp with relief.

'Do you think you can do something?' he asked timidly.

'I shall have to think carefully. Must exercise the intestines.'

'Intestines? You mean you wouldn't exercise your brain?'

The man did not reply. He said instead, 'Didn't I see Narahari Babu ride a horse yesterday in that field?'

'Which field? Oh, you mean Hamlatuni's Field?'

'The one that has a broken building in it.'

'Yes, yes. Is that where you stay?'

'My tridingipidi is lying just behind that building.'

Tipu could not have heard him right. But even if he had, he would probably have been totally unable to pronounce the word.

The man had started nodding again. This time he stopped after the thirty-first nod and said, 'There will be a full moon tonight. If you wish to see what happens then come to that field just as the moon reaches the top of the palm tree. But make sure no one sees you.'

Suddenly a rather alarming thought occurred to Tipu.

'You will not try to kill my maths teacher, will you?'

For the first time he saw the man throw back his head and laugh.

He also saw that there were two tongues in his mouth and no teeth.

'Kill him?' The man stopped laughing. 'No, no. We don't believe in killing. In fact, I was banished from my land because I had thought of pinching someone. The first set of calculations gave us the name "Earth" where I had to be sent. Then we got the name of this place and then came your own name. I will be set free as soon as I can wipe out the cause of your sadness.'

'All right then. See you . . .'

But the man had already taken another giant leap over the mulberry tree and disappeared.

The faint tingle that had set in Tipu's body stayed all evening. By an amazing stroke of luck his parents were going out to dinner that night. Tipu, too, had been invited, but his mother felt he should stay at home and study. His exams were just round the corner.

They left at 7.30. Tipu waited for about five minutes after they had gone. Then he set off. The eastern sky had started to turn yellow.

It took him almost ten minutes to reach Bishnuram Babu's house through the short cut behind his school. The horse was no longer there. It must be in its stable behind the house, Tipu thought. Light streamed through the open window of the living-room. The room was full of smoke from cheroots.

'Check.'

It was the voice of his maths teacher. He was obviously playing chess with Bishnuram Babu. Was he not going to ride the horse tonight? There was no way one could tell. But that man had asked Tipu to go to Hamlatuni's Field. He must go there, come what may.

It was a full moon night. The moon looked golden now, but would turn silver later. It would take another ten minutes to reach the top of the palm tree. The moonlight was not yet very bright, but things were fairly easily visible. There were plenty of plants and bushes. The derelict old factory stood at a distance. The man was supposed to be staying behind it. But where?

Tipu hid behind a bush, and prepared to wait. In his pocket was some jaggery wrapped in a piece of newspaper. He bit off a small portion of it and began chewing. He could hear jackals calling from the jungle far away. The black object that flew past must be an owl.

Tipu was wearing a brown shawl over his coat. It helped him merge into the darkness and kept him warm as well.

A clock struck eight somewhere, probably in Bishnuram Babu's house.

And, soon afterwards, Tipu heard another noise: clip-clop, clip-clop, clip-clop.

Was it the horse?

Tipu peeped from behind the bush and stared at the lane.

Yes, it was indeed the same horse with Narahari Babu on its back.

Disaster struck at this precise moment. A mosquito had been buzzing around Tipu's ears. He tried to wave it away, but it suddenly went straight into one nostril!

Tipu knew it was possible to stop a sneeze by pressing the nose hard. But if he did that now, the mosquito might never come out. So he allowed himself to sneeze, shattering the stillness of the night. The horse stopped.

Someone flashed a powerful torch on Tipu.

'Tarpan?'

Tipu began to go numb with fear. Why, why, why did this have to happen? He had gone and ruined whatever plans that man must have made. What on earth would he think of Tipu?

The horse began to trot up to him with his maths teacher on its back. But suddenly it raised its forelegs high in the air, neighed loudly, and veered off from the lane. Then it jumped into the field.

What followed took Tipu's breath away. The horse took off from the ground, flapping two large wings which had grown from its sides! Tipu's teacher flung his arms around the horse's neck and hung on as best as he could. The torch had fallen from his hand.

The moon had reached the top of the palm tree. In the bright moonlight, Tipu saw the horse rise higher and higher in the sky until it disappeared among the stars.

Pegasus!

It came back to Tipu in a flash. It was a Greek tale. Medusa was an ogress—every strand of whose hair was a venomous snake, the very sight of whom made men turn into stone. The valiant Perseus chopped off her head with his sword and from her blood was born Pegasus, the winged horse.

'Go home, Tarpan!'

That strange man was standing beside Tipu, his golden hair gleaming in the moonlight.

'Everything is all right.'

Narahari Babu had to go to a hospital. He stayed there three days, although there was no sign of any physical injury. He talked to no one. Upon being asked what the matter was, he only shivered and looked away.

On the fourth day he was discharged. He came straight to Tipu's house. What transpired between him and Father, Tipu could not make out. But, as soon as he had gone, Father called Tipu and said, 'Er . . . you may take your books from my cupboard. Narahari Babu said he didn't mind your reading fairy tales any more.'

Tipu never saw the strange man again. He went looking for him behind the old factory and passed Bishnuram Babu's house on the way. The horse was still tethered to the same post. But there was absolutely nothing behind the factory, except a chameleon—pink from head to tail.

Translated by Gopa Majumdar
First published in Bengali in 1982

Spotlight

We often came to this small town in Chhota Nagpur to spend our Puja holidays as many other Bengali families did. Some stayed in houses of their own, some rented a bungalow or went to local hotels. Ten days in a place like this was enough to add at least six months to an average lifetime. My father often said, 'The cost of living may have gone up a little, but the water you drink and the air you breathe are still free. And no one can say that their quality has suffered in any way.'

We usually arrived in a large group, so ten days went by very quickly, although there were no cinemas, theatres, markets or other attractions. If one were to ask whether what we did in these ten days varied from one year to the next, it would be difficult to find an answer, for we inevitably ate the same stuff every day: chicken, eggs, arhar daal, fresh milk, guavas and other fruits from our own garden; we followed the same routine—to bed at 10 p.m., wake up at 6 a.m., spend the afternoon playing cards and Monopoly, walk to Raja Hill after tea in the evening, have a picnic at least once during our stay, by the side of Kalijhora; everything we saw was always just the same: bright sunshine and fluffy white clouds; the birds, the animals, the insects, the trees, the plants and the flowers.

But not this time.

On this occasion, things took a different turn.

Personally, I had never liked Anshuman Chatterjee. But, of course, that did not stop him from being the most popular film-star in West Bengal. My twelve-year-old sister, Sharmi, had filled a whole scrapbook with pictures of Anshuman from film magazines. There were boys in my own class who were his admirers, and had already started copying his hair-style, his speech and mannerisms as well as his style of dressing.

The famous Anshuman Chatterjee was in the same town this time, staying in the house the Kundus owned. He had brought three of his sycophants with him in a yellow air-conditioned Mercedes with tinted glass windows.

Once, on our way to the Andamans, I had noticed how the smaller boats rocked and swayed in the huge waves that our own ship kept throwing up. Here, Anshuman became a ship like that. When he came out on the street, the other visitors simply drowned in the ripples he left behind.

There had never been such excitement in this small town. Chhoto Mama was not interested in films. But palmistry intrigued him.

'I must,' he declared, 'take a look at his fate line. I'd never get a chance back in Calcutta.'

Mother wanted to invite him to dinner. 'Sharmi,' she asked, 'do your film magazines ever mention what kind of food he prefers?' Sharmi promptly rattled off a long list that ended with '. . . but what he likes best is Chinese.' Mother sighed. Father said, 'I see no problem in asking him to dinner one evening. He might even accept. But I don't like those hangers-on . . .'

Chheni-da was a cousin of mine. He worked for a newspaper as a journalist and almost never got any leave. This time he had come with us only to write a feature on a festival of the local Santhals. He felt he had to corner Anshuman for an interview. 'That man has shooting three hundred and sixty-seven days a year. How on earth did he manage to come away on holiday? God, that itself would make a story!'

Chhoto-da was the only one who displayed no emotion. A student of Presidency College, he was a rather grave young man. He also happened to be a member of a film society and, having seen all kinds of German, Swedish, French, Cuban and Brazilian films, was now working on a critical thesis on the films of Bengal. He had spent three minutes watching Anshuman's *Sleepless Nights* on television, before saying 'Disgusting!' and leaving the room. It was his view that the film-star's arrival had spoilt the entire atmosphere of this beautiful place.

There were a few Bengalis who lived in the town permanently. Gopen Babu was one of them. He had lived here in a tiny house for twenty-two years and had a small farm. Slightly older than Father, he was a jovial old fellow. We all liked him.

He turned up a couple of days after our arrival, clad in a khadi kurta and a dhoti, a stout walking-stick in his hand, brown tennis shoes on his feet.

'Mr Chowdhury!' he yelled from outside, 'are you home?'

We were having breakfast. Father went out and escorted him in.

'Good heavens!' he exclaimed, 'what a spread! All I want is a cup of tea.' The last time we had seen him, he had a cataract in one eye. He had got it removed last March, he said. 'Now I can see things quite clearly.'

'Well, there's certainly a lot going on here,' said Father.

'Why?' Gopen Babu frowned.

'Haven't you heard? The stars from heaven have descended on earth!'

'Your vision cannot be clear enough,' said Chhoto Mama, 'if you haven't noticed the great hullabaloo over the arrival of the film-star.'

'Film-star?' Gopen Babu was still frowning. 'Why make a fuss over a film-star? They're all shooting stars, aren't they? They spend their lives shooting. You know what a shooting star is, don't you, Sumohan?' he said, turning towards me. 'Here today, gone tomorrow. Liable to slip from the sky any minute and burn to ashes. There wouldn't be anything left of it after that. Nothing at all.'

Chhoto-da coughed gently. Clearly, Gopen Babu's words had pleased him.

'This can only mean you haven't heard of the real star,' Gopen Babu added, sipping his tea.

'Real star?' asked Father. All of us stared at Gopen Babu.

'You must have seen the bungalow behind the church,' he said. 'You know, the one with a garden? That is where the gentleman is staying. His name, I think, is Kalidas . . . or is it Kaliprasad . . .? Something like that. The surname's Ghoshal.'

'Why do you call him a star?'

'Because he is one. Absolutely the pole star. Steady. Eternal. More than a hundred years old, but doesn't look it at all!'

'What! A centurion!' Chhoto Mama gaped, a half-eaten piece of toast stuck in his open mouth.

'Century plus twenty-six. He is a hundred and twenty-six years old. Born in 1856. Just a year before the revolt. A few years before Tagore. Tagore was born in 1861.'

We fell silent. Gopen Babu continued sipping his tea.

After about a whole minute of silence, Chhoto-da asked, 'How do you know his age? Did he tell you himself?'

'Yes, but not deliberately. He's a most unassuming man. I learnt of it by accident. We were sitting in the front veranda of his house. Through the curtain, I happened to catch a glimpse of a woman—grey hair, glasses in a golden frame, a sari with a red border. So I said, "I hope this climate here suits your wife?" Mr Ghoshal smiled at this and replied, "Not my wife. My grandson's." I was amazed! After a while I said, "Please forgive my asking, but how old are you?" Again he smiled and said, "How old do you think?" "About eighty?" I said. "Add another forty-six," he told me. Now you know. It's a simple calculation.'

None of us could eat our breakfast after this. A piece of news like this was enough to kill one's appetite. The very thought that the oldest man in the country—no, possibly in the whole world—was actually staying in the same town as us made my head reel.

'You must meet him,' said Gopen Babu. 'I couldn't keep this news to myself, so I told a few people before you came—Sudheer Babu, Mr Sen, Mr Neotia of Ballygunje Park. They've all visited him. Now it's just a matter of time before you get to see the attraction of a real star.'

'Is his health . . .?' asked Mama.

'A couple of miles. Twice a day.'

'You mean he *walks*?'

'Yes, he walks. He does take a walking-stick. But then, so do I. Just think—he's twice my age.'

'I must look at his life line . . .' muttered Mama, his mind running along the same old track.

'Yes, I'm sure he wouldn't mind you looking at his palm!'

Chheni-da was sitting quietly in a corner. Now he sprang to his feet.

'Story! I couldn't get a better story. This could be a scoop!'

'Are you going to meet him right away?' asked Father.

'Yes. If he's a hundred and twenty-six years old, I'm taking no chances.

Anything can happen to a man of that age, any time. He may not even have a period of illness before he dies. So, if I must interview him, I had better hurry before the word spreads.'

'Sit down,' Father ordered, 'we shall all go together. You're not the only one who'd like to meet him. You may bring your notebook and jot things down.'

'Bogus!' said Chhoto-da softly. Then he added with a little more force, 'Bogus! Fraud! Liar!'

'What do you mean?' Gopen Babu sounded annoyed. 'Look, Suranjan, you've read Shakespeare, haven't you? "There are more things in heaven and earth . . ." You do know the line, don't you? So you mustn't dismiss everything as bogus.'

Chhoto-da cleared his throat.

'Let me tell you something, Gopen Babu. It has been proved that those who claim to be more than a hundred are either liars or barbarians. Once there were reports of a group of people who lived in a village in Russia at a high altitude. A majority of them were supposed to have completed a hundred years and were still fit enough to ride. So there was an investigation and it showed that these people were all totally primitive. There was no record of their birth. When asked about things that had happened in the past, their replies were all mixed up. It's not easy to cross the nineties. There is a limit to man's longevity. That is how nature has created man. Bernard Shaw, Bertrand Russell, P.G. Wodehouse—none of them lived to be a hundred. Jadunath Sarkar in our own country couldn't. And here's your man saying he's a hundred and twenty-six. Ha!'

'Have you heard of Zoro Agha?' snapped Mama.

'No. Who's he?'

'Man from Turkey. Or maybe from Iran. Can't remember now. He died sometime between 1930 and 1935 at the age of a hundred and sixty-four. Every newspaper in the entire world covered the event.'

'Bogus!' said Chhoto-da adamantly.

However, when we left for Kali Ghoshal's house, he joined us, possibly only to have his scepticism reinforced. Gopen Babu led the group.

'It would be nice,' said Father, 'if you could introduce us. After all, we're just strangers, and we cannot drop in casually simply because we've heard about his age.'

Chheni-da did not forget to take a notebook and a ball point pen.

'You go first,' said Mother. 'I'll go and visit some other time.'

The front veranda of Kali Ghoshal's house was full of cane and wooden chairs and stools. Obviously, he had started to receive a large number of visitors. We had gone within an hour of breakfast as Gopen Babu said that was the best time to get him. He came out in answer to Gopen Babu's greeting spoken from the veranda, 'Are you home, Mr Ghoshal?'

A hundred and twenty-six? No, he really didn't look more than eighty. A clear complexion, a mole on his right cheek, a sharp nose, a bright look in his eyes and a bald dome, except for a few strands of grey hair over his ears. Of medium height, he must once have been good looking. Today he was wearing a white silk kurta and pyjamas and had white slippers on his feet. If his skin had wrinkles at all, it was only around the eyes and below the chin.

Introductions over, he asked us to sit down. Chhoto-da was probably planning to stand behind a pillar, but when Father said, 'Do sit down, Ranju,' he pulled up a stool and sat down. He was still looking grave.

'We are sorry to barge in like this,' Father said, 'but you see, none of us has been lucky enough to have met a man like you . . .'

Mr Ghoshal smiled and raised a hand in protest, 'Please do not apologize. I do realize my age is my only distinction and the only thing that makes me special. Once people learnt the truth about my age, I knew they would wish to come and take a look at me. It's only natural, isn't it? Besides, isn't it a privilege for me to have met all of you?'

'Well, then,' said Father, 'perhaps I should tell you something frankly. This nephew of mine, Srikanta Chowdhury, is a journalist. He is very keen to have our discussions published. If you have no objection, that is.'

'No, not at all. Why should I object?' said Mr Ghoshal, still smiling. 'If a certain amount of fame comes my way at this late age, I should consider myself lucky. I've spent most of my life living in a village. Have you heard of a place called Tulsia? You haven't? It's in Murshidabad. There is no connection by rail. One has to get off at Beldanga and travel further south for another seventeen kilometres. We used to be landowners in Tulsia. There is, of course, nothing left of our old glory, except the ancestral house. That is where I live. People there call me "Reject". Rejected even by death. And they're right. My wife died fifty-two years ago. I have no living children or brothers and sisters. All I have is a grandson, who was supposed to come with me. But he's a doctor, you see, and he had a patient in a rather critical condition. So he couldn't leave him and come away. I was prepared to come alone with a servant, but my granddaughter wouldn't let me. She came with me herself and has already settled down here comfortably.'

A ball point pen writes noiselessly. But I could see Chheni-da scribble furiously in his notebook. His tape recorder had no batteries, which was something he had discovered the day before we left. Everything, therefore, depended on how fast he could write. He had borrowed a Pentax camera from somewhere. No doubt it was going to be used at some stage. No article of this kind could be complete without a picture.

'Er . . . I happen to be interested in palmistry,' said Mama. 'Could I look at your hand, just once?'

'Of course.'

Kali Ghoshal offered his right palm. Mama bent over it eagerly and, after a minute's silence, nodded vigorously and said, 'Naturally. Naturally. Your life line could not have been longer than usual. It would have had to come right down to your wrist if it were to reflect your age. I don't suppose the human hand has any provision for those who live to be more than a hundred. Thank you, sir!'

Father took over again.

'Is your memory still . . . I mean . . .'

'Yes. I can remember most things.'

'Didn't you ever visit Calcutta?' asked Chheni-da.

'Oh yes. Certainly. I went to the Hare School and Sanskrit College. I used to stay in a hostel on Cornwallis Street.'

'Horse-driven trams—?'

'Yes, I often rode in them. The fare was just two paise from Lal Deeghi to Bhawanipore. There were no rickshaws. But there was a big *palki* stand just off the main crossing at Shyam Bazar. The palanquin bearers once went on strike—I remember that. And there were the scavenger birds. As common as crows and sparrows nowadays. Quite large in size, high enough to reach my shoulders. But perfectly harmless.'

'Do you remember any famous personalities of the time?' Chheni-da continued.

'I saw Tagore a few times, much later. I didn't know him personally, of course. Who was I, anyway, to get to know him? But I saw the young Tagore once, an occasion I remember very well. He was reading poetry at the Hindu Mela.'

'That's a very well known event,' said Father.

'I never saw Bankimchandra, which I might have done, had I stayed on in Calcutta. But I went back to my village soon after college. I did see Vidyasagar, though. That was a memorable incident. I was walking along the road with two other friends and Vidyasagar was coming from the opposite side, carrying an umbrella, a cotton *chadar* on his shoulder, slippers on his feet. His height must have been even less than mine. Someone had left a banana peel on the footpath. He slipped on it and fell. We ran and helped him to his feet. His umbrella rolled away. One of us collected it and returned it to him. Do you know what he did as soon as he was back on his feet? Only he could have done such a thing. He picked up the banana peel, threw it into a dustbin and calmly walked away, without showing the slightest sign of annoyance.'

We spent another half-an-hour with Mr Ghoshal. Tea was served and with it came home-made sweets, no doubt a contribution from the grandson's wife. When we rose to take our leave, Chheni-da had filled more than half of a brand new notebook with his scribbles. He had also taken at least ten photographs.

He posted a parcel to his office in Calcutta the same day. Five days later, a copy of his newspaper reached us, carrying the article he had written, together with a photo of Mr Ghoshal. The headline said, 'I had helped Vidyasagar'.

It was undoubtedly a scoop, and Chheni-da's office duly recognized his efforts. But soon after that, as many as seven different magazines and dailies from Calcutta sent their representatives to interview Kali Ghoshal.

Something else had happened in the meantime. Anshuman Chatterjee, the film-star, cut short his holiday and returned to Calcutta with his entourage. He was apparently called away for shooting. Sharmi did not seem to mind since she had already taken his autograph. To tell the truth, she had lost at least a quarter of her admiration for her hero the minute he had said to her, 'What's your name, little girl?' Besides, she was quite overwhelmed to have met the world's oldest man.

'I suppose,' said Father, 'the star felt offended at so much attention being paid to an old man.'

Kali Ghoshal and his grandson's wife dined with us the day before we returned. He ate very little, but with relish. 'I have never smoked in my life,' he told us, 'and I've always eaten moderately and walked as much as possible. Perhaps that is why death hasn't dared to approach me.'

'Were there others in your family who lived long?' asked Father.

'Oh yes. Both my grandfather and great-grandfather lived to be more than a hundred. The latter used to practise tantra. At the age of a hundred and thirteen, he called my grandfather one day and said, 'It is now time for me to go. Please make all the arrangements.' There was no sign of illness. His skin had no wrinkles, his teeth were intact, his hair only mildly touched with grey. But the arrangements for his funeral were made on the bank of the Ganga. Half immersed in water, Haranath Ghoshal closed his eyes, chanting hymns and breathed his last. I was standing by his side. I was then forty-two. I can never forget that scene!'

'Remarkable!' sighed Mama.

A week after our return to Calcutta, Chhoto-da arrived one evening with a large, fat book under his arm. But no, it was not really a book, but a few issues of a magazine called *Bioscope* bound together. The editor of *Navarang* magazine, Sitesh Bagchi, had taken a deposit of fifty rupees from Chhoto-da before letting him borrow the book for a day. A bus ticket flagged one of the pages. Chhoto-da opened the book at that page and threw it before me.

There was a still from an old mythological film, printed on glossy art paper. The film was called *Shabari*. The caption below the picture read, 'The newcomer Kalikinkar Ghoshal and Kiranshashi as Shree Ram Chandra and Shabari in Pratima Movietone's film *Shabari* still under production.'

'Check the resemblance, stupid,' said Chhoto-da.

I did. The man was of medium height, had a clear complexion, a sharp nose and a mole on his right cheek. He appeared to be a man in his mid-twenties.

The pit of my stomach suddenly felt empty. 'When,' I gasped, 'was this picture taken?'

'Sixty-eight years after the revolt. In 1924. It was a silent film. And Kalikinkar Ghoshal was its hero. That was the first and the last film he ever made. A review was published about three months later in the same magazine. Do you know what it said? "No difference would have been made if this newcomer had never made an appearance. He has absolutely no future as an actor in films."'

'Then . . . that means his age . . .'

'Yes, he is what he appears to be. About eighty. If he was twenty-five in 1924, then that lady who was with him must have been his own wife, not his grandson's wife. Gopen Babu was right.'

'Then the man must be . . .'

'Bogus. A cheat. A crook. But you know what? I shall do nothing to have him exposed. After all, he's got quite a sharp brain. One must appreciate that. In his youth he may have failed. But now, in his old age, just look at how, with a nice white lie, he snatched the spotlight from the top star and turned it on himself! Bravo!'

Translated by Gopa Majumdar
First published in Bengali in 1983

Uncle Tarini and Betal

It was a day in early August. It had been drizzling all day. Uncle Tarini turned up in the evening as soon as it got dark. He snapped shut his Japanese umbrella and propped it up against the door, before climbing on the divan to take his place. Then he pulled a cushion closer and said, 'Where's everyone else? Go and call them, and please tell Nikunja to put the kettle on. I'd like a cup of tea, and I want the water freshly boiled.'

As it happened, there was a power cut. The two candles burning in our sitting room created a specially spooky atmosphere.

Nikunja poured fresh water into a kettle, set it to boil, and went off to call the other boys from the neighbouring houses. Within minutes, Napla, Bhulu, Chotpoti and Sunanda arrived.

'On a dark, wet evening like this, in this flickering candlelight . . .' began Napla.

' . . . You'd like a ghost story?' Uncle Tarini finished.

'Yes, if you have any left in your stock.'

'My stock? What's left in my stock would make two Arabian Nights.'

'You mean two thousand and two nights?'

It was only Napla who could banter with Uncle. 'Yes, sir,' Uncle replied, 'but not all are ghost stories.'

Uncle Tarini's stories were always immensely interesting. What none of us had ever asked him was whether they were true, or if he simply made them up. We did know, however, that he had travelled very widely all over the country for forty-five years, and had had a lot of strange and exciting experiences.

'So what kind of a story are you going to tell us today?' Bhulu asked him.

'Well, you might call it a ghost story, or the story of a skeleton.'

'I didn't know a ghost and a skeleton were the same thing!' Napla exclaimed.

'How much do you know, young man? They may not be the same, but at times, they can merge and become one. At least, that's what I saw happen. If you think you have the courage to hear about it, I am prepared to tell you the story.'

'Of course we do! Yes, we do! Sure, we do!' the five of us chanted.

Uncle Tarini began his story:

'After a successful stint in buying and selling cardamom in Malabar,

I was at a loose end once again. From Cochin, I went to Coimbatore; from there to Bangalore; from Bangalore to Coonoor, and then to Hyderabad. My pockets were full at the time. So I travelled only by first class, stayed in good hotels, and if I wanted to travel within a city, took taxis everywhere. I went to Hyderabad chiefly to see the Salar Jung Museum. I couldn't have believed, until I saw it, that it might be possible for a whole museum to be filled with a single individual's personal collections.

'After seeing the museum, I went off to Golconda. Then I returned to Hyderabad and was planning another journey, when I saw an advertisement in the local press. An artist in Hyderabad, called Dhanaraj Martyand, was looking for a model for a painting with a mythological theme. Have you heard of Ravi Varma? He came from the royal family of Travancore. His mythological paintings made him quite famous towards the end of the nineteenth century. Many old palaces in India still have his oil paintings. Dhanaraj Martyand had a similar style to Ravi Varma's. At the time—about thirty-five years ago—Martyand was a well-known and a very busy artist.

'I found his advertisement most interesting. He had asked for a male model. The model had to be good looking, and should be able to sit for the artist every day. He would be handsomely paid. As I have told you before, when I was a young man, I used to look like a prince. Besides, regular exercise had kept me quite fit. If I donned a silk robe, wore a crown on my head and slung a sword from my waist, I could easily pass as a raja. Anyway, I applied and was called for an interview within a week.

'On the day of the interview, I shaved with a new blade, wore my best clothes and presented myself at Martyand's address. The house he lived in must have been a haveli, once owned by a nawab. Everywhere I looked, I saw marble and mosaic. Clearly, there was money to be made from mythological paintings.

'A bearer in uniform showed me into a room with rows of chairs. Five candidates were already sitting there, as if it was the waiting room in a doctor's surgery. One of them looked vaguely familiar, but I could not place him immediately. Within a minute of my taking a seat, the same man was called in. "Vishwanath Solanki!" cried the bearer. Now I could recognize him. I had seen his photos in film magazines. Why was he looking for a job?

'Curious, I asked the man sitting next to me: "Er . . . that man who just left . . . isn't he a film star?" The man smiled. "If he was, he wouldn't be here, would he? No, he tried to become a film star but three of his films flopped at the box office. So he's looking at alternatives."

'He told me something else. Apparently, Solanki came from a wealthy family in Hyderabad. Having squandered a lot of money in gambling, he had gone to Bombay to become a film hero. Now he was back where he belonged.

'My informant was a candidate, too. All five were here in the hope of becoming an artist's model, though it was only Solanki who was reasonably good looking. But he lacked what is known as manliness.

'I was the last to be called. It turned out that the room where interviews were being held was the studio. There was a large window on one side, an easel, and paints and brushes on a table. A desk had been placed in the middle of the room, with a chair on either side. Mr Martyand was seated on one of them. He had a hooked nose, a goatee, and his hair rippled down to his shoulders. I was struck by the dress he was wearing. It seemed likely that he had designed it himself, for I had never seen such an odd mixture of Japanese, European and Muslim styles of clothing. But he spoke well. His English was fluent, like a real Englishman's.

'We spoke for about five minutes. Then he asked me to take my shirt off. One look at my chest and my muscles settled the matter. I was selected for the job. For each sitting, I would be paid a hundred rupees. If he worked every day, then in a month I could make three thousand rupees. Today, that would be worth about fifteen thousand.

'The work began from the very next day. I was to be the model for the main male character, no matter what story he chose. His wife and their daughter, Shakuntala, acted as models for the female characters. There were plenty of other models to pose for minor male characters. Martyand had a huge stock of costumes to fit every part. There were turbans, crowns, robes, dhotis, cummerbands, amulets, necklaces and every conceivable item a figure from Indian mythology might wear. The first painting he started working on was going to show Arjun shooting the eye of a bird. Martyand had had a large and impressive bow made for this purpose.

'After getting this job, I moved to a new place, within walking distance from Hussain Sagar Lake. I took two rooms for a hundred and fifty rupees a month. My landlord, Mutalaif Hussain, was a very good man. I left each morning after breakfast—which usually consisted of toast and eggs—to report for duty at nine o'clock. I had to sit for the artist until one, except for a short tea break at eleven. After my work was over, I was free for the rest of the day. So I roamed all over the city, took a walk by the lake in the evening, and went to bed by ten. I had one other job besides this: it was to read the stories in our mythology to find suitable subjects for Martyand. He had read virtually nothing apart from the Ramayan and the Mahabharata and that too, not very thoroughly. The subjects he chose, therefore, inevitably became repetitive after a while.

'It was I who told Martyand about the stories of Raja Vikramaditya, some of which he liked very much. I knew my physical appearance was such that I would suit the part of Vikramaditya very well. But, as things turned out, I did not get to dress up as Vikramaditya. Let me tell you what happened.

'For four months, things went very well. I gave sittings every day, and the artist completed eight paintings in that time. Then, one evening, while walking back from the lake, someone hit me on the head. It was a quiet and lonely spot, not far from a mosque. I had just passed the mosque and was walking under a tamarind tree, when I was attacked. Just for a few seconds, bright stars flashed before my eyes, then everything went black.

'When I regained consciousness, I found myself in a hospital. A kind gentleman had found me lying unconscious by the roadside, and brought me to the hospital in his car. There was a great deal of pain in my head and in one of my arms. When I fell, my arm hit a large stone and my elbow was fractured. But that was not all. I had had one hundred and fifty rupees in my wallet; and on my wrist was an Omega watch, worth seven hundred rupees. Both the wallet and the Omega were missing. The police had been informed, but such an occurrence was so common that they did not hold out much hope of ever catching the culprit.

'For three weeks, I had to stay in bed with my arm in plaster. Four days after the incident, I sent a postcard to Martyand and told him what had happened. Martyand's reply arrived within three days, containing more bad news. He had been commissioned to do a whole series on Vikramaditya. Six paintings were required by a certain date, so he had been forced to employ another model. The new model was not as good as me, Martyand said, but he had no choice. He also said he would let me know when he finished the series.

'There was nothing for me to do. So, simply to pass my time gainfully, and to earn what little I could, I began to write for the *Andhra Herald*. Martyand would take at least three months to finish six paintings. Thanks to what a local hooligan had done to me, I was going to lose nine thousand rupees.

'However, barely a month later, Martyand rang my landlord and left a message for me. Apparently, he needed to see me urgently.

'Feeling quite curious, I went back to his studio. What did he want me for?

'"Can you get me a skeleton?" Martyand asked me. "I've asked a couple of other people, but they couldn't help. So I thought of you. If you can, I'll pay you a large commission."

'"A skeleton? Why do you need a skeleton?"

'Martyand explained that his next painting was going to be based on *Betal Panchavingshati*. Raja Vikramaditya was going to be shown with a skeleton on his shoulders. I do not know if children today read the stories of Betal. We used to enjoy them immensely. Vikramaditya once met a sadhu, who said to him: "Four miles from here, there's a cremation ground. A dead body is hanging from the branch of a tree over there. Go and get it for me." Vikramaditya had to obey the sadhu. So he went to the cremation ground and found the body, still hanging by its neck. He then cut the noose off with one stroke of his sword. The body dropped to the ground, and burst into laughter.

'When I was a child, I had seen a Hindi film called *Zinda Laash* (The Live Corpse). This was another *zinda laash*. It was a body occupied by an evil spirit. It is this body that's called Betal. Vikramaditya picked it up, and Betal promptly climbed on his shoulders. Then it said, "I know you have to take me to the sadhu. On the way there, I am going to ask you a number of riddles. If you can solve them all and give me correct answers, I will leave you and go back to the tree. If you can't, your heart will burst and you will die instantly."

'I could recall this story, but from what I remembered, Vikramaditya had found a corpse, not a skeleton. I said as much to Martyand.

'"I know," he replied. "If I can find a skeleton, in my painting I can turn it into a corpse. That's not a problem. The problem is finding a skeleton. I've got to have it!"

'"All right, but will your model agree to place it on his shoulders?"

'"Yes. I've already spoken to him, and he said he wouldn't mind at all. He's a brave man. Now you tell me if you can get me a skeleton."

'"I shall try my best. But it may cost you a great deal of money. And, once you've finished your painting, the skeleton may well have to be returned to the supplier."

'Martyand gave me two thousand rupees immediately. "That's how much I am willing to pay to hire a skeleton for a week. I don't wish to buy one. You will get two hundred."

'As you all know, it is not easy to get hold of a skeleton today. Virtually all available skeletons are exported abroad. Even in those days, particularly in a place like Hyderabad, I knew it was going to be difficult to find one. So, instead of wasting my time looking everywhere, I went straight to my landlord, Mr Hussain. He had lived in Hyderabad for forty-two years. He knew a lot about the city.

'On hearing my request, he frowned for a while. Then he said, "I know of a skeleton. What I don't know is whether it is a real one, or whether it is artificial; nor do I know if its owner has still got it."

'"Who is its owner?"

'"A magician. I don't know his real name, but he used to call himself Bhojraj. One of his items involved a skeleton. It sat with him at the same table, drank tea, played cards, and then got up and walked about the stage with Bhojraj. It was truly amazing. The man made quite a name for himself. Then he retired, and for nearly fifteen years now, I haven't heard of him."

'"Was he from Hyderabad?"

'"Yes, but I don't know his address. You can try asking the Andhra Association. They used to organize his shows every year."

'The Andhra Association were quite helpful. From them, I got the last known address where Bhojraj used to live. To my astonishment, I discovered that he had not moved. I found him in a two-room apartment in Chowk Bazar. Probably in his eighties, the man had a thick reddish-brown beard, a shiny bald dome, and skin as dark as ebony. He took one look at me, and said, "The Bangali babu seems to be going through a rough patch."

'How did he know? Was he a fortune teller? Anyway, I decided to come straight to the point. After explaining why I needed a skeleton, I said, "If you have still got it, could you lend it to me for a week? My luck might improve if you did. The man who wants to hire the skeleton is prepared to pay two thousand. Have you still got it?"

'"Got what? A skeleton? Why, I have two! Ha ha ha ha!"

'I stared, taken aback. "For that matter, babu, you have a skeleton, too," Bhojraj went on, "If you didn't, how could you move about? I can see your skeleton quite clearly. Your elbow cracked, then the doctors put it back together. The crack healed only because you are young. If a similar thing happened to me, do you think I'd ever recover?"

'I seized this chance to ask him a question: "Do you know who attacked me?"

'"A very ordinary goonda. What I don't know is whether there is someone else behind the attack. There may well be. My skeleton would know. It knows a lot more than me. I am prepared to lend it to you, babu. I haven't earned a penny for a long time. Two thousand rupees will settle all my debts. I can then die in peace. But there is something I would like you to know. The skeleton I will give you is no ordinary skeleton. It is that of a yogi. He had extraordinary powers. He could levitate six feet above the ground. He derived sustenance from the air, food for him was unnecessary. Once, while he was sitting in meditation outside his hut, a thief stole in and tried to remove some of his meagre possessions. The instant he stretched a hand to lift the first object, his hand was struck by leprosy. His fingers got twisted and bent. A cobra tried to bite this yogi, but just a glance from him reduced it to a handful of dust. He was so powerful."

'"But . . ." I couldn't help saying, "you managed to master his skeleton, didn't you? I've heard you could make it obey your every command. It performed a lot of tricks for you on the stage, didn't it?"

'"No," Bhojraj smiled. 'I was never the master of that skeleton. Whatever happened was simply because the yogi willed it. People thought the skeleton was mechanized, and that I had fitted gadgets inside it. That is not true. What happened was this: I was so impressed by the yogi's powers that I became his follower and, for ten years, did what I could to serve him. I was only a young man at the time. I had a certain curiosity about magic, but that was all. I could never have imagined that I would become a magician one day.

'"For ten years, Guruji took no notice of me. Then, one day, he suddenly looked at me and said, 'Beta, I am very pleased with you. But you must not think of leaving home. There's a lot for you to do. One day, you will become a king among magicians. You will be famous. I will help you in whatever you do, to repay you for all that you've done for me in the last few years. But I cannot do anything now. I can be of help to you only after my death.'

'"'How? How is that going to happen, Guruji?'

'"Guruji mentioned a date in the future. 'On this day,' he said, 'you must go to an old city called Mandhata, by the river Narmada, and find its cremation ground. There, you will see a woodapple tree. When you do, start walking to the west. Just follow the river, and count your steps. Nine hundred and ninety-nine steps should bring you to a forest. You should be able to spot a tamarind tree as soon as you enter the forest. Next to that tree, behind a bush, you will find a skeleton lying on the ground. That will be my skeleton. Take it with you, and use it in your work. It will perform with you on the stage, obey your commands, and help you win both fame and fortune. Then, when your work is over, throw it into a river. If there is still something that remains to be done, it will not sink. Pick it up again and bring it back with you.'"

'I remained silent when Bhojraj finished his story. After a few moments, I asked: "Isn't it time to throw it into a river?"

'"No, that time has not yet come. I did try, but it did not sink. So I brought it back. Now, I can see that it was simply waiting for you."

'"Me?"

'"Yes. Were you born under the sign of cancer?"

'"Yes."

'"On the fifth day after a full moon?"

'"That's right."

'"Well then, it has to be you. But even if your zodiac sign was different, it would not have mattered. It is clear to me that you are a good man. If Guruji can finally find peace through your hands, I should be very glad. He would have liked you. He could recognize good, honest men."

'"What do I have to do now?"

'"See that box over there? Go and open it."

'There was a large box—almost like a chest—standing in a corner. I went and lifted its lid. The skeleton lay on a piece of red velvet, with its knees bent. "Take it out and bring it here," said Bhojraj. I placed my hands on its ribcage and lifted it. All the bones were threaded delicately to one another with thin copper wires.

'"Put it down on its feet."

'I placed it on the floor, holding its arms to give it support. "Now let go of its arms," Bhojraj commanded.

'I removed my hands and saw, to my complete amazement, that the skeleton was standing straight without any support at all.

'"Now salute it. It is now your property. You are responsible for the final job."

'What final job? I had no idea, but decided not to take any chances. Instead of merely saluting it, I threw myself prostrate on the ground, to show my respect.

'"Do you realize the true significance of what you've taken on?" Bhojraj wanted to know. "Do you really believe everything you just heard?"

'"I keep an open mind about everything, sir," I replied. "I believe in afterlife, I believe in magic, I believe in science."

'"Good. Now arrange to take it away. Please see that Guruji gets what he wanted. When your work is done, throw it into the river Musi."

'Martyand was so pleased to get a skeleton that he paid me five hundred, instead of two. Then he said, "What are you doing this evening?"

'"Why do you ask?"

'"I will start the painting of Vikramaditya and Betal. I would like you to be there."

'"I thought you painted only during the day."

'"Yes, but this is a special case. The particular mood and atmosphere I need for this one will come more easily at night. I have arranged special lighting. I want you to see it."

'"But what if your model objects?"

'"He won't even know you are there. Come at seven o'clock, and stand quietly in that corner. All the lights will be focused on the model. He won't be able to see what's on the other side."

'I had once been in amateur theatre. I knew that, from the stage, it was impossible to see those sitting on the other side of the footlights. What Martyand was suggesting would be something similar. I agreed to return in the evening.

'When I turned up, with my heart beating just a little faster than usual, it was five minutes to seven. Martyand's servant, Shivsharan, opened the door and helped me slip into the studio quietly.

'The model had not yet arrived. But the lighting was ready. It was truly impressive: perfectly appropriate for a place where ghosts and spirits were supposed to converge.

'Martyand was sitting before the canvas, a strong light by his side. He glanced briefly at a door, to let me know that the model was in the ante-chamber, getting ready.

'Now I noticed something else. It was the skeleton. Martyand had hung it from a hat-stand. In the pale, ghostly light that fell on it, it looked as if it was grinning. I don't know if you've noticed it, but if you look at a skull, it will always appear to grin at you, possibly because its teeth are exposed.

'A faint click made me look at the other door that led to the ante-chamber. Vikramaditya emerged from it, wearing garments suitable for a king, a sword in his hand. He had a thick moustache, a heavy beard and long, wavy hair. Every little detail in his make-up and costume was in place. It was perfect. Just for a moment, I couldn't help feeling a pang of envy. I would have been wearing that costume, but for a stroke of misfortune!

'The model took his position under the lights, on what had become a stage. Martyand got up to make a few changes to his pose, then took the skeleton off the hat-stand. "Make it sit on your shoulders," he said to the model. "Bring its arms forward and hold them with your right hand. Get the legs to go round your waist, and grab the feet with your left hand."

'The model obeyed every instruction without any apparent discomfort. I had to admire his courage.

'Martyand began drawing. He would first do a charcoal sketch, then use colour. When I was his model, I never got the chance to see how he worked. This time, I had no difficulty in watching how swiftly and expertly he made his strokes.

'In less than five minutes, I heard a strange noise. It sounded like a moan, and it was coming from the stage. The artist was engrossed in his work. He did not appear to have noticed anything. All he said was, "Steady, steady!" He had to say this because the model had started to fidget a little.

'Then it became clear that, despite a word from the artist, the model could not stand still. He was turning and twisting, and the sound escaping through his lips could only be described as a groan, as if he was in pain.

'"What's the matter?" Martyand asked irritably. I could see what the matter was, clearly enough, though I could scarcely believe my eyes.

'The arms of the skeleton were no longer hanging down. They were raised, and placed round the model's neck, just under his chin. They were getting tighter and tighter, turning it into a horrific, ghostly embrace. But it was not just the arms. The legs round the waist had tightened, too, as if they could never be prised apart.

'The model looked a pathetic sight. The soft groans had turned into wild screams. He had thrown his sword away, and was tugging at the skeleton's arms with all his might, in a vain attempt to loosen its grasp.

'Martyand gave a sharp exclamation, and ran forward to help him. But their combined efforts failed. After a while, Martyand gave up, walked back with unsteady steps, then crashed against the easel, which overturned at once. Finally, he collapsed on the floor near me, leaning heavily against the wall.

'By this time, I had overcome my own shock and amazement. The model was now rolling on the floor, the skeleton still firmly attached to his body. "Do something!" I heard Martyand say hoarsely.

'I walked towards the stage. Something told me that the skeleton would do me no harm. It would not stand in my way.

'As I got closer, however, something else made my head start to reel once more. During the struggle, the model's wig, beard and turban had all fallen off. His face was fully exposed. I recognized it instantly. It was the face of the "flop-hero" Vishwanath Solanki.

'At once, I felt as if a curtain had been drawn aside before my eyes, and I could see the truth, clear as crystal. A cunning idea flashed through my mind in the same instant.

'I bent over Solanki. "Tell me, Mr Solanki, was it you who hired a goonda to attack me? There's going to be no escape, remember, unless you tell the truth."

'Solanki's eyes looked as if they would burst out of their sockets any minute. "Yes, yes, yes!" he gasped between short breaths. "Please save me. Please!"

'I turned to Martyand. "You heard him. Are you prepared to stand witness? I am going to hand him over to the police."

'Martyand nodded.

'I turned back and gently pulled at the skeleton's shoulders. It loosened its grasp instantly and slipped off the model's body.

'Solanki had to say goodbye to his career as an artist's model because, soon after this incident, he was forced to spend quite a long time in prison.

'The man who replaced him and dressed as Vikramaditya for the whole series was Tarinicharan Banerjee. Martyand was naturally deeply shaken by the episode, but he recovered within a week and began his work with renewed vigour.

'The day after the painting showing Vikramaditya with Betal was finished, I took the skeleton to the river Musi and threw it into the water.

'It disappeared without a trace even before I could blink my eye.'

Translated by Gopa Majumdar
First published in Bengali in 1983

Chameleon

Nikunja Saha occupied a chair in the New Mahamaya Cabin, ordered a cup of tea and a plate of potato fries, and looked around carefully. Were any of his acquaintances there in the restaurant? Yes, Rasik Babu and Sreedhar were already here. Panchanan would probably turn up in about ten minutes. The more the merrier. The success of his disguise lay in not being recognized by anyone who knew him.

But then, all his disguises had been remarkably successful so far. Today half his face was covered by a beard and the shape of his nose had been altered a little with the help of plasticine. But he had changed his gait and style of speech so completely that even Panchanan Gui, who had known him for ten years, could not recognize him when he came to ask for a match from Nikunja. Mustering all his courage, Nikunja had even ventured to speak, 'You may keep the whole box. I have another.' Panchanan had given no sign of recognition even at the sound of his voice. This was the essence of art.

For Nikunja all his other interests had waned. This passion for disguises had become almost an obsession. He had plenty of time, for he had given up the job he had before. He used to be a salesman in Orient Book Company on College Street. A childless uncle had died recently leaving Nikunja all the money he had made in the share market. The capital brought an interest of seven hundred and fifty rupees every month. He could, therefore, easily afford to leave his job.

The same uncle used to often tell him, 'Read, Nikunja, read as much as you can. There's nothing that one can't learn from books. You needn't go to a school, you needn't have a teacher—all you need is books. I have even heard that it is possible to learn to fly aeroplanes simply from instructions in a book.' There were two things his uncle himself had learnt quite well from books—palmistry and homoeopathy. Nikunja followed his advice and bought books on leatherwork and photography. Very soon, he managed to learn the rudiments of both.

About six months ago he had seen a fat American book on make-up on a footpath in College Street. Unable to resist the temptation, he had bought it and since then, this new interest had a firm grip on his mind.

The strange thing was that Nikunja was not interested in the one place where make-up was needed every day—in the theatre, although he did toy with the idea of utilizing his knowledge in a fruitful way. Who knows, he might even manage to make some extra money, he had thought.

He happened to know Bhulu Ghosh of the Naba Natta Company. Both were members of the East Bengal Club. One day, Nikunja went to Bhulu's house on Amherst Street and told him of his wish.

Bhulu, however, was not very encouraging.

'Why,' he asked, 'do you want to mess about in the theatre? We already have Aparesh Datta in our company. He's been our make-up man for thirty-six years. It's not going to be easy to replace him. He has the entire art of make-up on his fingertips. If you went and told him you've been dabbling in it for just over six months, he wouldn't even look at you. Forget about getting a break, Nikunja. You appear to be leading a fairly happy and carefree life. Don't get involved in something you don't know enough about!'

Nikunja dropped the idea of becoming a professional make-up man.

But what was he to do with his knowledge? On whom could he practise his skill? He could not, after all, open something like a hair-cutting salon where people would come and pay to have their appearances altered.

Then he had an idea. What about his own self? There were certain natural advantages in his appearance. Everything about him was average. He was of medium height, neither too dark nor very fair, his features neither sharp nor blunt. A straight, long nose could not be hidden. If one was tall, one's height could not be disguised. And the amount of make-up that was required to conceal a dark complexion was very likely to give the show away.

Nikunja studied his own appearance for two days and decided to start experimenting on himself.

But what after that? What could he possibly hope to achieve with his make-up and disguises?

Well, two things, certainly. The first would be to take his art to the very peak of perfection; and the second, to enjoy fooling all his friends.

Nikunja began buying materials for his make-up. He had read in the book that the best in the market was the pancake make-up produced by Max Factor. But it was not available in India. Nikunja, therefore, had to go to his neighbour, Dr Biraj Chowdhury. Dr Chowdhury had once treated him for jaundice. Nikunja knew that his son who was studying in America was supposed to be returning home soon to attend his sister's wedding.

Nikunja did not beat about the bush and came straight to the point.

'Could I request your son to bring me something from America? I shall pay him here as soon as he arrives.'

'What is it that you want?'

'Stuff for make-up. I've got the name written down. It's not available here.'

'All right. If you let me have the details, I shall certainly write to him.'

The Max Factor pancake make-up arrived within three weeks. Nikunja had already bought every other requisite— brushes, spirit gum, eyebrow pencils, black enamel paint to create missing teeth, white powder for grey hair and a number of fine nylon nets to help wear wigs. In addition to these, he had bought loose strands of hair which he fixed on some of the nylon nets one by one and made at least twenty different moustaches, twenty types of beards and various wigs: rough, smooth, straight, wavy, curly like Africans—the lot.

But, of course, it was not enough simply to change one's face. One had to have a change of clothes as well. Nikunja took about a week to make a round of New Market, Bara Bazaar and Grant Street to collect clothes of all kinds. Some of these had to be tailor-made since ready-made material was not always available. After sorting out his clothes, he turned his attention to other things he would wear and, eventually, managed to collect seven types of glasses, twelve pairs of sandals, ten different caps—including the cap of a police inspector. He also bought five types of fabric to make *pugris* and five wristwatches. The *kada* of Sikhs, the sacred thread of the Brahmins, the different prayer beads of the Vaishnavas and other religious groups, a wide assortment of medallions and talismans and, finally, paste diamond earrings to go with the attire of an *ustaad*—all were added to his collection.

A large mirror was bought and a strong bulb was fixed over it. In order to be able to work even during a power cut he also had to invest in a Japanese generator and teach his servant, Nitai, how to operate it.

He began practising from 16th November. He noted the date in his diary. At eight in the morning, he began working on his make-up and finished by 4 p.m. He knew it would be best if he dressed as someone from an average middle class background. There was no point in dressing as a beggar or a labourer, for the real test lay in being able to visit the New Mahamaya Cabin and having a cup of tea amidst his friends and acquaintances.

The very first day brought him success. He was made up as a solicitor: dark, bushy eyebrows and matching moustaches, white trousers, a much-used black gown, an old briefcase, a pair of worn out black shoes and loose white socks.

Panchanan came and sat at his table. The flutter in Nikunja's heart persisted for as long as he sat there, sipping a cup of tea. But he realized that day how totally incurious one could be about a fellow being, especially if one's attention was elsewhere.

Panchanan saw him all right, but took not the slightest notice. He kept reading the little race book he was holding in his left hand and with his right, tearing pieces from an omelette with a spoon, and stuffing them into his mouth. He did not glance at Nikunja even when he asked the waiter for his bill. This was an entirely new experience, a new thrill. Nikunja knew that from that day that this would be his only occupation.

Something rather funny happened that evening when he returned home. He really ought to have anticipated it, but the thought had not occurred to him.

Shashi Babu lived in the ground floor flat, right next to the front door. From his living-room it was possible to see all those who came in and went out of the building.

It was about a quarter-past-seven in the evening when Nikunja returned. The light in the passage was on.

'Who is it?' asked Shashi Babu as Nikunja stepped in, still dressed as a solicitor.

Nikunja stopped. Then he walked towards Shashi Babu's room. Now they were facing each other.

'Who are you looking for?' said Shashi Babu.

'Does Nikunja Saha live in this house?'

'Yes. Turn right as you go up the stairs. His is the first room.' Shashi Babu turned away to go inside. Nikunja removed his eyebrows and moustaches in an instant and said, 'I need some information.'

'Yes?' Shashi Babu turned back and grew round-eyed, 'Why—it's you, Nikunja!'

Nikunja went straight into Shashi Babu's room. Shashi Babu should be told about what he was doing. It might make things easier if someone in the building could be taken into confidence.

'Listen Shashi-da, you may find me returning like this now and then dressed differently. I may come as a solicitor or a doctor or perhaps a Sikh or a Marwari—do you understand? I'll go out in the evening and return at night. I'd like to come straight in here and remove my make-up. But this is just between you and me, all right?'

'How odd! When did you develop such a weird interest? Are you in the theatre?'

Shashi Babu was a true gentleman. He had read a lot and was the librarian of the local Bankim Library. He knew something of human nature. 'All right,' he said, 'as long as you don't do anything wrong, it's fine. Some people do have strange hobbies, I know.'

Nikunja knew he could not go out in disguise more than twice a week, since putting on the right make-up was a time-consuming task. So he decided to spend the rest of his time studying people. New Market was undoubtedly a gold mine for this purpose. Just one visit was enough to expose him to the wide variety of people who came there. Apart from New Market, he went to observe people at the stadium, and in queues for Hindi films. In his diary he noted down the details of all who struck him as interesting. On a few occasions, he even found an excuse to speak to them. Questions like, 'Could you tell me the time?' or 'Which bus do you think would take me to Gariahat?' often proved useful. On days when he happened to be free, he continued to visit the New Mahamaya Cabin, dressed in his own normal clothes to spend a few hours with his friends, discussing the world's problems. He would then return as usual to his flat in Vrindavan Basak Lane. His young servant, Nitai, knew about his master's disguises and seemed to enjoy the whole experience as much as Nikunja himself. But not much could be said of Nitai's own intelligence.

'Can you recognize me? Can you recognize me as your Babu?'

'But you are my Babu. I know it!'

'Does your Babu have moustaches like these? Is he bald? Does he wear such clothes? Such glasses? Does he wear a shawl?'

Nitai only smiled at these questions and kept leaning against the door, watching him. Nikunja realized his art was something a fool like

Nitai would never learn to appreciate. But was it enough simply to deceive a few close friends?

This question kept coming back to Nikunja. He discovered that a stronger ambition was rising in his heart. He must find out how his skill at make-up and disguise worked on a larger audience.

He found an opportunity soon enough.

One day, a few inmates of the house including Nikunja were gathered in Shashi Babu's room. Among the others was Bhujanga Babu who was interested both in religion and yoga. Rumour had it that he had once very nearly become a sanyasi. In fact, even now, he knew many sadhus and had been on a tour of Kedar-Badri, Varanasi and Kamakshya. It was he who happened to mention that a tantrik sadhu had arrived in Tarapeeth. He was reputed to have more supernatural powers than even the the sadhus of mythology whom one had read about.

'What name, did you say?' asked Harabilas, who worked in a bank.

'I didn't,' replied Bhujanga Babu, annoyed. His eyebrows had a habit of rising whenever he was irritated and his glasses would come slipping down his nose.

'Is it Hiccups Baba?' said Harabilas.

The papers had indeed carried a story on Hiccups Baba. It was said that he was given to having severe fits of hiccups while talking to his visitors, as though his end was near, but he recovered each time and resumed his conversation as if nothing had happened. Yet, doctors had confirmed that those hiccups were indeed of the variety that one might have just before dying.

Bhujanga Babu pushed his glasses back with a finger and said that the sadhu in question was called Kalikananda Swamy.

'Will you go and visit him?' asked Tanmay Babu, an insurance agent. 'I'll come with you, if I may. Being in the presence of a sadhu always gives me a feeling of . . . you know . . . of something. I'm disgusted with this wholesale filth in Calcutta.'

Bhujanga Babu mentioned that he did intend going one day.

Nikunja went back to his room without a word. His heart beat faster. He must check immediately what kind of things he would need to dress as a tantrik, and how many of those things he had already got.

He cast a quick glance through the description of a tantrik in Bankimchandra's *Kapalkundala*. Nothing had changed. Sadhus and sanyasis dressed today just as they had done hundreds of years ago. Nikunja had once gone to Varanasi. A look at the Dashashwamedh Ghat had given him a glimpse of ancient India.

He made his plans.

Tarapeeth was in Birbhum, near Rampurhat. He had a cousin living in Rampurhat. He would first go to his cousin's house with his make-up kit. He would get dressed there and then go to Tarapeeth. That was where the real challenge lay. He had to find out if he could mingle easily with the other sadhus. Besides, if Bhujanga Babu and the others were also going to be there, so much the better. It would give him added pleasure if they failed to recognize him.

Nikunja already had most of what was required. All he needed was a large walking stick, a pair of tongs and a copper bowl. He would also need a special wig, but that could be arranged quite easily.

Bhujanga Babu and his family were going to leave for Tarapeeth on Wednesday. Nikunja left the day before. He had already told his cousin, Santosh, of his arrival, although Santosh did not yet know the reason.

Santosh's father had been the owner of Purnima Talkies in Rampurhat. After his death the year before, its ownership passed on to Santosh who began to show popular Hindi films and earned a fair amount. Possibly as a result of his interest in Hindi films, he grew quite excited at the prospect of an adventure when he learnt of Nikunja's plans. 'Don't worry about a thing, Nikunja-da,' he said, 'I shall take you in my car and drop you near the cremation ground.'

Nikunja had forgotten that the cremation ground in Tarapeeth had a temple and it was in the cremation ground that the sadhus stayed. The famous tantrik, Bama Khepa, had lived here.

On Wednesday, Nikunja began working on his make-up quite early in the morning. The real Nikunja was wiped out the minute he fixed a long beard, moustaches and a wig. Long hair rippled down to his shoulders, his forehead was smeared with sandalwood paste with a vermilion mark in the centre; three rows of rudraksha beads were wound around his neck. When he finally slipped out of his own clothes and put on a saffron robe, Santosh jumped up and quickly touched his feet.

'Oh my God, Nikunja-da! This is perfect! No one on earth can recognize you now. I can tell only because I have been standing here throughout. Or I, too, would have been fooled!'

The experience of the last few months had taught Nikunja's hands to move faster. He was ready by half-past-two. The tongs and the copper bowl were brand new; so they, too, had to be made to look as though they had been used for some time. By 4 p.m., Nikunja Saha alias Ghanananda Maharaj was ready to depart. It was necessary to have a new name, but Nikunja had decided to speak as little as possible. Sadhus were different from ordinary folk. If a sadhu did not speak, no one would find it odd. The new name was Santosh's idea. 'When you get down from the car, Nikunja-da,' he said, 'people are bound to ask me who you are. You must have a name.'

Ghanananda had a deep, sombre ring to it. Santosh felt quite pleased.

Normally he drove himself. But, today, he took a driver.

'I shall have to go around with this sadhu baba,' he told the driver, 'you must keep an eye on the car.'

Here, Nikunja felt it was necessary to mention something to Santosh. 'I must be left alone when we reach there. I will try to get as close as possible to Kalikananda. I'm sure there will be groups of other sadhus near him. I will try to join one of these. You go and sit among the visitors.'

'All right. Don't worry, Nikunja-da, I'll manage.'

By the time Santosh's car reached the cremation ground in Tarapeeth, there was barely half-an-hour left before sunset. This place was no different from other holy places—a crowd outside the temple, little shops on both sides of the road selling flowers, vermilion, books, calendars, tea, biscuits, samosas and fly-ridden jalebis.

But Nikunja's experience here turned out to be very different from that in the New Mahamaya Cabin. It was amazing how a saffron-clad figure could arouse respect and admiration. The minute he came out of the car, people—young and old, men, women, boys and girls—started touching his feet. Nikunja's hand rose automatically in a gesture of blessing as he began to move forward. Soon, it became impossible to put his hand down even for a second. Had Santosh not been with him, he would probably have stayed rooted to the same spot all night. 'Please, please, make way,' said Santosh and pushed through the crowd. They finally managed to get inside and reach a relatively quiet corner. There were other sadhus, all dressed in saffron, so there was not much of a chance here for being singled out for attention.

Nikunja glanced around. A small crowd had gathered under a banyan tree at some distance. Not many were wearing saffron, so presumably they were ordinary people who had come to look at a sadhu.

'Wait here for a minute, Nikunja-da,' said Santosh, 'while I go and check if that is where Kalikananda is sitting. I will take you near him and then leave you. But I won't go far. Let me know when you wish to leave.'

Santosh returned a few moments later and confirmed that Kalikananda was indeed sitting under that tree and the crowd was listening to his words of wisdom.

'Go ahead, Nikunja-da. There's nothing to worry about.'

Nikunja made his way to the banyan tree. He was not worried. A feeling of complete satisfaction had enveloped his mind the minute he had set foot here. His make-up was flawless. He was the perfect artist, he felt convinced.

Kalikananda's discourse could be heard from where Nikunja had been standing. His voice grew louder as Nikunja came closer. Then he saw him. A strong personality, no doubt, made stronger by the tiger skin he was sitting on. What he was saying was nothing new, but the man was clearly a gifted speaker. There was something special in the way he spoke. And his eyes! The whites of his eyes were not really white. There was a tinge of pink in them. Could it be a result of smoking ganja? Possibly.

About fifty people were gathered around and the number was increasing steadily. There was Bhujanga Babu with his wife! Tanmay Babu must also be sitting somewhere in the crowd. Bhujanga Babu must have arrived quite early, for he was sitting right in front.

On both sides of Kalikananda and behind him, sat other sadhus. All had flowing beards, long hair, rudraksha beads round their necks and their bodies were smeared with ash. There was no difference at all between their appearance and Nikunja's.

Nikunja passed the crowd and moved towards this group of sadhus. From somewhere in the distance, came the faint strains of a bhajan.

Suddenly the song started to sound louder. The reason was simple. Kalikananda had stopped speaking.

Nikunja looked at the sadhu. Kalikananda's bloodshot eyes were fixed on him in an unblinking stare.

Nikunja stopped.

Everyone else turned their eyes on him.

This time Kalikananda spoke.

'A disguise, eh? Is a saffron costume all that is required to make a sadhu? And a few beads round one's neck? And ash on one's body? How dare you! What if I pulled at your hair? Do you realize what might happen? Could you still go on pretending?'

Santosh was beside Nikunja in a flash.

'That's enough, Nikunja-da. Back to the car. At once.' Nikunja's whole body felt numb. He had to lean on Santosh for support as they began walking towards the main gate. His eyes were virtually closed, but he could not shut his ears. Kalikananda's final words boomed in the air: 'Do you know the result of such deception, Nikunja Saha?'

Nikunja had to move into a new flat in Calcutta, far away from where he had lived before. Bhujanga Babu was a witness to the Tarapeeth episode. No doubt he would have gossiped and then it would have been quite impossible to face all the others who knew him. Luckily, he found a small flat in Bhawanipore. The rent was Rs 250 per month.

Even after his return to Calcutta, Nikunja shivered every time he thought of Kalikananda. Heavens—what acute perception that tantrik had! Nikunja got rid of all the 'religious' costumes he had. Dresses meant for priests, pandits, maulvis and monks were all thrown into the river.

It took him about three weeks to come back to his normal self. He had made a few friends in the meantime. There was another restaurant here, not very far from his house, called Parashar Cabin. The people he met here— Tarak Babu, Nagenda, Shibu—knew nothing of his scandalous past. Shibu, as a matter of fact, worked in a theatre. He took Nikunja with him one day to see his play, *Fiery Sparks*. 'You must see the first-class make-up I'm given,' Shibu said before they left.

Nikunja did not know whether to laugh or cry when Shibu's make-up was done. What kind of make-up was this? Had they never seen what really good make-up could be like? If they saw his own, they would be bound to feel ashamed!

The next instant he recalled the incident in Tarapeeth. But, then, tantriks did often have special supernatural powers. There was nothing surprising in that. Nikunja himself had made a wrong move, that was all.

Yes, that experience had been a frightening one. But surely that was no reason to give up his favourite occupation altogether? No that could never be. There were so many other different characters he had not tried his hand at. Why, he had not yet tried disguising himself as a criminal, had he? With the only exception of the tantrik, every other disguise he had donned was harmless and nondescript. No one would give such characters a second glance, anyway. The real challenge lay in disguising oneself as someone everyone would look at; yet they would fail to recognize the real person behind the make-up.

What should the criminal look like? Crew-cut hair, a heavy stubble, a scar under one eye, a broken nose—like a boxer—a tattoo on his hand, a chain round his neck, a buttonless checked shirt and a Burmese lungi.

After his Tarapeeth experience, Nikunja should not have gone anywhere near a disguise. But his passion had developed into a kind of addiction. He forgot the tantrik and began working with renewed enthusiasm.

Nikunja sat down before his mirror fairly early one morning soon after a cup of tea. He did not, therefore, get a chance to glance at the newspaper and so missed the news of the double murder in Kidderpore and the photograph of the absconding miscreant, Bagha Mandal. If he had seen it, no doubt he would have done his make-up a little differently.

A photograph of Bagha Mandal had been published about six months ago after a daring robbery. On that occasion, too, Bagha had managed to hoodwink the police. His photo had been published to warn the general public. Had Nikunja seen his photo at that time and had it, somehow, remained embedded in his memory? Why else should he start disguising himself to look exactly like Bagha Mandal?

But even if he had seen the photograph, he had obviously not grasped the significance of the story that had accompanied it. If he had, he would not have felt any surprise at the way people quickly left Parashar Cabin as soon as he came in and sat at a table.

What was the matter? Why was everyone behaving so strangely? Where did the manager disappear? Why had the waiter gone so pale?

How was Nikunja to know that the manager had gone to the chemist next door to telephone the police and that his phone call would bring the police van to Nikunja's neighbourhood?

But, at this critical moment, Nikunja's guardian angel stepped in. While he did not exactly offer a helping hand to get him out of the mess, he certainly offered a little finger. Nikunja's eyes suddenly fell on a newspaper that was lying on a vacant chair. The page it was opened at carried Bagha Mandal's photograph, together with a short, crisp write-up.

This was the face that had gradually come to life this morning in Nikunja's mirror.

Nikunja's limbs began to feel rather heavy. But he could not stop himself from grabbing the paper to read the article. Everything fell into place at once.

He forced himself to get up and walk out of the restaurant as casually as he could. Then he began walking towards his house as fast as his legs could carry him (running would attract attention). It took him ten minutes to reach his house. On his way, he heard the sound of a vehicle and assumed—correctly—that it was the police van, but paid no attention. Let them come. The police would be fooled. By the time they came up the stairs, Nikunja Saha's disguise would have vanished. It did not matter if the police found Nikunja Saha. After all, Nikunja was not the culprit.

He told his servant to make him a cup of tea and bolted the door. Oh no! There was a power cut. It would take him a little while to start the Japanese generator.

Never mind. There were candles. But first he must remove his clothes, and that could be done in the dark.

Nikunja slipped out of the lungi, shirt and the black jacket and threw them on his bed. Then he changed into his pyjamas and took a candle out of the drawer of his table. He lit it and placed it before his mirror.

There was still no sign of the police. Perhaps they were searching the whole area to see where Bagha was hiding. Certainly, no one in this building had seen him come in. But people from the neighbouring houses might have.

Nikunja started to remove his make-up. He must first take off his false moustaches.

False?

If the moustaches were false, why didn't they come off? Anything stuck with spirit gum usually came off at the first pull. Why didn't these?

Nikunja brought the candle closer to his face and peered at the mirror. His blood froze.

The moustaches were real. Each hair had sprung from his own skin. There was no sign of gum on them!

The wig was not a wig, either. It was his own hair. And the stubble, which he had created by pasting each individual hair, also appeared to be perfectly genuine.

And the scar? No artist on earth could have created that scar simply with the help of paint and plasticine. It was the result of the fight fought nineteen years ago with Badru Sheik in Entally. Bagha, who was then called Radhu Mandal, was still an apprentice in the world of crime and criminals, learning the tricks of the trade from Meghnad Rakshit . . .

The police had to break the door open. The inspector turned a powerful torch on the figure of Bagha Mandal, lying flat on the ground, unconscious.

'Does this man live in this house?' he asked Nitai.

'Yes, sir. He's my master.'

'What is he known as?'

'Nikunja Babu. Saha Babu.'

'Ha! Pretending to be a gentleman, was he?'

Then he said to his constable, 'Shake him. Shake him well, until he regains consciousness. Then we shall decide what to do with him.'

The inspector raised his revolver and aimed at the inert figure. The wig came off and fell on the ground with the first shake. Then came the moustaches. And then the scar slipped off, together with the nylon net and the extra bit of plasticine with which the shape of the nose had been altered.

By then, Nikunja was fully conscious.

A stern warning from the police had the effect a tantrik's threat had failed to produce.

Nikunja is now reading a lot on clay modelling. Since the river is not far away, it is possible for Nitai to bring him all the clay he needs. Nikunja plans to use Nitai as his first model.

Translated by Gopa Majumdar
First published in Bengali in 1983

The Citation

For about a minute, none among those present at the meeting of the Shatadal Club could utter a word when their secretary, Pranabesh Datta, dropped the bomb.

It was an emergency meeting, being held just five days before the Bengali New Year. Pranabesh did not tell anyone why he wanted them there. His note had only said that there was a crisis and a meeting of the members was essential.

Jayanta Sarkar was the first to speak.

'Are you absolutely sure?' he asked.

'Look at this letter if you don't believe me,' said Pranabesh. 'Here it is—Samar Kumar himself signed the letter. What better surety could you want?'

The letter made its rounds among the members and returned to Pranabesh.

No, there was no doubt. The signature was indeed Samar Kumar's. Thanks to the film magazines, there were very few people who had not seen that famous signature before.

'Did he give a reason?' asked Naren Guin.

'Shooting,' said Pranabesh, 'outdoor shooting in Kalimpong. Came up most unexpectedly. So he's very sorry, but . . .'

'Strange!' exclaimed Shantanu Rakshit. 'How could the man simply turn his "yes" into a "no"?'

Naren Guin remarked, 'I told you in the beginning not to get involved with film-stars. They never keep their word.'

'What a catastrophe!' said Jayanta. He liked being dramatic.

'Can you not think of an alternative arrangement?' asked Chunilal Sanyal, who taught Bengali at the local Vivekananda Institute.

'What alternative arrangement do you expect us to make, Chuni-da, at this last minute?' asked Pranabesh. 'Besides, I have already tried everything. I spoke twice to Nimu in Calcutta. Told him to get hold of someone else—it didn't matter if it was a singer or dancer or painter or sportsman. We've done all the publicity possible for our felicitation, we've got the citation written. We've held such felicitations regularly for the last ten years, it has become our tradition and we cannot do without it. But Nimu said, no chance. Seven felicitations have been arranged in Calcutta alone. There isn't much of a choice in the matter of candidates, is there? All the well-known people are already engaged. Paltu Banerjee is being felicitated twice on the same day. But he can manage it because both are in Calcutta. Shyamal Shome, Rajat Manna, Harabilash Gupta, Debraj Saha—everyone's been booked by some club or the other.'

'The citation you just mentioned,' said Indranath Ray, who happened to be the oldest among those present, 'well—how can you use a citation meant for Samar Kumar for someone else?'

'You haven't seen the citation, have you, Indra-da?'

'No.'

'That explains it. You see, it doesn't talk about films or film-stars. It begins with Dear Artiste. So it could be anyone.'

'May I see it now?'

Pranabesh took out a rolled parchment from a drawer.

'It took Monotosh a whole week to write it by hand. The language used was Chuni-da's.'

Chunilal coughed softly, a polite reminder of his presence.

'"We look at you, and our wonder knows no bounds" . . . why, I seem to have heard this one before!'

Indranath had unrolled the paper. His brows were puckered in a frown, his eyes fixed on Chunilal.

'So you have,' said Chunilal. 'Sir Jagadish Bose had once read an address at a reception given in honour of Tagore. This was the opening sentence. The speech had been written by Sarat Chandra.'

'And you just lifted it?'

'It's only a quotation, Indra-da. Surely no one can object to that? It's a famous line—every educated Bengali would recognize it. Besides, it makes such a good introduction.'

'How many other quotations have you got in this citation?'

'That's the only one. The rest is totally original.'

Indranath dropped the roll on the table, yawned and said, 'Well, then—you must decide on the next course of action.'

Akshay Bagchi was a rather grave and sombre man of about fifty. He now lit a cigarette and said, 'If you can give up the idea of having someone very well known, I can suggest a name. Since you must felicitate someone, you may wish to think about it.'

'Yes, it's obvious we can't get anyone all that well known,' said Pranabesh. 'But, at the same time, we can't get hold of any Tom, Dick or Harry, can we? The person you have in mind ought to have made some kind of fruitful contribution.'

'Yes,' said Akshay Bagchi, 'he has indeed.'

'Who are you talking about?' Pranabesh grew slightly impatient.

'Haralal Chakravarty.'

Silence fell. Clearly, nobody had heard the name before. Indranath Ray was the only person who frowned a little and then said, 'Haralal Chakravarty? You mean the illustrator?'

'Yes, that's right,' Akshay Bagchi nodded, 'we used to see his illustrations quite often in story-books when we were very young. Most of these were mythological in nature. He was once very popular. He even used to do illustrations for magazines. I think felicitating him is a better idea than doing something for people who are already quite successful.'

'Not a bad idea at all,' Indranath sat up. 'I quite agree with Akshay. Now I can recall those illustrations clearly. The edition of the Mahabharata we had at home had pictures drawn by Chakravarty.'

'Were they really good?' asked Jayanta Sarkar. 'I mean, this man in whose honour we'll arrange a reception—does he deserve it?'

This time Naren Guin said, 'Yes, I remember now. We had a copy of *Hatemtai*, and the illustrations were signed H. Chakravarty.'

'Any good?' Jayanta wanted to know.

'Yes, certainly better than the average kitsch,' said Naren and went out of the room. It was time for a smoke, but not where so many elders were present.

'Whether the pictures he drew were of a high standard or not is not really important,' said Indranath, 'what matters is that he worked continuously over a long period of time. He could not have done so if there was no demand for his work. So he must have earned a certain amount of popularity. But, as Akshay just said, true recognition never came his way. Our Shatadal Club can now give him that.'

'And the most important thing,' said Akshay Bagchi, 'also, if you like, the most convenient thing, is that he lives in this town. You don't have to run around Calcutta to get him.'

'Good heavens!' said Pranabesh. 'We didn't know that!'

The whole idea was so new that everyone started talking at once.

'But where does he live?' Pranabesh looked at Akshay Bagchi enquiringly.

'I know the place,' said Bagchi. 'If you go to the crossing at the end of Kumorpara and turn left, you will soon come to Dr Manmatha's house. He once mentioned that Haralal Chakravarty was his neighbour.'

'Do you know Haralal?'

'Well, I saw him once at the Mukherjees' about five years ago and that too, only for a few seconds. I think he was painting something for their family.'

'But . . .' Pranabesh still sounded a little doubtful.

'But what?'

'No, I mean, we shall have to announce his name if he accepts our proposal.'

'So what?'

'If no one has heard his name, then . . .'

'Then they'll wonder who on earth he is. Is that what you're worried about?'

'Exactly.'

'Don't worry. Just add "Distinguished Doyen of Illustrators" before his name. Those who haven't heard his name will get to know of it this way. Isn't that one of the aims of our club?'

'Yes, rescuing men from oblivion,' said Jayanta. 'A very good idea.'

Everyone agreed. The idea revived their waning enthusiasm and they had to admit that, if anything, such a step would only enhance the prestige of the club. What they were going to arrange was not just an ordinary reception, it was their commitment to society. This could well become their policy in future: to bring into the limelight once more, all those gifted sons of Bengal who were languishing in the darkness.

It was decided that Akshay Bagchi would call on Haralal Chakravarty, together with Pranabesh and some other members of the club. They would have to go the very next day for there was no time left. If Mr Chakravarty agreed, the name of Samar Kumar would have to be replaced on all the posters.

And, of course, one must not forget to add the words, 'Distinguished Doyen of Illustrators' before his name.

The pink house by the side of the road had a nameplate proclaiming 'Haralal Chakravarty, Artist'. This made their job a lot simpler. Akshay Bagchi was right. Dr Manmatha lived only two houses away. Akshay Bagchi and Pranabesh were accompanied by Chunilal Sanyal.

They opened the gate and went in.

There were a few flower beds in front of the house and an amra tree.

The surroundings were clean, but showed no sign of affluence. Obviously, Haralal Chakravarty had missed out not just on recognition, but also on earning a comfortable living.

There was no need to knock. Their arrival had probably been seen from a window. An elderly gentleman, wearing glasses and sporting a pair of grey moustaches, opened the door. He was clad in a dhoti draped like a lungi, and a vest with sleeves.

Akshay Bagchi greeted him with a namaskar and went forward.

'You may not remember, but we met briefly about five years ago in Dharani Mukherjee's house.'

'I see . . .'

'We . . . er . . . wanted to talk to you about something,' said Pranabesh. 'Could we come in?'

'Yes, of course.'

The living-room was to the left. There were a few framed paintings on the wall. At the bottom of each one, clearly visible, was the painter's signature: H. Chakravarty. Except for these, the room was devoid of any trimmings. The visitors sat on wooden chairs and a wooden bench.

'We have come from the Shatadal Club,' began Pranabesh.

'Shatadal Club?'

'Yes. It's a rather well-known club in this area. Barada Babu—you know, Barada Majumdar, MLA—is our President.'

'I see.'

'We have a function every year to celebrate the first of Baisakh. There's usually a musical performance, a one-act play and a reception given in honour of someone who has made a significant contribution to our art and culture. This time we thought of you. I mean—you live in the same town, and yet not many people know about you, so . . .'

'Hmm. The first of Baisakh, did you say?'

'Yes.'

'But that's only four days away.'

'Yes. Yes, I realize it's late. There were,' Pranabesh coughed, 'a few difficulties.'

'I see. But what does this reception really entail?'

'Oh, nothing much. We'll come and collect you at around six in the evening. Your reception will be the last item in our function. A citation will be presented, Mr Bagchi here will say a few words about you and, in the end, if you yourself could give a short speech, we'd all be very pleased. The whole thing would be over by 9 p.m.'

'Hmm.'

'Your family—I mean, your wife . . .'

'She suffers from arthritis.'

'Oh. But if there's someone else you'd like to invite . . .'

'Let me think about it.'

At this point, Akshay Bagchi raised a different issue.

'We would like an introduction about yourself.'

'All right. I shall write a few facts down. Please have it collected.'

'I shall come and collect it myself,' said Pranabesh.

The three members of the Shatadal Club rose to take their leave.

Haralal Chakravarty appeared to have finally grasped the significance of their proposal. His eyes seemed moist.

The Shatadal Club lived up to its reputation of being supremely efficient in organizing the New Year celebrations. The reception for Haralal Chakravarty was a resounding success. Those who had indeed asked, 'Who on earth is this man?' before the reception, ceased to raise questions afterwards.

Everyone learnt about how, after graduating from the Government Art School, Haralal had had to struggle to establish himself as a professional artist. Fifty-six books had been published in a mythological series that contained his illustrations, in addition to a large number of children's magazines that also published his pictures. Rai Bahadur L.K. Gupta had given him a silver medal. Finally, at the age of sixty-two, arthritis affected his right thumb, forcing him to retire.

When it was his turn to speak, Haralal expressed his appreciation for the efforts made by the Shatadal Club and said just one thing about himself: 'I do not deserve such praise.' His humility made a deep impression on the audience.

As he climbed into the car of Nihar Chowdhury, the Vice President of the club, carrying a garland and the citation, duly framed, it was difficult to tell who was more moved by the whole experience—Haralal himself or the members of the club.

Indranath had the last word.

'My dear Pranabesh,' he said, 'I suggest you give a reception for Bagchi next year. After all, wasn't it he who saved the prestige of the club this time?'

The next day, someone left a packet in the club office. It was addressed to Pranabesh. He opened it and found, to his utter surprise, the framed citation given to Haralal the day before.

It was accompanied by a note that said:

To the Secretary,
Shatadal Club

Dear Sir,
I could see when you called on me the other day that you were indeed in a difficult situation and had decided to give a reception for Haralal Chakravarty simply because there was no other alternative. I am very happy to have been able to play the role of your saviour. But I feel obliged to return the citation for two reasons. First, I can see that it may be used quite easily next year for a different person. All you need to do is change the name and the date. And, secondly, it is true that I do not really deserve it. The artist Haralal Chakravarty died three years ago in this town. He was my elder brother. I work as a clerk in the post office in Kanthi. I happened to be here on a week's holiday.

Yours truly,
Rasiklal Chakravarty.

Translated by Gopa Majumdar
First published in Bengali in 1983

Sadhan Babu's Suspicions

Sadhan Babu found a small twig lying on the floor of his room as he returned from work one evening. This made him frown for he was very fussy about cleanliness. Every piece of furniture in his room had to be spotless, as did all his bedclothes and embroidered tablecloths and curtains. It did mean paying rather a lot to the dhobi, but Sadhan Babu did not mind.

'Pocha!' he called out to his servant.

'Were you calling me, sir?' Pocha appeared.

'Why—do you doubt it?'

'No, sir. Why should I?'

'What is this twig doing here on the floor?'

'I don't know. A bird may have dropped it.'

'Why should a bird be allowed to come in and drop things in my room? Didn't you notice it when you swept the floor today? Or didn't you sweep it at all?'

'Oh, but I sweep your room every day, sir. When I did so today this twig wasn't there.'

'Are you sure?'

'Yes, sir.'

'How strange!'

The next day he noticed a sparrow sitting on his window-sill. This might be the bird trying to build a nest in his room and dropping bits and pieces on the floor. But where could it possibly build a nest? In the skylight? Perhaps.

Sadhan Babu began to think that something was amiss. There were seven rooms on the third floor of the building where he lived. Why was the bird trying to get into his? Did the room have something special to attract birds?

It could, of course, be the new ayurvedic hair oil he had started to use. It did have a rather strong smell and the bird may have come into his room because of it. The oil had been recommended by Nilmani Babu who lived in a flat on the second floor. Nilmani Babu dabbled in ayurvedic medicine and, according to him, this oil was the perfect remedy for dandruff. But could it be that he had played a practical joke on Sadhan Babu, trying deliberately to turn his room into a sanctuary for homeless birds?

The fact was that nearly everyone in the house was aware of Sadhan

Babu's suspicious nature and made fun of him behind his back. When he returned in the evening, very often he had to hear remarks like, 'So tell us about the new suspicions you had today!'

Some people pulled his leg in other ways. Nabendu Chatterjee lived on the ground floor. Sadhan Babu went to his house practically every evening to join the group that gathered there to play cards. Only the other day, Nabendu Babu had said to him as soon as he arrived, 'Take a look at this piece of paper. Does it tell you anything? Someone tossed it in through the window.'

It was only a page torn out of Nabendu Babu's daughter's maths exercise book. Sadhan Babu straightened it out, looked at it carefully and said, 'This seems to be a digital code of some kind.'

Nabendu Babu said nothing. Sadhan Babu went on, 'But we must have it decoded. It may be a sort of warning . . .'

Nobody had it decoded, of course. But they had achieved their goal, which was only to see in which direction Sadhan Babu's suspicions could be steered by just a piece of paper.

Sadhan Babu strongly believed that the entire city of Calcutta was filled with cheats and frauds and liars. No one here could be trusted. The only thing that could keep one going was one's own ability to question everything.

One day, Sadhan Babu returned from his office to find a large, square parcel lying on his table. His first reaction was to think it had come to him by mistake. Who would send him such a packet?

His belief grew firmer when he discovered the parcel bore no name on it.

'Who brought it here?' he asked his servant.

'Someone came this afternoon and left it with Dhananjay. He said it was for you.'

Dhananjay worked for another tenant on the first floor, Shoroshi Babu.

'Did he say who had sent it? What does it contain?'

'No idea, sir.'

'Well!'

Sadhan Babu sat down on his bed and stared at the packet. It seemed big enough to hold a large-sized football. But it was impossible to guess who had sent it.

He rose from the bed and picked it up. How heavy it was! At least five kilos.

Sadhan Babu tried to remember the last occasion when he had received a parcel. Ah yes, about three years ago, an aunt of his had sent him some mango cake. She had died six months later. He had no close relatives left. He never received more than a couple of letters a month. So a parcel was a rarity indeed. If only there was a note with it!

But who knows—perhaps the sender had indeed enclosed a note and Dhananjay had lost it. He must speak to Dhananjay.

Sadhan Babu went downstairs himself. Dhananjay was busy pounding spicy masala when Sadhan Babu found him. He left his work and came to meet Sadhan Babu.

'Er. . . did someone leave a parcel with you today saying it was for me?'

'Yes, sir.'

'Was there a note with it?'

'Why—no!'

'Did he say where he was from?'

'He did mention a name—Madan, I think he said.'

'Madan?'

'Yes, that's what he said.'

There was no one called Madan among Sadhan Babu's acquaintances. Heaven knows what the man had actually said. Dhananjay was undoubtedly an idiot.

'Was there no letter or any other paper with the parcel?'

'Yes, there was a receipt. My babu signed it.'

'You mean Shoroshi Babu?'

'Yes, sir.'

But Shoroshi Babu could not help either. He had indeed signed the receipt for Sadhan Babu, but did not notice the name of the place the parcel came from.

Sadhan Babu returned to his own room. It had grown quite cool in the evening. Winter was round the corner. And so was Diwali. Crackers and rockets had started to go off in all directions.

Boom! There went a cracker. And, in that instant a cold shiver went down his spine.

A time bomb!

Could there be a time bomb inside that parcel? God—it could go off any minute and end his days on earth!

There was a lot of talk nowadays about time bombs. They appeared to be the favourite weapon of terrorists.

But why should anyone send him a time bomb?

Why, one of his enemies, of course! His success as a businessman had caused great jealousy among his rivals. He had to keep all clients happy, just like the others. Yet, if a client chose to give him a contract, all the others immediately became his enemies. It happened all the time.

'Pocha?'

His voice sounded hoarse. His throat had become dry.

Pocha arrived.

'Did you call me, sir?'

'Yes . . . er . . .'

He stopped. Would it be a wise thing to do? He had wanted to ask Pocha to put his ear to the packet to see if it was ticking. Didn't all time bombs have a device attached that ticked? And didn't this ticking finally result in a huge explosion?

What if it exploded just as Pocha laid his ear against it? Sadhan Babu could not bear to think any more. But Pocha was still waiting for instructions. In the end, Sadhan Babu had to admit he had called him quite unnecessarily.

The night that followed left an indelible mark on Sadhan Babu's memory. He had spent sleepless nights before, especially during periods of illness. But never had he sat up all night feeling so utterly petrified.

His courage and common sense returned in the morning when it became clear that the parcel was not going to burst and go up in flames. 'I must open it this evening,' thought Sadhan Babu. Even to himself, his suspicions appeared to be crossing the limits of reason.

But something happened in the evening to stop him from unwrapping the parcel.

There are some people who have a passion for reading every word in a newspaper. Sadhan Babu did not fall into this category. He only looked at the headlines every day. This was probably why, that day, he missed the little news item about a murder in north Calcutta. He learnt about it in Nabendu Babu's house in the evening, when he arrived in the middle of a heated discussion.

The name of the deceased was Shibdas Moulik. He lived in Patuatola Lane. The very mention of the name brought back memories of his past that Sadhan Babu had quite forgotten.

He once knew a Moulik fairly well. Was his first name Shibdas? Yes, it was. Sadhan Babu used to live in the same Patuatola Lane in those days. Moulik was his neighbour. A few people went to his house every evening to play rummy. For some strange reason, everyone called Moulik only by his surname. There were two other men who came regularly. One was Sukhen Dutta and the other was Madhusudan Maiti. The latter turned out to be a dangerous crook. From the beginning Sadhan Babu had felt that Madhusudan cheated frequently at the game. One day he could not help mentioning it. Madhusudan's reaction at this was terrifying. No one had known until that day that he carried a knife in his pocket at all times. It had come flying out that evening. Sadhan Babu managed to escape unhurt only because Moulik and Sukhen Dutta stepped in just in time.

When his business began to prosper, Sadhan Babu left his little room in Patuatola Lane and moved into this apartment house in Mirzapur Street. He then lost all contact with Moulik and company. His fondness for playing cards remained, as did his habit of questioning and suspecting everything. But, apart from these, Sadhan Babu did indeed turn into a different man. The clothes he wore were now more stylish, he smoked cigarettes (having given up beedis) and often went to auctions to buy things like paintings, flower vases and fancy ashtrays for his house. All this had happened over the last six or seven years.

If the Shibdas Moulik who had just been murdered was the same Moulik that Sadhan Babu had once known, then the murderer was undoubtedly Madhu Maiti.

'How did the murder take place?' asked Sadhan Babu.

'Brutal! Oh, but it was really brutal,' said Nabendu Chatterjee, 'there was no way of identifying the body. They found his name from a diary in his pocket.'

'Why? Why was identification not possible?'

'They found the body, but not the head. So how could they identify the person?'

'What? You mean the head . . .?'

'Yes, the head . . . kaput!' Nabendu Babu raised both his hands above his head and then swung them down in a single movement. 'No one knows where the murderer hid the head,' he added.

'Does anyone know who actually committed the murder?'

'I believe a few people used to play rummy in Moulik's house. The police suspect it was one of them.'

As he went up the stairs to his own flat on the third floor, Sadhan Babu began to feel dizzy. He could vividly recall the events of that horrible day, soon after he had accused Madhu Maiti of cheating. The others did manage to stop Maiti from stabbing him, but he would never forget the look in Maiti's eyes.

'You have escaped today, Sadhan Majumdar,' Maiti had threatened, 'but you don't know me. One day I will settle scores with you—even if I have to wait for years!'

It was the kind of threat that curdled one's blood. Sadhan Babu had thought he had put the whole thing behind him after moving out of Patuatola Lane. But had he?

What if that parcel lying in his room had been sent by Madhu? Dhananjay had heard the fellow say 'Madan'; there was no doubt that Dhananjay was hard of hearing. There was not much difference between 'Madhu' and 'Madan', was there? Obviously it was either Madhu himself or someone deputed by him who had left the parcel.

And he had the receipt signed simply to make sure that it did reach Sadhan Babu.

That parcel must contain the hacked head of Shibdas Moulik!

The idea came to him suddenly and took a firm hold on his mind even before he stepped into his room. He could see the packet from the doorway. It was resting on his table, next to a flower vase. Its height and size were now a clear indication of its content.

Pocha looked curiously at his master as he saw him hovering near the door. With an enormous effort, Sadhan Babu pulled himself together, came into the room and asked Pocha to make him a cup of tea. 'Ah . . . did anyone come looking for me today?' he asked.

'No, sir.'

'Hmm.'

Sadhan Babu had had this wild vision of the police searching his house. The thought of what they might do to him if they found the head of the murdered man in his room made him break out into a cold sweat once again.

A little later, after a hot cup of tea, some of his courage seeped back. 'Well,' he thought, 'at least it's not a time bomb!'

But if he had to spend another sleepless night just staring at the parcel he knew he would go mad.

The answer, of course, was a sleeping pill. However, there was no escape from nightmares even if the pill did help him sleep.

In one he saw himself playing rummy with a headless Moulik. In another, the bodyless head of Moulik was saying to him, 'Get me out of this box, please—I'm getting suffocated!'

In spite of the pill, Sadhan Babu woke as usual at 5.30 in the morning. And the minute he opened his eyes, his mind hit upon a solution to his problem.

If the hacked head had been passed on to him, why should he not try to pass it on elsewhere? The main thing was to get rid of it, wasn't it?

Sadhan Babu put the parcel into a large shopping bag and set out, even at that early hour. He had to admit the packing had been done very well, for not a drop of blood had oozed out.

It took him twenty-five minutes to reach Kalighat by bus. He walked slowly towards the river and found a relatively quiet spot. And then, taking the parcel out of his bag, he threw it straight into the river.

It fell into the water with a loud splash.

The packet vanished and Sadhan Babu heaved a sigh of relief.

Thirty-five minutes later, he was back home. As he walked in through the front gate, he could hear the wall clock in Shoroshi Babu's house strike seven.

The sound of its chime suddenly shook Sadhan Babu into a new awareness.

For the last few days, there had been this niggling worry at the back of his mind that he was forgetting something he really ought to remember. Some people did, he knew, turn forgetful as they found themselves on the wrong side of fifty.

Upon being told about this, Nilmani Babu had prescribed a special herb.

But now the whole thing had come back to him and there was not a moment to be lost.

Sadhan Babu left home half an hour earlier than usual. He stopped at the auction house called Modern Exchange in Russell Street. Tulsi Babu, its owner, came forward to greet him, a broad smile on his face. 'I hope the table clock is working properly?' he asked.

'Did you send it?'

'Of course I did! Why, didn't it reach you?'

'Yes, yes, I mean . . . er . . .'

'Look, you gave me an advance of five hundred rupees and I promised to have it delivered to your house, didn't I? You're such an old client of mine. Would I not keep my word?'

'Oh yes. Oh yes. Of course. I mean to say, certainly . . .'

'That clock will keep excellent time—you mark my words. After all, it was made by such a famous French company! You got it for a song, I tell you. Very lucky.'

Tulsi Babu moved forward to welcome another customer. Sadhan Babu came out of the shop slowly. What he had got for a song now nestled below the rippling waves of the river.

No doubt Madhu Maiti had taken the most perfect revenge. No doubt, too, that what Dhananjay had heard as 'Madan' had, in fact, been 'Modern'!

Translated by Gopa Majumdar
First published in Bengali in 1983

Gagan Chowdhury's Studio

There are some apartments which appear to be quite satisfactory at first and one has to live in them to discover their little inconveniences. Sudheen Sarkar realized this when he moved into a flat in Bhawanipore. This was the only sphere where Lady Luck seemed not to have smiled kindly on him. In everything else she had given him all her support.

Take, for instance, the matter of his promotion. He was now the head of a department in his office. Not many could have made such rapid progress at such an early age. After all, he was only thirty-one. He had already climbed up to the shoulder of the department. The head was Nagendra Kapoor, forty years of age—tall, handsome, efficient. All eyes turned towards him as he entered the office, clad in a light grey safari suit. Who could have imagine that the same man would succumb to a cardiac arrest on a golf course?

That his death would lead to Sudheen's own promotion was only natural. And it was not just a matter of being lucky. No one could deny that Sudheen deserved it.

Then came the new flat. Sudheen's parents were keen to have him married. Sudheen knew it would be very difficult to live with someone else in the little pigeon-hole in Park Circus. It being generally a good phase in his life, he decided to start looking for a bigger flat. Life had become impossible in the old flat, anyway. There was a house nearby that was often let out for weddings. The sound of the *shehnai* on gramophone records played at full blast on loudspeakers was beginning to drive him mad.

The very first flat the house agent told him about was this one in Bhawanipore.

Situated on the first floor, the three large bedrooms, the two bathrooms, the veranda facing the south, the mosaic floors and the grills on the windows—all bore the stamp of careful planning and good taste.

The rent was eight hundred rupees a month. And the landlord seemed a good man. Sudheen did not have to look any further.

It was two weeks since he had moved in. He did not notice it at first, but one night he woke to find a bright light streaming in through his window and hitting his eyes directly. Where was it coming from at this time of night?

Sudheen went out on the veranda. The whole area was dark except for one room in the second floor of the house opposite. That was where the light was coming from, through an open window, past his veranda and straight on to his bed. Even if he changed his position on the bed, it would still shine in his face.

How annoying! How could anyone sleep in a room that wasn't totally dark? At least Sudheen couldn't. But was this going to trouble him every night?

A week later, Sudheen's suspicions were confirmed. Every night, the light was switched on around midnight and it stayed on until dawn. Sudheen couldn't bear the idea of closing his own window. A south-facing window had a special advantage in Calcutta, especially if there was no building in front to block the breeze. That was really another reason that had prompted Sudheen to take this flat. His veranda overlooked the garden of the opposite house. At least in the near future there was no chance of a new construction coming up here. It was really a rambling old mansion, probably once owned by a *zamindar,* lying now in a state of disrepair. By the look of things, its occupants were few.

But who used that room on the second floor?

Why did its occupant keep the light on all night?

Someshwar Nag lived in the flat downstairs. He had moved in four months before Sudheen. A man in his mid-fifties, he was a member of the Bengal Club where he liked to spend most evenings. Sudheen happened to run into him near the gate on a Saturday, and could not resist putting a question to him.

'Do you know who lives in that house opposite?'

'Mr Chowdhury. Why? Is anything wrong?'

'No, it's just that it doesn't seem as though too many people live in that house, and yet someone leaves a light on all night in a room on the second floor. Haven't you noticed it?'

'No, I can't say I have.'

'Does that light not get into your room?'

'No, that's not possible. You see, their terrace shields the room from a view of the ground floor. In fact, I didn't even know there was such a room!'

'You're lucky. I don't get any sleep because of that light.'

'Very strange. I've been told only a couple of people live in that house. It's owned by one Gagan Chowdhury. He doesn't go out much. At least, I have never seen him, but, apparently, he does exist. Perhaps he's grown quite old. I've heard that he used to paint once. Why don't you go and talk to him? He can at least keep his own window closed. Surely he wouldn't mind showing a little consideration for his neighbour?'

Yes, Sudheen certainly could go and talk to Mr Chowdhury, although there was no guarantee that his request would be granted. But what on earth went on in that room, anyway?

Sudheen realized that in addition to his discomfort over the business of the light coming in through the window, he was also getting quite intrigued by his neighbour's possible activities.

One of his friends, Mahim, often went to the races. He had a large pair of binoculars. Maybe that would help? A pair of binoculars were needed because the room was at some distance. The house Mr Chowdhury lived in was not exactly by the side of the road. There was an extension of the garden beyond the compound wall and a certain portion of the terrace had to be crossed to get to the room on the second floor.

Mahim's binoculars brought the window of the room a lot closer, but nothing could be seen beyond a portion of the wall over the top of a curtain. All he could make out was that a couple of oil paintings hung on the wall. Was this the studio of Mr Chowdhury? But did no one work in it now?

Yes, someone did. A shadow moved behind the curtain, passing from the right to the left. But it was impossible to see who it was.

After about fifteen minutes of looking through the binoculars, Sudheen began to feel tired. How silly to waste time like this and spoil whatever chances there were of getting some sleep!

Sudheen put the binoculars down on the table and went to bed. He had made up his mind.

He would go straight to Gagan Chowdhury and ask him to keep that particular window closed. If he agreed, well and good. If he didn't, Sudheen would have to learn to live with the situation. What kind of a man was Gagan Chowdhury? Sudheen wished he knew. It would be difficult to put up with fractious behaviour from a neighbour, no matter how old he was. But, in this case, that risk would have to be taken.

The gate was open and there was no chowkidar. This surprised Sudheen, though he was secretly quite pleased to have crossed the first hurdle so easily. He had decided to call on Mr Chowdhury at night simply so that he could actually show him how the light from the open window disturbed him.

It was around 11 p.m. The neighbourhood had fallen totally silent already. Last night there had been a full moon. Everything in the overgrown garden of the Chowdhurys was clearly visible in the moonlight. Sudheen passed a marble statue of a nymph and went across towards the dark, dank walls of the porch. The light on the second floor had not yet been switched on. With some luck, he would find Gagan Chowdhury downstairs.

Within seconds of his knocking on the front door, a middle-aged man opened it. He appeared to be a servant.

'Who would you like to see?' he asked.

'Mr Chowdhury—Gagan Chowdhury—has he gone to bed?'

'No.'

'Is it possible to meet him? My name is Sudheen Sarkar. I live in that house opposite. I've come on some urgent business.'

The man went inside and reappeared a few minutes later. 'Please come in.'

Everything was going smoothly. It was rather strange.

Sudheen crossed a landing and entered the living-room.

'Please sit down.'

A strip of moonlight had come in through a window and fallen on a sofa. Sudheen found his way to it and sat down. Why didn't the man switch on the lights? Surely there was no power cut?

He began to look around the room and, suddenly, his heart skipped a beat. Had he arrived amongst a room full of people? Who were all these people staring down at him?

But as his eyes grew used to the semi-darkness, Sudheen realized the eyes fixed on him were not men but masks. Every mask seemed to have turned its eyes on him. It was easy to tell that these masks had come from abroad. Most were from Africa, some may have been from South America. Sudheen himself had once been interested in painting. In fact, if his father hadn't put his foot down, he might have become a professional painter. He was still interested in art and handicrafts.

Sudheen could not help being impressed by his own courage. Anyone else would have had a heart attack sitting in a dark room, in this eerie atmosphere, surrounded by a gallery of fearsome masks.

He did not see anyone enter the room. The deep, sombre voice startled him.

He swivelled round and saw a man seated on the adjacent sofa. 'What brought you here so late?'

Sudheen raised his hands mechanically in a namaskar but failed to find words to answer the man.

There was no doubt that this man came from an aristocratic family. The expensive shawl he was wearing bore evidence of that. But Sudheen had never seen anyone so deathly pale and with such a piercing look. The first sight of a man like this would render anyone speechless.

The man continued to stare at him. It took Sudheen about a whole minute to pull himself together. Then, finally, he found his tongue.

'I . . . well, I have come to make a complaint. Please don't mind. You are Mr Gagan Chowdhury, I presume?'

The man nodded. His pepper-and-salt hair hung like the mane of a lion around his broad forehead. He must be about sixty-five, Sudheen thought.

'My name is Sudheen Sarkar,' he continued. 'I live in the first floor flat in the house opposite yours. The fact is . . . you see, the light in that room on your second floor disturbs me very much. It shines directly into my eyes. May I request you to keep your window closed? I can't sleep at all because of that light. You will appreciate how annoying that can be after a hard day's work . . .'

The man had not stopped gazing at him. Did this room not have even a single light?

Sudheen felt obliged to open his mouth once more. Perhaps he should take the matter a bit further.

'I realize,' he said, 'that an easy way of keeping the light out is to shut my own window. But since it faces the south, I am somewhat reluctant . . .'

'No, you don't have to close your window.'

'What?'

'I shall close mine.'

Sudheen suddenly felt as though a huge load had been taken off his shoulders.

'Oh. It is most kind of you. Thank you so much. I really am very grateful.'

'Are you leaving?'

Sudheen had half-risen from the sofa but, surprised by this question, sat down again.

'It's quite late, isn't it? I'm sure you'd like to go to bed?' he asked.

'I don't sleep at night.'

The eyes of the man were still fixed on Sudheen.

'Do you read a lot?' Sudheen asked. His throat was beginning to feel a little dry. Gagan Chowdhury's company in these weird surroundings was not really something that one might enjoy, he had to admit.

'No.'

'What do you do then?'

'I paint.'

Sudheen recalled having seen a couple of paintings through his binoculars.

Mr Nag, too, had mentioned that Mr Chowdhury used to paint once.

'Does that mean that room is your studio?'

'Yes, that's right.'

'But I don't think too many people in the neighbourhood know about it.'

Gagan Chowdhury gave a twisted smile. 'Do you have a little time to spare?'

'Time? Now? I mean . . .'

'Allow me to tell you a few things. I have wanted to speak for a long time, but never found the chance to do so. The words have been piling up.'

Sudheen realized it was quite impossible to ignore the man's request.

'All right,' he said.

'My neighbours don't know about my work because they are not interested. Nobody's even mildly curious about a man who has spent his whole life as an artist. There was a time when I used to have my own exhibitions. A few people saw what I drew, some even uttered words of praise. But when the trend began to change, when abstract art wiped out the old traditions in painting and portraits ceased to be appreciated, I withdrew. I have never been one for newfangled notions. In my heart, I looked upon da Vinci as my guru. I still do.'

But . . . what kind of things do you paint?'

'People.'

'People?'

'Portraits.'

'From your imagination?'

'No. I never learnt to do that: I cannot paint unless I have a model sitting for me.'

'In the middle of the night?'

'Yes, I do get models. Every night.'

Sudheen did not know wh... to say. What on earth was the man talking about? Was he, perhaps, slightly mad?

'You find that difficult to believe, don't you?'

There was a hint of a genuine smile on his lips this time. Sudheen remained silent.

'Come with me.'

Sudheen could not disregard the summons. There was something hypnotic in the man's eyes and his words. Besides, his curiosity had been aroused. What kind of portraits had been done? Who came for sittings in the dead of night? How did Mr Chowdhury get hold of them?

'I have retained an electric connection only in my studio,' said Gagan Chowdhury, as they began climbing up the wooden stairs in the hazy, yellow light of a kerosene lamp. 'I've had it disconnected everywhere else in the house.'

Sudheen was surprised to note that there was not a single painting on the landing, or the walls by the stairs or the living room. Were all his works kept together in his studio?

There was a door just as they turned left upon reaching the second floor. Mr Chowdhury pushed it open, went in with Sudheen, and then closed it again. Then he pressed a switch on the wall and the whole room was flooded with light.

This was obviously the studio. Every material an artist might need was strewn about the room. There was an easel under the lamp and on it a new white canvas. Mr Chowdhury was probably going to start on a new painting.

Apart from the material for painting, the other thing that claimed one's attention was the large number of portraits that hung on the wall. A lot more were piled up on the floor. There were at least a hundred of these. But it was not possible to see them unless one picked them up from the floor one by one. The ones staring at him were those that were placed on the wall. Most of them were portraits of men. Sudheen's experienced eye immediately caught the touch of an expert in the works, all done in the old traditional style. Once again, he felt as though he was surrounded by a lot of people, all of them alive. At least fifty pairs of eyes were looking straight at him.

But who were these people? A few faces did look vaguely familiar, but . . .

'How do you like these?' asked Gagan Chowdhury.

'The work of a master,' Sudheen had to admit.

'And yet, the whole tradition of oil painting is now extinct. In such a situation, can you imagine how artists like me had to struggle?'

'But, judging by what you've got in this room, it doesn't seem as though you lack work.'

'Yes, but I found work only recently. Before that, for fifteen long years, I kept advertising in the papers. Not a single person responded. In the end I had to give up.'

'And then? How did you happen to start again?'

'The circumstances changed, you see.'

Sudheen refrained from saying anything further for his whole attention was now fixed on the paintings. He had managed to recognize three people. One of them had died four months ago. He was the well-known singer, Anantalal Niyogi. Sudheen had been to a live performance and had heard him sing about eight years ago.

The second was Ashimananda Swami. He had once been a freedom fighter, but later became a sanyasi. He, too, had died a year ago. Sudheen remembered seeing his picture in newspapers.

The third man was a Bengali pilot of Air-India, Captain Chakravarty. He had been killed three years ago in an air crash on his way to London, together with two hundred and fifty others. Sudheen had met him once on a flight to Rome, where he was going on official work.

At this point, Sudheen could not help but ask a question. 'Did all these people come here simply to get their portrait done with no thought of owning them?'

For the first time, Sudheen heard Gagan Chowdhury laugh loudly.

'No, Mr Sarkar,' he said, 'none of these people needed a portrait for themselves. These were made only for my personal collection.'

'Do you mean to say someone or the other still comes and sits for you? Every night?'

'Yes, you will soon see what I mean. I am certainly expecting someone tonight.'

Sudheen's head began to reel.

'But . . . but . . . how do you contact all these people?'

'Wait, I shall explain it all to you. My system is a little different.'

Gagan Chowdhury brought down a ledger from a shelf. 'Open it and see what's inside.'

Sudheen took the ledger near the lamp and opened it.

It was really a scrapbook, each page of which was filled with clippings from newspapers. They were all obituaries. Some of them had a picture of the deceased. A few of these had a pencil mark against them.

'That mark means that a portrait has already been made,' said Mr Chowdhury.

'But you still haven't told me how you get in touch . . .'

Gagan Chowdhury took the scrapbook from Sudheen and put it back on the shelf. Then he turned around and said, 'Not many can do it. But I am an exception. It's not a matter of sending a letter or making a phone call. There is no way of reaching these people through such means. The place where they live has neither a telephone connection nor a postal system. I have to use a totally different way to get in touch.'

Sudheen's blood chilled, his throat was parched. But even so, he simply had to ask another question. 'Are you trying to tell me that you made these portraits after all these people died?'

'How could I have known about them unless they were dead, Sudheen Babu? I don't know many people in Calcutta. In any case, no one can be totally free before death. Only a man who is no more has endless freedom, boundless time and patience. He does not mind sitting in that chair for hours, quite motionless, until every detail in the portrait is perfect.'

A clock struck somewhere, shattering the stillness of the night. It must be the clock Sudheen had seen by the staircase.

'Midnight,' said Gagan Chowdhury. 'Time for him to come.'

'Who?' Sudheen's voice sounded abnormally hoarse. He had started to feel giddy.

'The man who will sit for me tonight. There—can you hear his footsteps?'

Sudheen's ears were still functioning. He could clearly hear the footsteps downstairs.

'Come and have a look!'

Gagan Chowdhury had moved towards an open window. 'If you don't believe me, come and see for yourself,' he said.

Again, Sudheen felt the hypnotic power behind his words. He moved liked a robot and stood beside Gagan Chowdhury. Then he looked down and screamed involuntarily, 'I know this man!'

The man had the same swift stride, the same height and was wearing the same grey safari suit. It was the same man who had, until recently, been Sudheen's boss—Nagendra Kapoor.

A wave of dizziness swept over Sudheen. He clutched the easel to stop himself from falling.

The footsteps were now coming up the stairs. The whole house seemed to echo with the sound of footsteps on the wooden stairs.

Then the sound stopped.

In the silence Gagan Chowdhury spoke again.

'Were you not talking about establishing contact, Sudheen Babu? It's very simple. They come just as I beckon at them. Like this.'

Before Sudheen's horrified eyes, Gagan Chowdhury took his right arm out of his shawl and stretched it towards him. It was the arm of a skeleton.

'The same hand that beckons also paints!' said Mr Chowdhury.

Just before he finally lost consciousness, Sudheen heard someone knock on the door.

Rap, rap, rap, rap . . .

Rap, rap, rap, rap . . .

'Dada Babu! Dada Babu!'

Sudheen woke with a start, squinting in the daylight. God—what a terrible dream that was!

'Open the door, Dada Babu!'

It was the voice of his servant, Adheer.

'Wait a minute.'

Sudheen rose from his bed and unlocked the door. Adheer came in looking deeply worried.

'It's so late . . .'

'Yes, I know. I overslept.'

'We had such a commotion in front of our house. Didn't you hear anything?'

'Commotion?'

'The old Mr Chowdhury passed away last night. Gagan Babu. He was eighty-four. He'd been ailing for quite some time. They left the light on all night in his room. Didn't you notice it?'

'You knew about his illness?'

'Of course! I used to meet his servant—Bhagirath—so often in the market.'

'Well!' said Sudheen, bereft of speech.

Translated by Gopa Majumdar
First published in Bengali in 1984

A Duel in Lucknow

'Do you know what the word "duel" means?' asked Uncle Tarini.

'Oh yes,' said Napla. 'Dual means double. Some actors play dual roles in films.'

'That's not what I meant,' Uncle Tarini said, laughing. 'D-U-E-L, not D-U-A-L. Duel means a fight between two persons.'

'Yes, yes, of course,' we all shouted together.

'I once read up on duels out of curiosity,' went on Uncle Tarini. 'The practice of duelling spread from Italy to the rest of Europe in the sixteenth century. Swords were then part of a gentleman's dress, and sword-play or fencing was part of their education. If a person was insulted by someone, he would immediately challenge the other to a duel in order to save his honour. Whether the honour was saved or not depended on the challenger's skill as a swordsman. But even if skill was lacking, the duel took place, because to swallow an insult was looked upon in those days as the height of cowardice.

'In the eighteenth century the pistol replaced the sword as the duelling weapon. This led to so many deaths that there was a move to pass a law against duelling. But if one ruler banned it, the next one would relax the law and duelling would rear its head again.'

Uncle Tarini took a sip of black tea, cleared his throat and continued.

'A duel was fought according to a set of strict rules. Both parties had to use identical weapons, each had to have his "second" or referee to see that no rules were broken, an obligatory gap of twenty yards was necessary between the two opponents, and both pistols had to be fired the moment the challenger's second gave the command.'

As usual we were impressed with Uncle Tarini's fund of knowledge, which was as rich as his fund of experiences. We knew that all this rigmarole—or 'instructive information', as Uncle Tarini called it—was a prelude to yet another episode from his colourful life. All we had to do was bide our time before we would be regaled with what Uncle Tarini called fact but which struck us as being stranger than fiction.

'I don't know if you are aware,' resumed Uncle Tarini, 'that a famous duel took place in our country—in fact, in Calcutta itself—two hundred years ago.'

Even Napla didn't know, so we all shook our heads.

'One of the two who fought was a world-famous person: the Governor General Warren Hastings. His adversary was Philip Francis, a member of the Viceroy's Council. Hastings had written an acrimonious letter to Francis which made the latter challenge him to a duel. You know the National Library in Alipur—the duel took place in an open spot not far from it. Since Francis was the challenger, a friend of his procured the pistols and served as his second. The pistols were both fired at the same time, but only one of the two men was felled by a bullet: Philip Francis. Luckily the wound was not fatal.'

'That's history,' said Napla. 'It's time we had a story, Uncle Tarini. Of course, living in the twentieth century, you couldn't possible have taken part in a duel.'

'No,' said Uncle Tarini, 'but I watched one.'

'Really?'

He took another sip of black tea, lit an export-quality beedi and began his story.

'I was then living in Lucknow. I had no regular job and no need for one because a couple of years earlier I had won a lakh and a half rupees in the Rangers Lottery. The interest on it was enough to keep me going. This was in 1951. Everything cost less then and, being a bachelor, one could live in comfort on six or seven hundred rupees a month. I lived in a small bungalow on La Touche Road, wrote occasional pieces for the Pioneer, and paid regular visits to an auction house in Hazratgunj. In those days one could still pick up objects belonging to the time of the great Nawabs. One made a sizeable profit by buying them cheap and selling them at a good price to American tourists. I was both a dealer and a collector. Although my sitting room was small, it was crowded with objects bought at this auction house.

'At the auction house one Sunday morning, I saw a brown mahogany box lying amongst the items to be sold. It was a foot and a half long, about eight inches wide and three inches high. I couldn't guess what it contained, and this made me very curious. There were other things being auctioned, but I had my eyes only on the mahogany box.

'After an hour of disposing of other objects, the auctioneer picked up the box. I sat up expectantly. The usual praises were sung. "May I now present to you something most attractive and unique. Here you are, ladies and gentleman, as good as new although more than a hundred years old. A pair of duelling pistols made by the famous firm of Joseph Manton. A pair without compare!"

'I was immediately hooked. I had to possess those pistols. My imagination had started working. I could see the duellists facing each other, the bullets flying, and the bloody conclusion.

'As my mind worked and the bidding went on, I suddenly heard a Gujarati gentleman cry out, "Seven hundred and fifty!" I topped it at once with a bid of a thousand rupees. This ended the bidding and I found myself the owner of the pistols.

'Back home, I opened the box and found that the pistols were even more attractive than I thought they were in the auction house. They were truly splendid specimens of the gunsmith's art. The name of the maker was carved on the butt of each pistol. From the little I had read about weapons, I knew that Joseph Manton was a most distinguished name among the gunsmiths of eighteenth-century Britain.

'I had arrived in Lucknow three months earlier. In the evenings, I usually stayed at home writing or listening to music on the gramophone. I had just sat down at my desk to write a piece on the Hastings—Francis encounter, when the doorbell rang. Perhaps a customer? I had already built up a small reputation as a supplier of antiques.

'I opened the door and found an Englishman standing outside. He was in his mid-forties and looked clearly like someone who had spent a long time in India. Indeed, he could well have been an Anglo-Indian.

'"Good evening."

'I returned his greeting, and he said, "Do you have a minute? There's something I wanted to discuss with you."

'"Please come in."

'There was no trace of an Indian accent in the man's speech. I could see him more clearly by the light of the lamp once he came in. He was a good-looking man with blue eyes, reddish-brown hair and a stout moustache. I apologized for not being able to offer him any liquor, and asked if he would care for a cup of tea or coffee. The man refused, saying that he had just had dinner. Then he came straight to the reason for his visit.

'"I saw you at the auction house in Hazratgunj this morning."

'"Were you there too?"

'"Yes, but you were probably too preoccupied to see me."

'"The fact is, my mind was on something which had caught my eye."

'"And you succeeded in acquiring it. A pair of duelling pistols made by Joseph Manton. You were very lucky."

'"Did they belong to someone you know?"

'"Yes, but he has been dead for a long time. I didn't know where the pistols went after his death. Do you mind if I take a look at them? I happen to know an interesting story about them . . ."'I handed him the mahogany box. He opened the lid, took out one of the pistols and held it in the light of the lamp. I could see that his eyebrows had gone up and a faraway look had come into his eyes. "Do you know," he said, "that these pistols were used in a duel which was fought in this very city?"

'"A duel in Lucknow!"

'"Yes. It took place a hundred years ago. In fact, it will be exactly a hundred years three days from now—on October the sixteenth!"

'"How extraordinary! But who fought the duel?"

'The Englishman returned the pistols and sat down on the sofa. The whole thing was so vividly described to me that I can almost see it before my eyes. "There was a very beautiful woman in Lucknow in those days. She was called Annabella, the daughter of Doctor Jeremiah Hudson. She was not only beautiful but also extremely gifted. She could ride a horse and wield a gun as well as any man. Besides this she was an accomplished singer and dancer. A young portrait painter, John Illingworth by name, had just arrived in Lucknow hoping for a commission for the Nawab himself. When he heard of Annabella's beauty, he turned up in the house of Doctor Hudson with an offer to paint her portrait. Illingworth got the commission, but before the portrait was finished he had fallen deeply in love with the sitter.

'"Some time earlier, Annabella had been to a party where she had met Charles Bruce, a captain in the Bengal Regiment. Bruce too had lost his heart to Annabella at first sight.

'"Soon after the party, Bruce called on Annabella at her residence. He found her seated on the veranda posing for her portrait to a stranger. Illingworth was an attractive young man and it took little time for Bruce to realize that he had a rival in the painter.

'"Now, Bruce regarded painters with scant respect. On this occasion he chose to make a remark to Illingworth in the presence of Annabella which clearly showed his disdain.

'"As befits the practitioner of a gentle art, Illingworth was of a mild disposition. Nevertheless, the insult in the presence of the woman he loved was something he couldn't swallow. He challenged Bruce to a duel forthwith. Bruce took up the challenge, and the date and time of the duel were settled on the spot. Now, I suppose you know that each participant in a duel has to have a second?"

'I nodded.

'"Usually the second is a friend of the challenger," said the man. "Illingworth's circle of acquaintances in Lucknow was not very large, but there was one whom he could call a friend.

'"This was a government employee by the name of George Drummond. Drummond agreed to be his second and to procure a pair of identical pistols. On the opposite side, Charles Bruce asked his friend Philip Moxon to be his second.

'"The day of the duel drew near. Everyone knew what the outcome would be, because Charles Bruce was a superb marksman while Illingworth was not nearly as adept with the gun as with the paint brush."

'He paused. Anxiously, I asked, "What happened next?"

'The Englishman smiled and said, "You can find that out for yourself."

'"How?"

'"Every year on October the sixteenth the duel is re-enacted."

'"Where?"

'"In the same spot where it took place. To the east of Dilkhusha, below a tamarind tree by the river Gomti."

'"What do you mean by re-enacted?"

'"Just what I say. If you were to come at six in the morning the day after tomorrow, you will see the whole incident before your eyes."

'"But that is impossible! Do you mean to say—"

'"You don't have to take my word for it. All you have to do is go and see for yourself."

'"I would very much like to, but I don't think I could find my way there. I haven't been here long, you know."

'"Do you know Dilkhusha?"

'"Yes, I do."

'"I will wait outside the gate of Dilkhusha at a quarter to six in the morning of October the sixteenth."

'"Very well."

'He bade me goodnight and left. It was then that it struck me that I hadn't asked his name. But then he hadn't asked mine either. Anyway, the name wasn't important; it was what he had said that mattered. It was hard to believe that Lucknow had been the scene of such chivalry and romance, and that I was in possession of a pair of pistols which had played such an important part in it. But who really won the hand of Annabella in the end? And which of the two did she really love?

'The alarm clock woke me up at five on the morning of the sixteenth. I had a cup of tea, wrapped a scarf around my neck and set off for Dilkhusha in a tonga. Dilkhusha had been at one time Nawab Sadat Ali's country house. There used to be a spacious park around it where deer roamed and into which an occasional leopard strayed from the forests nearby. Now only the shell of the house remained—and a garden which was tended and open to the public.

'At twenty to six I reached my destination. In my best Urdu, I told the tongawallah to wait as I would be going back home in half an hour's time.

'I had to walk only a few steps from the tonga to find the Englishman waiting for me under an arjun tree. He said he had arrived only five minutes ago. We started to walk.

'In a few minutes we found ourselves in an open field. The view ahead was shrouded in mist. Perhaps it had been misty on the morning of the duel too.

'Another minute's walk brought us to a dilapidated cottage which must have belonged to some Englishman in the last century. We stood with our back to the ruins and faced east. In spite of the mist I could clearly make out the huge tamarind tree at some distance from us. To our right, about twenty yards away, stood a large bush. Beyond the tree and the bush I could dimly discern the river, its water reflecting the eastern sky just beginning to turn pink. The surroundings were eerily quiet.

'"Can you hear it?" asked my companion suddenly.

'Yes, I could. The sound of horses' hooves. I can't deny that I felt a chill in my bones. At the same time, I was gripped by a keen anticipation of a unique experience.

'Now I saw the two riders. They rode down our left, pulled up below the tamarind tree and dismounted.

'"Are those the two duellists?" I asked in a whisper.

'"Only one of them," said my companion. "The taller of the two is John Illingworth, the challenger. The other is his friend and second, George Drummond. You can see Drummond is carrying the mahogany box."

'Indeed he was. I couldn't make out the faces in the mist, but I could clearly see the box. It gave me a very strange feeling to see it in the hands of someone when I knew the same box was at this very moment lying in my house locked in my trunk.

'Presently two more riders arrived and dismounted.

'"The blond one is Bruce," whispered my companion.

'Drummond now consulted a pocket-watch and nodded to the two duellists. The two men stood face to face. Then they turned right about and each took fourteen paces in the opposite direction from the other. Then they stopped, swung round and faced each other again.

'The pistols were slowly raised and they took aim. The next moment the silence was broken by Drummond's command: "Fire!"

'The shots rang out, and I was astonished to see both Bruce and Illingworth fall to the ground.

'But there was something else that caught my eye now. It was the hazy figure of a woman running out from behind the bush and disappearing into the mist away from the group around the tamarind tree.

'"Well, you saw what happened," said my companion. "Both men were killed in the duel."

'I said, "Very well, but who was the woman I saw running away?".

'"That was Annabella."

'"Annabella?"

'"Annabella had realized that Illingworth's bullet wouldn't kill Bruce, and yet she wanted both of them out of the way. So she hid behind the bush with a gun which she fired at Bruce the moment the command was given. Illingworth's bullet went wide off the mark."

'"But why did Annabella behave like that?"

'"Because she loved neither of the two men. She realized that Illingworth would be killed in the duel leaving Bruce free to court her against her will. She didn't want that because she loved someone else—someone she went on to marry and find happiness with."

'I could see the scene of a hundred years ago swiftly fading before my eyes. The mist was growing thicker by the minute. I was thinking of the extraordinary Annabella when a woman's voice startled me.

'"George! Georgie!"

'"That's Annabella," I heard my companion saying.

'I turned to him and froze. Why was he suddenly dressed in the clothes of a hundred years ago?

'"I haven't had a chance to introduce myself," he said in a voice which seemed to come floating across a vast chasm. "My name is George Drummond. It was me, Illingworth's friend, that Annabella really loved. Goodbye . . ."

'On getting back home, I opened the mahogany box and took out the pistols once more. Their muzzles were warm to the touch, and an unmistakable smell of gunpowder wafted up to my nostrils.'

Translated by Satyajit Ray
First published in Bengali in 1984

The Millionaire

Unable to contain his annoyance any longer, Tridib Chowdhury pressed the bell to call an attendant bearer. For quite some time now, he had had the feeling that his compartment was not as cool as it ought to have been. And yet, the three other passengers were already snoring. Tridib Babu failed to figure out how this could possibly happen. The basic problem, of course, was that no one ever thought of protesting against injustice. No wonder the entire race was going to the dogs.

There was a knock at the door.

'Come in.'

The door slid to one side and an attendant appeared.

'What is the temperature inside this room?' said Tridib Babu, somewhat aggressively.

'I don't know, sir.'

'Why? Why don't you know? Why should one make a booking in an air-conditioned coach and still have to suffer the heat? Do you not have a responsibility in this matter?'

What could the attendant say? He only looked on, smiling foolishly. Tridib Babu's voice had woken the South Indian gentleman on the upper berth. Tridib Babu had to swallow his anger.

'All right, you may go. Don't forget to bring me a cup of tea exactly at six-thirty in the morning.'

'Very well, sir.'

The attendant left. Tridib Babu closed the door and lay down. He would not have had to suffer such inconveniences if he had gone by air. People like him would normally fly if they had to go to a place like Ranchi from Calcutta. But Tridib Babu suffered from an abject fear of flying. About twelve years ago he had flown to Bombay. What a terrible experience that had been! The weather was awful that day, and the bumping that started as soon as the plane took off did not stop until it had actually landed. Tridib Babu had vowed that day never to ride a plane again. When it became necessary to go to Ranchi on this occasion, he booked himself on the Ranchi Express straightaway. But now it was obvious that all thoughts of comfort in an air-conditioned coach would have to be abandoned. Tridib Babu closed his eyes in the darkened room and was left alone with his thoughts.

Thoughts of his childhood came back to him. He was born in Ranchi. His father, Adinath Chowdhury, was a well-known doctor. After finishing school, Tridib Babu went to Calcutta for further studies. He stayed in an uncle's house there and completed his graduation. Soon afterwards, a Marwari friend advised him to start his own business. A small beginning—dealing with scrap metal—showed him that Lady Luck was certainly going to smile on him. Money began pouring in. He stayed on in Calcutta, though his parents continued to live in Ranchi.

At first he took a flat on Sardar Shankar Road. Then, as his income grew, he shifted to a ground floor flat in a two-storey house on Harrington Street. But he stayed in touch with his parents. He went back to Ranchi once every year and spent at least a week with them. At his parents' request, he married when he was twenty-six. A couple of years later his son was born—he was now studying in America. Tridib Babu had no other children. His wife had died three years ago. He lost his mother in 1972 and his father two years later. The house in Ranchi was looked after by a servant and a gardener. Tridib Babu had been paying them regularly for the last ten years. The aim behind keeping the house was simply to have somewhere to go and rest for a few days. But his busy life very seldom gave him the opportunity to do so. Besides, being away even for three days meant a loss of at least five thousand rupees. For a man whose sole mission in life was to make money there was no question of taking a break. Tridib Babu was a millionaire today, a living contradiction to the general belief that Bengalis could not flourish in private enterprise.

His visit to Ranchi this time was also connected with his business. There were great possibilities in the business of lac. Tridib Babu was going to examine these. He would stay in his own house, and thought he'd be able to finish his work in two days. He had written to his childhood friend Prashant Sarkar. He would tell his servant and make all arrangements. Prashant now taught in a missionary school in Ranchi. It was not as if the two of them were in regular contact, but Tridib Babu knew that if requested, Prashant would readily do this for an old friend.

Tridib Babu's mind jumped from one thought to another. He could not tell when he finally fell asleep. Nor did he realize that, in his sleep, he joined the chorus of the other three passengers, snoring in harmony.

The Ranchi Express was scheduled to arrive at a quarter past seven in the morning. Prashant Sarkar reached the station ten minutes before its arrival to greet his friend. He had been quite close to Tridib, alias Montu, when they were in school. They wrote to each other regularly even after Tridib Babu went to Calcutta. But soon after he left college, their intimacy began to wane. Tridib Babu, of course, was largely to blame. On the few occasions he came to Ranchi to see his parents, he would arrive without telling Prashant. As a result, most of the time, the two could not even meet for a chat. Prashant could not at first understand the reason behind the change in his friend's behaviour. Then he read in the papers that Tridib had become an important businessman, which meant that he was now beyond Prashant's reach—member of a different class. This was made more obvious by the dry and matter-of-fact tone of the brief letter Tridib had sent him.

Prashant Babu felt sad at this change in his friend. The millionaire T. Chowdhury of today was indeed different from the simple, fun-loving Montu he had once known. Did people really change so much over a period of time? It was true that Tridib Chowdhury's financial status had changed dramatically. But Prashant Sarkar was not a man who judged people by their possessions. This aspect of his character was something he inherited from his father. Pramatha Sarkar, Prashant's father, had been a believer in Gandhian principles. There had been no major upheaval in Prashant's own life. After all, a schoolmaster's life did not have much scope of being filled with new excitements. It was, therefore, not difficult to place him as the Panu one had known as a child. But could the same be said about Tridib Chowdhury? Prashant waited eagerly to find out. If Tridib had indeed turned into a snob, Prashant would find that difficult to put up with.

The train was late by ten minutes. Since the visit was going to be a short one, Tridib Babu had brought nothing except a small suitcase and a flask. Prashant Babu took the suitcase from his hand, despite his protests. Then they both began to walk towards the taxi-stand.

'Did you have to wait for a long time?' Tridib Chowdhury asked.

'Just about twenty minutes.'

'I did not expect you to come to the station. There was no need. After all, this is not my first visit to Ranchi.'

Prashant Babu smiled but did not comment. He had not failed to note the slightly formal tone his friend was using.

'Are things all right here?' asked Tridib Babu.

'Yes, everything's arranged. Your gardener and Chintamani are both very excited at the thought of their Babu returning to the house.'

Chintamani was the cook-cum-chowkidar.

'Is the house still liveable? Or has it turned into a haunted house?'

Prashant Babu smiled again. Then, after a few moments of silence, said, 'I don't know about the house being haunted, but there's something I ought to tell you. I saw a little boy playing in your garden the other night as I was passing by.'

'At night?'

'Yes, it was pretty late. About eleven-thirty. I was startled. It seemed as though the ten-year-old Montu had come back!'

'Anyway, obviously it wasn't a ghost. My father had this house built, so I know all about those who lived and died here. What I'm more concerned about is whether they've kept it clean.'

'It's spotless. I saw that for myself yesterday. Well—what do you have to do now? Where do you have to go?'

'I need to go to Namkan today after lunch. There's a man called Maheshwar Jain there dealing with lac. My appointment is for two-thirty.'

'All right. You can keep the same taxi that we will take now. It can come back after lunch and take you to Namkan. Shouldn't take you more than ten minutes to get there.'

Both men got into the taxi. Prashant Sarkar came to the point a little later.

'Er . . . how long are you here for?'

'If I don't finish the business dealings with Jain today, I'll have to go back tomorrow. Then I'll return to Calcutta the day after.'

'You seem so different . . . one feels hesitant to talk to you.'

'Tell me what you have to. Don't beat about the bush. I get suspicious when people do that.'

'It's nothing much, really. Just a request. If you agree, this childhood friend of yours would feel most grateful.'

'What is it?'

'Do you remember Father William?'

'William? Willie . . . the red beard?'

'Yes, the red beard. About five years ago, he opened a school for poor children. All kinds of children go there regardless of what families they come from—Hindus, Muslims, Christians. Father William's worked really hard to get it going. He's very keen that you go and visit the school. It shouldn't take you more than half an hour. He'd feel very encouraged if you went.'

'Going there means being offered a begging bowl.'

'Meaning?'

'Do you not know the real reason behind such an invitation? A new institution, need for funds, a wealthy client and a begging bowl. If I must give my money away in the name of charity, I shall do so in my old age, when it's time to think of the other world. But now is not the time for this. This is the time to save. If it gets known that I am the loving and giving kind, there shall be no end to appeals for help. So don't try to make a request like this. I shall pay no attention. I'm sure if you explained things to Father, he'll understand. All I want to do here, apart from making a business deal, is to rest. I don't get much relaxation in Calcutta.'

'All right.'

Prashant had not expected such a violent reaction. But perhaps it was natural enough. This man was not the Montu he had once known. He was a stranger.

But the sight of the place he was born in made Tridib Babu grow a little less pompous and more cheerful. Prashant Babu took this opportunity to make the second request.

'You rejected one of my proposals, dear friend, but you've got to accept this one. My wife gave me strict instructions to bring you over to our house for dinner tonight. We are not very wealthy ourselves, but I can say with full confidence that no one in my house shall greet you with a begging bowl.'

Tridib Babu accepted his invitation readily enough. Was it simply out of pity? Prashant Babu chose not to brood on the issue. He had a lot of work to do now—finish all the shopping, go back home, take a bath, then a meal and then go to his school.

'I will come myself to fetch you at around eight,' he told Tridib Babu as they parted, 'and I promise to drop you back by ten o'clock.'

It was proved once more that day that it was the personality of Tridib Chowdhury and his sharp communications skills that were responsible for his success. His visit to Ranchi resulted in the addition of a new side to his business—the development of trade dealing with lac. No doubt this also meant additional complications, but they seemed insignificant when one considered the extra income that would be generated.

Tridib Babu returned home at about five in the evening, just in time for a cup of tea. Then he moved about in the house, looking carefully at everything. This was where he was born. The ground floor had the living- and the dining- rooms, a guest-room and the kitchen. There were two bedrooms on the first floor, a bathroom and a covered veranda facing the west. The smaller of the two bedrooms had been his own.

The room seemed much smaller than he remembered possibly because he had grown in size. He stared for a few minutes at the bed and decided to sleep in the same room. Chintamani had already asked him once, but he had been undecided. He called the servant before setting out with his friend and told him to make his bed in the small bedroom.

Prashant Sarkar's wife, Bela, was not only an efficient housewife but also an excellent cook. The dinner, therefore, was a success. Prashant Babu had spared no expense to feed his friend well—there were meat and fish dishes of more than one kind, pulao, puris and sweets. Tridib Babu ate everything with relish but did not stay for more than ten minutes after dinner. Prashant Babu did not get a single opportunity to ask him about his present position in society and how he had got there. Tridib Babu returned to his own house at a quarter to ten.

The house was in a relatively quiet locality. All was silent when he reached home. As Tridib Babu began to go up the stairs, the sound of his footsteps, even to his own ears, seemed unnaturally loud.

His bed had been made in the same room where he had spent his childhood. It was too soon after dinner to go to sleep. Tridib Babu decided to rest for a while in an easy chair on the veranda.

In less than half an hour he realized all his fatigue had vanished. He began to feel fresh and totally relaxed. There was a pale moon in the sky and, in its light, he could see the dark branches of a bare shirish tree. He could even hear himself breathe. It seemed as though that was the only sound on earth.

But was it?

No, the sound of something else was added to it. A faint voice. Difficult to say where it was coming from.

Tridib Babu listened carefully. A little boy was reciting a poem. A well-known nursery rhyme that Tridib Babu recognized at once.

The voice still came only faintly, but the words were clear.

Baa baa black sheep
Have you any wool?

It was as though these few lines had been hiding in a corner of his mind. The voice made them leap out of memory.

The voice grew fainter. Tridib Babu rose. It was no use looking back. What mattered in life was the future, not the past. He knew he had to make a lot more money in future, climb higher on the social ladder, become a billionaire. The past made a man weak. Thoughts of the future, on the other hand, would give him new strength.

He went into the room and frowned. There was a power cut. A candle flickered on a table by the bed. Even in its dim light, he could see clearly that the bed had not been properly made. The bed-sheet and the pillow case were both wrinkled. He straightened them and took off his kurta. Then he lay down. Should he let the candle burn? No, there was no need. He snuffed it out. The pungent smell of burnt wax hung in the air for a few minutes before fading away gradually. The window was open. Through it, he could see the sky. The moonlight seemed brighter. From where he lay, he faced the door. That too, was open. A portion of the veranda and the staircase could be seen. There was really no reason for him to look at the stairs, but something made him do so—it was the strange sound of bare feet coming up the stairs.

But no one actually arrived. The sound stopped in the middle of the staircase.

Tridib Babu suddenly felt he was being very foolish. The whole thing was no more than his imagination. He removed all fanciful thoughts from his mind and closed his eyes determinedly. The Japanese clock in the dining-room downstairs struck eleven. It had stopped working but, this morning, Tridib Babu had got it going again.

The silence seemed to deepen as the last chime of the clock faded away.

Even with his eyes closed, Tridib Babu began to see things—broken little pictures, disjointed pieces of a dream. He knew he would soon fall asleep. Just as a singer hummed a tune quietly to himself before starting a song, these broken dreams were a prelude to slumber.

But he was not quite asleep yet. In spite of his closed eyes, his sixth sense told him someone had entered his room. No, it was not just his sixth sense. His ears, too, said the same thing. He could actually hear someone breathe. It sounded as though someone had come running up the stairs and was now panting in the room.

Tridib Babu opened his eyes, convinced he would actually be able to see this person. He was not mistaken.

A boy was standing at the door, his right hand resting lightly on the doorknob, his left foot slightly raised, as though the sight of another person in the room had startled him into halting in his tracks.

Tridib Babu realized that a cold shiver was working its way up his legs, past his spine and on to his head! Prashant had said he had seen a boy in the garden . . . a little boy . . . the Montu of his childhood . . .

His limbs froze, a nerve throbbed at his temple. He thought he would faint, his mounting terror choked him.

The boy took a step forward. He was wearing a purple shirt . . . why, this was the same shirt . . .

Just before passing into oblivion, he heard a question, spoken in a sweet, boyish voice:

'Who is sleeping in my bed?'

Tridib Babu woke as usual at half-past six in the morning. He could not recall when he had regained consciousness at night and when he had dropped off to sleep again.

Prashant had said he could come and have breakfast with him at seven-thirty. Tridib Babu could not focus on any of his routine activities. What happened last night had left him feeling totally shaken. Never before in his life had such a thing happened.

That nursery rhyme he had heard last night was one that he had recited in class when he was very young and even won a prize for. And the second prize? That had gone to Prashant Sarkar. Montu had been displeased at this.

'What fun we would have had if we had both won the first prize!' he had said to his dearest friend, Panu.

He had not looked at the face of the boy who had come into his room last night, but he had definitely noticed the shirt the boy was wearing. It was the same purple shirt his aunt had given him. It was his favourite shirt. The first time he wore it to school, Panu had said, 'Good heavens—you look like a European today!'

The meaning of the incident last night was clear enough. The Tridib Chowdhury of today was definitely not the Montu he had once been. The child Montu was no more. It was his ghost that had come the night before and told him that the new Tridib Chowdhury—the great millionaire—was an obnoxious idiot. He could not be tolerated.

Tridib Babu did not say anything to Prashant about his experience. But he knew that he was still tense and nervous and quite unable to relax. It was possibly because of this that Prashant Babu, after a while, happened to remark, 'What is the matter with you? Didn't you sleep well last night?'

'No . . . Uh . . . I mean, since I've finished all my work already, couldn't we go and visit Father William's school today?'

'Excellent idea,' said Prashant Sarkar cheerfully.

But he had to hide a smile. His plan had worked beautifully. He must drop in at his neighbour's house on his way back and tell his son, Babu, that his recitation and acting the night before had been just perfect. And, of course, Chintamani would have to be given a fat tip for his contribution!

Translated by Gopa Majumdar

First published in Bengali in 1985

I Am a Ghost

I am a ghost. I was alive three years ago. Then, one day, I was burnt to death in this house, in Deoghar. The house is called Lily Villa. I was here with a friend, on holiday. That morning, as I lit the stove to make a cup of tea, it burst into flames and my clothes caught fire. The flames also seared my face. That much I do remember. But I cannot recall anything else. I have been living in this house since that day. I cannot tell what I now look like, for as a ghost, even if I were to go and stand before a mirror, I could not see my reflection. I've tried peering into the water in a pond, but that did not work either. But I know I am not really anything much to look at.

Two years ago, a family came to Lily Villa to spend a few days. The head of that family happened to come face to face with me. I saw his eyes bulge with horror, and he promptly fainted. It was actually my own fault. A ghost can choose to remain invisible, and to be honest, it was my intention to keep myself that way. But I was a bit preoccupied that day, and not really paying much attention to what I was doing. So, just for a moment, I had become visible to that gentleman. Judging by his reaction, my turning into a ghost had done nothing to alter my appearance. Obviously, I still had a badly burnt face.

After that incident, people stopped coming to this house. Lily Villa has come to be known as a haunted house. I am quite sad at this turn of events, for I liked watching and being with the living. Now I feel very lonely. There are other ghosts in the neighbourhood, but none in this house. No one except me died an unnatural death here. Besides, I don't like many of the other ghosts in Deoghar. Some of them are really quite wicked. Naskarda, for instance. His name used to be Bheem Naskar when he was alive. I've never known a ghost more cunning or malicious.

A postmaster called Laxman Tripathi used to live in Deoghar. He and Kantibhai Dubey, who worked for the State Bank, could not get on at all. One evening, as Laxman Tripathi was returning home from the post office, the ghost of Bheem Naskar decided to attack him. Just as Tripathy had gone past the house of the Shahs and reached an open field, Naskar slipped down from a tamarind tree and broke Tripathy's neck. What a ruckus that kicked up! The police came, arrests were made, cases were fought and eventually a man was hanged! Which man? None other than Tripathy's sworn enemy, Kantibhai Dubey. He had to pay for Naskarda's misdeed. Naskarda knew this would happen, so he had deliberately killed Tripathy. That time, I felt I had to speak to Naskarda. 'What you did was wrong,' I told him. 'Just because you are a ghost now does not mean that you have the right to meddle with other people's lives, and harm them. Why don't you simply mind your own business, and let the living mind theirs? Our two worlds are different, Naskarda. If one interferes with the other, there can only be disaster and calamity.'

I have never harmed anybody. Not consciously, anyway. Ever since I learnt that my appearance was likely to frighten people, I have become extremely cautious. There is a broken-down and abandoned room at the far end of the garden in Lily Villa, behind some mango and jackfruit trees. I believe the room was once used by a mali. That is where I now spend most of my time. Not that there is anyone in the main building who might see me. Lily Villa has been lying empty for a long time. But, sometimes, children from the neighbouring house of the Chowdhurys come here to play hide-and-seek. Surprisingly, they do not appear to be afraid of ghosts at all. Or perhaps they come because they expect to see one. But I take great care to remain invisible while they are here. If the sight of my face could make an adult faint, what effect would it have on children? No, I could never take any risks.

However, this does mean that I must continue to be lonely. Yes, ghosts feel lonely, too. Well, if I am alone, I have only myself to blame. It is because of my own mistake that Lily Villa is now known as a haunted house. No one wants to come and live here; and so I cannot hear human voices any more, see them move, or sing, or laugh. This makes me feel very depressed at times. If the living knew how much the spirit of the dead craved their company, would they be afraid of ghosts? Of course not.

One day, however, a visitor turned up in Lily Villa. I heard the horn of a cycle rickshaw one morning. So I peered out and saw that someone's luggage was being taken out of the rickshaw. How many had arrived? Two, as it turned out. The visitor was accompanied by a servant. That was good enough for me. I did not need a large number of people. Something, I felt, was better than nothing.

Since ghosts can see clearly even from a long distance, I could catch every detail of the visitor's appearance: he was close to fifty, short, bald, had a bristly moustache, thick eyebrows, and his eyes held a stern look. The first thing he said to his servant upon entering the house was, 'Get cracking. I need a cup of tea in half an hour. Then I'll start working.'

Needless to say, I could hear every word from my own room. A ghost's hearing is as good as his sight. His eyes and ears both work like binoculars.

The servant was most efficient. He brought his master a cup of tea and a plate of biscuits in half an hour. The visitor was in the room that overlooked the garden, unpacking and putting his things away. There was a desk and a chair near the window. I noticed that he had placed a sheaf of papers, pens and an inkwell on the desk.

That meant he was a writer. Was he famous?

Yes. Within an hour of his arrival, about eight local residents turned up to meet him, and I learnt his name. He was called Narayan Sharma. I could not tell whether it was his real name, or a pseudonym, but that was how everyone addressed him. The locals were very pleased to find him in their midst. After all, it was not every day that a celebrity came to Deoghar. So, they said, if Mr Sharma had no objection, they would like to hold a reception in his honour.

Narayan Sharma, I could see, was not a man with a soft and gentle disposition. He said, 'I left Calcutta and came here simply to work undisturbed. And you're already making impositions on me!'

The others looked suitably abashed. That made Mr Sharma relent somewhat. 'Very well,' he said, 'Give me at least five days of peace and quiet. Then we'll think about a reception, all right? But if you start putting any pressure on me, I'll just pack my bags and go back to Calcutta.'

At this moment, Nitai Ghosh from the group suddenly asked a question that I did not like at all. 'Why did you choose Lily Villa, of all places? There are so many other houses in Deoghar.'

For the first time, a smile appeared on Mr Sharma's face. 'You are saying that because this house is supposed to be haunted, isn't that right? Well, I wouldn't mind seeing a ghost. He could keep me company.'

'You're not taking this seriously, are you?' said Haren Talukdar. 'Once a doctor from Calcutta came to stay here for a few days, with his family. He saw the ghost. It was apparently a horrific sight. He was unconscious for almost fifteen minutes. Tell you what. There's a very good dak bungalow here. Its manager is a fan of yours. He'd be prepared to make every arrangement for your stay. It's just a matter of telling him. Please, you must get out of Lily Villa.'

In reply, Narayan Sharma said something very strange. 'Perhaps you are not aware that very few people know as much as I do about spiritualism. In fact, I have come here to write on this subject. I can assure you that I will not end up like your doctor. He had taken no precautions against ghosts, had he? I will. No ghost could do me any harm. I realize you have all got my best interests at heart, but I want to stay and work in Lily Villa. You see, I have stayed in this house before, as a child. I have many fond memories of that time.'

This was the first time I'd heard anything about precautions against ghosts. I did not like it at all. And spiritualism? How could spirits and spooks be a subject for study? What was Narayan Sharma talking about?

There was no point in pondering over this now. I would have to wait until it got dark. After that, I was sure to get all the answers.

There was one thing I wanted to do, however. I felt I had to pass on whatever I had heard so far to Bheem Naskar, if only as a joke, to see his reaction. He had once broken a man's neck. What would he say to all this?

As the day wore on, I grew increasingly restless. In the end, I could contain myself no more. I left Lily Villa, taking great care to remain invisible, and went to the derelict old house owned by the Malliks. It was said to be two hundred years old.

'Naskarda!' I called.

He came floating down from a broken, roofless room on the first floor, and said irritably, 'What do you want at this odd hour?'

I told him about Narayan Sharma. Naskarda's frown deepened ominously. 'Really? Is that so? Tell me, does he think he is the only one who can take adequate steps? Can't we?'

'Take steps? What do you propose we do?' I asked a little nervously. I could see that a plan was already taking shape in his mind.

'There's one thing I could do quite easily. When I was alive, for thirty-two years, I exercised regularly. Push-ups, heavy clubs, dumb-bells, chest-expanders . . . you name it, I had used them all. You think I haven't got the strength to break this Narayan's neck?'

It was true that Naskarda was once a bodybuilder. He had died by swallowing poison, which meant that his appearance had remained unchanged. Even now, when he moved, muscles rippled all over his body.

'Well, what does that mean?' I asked. If I still had a heart, I am sure it would have started thudding madly by now.

'Only this: tonight, at twelve o'clock, Narayan Sharma's life is going to come to an end. If he thinks he can mess around with ghosts, no ghost worth his name is going to let him get away with it.'

Only I know how nervously I passed the rest of the day. Narayan Sharma spent most of his time writing in his room. Some time before the sun set, he went for a long walk along the street going to the north. He returned a little before the evening star appeared in the sky. It was going to be a moonless night.

I could see everything from my little den. Now I saw Narayan Sharma do something rather strange. He opened his suitcase and took out a handful of powder from a bag. Then he poured it into an incense-burner, lit it and placed it just outside the threshold to his room. Smoke began billowing from it very soon, and a southern breeze brought the smoke into my own room.

Oh my God, was this his 'precaution'? If so, it was undoubtedly most effective. With the smoke had come a smell. Normally, one wouldn't expect a ghost to be able to smell anything, but this smell was so strong that it seemed to burn not just my nose, but the inside of my head as well. It was terrible. Even Naskarda would find it difficult to make his way through this powerful stuff. How would he get anywhere near this house?

My fears were confirmed, a few hours later. Around midnight, I heard a hushed voice call from the other side of the garden wall: 'Sudhanya! Are you there?'

Sudhanya was my name. I went out. Naskarda was sitting by the road, on the grass, clutching his nose. His voice sounded nasal when he spoke.

'I died twenty-one years ago. This is the first time that I've been beaten by a live man. Who knew man had learnt to use such contraptions?'

'That particular man has studied his subject thoroughly, Naskarda.

He knows a lot.'

'How sad . . . how absolutely awful. Just think what fun I might have had, breaking his neck!'

'Yes, but that is not going to happen. You do realize that, don't you?'

'Yes, I most certainly do. I'd better go now. This has been a totally new experience for me.'

Naskarda left, and I returned to my room. Only a minute later, I suddenly discovered that I was feeling extremely sleepy. This was incredible, completely unheard of. A ghost never feels sleepy. But tonight was obviously going to be an exception. That powder in the incense-burner clearly contained something that put ghosts to sleep, even though the best time for them to move about was during the night.

I could not keep my eyes open any longer. Feeling dazed, I lay down on the floor.

The sound of someone's voice woke me. It was morning.

I sat up hastily. At once, my eyes fell on the man who had entered my room. I could only stare at him in disbelief. How did he . . .?

It was Narayan Sharma, that much was clear. But what had happened to him?

Narayan Sharma answered my unspoken question. 'My servant was still asleep when I woke. So I thought I'd make myself a cup of tea. I tried to light the stove, and it burst in my face. At this moment, I think everyone's trying to arrange my funeral. I came here looking for somewhere to live. I like this place. Do you think there's enough room here for a second person?'

'Of course!' I replied, feeling very pleased.

I had company at last. There was no doubt in my mind that one charred face would get on very well with another.

Translated by Gopa Majumdar
First published in Bengali in 1985

The Two Comedians

'Today, I'm going to talk about a film star,' said Uncle Tarini, sipping his tea.

'Which film star? What's his name?' we cried in unison.

'You wouldn't have heard of him,' he replied. 'You were probably born only after he retired.'

'Even so, do tell us his name,' Napla insisted, reluctant to give up easily. 'We often see old films on TV, and know the names of many old stars.'

'All right, his name was Ratanlal Raxit.'

'Yes, I know who you mean,' Napla nodded sagely. 'I saw a film called *Joy Porajoy* (Victory and Defeat) on TV about three months ago. Ratan Raxit played the hero's father.'

'Well then, if you have seen him in a film, you'll be able to enjoy the story all the more.'

'Is it a ghost story?'

'No, but it is about something dead and gone. In that sense, I suppose you could call it a ghost story. It concerns the past; events from days gone by.'

'Very well. Please begin.'

Uncle Tarini pulled a bolster closer to lean against, and began his story:

'Ratanlal Raxit retired in 1970, at the age of seventy. His health was not very good, so his doctor prescribed complete rest. He had worked in films for forty-five years, right from the era of silent films. He had made a great deal of money, and knew how to put it to good use. He had three houses in Calcutta and lived in the one in Amherst Street. The others he let out on rent.

'One day, after his retirement, Ratanlal put an advertisement in the papers for a secretary. I was in Calcutta then, and was almost fifty years old at that time. Having spent all my life travelling and trying my hand at a variety of jobs, I was wondering whether it was time to settle down once and for all in my own homeland, when I spotted that ad. So I applied. The name of Ratanlal Raxit was well known to me. I had seen many of his films and, besides, you know I have a special interest in films.

'I received a reply within a week. I was to appear for an interview.

'I went to Mr Raxit's house. I knew he was unwell, but there was no sign of illness in his appearance. His skin was smooth, and his teeth appeared to be his own. The first thing he asked me was whether I had seen any of his films. I told him that I had, not just his later films, but also some of the earliest ones, made in the silent era, when Mr Raxit used to act in comedies.

'My answer seemed to please him. He said, "I have managed to collect, over the last few years, copies of most of my silent films. A room in this house now acts as a mini-cinema. I've got a projector in that room, and appointed someone to run it. It is very difficult to get hold of silent films. Perhaps you know about the fire in the main warehouse that destroyed copies of most silent films in Bengal? It happened not once, but twice. As a result, it is almost impossible to find prints of those films. But I refused to give up without trying. I advertised in the papers, and came to know eventually that many of my films were kept safe in the warehouse of one of my producers called Mirchandani. The reason for this was simply that Mirchandani was not just the producer, but also a fan of mine. He died four years ago. I spoke to his son, and bought from him what films he had. Then I advertised again, and over a period of time, collected the rest. My failing health has forced me to retire, but I cannot possibly stay away from films. So I watch my own films, and pass a pleasant evening every day. Your job will be to look after my film library, make a catalogue of all my films, and find out which ones are missing from my present collection. Can you do it?"

'I said I would certainly do my best. It would not be too difficult to make a catalogue of the films he already had. Looking for the ones he didn't would naturally be a bigger challenge. "I am not talking only of my silent films," Mr Raxit added. "Some of the early talkies are missing as well. But I think if you went to the offices of a few producers and distributors in the Dharamtola area, you'd definitely be able to get copies of what you need. I want my collection to be complete, with not a single film missing. In my old age, I wish to entertain myself only by watching my own films."

'I got the job. Mr Raxit was an unusual man. His wife had died fifteen years ago. He had two sons, both of whom lived in south Calcutta. His only daughter was in Allahabad. Her husband was a doctor there. Occasionally, his grandchildren came to visit him. So did his sons, at times, but Mr Raxit was not really in close contact with his family. He lived with two servants, a cook, and a special personal bearer called Lakshmikant. Lakshmikant was in his sixties, and totally devoted to his master. Mr Raxit was lucky to have someone like him.

'I began my work, and with Lakshmikant's help, managed to produce a catalogue of all the films in the collection within ten days. Then I made a round of the film distributors' offices in Dharamtola and located many of the early talkies Mr Raxit had featured in. He bought a print of each.

'I worked from ten in the morning to five in the evening. But sometimes, I spent the evening with Mr Raxit, instead of going home at five. He usually started seeing his films at half past six, and finished at eight-thirty. The projectionist was called Ashu Babu, a cheerful man. The audience comprised only three people—Mr Raxit, Lakshmikant and myself. The bearer had to be present, for Mr Raxit liked smoking a hookah. Lakshmikant was required to take it away from time to time to refill it. Although it was always dark in the room, I could tell by glancing at Lakshmikant's face that he enjoyed watching the films very much.

'The silent films were the best of all. I've told you already that Mr Raxit had acted in comedies in the silent era. Many of these were short films. There were only two reels, which ran for twenty minutes. They showed the escapades of a duo called Bishu and Shibu, a bit like Laurel and Hardy. Mr Raxit played Bishu, and Shibu was played by an actor called Sharat Kundu. Twenty minutes simply flew when we began watching the antics of these two. In some films they appeared as businessmen, or gamblers. In others, they were clowns in a circus, or a zamindar and his hanger-on. I knew how popular they were in their time. These short films were often shown before a longer feature film.

'What I enjoyed watching more than these films, however, was Mr Raxit's response to his own acting. He would roll around laughing every time he saw himself clowning on the screen. Sometimes, I found it hard to believe that a comedian could laugh so much at his own acting. Naturally, I had to laugh with him. He said to me at times, "You know, Tarini, when I acted in these films, I did not find them funny at all. In fact, they struck me often as slapstick, and the humour seemed forced. It used to annoy me. But now, I can see that these films contain a lot of pure, innocent fun which is far better than what you get to see in modern comedies."

'One day, I asked him something that had been bothering me for some time. "I am very curious about one thing, sir," I said. "You played Bishu. But what about Sharat Kundu, who played Shibu? What happened to him? Aren't you in touch?"

'Mr Raxit shook his head. "As far as I know, Sharat Kundu stopped acting in films when the talkies started. We were quite close when we worked together. We used to rack our brains and plan our acts ourselves. There was a director, but only in name. We did everything, including providing the props and costumes. Then, one day, we read in a press report that films in Hollywood were being made with sound; so when the characters spoke, the audience could now hear their voices. That was in either 1928 or 1929. Three or four years later, the same thing happened in Indian films. It created a major stir. The entire process of film-making changed, as did the style of acting. Personally, I did not find that a problem. I had a good voice, so the talkies could do me no harm. I was then in my early thirties. The film industry in Bengal needed a hero with a good voice, and I had no difficulty in meeting that demand. That put an end to clowning around for twenty minutes. I became a hero. But, for some reason, Sharat Kundu disappeared. I asked a few people about him, but no one could tell me where he was. God knows if he died young."

'If that was the case, naturally, there would be no point in looking for him. But something told me I should make a few enquiries about Sharat Kundu. Judging by those twenty-minute films, he was no less gifted an actor than Ratanlal Raxit.

'I went to Tollygunj and asked a few people I knew. I learnt that a journalist called Naresh Sanyal was doing research on the very early films made in Bengal, with a view to writing a definitive book on them and their makers. I managed to get his address, and turned up at his house one Sunday morning. Mr Sanyal admitted to knowing a few things about Sharat Kundu. Apparently, about five years ago, he had obtained Sharat Kundu's address, after considerable difficulty, and visited him to conduct an interview. "Where did you find him?" I asked.

'"In a slum in Goabagan," Mr Sanyal told me. "He was almost a pauper at the time."

'"Are you interviewing all the actors who had appeared in silent films?" I wanted to know.

'"As many as I can. Very few are still alive," Mr Sanyal replied.

'I told him about Ratanlal Raxit, adding that I could arrange an interview with him. Mr Sanyal greeted this news with great enthusiasm.

'Now I asked him what I really wanted to know: "Did Sharat Kundu stop acting once the talkies started?"

'"Yes. He was rejected after a voice test. He did not tell me how he survived after that, possibly because he did not want to talk about a bitter struggle. But I learnt a lot of facts about the silent era from him."

'After that, I went back to Tollygunj and spoke to some other people. It turned out that Sharat Kundu had continued to visit the studios for quite a while, even after it became clear that there was no future for him in the talkies. His financial situation had become grave. The manager of the Mayapuri Studio in Tollygunj told me that, just occasionally, Sharat Kundu was given a role as an extra, which brought him an income of just a few rupees. An extra is usually required to stand in the background in a crowd. He does not have to speak.

'It was in the same Mayapuri Studio that I learnt something else from an old production manager called Dwarik Chakravarty. "Go to Nataraj Cabin in Bentinck Street," he said. "I saw Sharat Kundu there, just a few years ago."

'By this time I was determined to drag Sharat Kundu out of oblivion. So I went to Nataraj Cabin. Before doing so—I forgot to mention this—I had been to Goabagan and learnt that he no longer lived there. Needless to say, in my efforts at rediscovering Sharat Kundu, I had the full support of Ratanlal Raxit. He was as enthusiastic as me, and seemed to have caught my obsession for Sharat Kundu, as if it was some sort of a contagious disease. He began telling me about their close friendship, and how popular their short films had been. When people went to the cinema, they were more interested in watching Bishu and Shibu than the main feature film. They had been an enormously popular duo, but now only one of them was around. This was not fair. The other had to be found.

'Pulin Datta, the manager of Nataraj Cabin, said to me, "Three years ago, Sharat-da was a regular visitor here. But I haven't seen him since."

'"Did he have a job?"

'"I don't know. I tried asking him, but never got a straight answer. All he ever said was, 'There's nothing that I haven't done, just to keep myself from starving.' But he stopped working in films, or even watching films, for that matter. Perhaps he could never forget that the arrival of talkies destroyed his career."

'A month passed after my meeting with Pulin Datta. I made some more enquiries, but drew a blank everywhere. Sharat Kundu seemed to have vanished into thin air. Mr Raxit was genuinely disappointed to hear that I had failed to find him. "He was such a talented actor!" he lamented. "Finished by the talkies, and now totally forgotten. Who would recognize his name today? Isn't it as bad as being dead?"

'I decided to drop the subject of Sharat Kundu since there was nothing more that I could do. I broached a different matter. "Would you mind giving an interview?" I asked.

'"An interview? Who wants it?"

'I told him about Naresh Sanyal. Mr Sanyal had called me that morning saying he wanted to come the next day.

'"All right, tell him to come at ten. But I cannot spend a long time talking to him, tell him that." I rang Naresh Sanyal, and passed on the message.

'That evening, I remained in the projection room to watch the antics of Bishu and Shibu. There were forty-two films in all. Thirty-seven of them were already in Mr Raxit's collection when I started my job. I had managed to get the remaining five. That day, watching some of these films, I was struck again by Sharat Kundu's acting prowess. He was truly a gifted comedian. I heard Mr Raxit click his tongue in regret at the disappearance of his partner.

'The following morning, Mr Sanyal turned up within ten minutes of my own arrival. Mr Raxit was ready to receive his visitor. "Let's have some tea before our interview," said Mr Raxit. Mr Sanyal raised no objection.

'It was our daily practice to have a cup of tea at ten o'clock. Usually, this was the time when Mr Raxit and I discussed what needed to be done. Then I started on my job, and he went back to his room to rest. I had finished making the catalogue. Now I was making a synopsis of each of the films featuring Bishu and Shibu, and a list of other actors, the director, the cameraman and other crew. Such a list is known as filmography.

'Anyway, today a plate of hot kachauris arrived with the tea, in honour of our visitor. Mr Sanyal was speaking when the tea was brought. He broke off abruptly the instant the tray was placed on the table. I saw him staring at the bearer who had brought it in. It was Mr Raxit's personal attendant, Lakshmikant.

'I, too, found myself looking closely at him; and so did Mr Raxit. Lakshmikant's nose, his chin, his broad forehead, and that sharp look in his eyes . . . where had I seen those before? Why, I had never looked properly at him in all these months! There was no reason to. When do we ever look closely at a servant, unless there is a specific reason to do so?

'The same name escaped from our lips, almost in unison: "Sharat Kundu!"

'No, there could possibly be no doubt about it. Sharat Kundu, once his partner, was now Mr Raxit's personal attendant.

'"What is this, Sharat?" Mr Raxit shouted. "Is it really you? All this time . . . in my house . . .?"

'Sharat Kundu took some time to find his tongue. "What could I do?" he said finally, wiping his perspiring forehead. "How was I to know this gentleman would recognize me? If he didn't, you certainly wouldn't have. You didn't realize who I was, did you? How could you, it's been forty years since you last saw me. What happened was simply that I went to Mirchandani's office one day to look for a job. There I heard that you had bought copies of all our old films. So I thought I might get the chance to watch my own films again, if I could work for you in your house. I didn't even know those films were still available. So I came here and asked if you needed a bearer. Luckily for me, you did. So I got the job, although you did not recognize me. I did not mind at all. I have worked as a coolie in the past. The job of a bearer is sheer heaven after that, I can tell you. Besides, I really enjoyed being here. All those films that we made before the talkies started . . . they weren't bad, were they? But now, I guess I won't get to see them any more."

'"Why? Why shouldn't you?" Mr Raxit jumped to his feet. "From now on, you are going to be my manager. You will sit in the same room as Tarini, and you'll live here with me in my house. We'll watch our films together every evening. A stroke of misfortune may have broken the famous duo, but that breakage has now been put to right. What do you say, Tarini?"'

'I looked at Naresh Sanyal. I had never seen anyone look so totally dumbstruck. But what could be a better scoop, from a journalist's point of view?'

Translated by Gopa Majumdar
First published in Bengali in 1985

A Dream Come True

No one is ever fully satisfied with his appearance. Ram might wish he had a little more flesh on his body—all his bones stuck out so! Shyam might wonder why he could not sing, when the fellow next door played the harmonium every evening and sang to his heart's content. Jodu might say—if only I could be a sportsman! Look at Gavaskar, he has created so many records and become so famous. Modhu's wish might be to become a film star in Bombay. If he could have his wish, money and glamour would both come pouring in.

Like most people, Nidhiram Datta too had a lot of unfulfilled desires. To start with, there were many things about himself that he did not like. For instance, he could see others eating fruit and enjoying it. Mangoes, lychees, apples, grapes . . . each fruit was well known for its taste and good qualities. People who ate them found such nourishment from each of them. But Nidhiram? He did not like eating fruit at all. He just wasn't interested. Why did God have to make him such a strange exception?

He was not happy with his appearance, either. He was reasonably good looking, but not very tall. Once he had got his height measured. It was five feet six inches. One of his colleagues was six feet tall. Nidhiram often looked at him and his heart filled with envy. If only he could gain a few inches!

Nidhiram worked in the office of Mukherjee Builders & Contractors. He had been there for the last fourteen years. His employers were quite happy with him. His salary was enough to keep him, his wife and his two children in reasonable comfort. But the truth was that Nidhiram did not like the idea of doing a job. So many people made a living by writing novels and stories. Of course they had to work hard, but they were not forced to spend several hours, from ten in the morning to five in the evening, bent over a desk. Besides, one could make a name for oneself only by becoming a writer, or artist, or musician, not by doing a job in an office. But that was all Nidhiram felt he was destined to do. He would never know what it meant to bring joy to a large number of people. It was, to him, a great cause for regret.

One of his friends, Manotosh Bagchi, was an actor. He was really quite gifted, and had joined the theatre as a professional actor. He played the lead most of the time, and had, by now, become quite well known. Nidhiram had said to him, more than once: 'Why don't you teach me how to act, Manotosh? I really want to learn. If I could get even a couple of small roles in amateur theatre, people would come to know me!'

Manotosh's reply had been, 'Not everyone can do it, Nidhiram. You need a good, powerful voice to be an actor. You haven't got that. If people in the back rows couldn't hear you, they'd boo so loudly that you'd forget all your lines!'

This year, Nidhiram went to Puri during the Puja holidays. There, he found a sadhu baba. The baba was standing on the beach, surrounded by a group of about twenty men and women. The sight of a sadhu always made Nidhiram curious. This one, in particular, looked so powerful that he felt he had to go and see him more closely.

Nidhiram pushed his way through the crowd. Babaji's eyes fell on him almost at once.

'What are you trying to do, Nidhiram?' he asked. 'Why do you wish to be what you are not?'

Nidhiram's jaw fell open. How did the sadhu learn his name? Clearly, he had some psychic powers. 'Why, n-no, I mean . . .' Nidhiram faltered.

'No? Are you denying it?' the sadhu cut him short. 'I can see it all so vividly. Your body has been divided into two. One is what you are. The other is what you desire to be. It is your desire that's getting stronger. What are you going to do?'

'You tell me!' Nidhiram cried. 'Please tell me what's going to happen. I am a simple man, Baba, I know nothing.'

'You will get what you want,' the sadhu replied. 'But not right away. It will take time. After all, the whole thing must be uprooted. Then new roots must grow, and spread under new earth, to gain a foothold. It won't be easy. But, as I just said, one day it will happen.'

Nidhiram returned to Calcutta a few days after this incident. One day, soon after his return, he suddenly felt like eating a banana. He spotted a man selling a whole basketful at the crossing of Bentinck Street. Nidhiram bought one from him, ate it, and found it quite tasty. Could this mean that, even at the age of thirty-nine, one might find one's tastes changing? Nidhiram did not, at the time, think that this had anything to do with what the sadhu had said. But this was the first of the many changes that slowly came over him.

He went back to his office but, for several days, could not concentrate on his work. His mind kept going back to what the sadhu had told him in Puri. One day, Phoni Babu, his colleague who sat at the next table, lit a cigarette when it was time for their lunch break, and said, 'Why are you so preoccupied, Mr Mitter? What's on your mind?'

Then he inhaled deeply, letting out in the next instant a cloud of smoke, which got into Nidhiram's throat and made him cough. This was surprising, since Nidhiram often smoked himself. He was used to it. Why then did it upset him today? Why, he had a packet of Wills in his own pocket! It suddenly occurred to him that he had not had the cigarette he normally had at around eleven, after a cup of tea. This had never happened before. So here was another change—a big one—that had crept into his daily habits. Nidhiram realized it, but said nothing about it to Phoni Babu.

After that day, Nidhiram began to change very quickly. He gave up wearing a lungi at home, and began wearing dhotis. Then he became a vegetarian, and started going to a homoeopath instead of his own doctor. He even switched the parting in his hair from the left to the right. He had always been clean shaven. Now he grew a small, thin moustache. His hair grew longer, over his neck.

One Saturday, Nidhiram took his wife to see a play. His friend, Manotosh Bagchi, was playing the hero. Nidhiram realized what a capable actor he was. He knew how to impress the audience; and the audience, too, showed its appreciation by breaking into frequent spontaneous applause.

Nidhiram felt a fresh longing to become an actor. He went to see his friend backstage after the show, and praised his acting prowess with the utmost sincerity. Then he added a few words of regret about his own failure to appear on the stage. Manotosh slapped his back. 'Why do you wish to invite trouble, my friend? Do you realize how uncertain things are in the theatre?' he asked. 'I may be here today, but tomorrow I may well be gone. You are better off with your steady job, far more secure.'

Nidhiram had gone to the matinee show. On his way back from the theatre, he stopped in College Street and bought a few plays, as well as books on the theatre. Manorama, his wife, asked, 'What will you do with these?'

'Read them,' Nidhiram replied briefly.

'But I've never seen you read plays!'

'Now you shall,' said Nidhiram.

Manorama had not failed to notice the changes her husband had undergone. But she had not commented on them. She did not know anything about the sadhu or what he had told Nidhiram, for she had not accompanied him to Puri. On that occasion, she had had to go back to her own house to look after her ailing father. Nidhiram had decided not to tell her anything, either.

However, so many changes had occurred over the last few months that they were bound to attract his wife's attention. To tell the truth, she was happy with these changes, for they were all for the better.

Nidhiram read all his new books over the Christmas holidays. Then he learnt a number of lines the hero of one of the plays was supposed to speak, and held a little performance for his wife. Manorama's eyes nearly popped out. She could never have imagined that such talent was hidden within her husband.

Nidhiram was thirty-nine years old. No one at that age can possibly grow taller. The average male grows in height up to the age of twenty-five, at the most. But Nidhiram noticed one day that the sleeves of his shirts appeared shorter. He measured his height once more. It was now five feet nine inches. He did not disclose this extraordinary occurrence to anyone except his wife. Manorama had to be told because he needed to get new clothes made. It proved to be an expensive business, but overjoyed by this unexpected turn of events, Nidhiram did not mind spending the extra money. Besides, it was not just his height that had improved. His complexion now looked clearer, and his physical strength had increased considerably.

One day, he returned from work and spent a long time standing before the mirror fixed on his wardrobe. Then he took a decision. He would go to Shambazar, where most of the theatre companies had their offices. He had heard that the Samrat Opera Company had recently lost Moloy Kumar, who used to play their male lead. Nidhiram would go and talk to the manager of Samrat.

He did not waste any time. Soon, he was sitting face to face with the manager, Priyanath Saha. 'Have you had any experience?' the manager asked.

'No, none,' Nidhiram admitted frankly, 'but I can act. Would you like me to show you? I know all the lines Moloy Kumar spoke in your play *Echoes*.'

'Really?' said Priyanath Saha. 'Akhil Babu!' he called a second later. A bald, middle-aged man lifted a curtain and entered the room.

'Did you call me?' he asked.

'Yes. Arrange an audition for this man. He says he knows Moloy's lines. See if he'll do.'

It did not take them long to find out. In only a few minutes, Nidhiram proved that he was not just good, but in fact, much better as an actor than their departed hero.

On the first of January, he resigned from his job and joined Samrat. His starting salary was two thousand five hundred. If the audience liked him, it would go up soon, he was assured.

No one in his old office had ever thought that he might leave them one day. 'Well, change is inevitable, isn't it?' Nidhiram said to his colleagues philosophically. 'It would be a mistake to assume that every man would remain the same, or do the same thing, all his life!'

Even so, he could not cut himself off completely from his old friends and colleagues. One Monday, he turned up during their lunch hour for a chat, and learnt that his vacant post had been filled. It was Phoni Babu who gave him this news. 'This new man,' he said, 'is your opposite. I believe he used to be an actor before.'

Nidhiram felt curious. 'An actor? What's his name?'

'Manotosh Bagchi. Apparently, he had met a sadhu in Puri. This sadhu told him that a lot of changes were in store for him. The man was quite tired of his life in the theatre. He says he's far happier now with a quiet, steady job!'

Translated by Gopa Majumdar

First published in Bengali in 1986

Nitai and the Holy Man

It has been said, by someone wise, that the category most human beings fall into can only be called average. These words may be true, but the category Nitai fell into was not even that. He was inferior in many ways to most people. Not only did he lack in height, but the growth and development of his mind had also remained stunted, ever since his childhood. He had just turned thirty-eight. His job in a bank—he worked as a petty clerk—was wholly insignificant. What he earned was barely adequate for him to support his wife and his thirteen-year-old son. Fortunately he did not have a daughter. If he did, he would have had to sell all his possessions just to get her married. Needless to say, his wife nagged and cursed him a good deal. Soudamini was a real shrew.

It simply meant that both at home and at work, Nitai had to tread cautiously. At home, there was Soudamini. At work, he had all his bosses to consider. How nice it would be if he could do something in life that he could be proud of, that might earn him a lot of praise! But no, Nitai did not think he could ever get that lucky. It was his belief that when God created him, He had something else on His mind, and so failed to pay enough attention to the job in hand. That was the reason why Nitai could never be a success.

Who were the people to whom God had been kind? What were they like? Well, Nitai knew one of them. If asked, he would have immediately cited this man's name as an example. A few days ago, a new sadhu baba had arrived in Calcutta—Jeevananda Maharaj—who had endless followers. The man spoke well, had a good voice, often enchanted people with his explanations of the Gita, and commanded such a lot of respect that people queued up just to touch his feet. He was, it appeared, an incarnation of God Himself. Jeevananda Maharaj had arrived from Krishnanagar, and was staying at the house of a follower in Harrington Street. The whole city was talking about him. There had been holy men before, but none as powerful as him. Not for a long time, anyway.

Nitai and Soudamini both wanted to see him, but according to all reports, for ordinary people like them, that would be very difficult indeed. There was an open patch of ground in front of the house where he was staying. A shamiana had been put up there, and a dais built. Jeevananda sat there before his audience, every morning and evening, and spoke wisely on various spiritual matters. Only the very fortunate could get to sit in the front rows. If it took Jeevananda's fancy, he sometimes called a few of these people and talked to them individually, which doubled their devotion to him.

Nitai could not have dreamt that, one day, he would get the chançe not just to visit this holy man, but to sit in the first row. But it happened, thanks to his brother-in-law, Rasiklal Bose. Rasik was married to Soudamini's sister. He had a good job in a big company, but he had no airs. He visited Nitai and his family often, and always spent a long time laughing and chatting with them. He had always been interested in sadhus and other holy men; so it had not taken him long to join Jeevananda's band of followers, and become one of the few who were closest to him. One Saturday, Rasiklal arrived in Nitai's house and said, 'If you want to see a truly great man, I can take you to him.'

'Who do you mean?'

'Who? There's only one man, my friend. He's staying in Harrington Street. The look in his eyes would tell you what our ancient sages were like. Not being able to see him would really be a big loss for anyone.'

'I know. But I believe it's impossible to get within a hundred yards of that man.'

'Yes, that's true. That applies to most people. But I am very lucky, I am allowed to sit in the front. Babaji seems to have grown rather fond of me. When he speaks, he almost always looks straight at me. It gives me goosepimples sometimes. Would you like to go with me one day?'

'Of course! I never imagined I'd get such a chance.'

'He spent twenty-five years simply in meditation, you know, somewhere in the Himalayas. Near Gangotri, I believe. One look at him will tell you he is totally genuine. Here's one man who has found the truth.'

They fixed a date and time. It was agreed that Rasik would come again at half past six the following Tuesday to collect Nitai and his wife.

'Shall we really get to sit in the front row?' Nitai asked, still unable to believe his luck.

'Absolutely. I guarantee it,' Rasik said emphatically. 'Oh, by the way,' he added, 'wear a little attar, if you can. Babaji is very fond of attar.'

The month being October, it grew dark by six o'clock. Nitai and Soudamini arrived at the house of the barrister, Jatish Sengupta, in Harrington Street. The shamiana under which Jeevananda was sitting had fluorescent lights fixed here and there. The sadhu was visible to all, easily and clearly. At first, Nitai felt somewhat overwhelmed by the presence of a lot of well-dressed men and women; but Rasik dragged him to the front row. He threw himself prostrate on the ground before the sadhu, which meant that Nitai and his wife also had to show their respect and touch the feet of the holy man. Then Nitai took his seat among the fortunate few in the front row, and could finally look properly at Jeevananda.

He did cut a rather impressive figure. There was no doubt about that. His long beard touched his chest, wavy salt-and-pepper hair rippled down to his shoulders; he was wearing a long saffron robe, and three strings of large rudraksha beads round his neck. By his side rested a small heap of garlands made of white, fragrant bel flowers. Obviously, they had been presented by some of his followers. Nitai was not wearing attar or any other perfume, but he realized that many others in the vicinity were. Added to this was incense, burning in a corner. Its smell, combined with different types of perfume, had made the air quite heady.

The sadhu broke his silence by chanting a few lines from the Gita. Then he began explaining their meaning.

Nitai's eyes remained fixed on Jeevananda. There was, in fact, a specific reason for this. Two reasons, to be precise. The first was simply that he appeared to have a slight squint. And the second was a big mole on his left cheek, just under his eye.

These two things made Nitai grow a little distracted. That squint and that mole.

He looked more carefully at Jeevananda's face. He was well into his explanatory speech by this time. He had a melodious voice; it was likely that he was a good singer, too. The harmonium and drum placed beside him indicated that music would follow the discourse, and Babaji would sing.

Suddenly, he stumbled over a word. Only for a second, but the stammer was unmistakable. A thought flashed through Nitai's mind, with the speed of lightning. Involuntarily, a name escaped through his lips, quite loudly: 'Chheno!'

His voice rose higher than the sadhu's. Many people exclaimed, a mixture of surprise and annoyance in their tone. Who was this thoughtless, ill-mannered brute, who could shout like that during an important religious discourse?

Rasiklal, like everyone else, was perfectly taken aback. What was the matter with his brother-in-law? Had he gone mad? Who was Chheno, anyway?

Having uttered that one single word, Nitai had fallen silent. But so had Jeevananda. He was staring straight at Nitai.

What followed was something Nitai was not prepared for. Perhaps he should have been. The two chief followers who were seated beside Jeevananda got up, walked over to Nitai and said, 'You'll have to leave. Babaji's instruction. He does not allow anyone to interrupt him.'

Nitai and his wife rose. Rasik was left with no choice but to follow suit. When they were outside the main gate, Rasik turned to Nitai. 'What happened to you? I gave you the chance to sit so close to Babaji, and you ruined everything!' he said.

'But . . . but . . . it's true!' Nitai protested. 'Your Babaji is Chheno. His real name is Srinath. He and I were in the same class in school, in Katwa.'

It was not possible to explain the whole thing standing in the street. They returned to Nitai's house in Nilmoni Acharya Lane. There, seated on a divan, Nitai told them the whole story.

Srinath, alias Chheno, was a pest, infamous in the entire school. He was older than Nitai, but having failed in his exams three times in a row, he studied in the same class with him. Chheno had a slight squint in one eye, a mole on his left cheek, and stuttered occasionally. But he was good looking, could sing well, and was a good actor. It was because of his ability to sing and act that the school had allowed him to remain in the same class, year after year. If he did not have these redeeming qualities, he would have been rusticated long ago.

The same Chheno had turned into Jeevananda Babaji, who had countless followers, whose discourses were so good that people actually spent hours listening to him, or thought that their lives were fulfilled if they so much as caught a glimpse of the man.

Rasiklal heard him in silence. Then he said, 'Look, it doesn't matter what your Chheno did in school. Anyone can change. I have no doubt that today he is a truly knowledgeable man. Forget what happened in school. We can go back to him tomorrow, and you can beg to be forgiven. Baba is infinitely kind. I am sure he will forgive you.'

But Nitai could not agree. Memories of his school days came rushing back. He had been a simple boy, and Chheno was extremely clever. He had teased and bullied Nitai endlessly. Nitai could never forget how he had suffered at Chheno's hands. At the time, he had been totally unable to defend himself or settle scores. Chheno was far too cunning. And yet, today it was the same Chheno who . . .

Nitai could think no more. He realized he should not have shouted his name like that in front of so many people, but he did not do it purposely. It just happened. After all, how could anyone always behave with propriety, without making a single slip, ever?

Going back to Chheno to apologize was out of the question. No, Nitai could not do it.

The next day was Wednesday. Nitai's office started at ten o'clock. He usually left his house at half past nine. At seven o'clock, when he had just had his tea and opened the morning newspaper, someone knocked on his door. The door opened to the main street. Nitai found a smart and bespectacled young man standing outside.

'You are—?' he began.

'I work for the *Daily News*,' the man said, 'My name is Debashish Sanyal. I am a reporter. I was present in the audience yesterday, when Jeevananda was speaking. I saw what happened. Then I followed you all the way here, just to see where you lived.'

'Really? Why?'

'Because I want to know what made you shout like that, and why you were removed from there. I'd like to record everything you tell me, and then write a report on the whole incident.'

It suddenly dawned upon Nitai that he had acquired an extraordinary power. It was an amazing thing for an ordinary, insignificant man like him. If he spoke to this reporter and told him the full story, he could expose the famous Jeevananda. What a furore that would create among his followers!

Should he do that? Should he unmask the great sadhu for the cheat and the fraud that he was? All he had to do was tell this man something about Jeevananda's school life.

In the next instant, Nitai realized something else. The real reason why he wanted to expose Chheno was simply that, today, somehow, he had become an eminently successful man. Nitai was envious of his success. But that was not all. He could not forget the way Chheno had tormented him. In wishing to talk to this reporter, there was a strong element of wanting to take revenge, to pay Chheno back for what he had done in the past.

No, revealing Jeevananda's past was not going to bring Nitai any pride and glory. There was no reason to take away his success, just because Nitai himself had not been successful in life. Besides, it was true that people changed with age. Who could say for sure that Chheno had not changed completely over the years? The way the human mind worked was so complex, so difficult to grasp. Perhaps Chheno had become a better person? Who knew?

The reporter was looking anxiously at him, waiting for his reply.

Nitai shook his head. 'No, I don't have anything to say about what happened yesterday. It's nothing worth reporting.'

'Nothing?' the young man sounded openly disappointed. 'Surely you have got something to say?'

'No. I just told you. I have nothing to say, nothing at all.'

Needless to say, the *Daily News* did not publish the story. Strangely enough, Jeevananda Babaji, who was supposed to remain in Calcutta for another week, suddenly announced the day after this incident that he had received an urgent telegram and was obliged to leave at once for Patna.

Two years have passed since that day. Jeevananda has not returned to Calcutta.

Translated by Gopa Majumdar
First published in Bengali in 1986

Uncle Tarini, the Maharaja

'Why are you frowning, Uncle?' asked Napla. We had noticed it, too. Uncle Tarini was sitting crosslegged on a divan, his right hand placed on one foot, and was rocking himself gently, backwards and forwards. Between his eyebrows lay a deep crease.

'On a wet evening like this,' Uncle replied, 'until you can provide me with a hot cup of tea, boys, that frown will remain where it is.'

Tea had been ordered only a few minutes ago, as soon as Uncle Tarini had made an appearance. Even so, I raised my voice and called out to our cook to remind him.

'Have you finished concocting a story?' Napla went on. There was no end to his impertinence.

'I do not concoct my stories!' Uncle snapped, pulling a face. 'I have had such a lot of strange and wonderful experiences that if I were to relate each one, it would take me years to finish. You'd be an old man by then.'

The tea arrived. Uncle took a noisy sip, and began: 'You may have heard of the man who became a sultan just for a day. It happened during the time of Humayun. I had a similar experience once. Did I ever tell you the story of how I spent five days as the Maharaja of a princely state?'

'No!' we cried.

'Did you actually have to sit on the throne?' Napla wanted to know.

'No, sir. It happened in 1964. Rajas had stopped sitting on thrones by then. It was a long time after India's independence. However, Raja Gulab Singh was still pretty well known. Everyone in his state addressed him as Maharaja. Anyway, let me get on with my story.'

Uncle Tarini gulped down some more tea and continued:

'I was in Bangalore at the time, looking for something to do. I had worked as the manager of a hotel in Madras for two years, but was now at a loose end once more, roaming like a vagabond. One day, my eyes fell on an advertisement in a newspaper. It was rather peculiar. I had never seen anything like it before. There was the picture of a man. Underneath it, in large letters, it said: "REWARD OF RS 10,000". Then, in smaller letters, it went on to say that if anyone thought their appearance was similar to that of the man in the picture, they should apply with a photo. If found suitable, they would then be called for an interview. The address given was: Bhargav Rao, Diwan, Mandore State,

Mysore. I had heard of Mandore, and knew that it was a princely state. But who was the man in the picture? I had no idea, but realized immediately that I did not look all that different from him. In fact, if I trimmed my moustache a little, there would be hardly any dissimilarities left.

'So I trimmed my moustache, and went to Victoria Photo Studio to get a passport-size photo taken. Then I sent it to Mandore with an application. Ten thousand rupees in those days was a lot of money. It was difficult to resist the temptation.

'A reply came within a week. I had been selected for an interview. All expenses for my travel, board and lodging would be met by the advertisers. All I was required to do was leave for Mandore without a moment's delay. The letter also stated that I should pack enough clothes for ten days.

'I sent them a telegram the next day and left Bangalore. Mandore was only a couple of stations from Hubli. I was going to be met upon arrival. It was a long journey, so I had a lot of time to think. What puzzled me the most was the purpose of the advertisement. What could it mean? The man in the picture appeared to be from a well-to-do family. But why was it suddenly necessary to find his double? It just did not make any sense.

'I got off the train at Mandore clutching my suitcase, and began looking around. Soon, a man in his sixties approached me. "You are Mr Banerjee?" he asked, stretching his right hand towards me. It was clear that the man was startled by my appearance.

'"Yes, I am Banerjee," I said, shaking his hand.

'"My name is Bhargav Rao," the man replied. "I am the Diwan of Mandore. We are fortunate indeed, sir, to have found a candidate like you."

'"A candidate for what?"

'"Let's get into the car. I'll explain everything on the way. The palace is seven kilometres from here. I believe I shall be able to answer all your questions in the time it takes us to get there."

'We got into an old-fashioned but large and comfortable Armstrong Siddeley. The Diwan sat in the back with me. I could see a range of hills through the window; it was most picturesque.

'The Diwan started unravelling the mystery as soon as the car started.

'"You see, Mr Banerjee, we are facing an extremely tricky situation here in Mandore. Call it an accident, if you like; but our Maharaja, Gulab Singh, has suddenly gone insane. He's had to be hospitalized. A well-known doctor from Mysore has arrived to treat him, but I don't think he is going to recover soon. The problem is that in just three days we are expecting a very important visitor from America—the millionaire, Mr Oscar Horenstein. He collects antiques and other objects of art, and spends thousands of dollars on them.

'"Our Raja has a number of antiques in his possession. He wanted to sell some of those to Horenstein because our treasury is in urgent need of money. We have been losing money for some time. There are half a dozen palaces, of various sizes, on the land owned by the Raja. One of them is going to be turned into a hotel. It was the Raja's decision. There is plenty to see in Mandore: a lake, hills, and quite a lot of wildlife in the forests. We have deer, tigers and elephants. Besides, the air here is clean and healthy. So, if there is adequate publicity, there is no reason why a hotel should not turn out to be a profitable business. However, before that business can actually start, we were hoping to get a substantial amount from this Horenstein. That's why we did not tell him about Raja Gulab Singh's illness, or ask him to cancel his visit. You do understand, don't you?"

'I did indeed. "That means that picture in the advertisement was of the Raja, and now I am to play that role. Is that right?"

'"Yes, but only during Horenstein's stay."

'"Where did he meet the Raja?"

'"Minneapolis, in America. The Raja went there in March to visit his son, Mahipal. Mahipal works there as a doctor. There, he met Horenstein at a party, and invited him here. Horenstein, I believe, is also interested in shikar. So we'll have to make arrangements for that as well. Can you shoot?"

'"Yes, though I haven't been out hunting for ten or twelve years."

'"You will be on an elephant here. That is relatively safe."

'"You mentioned something about the Raja's collection. What sort of things has he got?"

'"Mainly weapons. Daggers, swords, shields and pistols—there are plenty of those. You'll be able to see for yourself how valuable they are. Besides, he has old containers of perfume, hookahs, vases and paintings. I don't think Horenstein will need much persuasion from you. From what I've heard, he is already quite interested in buying some of it. The Raja made a list of prices when he heard Horenstein was going to come. I'll pass that on to you."

'Now I had finally grasped what I was required to do. Instead of just for a day, I was to be a sultan for five days. After that, naturally, I would have to go back to being my insignificant self. But the amount offered was not insignificant at all. Ten thousand rupees in 1964 was five times its value today.

'When the car swept in through the huge gate of the palace, I could feel my heart beat faster. But, to tell you the truth, I was not actually nervous. I had caught the Diwan glancing curiously at me several times during our journey. "I could not have dreamt," he finally said, "that we would find a double for the Raja. I had assumed the advertisement would not work, and we would have to ask Horenstein not to come. Now, I am beginning to hope that we will get what we want, without having to reveal the truth."

'The American was expected to reach Mandore on Wednesday. I got there the preceding Sunday. I was told to spend the next three days reading the Raja's diaries, and listening to his voice on a tape recorder. Three of his speeches, delivered in English, were recorded on different tapes. The

Diwan handed them to me, together with leather-bound volumes of the Raja's diaries, maintained over the last ten years. I went through them briefly. The entries had been made in English. The Raja's language was clear and lucid. Details of his daily activities were described in his diaries. I learnt what time he liked to get up in the morning, what exercises he took, what he liked to eat, what he preferred wearing, and that he was not fond of music.

'He had lost his wife three years ago. For two weeks after her death, all the pages in his diary were blank, bearing evidence of his shock and grief. For me, it was a useful discovery.

'On the third day, I told the Diwan that I was ready for the job. Then I added something I had been meaning to say after my first night in the palace. "Diwanji, I am perfectly satisfied with every arrangement, but I cannot continue to sleep in the Raja's bed. It's too soft. I cannot sleep on such a soft mattress."

'"Well then, where are you going to sleep?" he asked.

'"Why, you have so many smaller palaces here. Lal kothi, peeli kothi, safed kothi. Couldn't I stay in one of those?"

'"Yes, you could," replied the Diwan, looking faintly concerned. "Lal kothi would be most suitable for you, I think. It has quite a comfortable bedroom. Gulab Singh's father used to stay there sometimes. Shatrughna Singh did not like staying in the same building for long. So various small houses had had to be built for him."

'"Very well. I will stay in lal kothi."

'"Yes, but . . ."

'"Why, is there a problem?"

'"There is just one thing . . ."

'"What is it?"

'"Well, you see, at the age of fifty, Shatrughna Singh lost his mind. He killed himself—put a gun to his head—in that bedroom in lal kothi."

'"So you think that room is haunted?"

'"I don't know. No one has ever slept in it since Shatrughna Singh's death."

'"Never mind. That's where I'll stay. I don't want to miss such an experience. I have stayed in haunted houses before, even seen some ghosts. So I'm not afraid of them. But please make sure that my bed is not so soft."

'The Diwan agreed to make the necessary arrangements. From the look on his face, he seemed surprised at my words. Perhaps he had not expected a Bengali to show such courage.

'The American arrived that afternoon. About fifty years of age, he was taller than me by about three inches; his face looked as if all the flesh that should have been evenly spread over it was concentrated only on his chin; his blue eyes stared out of glasses with a golden frame. His salt-and-pepper hair was brushed back.

'"Let him go to safed kothi and rest for a while in his room. There's no need to bring him to see you right away," the Diwan said to me. "We don't wish to appear too eager, there's our prestige to consider. But I must warn you that he appears somewhat short-tempered. The car got a puncture on the way from the station. That seemed to annoy him a lot."

'"I decided to remain calm, even if Mr Horenstein appeared cross. When I finally met him, he said, half jokingly and half reprovingly: "Well, Maharaj, what kind of a welcome is this? I was made to stand in the hot sun for fifteen minutes on my way here!"

'I apologized as much as I could, giving him my word that such a thing would not happen again during his stay. The man took a chair, and picked up a glass of sherbet. The cool drink seemed to calm him down a little.

'"Do tell me what you'd like to do here," I said after a while. "I have a pretty good idea, and I've had all the arrangements made. But even so, I would like to hear it from you."

'"Well, I like hunting. I want to look for a tiger . . . have you arranged for that?"

'I nodded. He went on, "And I want to buy a few things from your collection. My silver wedding anniversary is coming up. I'd like to buy something nice for my wife. I hope you've got some pretty things?"

'"You can see for yourself what I've got. There's some very good stuff in our collection, some of it a hundred and fifty years old."

'We took him to the museum after lunch. This was my first visit, too. What I saw was a treat for the eyes. But my heart felt heavy at the thought of losing some of those beautiful things. Horenstein turned out to be quite a good connoisseur of antiques. Quickly, he began to separate those that he wished to buy. Soon, he had made a pile worth about a million rupees. Even so, there was a frown on his face. What was wrong? "All this is fine," he said eventually, "but I still haven't found anything suitable for Cathleen. Don't you have a diamond brooch or something? My wife is crazy about stones. If only I could get a nice stone for her here!"

'I shook my head. "I'm very sorry, Mr Horenstein. If I had a stone worth selling, most certainly I'd have shown it to you."

'The rest of the day was spent in taking the American around in the Raja's Lagonda, to show him all the sights of Mandore. In the evening, we had a game of chess. I could see that Horenstein was still upset about not getting anything for his wife. Perhaps that was the reason why he kept making mistakes. Bearing in mind that he had a quick temper, I deliberately played badly and let him win.

'At nine o'clock that evening, we finished a large and sumptuous meal, which was followed by coffee and brandy. Horenstein lingered over the latter, but eventually retired for the night in safed kothi. Raja Gulab Singh did not drink, and nor did I—so there was something else we had in common. I had a cup of coffee and a Havana cigar, and then rose to go to lal kothi. The Diwan himself decided to accompany me.

'"How is Gulab Singh today?" I asked him.

'He shook his head and clicked his tongue regretfully. "He's still the same. Raving and ranting, and driving the nurses up the wall. Even the doctors are having a difficult time."

'The bed in the new palace proved to be quite satisfactory. The Diwan said before leaving me, "You are indeed a brave man, Mr Banerjee. This is the first time anyone has offered to sleep in this room since Shatrughna Singh's death."

'"Please don't worry about me, sir. I can look after myself under any circumstance."

'There was a bedside lamp. I switched it on and began reading a book on the history of Mandore. Then, at around half past eleven, I switched the light off. There was a large window on the western side, through which came moonlight and a soft breeze. It did not take me long to fall asleep.

'When I woke, the moon had moved further and the room was filled with a hazy light. The minute I opened my eyes, I realized I was not alone in the room. The door was still bolted from inside, but a man was standing near the window, looking straight at me. He was tall like me, and his general appearance was similar to mine, except that his moustache was thicker. The light was not good enough to see clearly, but I realized that the man was dressed in a dark suit.

'I propped myself up on an elbow and sat up. There was a slight tremor in my heart, but I refuse to call it fear. I did not have to be told that the intruder was not alive. It was the ghost of Gulab Singh's father, Shatrughna Singh, who had committed suicide in the same room. There could be no doubt about that.

'"I have come to tell you something," said the figure, in a deep voice.

'"What have you got to say?"

'"Thirty years ago, I bought an extremely valuable stone in Vienna. It was an emerald. It was called the Dorian Emerald. You don't often get to see a stone like that."

'"What happened to it?"

'"It's still there, in a drawer in my son's wardrobe. It's kept in a red velvet box. Sell it, if you can. Since you've found a buyer, don't miss this chance."

'"Why are you saying this?"

'"That stone is cursed. I did not know that when I bought it. Its first owner was Count Dorian of Luxemburg. He committed suicide by jumping off the roof of his castle. Every single bone in his body was broken. After this, that emerald changed hands nineteen times. Each of its owners killed himself. I eventually came to know this fact, but still could not believe that such tragedy could be linked with a beautiful object like that. But now I know beyond any doubt that it was the emerald that was responsible for my death. If my son has lost his sanity today, it is because of that stone. Only, nothing has happened to my grandson. At least, not yet. But what if in the future . . .?" the ghost stopped.

'"You need not worry any more," I reassured him. "I am absolutely sure that I can get rid of that stone."

'"In that case, I had better go. Goodbye."

'The figure dissolved into the faint moonlight. I remained awake for the rest of the night.

'The next morning, I told the Diwan about my encounter with Shatrughna Singh. He stared at me, totally amazed. "But I have never even heard of such a stone!" he exclaimed.

'"Maybe not. Nevertheless, we must open the Raja's wardrobe and look in all the drawers."

'Finding the small red velvet box proved quite easy. The emerald in it left me bereft of speech. I had never seen a stone like that in my life.

'I sent word to Horenstein. "Look," I said to him when he arrived, "you wanted a stone, didn't you? There is a stone in my private collection. I did not mention it to you before because my father had bought it, and I wanted to treasure his memory. However, I've now thought things over, and seeing that you are our distinguished guest, and you have travelled thousands of miles to visit us, I don't think you should go back empty-handed. See if you like this emerald."

'The American's eyes nearly popped out of their sockets when he saw the stone. "It's a beauty . . . a beauty!" I heard him mutter under his breath. Then he added, "I don't want to take anything else."

'The emerald was handed over to Horenstein. In return, he wrote a cheque and passed it to us.

'Surprisingly enough, the hospital informed us that evening that the Raja was feeling a lot better.

'We went to find a tiger the next day, but things did not go very well for Horenstein. The beaters managed to make a tiger run out of the forest and emerge quite close to the elephant Horenstein was riding. Despite that, he missed it when he fired. In the end, it was a bullet from my gun that killed it.

'Horenstein left for Delhi the following day.

'Two days later, I read in the papers that a Pan Am flight had run into problems just as it had taken off. Apparently, somehow a vulture got into its engine at the moment of take off. The engine packed up, and the plane crashed. Luckily, no one was hurt, but about twenty-five passengers had to be taken to a hospital for treatment of nervous shock. Among them was the American millionaire, Oscar M. Horenstein.'

Translated by Gopa Majumdar
First published in Bengali in 1986

Anukul

'He's got a name, hasn't he?' Nikunja Babu asked.

'Oh yes, he has.'

'What is it?'

'Anukul.'

A robot supplying agency had opened in Chowringhee about six months ago. Nikunja Babu had always wanted a mechanical servant. His business had lately been doing rather well, so he could now afford to fulfil his little desire.

Nikunja Babu looked at the robot. It was an android, which meant that it looked exactly like an ordinary human being although it was really a machine. It had a pleasant appearance, its age was around twenty-two.

'What kind of work will this robot do?' Nikunja Babu asked.

The man behind the counter lit a cigarette and replied, 'He'll do more or less everything an ordinary servant does. The only thing he doesn't know is how to cook. Apart from that, he can do the washing and cleaning, make the beds, make tea, open doors and windows—just about everything. But don't send him out. He can manage everything in the house, but he couldn't go and do your shopping. And . . . er . . . you must talk to him politely. He expects one to say "please" and "thank you".'

'He's not ill tempered, I hope?'

'No, no. You'll find him troublesome only if you raise your hand. Our robots cannot stand physical assault.'

'There is no likelihood of that. But suppose someone gives him a slap. What will he do?'

'He will take revenge.'

'How?'

'He might use the middle finger of his right hand. He can give a high voltage electric shock with that finger.'

'Can that result in death?'

'Certainly. And the law cannot do anything about this for a robot cannot be punished like a normal human being. But I must say there has never been a case like this so far.'

'Does he sleep at night?'

'No. Robots don't sleep.'

'What does he do then all night?'

'He just sits quietly in the corner. Robots don't lack patience.'

'Does he have a mind?'

'Robots can, at times, feel and understand things that a human being can't. But then, not all robots are so sensitive. It's a matter of luck, really. Only time can tell how gifted a robot is.'

Nikunja Babu turned towards the robot and said, 'Anukul, you have no objection to working for me, have you?'

'Why should I object?' said Anukul in a perfectly normal voice. He was wearing a blue striped shirt and black shorts. His neatly brushed hair had a side parting, his complexion was fair, his teeth bright and clean and his mouth parted in a half smile. His whole appearance inspired confidence.

'Come along then.'

Nikunja Babu's Maruti van was waiting outside. He paid for Anukul by cheque and came out with him. Anukul's movements were no different from those of an ordinary man.

Nikunja Babu lived in Salt Lake. He was not married. A few of his friends dropped in to play cards in the evening. They had already been told about the arrival of a mechanical servant. Nikunja Babu had, in fact, done some research before acquiring Anukul. Quite a number of people amongst the upper classes of Calcutta had already got robots to work for them. Mr Mansukhani, Girija Bose, Pankaj Datta Roy, Mr Chhabria—everyone said they were very satisfied and that their servant gave them no trouble at all.

'Our Jeevanlal does everything immediately, just as he's told,' said Mr Mansukhani. 'I'm convinced he's not just a machine—he must have a real brain and a heart!'

Nikunja Babu formed a similar opinion within seven days. Anukul's way of working was just perfect. He seemed to have grasped fully the logical link between one task and another. If asked whether the water for his bath was ready, he would not only bring the water immediately but would also provide a soap and a towel for his master. He would then get his master's clothes and shoes and everything else that might be needed. And he did everything so willingly that there was no question of being impolite to him.

Nikunja Babu's friends took a little time to get used to Anukul, especially Vinay Pakrashi. He often spoke rather rudely to his own servants and, on one occasion, he happened to address Anukul a little harshly. Anukul did not lose his calm. 'If you are rude to me, old boy,' he said quietly, 'I am going to be rude to you!'

Vinay Babu did not make the same mistake again.

Nikunja Babu formed a very good relationship with Anukul. Anukul began to do things for him without being told. His master found this surprising, but recalled that the man in the robot supplying agency had indeed told him that certain robots had something akin to a brain and could think. Anukul must belong to that category.

But what was most difficult to believe was that Anukul did not sleep at all. He was so much like a real human being, surely he slept a little at night? Nikunja Babu decided to check this out one night. Just as he peeped into Anukul's room, he heard Anukul say, 'Do you want anything, sir?'

Embarrassed, Nikunja Babu said, 'No,' and retraced his steps. It was possible to converse with Anukul on a wide range of subjects. He appeared to know a lot about sports, cinema, theatre, literature. He seemed to be better informed about most things than his master. Nikunja Babu marvelled at the extent of his knowledge and the skill of the robot makers.

But all good things come to an end.

Nikunja Babu happened to make a few wrong moves in his business and, within a year of Anukul's arrival, his financial situation deteriorated. He continued to pay the hire charges for Anukul, which was two thousand rupees a month. But if his financial situation did not improve, who knew when he would have to stop? The robot supplying agency had told him Anukul would be taken away if the monthly payment was not made. Clearly, Nikunja Babu would have to be very careful with his money.

But something happened at this time to upset all his plans.

One fine day, Nikunja Babu's uncle turned up. 'I was getting rather bored in Chandan Nagar all by myself—so I thought I'd come and spend a few days with you,' he said.

This uncle of Nikunja Babu—called Nibaran Banerjee—came occasionally to stay with his nephew. Nikunja Babu had lost his father many years ago and Nibaran was the only uncle left among the three he had had. An irascible old man, he was reported to have made a lot of money as a lawyer, although that was impossible to tell from the way he lived. The man was indeed a miser.

'You're very welcome to spend a few days here, Uncle,' said Nikunja Babu, 'but I must tell you something right away. I have now got a mechanical servant. You must have heard of the companies that are making robots in Calcutta.'

'Yes, I've seen the advertisements. But where is your servant from? You know I'm a little fussy in this matter. Is this new servant doing the cooking?'

'No, no, no,' reassured Nikunja Babu, 'I've still got the old cook. So you needn't worry. The new one is called Anukul and . . . er . . . you must speak to him politely. He doesn't like being shouted at.'

'Doesn't like it, eh?'

'No, he doesn't.'

'Do I have to act according to *his* likes and dislikes?'

'That applies to everyone, not just you. But you won't find fault with his work.'

'Why did you have to get into this mess?'

'I've told you already—he is a very good worker.'

'Well, then call him. Let's see what he's like.'

'Anukul!' Nikunja Babu called out. Anukul arrived immediately.

'Meet my uncle,' said Nikunja Babu, 'he's going to stay here for some time.'

'Very good, sir.'

'My goodness—he speaks just like a man,' exclaimed Nibaran Banerjee. 'All right then, could you please give me some hot water? I'd like to have a bath. It's turned a little cool after the rains—but I am so accustomed to having a bath twice a day.'

'Yes, sir.'

Anukul left to carry out the instructions.

Nibaran Babu's arrival did not result in any improvement in his nephew's financial status. All that happened was that Nikunja Babu's friends stopped coming in the evening. It was not proper to play rummy or poker in front of an uncle; besides, Nikunja Babu could no longer afford to gamble.

It was difficult to tell how long his uncle would stay this time. He usually came and went just as he liked. This time it seemed as though he was nicely settled for a while—and the reason was Anukul. The mechanical servant appeared to be attracting and repulsing him equally. He could not deny that Anukul's efficiency as a worker was irreproachable. At the same time, however, he could not quite accept the fact that one was expected to be careful in one's behaviour when dealing with a mere servant.

He said to his nephew one day, 'Nikunja, this servant of yours is giving me a lot of trouble at times.'

'Why, what happened?' Nikunja Babu asked, worried.

'I was reciting a few lines from the *Gita* the other day and that damned servant had the cheek to correct what I was saying. Even if the words I had spoken were wrong, it's not for him to correct me, is it? Isn't that a bit too much? I felt like giving him a tight slap. But, I managed to control myself with difficulty.'

'No, no, Uncle, you must never raise your hand—it can have a disastrous effect. The suppliers told me so. The best thing would be not to speak at all when he's around.'

Nibaran Babu went away muttering to himself.

As the days went by, Nikunja Babu's earnings grew less and less. He began to find it very difficult to make the monthly payment for Anukul. He could not help mentioning this to Anukul one day.

'Anukul, my business isn't doing very well.'

'I know.'

'Yes, perhaps you do. But what I don't know is how long I shall be able to keep you. I don't wish to part with you, and yet . . .'

'Let me think about it.'

'Think about what?'

'If there's a solution to the problem.'

'How is your thinking going to help? Running a business is not your line, is it?'

'No, but do let me try.'

'All right. But it may not be possible for me to keep you for very long—I just wanted to warn you.'

'Yes, sir.'

Two months passed. It was a Sunday. Nikunja Babu's careful calculations showed that he could, at the very most, afford to keep Anukul for another two months. After that, he would have to look for a human servant. In fact, he had already started looking for one. The whole thing depressed him no end. And, to make matters worse, it was pouring cats and dogs.

Nikunja Babu pushed the newspaper aside and was about to call Anukul to ask for a cup of tea when Anukul appeared.

'What is it, Anukul?'

'There's been an accident, sir.'

'Accident? What happened?'

'Your uncle was standing near the window and singing a Tagore song about the rain. He got some of the words wrong, so I felt obliged to correct him. He got so angry at this that he gave me a slap. So I had to pay him back.'

'Pay him back?'

'Yes. I had to give him a high voltage shock.'

'Does that mean . . .?'

'He is dead. But there was a clap of thunder just as I gave him the shock.'

'Yes, I heard it.'

'So you needn't tell people the real reason for his death.'

'But . . .'

'Don't worry, sir. This will do you a lot of good.'

And so it did. Two days after his uncle's death, Nikunja Babu got a call from his uncle's lawyer, Bhaskar Bose. Nibaran Babu had left all his property to his nephew. Its total value was a little more than a million rupees.

Translated by Gopa Majumdar

First published in Bengali in 1986

The Scarecrow

Mriganko Babu's suspicions were confirmed just as they were about to reach Panagarh. His car ran out of petrol. The petrol gauge had not been functioning properly for quite a while. He had pointed this out to his driver, Sudheer, before they set out this morning. But Sudheer had paid no attention. There had, in fact, been less petrol in the tank than the gauge had shown.

'What are you going to do now?' Mriganko Babu asked.

'I'll walk to Panagarh, and come back with more petrol,' Sudheer replied.

'How far is Panagarh?'

'About three miles.'

'That means I must wait here for at least two and a half hours. It's all your fault. What am I going to do? Have you thought of that?'

Mriganko Babu was an amiable man. He did not usually snap at his driver or servants. But the thought of sitting alone in his car for more than two hours, in the middle of nowhere, made him irritable.

'Well, you'd better leave. Can we make it back to Calcutta by eight o'clock? It's now half past three.'

'Oh yes, sir. We'll certainly be back by eight.'

'Here's the money for the petrol. Don't make this mistake again. You must never take such a risk on a long journey.'

Sudheer took the money and left for Panagarh.

Mrigankoshekhar Mukhopadhyay was a famous and popular writer. A club in Durgapur had invited him to a cultural function, in order to felicitate him. He could not get a reserved seat on the train, hence his departure by car. He had left for Durgapur quite early in the morning, soon after a cup of tea. He was now on his way back. He was not one to believe in superstitions, and certainly he never consulted the almanac before travelling anywhere. However, now it did occur to him that if he had bothered to look at the almanac today, it would not be surprising to find that it forbade long journeys.

He got out of the car, stretched, and lit a cigarette. Then he looked around.

It was the end of January. All the crops had been removed from the fields. The empty, barren fields stretched for miles. In the far distance, a small hut could be seen standing next to a tamarind tree. There was no other sign of habitation. Still further stood a row of palm trees, beyond which lay a dense, dark forest. This was the scene that greeted him on one side of the road—on the eastern side, that is.

On the western side, things were not all that different. About forty feet away from the road was a pond, but it did not have a great deal of water in it. The few trees that were visible were all quite far, except some thorny bushes. There were two huts, but no sign of people. In the middle of the field was a scarecrow. To the north, in the sky, there were clouds; but it was quite sunny where Mriganko Babu was standing.

Although it was winter, Mriganko Babu began to feel warm in the sun after a while. So he returned to the car, took out a detective novel from his bag and began to read it.

In the last few minutes, two Ambassadors and a lorry had gone past, one of the cars in the direction of Calcutta. None of the drivers stopped to ask if he needed any help. All Bengalis are selfish, Mriganko Babu thought. They would never think of considering the welfare or convenience of others—at least, not if it meant causing themselves any inconvenience. Would he have done the same? Perhaps. After all, he was a Bengali, too. He might be a well-known writer, but his fame could not have removed the faults inherent in him, surely?

Rather unexpectedly, the clouds from the north spread quickly and covered the sun. At the same time, a cool breeze started blowing. Mriganko Babu took out a pullover from his bag and slipped it on. The sun would set by five o'clock. It would grow cooler then. Oh, what an awful situation Sudheer had landed him into!

Mriganko Babu discovered that he could not concentrate on his book. Perhaps he should try to think of a new plot for a story. The *Bharat* magazine had asked for a story, but he had not yet written one for them. A plot had started to form in his head, even during the short journey from Durgapur. Now he took out his notebook and jotted a few points down.

No, sitting in the car was boring.

He put his notebook away, climbed out and lit another cigarette. Then he walked a few paces and stood in the middle of the road. It seemed as if he was the only human being in the whole world. He had never felt so completely desolate.

But no, there was someone else.

It was that scarecrow.

There was a small patch of land where someone had grown some plants, perhaps more winter crop. The scarecrow was standing right in the middle of it. A bamboo pole had been fixed vertically on the ground, and another was placed horizontally across it. The two ends of the second pole stretched out like two arms. A shirt had been slipped onto this structure. Its sleeves covered the 'arms'. Over the free end of the vertical pole, an earthen pot had been placed, upside-down. It was not very easy to see from this distance, but Mriganko Babu could guess that the pot had been painted black, and huge eyes had been drawn on it with white paint. How strange—it was this weird figure that birds mistook for a real person, and were frightened enough not to cause any harm to the crop. Were birds really that foolish? Why, dogs didn't get taken in! They could, of course, smell a real person. Didn't crows and sparrows have a similar sense of smell?

Sunlight appeared through a crack in the clouds and fell on the scarecrow. Mriganko Babu saw that the scarecrow was wearing a printed shirt. He had seen that torn, red and black printed shirt before. Or, at least, it reminded him of someone. Who could it be? Mriganko Babu tried very hard, but failed to remember. Yet, he felt sure that he had seen someone wear such a shirt, a long time ago.

Mriganko Babu looked at his watch. It was twenty minutes past four. There was tea in a flask in the car. He could help himself to some of it now. He returned to the car, poured tea into the cap of the flask and drank it. Now he felt a little warmer.

The sun peered again through the dark clouds. It was just over the trees on the western side. In about five minutes, it would set. A reddish light fell on the scarecrow.

Another Ambassador passed Mriganko Babu's car. He drank some more tea, then got out again. Sudheer was not going to be back for another hour. How could he spend that time?

The western sky had turned crimson. The clouds had moved away. The red disc soon sank into the horizon. It would not be long before dusk fell.

That scarecrow. For some unknown reason, Mriganko Babu continued to feel strangely drawn towards that figure. He looked steadily at it. In a few minutes, he noticed a few things that made his heart beat faster.

Had its appearance changed somewhat? Had the two arms been lowered a little?

Wasn't it standing a little less stiffly, and more like a real man?

And what was that? Was there a second pole, standing upright, next to the first one? Or were those not bamboo poles at all, but legs?

The black pot, too, seemed much smaller.

Mriganko Babu normally did not smoke heavily. But, at this moment, he felt the need to light another cigarette. Standing here in this remote spot, he was seeing things.

Could the figure of a scarecrow come to life? No, of course not. But . . . Mriganko Babu's eyes went back to it. Now there could be no doubt at all. It had moved forward. No. It was more than that. The scarecrow was moving, advancing towards him.

It was walking with a limp, but most certainly it had two legs. Instead of an earthen pot, it had a human head. But it still had the same shirt on; and a short, slightly dirty dhoti.

'Babu!' A tremor shot through Mriganko Babu's body. The scarecrow had actually spoken with a human voice, and he had recognized it. It was the voice of Abhiram, who had been Mriganko Babu's servant, many years ago. His village used to be somewhere in this region. Mriganko Babu had once asked him where he came from, and he had said his village was next to Mankar. Why, Mankar was the name of the station that came before Panagarh!

Terrified, Mriganko Babu took a few steps backwards and stood leaning heavily against his car. Abhiram was now much closer, standing only about ten yards away.

'Can you recognize me, Babu?' he asked.

Mriganko Babu mustered all his courage and said, 'You are Abhiram, aren't you?'

'Yes. So you did recognize me, even after all these years.'

Abhiram looked no different from an ordinary, normal man. Perhaps that was why Mriganko Babu could find the courage to speak. 'Yes,' he said, 'it was your shirt that reminded me of you. Didn't I buy you that shirt?'

'Yes, that's right. You did a lot for me, Babu. But why did it all have to end so badly? I was perfectly innocent. Why didn't you believe me?'

Mriganko Babu recalled what had happened, three years ago. Abhiram had worked for his family for twenty years. Everyone trusted him. However, one day he seemed to have lost his head. He stole the gold watch Mriganko Babu had been given as a wedding gift. Abhiram denied the charge, of course, but he had had both the time and the opportunity to remove the object. Besides, when Mriganko Babu's father called a local witch doctor who cast a spell and made an ordinary wicker tray spin and rotate until it stopped, pointing at Abhiram, there could possibly be no doubt about his guilt. Abhiram lost his job.

'Do you know what happened to me after I left?' he now asked. 'I never worked anywhere else. I couldn't, because I fell ill. I got dropsy, and it became serious. But I had no money to go to a doctor, or buy medicines, or even eat properly. I never recovered. My son kept this shirt. He wore it for some time, then it got torn. So it became something a scarecrow could wear. And I became that scarecrow. Do you know why? Because I knew that one day I would meet you again. My heart longed—yes, even a dead man can have a heart—to tell you what I learnt after death.'

'What did you learn, Abhiram?'

'When you go home tonight, look under your wardrobe. That's where you'll find your watch, pushed to the back. It has been lying there for the last three years. Your new servant does not sweep every corner, so he did not find it. When you get it back, you will know that Abhiram was not a thief.'

The figure of Abhiram became hazy. It was already quite dark. Mriganko Babu heard his voice once more: 'Now I have found peace. After so many years, at last I've been able to tell you the truth. Oh, it's such a relief! . . . Goodbye, Babu. I must go.'

Abhiram disappeared before Mriganko Babu's eyes.

'I've brought the petrol, sir!'

The sound of Sudheer's voice woke Mriganko Babu up. He had fallen asleep in the car, thinking of a suitable plot for a story. In his hand he still held his pen. As soon as he opened his eyes, he glanced quickly at the scarecrow. It was still standing in the distance, exactly as he had seen it before.

On reaching home, Mriganko Babu went straight to his room and searched under his wardrobe. He had no difficulty in finding his watch. He decided that if something ever got stolen from his house, from now on, he would never seek a witch doctor's help.

Translated by Gopa Majumdar
First published in Bengali in 1987

Kutum-Katam

'Where did you find this?'

'Quite near my house,' Dilip replied. 'There's some empty land, you see; all it has are a few trees and bushes. I found it lying under a tree. I saw in Alok's house that he had found a tree trunk and fixed a round sheet of glass on top and was using it as a table. So I thought perhaps I could do something similar. Well, I didn't find a tree trunk, but this.'

'This' was just a part of a broken branch. Held at a certain angle, it looked like a four-legged animal. One could even make it stand on its four legs, although one of the legs being smaller than the rest, it leant to one side. Its back was arched like a bow. It had a long neck, and it was not altogether impossible to imagine the uneven portion at its end as some sort of a face. It also seemed to have a thick tail, about an inch long. All things considered, it was something worth looking at. I was surprised that Dilip had noticed it lying on the ground. But then, he had always had a special eye, the eye of an artist. When we were in school, he used to place petals or bits of fern between the pages of his books. There were various little artistic objects strewn all over his house which bore evidence of his refined taste. Once, he had gone from Bolpur to a place called Gushkora to see how the blacksmiths there made dhokra figures. He had brought back samples of their work for all of us—owls, fish, a figure of Ganesh, and a bowl. They were beautiful.

'This is nice, but you are not the first to pick up something like this. Someone else was known to collect broken branches with strange shapes, long before you started,' I told him.

'I know. Abanindranath Tagore, wasn't it? Rabindranath's nephew? I believe he used to call his pieces "kutum-katam". But what about this one? What kind of animal does it remind you of? What can we call it? A fox? A pig? A dog?'

'We'll think of a name. Where are you going to keep it?'

'On the shelf in my bedroom; for the time being, anyway. I only found it yesterday. I showed it to you because you happened to drop by.'

I work in an advertising agency. Dilip has a job in a bank. He has not married. I, on the other hand, have a family. My son is five years old and has just started going to school. A couple of our friends—Sitangshu and Ranen—join us occasionally, and we play bridge in Dilip's house.

A few days after that day, Dilip showed the branch to the others. Ranen, matter-of-fact and devoid of any imagination, remarked: 'Why are you filling your house with such rubbish? How can you say it looks like an animal? Why, I can't see anything! Throw it away, do you realize it may be full of germs? Look, there are ants crawling all over it!'

No one paid him any attention. We played until half past nine that evening. Then, as the others took their leave, Dilip made a slight gesture to indicate that he would like me to wait.

'What is it?' I asked, when he returned after seeing the others to the door. 'You look as if there's something on your mind.'

Dilip took a deep breath before making his reply. 'You will laugh the whole thing off, I know. But I have to tell you.'

'Tell me what?'

'About that branch. I don't believe in supernatural things. Yet, I don't know what else to call it.'

'What are you talking about?'

'In the middle of the night . . . I can hear a strange sound. It comes from the shelf in my room where I've put that animal.'

'What kind of sound?'

'It's a sort of whistle. You know, the kind of noise you might hear if wind blew through a small hole. But it sounds kind of sad, rather pathetic. As if someone's crying.'

'What do you do when you hear that noise?'

'It doesn't continue for very long. But that isn't all. I keep that thing propped up on its legs. This morning, I found it lying on the shelf.'

'It might have fallen. Why, a strong gust through the window would have been enough to knock it down!'

'True. But how do you explain the crying? I used to boast about my courage. I wouldn't any more. I could, of course, get rid of it. But I don't want to. I seem to have grown quite attached to that funny little thing.'

'Well, see how things go in the next couple of days. Tell me if this continues. I think you are quite mistaken in thinking the noise is coming from the animal. Maybe you simply had a dream.'

Honestly, what Dilip had just told me sounded like the ramblings of a lunatic. He always was very imaginative. Anyway, he agreed to wait and watch for a few days before drawing any firm conclusions.

Only two days later, he rang me at work. 'Is that you, Pramod?' he asked.

'Yes. Dilip? What's up?'

'I need to see you. Today.'

I presented myself at his house in the evening. 'Ring your wife,' Dilip said on seeing me.

'Ring my wife? What for?'

'Tell her you're going to spend the night here. You can explain the reason tomorrow, when you go back.'

Dilip appeared to be absolutely serious, so I could not refuse. However, he did not say much more on the subject, even when I asked. But I could guess that the problem involved that animal.

It was very difficult to accept that something extraordinary was happening here in New Alipur, in the twentieth century; but I had read, more than once, that if a supernatural event had to occur, time and place were of no consequence.

When we retired to his room after dinner, Dilip said, 'The more I see it, the more I like that animal. If only it didn't behave so strangely!'

'Are we to keep awake all night?'

'Yes, I think so, if you don't mind. It probably won't be long before something happens. I haven't slept for many nights.'

I said nothing more to Dilip. Whatever happened, this time I would see and hear it for myself.

We sat on his bed. Dilip switched off the light. There was plenty of moonlight. In just two days, we would have a full moon. Some of its light poured in through a window and fell on the floor. In its reflected glow, I could see the animal quite clearly on the shelf.

'May I smoke?' I asked Dilip.

'Of course.'

Dilip himself did not smoke. He did not even drink tea, or chew paan.

I had my first cigarette at eleven. At half past twelve, just as I was about to light my second, I heard the noise. It did sound like wind whistling. Faint, thin, but not without a definite tone. The best way to describe it would be to call it a wail. There was no doubt that the noise was coming from the shelf.

Then I noticed something else. It seemed as if the animal was moving. It kept bending low to raise its hind legs and strike the shelf with them. As a result, there was a tapping noise as well.

Now I could no longer doubt Dilip's words. I could see everything with my own eyes. Dilip was sitting very still next to me, clutching my sleeve with his left hand. He seemed absolutely terrified. Seeing him like that, my own fears diminished somewhat, although I could still feel my heart galloping away.

However, neither of us was prepared for what followed next. It chilled my blood.

The animal suddenly leapt from the shelf and landed on Dilip's chest. Dilip screamed. I managed to reach over and pull it away. But I could feel it struggling in my grasp. Even so, gathering all my courage, I held it tightly in my hand. Slowly, its struggles ceased and it became inert once more.

I rose and put it back on the shelf.

What remained of the night passed without further event, although neither of us could sleep. As soon as dawn broke, Dilip said: 'I am going to take it back and leave it where I had found it.'

I said, 'I've got a different idea.'

'What is it?'

'I didn't think of taking it back. But we need to visit that spot immediately.'

Dilip had not fully regained his composure as yet. I saw him shudder a couple of times. 'Yes, isn't that what I just said? We must go back, and leave it there!' he said.

'Whether or not we must get rid of it is something we can decide later. Let's just go there.'

'With the branch?'

'No. There's no need to take it with us. Not yet, anyway.'

We left. The empty plot of land was within five minutes' walking distance. There were buildings on three sides of the plot. In it, I could see a palm, a jackfruit and another tree, which I failed to recognize. There were several shrubs and bushes, too. Dilip pointed at a particular bush and said, 'That's where I found the branch.'

I began looking around. It did not take me long. Only about three minutes later, I picked up another branch, which might have been a twin of the first one. The only difference was that this one did not have a tail.

'What will you do with it?' Dilip asked.

'I shall do nothing. You, my dear, will take it and keep it together with the other one, on the same shelf. I'll spend another night in your house. Let's see what happens.'

Both animals stood quietly, side by side, the whole night. There was no problem at all.

'It's clear that the two are friends,' I said to Dilip the next morning. 'You separated them. Hence all that wailing.'

'But . . . but . . . how is it possible? In this day and age?'

In reply, I quoted the famous lines from Shakespeare:

There are more things in heaven and earth, Horatio,
Than are dreamt of in your philosophy.

'But what am I going to call them?' Dilip wanted to know.

'Kutum and Katam.'

Translated by Gopa Majumdar
First published in Bengali in 1987

The Case of Mriganko Babu

It was from his colleague, Salil Basak, that Mriganko Babu first learnt about man's evolution from a species of apes. Today, every educated person is aware of this fact; but, somehow, Mriganko Babu had never heard such a thing before. As a matter of fact, his knowledge about most things was extremely limited. As a student, he had been just about average. He never read anything except the books in his syllabus, and even in later life, failed to find any interest in reading.

'What! You don't say. Man has evolved from monkeys?' he asked in profound amazement. 'That's right,' said Mr Basak. 'Millions of years ago, man was a four-legged creature. You can still find apes, but that particular species from which the human race evolved has become extinct.'

Mriganko Babu and Salil Basak worked as clerks in Hardinge India Company. Mriganko Babu had been there for the last twenty-two years, and Salil Basak for fifteen. They sat next to each other, which was why a friendship had developed between them. Generally speaking, Mriganko Babu was not a person who could make friends easily.

What he learnt that day about men and apes made a deep impression on his mind. He went to a book shop in College Street and, after rummaging around for a while, found a book on evolution. He realized after reading it that Salil was right. Seeing his friend's words in black and white, Mriganko Babu could no longer question what he had said. How very strange—why did it take a few million years for apes to turn into men? And his book said that there were still some areas about which not enough was known, but that anthropologists were still engaged in research. He also learnt that there was something called the 'missing link', which referred to the stage just before the emergence of the human form.

Mriganko Babu was not fully satisfied with what was written in the book. He went to the museum to find out more. One look at a picture of ancient man and the bones that had been discovered told him that his early ancestors had indeed borne a strong resemblance to monkeys. He then went to the zoo, and spent a long time inspecting the primates. Monkeys had tails, he realized; the ones without tails were called apes. There were several species of these animals. In addition to Indian monkeys and langoors, there were gorillas from Africa, as well as chimpanzees and baboons. There were also the orangutans from Sumatra.

African chimpanzees struck him as being the closest to human beings.

Not only that, one particular chimpanzee seemed quite interested in him. It cast frequent glances at him, then came closer and stood staring straight at him through the iron bars in its cage. It even made faces and, finally, grinned at him. Mriganko Babu could not help feeling as if he had known the animal for years.

He spent an hour in the zoo. On his way back from there, he suddenly thought of an uncle of his, who he called Kalumama. When Mriganko Babu was about twenty-five years old, Kalumama had once visited his house. He had, on that occasion, addressed Mriganko Babu as 'markat'. 'Hey, markat, go and get me a packet of cigarettes from the corner shop,' he was often heard saying.

One day, Mriganko Babu felt he had to ask his uncle to explain. 'Why do you call me markat?' he asked.

Pat came Kalumama's reply: 'Because you look like one. Don't you ever look at yourself in the mirror? You have a small forehead, tiny eyes, such a big gap between your nose and your mouth . . . what else can I call you but a markat? Don't you know what it means? A markat is a monkey. That blue ring that you wear . . . I can see that the letter "M" is engraved on it. Well, I think it stands for "monkey", not "Mriganko". You'll never have to look for a job, there will always be a vacancy for you in the zoo!'

After this, Mriganko Babu spent a long time studying his face in a mirror. Having done that, he had to admit that Kalumama was right. There were discernible resemblances between his face and that of a monkey. Then he remembered a teacher in his school called Mahesh Sir. He had sometimes said to him, 'Oy you, stop monkeying around.' Mriganko Babu was only twelve or thirteen at the time. It had not occurred to him till then that he might actually look like a monkey.

It was not just his face, either. The way he slouched, and the abundance of hair on his body also gave him quite a simian-like look. He thought again of what Salil had said. There were traces of the ancient ape in Mriganko Babu's body, the same ape from which the human race had evolved. The more he thought about it, the more uncomfortable did he feel. Even when he was typing in his office, he couldn't help thinking: 'I am not fully evolved, I am still partly an ape.' But, in the next instant, he would think: could an ape sit at a desk and type? If he looked like a monkey, surely it was only by chance? Other men bore resemblances to animals, too. Why, Suresh Babu in their accounts department looked so amazingly like a mole! No, Mriganko Babu was a man. One hundred per cent human. There could be no doubt about that.

Only a few days later, however, he suddenly realized that he had a special fondness for bananas and peanuts. On his way back from his office, almost every day, he bought either a banana or a packet of peanuts. Weren't monkeys too fond of these? Was this similarity also an accident? It had to be. Plenty of other people like eating bananas and nuts. They weren't all monkeys, were they? Mriganko Babu tried to push the thought away, only to discover that it would not go. 'Man came from apes . . . apes became men . . . am I a complete man, or is there something of an ape still left in me?'

He began making mistakes in his work. His boss called him into his room one day. 'Your typing has always been flawless. Why have you suddenly started making mistakes?' he asked. Mriganko Babu hardly knew what to say. 'I . . . I haven't been feeling too well, sir,' he mumbled.

'In that case, see a doctor. We have our own doctor, don't we? Speak to Dr Gupta.'

'No, sir. I am all right now. I don't have to see a doctor. There won't be any more mistakes in my typing, I promise. Please forgive me, sir.'

His boss agreed to drop the matter. But Mriganko Babu himself could find no peace. He decided to see Dr Gupta, anyway. 'Please give me something to help me concentrate more on my work,' he said. 'I have been feeling quite distracted lately. It's affecting my job.'

Dr Gupta stared at Mriganko Babu for a few seconds. Then he said, 'You don't look well. You have lost weight, and there are dark circles under your eyes. Medicines alone can't help. Can you take some time off?'

'Yes. I haven't taken any leave at all in the last couple of years.'

'Well then, I suggest you take a week off and have a holiday. You need a change of air. I will prescribe some tablets for you, but going out of town is more important.'

Mriganko Babu took ten days' leave. Where could he go?

A cousin of his lived in Varanasi, near a ghat. The fresh air from the river might do him good. This cousin had invited him to visit Varanasi several times in the past, but Mriganko Babu had not been able to go. Now, he decided, it was to Varanasi that he would go.

What he did not know was that Varanasi was full of monkeys. In the streets, on the ghats, roofs of buildings, trees, even in temples—no matter where he looked, there were monkeys everywhere. Mriganko Babu couldn't help commenting on it. 'This is nothing!' his cousin, Neelratan, said with a laugh. 'I'll take you to Durgabari. Then you'll know what a monkey-infested area looks like!'

The sight of Durgabari left Mriganko Babu quite speechless. More than fifty monkeys ran and surrounded him as soon as he walked in through the gate. Their constant screeching wiped out any other noise. 'Wait, let me go and get some peanuts,' said Neelratan.

Strangely enough, Mriganko Babu did not feel uncomfortable at all in the company of so many monkeys. On the contrary, he felt quite at home, as if he knew them all, and was back with his own people after a long time.

This happened on the third day after his arrival in Varanasi. On the fifth day, he realized that he was beginning to lose the thread of his conversation. Very often, he was having to stop and say, 'Er . . .' Simple, ordinary words appeared meaningless. Neelratan said to him, 'Mrigankoda, when I come back from work this evening, I'll take you to Dashashwamedh Ghat. A group there will sing keertan. They're quite good.'

Mriganko Babu found the word 'keertan' hard to understand. 'Where will you take me?' he asked.

'Dashashwamedh Ghat. Will you go?'

'Er . . . Dash . . . Dashashwamedh? Why?'

'I just told you. There will be keertan this evening. You'll enjoy it. You like keertan, don't you? At least, you did once!'

'Oh. Er . . . keertan? I see. But . . . those who'll take part in this . . . I mean, the singers . . . will they be human?'

'Human? What are you talking about? Of course they'll be human. You don't expect a group of monkeys to sit and sing devotional songs, do you?'

'Er . . . but in the past . . . weren't all humans monkeys?'

'Now you're talking utter rubbish. Is this your idea of a joke? No, Mrigankoda, I can't say I appreciate your humour. I'm off to work now. I'll come back at half past five, and then we'll both go. All right?'

Mriganko Babu went with his cousin to hear the singers in the evening. He had an extraordinary experience there. It seemed to him, every now and then, as if it was a group of monkeys that was singing, beating the drums and cymbals and playing the harmonium. Mriganko Babu hardly knew what to do.

On returning home, Neelratan declared after dinner that he had to visit his doctor in Bangalitola. 'I'll be back in half an hour. He's a homoeopath, you see. I've run out of my medicine. He'll prepare it himself.'

Soon after Neelratan's departure, Mriganko Babu was suddenly seized by the desire to walk like a monkey. He climbed down from his bed, and began crawling on all fours on the floor, going round and round the bed. He had done this about four times, when he realized that Neelratan's servant, Ramlal, was standing across the threshold, staring at him wide-eyed.

Mriganko Babu scrambled to his feet. Then he faced Ramlal and said, 'What's so amazing about this? You live here in Varanasi. Haven't you seen a monkey before?'

Without uttering a word, Ramlal came into the room and began making the bed.

Mriganko Babu spent the remainder of his stay in almost complete silence. Neelratan remarked on it one day. 'What's the matter, Mrigankoda?' he asked. 'Why are you so quiet? Are you feeling unwell or something?'

'Un-unwell? N-no, I don't think so. I mean, the th-thing is, if monk-monkeys could become men, m-men could become monkeys, couldn't they? Ev-evolution in rev-reverse?'

Neelratan was perfectly taken aback, but chose to say nothing. Mriganko Babu's behaviour was distinctly odd. Should he perhaps consult his homoeopath?

Two days later, Mriganko Babu returned to Calcutta. His servant, Dasharathi, was the first to greet him when he reached his house in Hajra Lane, suitcase in hand. Dasharathi was an old servant, he had worked for Mriganko Babu for years. 'Oh, you're back, babu!' he smiled in welcome. 'All went well, I hope?'

Mriganko Babu said, 'Hoop!'

Dasharathi burst out laughing. 'That was very good, babu. You sounded exactly like a monkey. I went to Varanasi once in my childhood. It's packed with monkeys, isn't it?'

In reply, Mriganko Babu said, 'Hoop! Hoop!'

Four days later, an event hit the headlines in every newspaper. At dawn the previous day, an employee of the zoo had found a strange creature lying on the ground just outside the cage of a chimpanzee. It appeared to be asleep. Quite possibly, it had jumped over the wall in the middle of the night. The superintendent of the zoo had stated that the creature seemed to be a monkey, but from a totally new species, hitherto unseen. Just as a mule is a cross between a horse and a donkey, this animal seemed a mixture of a man and a monkey. It was still alive, screeching and making noises very much like a monkey.

The most amazing thing was that on the third finger of its left hand was a blue ring. In its centre, engraved in white, was the letter 'M'.

Translated by Gopa Majumdar
First published in Bengali in 1988

The Promise

Mahim glanced at his watch. Seven minutes to twelve. It was a quartz, so the time had to be accurate. Over the last few minutes his heart had started gallcping. It was only natural. Twenty years! Today, it was 7 October 1989. That day, it was 7 October 1969. Mahim remembered the day so well. The question was, would Pratul? Well, in another seven minutes, that question would be answered.

Mahim looked around, simply to pass the time. He was standing in the lobby of the Lighthouse cinema, opposite the ticket windows. Pratul was supposed to come and meet him here, at this very spot. Through the open door in front of him, Mahim could see the street outside. A knot of people had gathered around a book stall on the opposite pavement. Four Ambassadors of different colours were parked in the road. And there was a cycle rickshaw. Mahim's eyes moved above the door. There was a poster of the film currently running at the cinema. The figure that stood out most prominently was the villain, Kishorilal, with his thick moustache, its points upturned. Mahim did not watch Hindi films. These days, videos were so common that most people liked watching films at home, anyway. Besides, the cinemas were in an awful state. Mahim had heard his father say that once the Lighthouse was the city's pride and joy. Today, just looking at it was bound to bring tears to his eyes.

Staring at the stream of people that flowed past the ticket windows, Mahim's mind drifted back to the past.

Mahim was then fifteen years old, and Pratul was older by a year. How clearly he remembered that particular day! It was their lunch break. The two friends were sitting under a tree, having a quick snack. They were bosom pals. Both were famous for the mischief they could get up to. They were not afraid of a single teacher, not even Karali Babu, who taught maths and had succeeded in terrorizing the rest of the school. Karali Babu punished them often. When everyone else was sitting peacefully in their class, Mahim and Pratul were seen standing on a bench. But that made no difference to them. They went back to their pranks in the very next class.

However, both boys were reasonably intelligent. Neither of them ever spent a lot of time studying, but when the final exam results came out, Mahim always managed to secure a position somewhere in the middle ranks. Pratul did not fare so well; but he never failed in any subject, either. Pratul's father worked for the railways, and had a transferable job. In 1969, he was transferred to Dhanbad. Pratul, naturally, had to go with his father, which meant an end to his friendship with Mahim. The two boys discussed this that day before Pratul left.

'Who knows when we'll meet again?' said Pratul. 'If we leave Calcutta permanently, I can't come back even for a short visit. But if you go to Dhanbad, we can get together again.'

'Dhanbad? No, I don't think so. My father will never consider spending our holidays there. He always chooses either Puri or Darjeeling. We've never gone anywhere else.'

Pratul sighed, staring at the grass. After a while, he asked, 'Have you decided what you'd like to be when you grow up?'

Mahim shook his head. 'No. I've got plenty of time to think about that. My father's a doctor, so he'll be pleased if I study medicine. But I have no such desire. Why, have you decided what you want to be?'

'No.'

Both fell silent after this. It was Pratul who broke the silence. 'Listen!' he said, 'Why don't we do something?'

'What?'

'We're friends, aren't we? So I was thinking of testing our friendship.'

Mahim frowned. 'Testing our friendship? What nonsense are you talking?'

'It isn't nonsense at all. I've read about this. It's been done before.'

'What's been done before?'

'When two friends part, they promise to meet each other again, at a certain time, on a certain date.'

Now Mahim could grasp his friend's intention. 'All right,' he said, thinking it over, 'I am quite prepared to make such a promise. But when should we meet? After how many years?'

'Say, twenty? It's 7 October today, and the year is 1969. We'll meet again on 7 October 1989.'

'At what time?'

'Twelve o'clock in the afternoon.'

'All right. But where?'

'It has to be a place we'd both be familiar with.'

'What about a cinema? We've seen so many films together.'

'Very well. Let's meet in twenty years, at the Lighthouse, opposite the ticket windows.'

'All right, that's a promise.'

The two friends parted company. Mahim did wonder at times whether he would be able to remember his promise. Funnily enough, in the last twenty years, he had not forgotten about it even once.

After Pratul left Mahim began to change very much for the better, possibly because he had no other close friend. His behaviour in class improved, as did his results. He came to be known as one of the good students of his school.

He began writing when he went to college. Soon, his stories, essays and poetry began to appear in magazines. When he was only twenty-three—that was in 1977—he wrote his first novel. A well-known publisher published it, and it got good reviews. Eventually, it even won a literary award. Today, Mahim Chatterjee was a famous figure in the world of literature. Most critics rated him among the best contemporary novelists.

In the last twenty years, he had had no contact with Pratul, except the few letters he wrote at first. Pratul had written to say that although he had made a few friends in Dhanbad, no one could take Mahim's place. He had sent him four letters in the first six months, but that was all. This did not surprise Mahim. He knew Pratul was extremely lazy when it came to writing letters. It struck him as a chore that he wanted to avoid most of the time. Mahim did not mind writing letters, but he could not keep up the flow of correspondence singlehanded.

It was now two minutes after twelve. Pratul must have forgotten his promise. Even if he hadn't, he could well be in a different city, thousands of miles away. One could hardly expect him to rush back to Calcutta just to keep an appointment made twenty years ago. Besides, there was something else to consider. Pratul might be in Calcutta, he might have remembered his promise, but it could well be that he was held up in a traffic jam.

Mahim decided to wait for another ten minutes before going home. Thank goodness it was a Sunday today, or he would have had to leave his office an hour before lunch. Mahim earned well enough as a novelist, but he had not given up the job he had in a private firm. He had made a lot of new friends, too, in the course of time. But he could not forget his days at school, filled with laughter and mischief.

'Excuse me!' said a voice, bringing Mahim out of his reverie. He turned, to find a boy of about sixteen looking at him. In his hand was an envelope.

'Are you Mahim Chatterjee?' he asked.

'Yes. Why do you ask?'

'Here's a letter for you.'

The boy passed the envelope to Mahim. Then he said, 'I need your reply,' and waited.

Slightly taken aback, Mahim took the letter out and read it quickly. It said:

> Dear Mahim,
> If you have not forgotten the promise we made to each other, you will get this letter. I am in Calcutta, but there is no way I can meet you at the Lighthouse. I wanted to let you know that, and ask to be forgiven. I have not forgotten you; nor did I forget our appointment. I would like to go to your house to meet you. If you write your address on the other side of this sheet, and also let me know the date and time that might be convenient, I will call on you. With good wishes,
> Your friend,
> Pratul

Mahim had a pen in his pocket. He scribbled his address on the letter as instructed, and wrote, 'Next Sunday, between nine and twelve o'clock'. Then he returned the letter to the boy. He took it silently, and went out of the door.

There was no need for him to linger in the lobby. Mahim left the cinema, and went to find his new blue Ambassador, parked in Humayun Court. The important thing was that Pratul had not forgotten. But why couldn't he have come today, when he was in town? Mahim felt quite mystified. There was no mention of Pratul's address on the letter, so Mahim could not contact him. He could have asked the boy, but the thought had not occurred to him at the time. The letter was written on an ordinary piece of paper, torn out of an exercise book. Could that mean that Pratul had fallen on hard times, and did not want his friend to find out? But he had offered to come to his house. Well, Mahim would have to wait until he arrived to learn the truth.

When he returned home, his wife Shubhra asked, 'Did you meet your friend?'

'No, but he sent me a letter through someone. He remembered our appointment, that's the main thing. I would never have believed such a thing was possible if I hadn't done it myself. In fact, even at the time we made that promise, I had wondered whether we'd remember it in twenty years' time!'

The following Sunday, Mahim's door bell rang at ten o'clock. He was in his living room, reading the newspaper. His bearer, Pashupati, opened the door. 'Is your babu at home?' Mahim heard the visitor ask. 'Yes, sir,' replied Pashupati. A gentleman walked in through the door a second later. He had an outstretched arm, and on his lips was a big smile.

Mahim stretched his own arm and clasped the man's hand firmly. 'Pratul?' he said wonderingly, smiling back. 'Why, you haven't changed! I mean, you've grown older, obviously, but that's about all. Do sit down.'

Pratul sat down on a sofa, still smiling. 'What better proof of friendship could you ask for?' he said.

'Exactly.'

'You're a writer, aren't you?'

'Yes.'

'You won an award . . . I saw it in the papers.'

'Yes. But what about you? You seem to know enough about me!'

Pratul stared at Mahim for a few moments. Then he said slowly, 'I am . . . getting along. Yes, I am doing all right.'

'Do you live here in Calcutta?'

'Not all the time. I have to travel.'

'Are you a travelling salesman?'

Pratul gave a slight smile in reply, but remained silent. 'You still haven't told me!' Mahim complained.

'What?'

'Why you didn't come to the Lighthouse that day. What was the reason, you idiot? Why did you have to send a letter through someone else?'

'I had a problem.'

'What problem? Come on, tell me. I can—'

Mahim stopped. His eyes moved towards the window that overlooked the street. A large number of youths had gathered outside and were making a lot of noise. Irritated, he went to the window and lifted the curtain to have a look. Then he said, sounding incredulous, 'Is that car yours?' He could not remember having seen a bigger car anywhere in Calcutta. 'And why are these boys making such a racket?' Mahim turned back as he asked the second question. Immediately, his jaw fell open.

Pratul was grinning at him. But now, under his nose sat a thick moustache, its points turned upward.

'Kishorilal!' Mahim almost shouted.

Pratul peeled the moustache off and put it in his pocket. 'Now can you understand why I couldn't go to the Lighthouse? It's the price of fame. I cannot go anywhere without being recognized.'

'My God!'

Pratul rose. 'I should not stay here any longer. If I do, that crowd might get quite out of control. So I'll go now. You haven't seen any of my films, I take it?'

'No, I am afraid I haven't.'

'You ought to see one. Please. I'll have a couple of seats reserved for you at the Lighthouse.'

Pratul made his way to the front door, followed by Mahim. The crowd roared as soon as the door was opened. 'Kishorilal! Kishorilal!' they began chanting. Pratul somehow managed to push his way through the crowd and got into the car. His driver started it at once. Mahim saw his friend waving at him. He raised his own hand to wave back.

A boy emerged from the crowd and approached Mahim, his eyes wide with amazement. 'Kishorilal . . . Kishorilal is known to you?' he gasped.

'Yes. Yes, he's my friend.'

It was easy enough to guess what was now going to happen. Mahim knew that, from now on, his own name would get wiped out. The local boys would refer to him simply as 'Kishorilal's friend'.

Translated by Gopa Majumdar
First published in Bengali in 1990